NATURE, JUSTICE, AND RIGHTS
IN ARISTOTLE'S *POLITICS*

Nature, Justice, and Rights in Aristotle's *Politics*

FRED D. MILLER, JR.

CLARENDON PRESS · OXFORD

Oxford University Press, Walton Street, Oxford OX2 6DP
Oxford New York
Athens Auckland Bangkok Bombay
Calcutta Cape Town Dar es Salaam Delhi
Florence Hong Kong Istanbul Karachi
Kuala Lumpur Madras Madrid Melbourne
Mexico City Nairobi Paris Singapore
Taipei Tokyo Toronto
and associated companies in
Berlin Ibadan

Oxford is a trade mark of Oxford University Press

Published in the United States by
Oxford University Press Inc., New York

First published 1995

British Library Cataloguing in Publication Data
Data available

Library of Congress Cataloging in Publication Data
Miller, Fred Dycus, 1944- .
Nature, justice, and rights in Aristotle's Politics / Fred D.
Miller, Jr.
Includes bibliographical references.
1. Aristotle. Politics. 2. Aristotle—Contributions in political
science. 3. Civil rights. 4. Justice. 5. Natural law. I. Title.
JC71.A7M55 1995 323—dc20 94-45696
ISBN 0-19-824061-9

3 5 7 9 10 8 6 4 2

Printed in Great Britain
on acid-free paper by
Biddles Ltd., Guildford and King's Lynn

To my mother
and the memory of my father

Preface and Acknowledgements

Aristotle maintains that there is only one constitution which is everywhere according to nature the best (*EN* V 7 1135ª5). This book is a study of what I take to be the central argument of his *Politics* in support of this thesis: that constitution is best according to nature which is unqualifiedly just and which guarantees the rights of its citizens according to this standard. The best constitution serves as a standard by which politicians can establish, preserve, and reform different political institutions appropriate to a wide variety of social circumstances. I offer a reconstruction of Aristotle's political philosophy based upon an examination of his texts, along with an assessment of his argument in the light of modern theories and concerns. I argue that Aristotle is a precursor of modern theorists of justice, that it is not anachronistic to understand him as concerned with individual rights, and that he makes an important contribution to our understanding of these concepts.

This book is intended not only for specialists in Aristotle, but also for readers who have a general interest in theories of justice and rights, in the history of ethics, political theory, and jurisprudence, or in ancient Greek political history. All Greek text in this book is translated; and, unless otherwise explicitly indicated, the translations are mine. All Greek terms are transliterated, with the following conventions: upsilon is transliterated as 'u'; eta as 'ē'; omega as 'ō'; and iota subscript is rendered by an 'i' following the subscripted vowel. I have relied primarily on Dreizehnter's edition of the *Politics* and the Oxford Classical Texts of the *Nicomachean* and *Eudemian Ethics*, although I have noted some departures from these. Sigla for manuscripts are from these editions. I have found especially valuable Lord's translation of the *Politics*, Irwin's translation of the *Nicomachean Ethics*, and Barnes's revised edition of the Oxford translations of Aristotle. Throughout the project I relied constantly on Newman's magisterial four-volume commentary of the *Politics*. I have also made frequent use of the other critical editions, translations, and commentaries for these and other Aristotelian writings, which are listed by the name of editor, translator, or commentator in the Bibliography.

Some of the material in this book appeared earlier in another form, but it was all reworked (for the most part extensively) in order to be incorporated into this book. Parts of Sections 1.2 and 1.5 are based on the introduction to David Keyt and Fred D. Miller, Jr. (eds.), *A Companion to Aristotle's Politics* (by permission of Basil Blackwell © 1991). Sections 2.1–4 are revised from 'Aristotle's Political Naturalism', in Terry Penner and Richard Kraut (eds.), *Nature, Knowledge, and Virtue: Essays in Memory of Joan Kung* (by permission of Academic Printing and Publishing © 1989). Sections 3.3–5 are descended from 'Aristotle on Nature, Law, and Justice', *University of Dayton Review*, Special Issue on Aristotle, 19 (1988–9), 57–69 (by permission of *University of Dayton Review*); and 'Aristotle on Natural Law and Justice', in *A Companion to Aristotle's Politics* (by permission of Basil Blackwell © 1991). Chapter 9 appeared in an earlier form as 'Aristotle on Property Rights', in John Anton and Anthony Preus (eds.), *Essays in Ancient Greek Philosophy*, iv (by permission of State University of New York Press © 1991). Section 10.2 is partly based on Michael Bradie and Fred D. Miller, Jr., 'Teleology and Natural Necessity in Aristotle', *History of Philosophy Quarterly*, 1 (1984), 133–46 (by permission of Nicholas Rescher). Section 10.4 also draws upon 'The State and Community in Aristotle's *Politics*', *Reason Papers*, 1 (1974), 61–9 (by permission of Tibor Machan). I am also indebted to Kurt Luckner of the Toledo Art Museum for assistance with the cover art.

I have many people to thank, beginning with my wife Kathryn for her love, encouragement, and patience throughout this project. I am grateful to the Earhart Foundation for two grants in support of my research and to Dean Louis Katzner and Bowling Green State University for a research leave. I also acknowledge the warm hospitality of John Gray and the Fellows of Jesus College, Oxford, where I visited in 1989. Special thanks are also due to my co-directors at the Social Philosophy and Policy Center, Ellen F. Paul and Jeffrey Paul, who have offered continuing encouragement. I have also received unflagging support from the Center's staff, including Kory Swanson, Terrie Weaver, Tamara Sharp—and especially Mary Dilsaver for years of meticulous typing.

During the decade I have worked on this book, I have benefited greatly from the generous assistance, suggestions, and criticisms of many other persons. I received helpful reactions from commentators and audiences when presenting earlier drafts of chapters and sections at meetings of professional societies, including the American Philosophical Association, the American Political Science Association, the Society for Ancient Greek Philosophy, the American Association for the Philosophic Study of Society, the Greater Philadelphia Philosophy Consortium, and an NEH summer institute on Aristotle directed by John M. Cooper, Michael Frede, and Allan Gotthelf, as well as in symposia, colloquia, and seminars at the

University of Colorado at Boulder, the University of Dayton, the University of Manchester, the University of Waterloo, and Bowling Green State University.

In addition to many individuals who have discussed the project with me, the following individuals generously made written comments and criticisms on earlier drafts: Julia Annas, Larry Arnhart, Neera Kapur Badhwar, Thomas Banchich, John Boler, Sterling Burnett, David Charles, John M. Cooper, Kenneth Cust, Douglas J. Den Uyl, David Depew, Harold C. Dolan, Thomas A. Fay, Don Fowler, R. G. Frey, David Gordon, Daniel Greenberg, Charles Griswold, John Gray, John Haldane, Waldemar Hanasz, Maureen Kelley, Irfan Khawaja, Richard Kraut, Lawrence Jost, Lindsay Judson, Joan Kung, James G. Lennox, Anthony J. Lisska, Loren Lomasky, Robert Mayhew, Eugene F. Miller, Phillip Mitsis, Jan Narveson, John O. Nelson, Ronald Polansky, Anthony Preus, Douglas B. Rasmussen, A. E. Raubitschek, D. A. Rees, Meyer Reinhold, Gerasimos Santas, Christopher Shields, Peter Simpson, Steven B. Smith, James Sobredo, Hillel Steiner, James Stuart, Brian Tierney, Henry B. Veatch, Lloyd L. Weinreb, Carrie-Ann Zinaich, Samuel Zinaich, Catherine H. Zuckert, Michael P. Zuckert, and two anonymous referees for Oxford University Press. I also received valuable assistance in preparing the indices from Mary Dilsaver, Tamara Sharp, and Carrie-Ann and Samuel Ziniach. My greatest debt is to my teacher and mentor, David Keyt. It was my good fortune that we developed a fascination with Aristotle's *Politics* at the same time, for David has been a stimulating interlocutor, supportive collaborator, and unrelenting critic over the past decade. Of course, none of the above individuals necessarily agrees with all my conclusions (indeed, some vehemently disagree!), and the sole responsibility for any residual errors is mine.

Finally, this book is dedicated to my late father, Fred D. Miller, Sr., who introduced me to ancient history.

F. D. M.

Contents

List of Figures

List of Tables

List of Abbreviations

ARISTOTLE

An. Post.	*Analytica Posteriora*
An. Pr.	*Analytica Priora*
Ath. Pol.	*Athēnaiōn Politeia*
Cat.	*Categoriae*
DA	*de Anima*
DC	*de Caelo*
DI	*de Interpretatione*
EE	*Ethica Eudemia*
EN	*Ethica Nicomachea*
GA	*de Generatione Animalium*
GC	*de Generatione et Corruptione*
HA	*Historia Animalium*
IA	*de Incessu Animalium*
MA	*de Motu Animalium*
MM	*Magna Moralia*
Met.	*Metaphysica*
Meteor.	*Meteorologica*
Oec.	*Oeconomica*
PA	*de Partibus Animalium*
Phys.	*Physica*
Poet.	*Poetica*
Pol.	*Politica*
Probl.	*Problemata*
Protr.	*Protrepticus*
Rhet.	*Rhetorica*
Rhet. Al.	*Rhetorica ad Alexandrum*
SE	*Sophistici Elenchi*
Somn.	*de Somno et Vigilia*
Top.	*Topica*

PLATO

Apol.	*Apology*
Charm.	*Charmides*

Gorg.	*Gorgias*
Hip. Maj.	*Hippias Major*
Laws	*Leges*
Parm.	*Parmenides*
Phdo.	*Phaedo*
Phlb.	*Philebus*
Prot.	*Protagoras*
Rep.	*Republic*
Soph.	*Sophist*
Statesman	*Politicus*
Theaet.	*Theaetetus*
Tim.	*Timaeus*

XENOPHON

Anab.	*Anabasis*
Apol.	*Apology*
Cyrop.	*Cyropaedia*
Hell.	*Hellenica*
Mem.	*Memoribilia*
Oec.	*Oeconomica*

MISCELLANEOUS ABBREVIATIONS

CIAG	Prussian Academy (1882–1909), *Commentaria in Aristotelem Graeca*, 23 vols. (Berlin)
DK	H. Diels and W. Kranz (1952), *Fragmente der Vorsokratiker*, 3 vols. (6th edn., Berlin)

Introduction

I

The Argument of Aristotle's *Politics*

1.1. ARISTOTLE AND THE POLIS

Aristotle of Stagira (384–322 BC) wrote the *Politics* in the latter half of the fourth century BC, as an unprecedented period of political experimentation was drawing to a close. King Philip of Macedon defeated an alliance of Greek city-states led by Athens and Thebes in the battle of Chaeronea in 338 BC, a disaster the Greeks called 'fatal to liberty', and asserted hegemony over most of Greece. Philip then announced his plan to invade the Persian Empire, ostensibly in order to liberate the Greeks in Asia Minor, but he was assassinated in 336 BC[1] and succeeded by his son Alexander the Great. Throughout Aristotle's final stay in Athens (335–323 BC), his former pupil Alexander carried out the conquest of the Persian Empire and prepared the way for the new Hellenistic empires, which were to eclipse the old-fashioned city-states. In retrospect, it may seem ironic that it was the waning city-state that provided the subject-matter for the *Politics*. Nevertheless, Aristotle's theorizing about Greek politics contained many ideas of enduring significance. Perhaps the most fundamental of these is the idea that the faculty of human reason could, and should, guide the activities of establishing, governing, and altering human communities.

One factor that encouraged the development of this idea was the character of the city-state or polis itself. The word 'polis'[2] originally referred to a high stronghold or citadel to which the Greeks of the dark ages repaired when their villages were under attack.[3] The related word

---

[1] This is the latest event mentioned in the *Politics*, at V 10 1311^{b}1–3.

[2] Henceforth, I use the Anglicized word 'polis' (plural, 'polises'), rather than the common translations 'city', 'state', or 'city-state', to emphasize that the Greek word *polis* refers to an actual historical phenomenon with important features that distinguish it from other types of political organizations. Moreover, the use of 'polis' helps to emphasize the central place of this historical phenomenon in the science which Aristotle calls 'politics'. Valuable introductions to the history and character of the Greek polises include Sealey (1976) and Ehrenberg (1964). Busolt and Swoboda (1920) offer a detailed account of the political institutions in the different polises.

[3] The acropolis of Athens was still called 'the polis' in the late 5th cent. (Thucydides, II 15 6).

politēs originally designated a look-out for the polis; later it meant 'citizen'. The polis came to include the households and businesses gathered around the citadel and later the surrounding territory. The word *astu* was used in Attica to denote the town or city of Athens proper, in distinction from the countryside (*agros* or *chōra*). During the sixth and fifth centuries BC, the polis developed into a distinctive political community, for its small size and compactness made possible an unusual level of direct political participation by the citizens. Attica, the most populous polis, had in Aristotle's time a population of about 300,000, including 30,000 adult male citizens, 70,000 female citizens and children, 10,000 metics (resident aliens), and over 150,000 slaves. The polises were so numerous that Aristotle and his pupils at the Lyceum were able to assemble descriptions of 158 constitutions, which exhibited many similarities and differences.[4] Despite fundamental similarities, the polises displayed great variety in size, location (on the coast, inland, or on an island), economic activity (agricultural or mercantile in varying degrees), customs, and temperament. Each polis was a microcosm, geographically distinct, and, to a significant extent, economically self-sufficient and politically independent. The polis, like Heraclitus' river, exhibited constancy as well as flux. For although its members remained tightly intertwined by relationships of kinship, economic exchange, custom, and religious practice, there were also powerful social forces perpetually at work producing instability, change, and faction. Moreover, as the Greeks established new colonies around the Mediterranean and the Black Sea, they were constrained to address basic constitutional issues: Who should be recognized as a citizen? What governmental offices and bodies should exist? Who should have the right to participate in them?

These political realities made it difficult to sustain the myth that the constitution and the laws were the sacrosanct bequest of a hero or divinity in the remote past (cf. Plato, *Laws*, IX 853^{c}3–7). The increasingly influential notion that politics could be an expression of human reason arose in part out of the legend of the Seven Sages, wise men who provided the Greek polises with practical political guidance.[5] One such sage (*sophistēs*) was Solon of Athens, whose constitutional reforms in the early sixth

---

[4] Of these the *Constitution of Athens* was discovered in papyrus form in 1890. As for the rest, there are only brief fragmentary quotations by ancient authors: see Rose (1886), fr. 381–644, partially trans. in Barnes (1984), ii. 2453–8. Other authors were probably influenced by Aristotle, e.g. the description of the Spartan constitution in Plutarch, *Lives*, Lycurgus: cf. Forrest (1968), 41. The total number of polises has been estimated at about 750, but many were tiny: cf. Hansen (1991), 54.   [5] See Meier (1990), 40–52.

century, although short-lived, paved the way for the democratic reforms of Cleisthenes at the end of the century.[6] The study of political reforms was a central theme in the writings of fifth-century intellectuals such as Protagoras of Abdera, who drew up a code of laws for the colony of Thurii (444 BC), Thucydides of Athens, and Democritus of Abdera. It became more credible to view the lawgiver or politician as a craftsman,[7] like a doctor, architect, athletic trainer, or weaver. Philosophers and rhetoricians encouraged the view that there was an art of the polis, a political craft (politikē technē).[8] This craft involved the application of an organized body of expert knowledge to the issues involved in governing the polis. To be sure, the Greeks resolved many questions of governance in the manner of 'barbarians' before and after them: by duplicity, Realpolitik, sheer force, or unquestioning adherence to tradition and superstition. Yet to an unprecedented extent their political life was subject to rational reflection, criticism, and prescription.

The elevation of reason in politics is especially pronounced in the dialogues of Plato (c.427–c.347 BC). For example, in the Gorgias Socrates contends that one should be guided not by the opinions of the many but by knowledge which may belong to only one person (471^{e}2–472^{d}4). The implication is that by Socratic reasoning one could discover a standard of justice on the basis of which the polis should be governed.[9] Indeed, Socrates claims in the Gorgias that he, not the sophist or rhetorician, possesses 'the true political craft' (521^{d}7). Plato's Republic goes much further, depicting the ideal of philosophers as rulers and craftsmen of a virtuous citizenry (VI 500^{d}4–8). Although Aristotle took issue with Plato's conception of rationality and with many of his political prescriptions, he followed Plato on the most important point: Politics ought to have the character of a science (epistēmē), with the aim of establishing and preserving a just polis.

1.2. THE SCIENCE OF THE POLIS

The special science devoted to the polis is called 'political science' (hē politikē epistēmē), or 'politics' (hē politikē) for short. It falls into the second

---

[6] Ath. Pol. VI–XII on Solon's reforms, and XXI 1–XXII 4 on Cleisthenes' reforms. On more radical democratic changes to the Athenian constitution due to Ephialtes and Pericles in the mid-5th cent. BC, see Ath. Pol. XXIII–XXVII. Cf. Pol. II 12 1273^{b}35–1274^{a}21.

[7] Cf. Pol. III 2 1275^{b}26–30. Dēmiourgos, 'craftsman', was the title of a magistrate in some polises (cf. Hesychius, Lexicon, s.v.).

[8] See Democritus, DK 68 B 157; Plato, Prot. 319^{a}4. Cf. Farrar (1988).

[9] Cf. also Xenophon, Mem. III 9 10.

of the three main Aristotelian divisions of the sciences: the contemplative, the practical, and the productive (*Top.* VI 6 145ª15–16; *Met.* VI 1 1025ᵇ25, XI 7 1064ª16–19; *EN* VI 2 1139ª26–8). These three types of science or discipline are distinguished by their ends or goals. The end of contemplative thought is knowledge; the end of practical thought is good action; and the end of productive thought is the production of objects distinct from the activity producing them.

Contemplative[10] thought is subdivided into three main subtypes: first philosophy (theology), natural philosophy, and mathematics (*Met.* VI 1 1026ª18–19, XI 7 1064ᵇ1–3; cf. *EN* VI 8 1142ª17–18). Natural philosophy or science includes a number of specific disciplines: e.g. physics, biology, psychology, and astronomy (*Phys.* II 1 192ᵇ8–12, *DC* III 1 298ª27–32, *DA* I 1 403ª27–ᵇ2). Practical thought also has three subtypes, which deal respectively with the individual, the household or family, and the polis: prudence (i.e. individual practical wisdom), household science, and politics (*EE* I 8 1218ᵇ12–14; *EN* VI 8 1141ᵇ29–32). Politics itself is divided into legislative science (*nomothetikē*) and politics in the more pedestrian sense, i.e. which is concerned with particular everyday political activities such as the preparation of decrees. The latter is further divided into parts concerned with deliberation and adjudication (see *EN* VI 8 1141ᵇ32–3). Finally, productive thought (also called *technē*, craft or art) is either useful or mimetic. The useful crafts are such things as shipbuilding, weaving, gymnastics, medicine, and agriculture, whereas the mimetic arts include painting, sculpture, music, dance, and poetry (see *Rhet.* I 11 1371ᵇ4–8, *Poet.* 1). Aristotle does not locate logic within this scheme, but seems to suggest that it is presupposed by the particular sciences since it can be applied to any subject-matter (*Met.* IV 3 1005ᵇ2–5). Later Aristotelians characterized it as the instrument (*organon*) of all the sciences, rather than as one science among many. Given this, Aristotle's classification may be represented as in Fig. 1.1.

[10]   The adjective *theōrētikos* is related to the verb *theōrein* (to contemplate, study, etc.) and the noun *theōria* (the activity of studying, contemplating, etc.). The verb has the sense of beholding something clearly and thus is not quite captured by the English term 'theorize'. The verb *theōrein* sometimes has a broader sense which includes the practical study of practical objects (see *EN* VI 1 1139ª6–8), but the adjective *theōrētikos* often contrasts with *praktikos*. When *theōrētikos* and related forms are used in the latter narrow sense, I shall translate them as 'contemplative', etc.: e.g. *ho theōrētikos bios* as 'the contemplative life'. I shall use 'theorize' or 'study' for the broader sense of *theōrein* which includes practical and productive applications, e.g. *politikē theōria* at *Pol.* VII 2 1324ª19–20. (Note that English translations of Aristotle often use 'theoretical' for the narrow sense, especially in connection with his metaphysics and epistemology.) *Praktikos* also has a wider sense which includes contemplative activity in *Pol.* VII 3 1325ᵇ16–21 (in which case I translate it as 'active').

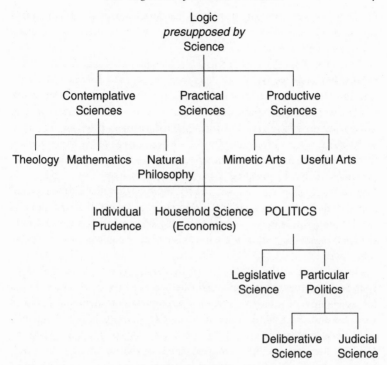

Logic
presupposed by
Science

Contemplative Sciences — Practical Sciences — Productive Sciences

Theology Mathematics Natural Philosophy Mimetic Arts Useful Arts

Individual Prudence Household Science (Economics) POLITICS

Legislative Science Particular Politics

Deliberative Science Judicial Science

FIG. 1.1. The Aristotelian Sciences

In defining politics as a science, Aristotle is also assigning it a place among the human virtues or excellences. His account of the virtues proceeds from his claims that the function of a human being is activity of the soul in accordance with reason, and that the function of the excellent (*spoudaios*) person is to perform the function of reason nobly and well (*EN* I 7 1097[b]33–1098[a]18). His analysis of the virtues accordingly presupposes a division of the soul into rational and non-rational parts (see *EN* I 13, *EE* II 1, *Pol.* I 13, VII 15). The non-rational part is further subdivided: the first subdivision (called the vegetative part), which governs the growth and nutrition of the organism, is found in all living things. But it does not share in rationality at all and is not naturally a part of human virtue (*EN* I 13 1102[b]12, 29–30). The other non-rational subdivision (called the desiring part), which motivates a human being to act, partakes of reason in some sense, for it can obey or 'listen to' the commands of reason (cf. *Pol.* VII 15 1334[b]17–20). In an incontinent person, the desiring part opposes reason and the agent thus fails to act rationally; in a

continent person, this part 'listens to' reason even though he is tempted
to do otherwise; and in a virtuous agent, the desiring part is in complete
agreement with reason.

The other main division of the soul, the part possessing reason, is also
subdivided into two parts. The superior subdivision (which I shall call
'the rational faculty') possesses reason with authority and within itself,
whereas the other part possesses it by listening to reason (1103^a2-3). The
inferior rational subdivision (evidently the desiring part of the soul, in so
far as it obeys the rational faculty) 'possesses reason' in the way a person
listens to advice from a parent or a friend, not in the way a mathematician
possesses reason in grasping a mathematical principle (cf. 1102^b31-3).
It is by exercising the rational faculty directly that the mathematician
apprehends and applies rational principles. In saying that the rational
faculty possesses reason with authority (*kuriōs*), Aristotle implies not only
that it possesses it within itself but, also, that it has authority over the
other part.

On the basis of these divisions of the soul, Aristotle begins his analysis of the virtues. He first distinguishes between the intellectual virtues
(or excellences of thought), such as contemplative wisdom and practical
wisdom, and the ethical or moral virtues (or excellences of character),
such as generosity and courage (see *EN* I 13 1103^a4-7; *EE* II 1 1220^a5-
6). The intellectual virtues are excellences of the rational faculty itself,
whereas the ethical virtues consist in the responsiveness of the second
rational subdivision (the desiring part) to the correct guidance of the
rational faculty.

The ethically virtuous person must also be in a certain condition when
he acts: 'first he must have knowledge, second he must choose [his acts]
and choose them for their own sakes, and third he must do them from a
firm and unchanging condition' (*EN* II 4 1105^a29-33). An ethical virtue
is 'a state (*hexis*) which makes a human being good and which makes
him perform his function well' (6 1106^a22-4). Virtuous agents find the
appropriate mean between extremes. For example, people can be afraid
or feel confident too much or too little, but courage enables them to have
the appropriate feelings when they ought to, about things which they
ought to, towards persons when they ought to, and for the sake of ends
and in the manner in which they ought to. Similarly, actions (like giving
to others and taking from them) admit of excess and deficiency, and the
virtue of generosity enables an agent to find the appropriate intermediate
action (see 1106^b16-24). In general, an ethical virtue is 'a state involving

choice, found in a mean which is relative to us, defined by reason and in the manner in which the person with practical wisdom would define it' ($1106^b36-1107^a2$).

The rational faculty is itself distinguished into two parts with distinctive functions: the scientific part (*to epistēmonikon*), with which we theorize about things whose principles cannot be otherwise; and the calculative part (*to logistikon*), with which we theorize about things whose principles can be otherwise (*EN* VI 2 1139^a6-8).[11] Each part has a distinctive set of intellectual virtues. The virtues of the scientific part involve the grasping of true principles. These include *nous* (intelligence, intuition, understanding) by which one grasps the true ultimate principles concerning unchangeable objects, and *epistēmē* (knowledge, science), by which one apprehends true conclusions concerning these objects. The union of these two virtues is *sophia* (contemplative wisdom) (see *EN* VI 7 1141^a17-20; *An. Post.* II 19 100^b5-12). The calculative part, which involves reasoning concerned with means and ends (*DA* III 10 433^a14), admits of yet another subdivision, because things which can be otherwise include the results of production and of action. Although Aristotle often uses *prattein* (to act) and *poiein* (to do, make, produce) in a broad sense in which the two are roughly interchangeable, he also uses them in a strict sense in which they are mutually exclusive (see *EN* VI 4 and *Pol.* I 4). In this strict sense, production (*poiēsis*) is an activity, such as housebuilding or shoemaking, carried out solely to produce an object which is distinct from the activity of producing it; whereas action (*praxis*) is performed for its own sake (*EN* VI 5 1140^b6-7).[12] The virtue concerned with production is *technē* (craft or art), identified with 'a state [of the soul] concerned with production which involves true reason' (*EN* VI 4 1140^a10, cf. 2 1139^b12-3 1139^b18).

Every craft is concerned with coming-to-be, that is, contriving or studying how something may come to be which is capable of being or not being, and which has its origin in the producer rather than in the product; for a craft is not concerned with things that are or come to be by necessity, nor with things that are or come to be by nature, for these have their origin in themselves. (1140^a10-16)

---

[11] *Met.* VI 1 1025^b18-28 marks the distinction somewhat differently: contemplative thought includes natural science (e.g. physics) which theorizes about things that change, but which have their principle of movement or rest in themselves. In the case of production and action the source of change is not in the object but in the producer or agent, respectively.

[12] Such acts (e.g. generous or courageous deeds) are done for the sake of the noble (IV 1 1120^a23-4) but they may also be, and often are, performed for the sake of another end, namely, happiness (see *EN* I 7 1097^b1-5) and the well-being of friends and homeland (IX 8 1169^a18-20).

To possess a craft or art is to apprehend universal principles. A craft is acquired through experience of individuals, and experience is needed to apply it to particular cases (*Met.* I 1 981ᵃ12–981ᵇ9). Finally, the other virtues of calculative reason are practical, that is, concerned with action (*praxis*).

The most important of these is practical wisdom (*phronēsis*), which is defined as 'a state [of the soul] involving truth and reason concerned with action regarding things that are good and bad for a human being' (*EN* VI 5 1140ᵇ4–6). A practically wise person (*phronimos*) deliberates nobly or well concerning what is good or advantageous in the sense of what promotes the good life as a whole.¹³ Practical wisdom is inseparable from ethical virtue (13 1144ᵇ30–2). This implies the unity of ethical virtue, for when practical wisdom is present all the ethical virtues are as well (1144ᵇ35–1145ᵃ2). Aristotle treats politics as a form of practical wisdom, saying that they are the same state but different in being (VI 8 1141ᵇ23–4). By this he evidently means that practical wisdom in general is concerned with deliberating about the good life, but this virtue takes different specific forms depending on *whose* life is in question. One form, prudence,¹⁴ is concerned with the well-being of the individual agent, but there are other specific forms: household science is concerned with the family, and politics with the polis as a whole (1141ᵇ30–3). Practical wisdom in all its forms is closely related to (indeed, may include) the practical virtue of *nous* (intelligence, intuition, understanding), which apprehends the particular circumstances of action, thus enabling agents to carry out their life-plans (*EN* VI 11).¹⁵ Other related virtues are *sunesis* (understanding, comprehension) which enables one to judge well or nobly whether the prescriptions of others are practically wise, and *gnōmē* (judgement, consideration) which enables one to judge others well, taking into account the particular circumstances in which they have made decisions and acted

---

¹³ Commentators disagree over whether Aristotle holds that practical wisdom has among its functions the correct apprehension of the ultimate ends of human action, or he thinks that its operations are confined to identifying means to ends embraced by the agent as a result of moral habituation. Allan (1953) argues persuasively for the former view and Bodéüs (1993: 27–38) for the latter; the issue continues to be hotly debated. My own interpretation here minimally assumes that practical wisdom involves a correct understanding (arrived at by some means or other) of the ultimate human end.

¹⁴ I translate *phronēsis* in the general sense as 'practical wisdom' and in the specific self-regarding sense as 'prudence'. The term 'prudence' suggests the ability to exercise sound judgement in practical matters, e.g. in selecting a course of action or policy, but it has a connotation of self-interestedness. On practical wisdom and prudence generally, see Den Uyl (1991).

¹⁵ *EN* VI 12 1143ᵃ35–ᵇ5 contrasts the contemplative form of *nous*, which is concerned with the first principles of demonstrative science, and the practical form, which is concerned with the contingent features of particular circumstances and is closely tied to perception.

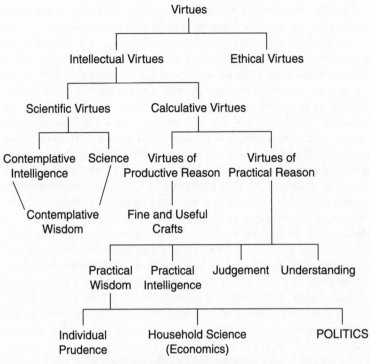

FIG. 1.2.   The Aristotelian Virtues

(*EN* VI 10–11). The latter two virtues are exercised in correct judgement (*krisis*), for example, by a jury member.

Fig. 1.2 illustrates Aristotle's distinctions among the various forms of virtue. With Fig. 1.1, this highlights some noteworthy features of Aristotelian politics. Although it is 'political science', it is not a science in the strict, narrow sense of *Nicomachean Ethics*, VI 3.[16] Because of the fluctuation and variety of its subject-matter, political science admits of much less precision (*akribeia*) than a strict science such as mathematics (I 3 1094^{b}11–27). Nor is politics a craft, because it is primarily concerned with action rather than production. Further, politics is distinguished from the individual exercise of prudence, which is concerned with the good life for the agent and which corresponds roughly to what some modern normative theorists call 'ethics' as distinguished from political or social philosophy.

---

[16] Henceforth, I use 'science' in the broad sense including political science, and 'strict science' for the narrower sense of *EN* VI 3.

However, this simplified picture needs to be qualified in several ways. First, practical wisdom generally and politics in particular share an important feature with the strict sciences: they involve an apprehension of universal principles (*EN* X 9 1180^{b}20–5).[17] For example, Aristotle's *Politics* begins with a general account of the elements contained in the composition and development of political communities. He also describes politics quite broadly as 'the philosophy of human affairs' (*hē peri ta anthrōpeia philosophia*, *EN* X 9 1181^{b}15; cf. I 2 1094^{a}26–^{b}11). As noted above, politics presupposes a knowledge of the general features of human nature, such as the parts of the soul. However, although it is based on universal truths, politics is not a 'deductive' science, but must deal with particular situations through deliberation. The nature of deliberation for Aristotle is much disputed, but the following seems to be a defensible account: The exercise of practical wisdom in the process of planning or deliberation can be completed only at the time of action. Practical intelligence brings deliberation to completion through the identification of suitable means. Practical wisdom and deliberation involve sense-perception by the agent of particular objects in the field of action, and perception of them as means of furthering the agent's ends.[18] For example, a politician might determine that a political crisis could be alleviated through the introduction of a new office which permitted the participation of formerly disenfranchised persons.

Second, although Aristotle distinguishes politics as a practical science from the productive crafts, he also compares it with crafts such as gymnastics, medicine, shipbuilding, and weaving (*Pol.* IV 1 1288^{b}19–21; VII 4 1325^{b}40–1326^{a}5; cf. I 2 1253^{a}30–1). He even counts politics as a productive science because it has good law (*eunomia*) as an end (*EE* I 5 1216^{b}16–19). Yet its highest end is not a product *per se* but noble action (*Pol.* III 9 1281^{a}2–3). The task of politics is to assist communities in attaining this end: 'to see how a polis, a class of human beings, and every other community will share in the good life and in the happiness that is possible for them' (*Pol.* VII 2 1325^{a}7–10; cf. I 2 1252^{b}30). This is done through good law: by framing a constitution and appropriate laws, by preserving the constitution and laws, and by correcting them if necessary. But in so far as its ultimate end consists in a certain form of human action (*praxis*), politics is a practical science.

---

[17] See Reeve (1992), 67–98.
[18] See F. D. Miller (1984), Den Uyl (1991), 73–8, and Reeve (1992), 67–73.

Third, Aristotle conceives of politics more broadly than moderns think of 'political philosophy'. For politics encompasses not only the thought expressed in the work we call the *Politics*[19] (see I 1 1252ᵃ15, 10 1258ᵃ22; IV 1 1288ᵇ22, VII 2 1324ᵇ32, VIII 4 1338ᵇ35) but also that of the ethical treatises (*ēthikoi logoi*), including the account of the ethical and intellectual virtues (see *EN* I 2 1094ᵃ27–8, ᵇ10–11; 3 1094ᵇ14–15, 1095ᵃ2; 4 1095ᵃ15–17, 13 1102ᵃ7–10; and cf. *EE* I 6 1216ᵇ37; VII 1 1234ᵇ22). Because it aims at the good life, politics, as Aristotle conceives of it, includes ethics as he understands it (see *EN* I 1–2).[20]

Politics aims at 'the highest goods attainable by action' (see *EN* I 4 1095ᵃ14–17; cf. 2 1094ᵃ18–28, 3 1095ᵃ5–6) and seeks to make the citizens of the polis virtuous (*EN* I 13 1102ᵃ5–15). The practitioner of this science is called 'the true politician' (*ho kat' alētheian politikos*). Aristotle acknowledges that most so-called politicians 'are not truly so called; they are not in truth politicians, for the politician is one who is disposed to choose noble acts for their own sake, while most take up the political life for the sake of money and excessive possession' (*EE* I 5 1216ᵃ23–7; cf. *EN* VI 8 1142ᵃ1–2).[21] The true politician fashions or refashions the polis in accordance with practical wisdom and the ethical virtues, particularly justice (see *Pol.* III 4 1277ᵇ25–6, VII 2 1324ᵇ32–6). Hence, Aristotle also refers to politics as political virtue (*politikē aretē*), which is exercised in political rule (*politikē archē*). This is rule over persons who are free, similar, and equal, and typically all the citizens share in ruling (*Pol.* III 4 1277ᵇ7–9; see 6 1279ᵃ8–10).

Aristotle states that 'justice is a communal virtue (*koinōnikē aretē*), which all the other [virtues] necessarily follow' (III 13 1283ᵃ38–40). In particular, to the extent that the citizens are just, they also manifest the virtue of friendship towards each other (*EE* VII 9 1241ᵇ12–17, *EN* VIII 9 1159ᵇ25–31). The treatise on justice refers to the form of justice that

[19] Either Aristotle or his ancient editors gave the work the Greek title TA POLITIKA, literally, 'the things pertaining to the polis'.

[20] See Newman (1887), ii, app. A. *An. Post.* I 33 89ᵇ9 does refer to ethical theory (*ēthikē theōria*), but this may refer to the theorizing about moral character, virtue, and practical wisdom which belongs to political science. See Bodéüs (1993), 40. Contrast John Locke: 'true politics I look on as a part of moral philosophy' (Letter to Lady Peterborough, cited by Simmons (1992), 12. n. 9).

[21] *Politikos* is also translated as 'statesman'. I use 'politician' to emphasize the link with *polis* and to keep in view that Aristotle's confidence in the *politikos* was controversial even in his own day. The politician who frames the constitution and 'lays down laws' is called a lawgiver (*nomothetēs*) (see VII 14 1333ᵃ37). It is assumed henceforth that politics includes the function of legislation.

belongs to the polis as 'political justice' (*to politikon dikaion*): 'which is present among persons who have their life in common[22] with a view to self-sufficiency, who are free and equal either proportionately or numerically' (*EN* V 6 1134ª26–8). Justice belongs to those who have law in their relations to each other, since law and the administration of justice (*dikē*) judges what is just and unjust (1134ª30–2). Hence, political justice involves 'the rule of law': 'Therefore, we do not allow a human being to rule but rather law,[23] because a human being does this [i.e. acts unjustly] for himself and becomes a tyrant. But the ruler is the guardian of justice and hence of equality' (1134ª35–ᵇ2). Summarizing this discussion, he remarks that political justice 'was according to law, and belonged to those who were naturally (*epephukei*) fitted for law, and these were persons who possessed equality in ruling and being ruled' (1134ᵇ12–15).

This important passage foreshadows the central argument of Aristotle's *Politics*. The proper aim of the polis is the happiness of its citizens, and the proper task of the science of politics is to perfect them by providing them with a just political order embodied in a constitution and laws. In order to establish and preserve such an order, the lawgivers and politicians must have a true understanding of the nature of the human beings who are to share in the polis. Proceeding from this understanding, they can form a correct conception of justice which will guide the process of legislation so that the citizens of the polis will possess rights or claims of justice which are in accordance with nature. The main task of the rest of this book is to examine this central argument of the *Politics*, which is summarized more fully in the following section.

1.3. OVERVIEW OF ARISTOTLE'S ARGUMENT

The principal task of politics as a practical science is to determine what is the best constitution *simpliciter* or, failing that, the best constitution for a given polis, taking into account its population and natural resources. Another function of politics is to study the inferior types of constitution, how they arise and how they may be preserved or corrected.[24] Politics

---

[22] I generally translate *koinōnein* as 'to have in common', in order to retain the connection with *koinon*, 'common', *koinōnia*, 'community', and so forth. Where this translation is too cumbersome, I use 'to share', 'to participate', etc.

[23] Reading *nomon* with manuscript Mᵇ, rather than *logon*.

[24] These functions of politics, set forth in *Politics*, IV 1–2, are discussed more fully in Sect. 5.6 below.

discharges these practical tasks in order to promote the good life for human beings (see *Pol.* VII 1 1323ᵃ14–16; cf. IV 11 1295ᵃ25–31) and pre-supposes a theory of human nature. Hence Aristotle's frequent appeals, explicit and implicit, to the concept of nature (*phusis*) in the *Politics*, especially in its opening chapters.

Of paramount importance for Aristotle's political theory are the doctrines defended in *Politics*, I 2, that human beings are by nature political animals and that the polis exists by nature (see Chapter 2). Both claims presuppose that the polis is a community in which individuals must co-operate in order to attain self-sufficiency and thereby lead the good life. There are important similarities between a polis and a living organism, which is for Aristotle the cardinal example of a thing that exists by nature. An organism such as a human being or a horse has within it an organizing and guiding formal principle: its soul. The polis also has within it a formal principle by which it is organized and governed: its constitution. As the orator Isocrates (436–338 BC) pronounced, 'The soul of a polis is nothing other than its constitution.'²⁵ An organism can function well and be healthy, or function badly and be sick; hence, it can live in a natural condition (*kata phusin*) or in an unnatural condition (*para phusin*). Similarly, the polis can exist in a natural condition or an unnatural condition. Thus Aristotle's evaluation of the polis appeals to an objective normative principle, not merely to convention or opinion.

This principle is expressed in his theory of justice (see Chapter 3). A constitution is the particular embodiment of a general standard of justice. If this standard conforms to natural justice, the constitution is 'correct'; if not, it is 'deviant'. As a practical science, politics is intended to provide guidance to politicians and lawgivers: i.e. to enable them to determine what would be the best possible constitution in the most favourable of circumstances ('the polis of our prayers'); what would be the best con-stitution that most existing polises could practically strive to attain; how to improve existing constitutions; and how to preserve constitutions once they have been established. In each instance the politician should, as far as is feasible, bring the polis into a natural condition or maintain it in this condition. A polis is in a natural condition when it aims at justice and the common advantage. Aristotle represents the basic problem of politics as a dispute over who in the polis has a just claim or right to be a citizen and over what rights the citizens should have. Political philosophy solves this

---

²⁵ *Areopagiticus* 14 1. Cf. Aristotle, *Pol.* III 3 1276ᵇ7–8 and IV 4 1291ᵃ24–8. The analogy between soul and constitution is also central to Plato's *Republic*.

problem by providing the correct theory of justice. On this basis true politicians can establish a constitution and laws protecting individual rights
which are based on nature and justice (see Chapter 4).

The implications of this argument are developed in Aristotle's constitutional theory (see Chapter 5). The polis is a multitude of citizens under
a constitution, and citizens are defined as members of the polis possessing in common specific political rights and functions. The constitution is
distinguished into parts—deliberative, official, judicial—which are themselves composed of modes, i.e. specific ways of assigning political rights
and duties to the citizens. These modes may be evaluated in terms of
Aristotle's theory of justice and constitutional correctness. The best constitution will serve the common advantage in the sense of promoting
the happiness of each and every citizen. The ends of some of the members
of the polis must not be advanced at the expense of others; thus the ends
of the ruled must not be sacrificed in order to benefit the rulers. In this
sense, political justice has a fundamentally individualistic character (see
Chapter 6). Even in the case of inferior constitutions the politician should
be guided by considerations of justice and rights, and, as a practical matter, Aristotle believes that injustice is a destabilizing property of political communities (see Chapters 7–8). In addition to defining political
institutions, the correct constitution and laws should also protect other
rights such as private property (see Chapter 9).

According to the foregoing overview, Aristotle takes seriously the question of whether political systems respect the rights (just claims) of individuals, and he distinguishes between 'natural' and merely conventional
rights. However, this interpretation needs to be qualified.[26] For Aristotle's
emphasis on natural justice and rights is not intended to deny the contribution of human reason or even of convention and contingency. Nor does
the concern for justice override all other considerations on Aristotle's
view, for he is prepared to accept 'second-best' or even worse solutions
when there are exorbitantly high costs or risks involved in trying to attain
the best constitution, which would, ideally, respect all of the (naturally)
just claims of the citizens. Nevertheless, the Aristotelian argument supports
a theory of natural justice which politicians should employ as far as is
feasible in their deliberations.

Moreover, it would be misleading to ascribe to Aristotle a theory of
'natural rights' in the same sense as modern theorists like John Locke.
Aristotle would not agree that individuals start from a non-political state

---

[26] See also Sect. 4.1 below.

of nature in which they already possess a robust set of natural rights merely by existing, or that these natural rights are pre-existing claims which must be subsequently recognized by a political constitution. Rather, on his view, the political community is a naturally existing phenomenon which may be in a natural or unnatural condition. When the polis is in a natural condition, it is governed according to natural justice and its citizens possess rights 'based on nature' (*kata phusin*). In this qualified sense, Aristotle is an ancestor of the natural-rights tradition.

Many writers object that it is misleading and anachronistic to impute 'rights' in any sense to Aristotle; they contend that he does not speak in terms of 'rights' and that any concept of rights is alien to his thought. This book argues that this objection is fundamentally mistaken. Chapter 4 in particular exhibits a number of Aristotelian locutions which have a logical force comparable to modern 'rights' terms and shows that these locutions were used to make rights claims in legal and political contexts. On a deeper, theoretical level this book as a whole argues that rights have a central place in Aristotle's politics because he understands justice as the virtue permitting co-operation for mutual advantage. As a co-operative association a just polis must recognize the claims of each of its contributing members. To recognize 'rights' in Aristotle is to acknowledge the respect for individuality which is a central theme of his political theory.

1.4. ARISTOTLE'S PRESUPPOSITIONS

The argument outlined in the preceding section presupposes central doctrines in Aristotle's political philosophy. Several of these principles make their presence felt in the opening lines of the *Politics*:

Since we see that every polis is a sort of community and that every community is established for the sake of some good (for everyone does everything for the sake of what they believe to be good), it is clear that every [community] aims at some good, and the [community] which is most authoritative of all and includes all the others [aims at a good] most of all and [aims at] the most authoritative good. This is what is called the polis or political community. (I 1 1252ᵃ1–7)

Four doctrines implicit here are of special importance: (1) human beings have natural ends or functions (the principle of teleology); (2) the most authoritative good for human beings consists in the fullest possible realization of their nature (the principle of perfection); (3) the community should have authority over its members (the principle of community); and (4) the community can attain its ends only through rule by human agents (the principle of rulership). This section briefly introduces each of these presuppositions, though their full import will become evident only as the argument unfolds in subsequent chapters.

The principle of teleology

According to Aristotle substances or primary existents have a nature, i.e. an end or *telos* (*Phys.* II 1 192^{b}32–3, 2 194^{a}28–9). Following tradition I refer to this as their 'natural end'. The natural end is a causal principle used in Aristotle's strict sciences to explain how a thing comes into being and maintains itself (8 199^{b}15–18). The end of a thing is also identified with its function (*ergon*) (*EE* II 1 1219^{a}8; cf. *DC* II 3 286^{a}8–9, *PA* IV 12 694^{b}13–14). Further, Aristotle states that everything is defined in terms of its function (*Meteor.* IV 12 390^{a}10–11). Natural teleology also has an important place in Aristotle's practical science. For example, the definition of the human good or happiness in the ethical treatises proceeds from an analysis of the function of a human being (*EN* I 7 1097^{b}24–5) or the function of the soul (*EE* II 1 1219^{a}5). Again, the *Politics* claims that the polis exists by nature because it is in a sense an end or nature (I 2 1252^{b}30–2), that 'nature does nothing in vain' (1253^{a}9), and that everything (including a human being) is defined by its function and power (1253^{a}23). The import of these claims is investigated in Chapter 2.

The principle of perfection

A second presupposition of Aristotle's argument is that the best life for human beings consists in the attainment of their natural ends, i.e. in the full realization of their nature. This normative ideal is explicitly endorsed in the *Politics*: 'What is most choiceworthy for each individual is always the highest it is possible for him to attain' (VII 14 1333^{a}29–30; cf. *EN* X 7 1177^{b}33–4). This state of full self-realization is perfection or completeness (*teleiotēs*), which is the full normal functioning of a thing relative to the capacities specific to its natural kind.[27] The prescription that one ought to strive for perfection may be called 'the principle of perfection'. Aristotle's application of this to human affairs may be called 'the principle of *eudaimonia*' because he regards human perfection as consisting

---

[27] 'Perfect' (*teleion*) is opposed to 'mutilated' or 'defective' (*pēron*, *pērōmon*) (see *DA* II 4 415^{a}27). This contextual use of 'perfection' contrasts with the common English use of 'perfectionist', implying a demand for more than can be realistically expected.

in *eudaimonia* (happiness or flourishing). Happiness is the activity of the soul according to reason (or not without reason), i.e. activity in accordance with the most perfect (or complete) virtue or excellence (*EN* I 7 1098ᵃ7–17).²⁸ The general principle of perfection has two types of practical application: when human beings act as individual agents, they ought to strive for their own perfection (individual perfection); when they co-operate with each other in a polis, they ought to strive in concert for the perfection of the whole polis (political perfection). Aristotle evidently endorses both applications of the principle of perfection when he says, for example, 'that way of life is best, both separately for each individual and in common for polises, which is equipped with virtue . . .' (*Pol.* VII 1 1323ᵇ40–1324ᵃ1; cf. 2 1324ᵃ23–5 and 1325ᵃ7–10).²⁹ Aristotle recognizes that a thing may fall short of perfection in varying degrees. He accordingly endorses a related normative doctrine which may be called 'the principle of proximity': It is best to attain perfection, but, failing that, a thing is better in proportion as it is nearer to the end (see *DC* II 12 292ᵇ17–19;³⁰ cf. *GA* II 1 731ᵇ24–732ᵃ11).

The principle of community

On Aristotle's view, the community which is the most inclusive is also the most authoritative. This is explicitly asserted in the opening lines of the *Politics* cited above. A community (*koinōnia*) is a group which co-operates for the sake of some common good, e.g. meals or property (I 1 1252ᵃ2, VII 8 1328ᵃ25–6).³¹ The claim that the polis is the most inclusive community is crucial for the argument that the polis is 'complete' and attains 'the goal of self-sufficiency', so that it can 'exist for the sake of the good life' (*Pol.* I 2 1252ᵇ27–30). A thing is self-sufficient (*autarkēs*) if, when isolated, it is lacking nothing in order to perform its function (cf. *EN* I 7 1097ᵇ14–15, *Pol.* VII 5 1326ᵇ29–30). The polis is self-sufficient in that it provides the citizens not only with the necessary equipment but also, more importantly, the habituation required for a virtuous life. As the poet Simonides

²⁸ *Teleion* often implies 'complete' as well as 'perfect', especially when it involves self-sufficiency. In some contexts, however, it is disputed as to whether *teleion* entails 'complete', for example, when Aristotle applies the superlative form to happiness and contemplation. On the senses of *teleion* see Richardson (1992).

²⁹ This statement implies that individual perfection and political perfection are in a sense the same; the sense in which they are the same is considered in Sect. 6.6 below.

³⁰ Roderick Long called this passage to my attention.

³¹ On Aristotle's concept of community, see Finley (1977), 144, and Yack (1993), ch. 1.

(*c*.556–*c*.468 BC) said, 'The polis teaches the man.'[32] To secure the good
life, it must include the basic relationships of the household and villages,
as well as many other forms of community: schools and educational
groups, fraternal associations, religious communities, and, most importantly
for Aristotle, close personal friendships. In speaking of the polis as 'most
authoritative', however, he implies that the individual should be subject
to the authority of the political community (the principle of community).
Because he views the polis both as the most inclusive community and as
the most authoritative, it is apparent that he does not draw the distinction
between state and society which is made by many modern political theorists.
For example, Max Weber defines the state as an association possessing a
monopoly over the legitimized use of coercive force within a definite geographical area.[33] So understood, the state is but one part of the society,
the all inclusive community which does not, as such, have an authoritative
organization. In contrast, Aristotle's concept of polis is, in effect, a 'fused'
concept, combining features of the state and society as moderns understand
them.

The principle of rulership

On Aristotle's view, the good polis is a well-ordered community, and the
political order must be produced and maintained by a ruler (*archōn*) who
is in a position of authority. The assumption is easy for Aristotle to make,
especially given the link between the Greek word for 'order', *taxis*, and
the verb, 'to order', *tassein* (*tattein* in Attic Greek). A typical example of
a *taxis* is the order of an army which is imposed by a commander (see
Met. XII 10 1075ª11–25). Throughout the *Politics* Aristotle assumes that
order within the polis depends on the exercise of political authority by
some individual or group of individuals (the principle of rulership). The
principle of community and the principle of rulership are distinct but complementary doctrines: the former states that individuals should be subject
to the authority of the community, whereas the latter holds that some
individual or group should rule or govern over the other members of the
community. A theory of popular sovereignty might accept the former principle but not the latter, but Aristotle believes that an authoritative order
requires a ruling principle at the head. Similarly, in his natural philosophy
Aristotle maintains that a complex whole must be unified by a principle
which is a ruler or natural authority (*kurios kata phusin*). The soul serves

---

[32] Simonides, fr. 95 (Edmonds).   [33] Weber (1947), 156.

as such an authority over the material elements in a living organism (see *DA* I 5 410ᵇ10–15, and cf. *Pol.* I 5 1254ᵃ34–6).

These four principles of teleology, perfection, community, and rulership are major presuppositions for the central argument of Aristotle's *Politics*, which is outlined above in Section 1.3. The following Chapters 2–9 offer a detailed reconstruction of this argument. Chapters 2–4 examine the theoretical foundations, focusing on three central elements: nature, justice, and rights. Chapters 5–9 consider how the theory is supposed to be applied to particular political circumstances in framing constitutions, establishing laws, and solving the particular problems of political governance. This discussion accepts without reservation the four underlying doctrines discussed in this section: teleology, perfection, community, and rulership. However, these doctrines were controversial in Aristotle's own time, and they have frequently been assailed by modern political theorists. Chapter 10 accordingly offers a critical assessment of these underlying doctrines from the standpoint of modern philosophy and science. The final chapter also reconsiders Aristotle's distinctive contribution to the theory of human rights.

1.5. ON INTERPRETATION

There are different ways of seeking to interpret and assess the writings of an ancient thinker such as Aristotle. One method, that of the strict commentator, is to try as far as possible to explicate his thought in his own terms and within his own context. On this approach one tries to state the problems as Aristotle understood them and to explicate concepts and to fill out or extend arguments using notions and techniques that would have been familiar to him. Criticisms of his analyses and arguments should also be framed in a way that would, or should, have been comprehensible and credible to him. There is an obvious need for literal exegesis of the sort to which nineteenth- and twentieth-century commentators have aspired. A second method, which may be called 'reconstruction' (also called 'philosophical scholarship' or 'doxography'), is to try to understand the text not only on its own terms but also by applying external concepts, theories, and techniques. This often includes a comparative methodology, exploring similarities or differences with other modes of thought, such as modern viewpoints. One may also consider the further implications of a philosopher's thought, at times pressing it beyond the point he might have considered necessary or even possible. A third approach is to philosophize in the tradition, more or less broadly understood, of a given philosopher. One adopts certain distinctive principles or methods and treats them as points of departure, not concerning oneself overly with issues of accurate exegesis or anachronism. Such theorizing is often denoted with the cautionary prefix 'neo-', e.g. 'neo-Aristotelian'.

There are in fact no sharp lines between these three hermeneutical methods, and many studies of Aristotle use more than one method.[34] For example, recent essays on *De Anima* combine close textual exegesis with debate over whether Aristotle can be described in modern terms e.g. 'materialist', 'dualist', or 'functionalist'. This study of Aristotle's political philosophy also combines these different methods, but it is for the most part a work of reconstruction. I think that it is correct to view Aristotle as a forerunner of modern theorists of justice, and, as indicated above, I argue that it is not anachronistic to attribute to him a concept of rights. The method assumes that a concept or a claim may have a place in a philosopher's thought even though it may not be articulated in terms corresponding precisely to ours. Admittedly, the method of reconstruction runs the risk of misrepresenting or distorting Aristotle by importing ideas or imposing structures that are inimical to his thought. I have been wary of this hazard throughout the writing of this book, but the reader must judge whether I have successfully avoided it. Only the last chapter is primarily concerned with the 'neo-Aristotelian' project.

This study focuses on the writings of Aristotle although I frequently compare him to other thinkers both ancient and modern. Although my principal text is the *Politics*, I also make frequent reference to other works of Aristotle, especially the *Nicomachean Ethics* and *Eudemian Ethics*. The relations among these three works (all of which belong to 'politics' or political science in Aristotle's sense) are controversial. Many scholars hold that the *Eudemian Ethics* was written before the *Nicomachean*, and that the 'common books' (*EN* V–VII = *EE* IV–VI) originally belonged to the *Eudemian Ethics* and were later transposed to the *Nicomachean*. These common books include two books especially relevant to the study of Aristotle's politics: a treatise on justice (*EN* V = *EE* IV) and a treatise on intellectual virtue (*EN* VI = *EE* V). I follow the practice of referring to the common books as part of the *Nicomachean Ethics* (while keeping in view their likely connection with the *Eudemian*). There is also some

---

[34] A similar threefold distinction is made by Charles (1984), pp. ix–x, and by Rasmussen and Den Uyl (1991), p. xv.

evidence that the *Politics* was written after the *Eudemian Ethics* and before the *Nicomachean.*[35] However, Aristotle seems to have intended the *Nicomachean Ethics* to be read before the *Politics,* which is partially described in the final lines of the *Nicomachean.* In addition, I refer to the *Magna Moralia,* which was probably by an early Peripatetic rather than Aristotle, but which may be used 'with the necessary circumspection' (Cooper (1975), p. xi). Finally, I make reference to the papyrus text, which is widely thought to be the *Constitution of Athens* attributed to Aristotle by ancient tradition. However, the *Constitution* differs from the *Politics* in style and some details, and may well be by a pupil of Aristotle. None the less, because it was evidently written during Aristotle's final stay in Athens and it shows his influence, it is a valuable source for a study of his political theory.[36]

There are also scholarly controversies concerning the *Politics* itself, as to how Aristotle himself intended the treatise to be organized. Based upon cross-references within the *Politics,* Book III is, as W. L. Newman remarks, 'the centre round which the whole treatise is grouped',[37] for the other books, except the first and last, refer to it. Books I–II–III form a continuous sequence as do Books IV–V–VI and Books VII–VIII. However, there are no certain references between the latter two sequences so that Aristotle himself may not have settled on their mutual relation. As an added complication the final sentence of Book III resembles the first sentence of Book VII, prompting scholars in the past to conjecture that Book VII originally followed III, but subsequently Books IV–V–VI were for some reason inserted between them.[38] At any rate, the books do not form a strict linear sequence but only the partial ordering shown in Fig. 1.3. This partial ordering follows the internal logic of the treatise, stays within the pattern of cross-references, and emphasizes the central position of Book III.

Ulrich von Wilamowitz-Moellendorff suggested that the difficulties in

---

[35] The *Politics* contains six references to 'the ethical treatises' (*ta ēthika, hoi ēthikoi logoi*), of which four are to the 'common books' (II 2 1261ᵃ31 is to *EN* V 5 1132ᵇ31–4; III 9 1280ᵃ18 is to *EN* V 3 1131ᵃ14–24; III 12 1282ᵇ20 is to *EN* V 3 1131ᵃ11–14; and IV 11 1295ᵃ36 is to *EN* VII 13 1153ᵇ9–21), and two are probably to the *Eudemian Ethics* (VII 13 1332ᵃ8 most probably refers to *EE* II 1 1219ᵃ38–9, ᵇ1–2, though it may refer to *EN* I 7 1098ᵃ16–18, 10 1101ᵃ14–16; VII 13 1332ᵃ22 most probably refers to *EE* VIII 3 1248ᵇ26–7, but it may refer to *MM* II 9 1207ᵇ31–3).

[36] See Rhodes (1981), 58–63. A papyrus text of the *Constitution of Athens* was acquired by the British museum in 1888–9 and published by F. G. Kenyon in 1891.

[37] Newman (1887–1902), ii. p. xxxi.

[38] Some editors, including Newman, rather confusingly alter the ordering of the books, renumbering VII–VIII as 'IV–V' and IV–V–VI as 'VI–VII–VIII'.

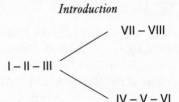

FIG. 1.3. Order of Books of Aristotle's *Politics*

the organization of the *Politics* stemmed from the fact that the central books IV–V–VI were written later than Books VII–VIII. This idea was developed in detail by Werner Jaeger and issued in a flood of ink over whether different chronological strata are detectable in the *Politics*.[39] The aim of such investigations is to reconcile alleged inconsistencies of approach or of doctrine in a given work. However, although I am inclined to agree that Books IV–V–VI do contain later material (for example, regarding the classification of constitutions), I am not convinced that there are major inconsistencies involving fundamental principles in the *Politics* requiring the postulation of different chronological strata to explain them away.[40] The fact that Aristotle uses a variety of different approaches in the *Politics*—historical, aporetic, classificatory, expository—does not in itself pose a difficulty, because he could very well have taken a variety of them without contradicting himself. Moreover, different problems arising in different contexts may call for different but compatible solutions. The following chapters seek to show that despite some discrepancies the different parts of the *Politics* belong to a unitary and coherent argument.

[39] See Wilamowitz (1893), i. 355–6, and Jaeger (1948), ch. 10. Schütrumpf (1980) (1991), i. 60–6, is a recent defender of the developmental interpretation. Rowe (1991) provides an overview of the controversy. [40] See Sect. 5.6 below.

PART I

Political Theory

2

Nature and Politics

2.1. ARISTOTLE'S POLITICAL NATURALISM

Aristotle's politics may be characterized as 'naturalistic', in the sense that it assigns a fundamental role to the concept of nature (*phusis*) in the explanation and evaluation of its subject-matter. Indeed, naturalism, in this sense, is a dominant theme throughout his philosophy. This chapter considers whether the main claims about nature in Aristotle's politics are consistent with each other and with his general philosophy of nature. This introductory section points out some of the difficulties which need to be addressed by a satisfactory interpretation.

In Aristotle's metaphysics, substances, the entities which have primary reality, exist by nature or have an internal source of change (*Phys.* II 1 192^{b}32–3; cf. *Met.* VII 7 1032^{a}12–19).[1] This is a teleological doctrine, because things that exist by nature (of which the central cases are living organisms) act for a final cause (II 8 199^{b}15–18). 'Final cause' is an expression devised by the Latin philosophical tradition to translate the Greek *telos* (end) and *aitia* (cause). Aristotle also equates the end with that-for-the-sake-of-which (*hou heneka*) or the good (*agathon*).[2] The use of 'cause' is somewhat misleading because when we think of different causes, we think of competing incompatible explanations (e.g. was the death a murder, suicide, or an accident?). In Aristotle's sense of 'cause', the same thing or state of affairs can have several different causes at once. For example, a statue has a material cause (the bronze from which it is

---

[1] This needs some qualification. A natural substance is a compound of matter (ultimately of the basic elements) and of form. The nature or internal cause of a thing is its form (*Phys.* II 1 193^{a}30–^{b}18). In living organisms this form is their soul (*DA* II 1 412^{a}19–21). The *Metaphysics* argues further that the form or essence of a natural substance is its substance (VII 17 1041^{b}27–33), implying that on the deepest level form is the primary reality. Further, naturalism applies only to substances other than God, who is immaterial and immutable (*Met.* XII 7 1073^{a}3–13).

[2] All three descriptions occur at *Phys.* II 3 195^{a}23–5. Aristotle also identifies the end of a thing with its function (*ergon*). There is a dispute among interpreters as to whether Aristotle thinks that X is a final cause because X is good, or vice versa. See Gotthelf (1988) and Sect. 10.2 below.

cast), a formal cause (its shape), an efficient or moving cause (the sculptor), and a final cause (the purpose of the sculptor). Aristotle applies the language of final cause to two different sorts of cases: to actions done consciously for some purpose, e.g. a polis goes to war in order to rule over another polis (II 7 198^{a}19–20); and natural processes which are not the result of deliberation or thought, e.g. plants send their roots down rather than up in order to obtain nourishment (8 199^{a}26–30). Aristotle emphasizes the parallels between these two sorts of final causation (*DA* II 4 415^{b}15–22), but he also distinguishes them.[3] In conscious production there is a form in the soul of the human producer, but, in natural processes, there is a form in the parent and a potential to develop into a form, which is internal to the offspring. An olive seed grows into a mature olive tree because it contains a potential to develop in this way which it inherited from previously existing olive trees, and the form or potential for form is distinct from the elements (earth, air, fire, and water) which are present in the olive tree at any stage of its development (see *DA* II 4 415^{b}28–416^{a}18; *PA* I 1 640^{a}19–26). Hence, things existing by nature (in particular, all ensouled organisms) are said to have an internal source of movement or change, which guides them to the end which is specific to their natural kind.

In Aristotle's politics, the polis or political community exists by nature (*Pol.* I 2 1252^{b}30), a view closely connected with the thesis that human beings are by nature political animals (1253^{a}1–3). Like other naturally existing things, a polis possesses a form, its constitution (III 3 1276^{b}1–11). To the extent that this constitution is in a natural condition (*kata phusin*), it is correct or just, and to the extent that it is in an unnatural condition (*para phusin*), it is deviant or unjust (III 6 1279^{a}17–7 1279^{b}10; cf. 17 1287^{b}39–41). Aristotle further claims that the polis is by nature prior to the individuals which constitute it (I 2 1253^{a}25–6). It remains to be seen whether his political naturalism commits him to the thesis that the polis possesses a nature of its own, as natural substances do, which is separate from the natures of the individuals which constitute it (see Section 2.3). But it is clear, at any rate, that he regards political life as deeply rooted

---

[3] See Gotthelf (1987) for an illuminating discussion of this distinction. Aristotle's teleology has been frequently misunderstood by critics who have taken him to be imputing consciousness to natural processes; cf. Lennox (1992). This confusion is encouraged in the original Oxford translation: cf. the translation of *Phys.* II 5 197^{a}7–8, 'purpose (*prohairesis*) involves intelligent reflection', with that of II 8 199^{b}26–8, 'It is absurd to suppose that purpose (*heneka tou*) is not present because we do not observe the agent deliberating.' In the former passage Barnes (1984) has replaced 'purpose' with 'choice'.

in human nature and human nature as requiring political life for its fulfilment.

The difficulties in interpreting Aristotle's political theory become evident when one compares his views to those of modern political philosophers. During the Renaissance the idea gained currency of 'the state as a calculated conscious creation, as a work of art'.[4] This is also a fundamental theme of the *Leviathan* of Thomas Hobbes (1588–1679).[5] Rather than treating the political state as natural, he contrasts it with a state of nature, a theoretical construct which is supposed to be independent of and prior to the political state. In this state of nature, individuals are supposed to be governed by natural law and to possess natural rights. The political state is justified only if it would be rational for individuals to move from the hypothetical state of nature to the political state. Hobbes's state-of-nature analysis thoroughly contradicts Aristotle's political theory. For it maintains that human beings are *not* political animals by nature; on the contrary, they are unqualifiedly capable of living outside a political context, endowed with natural rights. It also implies that it is possible for individuals to start from a non-political condition and then bring the state into existence. Hence, it implies that individuals are prior to the state, rather than vice versa. Finally, it asserts that the political community is a human creation or artefact, a point which Hobbes makes at the outset of *Leviathan*: '. . . by Art is created that great LEVIATHAN called a COMMON-WEALTH, or STATE, (in latine CIVITAS) which is but an Artificial Man . . .'[6] This seems flatly inconsistent with the Aristotelian claim that the polis exists by nature.

However, these seemingly clear differences become muddied by other features of Aristotle's account. In the same sentence in which he concludes his argument for the naturalness of political life, he praises the human founder of the polis as a great benefactor (*Pol.* I 2 1253ᵃ29–31). The polis is brought into being when its constitution is established, and this is the work of practical rationality embodied in the lawgiver (i.e. politician). Aristotle's description of the lawgiver as a craftsman (*dēmiourgos*), which implies that politics is like a craft (*technē*), seems to agree with Hobbes's view of the state as an artefact (see *Pol.* II 12, VII 4). The argument in

---

[4] Burckhardt (1960), 41.

[5] John Locke (1632–1704) agrees with Hobbes on many points, particularly in using state-of-nature and social-contract analyses as points of departure for political theory. Nevertheless, Locke's view is closer to Aristotle's in some respects (see Sects. 2.6 and 4.5–6 below).   [6] Hobbes, *Leviathan* (1968), Introd., 1.

Politics, I 2, that the polis emerges out of pre-existing communities, also seems to be in curious agreement with the state-of-nature hypothesis. Further, Aristotle is cognizant of ancient Greek counterparts to Hobbes's social-contract theory (see III 9 1280^{b}10–11). From Hobbes's point of view, Aristotle seems confused. If the polis is a product of human reason, how can it be due to nature? And if human beings can exist outside a political community, which is itself a human creation, how can they be political animals and how can the polis be prior by nature to them? These are not easy questions to answer. Indeed, in a recent article David Keyt has sided with Hobbes, concluding that the problems are intractable and that 'there is a blunder at the very root of Aristotle's political philosophy'.[7] On the other hand, we should not forget Aristotle's admonition that political science, due to the complex and fluctuating character of human affairs, possesses less precision (*akribeia*) than a science like mathematics (*EN* I 3 1094^{b}11–27). Certain terms such as 'nature', 'prior', and 'political' may be used in an imprecise manner. Keeping this observation in view, the remainder of this chapter expounds and defends Aristotle's main claims within the context of his philosophy of nature.

2.2. HUMAN NATURE AS POLITICAL

The precise meaning of Aristotle's thesis that a human being is by nature a political animal is the subject of controversy, since Aristotle evidently advances the claim in different ways in different contexts.[8] Scholars disagree over whether 'political animal' should be interpreted in a narrow or a broad sense.

According to the narrow interpretation a *politikon zōion* is a polis-dwelling animal, or an animal capable of dwelling in a polis. In this sense, only human beings are political animals. (Indeed, in the strictest sense, some human beings, such as barbarians, would not even be 'political' in this sense; see *Pol.* III 9 1280^{a}32–4.) In speaking of animals such as bees or ants as political animals, Aristotle must be 'speaking loosely' or equivocally. This interpretation[9] has in its favour the etymological connection

---

[7] Keyt (1991*b*), 118. Ambler (1985) also alleges a conflict between the apparent naturalism in *Pol.* I and Aristotle's account of political authority.

[8] *Pol.* I 2 1253^{a}1–3, 7–9; III 6 1278^{b}17–21; *HA* I 1 487^{b}33–488^{a}14; *EN* I 7 1097^{b}8–11; VII 12 1162^{a}17–19; IX 9 1169^{b}17–19; *EE* VI 10 1242^{a}22–7.

[9] Favoured by Arendt (1958), 27; Mulgan (1977), 23–4; Schütrumpf (1991), i. 215–19, and Keyt (1991*b*), 123–4.

between *politikon* and *polis*,[10] but it has the difficulty that Aristotle evidently uses 'political animal' in the broader, biological sense at *Pol.* I 2 1253ᵃ7–9: 'That a human being is a political animal more (*mallon*) than any bee or gregarious animal is clear' (cf. the use of *mallon* at *Met.* VII 3 1029ᵃ29–30). This implies that 'political animal' is applicable to animals other than humans.[11] This difficulty can evidently be avoided by adopting a wider, biologically based understanding of 'political animal'. This interpretation[12] relies on the account of *HA* I 1 488ᵃ7–10. 'Political [animals] are those of which the function [*ergon*] becomes some one common thing, which not all the gregarious animals do. Such are the human being, the bee, the wasp, the ant, and the crane.' On this interpretation, 'political' applies to other kinds of animals besides humans, but human beings allegedly satisfy the definition more fully.

Nevertheless, the problem seems to remain that, in the claim that *humans* are political animals, the scope of 'political animal' seems to shift in different contexts. In some cases 'political animal' seems narrowly tied to the polis, as when it is contrasted with 'household animal'. If these shifts are merely arbitrary and equivocal, it would seem impossible to determine which interpretation best fits *Politics*, I 2. However, the comparative expression 'more political' at 1253ᵃ7–9 suggests a solution. It is possible to satisfy the definition of 'political' as 'having some one common function' to a greater or lesser degree. Having a common function involves co-operation, and it is possible to engage in more complex and effective forms of co-operation to the extent that the co-operative group's members are rationally co-ordinating their activity. A beehive satisfies the definition to some extent, a human household satisfies it to a greater extent, and a human polis satisfies it most of all. (The argument for this is examined below.) The same thing may be called 'large' in one context and not 'large' in another—e.g. when it is contrasted with an even larger object. Similarly, a human being *qua* member of a household may be described as political, but when there is a contrast with a human being *qua* member of a polis, we may call the former a 'household' animal and the latter a 'political' animal. To interpret the claim that a human is a

---

[10] See also *EN* VII 12 1162ᵃ17–18 where *politikon* is contrasted with *sunduastikon* (capable of coupling or mating), and *EE* VII 10 1242ᵃ22–7 where it is opposed to *oikonomikon* (capable of living in a household) and *koinōnikon* (capable of community).

[11] Mulgan (1977) contends that Aristotle has conflated the two senses in this passage.

[12] Favoured by Kullmann (1991), Cooper (1990), and Depew (forthcoming*a* and forthcoming*b*).

political animal, therefore, we must take into account the specific context of the claim.

What, then, are the grounds for the claim that human beings are *by nature* political animals? It is noteworthy that Aristotle's argument proceeds from the teleological premiss that 'nature, as we say, does nothing in vain' (*Pol.* I 2 1253ᵃ9). The claim thus presupposes Aristotle's natural teleology. The nature of a thing is an internal causal factor with an end or final cause (see *Phys.* II 7 198ᵇ1–9; 8 199ᵇ32–3). The growth of a living organism from embryo to adult is explained in terms of potentialities within it which are actualized when it is fully developed. Analogously, Aristotle's argument that human beings are by nature political depends upon the claim that they possess innate potentialities for the political life. The latter claim is complex, involving two distinct components: that human beings possess innate capacities essential for the political life (see *Pol.* I 2 1253ᵃ7–18), and that they have the innate impulse to live in political communities (see 1253ᵃ29–30; cf. III 6 1278ᵇ15–30).

The argument from political capacities

The argument at I 2 1253ᵃ7–18 explicitly invokes Aristotle's natural teleology: nature does nothing in vain. Only humans have speech (*logos*);[13] other animals have mere voice. The nature of non-human animals has developed sufficiently so that they have a perception of the painful and pleasant and the capacity to signify them to one another; e.g. because nature has given a young animal the capacity to perceive pain, nature has also given it voice so that it can communicate this perception to its parents. Human speech exists in order to reveal the advantageous and harmful, and hence also the just and the unjust; for human beings, in distinction from other animals, have a perception of good and bad, just and unjust. The community of good and bad, just and unjust, etc., is the basis for a household and polis. This is evidence that a human being is a political animal more than any bee or any gregarious animal.

In this argument 'political animal' can be understood in terms of the broader, biological sense.[14] Political animals are able to co-operate with a view to a common end or function, and through communication humans are able to co-operate more effectively and at a higher level than other animals. For human beings alone possess moral perception, and above all

---

[13] *Logos* can mean 'reason' as well as 'speech' or 'language'. The context indicates that human speech involves practical rationality.

[14] As argued in Cooper (1990) and Depew (forthcoming*b*).

the perception of advantage and justice.[15] This enables human beings to co-operate in the pursuit of goods higher than mere pleasure and pain (most notably, ethical and intellectual virtues), and to do so by means of far more complex and effective social arrangements than bees or ants. Aristotle's claim that it is nature that has endowed human beings with the capacity for speech and moral perception seems open to criticism.[16] For he holds that moral perception—the ability to perceive the just decision or morally correct course of action—differs from sense perception. Humans possess moral perception only if they to some extent possess ethical virtue and practical wisdom, which they acquire not by nature but through habituation.[17] Further, moral habituation and education are normally fostered by the laws of the polis (*EN* X 9 1180ᵃ14–ᵇ28), so that humans could not possess them by nature.

This is a serious internal criticism, but Aristotle has resources to respond to it, for he distinguishes different levels at which a capacity or potentiality may be actualized. He illustrates this with the example of knowledge.[18] A human being's capacity for geometrical knowledge may exist on three levels. Consider the example of Euclid the geometer:

I   Euclid has the capacity to know that when equal angles are subtracted from equal angles, the remainders are equal, because he is a human being and human beings are able to acquire geometrical knowledge.

At this level he has an innate epistemic ability which he has not yet developed. But through perception, memory, experience, and induction,[19] he reaches the following level:

II   Euclid, having become a geometer, acquires this knowledge through induction.

This is a first-level actualization of his epistemic capacity. He can consider this knowledge and use it whenever he wants to, but he does not necessarily do so. For example, he might not use it because he is asleep or thinking about something else. Finally,

III   Euclid actually uses this knowledge, e.g. to prove that, when two lines intersect, the opposing angles are equal.

---

[15] The connection between the advantageous (*to sumpheron*) and the just (*to dikaion*) is discussed in Sects. 3.1 and 6.2 below.   [16] See Keyt (1991*b*), 134–5.
[17] See *EN* II 1 1103ᵃ18–ᵇ6; VI 9 1141ᵇ14–22; 1142ᵃ20–30, 13 1144ᵇ1–14.
[18] See *DA* II 5 417ᵃ21–ᵇ2, *GA* II 1 735ᵃ9–11. Cf. Lear (1988), 119.
[19] See *An. Post.* II 19 99ᵇ34–100ᵃ6; *Met.* I 1 980ᵃ27–981ᵃ12.

This is the highest-level actualization of the epistemic capacity which was only partially actualized at II.

We should similarly understand a moral capacity as developing through three levels. Consider Aristides the politician:

> I   Aristides, as a young child, has the capacity to perceive justice, because he is a human being and human beings are able to acquire ethical virtue and practical wisdom and thereby perceive justice.

Aristides at this stage has a first-level potential or capacity to perceive justice and the good. However, this is not yet developed into a capacity to perceive justice and good which Aristides may exercise as the occasion arises.

> II   Aristides has the capacity to perceive justice and the good, because he has undergone moral education and habituation and has experience making correct moral choices.

Aristides now has a higher-level potential or capacity for moral perception: the ability to recognize the just or good decision or course of action. In one sense, his potential has been actualized. But it is only a first-level actualization, because he may not now need to make a decision, he may be asleep, etc.

> III   Aristides is now perceiving the just thing to do.

This, again, is the highest-level actualization of the moral capacity which existed in different forms in the previous stages and which was partially actualized at II.

Aristotle's argument at *Pol.* I 2 1253ᵃ7–18 only needs to assume that human beings possess a first-level capacity for moral perception, requiring habituation and education to attain the higher levels. They thus differ from a colony of bees held together by a natural behavioural instinct.[20] However, nature has endowed human beings, alone of all the animals, with the first-level potential to acquire the ethical virtue that makes the

---

[20] Keyt (1991*b*), 134–5, objects that this disanalogy between a polis and a beehive effectively undermines Aristotle's other claim that the polis exists by nature, for this argument represents the polis as held together by artificial rather than natural bonds. However, this objection assumes that when Aristotle claims that the polis 'exists by nature', he means that it has an innate internal cause holding it together. In Sect. 2.3 below, I criticize this interpretation and defend an alternative account of the natural existence of the polis which is consistent with the construal of political animals advanced here.

polis possible. Invoking his teleology, Aristotle theorizes that nature has uniquely adapted them for political activity. This is what he means when he elsewhere states, 'politics does not make human beings but uses them having received them from nature' (*Pol.* I 10 1258ᵃ21–3).

The argument from political impulses

Aristotle also infers 'Therefore, the impulse (*hormē*) to such a community [i.e. the polis] is in everyone by nature' (I 2 1253ᵃ29–30). The term *hormē* refers to the innate tendency of a thing to attain a specific condition (cf. *Phys.* II 1 192ᵇ13–27). Just as a seed has an innate impulse to develop into a tree, human beings have an innate impulse to live in communities. This inference is actually defended in *Pol.* III 6 1278ᵇ17–30, which identifies three motivations for political life, including prereflective desires as well as rational choices: (1) humans desire to live together even when they do not need mutual assistance; (2) the common advantage brings them together, in so far as a part of the noble life falls to each of them; and (3) they come together and maintain the political community for the sake of life itself, because there is perhaps a noble element and natural sweetness in living as such (provided life does not involve excessive hardship).

Of these motivations, only (3) would be countenanced as well founded by Hobbes.[21] It appeals to self-interest and the desire for survival, which can be most efficiently secured by entering into social co-operation and agreeing to refrain from mutual aggression. Yet it would not be a fully satisfactory reason for Aristotle, because it could only justify entering into a mutual non-aggressive alliance, not a fully developed polis (see *Politics*, III 9).

Motivation (2) encapsulates much of the argument of *Politics* I 2: It is rational for human beings to choose the political life because this will enable each of them to realize his natural end. Individual human beings as individuals are not self-sufficient, i.e. they cannot attain their natural ends on their own (1252ᵇ27–30, 1252ᵇ34–1253ᵃ1, 1253ᵃ26–9). Only collectively, as members of the polis, do they achieve 'the goal of self-sufficiency', for only through such co-operation do they have the resources to live the good life.[22] This involves, of course, the idea that the polis can

---

[21] e.g. in *De Cive*, I I 2: 'We do not therefore by nature seek society for its own sake, but that we may receive some honour or profit from it; these we desire primarily, that secondarily'.

[22] See *EN* I 7 1097ᵇ8–13, 8 1099ᵃ31–ᵇ6.

provide more resources and better security for its members than can a household or village. But Aristotle argues further that humans need the polis in order to develop their moral capacities and to realize their natural ends (see Section 2.5 below).

Motivation (1) is the natural prereflective desire of individuals to live together regardless of any further benefits from communal living. Aristotle makes a similar point at *EN* IX 9 1169^{b}17–19; 'no one would choose to have all [other] goods although he is by himself; for a human being is political, tending by nature (*pephukos*) to live together with others.' He argues that this propensity for communal living is not merely an unreflective, irrational desire; rather, the company of others is a necessary component of the good life, because we benefit from the presence of other persons who share with us in the good life. Each of these motivations reflects the fact, also noted at *EN* VI 9 1142^{a}9–10, that an individual's well-being requires a polis and a constitution (see Section 4.7 below). Aristotle's claim that the political impulse is present by nature in all human beings is thus open to a teleological explanation: nature endows human beings with the desire for political communities, because life in such communities is necessary for full human self-realization.

A charitable interpretation of Aristotle's reasoning would take the foregoing arguments from innate capacities and innate impulses together as providing evidence for the claim that human beings are by nature political animals. If he were simply claiming that the possession of either a first-level political capacity or of an innate political impulse was sufficient to make one a political animal by nature, his argument would be vulnerable to obvious counter-examples. From the mere fact that an individual has a first-level capacity to be a shoemaker it does not follow that he is by nature a shoemaker, and from the mere fact that an individual has a desire to be an Olympic champion it does not follow that he has even the first-level capacity to be one. However, Aristotle is arguing that human beings as such have both the innate first-level capacity and the innate impulse for the political life. According to his teleological theory, this universal human trait (found in all except bestial and godlike persons, 1253^{a}27–9) is best explained as present for the sake of political co-operation and, in turn, for the sake of full human perfection. No doubt Hobbes would reject a number of Aristotle's assumptions, including his natural teleology and his claims about human political impulses. But, given these assumptions, his argument that human beings are by nature political animals is intelligible and plausible. The assumptions themselves are discussed more fully in Section 2.6 below.

2.3. THE NATURAL EXISTENCE OF THE POLIS

The thesis that the polis is (or exists) by nature is the core of Aristotle's political naturalism. It is clearly a response to those, like the sophists, who claim that the polis—together with its laws and justice—exists by convention rather than by nature.[23] Less clear, however, is the precise meaning of Aristotle's thesis. I consider here two interpretations.

The internal-cause interpretation

The phrase *esti phusei*, 'is (exists) by nature', is used in a narrow technical sense in *Physics*, II, and, on this interpretation,[24] Aristotle uses it in the same sense in the *Politics*. In this strict sense a thing exists by nature if, and only if, it has a nature, in the sense of a source or cause of moving or being at rest, which is internal to it as such (*Phys.* II 1 192^{b}21–3; cf. *Met.* V 4). Paradigms of natural existents are animals and plants which grow and move due to their souls, which function as internal causes. Aristotle begins the *Physics*, II, discussion: 'Of things that exist, some exist by nature, some from other causes.' This implies that a thing exists by nature if, and only if, it comes to be by nature and not by some other cause.[25] Indeed, the major theme of *Physics*, II, is the distinction between natural coming-to-be, involving teleology, and coming-to-be due to other causes, viz., craft, chance, or spontaneity.

The internal-cause interpretation, then, states that 'exists by nature' has the same sense in *Politics*, I 2, as in *Physics*, II 1. This interpretation has several advantages: (1) The first is simplicity, because it provides for a clear continuity between Aristotle's metaphysical naturalism and his

---

[23] Aristotle alludes to this line objection at *EN* I 3 1094^{b}16, V 7 1134^{b}24–5; *Pol.* I 3 1253^{b}20–1. Cf. especially the argument of Callicles in Plato, *Gorgias*, 482^{c}4–484^{c}3.

[24] Defended by Keyt (1991*b*), 122–3. Cf. Ambler (1985), 168–9.

[25] Keyt (1987), 60, points out exceptions: e.g. the celestial bodies in Aristotle's cosmos exist by nature but being eternal do not come to be (see *DC* III 1 298^{a}27–31; I 12 281^{b}25–7, 282^{a}21–3). However, this exception may be safely ignored, since the polis belongs to the sublunary region. I am not convinced by Keyt's other counter-examples. Spontaneously generated plants and animals, he says, exist by nature but are not generated by nature; however, he cites no passage in which a spontaneously generated organism is said to exist by nature. Further, Aristotle in arguing against Empedocles in *Phys.* II 8 maintains that things which are by nature (*esti phusei*) are for an end and not due to spontaneity (see 199^{a}3–8). I also question (see n. 36 below) his alleged examples of things which are generated by nature but do not exist by nature. However, Keyt also remarks, 'Aristotle's claim that the polis exists by nature implies a belief that it also comes to be by nature' (58), because the counter-examples are anomalous and can, Keyt thinks, be disregarded in the context of *Pol.* I 2.

political naturalism. (2) In view of the fact that naturally existing things are naturally generated, one is led to expect Aristotle to consider the polis as a thing which is naturally generated. This seems to be what he does: '[I]f one were to consider things developing naturally (*phuomena*) from the beginning in these things [viz., political] as in others, one would theorize about them in the most noble way' (*Pol.* I 2 1252ª24–6). Although he does not explicitly say that the polis comes to be by nature,[26] he does describe how it comes to be and concludes that it exists by nature (1252ª26–ᵇ31).

Nevertheless, there are serious difficulties associated with the internal-cause interpretation: (1) Aristotle shows no interest in establishing that the polis in fact satisfies this definition of natural existence; i.e. he does not try to show that the polis exists by nature *because* it has an innate impulse to change or remain at rest.[27] (2) The thesis, so construed, leads directly to inconsistencies with other Aristotelian positions, most remarkably in the following nature–craft dilemma:[28]

(*a*)   The polis exists by nature.

(*b*)   The polis is brought into being by a lawgiver (i.e. politician) who is a craftsman (*dēmiourgos*).[29]

(*c*)   That which exists by nature cannot also be an artefact.[30]

In *Physics*, II 1, natural existence is tied to natural generation and cannot result from other types of causation, including craft. Craft involves a human agent who possesses the form of a product in his soul and then imposes the form upon a material which is inert in so far as that specific form is concerned (see 192ᵇ16–20). A craftsman—e.g. a weaver, potter, shipbuilder, carpenter, etc.—makes a product or artefact by imposing a specific form of a blanket, bowl, trireme, house, etc., upon the appropriate materials—e.g. thread, clay, wood, bricks, etc. An artefact thus lacks an internal cause and cannot exist by nature in the internal-cause sense. The evidence for (*b*) consists of Aristotle's frequent comparisons of politics

[26] A polis does not necessarily come to be from a polis, as a horse is begotten from a horse.

[27] Keyt (1991*b*), 123, acknowledges that 'it is curious that Aristotle, in attempting to prove the naturalness of the polis, never appeals to his definition of natural existence'; although, in Keyt's view, he could have done so: the polis can change locations, it can control its own size, and can perceive and think through its officials.

[28] See Ambler (1985), who infers that nature as understood in *Politics*, I, does not provide a standard for Aristotelian political practice.

[29] *Pol.* VII 4 1325ᵇ40–1326ª5, II 12 1273ᵇ32–3, 1274ᵇ18–19.

[30] *Phys.* II 1 192ª17–19; *Met.* VII 7 1032ª12–13, XI 8 1065ᵇ3–4, XII 3 1070ª6–9; *EN* III 3 1112ª31–3, VI 4 1140ª14–16; *Pol.* VII 14 1333ª22–3; *Rhet.* I 4 1359ª30–ᵇ2.

to the crafts. Like a craftsman, the lawgiver imposes a form, i.e. a constitution, upon materials, i.e. a given population and territory (see *Pol.* III 3 1276^{b}1–11, VII 4 1326^{a}35–8). 'By the analogy, then, a polis is an artefact of practical reason just as a ship or a cloak or a sandal is an artefact of productive reason.'[31] The argument of *Politics*, I 2, itself contains an indication that the lawgiver plays an indispensable role in the creation of the polis (1253^{a}30–1). But as we have seen, the internal-cause interpretation implies an incompatibility between the natural existence of the polis and any such role for the lawgiver.

(3) Aristotle's main argument that 'the polis exists by nature', becomes incredibly feeble on this interpretation: the polis develops out of more basic communities which exist by nature. The first communities are the combination of male and female, which results not from deliberate choice but from a natural (*phusikon*) striving to leave behind offspring like oneself, and the combination of natural ruler and ruled for the sake of preservation and mutual advantage. The household consisting of these communities is itself a community established according to nature (*kata phusin*) for everyday needs. The village comes to be out of several households for non-daily (i.e. higher) needs as a natural extension (*apoikia*, 'colony') of the household. Finally, the polis is the community which comes to be from the villages and is complete (*teleios*), attaining the goal of self-sufficiency; hence, although it comes to be for the sake of life, it exists for the sake of the good life. 'Therefore every polis exists by nature, since the first communities are also such. For it is their end, and the nature is an end: what each thing is when its coming to be is completed we call its nature, for example, of a human being, a horse, or a household' (1252^{b}30–4).

How could such an argument be supposed to support the claim that the polis exists by nature in the sense of having an internal cause? It has been suggested[32] that Aristotle's argument relies upon a tacit premiss: If entity$_1$ is prior in completeness[33] to (i.e. more complete than) entity$_2$, but entity$_2$ exists by nature, then entity$_1$ also exists by nature (the transitivity of naturalness principle). Hence, since the polis is prior to or more complete than its constituent communities, which exist by nature, the polis must also exist by nature. However, this principle is clearly false even for

---

[31] Keyt (1991*b*) 119. The analogy of politics and crafts is suggested at *EN* I 2, VI 8, 13 1145^{a}6–11, X 9 1180^{b}23–1181^{b}12; *Pol.* I 10 1258^{a}21–3, II 8 1268^{b}34–8, III 12 1282^{b}14–16, 22–3, VII 14 1333^{a}22–3; *Rhet.* I 4 1359^{a}30–^{b}2.　　　　[32] Keyt (1991*b*), 129.
[33] Although Keyt refers to this as 'priority in substance', I use 'priority in completeness' for reasons discussed in Sect. 2.4.

Aristotle. As Keyt objects, 'a house is prior in substance to the materials of which it is composed (*PA* II 1 646ᵃ24–9); and all of these materials are ultimately provided by nature—lumber comes from trees, bricks from clay and straw, and so forth—but houses exist by craft, not by nature'.[34] The transitivity principle fails because it does not follow from the fact that the parts of a whole have internal principles of motion that the whole as such has an internal principle of motion, even if the whole is more complete than the parts.

It is evident from the foregoing that the internal-cause interpretation leads to many serious difficulties. Aristotle's theory that the polis exists by nature may ultimately turn out to be a hopeless muddle, but we ought first to re-examine the offending phrase 'exists by nature' and consider whether it is open to an alternative interpretation.

The teleological interpretation

The internal-cause interpretation contains an important kernel of truth, viz., that on Aristotle's view the existence of the polis is natural because it is grounded in nature. However, the ultimate basis for Aristotle is not the nature of the polis but *human* nature. His claims about the polis must be understood within the context of his teleological account of human beings as having natural ends.[35] On such an account, humans have innate impulses for communal and political life *because* these will serve to promote their natural ends. It should be noted that Aristotle uses the phrase 'exists by nature' in the *Physics* not only for things which contain internal impulses but also in an extended sense for all things which result from such impulses for the sake of something: 'all such things exist by nature' (*Phys.* II 8 199ᵃ6). For example, birds' nests and spiders' webs, like birds and spiders themselves, are due to final causality, and thus qualify as 'things which come to be and exist by nature' (199ᵃ7–8, 29–30).[36] Nests and webs differ from products of human craft such as houses and clothing, because the latter are not the result of innate impulses. This suggests the following extended sense of 'natural existence':[37] a thing exists by nature if, and

---

[34] Keyt (1991*b*), 130–1.

[35] The importance of the idea of natural ends for Aristotle's political theory is rightly emphasized in Polansky (unpublished). Polansky's interpretation differs from mine in that it takes 'natural' to mean merely 'necessary for realizing one's natural ends' and not to have any causal significance.

[36] Keyt denies this in (1987), 59–60, but abandons his denial in (1991*b*).

[37] This is the traditional interpretation offered by the major commentators; e.g. Susemihl and Hicks: '[Aristotle] proclaims a truth as novel as it was important that man, and properly

only if, it has as its function the promotion of an organism's natural ends and it results, in whole or in part, from the organism's natural capacities and impulses. The polis satisfies both of these conditions for natural existence. First, it has as its function or end the promotion of human natural ends; in fact, it is only in the polis that humans can attain the level of self-sufficiency needed for them to achieve the good or full self-realization. Second, its natural existence is due, in part, to the natural impulse that human beings have to live in communities. This is consistent with acknowledging an indispensable causal role on the part of the lawgiver or politician.[38] On this interpretation, the thesis that the polis exists by nature is based on the thesis that human beings are by nature political animals. For the latter claims that human beings have natural capacities and inclinations for political life, and the former relies upon this claim in order to argue that the existence of the polis is in part due to human natural potentials.[39]

This interpretation, because it includes a causal condition, is supported by the same evidence as the internal-cause interpretation: (1) Aristotle's emphasis on all human beings having an impulse (*hormē*) for living in political communities, and (2) his interest in the process by which the polis develops out of more basic communities; (3) but it has the additional advantage of giving proper weight to Aristotle's concern with human natural ends, i.e. to his emphasis on the polis providing for self-sufficiency and existing for the sake of the good life.

However, the teleological interpretation adopts a weaker causal requirement, viz., that the existence of the polis is due at least in part to a natural impulse, so that it does not fall prey to the nature–craft dilemma[40] in the

---

speaking he alone of all creatures on earth, is a being destined by nature for political society. Nevertheless, the actual combination to form the state appears . . . to be man's own spontaneous act, quite as much as the actual function of poetry out of its germs in man's inner nature and the first rude attempts to develop them' (1894: 23–34). Cf. Newman (1887), i. 20; Bradley (1991), 25–6; and Barker (1946), 7 n. 1. I do not claim that the teleological interpretation is original, but only that it is correct.

[38] Cf. Barker: '. . . art co-operates with nature: the volition and action of human agents "construct" the state in co-operation with a natural immanent impulse' (1946: 7 n. 1). Barker correctly (in my view) insists that there is no contradiction in Aristotle's account (pp. xlix–l).

[39] Contrast Keyt (1991*b*), 132, who treats the political animal thesis as a corollary of the natural existence of the polis. Interpretations similar to mine are offered by Everson (1988), 95, and Yack (1993), 95.

[40] Polansky (unpublished) seeks to avoid the dilemma by weakening claim (*a*) that the polis exists by nature, and Depew (forthcoming*a*) by weakening claim (*b*) that the polis is brought into being by a lawgiver. Both these interpretations must disregard textual evidence presented by Keyt. My strategy is to go between the horns and deny claim (*c*) that the polis cannot be causally due to both nature and human reason.

way the internal-cause interpretation does: (4) it is possible for human reason and natural impulses to function jointly as causes of a product. The existence of the polis is therefore due to two distinct causal factors: the aptitude and inclination of a given population for political life, and the application of politics by the politician. Each of these is a necessary condition, but they are not conjointly sufficient (because the formation of the polis requires favourable resources, the absence of enemies, etc.). However, the sufficient condition for the polis will include these two factors. Accordingly, Aristotle can consistently affirm the causal contributions both of the natural communal impulse and of the legislator, who is called 'the cause (*aitios*) of very great goods' (1253^a29-31).

(5) This interpretation provides a way of understanding Aristotle's argument for the natural existence of the polis so that it is plausible given his assumptions. Recall that his argument relies on the idea that one community may be a natural extension of another. The context indicates that we may explicate this notion as follows:

'Community C_2 is more complete (or final) than community C_1 if, and only if, C_2 serves natural ends which are of a higher order or more inclusive than the natural ends served by C_1.

C_2 is a natural extension of C_1 if, and only if, C_2 contains and comes to be from C_1, and C_2 is more complete (or final) than C_1.

Thus, the village is more complete than the household because it is not confined to daily needs, and the polis is more complete than its predecessors because it promotes the good life. Further, the communities discussed are so ordered that each comes to be from and contains its predecessor. Finally, the tacit transitivity of naturalness principle will be restricted to natural extensions:

If C_1 exists by nature and C_2 is a natural extension of C_1, then C_2 also exists by nature.

This principle is plausible on the teleological interpretation, because the antecedent supplies what is needed for the consequent: given that C_2 comes to be from C_1 and that C_1 is caused at least in part by natural potentials, then C_2 is also caused at least in part by a natural potential. Further, it is plausible to speak of the self-sufficient natural extension of C_1 as the end (and hence nature) of C_1, as Aristotle does at 1252^b31-4. Aristotle will understand the transitivity principle as restricted to communities which serve human natural ends: it will include villages and polises but not associations for vulgar pleasures or retail businesses established to make financial gains. This is what Aristotle has in mind when he says that the polis exists by nature if the first communities do (1252^{b}30–1).

In spite of these advantages, the teleological interpretation may seem to face objections of its own: (1) The first is that this interpretation ascribes to Aristotle a weaker claim than the evidence warrants, because he maintains that the polis has a nature of its own, distinct from the natures of the individuals who compose it, e.g. at *Pol.* I 2 1252^{b}31–1253^{a}2. However, Aristotle does not go that far. Rather, he states here that the polis *is* the nature of its component communities. The point is that the polis is the end of these communities. Their coming-to-be is completed in the polis, because it also reaches the level of self-sufficiency necessary for its members to attain the good life, i.e. for them to realize their natural ends.[41] This is confirmed at *Pol.* II 2 1261^{a}18, which says that 'the polis is in its nature (*tēn phusin*) a certain multitude' rather than a unity like a human being. Here the polis is a collective entity, its nature inseparable from the natures of its members.

(2) A second objection is that Aristotle's concept of nature excludes the solution to the nature–craft dilemma proposed here. However, as I have argued above, Aristotle speaks of 'natural existence' in an extended as well as a strict sense, and it is only the strict sense (i.e. having an internal cause) that excludes production by craft. It is noteworthy that the *Physics* allows that craft may co-operate with nature: 'generally craft in some cases completes what nature cannot bring to a finish, and in others imitates nature' (II 8 199^{a}15–17). For example, a doctor may produce health in a patient in whom the natural processes have failed. The medical craft requires a knowledge of health and of material factors such as bile and phlegm (see II 4 194^{a}21–2). In such a case we may speak of craft as co-operating with nature to produce health.[42] Aristotle makes a similar point in *Pol.* VII 17 1336^{b}40–1337^{a}3, when he suggests that in designing an educational system, 'one should follow the distinctions of nature, for all craft and education want to supply that which is missing in nature'. This indicates both that craft and education must sometimes complete what nature does not and they must 'follow' nature.[43] Like the educator, the politician must use politics to complete what nature has left undone while following nature's direction.

[41] Cf. *telestheisēs* at ^{b}32 with *teleios* at ^{b}28.

[42] Cf. Veatch (1985), 65. For a similar view, cf. Plato, *Laws*, X 889^{d}4–6.

[43] Cf. the discussion at VII 15 1334^{b}14–25. The context of these passages is discussed in Sect. 6.7 below.

Nevertheless, it may still be objected that this interpretation overlooks
a disanalogy between the medical case and those of education and politics.
In cases like medicine, the end (health) which is attained by craft co-
operating with nature is an end which nature 'always or for the most part'
attains all by itself. This is not the case for education and politics. However,
Aristotle offers another parallel (mentioned above in Section 2.2), viz.,
the acquisition of language. The use of language is part of the natural
end of human beings: 'nature has given this faculty [viz., of voice] to the
human being because he alone of animals makes use of speech (*logos*) and
voice is the material of speech' (*GA* V 7 786^{b}19–22; cf. *PA* II 16 659^{b}30–
660^{a}2 and 17 660^{a}17–23). However, the linguistic potential has to be developed through learning and instruction, and the same is true of lower
animals such as birds, which use their voice to communicate in a more
rudimentary way (*HA* IX 1 608^{a}17–21; cf. IV 9 536^{b}17). But human
beings learn to speak a particular dialect such as the Greek spoken by
Aristotle. Because of the wide variation, there is no 'natural' dialect, but
various dialects can be produced by 'shaping' or training (*plattesthai*); and
Aristotle notes similar variation and instruction in connection with bird
songs (536^{b}14–20). Linguistic capacity is a natural, universal trait among
human beings (as with singing in birds), but language also takes the form
of particular dialects because humans (analogously with certain animals)
must learn through education to distinguish particular sounds in a dialect
and what they signify (cf. IX 1 608^{a}20–1 and *DI* 1 16^{a}3–8). The dichotomy
between instinct and learning is thus a false one in the case of higher animals as well as human beings.[44] For in language nature must co-operate
with human inventiveness in order to attain its end. In general, the natural
ends of human beings (and certain higher animals) involve intelligence
and rationality, and the realization of such ends requires the contribution
of humans themselves (and of the other animals) through education and
habituation.

(3) It might also be objected that the teleological interpretation does
not account for the evident discrepancy between Aristotle's arguments in
Politics, I 2, that the polis exists by nature and his argument in *Nicomachean
Ethics*, II 1, that ethical virtue does not exist by nature:

Ethical (*ēthikē*) virtue comes about as a result of habit; hence its name involves a
slight variation from that of habit (*ethos*). From this it is also clear that none of the
ethical virtues arise in us by nature; for none of the things that exist by nature can
become other [than its nature] by habituation. For example, a stone which moves
downward by nature could not be habituated to move upward, not even if you

----

[44] Cf. Arnhart (1993), 49–55.

threw it up ten thousand times in order to habituate it, nor could fire be habituated to go downward nor could anything else that naturally [does a specific kind of thing] be habituated to act otherwise. Therefore, the virtues do not arise either by nature or against nature, but we are naturally able to acquire them and we are perfected [or completed] through habit. ($1103^{a}17-26$; cf. *EE* II 2 $1220^{a}39-^{b}5$)

It is evident that this passage uses 'by nature' in the strict sense, because earth and fire are moved down and up as a result of internal causes (*Phys.* II 1 $192^{b}8-23$). Virtue does not arise 'by nature' in this strict sense, because it requires the additional contribution of human beings in the form of habituation and reasoning (see *Pol.* VII 13 $1332^{a}39-^{b}11$). Similarly, no one possesses the intellectual virtue of contemplative wisdom (*sophia*) by nature (cf. VI 11 $1143^{b}6-7$).

However, Aristotle also uses 'nature' (*phusis*) in another sense in his ethical and political writings, for a human being's final cause or end, what it is when it is perfected.[45] In this latter sense, a human being is one of the things excellent by nature (*EE* VII 2 $1237^{a}16$; 6 $1240^{b}20-1$). 'Reason and intellect are for us the end of nature, so that birth and the care for habits ought to be arranged with a view to these' (*Pol.* VII 15 $1334^{b}14-17$). In this sense nature serves as a standard of value: 'what is proper to each thing by nature is best and pleasantest for it' (*EN* X 7 $1178^{a}5-6$; cf. I 9 $1099^{b}21-2$; IX 9 $1170^{a}13-16$, $1170^{b}1-2$, 15). This is also implicit in the argument that happiness is defined by reference to the distinctive function of human beings (*EN* I 7 $1097^{b}24-5$, cf. *EE* II 1 $1218^{b}38-1219^{a}1$). It is in this sense that happiness constitutes the natural end of human beings. On Aristotle's view the natural end of human beings can be fully realized only through habituation and education. Hence, this sense of 'nature' as a natural end is closely related to the extended sense in which the polis exists 'by nature' in *Politics*, I 2: the polis arises out of human nature (in the strict sense) and is also necessary for the fulfilment of human nature (in the sense of an end). Aristotle's failure to distinguish explicitly these different senses of 'nature' is a source of misunderstanding, but, given the above implicit distinctions, his theory that the polis exists by nature is internally consistent.

2.4. THE NATURAL PRIORITY OF THE POLIS

The thesis that the polis is prior by nature to the individual has been called 'undoubtedly the most provocative assertion in the *Politics*'.[46] To

---

[45] The two 'aspects' of Aristotle's concept of nature are distinguished by Irwin (1985a), 416–17. Cf. Annas (1993), 142–58, Schütrumpf (1991), i. 209, and Nichols (1992), 18, on the different senses of 'natural'. [46] Keyt (1991b), 139.

modern readers, the thesis may evoke the statist ideologies used to rationalize the political horrors of the twentieth century. The fact that Aristotle defended this thesis seems to lend credence to Karl Popper's claim that Aristotle is, with Plato, a precursor of modern totalitarianism.[47] Aristotle's arguments for this doctrine have also seemed to critics to be seriously flawed. However, before this thesis can be properly evaluated, it must first be understood, and this is difficult, because it is fraught with imprecision and even ambiguity. For Aristotle speaks of one thing as prior to another in several different senses, and it is hard to determine from the context of *Politics*, I 2, which sense he intends. Nor is it obvious what important normative implications Aristotle takes the thesis to have for his political theory.

Four concepts of priority

Aristotle makes the claim that X is prior to Y in several different ways:[48] (*a*) 'X is closer to the beginning than Y'. The beginning may be either absolute or relative, and it may be a place, a time, a movement, etc.: e.g. the morning is prior to the afternoon. The temporal version of this is 'priority in generation (*genesei*)'. (*b*) 'Knowledge of X is required for knowledge of Y, but knowledge of Y is not required for knowledge of X'. This is 'priority in knowledge' and may be due to the fact that Y is referred to in the formula of X but not vice versa; e.g. musical is prior to musical man. (This is 'priority in formula'.) Or it may be because we know Y as a result of perceiving X; e.g. we know the universal horseness as a result of perceiving particular horses. (*c*) 'X is more complete or more perfect (*teleioteros*) than Y'. Aristotle remarks a number of times that that which is posterior in generation is prior in this sense. He illustrates this with artefacts: e.g. bricks are prior in generation to a house, but the house is prior in sense (*c*); and he uses it with natural, living things: e.g. the seed is prior in generation to the plant, but the plant is prior in sense (*c*).[49] (*d*) 'X can exist without Y, but Y cannot exist without X'. In this sense,[50]

---

[47] Popper (1962), ch. 11. Cf. Barnes (1990*a*) and Holmes (1979).

[48] Several senses of 'prior' (*proteron*) and 'posterior' (*husteron*) are distinguished in *Met.* V 11 and *Cat.* 12. There are briefer discussions in *Phys.* VIII 7 and 9, *PA* II 1, *GA* II 6, *Met.* I 8, VII 1 and 13, IX 8, XIII 2, *Rhet.* II 19. For summaries of these senses, see Ross (1948), ii. 317–18, and Keyt (1991*b*), 126–7.

[49] Aristotle seems to have this sense of priority in mind in *Pol.* III 1 1275ᵃ38–ᵇ3, when he says that the correct constitutions are prior and the deviant ones are posterior. In the political contexts discussed in this section, *teleion* connotes both 'perfect' and 'complete'.

[50] Aristotle (*Met.* V 11 1019ᵃ4) attributes this to Plato; although the source is uncertain. Perhaps it pertains to the claim that the forms are separate in that they can exist without particulars, but not vice versa.

one of Socrates' sandals is prior to the pair consisting of both his sandals. Somewhat confusingly, Aristotle refers to both senses (*c*) and (*d*) on different occasions as 'priority in substance' (*ousiai*) and 'priority in nature' (*phusei*). To avoid this ambiguity, I shall refer to sense (*c*) as 'priority in completeness' and to (*d*) as 'priority in separateness'.

It is apparent that the polis is prior neither (*a*) in generation nor (*b*) in knowledge. Regarding (*a*) both the individual and the household are treated as prior in generation to the polis, since it comes to be out of villages which are themselves formed from conjunctions of households, which arose from primitive forms of communities of individuals. Regarding (*b*), it might be argued that the polis is prior because a human being is by nature a political animal;[51] however, the formula of the polis makes reference to the individual, since it is a certain multitude (*ti plēthos*) of citizens, which must be defined in terms of its constituent members rather than vice versa (see *Pol.* III 1 1274ᵇ38–1275ᵃ2, 6 1279ᵃ21). It would seem that neither polis nor individual is prior in sense (*b*).

However, there is some plausibility in supposing either (*c*) priority in completeness or (*d*) priority in separateness to be relevant to the claim that the polis is prior.[52] The argument turns on the point that the polis is self-sufficient whereas the isolated individual is not, and this is connected with the idea that only the polis is complete—suggesting sense (*c*)—and that the individual cannot, in some sense, exist in separation from the polis—suggesting sense (*d*). This section will examine the evidence for each line of interpretation of the priority claim and then consider the implications of this claim for Aristotle's theory.

The separate-existence interpretation

On this view[53] the crux of Aristotle's argument is an analogy between an organism and its individual organs on the one hand, and a polis and its individual members on the other. Individual body parts such as a finger or a hand are posterior in separateness to a whole animal, because the whole can exist without them but they cannot exist without the whole. As Aristotle states at *Met.* VII 10 1035ᵇ23–5: 'For [the parts] cannot even

---

[51] See Barker (1906), 278.

[52] Cf. Mulgan (1977), 31: 'The polis is prior in both of these specialized senses.' Keyt (1991*b*), 136, contends that in the argument at 1253ᵃ18–33, it is clear from the opening sentence, 'And a polis is prior in nature to a household and to each of us', Aristotle specifically intends sense (*d*). However, as noted above, Aristotle uses 'in nature' in connection with both senses (*c*) and (*d*).

[53] This interpretation is offered by Newman (1887), ii. 125–7, who is followed by many other commentators including Keyt.

exist if separated [from the whole]; for it is not a finger in every state that is the finger of an animal, but a dead finger is a finger only homonymously.'[54] Similarly, the polis can exist without the individual member but the individual member cannot exist without the polis; thus, the polis is prior in separateness.

This interpretation gains considerable support from the text of *Pol*. I 2 1253ᵃ18–33, where Aristotle compares the individual member of the polis to a hand or a foot. According to this interpretation, the argument proceeds as follows:

(1) Everything is defined by its function and capacity; without them it can no longer be called the same thing except homonymously.

[(2) A part of a whole has its defining function and capacity only when it is part of the whole.][55]

(3) Therefore, the part can no longer exist if it is removed from the whole, except in a homonymous sense.

[(4) The whole can exist apart from the part.]

(5) Therefore, the whole is prior (in separateness) to the part.

(6) The individual when separated from the polis is not self-sufficient.

(7) Therefore, the individual stands to the polis like other parts to wholes.

(8) Therefore, the polis is prior (in separateness) to the individual.

Step (1), which is explicitly assumed at 1253ᵃ23–5, echoes a statement at *Meteor*. IV 12 390ᵃ10–13: 'All things are defined by their function: for things which are able to perform their function are each truly [what they are], e.g. an eye, if it sees. But that which cannot [perform that function] is [what it is] homonymously, like a dead eye or one made of stone, just as a wooden saw is no more a saw than one in a picture.'[56] Step (2) is a tacit premiss; and, unless qualified, it is false, even for Aristotle. For he recognizes that when an artificial whole such as a house is disassembled into its parts, these can continue to be called beams, bricks, doors, and so forth without homonymy, unless they have actually been damaged in the process of disassembly.[57] Hence, the house will not be prior in separateness

[54] Cf. *Met*. VII 11 1036ᵇ30–2, 16 1040ᵇ6–8; *DA* II 1 412ᵇ17–22; *PA* 1 1 640ᵇ35–641ᵃ5. Things are homonymous if they have the same name but different definitions (*Cat*. 1 1ᵃ1–6).

[55] I use brackets for steps of arguments which, although unstated, are imputed to Aristotle.

[56] See Shields (1990) on the significance of this passage for Aristotle's psychology. Cf. also *DA* II 4 416ᵇ23–4.

[57] This is recognized at *Top*. VI 13 150ᵃ33–6, as is noted by Newman (1887), ii. 127.

to a particular part.[58] In this respect an artefact differs fundamentally from an organism. Aristotle needs to qualify (2), therefore, in such a way that it will hold for organisms but not artefacts. On this interpretation, the premiss must be restricted to natural wholes, i.e. to wholes which are also 'natural entities' (things which exist by nature in the internal-cause sense).[59] Similarly, the inferences to (3) and subsequently to (5) will follow only if they are restricted to natural wholes and their parts. Step (4), it should be noted, is also a tacit premiss. It may seem to be supported by the idea that a human being can continue to exist minus a hand, a foot, or an eye. Step (6) is a premiss (stated at 1253ª26) providing the basis for the analogy between the organism and the polis. Individuals apart from the polis are not self-sufficient. An individual would be self-sufficient (*autarkēs*) if he needed nothing in order to attain his ultimate good (1253ª28, cf. *EN* I 7 1097ᵇ14–15). Hence, individual human beings are not able to realize their natural ends or functions apart from the polis. Premiss (6) thus implies that individuals cannot exist apart from the polis except in a homonymous sense. It can then plausibly be inferred (7) that the polis stands to individuals like an organism to its organs. It can exist without them, but they cannot exist without it. On this interpretation the polis is literally a 'social organism'. It is a short step to (8), the conclusion that the polis is prior in separateness to individual human beings.

Given the separate-existence interpretation, Aristotle's polis resembles a Hegelian social organism with its political connotations. However, the resulting thesis seems vulnerable to the sort of counter-example offered by Keyt:

Suppose that a person—call him 'Philoctetes'—is forced to live in isolation because he is suffering from a snake bite that will not heal and which gives off a stench that no one can stand. Suppose, further, that Philoctetes is less than a god and, consequently, is not the sort of person who 'has no need [to share in a polis] since he is self-sufficient' (1253ª28). Now, the priority thesis entails that any given polis can exist without Philoctetes but not Philoctetes without a polis. To say that Philoctetes cannot exist without a polis is not to say that, like a honey bee separated from its colony, he would perish without a polis but that he would cease being a human being and sink to the level of a lower animal. . . . (1253ª27–9) Thus in respect of the species to which he belongs Philoctetes would be, like a eunuch in respect of his sex, a man in name only.[60]

---

[58] It does not follow that the part is prior in this sense to the artefact, because, for example, a house might still be a house even if its door was removed.
[59] Keyt (1991*b*), 136.   [60] Ibid. 139.

Keyt objects that this consequence is false by Aristotle's own principles. 'For Philoctetes' inability to share in a polis is not the sort of inability that destroys humanness.' A person—e.g. a carpenter—may lack the ability to do *F* because he lacks the capacity or skill to do *F* or because he lacks the opportunity to do *F*. The former inability entails that a person is not a carpenter; a person with the latter inability is simply a carpenter out of work. Analogously, 'Philoctetes living in isolation is like a carpenter out of work. Since he is polisless through misfortune rather than through lack of capacity to live with others, he remains a human being just as a carpenter out of work remains a carpenter.' Aristotle seems to concede (at least tacitly) this point when he speaks of the pre-political existence of human beings and when he distinguishes between those who are without a polis 'by chance' rather than 'due to nature' (1253^a3–4).

The completeness interpretation

On this view,[61] the polis is prior in completeness to the individual: it represents a complete and self-sufficient whole, whereas individuals taken by themselves and apart from the polis are not complete and self-sufficient. In general, Aristotle views self-sufficiency (*autarkeia*) as a property of the polis rather than of its individual members. It might be thought that if self-sufficiency characterizes happiness, then a happy person should be able to be happy in a completely solitary condition. Aristotle denies this: 'Now what we count as self-sufficient is not what suffices for a solitary person by himself, living an isolated life, but what suffices also for parents, children, wife and in general for friends and fellow citizens, since a human being is a naturally political [animal]' (*EN* I 7 1097^b8–13). Therefore, rather than self-sufficiency implying solitariness, human beings can attain self-sufficiency in communities, by co-operating with others (cf. *Pol.* I 2 1253^a26–8; *EE* VII 10 1242^a7–8).[62]

The analogy with the parts of a whole rests on the deep dependence of individuals on the polis, but Aristotle does not need to prove that the polis is prior in separability. The argument of 1253^a18–33 will, instead, be understood as follows.

---

[61] This is the interpretation of Aquinas, *Commentary on the Politics*, 38: the polis is 'prior in the order of nature and perfection'. Cf. Barker (1906), 277–8.

[62] Schütrumpf (1991), i. 203–6, argues that *autarkeia* in *Pol.* I 2 pertains to the ability of the polis to provide sufficient resources and not to inner freedom. Also, Kelley (forthcoming) argues persuasively against Cole's (1988) thesis that *autarkeia* corresponds to the modern notion of autonomy.

(1) Everything is defined by its function and capacity; without them it can no longer be called the same thing except homonymously.

(2) A part of an organism is corrupted when the whole perishes.

(3) Therefore, the part cannot perform its defining function if it is removed from the whole.

[(4) Therefore, the part as such is not self-sufficient.]

[(5) The whole is self-sufficient (or more so than the part).]

(6) Therefore, the whole is prior (in completeness) to the part.

(7) The individual human being, when separated from the polis, is not self-sufficient.

(8) The individual is a part of the polis.

(9) Therefore, the individual, when separated from the polis, is not able to perform its defining function (by analogy to organic parts).

[(10) The polis is self-sufficient (see 1252ᵇ27–1253ᵃ1).]

(11) Therefore, the polis is prior (in completeness) to the individual.

This reconstruction requires the addition of inference (4) and premiss (5)—additions which seem reasonable given Aristotle's definition of 'self-sufficient' as 'needing nothing in order to fulfil its function or end' (cf. VII 5 1326ᵇ29–30, *EN* I 5 1097ᵇ14–15, *Rhet.* I 7 1364ᵃ8–9). They make explicit the basis for the analogy between the polis and other wholes: because the polis is more self-sufficient than the individual, it is prior in completeness to the individual. The point of the analogy is that a human being resembles a hand or foot in that, if it is separated from the polis, it will be corrupted (*diaphthareisa*) and hence a human being only homonymously. The verb *diaphtheirein* often means 'to destroy or to kill' but it also has the meaning 'to ruin or to corrupt'. In the latter sense Aristotle contrasts things which are in a corrupted condition (*diephtharmena*) with things that are in a natural condition (*kata phusin*) (*Pol.* I 5 1254ᵃ36–7). The latter interpretation has the advantage that it provides a smoother transition to the following argument and, in particular, to the claim that 'just as a human being is the best of animals when completed or perfected [*teleōthen*],[63] when separated [*chōristhen*] from law and the administration of justice he is the worst of all' (2 1253ᵃ31–3). This argument obviously assures that human beings *can* exist in separation from the polis, but that they exist in an imperfect, debased, corrupted condition.[64] This assumption

---

[63] I read *teleōthen* with the manuscripts. The term means 'having attained its end (*telos*)'.

[64] Cf. Aquinas, *Commentary on the Politics*, 39: 'just as a hand or foot cannot exist without a human being, so also one human being cannot live self-sufficiently by himself if he is separated from the city'.

is consistent with the completeness interpretation of the priority of the polis, but not with the separate-existence interpretation.

Although this interpretation does not saddle Aristotle with the claim that the polis is prior in separability, there remains the Philoctetes problem. In so far as Philoctetes resembles an organ such as a hand or a foot, he can be called 'human being' only in a homonymous sense when he is separated from the polis. This seems absurd even by Aristotle's lights. However, we may think of human nature as involving successive stages of potentialities and actualizations (see Section 2.2 above):

I   Philoctetes, as a young child, has the capacity to acquire ethical and intellectual virtue, because he is a human being.

II   Philoctetes has the developed capacity for noble action and contemplation because he has acquired ethical and intellectual virtue.

III   Philoctetes is engaging in noble action and contemplation.

Certainly Aristotle would recognize that Philoctetes could exist apart from the polis at stage I. Philoctetes might have been lost as an infant, raised by wild animals, and have lived in a brutish condition with thoroughly unrealized human capacities. Otherwise, Aristotle could not distinguish between beasts or gods who are without a polis by nature from humans who are without it by chance (1253ᵃ3–4).[65] However, he would contend that Philoctetes could not progress from I to II without the polis and its institutions: the household, education, and the laws.[66] He would also argue that Philoctetes could not move fully from II to III without the polis and its institutions: the family, the constitution, and friendship relations.[67] Presumably, then, he could respond to the Philoctetes problem on two levels. First, although Philoctetes could live alone on the island at stage II with the developed potential for virtuous activity, he could not have developed this potential initially without the polis. Without the polis he could not even reach the stage of 'the carpenter out of work'. Second, even if he had acquired the virtues before he was alone on his island, he could not exercise them fully while he was apart from the polis. He would fall short of the 'complete exercise' of virtue. Given Aristotle's teleological

---

[65] See also *HA* I 1 488ᵃ7 which implies that a human being dualizes (*epamphoterizei*) between being political and being solitary. Cooper (1990), 222 n. 5, argues persuasively that Aristotle's meaning is that 'human beings dualize between living in large groups and solitarily, but the latter is an exception and a departure from the norm'. Cf. Salkever (1990), 71.   [66] See e.g. *EN* X 9 1179ᵇ20–1180ᵇ28 and *Pol.* VII 17 1336ᵇ40–1337ᵃ3.

[67] The importance of family, friendship, and political relations for happiness is implied at *EN* I 7 1097ᵇ8–11, and argued for in *EN* IX 9 and *EE* VII 12. This thesis is supported by many passages in the *Politics*, e.g. III 6 1278ᵇ21–4. See also Sect. 4.7 below.

view, the nature (*phusis*) of Philoctetes requires that he be a citizen, even when he is excluded from the polis by law (*nomōi*). If we recognize different levels or degrees of being human, then there is a plausible sense in which a Philoctetes stalled at level I or even at level II has failed to realize his humanness and is 'less than human'.

We are now in a better position to appreciate the relationship between the doctrines that the polis exists by nature and that the polis is by nature prior to the individual, which are both served up as conclusions at 1253ᵃ25–6.[68] The two theses make complementary claims based on the arguments of *Politics*, I 2: 'The polis exists by nature' makes, in part, the claim that in order to promote the natural ends of its members, the polis attains self-sufficiency, providing them with everything they need in order to realize their natural ends; 'the polis is prior by nature to the individual' makes, in part, the complementary, but distinct, claim that human beings cannot realize their natural ends without the polis. The difference between the two claims corresponds, very roughly, to a distinction between sufficient and necessary conditions for leading the good life.[69]

Organisms and communities

The priority of the polis is sometimes taken to imply that the polis contains individual human beings in the same way that a substance (i.e. an organism) contains its parts. Such a view has obvious affinities with the internal-cause interpretation of natural existence. However, the interpretation of Aristotle's priority thesis is complicated by the fact that he speaks of two quite different relations of part to whole. In the first, the part stands to the whole as an 'organ' of it. In ordinary Greek, *organon* means a tool or instrument such as an axe or a saw. In *De Anima* Aristotle extends it to bodily organs such as the eye, and speaks of plant and animal

[68] The major editors (Bekker, Newman, Immisch, Ross, and Dreizehnter) all take the text to say, *hoti men oun hē polis kai phusei kai proteron ē hekastos, dēlon*. It should be noted, however, that there is disagreement among the manuscripts: the first *kai* is omitted in the entire π¹ family and the second *kai* in various π² family manuscripts. But even if we follow the editors, it is not necessary to understand this clause as asserting that the natural-existence thesis is a conclusion of the argument at 1253ᵃ18–29. Aristotle may simply be summing up the two main conclusions of *Pol.* I 2 as a whole up to this point. In contrast, Keyt (1991*b*), 138, claims that the natural-existence thesis is a premiss for the priority thesis, because he adopts the internal-cause interpretation of the former and the separate-existence interpretation of the latter.

[69] Very roughly, in part because merely living in a polis, even the polis of our prayers, is not a guarantee of a good life. 'For Aristotle, *eudaimonia* is necessarily the result of a person's own efforts', as Cooper (1975), 123–4, correctly emphasizes (citing *Pol.* VII 1 1323ᵇ24–9). Self-sufficiency (*autarkeia*) means that agents are lacking nothing they need in order to act, not that their action is necessitated in a deterministic sense.

bodies as *organikon*—i.e. consisting of parts which are tools with specific functions: 'Also the parts of plants are *organa*, although entirely simple ones—e.g. the leaf is a covering for the pod, and the pod for the fruit; and roots are analogous to the mouth, for both draw in food' (II 1 412^{b}1–4). I refer to such cases as 'organisms' and 'instruments'.

In the second relation, the part stands to the whole as a member or subset of a group. The whole is a group of individuals which have something in common (*koinon*), such as land, food, or some other good. Individuals must have this thing in common (that is, share or participate in, *koinōnein*)[70] in order to be a part of the whole. The whole is accordingly called a community (*koinōnia*) and its members are called 'those who have [something] in common' (*koinōnoi*). I shall refer to such cases as 'communities' and 'members'.

To be sure, Aristotle recognizes important similarities between organisms and communities: 'One should suppose that an animal is established like a polis under good laws' (*MA* 10 703^{a}29–30). In particular, certain communities—viz., the household, village, and polis—share an important feature with organisms: viz., the parts cannot realize their natural function or end outside of the whole. This is the point of the natural priority thesis in *Politics*, I 2.

However, there are also important differences between organisms and communities. In the former, the part typically has a function or end which is distinct from and subordinate to the end of the whole. For example, the primary end of Socrates' eyebrows is to protect his eyes (see *PA* II 15 658^{b}14–15) and the end of his lungs is to breathe or provide the body with air (*PA* III 6 669^{b}8), whereas the end of Socrates himself is rational activity (*Pol.* VII 15 1334^{b}14–15). But in the community the end of the whole is a common good in which the parts must directly share in order to qualify as parts: 'For there must be some one thing that is common and the same for those who have [something] in common (*tois koinōnois*), whether they partake [in it] equally or unequally, e.g. food, an amount of land, or something else of this sort' (*Pol.* VII 8 1328^{a}25–8). Hence, the realization of the end of the whole must *include*, rather than transcend or supersede, the fulfilment of the ends of the parts.[71] Aristotle distinguishes between the community proper and what might be called an

---

[70] As noted in Ch. 1, I generally translate *koinōnein* as 'to have in common' to preserve the link with *koinon* and *koinōnia*. The verb generally takes the genitive case for that which is had in common, and the dative case for those with whom one has it in common. I use a bracket when the object is tacit. The verb is also frequently translated 'share' or 'participate'. The participle is also translated 'partner' in a business context.

[71] The force of 'includes' depends on the type of community in question. A poker game's end might include the players' ends in a fairly weak sense. However, as argued in Ch. 6

'extended community', which includes adjuncts that perform functions necessary for the community as a whole but which do not share directly in the common end of the community. An example of such a community proper might be the partners in a business venture, such as a caravan, and the extended community might include their slaves or paid labourers.

Politics, VII 8, makes clear that the polis is a community rather than an organism. For individuals do not qualify as members of the polis unless they can partake of the way of life which is the natural end of the polis. This is why, in Aristotle's view, natural slaves do not qualify as members of the political community, even though they are necessary for its existence, because they are unable to partake of happiness and the activity of virtue (1328^a33-5: slaves are included in the 'ensouled parts of property'; cf. I 4 1253^b32).

Aristotle also rules out the organic interpretation of the polis, in the course of his criticisms of Socrates' ideal constitution as depicted in Plato's *Republic*. Aristotle ascribes to Socrates the hypothesis that it is best for the polis to be as far as possible one, which he objects will destroy the polis: '. . . for the polis is with respect to its nature a sort of multitude [*plēthos*], and if it becomes more one it will become a household instead of a polis, and a human being instead of a household; for we would say that a household is more one than a polis and one human being is more one than a household . . .' (II 2 1261^a18-21). It is evident from this that a polis does not possess the innate unity which is characteristic of an Aristotelian substance. Its superiority lies instead in its complete-ness and self-sufficiency (1261^b10-15).

As noted above, Aristotle sometimes speaks as if the polis were related to its parts in the manner of an organic body (IV 4 1291^a24-8, V 3 $1302^b33-1303^a2$); cf. *MA* 10 703^a29-^b2 and *EN* IX 8 1168^b31-3). It is not, however, necessary to take these passages as inconsistent with the view that the polis is a whole *qua* community. Indeed, the comparisons with organic wholes may be regarded simply as resulting from the above-mentioned fact that communities resemble organisms in certain respects.[72] For example, a polis must grow in a proportionate manner as an organic body should, if it is to achieve the end of self-sufficiency necessary for

below, Aristotle endorses the strong requirement that a polis is in a natural condition only if each of its members is in a natural condition.

[72] Similarly, although Hobbes regards the commonwealth as an artefact, he repeatedly avails himself of analogies between 'the Body Politique' and an animal: e.g. between social systems and 'the similar parts, or Muscles of a Body naturall', between public ministers and 'the parts Organicall', its economic affairs and 'Nutrition and Procreation', and so forth (*Leviathan*, II. 22–4).

all its members to achieve the good life; conversely, if some part of the community grows too large or powerful—e.g. the rich or the poor—the community may be unable to serve the ends of all its members.[73]

In conclusion, Aristotle's provocative claim that the polis is prior by nature to the individual does not entail that he views the polis as an organism or substance. Rather, the priority claim rests on the principle of community that individuals can realize their potential only if they are subject to the authority of the polis (see *Pol.* I 2 1253ª31–9, discussed in the following section). The polis is a whole in the sense of a community: its natural end is a common good in which the individual members directly participate.

2.5. THE POLIS AS HUMAN PRODUCT

The sentence concluding Aristotle's argument for political naturalism also asserts that the polis is a human creation: 'Therefore, the impulse for the [political] community is in everyone by nature; and he who first established it is the cause of very great goods' (1253ª29–31). The phrase 'he who first established [it]' is evidently a reference to the lawgiver. The argument at 1253ª31–9 contends that justice is of paramount importance, in that human beings cannot achieve perfection without it; that justice itself is political, that is, dependent on the polis; and political things (i.e. things of the polis) are due to the lawgiver. The argument thus implies that the polis is a human artefact as well as due to nature. The argument at 1253ª31–9 rests upon three main premises: (i) justice is a very great good, (ii) justice is political, and (iii) political things are caused by the lawgiver. I shall examine the arguments for these premises in turn.

Justice is a very great good

This is the claim that justice has a high place among human goods.[74] The argument is based upon Aristotle's perfectionism:

(1)   The things which enable human beings to be perfected are very great goods, whereas those which impede these ends are very great evils.

---

[73] Aristotle uses similar reasoning in apparent defence of ostracism (see III 13 1284ᵇ7–13 and Sect. 6.9 below).

[74] The superlative *megistōn* need not imply uniqueness. Cf. *EN* VIII 12 1162ª6–7: the parents confer very great (*ta megista*) benefits 'since they are causes of [the children's] being and nature and of their education after they are begotten'.

(2) Justice enables human beings to be perfected, whereas injustice impedes this.

(3) Therefore, justice is a very great good, and injustice a very great evil.

The first premiss assumes the principle of perfection: a thing is better to the extent that it promotes human natural ends. Premiss (2) makes a further, obviously controversial claim. The argument for it turns on the idea that human beings naturally develop (*phuetai*) the possession of arms or weapons used for practical wisdom and virtue, but these arms are also especially useful for the opposite traits, those of vice. By this Aristotle presumably means that humans are innately equipped with physical strength, intelligence, and aptitudes needed to exercise the ethical virtues and to enforce justice. Throughout this argument Aristotle evidently uses 'justice' in the universal sense identified with the lawful (*nomimos*), and this type of justice is concerned with producing and safeguarding the happiness of the polis (*EN* V 1 1129^b11–19; see Section 3.1 below). Without justice or ethical virtue, human beings use their natural arms for unjust ends, falling into conflict, especially regarding bodily objects such as food and sex, and descending to a savage level of existence (1253^a33–7).[75] Aristotle's observation here resembles that of Hobbes, who remarks 'that during the time men live without a common power to keep them in awe, they are in that condition which is called Warre; and such a warre, as is of every man, against every man'. War, for Hobbes, consists not only in the act of fighting but also the disposition of humans to fight when there is no mutual assurance that the parties will restrain themselves. Hobbes continues with a famous paragraph:

Whatsoever therefore is consequent to a time of Warre, where every man is Enemy to every man; the same is consequent to the time, wherein men live without other security, than what their own strength, and their own invention shall furnish them with all. In such condition, there is no place for Industry; because the fruit thereof is uncertain; and consequently no Culture of the Earth; no Navigation, nor use of the commodities that may be imported by Sea; no

---

[75] Aristotle's argument seems to echo an argument of the Athenian Stranger in Plato's *Laws* as to why the lawgiver should give priority to the education of the citizens: 'Whatever the creature—whether plant or animal, tame or wild—if its early growth makes a good start, that is the most important step towards the happy consummation [*telos*] of the excellence [*aretē*] of which its nature is capable. Now man we hold to be a tame animal; all the same, while with correct training and a happy disposition, he will turn into the most divine and gentlest of creatures, if reared carelessly or ill, he is the fiercest creature upon earth (VI 765^c3–766^a4; trans. England; cf. IX 874^c8–875^a1).

commodious Building; no Instruments of moving, and removing such things as require much force; no Knowledge of the face of the Earth; no account of Time; no Arts; no Letters; no society; and which is worst of all, continuall feare, and danger of violent death; And the life of man, solitary, poore, nasty, brutish, and short.[76]

Aristotle's analysis of this problem is, of course, quite different from that of Hobbes, since Aristotle assumes a natural teleology and a perfectionist theory of the good, contending that humans can attain the objective good only if the arms with which they are naturally endowed are used in a just or virtuous manner.

Justice is political

Aristotle offers the following argument for this premiss:

(1) The administration of justice (*dikē*) is the order or organization (*taxis*) of the political community.

(2) The administration of justice (*dikē*)[77] is judgement of what is just (*to dikaion*) (cf. *EN* V 6 1134^{a}31–2).

(3) [Judgement of what is just is necessary for the habituation of justice.]

(4) Therefore, justice (*dikaiosunē*) is political.

The argument is loosely stated, so that its precise logical form is somewhat elusive. Three different terms for justice appear in the argument, and it is not altogether clear how they are to be connected. It seems plausible, however, that in the conclusion *dikaiosunē* refers to the virtue of justice which should be possessed by the citizens of the polis. The expression *to dikaion*, 'the just' in premiss (2) probably refers to just actions or claims which are the subject of judgement. *Dikē* can be equivalent to *dikaiosunē*, but here the former term seems to refer to the implementation of justice in a legal or broader political context. Thus, *dikē* here is translated as 'the administration of justice'.[78] The general point of the argument, then, is that the virtue of justice is inculcated in individuals through institutionalized modes of judgement about the actions or claims of individuals.

Premiss (1) identifies the administration of justice (*dikē*) with *taxis*, a way of ordering or organizing the polis. Aristotle also connects *dikē* with

---

[76] *Leviathan*, I. 13 (1968: 62).

[77] I read *dikē* with the manuscripts. Ross (1957) substitutes *dikaiosunē*.

[78] Following Jowett in Barnes (1984); cf. 'judicial procedure' in Rackham (1932), and 'adjudication' in Lord (1984).

law (*nomos*) at 1253ᵃ32–3. Elsewhere, the constitution is defined as a *taxis*, or way of ordering the offices in polises, which also determines the end of the political community (IV 1 1289ᵃ15–18; cf. 3 1290ᵃ7–11). The constitution in turn determines the laws.[79] Accordingly, Aristotle also speaks of law, perhaps in a derivative way, as a *taxis*, and of good law (*eunomia*) as good order (*eutaxia*) at VII 4 1326ᵃ29–31 (cf. III 17 1287ᵃ18). Premiss (2) states that the administration of justice involves judgement or decision (*krisis*) about what is just and unjust. The term *krisis* can be used in non-legal contexts, as when one makes a judgement about a friend's moral character (cf. *EN* VIII 8 1159ᵃ24), but in the present context it clearly refers to a legal judgement or at least a political judgement. The argument also relies on tacit premiss (3) that legal judgement is indispensable for the habituation and moral development of the citizens. Hence, human beings require a legal and political system in order to acquire ethical virtue. (On the educative function of law, see also *Pol.* II 7 1266ᵇ31–8; III 16 1287ᵇ25–6; *EN* V 2 1130ᵇ25–9.) There is an argument for this in *EN* X 9 1179ᵇ20–1180ᵃ24, which contends that moral education requires the preparation of the soul by means of habituation of feelings, 'like ground that is to nourish seed'. Young persons should be taught to enjoy or disdain the appropriate sorts of activities. Otherwise, they will take pleasure in the wrong things and be unreceptive to moral reasoning (cf. Plato, *Laws*, II 653ᵃ5–ᶜ4). This preparation must be done through the laws, for two reasons. First, habituation requires the use of coercion, but parents and private individuals generally lack the influence and compelling power of the laws. Second, individuals are more inclined to resist others who oppose their impulses, even when those others are right, than they are to resist rules. This stretch of argument clearly supports the principle of community, i.e. that individuals can become good only if they are subject to the authority of the community. Aristotle's principle of rulership comes to the fore in the next part of the argument.

Political things are caused by the lawgiver

Aristotle speaks of the lawgiver, i.e. politician, as a craftsman who shapes material (population and land) into a finished polis (see *Pol.* VII 4 1325ᵇ40–1326ᵃ5). He mentions Lycurgus and Solon as craftsmen of the constitutions

---

[79] Cf. IV 1 1289ᵃ13–15: 'For the laws should be enacted relative to constitutions, and they all are, but constitutions should not be enacted relative to laws.' See Sect. 3.4 below.

of Sparta and Athens respectively (II 12 1273^{b}32–3). When Aristotle speaks of the politician as making the citizens good by habituating them (see *EN* I 9 1099^{b}29–32, 13 1102^{a}7–10; II 1 1103^{b}3–6; X 9 1180^{a}29–34; cf. *EE* VII 1 1234^{b}22–3, 2 1237^{a}2–3), he does not imply the exclusion of nature. Although the ethical virtues do not arise 'by nature' in the strict sense of *Physics*, II 1, they are natural in an extended sense which refers to the natural end of human beings: e.g. 'reason and intellect are the end of our nature' (*Pol.* VII 15 1334^{b}14–15). He also says that 'we naturally (*pephukosi*) acquire [the virtues], and are perfected through habit' (*EN* II 1 1103^{a}23–6). Again, he speaks of persons who 'naturally' (*epephukei*) have law (V 6 1134^{b}12–15). Further, the *Eudemian Ethics* says, '. . . as will be said later, each virtue is in a way both natural (*phusikai*)[80] and otherwise, i.e. with practical wisdom' (III 7 1234^{a}23–33). This is evidently a forward reference to a distinction in the common books (*EN* VI = *EE* V), between natural virtue (*phusikē aretē*) and ethical or 'authoritative' virtue (*kuriē aretē*):

everybody thinks we possess each type of character in a way by nature (*phusei pōs*), for we are just, brave, temperate, and the rest directly from birth. But we are still seeking some other condition as the authoritatively good, for we are also seeking to possess such characteristics in another way. For the natural states (*phusikai hexeis*) belong to children and to beasts as well [as to adults], but without intelligence (*nous*) they are evidently harmful. (VI 13 1144^{b}4–9)

On this account, humans are 'by nature' reasonable and virtuous, but their character still needs to be properly developed through moral education (cf. *Pol.* II 7 1267^{b}6). Without practical wisdom the child's naturally virtuous actions might be as unintelligent as those of a dog which prevents a doctor from attending its injured owner.[81] Aristotle observes that human beings become good and excellent through three features: nature, habit, and reason (*Pol.* VII 13 1332^{a}38–40). The *Politics* treats the three as forming a natural hierarchy:[82] 'The other animals live mostly by nature, although in some slight ways by habits as well, but a human being also lives by reason, for he only has reason' (1332^{b}3–5). In contrast to inborn natural traits, habits and rational capacities have to be acquired through education (*paideia*) or (*mathēsis*), which takes two forms: habituation and lecturing (1332^{b}10–11). The design of a system of education is a primary

---

[80] I read *phusikai* with the manuscripts. Walzer and Mingay (1991) read *phusei kai*, following Spengel.

[81] White (1992), 103–7, offers a persuasive reconstruction of the argument.

[82] Murphy (1993), ch. 4. But see *EN* X 9 1179^{b}20–31, which emphasizes the importance of habituation for moral education.

aim of the lawgiver (14 1333ᵃ14–16; see Section 6.7 below). Such education complements the nature, i.e. innate capacities and inclinations, of human beings and enables them to realize their nature, i.e. natural end.

2.6. NATURE AND POLITICS: MODERN ECHOES

Aristotle's view that the political community results in part from a natural human inclination is opposed by theorists who regard it as purely a contrivance of reason, for example, the ancient sophists and Hobbes. However, Aristotle's view is shared by a number of modern theorists. For example, John Locke (1632–1704) agrees with 'the judicious Hooker' that 'we are naturally induced to seek communion and fellowship with others . . .'[83] Similarly, Hugo Grotius (1583–1645) concurs with the ancient stoics that man is a 'sociable' animal, for 'among the traits characteristic of man is an impelling desire for society, that is, for the social life—not any and every sort, but peaceful, and organized according to the measure of his intelligence'.[84] Samuel von Pufendorf (1632–94) also calls 'man a sociable animal because men are so constituted as to render mutual help more than any other creature', noting similar views in Seneca and Cicero.[85]

More surprisingly, David Hume (1711–76), not generally noted for his Peripatetic views, distinguishes between two sorts of virtues, the natural and the artificial. Natural virtues (e.g. benevolence, beneficence, generosity, and moderation) are those which human beings naturally and normally possess, and of which they naturally tend to approve. Artificial virtues (e.g. justice, modesty, chastity), on the other hand, are those which they possess and commend 'by means of an artifice or contrivance, which arises from the circumstances and necessity of mankind'. Hume argues that 'the sense of justice and injustice is not deriv'd from nature, but arises artificially, tho' necessarily from education, and human conventions'.[86] However, he qualifies this conclusion:

To avoid giving offence, I must here observe, that when I deny justice to be a natural virtue, I make use of the word, *natural*, only as oppos'd to *artificial*. In another sense of the word; as no principle of the human mind is more natural

---

[83] Locke, *Second Treatise*, II. 15, quoting Richard Hooker (1554–1600), *Laws of Ecclesiastical Polity* I. 10. Cf. *Second Treatise*, VII. 77.   [84] Grotius, *De jure belli ac pacis*, Prol. 6.

[85] Pufendorf, *De jure naturae et gentium*, II. 3. 16; citing Seneca, *Epistle* XCV, and Cicero, *De finibus bonorum et malorum*, III 20, and *De officiis*, I 44.

[86] Hume, *A Treatise of Human Nature*, III. II. I (1973: 477, 483).

than a sense of virtue; so no virtue is more natural than justice. Mankind is an inventive species; and where an invention is obvious and absolutely necessary, it may as properly be said to be natural as any thing that proceeds immediately from original principles, without the intervention of thought or reflection. Tho' the rules of justice be *artificial*, they are not *arbitrary*. Nor is the expression improper to call them *Laws of Nature*; if by natural we understand what is common to any species, or even if we confine it to mean what is inseparable from the species.[87]

In another passage reminiscent of the closing lines of Aristotle's *Politics*, I 2, Hume describes the co-operation of nature and politicians:

Tho' this progress of the sentiments be *natural*, and even necessary, 'tis certain, that it is here forwarded by the artifice of politicians, who, in order to govern men more easily, produce an esteem for justice, and an abhorrence of injustice. This, no doubt, must have its effect; but nothing can be more evident, than that the matter has been carry'd too far by certain writers on morals, who seem to have employ'd their utmost efforts to extirpate all sense of virtue from among mankind. Any artifice of politicians may assist nature in the producing of those sentiments, which she suggests to us, and may even on some occasions, produce alone an approbation or esteem for any particular action; but 'tis impossible it should be the sole cause of the distinction we make betwixt vice and virtue. For if nature did not aid us in this particular, 'twou'd be in vain for politicians to talk of *honourable* or *dishonourable*, *praiseworthy* or *blameable*. These words wou'd be perfectly unintelligible, and wou'd no more have any idea annex'd to them, than if they were of a tongue perfectly unknown to us. The utmost politicians can perform, is, to extend the natural sentiments beyond their original bounds; but still nature must furnish the materials, and give us some notion of moral distinctions.[88]

Here Hume offers an instructive parallel with Aristotle.[89] Just as Aristotle contends that human beings acquire the ethical virtues through habituation and the influence of the laws, Hume maintains that the progress or development of the moral sentiments requires the artifice of politicians. Hume further agrees with Aristotle that the moral development of individuals within civil society requires the co-operation of nature, which disposes human beings to be receptive to moral habituation. Hume thus evidently rejects the Hobbesian view that justice and other moral virtues are conventional or artificial. The Hobbesian, like the ancient sophists, asserts a fundamental dichotomy between *phusis* and *nomos*, or between nature and nurture, so that ethics can only be based in one or the other.

---

[87] Hume, *A Treatise of Human Nature*, III. II. I (1973: 484).

[88] Ibid., III. II. II (1973: 500).

[89] The parallel was pointed out to me by John Gray. It is also evident in McShea (1990) and Wilson (1993).

Hume, in contrast, agrees with Aristotle that human moral development and the existence of civil society require the co-operation of these two factors. On this issue Hume is closer to Aristotle than he is to Hobbes.[90]

Again, John Stuart Mill (1806–73) argues that morality has a 'basis of powerful natural sentiment'. He adds, 'This firm foundation is that of the social feelings of mankind; the desire to be in unity with our fellow creatures [is] a powerful principle in human nature . . . The social state is at once so natural, so necessary, and so habitual to man, that . . . he never conceives himself otherwise than as a member of a body . . .'[91] Charles Darwin (1809–82) notes with approval Mill's statement that the moral faculty is rooted in human nature, but he chides Mill for hedging his endorsement of naturalism by adding, 'if, as in my own belief, the moral feelings are not innate, but acquired, they are not for that reason less natural'. Darwin replies, 'It is with hesitation that I venture to differ at all from so profound a thinker, but it can hardly be disputed that the social feelings are instinctive or innate in the lower animals; and why should they not be so in man?' Darwin argues that sociability is an innate trait of humans and of animals of many kinds. Although Darwin makes no reference here to Aristotle (apparently seeing political naturalism as instead originating with Marcus Aurelius) his arguments that 'man is a social animal' resemble Aristotle's in many respects. It is especially revealing to compare Darwin's account of the development of the moral sense with Aristotle's linguistic argument in *Politics*, I 2. First, 'the social instincts lead an animal to take pleasure in the society of its fellows, to feel a certain amount of sympathy with them, and to perform various services for them'. Second, with the development of the higher faculties, individuals would have images of past actions and motives, and would feel dissatisfaction or pain for any unsatisfied instinct. Third, 'after the power of language had been acquired, and the wishes of the community could be expressed the common opinion how each member ought to act for the public good, would naturally become in a paramount degree the guide to action'. Last, 'habit in the individual would ultimately play a very important part in guiding the conduct of each member; for the social instinct, together with sympathy, is, like any other instinct, greatly strengthened by habit'.[92]

[90] This is not by any means to discount the differences between Hume and Aristotle. Aristotle's natural teleology is opposed by Hume's explanation of human behaviour in terms of his own theory of the passions, modelled after Newton's mechanistic physics. Hume also expresses scepticism as to the possibility of moral knowledge in the traditional sense.

[91] Mill, *Utilitarianism*, ch. 3 (1969: 230–1).

[92] Darwin, *Descent of Man*, ch. 4. Cf. Arnhart (1984; 1994).

More recently, a number of biologists and social scientists have offered accounts similar to that of Aristotle regarding the contribution of human nature to social and political co-operation.[93] The development of social relations played an indispensable role in the evolution of the human species, and indeed of all surviving primate species. Rather than depending on instincts and 'hard-wired' behavioural responses to environmental inputs, they had the advantage of much larger brains which enabled them to react to the opportunities and dangers they confronted far more successfully than other animals; but in order to use their larger brains they required extended care within a family in which they were educated in how to sustain their own existence and how to reproduce and rear their own young. Primates deprived of maternal care behave in a dysfunctional and psychotic manner, as do human children raised in isolation from other humans. Moreover, human beings discovered the use of language and technology and were able by means of social life to transmit these discoveries to their offspring and gradually add to these collective discoveries. Archaeological evidence indicates that early human beings and their australopithecine ancestors were social animals, although the character of their communities has varied widely over time and place. As Aristotle observes, human beings have a natural propensity to co-operate with other human beings although co-operative behaviour is a learned trait.

To be sure, there is also evidence for Hobbes's view that conflict has characterized human existence from time immemorial. But this need not support his conclusion that humans have a natural mutual antipathy[94] or that our species should be called *homo necans*. It is more accurate to say that aggression, like co-operation, is rooted in natural impulses as well as resulting from habituation and education. It should not be overlooked that conflict is itself commonly a social phenomenon, for violence is often employed in order to promote or defend the interests of one's group against other groups. Indeed, human beings are vastly more effective in perpetrating violence when they do so in co-operation with others; submitting to the authority of the group may make one more inclined to use aggression against members outside the group. Further, given the

[93] Masters (1975; 1987; 1989a; 1989b; and 1990) details these parallels. The following two paragraphs are based on Masters's research.

[94] Hobbes, *Leviathan*, I. 13 (1968: 61) states, '. . . men have no pleasure, (but on the contrary a great deal of griefe) in keeping company, when there is no power able to overawe them all'. The causes of war inherent in 'the nature of man' are competition, diffidence (i.e. mutual distrust), and glory.

complexity of the human brain and the vagaries of the process by which human beings are habituated to social existence, there are many ways the process can fail, so that individuals inflict violence on members of their own group. As Aristotle observes, the weapons which are needed to sustain the co-operative life of the polis are the weapons which can make humans the most destructive of animals. However, the facts of human violence do not establish that social co-operation is artificial or conventional as opposed to natural. Surely the correct view is that of Aristotle: humans have a natural propensity to engage in co-operation and to show mutual concern, but the virtues, specific dispositions for mutually advantageous co-operative behaviour, have to be acquired through learning and habituation.

Recently, some political scientists, including James Q. Wilson, have argued that a neo-Darwinian social theory can support a neo-Aristotelian naturalism in the social sciences. Wilson, for example, defends Aristotle's claim that 'man is by nature a social animal' and that 'our moral nature grows directly out of our social nature', drawing evidence from a variety of disciplines, including evolutionary biology, primatology, anthropology, and the social sciences. He also agrees with Aristotle that moral 'habituation operates on a human nature innately prepared to respond to training'.[95] Larry Arnhart also argues that Darwinian biology, by offering an evolutionary account of social behaviour, provides a way of overcoming the Hobbesian dichotomy between nature and culture.[96]

Another, less explicit parallel is found in contemporary sociobiology.[97] For example, E. O. Wilson states,

> We should first note that social systems have originated repeatedly in one major group of organisms after another, achieving widely different degrees of specialization and complexity. Four groups occupy pinnacles high above the others: The colonial invertebrates, the social insects, the nonhuman mammals, and man.[98]

Wilson remarks that 'human societies approach the insect societies in co-operativeness' despite the fact that among mammals including humans 'selfishness rules the relationships between members'. Mammals display a greater degree of innate individualism because there is a greater genetic investment in each individual organism: i.e. the strategy they have adopted for propagating their genes is 'to "invest" energy and resources in individual organisms that compete with each other, since the species has approached the greatest possible exploitation of relatively stable environmental

---

[95] Wilson (1993), 121, 235–7, 244, commenting on *EN* II 1 1103ª23–ᵇ2.
[96] Arnhart (1994).   [97] See Ruse (1990).   [98] Wilson (1975), 379.

resources'.[99] Human beings differ from other social animals, in the extent
to which they have managed to reconcile their individual genetic goals
with a high level of co-operation:

Man has intensified [his] vertebrate traits while adding unique qualities of his
own. In so doing he has achieved an extraordinary degree of co-operation with
little or no sacrifice of personal survival and reproduction. Exactly how he alone
has been able to cross to this fourth pinnacle, reversing the downward trend of
social evolution in general, is the culminating mystery of all biology.[100]

Aristotle's political naturalism may be viewed as an early attempt to
fathom this mystery. Although his theory suffers from some fundamental
deficiencies—including most notably the failure to include an evolutionary theory—he shares with many modern theorists a conviction that the
disposition to co-operate for mutual advantage is rooted in human nature.

[99] Wilson (1975), 380.   [100] Ibid. 384.

3

Justice

3.1. JUSTICE AND POLITICS

Aristotle's defence of political naturalism in *Politics*, I 2, contains two important references to justice. First, in his argument that human beings are by nature political animals (1253^a7–18), there is the claim that human beings are uniquely endowed by nature with the ability to form the concept of justice and hence with the capacity for political co-operation (cf. *EE* VII 9 1241^b14–15). Second, the argument that the lawgiver is a great benefactor (1253^a31–9) contains the claims that human beings become perfected only by acquiring virtue and practical wisdom, and that this requires the administration of justice in the polis. When separated from the law and justice, humans are the worst of all animals; they sink into a savage existence and are unable to fulfil their nature. Thus, justice, along with virtue and practical wisdom, is necessary for the full realization of human nature.

The centrality of justice to Aristotle's political theory is confirmed by his theory of constitutions: 'All constitutions are a form of justice, for [a constitution is] a community, and everything common is established through justice' (*EE* VII 9 1241^b13–15). His classification of constitutions distinguishes, most importantly, between just and unjust arrangements (*Pol.* III 6 1279^a17–21). He views the disputes within the Greek city-states over which constitutional form is correct as turning, ultimately, on their competing theories of justice (III 9 1280^a7–22, 1281^a8–10; 12 1282^b14–23; V 1 1301^a25–8). These discussions in the *Politics* presuppose Aristotle's treatise on justice,[1] which makes the important claim that there is only one constitution that is the best everywhere according to nature (*EN* V 7 1135^a5). This chapter, accordingly, offers a synoptic account of Aristotle's theory of justice and its political applications. Section 3.2 discusses his distinction of justice into universal and particular forms, Section 3.3 his

---

[1] *Pol.* III 9 1280^a18 refers to *EN* V 3 1131^a14–24, and *Pol.* III 12 1282^b20 refers to *EN* V 3 1131^a11–14. Also, *Pol.* II 2 1261^a31 refers to *EN* V 5 1132^b31–4. References in Sects. 3.2 and 3.3 are to *EN* V unless otherwise noted.

analysis of political justice into natural and legal (i.e. conventional) spheres, and Section 3.4 his political applications of justice. In addition, Section 3.5 explores some of Aristotle's hints concerning possible extensions of justice beyond the confines of the polis.

3.2. UNIVERSAL AND PARTICULAR JUSTICE

Aristotle's treatise on justice deals not only with the virtues of justice, but also with what might be called 'formal' principles of justice, i.e. abstract principles admitting of different, correct as well as incorrect, applications. Aristotle begins by distinguishing between universal and particular justice (EN V 1 1129^{a}26$-^b$11). The just and unjust are spoken of homonymously, he says, but this escapes notice because the different cases are in close proximity. The ambiguity is detected by considering two forms of injustice: lawlessness and inequality. These are opposed to two distinct forms of justice: lawfulness and equality, which Aristotle calls, respectively, universal justice and particular justice. 'Equal' (*isos*) and 'unequal' (*anisos*) have the connotation of 'fair' and 'unfair' in this context. The unfair person is excessively possessive or greedy (*pleonektēs*), seeking more than his fair share of the goods of fortune such as property and honour.

The identification of universal justice with lawfulness is explained teleologically: the just in the sense of the lawful promotes the happiness of the political community in some sense. This formal principle can have different specific applications, because the law may aim at the happiness (or parts of happiness) of the community as a whole or of parts of the community.

Since the lawless person [as we said] was unjust and the lawful person just, it is clear that all lawful things are in a way just; for the things defined by legislative science are lawful, and we say that each of these is just. Now the laws in dealing with all matters aim at the common advantage either of all or of the best or of those who have authority either based on virtue[2] or on some other such basis; so that in one way we call just the things that tend to produce and safeguard happiness or parts of happiness for the political community. (EN V 1 1129^{b}11–19)

Universal justice applies to any polis with laws. In a correct constitution, the just (*qua* lawful) promotes and protects the common advantage of

[2] Editors have been troubled by the expressions *tois aristois* (the best) and *kat' aretēn* (based on virtue), and have recommended the deletion of one or the other. (The latter is absent from manuscript K^b.) However, Stewart (1892), 390–1, suggests that the terms be understood as 'relative to a hypothesis' rather than 'without qualification'. If Stewart is correct, the expressions pertain to deviant constitutions and deletion is unnecessary.

everyone. In a deviant constitution, the just (*qua* lawful) promotes the advantage of the ruling class, for example, by protecting the property of the wealthy class in an oligarchy.

Moreover, the law commands all the virtuous acts that contribute to the happiness of the political community. Therefore, universal justice is not a particular virtue but includes all of virtue. A person who is just in this sense will act courageously (e.g. not deserting his post), temperately (e.g. not committing adultery or acts of insolence), and so forth. For the laws should require such acts and forbid their opposites (1129^b19-25, 2 1130^b22-4). Further, Aristotle argues ($1129^b25-1130^a13$) that this form of justice is to be identified with perfect (or complete) virtue, not without qualification but in relation to others. Universal justice and ethical virtue are the same state, but they differ in being or essence, in that justice has the qualification 'in relation to another'. A person may exercise ethical virtue in his personal affairs but be unable do so towards others. The worst person acts wickedly towards both himself and others, whereas the best person acts virtuously not only towards himself but also towards others.[3]

Aristotle says that the homonymy of universal and particular justice and injustice is close (1129^a27). Particular injustice is a part of universal injustice, for the latter can include other vices: cowardice, self-indulgence, bad temper, and excessive possessiveness (2 1130^a14-^b5). Excessive possessiveness (*pleonexia*), a form of particular injustice, differs from other vices in its peculiar objects (honour, money, security) and its specific pleasure (from gain). But, like universal injustice, particular injustice is essentially detrimental to the community.[4] Conversely, justice in both senses is concerned with the good of others (1 1130^a3, cf. *Rep.* I 343^c3-5). Accordingly, the *Politics* calls justice the 'communal virtue' (*koinōnikē aretē*) (III 13 1283^a38-9). Both universal and particular justice are concerned with human beings provided they have something in common (*koinōnousi*) or form a community (*koinōnia*). Universal justice includes any ethical virtue in so far as it promotes and protects the good of the

---

[3] According to Aquinas, Aristotle is distinguishing between virtue 'inasmuch as it aims to perform actions useful to another, viz., to the community or the ruler of the community' and virtue in so far as it aims to achieve an individual's own good (*Commentary on Aristotle's Nicomachean Ethics*, 909).

[4] Williams (1980) objects that *pleonexia* is too narrow to be a vice opposed to particular justice. Irwin (1988), 624 n. 6, plausibly replies that there is a distinction between mere unconcern with justice and the positive injustice exemplified by the person who seeks to gain an unfair comparative advantage over others (regarding honours, property, etc.). It is the latter which Aristotle emphasizes.

community, whereas particular justice involves specific sorts of actions affecting the common advantage.

Particular justice itself takes different specific forms, each of which promotes the common advantage in a distinctive way. Distributive justice is concerned with the distribution of a common asset, such as honour or property among those who have a constitution in common (*tois koinōnousi tēs politeias*). Corrective justice is concerned with rectifying previous unjust transactions between them. Corrective justice has further subparts involving either voluntary transactions (e.g. selling, buying, renting, hiring) or involuntary transactions (including acts of secrecy, e.g. theft and adultery; and acts of force, e.g. assault and murder) ($1130^b30-1131^a9$). Aristotle also speaks of a third form, reciprocal (or commutative) justice, which is found in communities of exchange (*en tais koinōniais tais allaktikais*), e.g. when a farmer and a shoemaker exchange food for shoes ($5\ 1132^b31-3$). It is noteworthy that Aristotle's use of distributive justice is narrower than what recent theorists call 'justice in holdings', since the latter includes corrective and commutative justice as well as distributive justice. There is an overview of these three forms of particular justice in *Nicomachean Ethics*, V 3–5.

Distributive[5] *justice* involves the assignment to individuals of a fair or equal share (*to ison*) of a common asset such as property or honour. According to the theory of the mean, a just share is a mean between a share that is too large or too small.

Therefore, the just must be a mean and equal and relative to something (that is, for some persons); and in so far as it is a mean it is between things (that is, greater and less), in so far as it is equal, it is of two things, and in so far as it is just, it is for some people. Therefore, the just must involve four things at least; the persons for whom it is just are two, and the things which it involves are two. (1131^a15-20)

In a just relationship, the equality of the persons will be the same as the equality of the things (1131^a20-1). That is, X and Y will have equal things if, and only if, X and Y are themselves equal. There will be an unjust distribution when equal persons receive unequal things or unequal persons receive equal things. Aristotle calls the governing principle here 'geometrical proportion' (1131^b12-13).[6] The passage cited above (1131^a15-

---

[5] The adjective *dianemētikos*, 'distributive', is associated with the nouns *nomē* and *dianomē*, 'distribution', and the verbs *nemein*, *dianemein*, and *aponemein*, 'to distribute'.

[6] The idea that justice consists in proportionate equality is found in Aristotle's predecessors: e.g. the Pythagoreans (referred to at $5\ 1132^b21-2$), Isocrates (*Nicocles*, 15, and *Areopagiticus*, 21–2), and Plato (*Laws*, VI 757^c1-7).

20) suggests that this proportion consists in the following equality of ratios:

$$\frac{\text{Person } X}{\text{Person } Y} = \frac{X\text{'s share}}{Y\text{'s share}}$$

However, this is a purely formal principle until the respect in which the persons, on the one hand, and the things, on the other, are being compared is specified. Aristotle's formula assures that the persons are being compared on the basis of their *axia* (merit, worth, or desert) and that the things are compared on the basis of their value or choiceworthiness ($1131^a25–6$, $^b19–23$).[7] The proportion involved may thus be restated as follows:

$$\frac{\text{Merit of } X}{\text{Merit of } Y} = \frac{\text{The value of } X\text{'s share}}{\text{The value of } Y\text{'s share}}$$

Distributive justice presupposes a partitioning of a common asset into portions (e.g. parcels of property or political offices). A distribution (*dianomē*) is a function which assigns to each person in a given domain one of these portions. The result is that each person has a just claim or right[8] to a portion of the whole. Justice requires that rights be proportional to the merit of the right-holders:

$$\frac{\text{Merit of } X}{\text{Merit of } Y} = \frac{\text{The right of } X}{\text{The right of } Y}$$

For example, if X contributes one mina to a business venture while Y contributes ninety-nine, X has a just claim to only one-hundredth of the net earnings (see *Pol.* III 9 $1280^a25–31$). When the distribution does not conform to this principle—when individuals receive something other than what they have a right to—there will be justified complaints. If X contributes less than Y to the venture but receives the same share, then Y will justifiably complain. Or if X contributes the same but receives a smaller share, X will justifiably complain. In each case the complaint will be that the other party possesses more (*pleon echein*) than he has a right to.

Corrective[9] *justice* aims at the rectification of past losses due to the

[7] Illuminating reconstructions of Aristotle's formal principle of distributive justice are provided by Keyt (1991*a*) and Galston (1980), 145–50.

[8] Section 4.3 below defends the ascription of rights claims to Aristotle.

[9] The adjective *diorthōtikon* is associated with the adjective *orthos*, 'correct', and the verbs *diorthoun* and *epanorthoun*, 'to correct'.

injustice of others. Unlike distributive justice, corrective justice treats the parties involved as if they were numerically equal, because it is not concerned, as distributive justice is, with the distribution of a common asset. Rather it is concerned with repairing losses incurred in individual transactions.[10] In such a case the aim of the judge is to restore an unjust situation to a just one by restoring a sort of numerical equality between the parties (*EN* V 4 1131^{b}27–1132^{a}7). However, corrective justice resembles distributive justice in that a just claim consists in the mean between more and less:

Thus, the equal is a mean between the greater and the less, but profit and loss are more and less in opposite ways, since more of good and less of evil is a profit, and the opposite is a loss. And the equal, which we call just, is a mean. Corrective justice is thus the mean between profit and loss. (1132^{a}14–19)

If one party inflicts a loss on another, e.g. by taking the other's property, this produces an inequality. The wrongdoer has too much. This can be rectified only by the transfer of the property (or some equivalent) back to the original owner. The parties involved in a dispute typically turn to a jurist, whose task it is to determine the right (*to dikaion*) of each party, that is, what is his own (*to hauton*). Aristotle uses the analogy of adding and subtracting line segments. He seems to have the following in mind. Suppose *W* the wrongdoer has exacted an unfair gain from *V* the victim. The judge should bring about the following:

Before correction	*Transfer*	*After correction*
W's unjust share	Minus *W*'s unfair gain	What *W* has a right to
V's unjust share	Plus *V*'s unfair loss	What *V* has a right to

Here the equal is a mean between having more or less than one is entitled to. It has been complained that Aristotle's theory of corrective justice is unsatisfactory as a theory of punishment because it omits a criminal penalty.[11] On the other hand, it does emphasize compensation and the need to make the victim whole, which are essential to a theory of punishment.[12]

Aristotle's account of corrective justice presupposes an unspecified

---

[10] These are often private transactions, but in some cases the injured party is a public official (see *EN* V 5 1132^{b}23–30) or the polis itself (see 11 1138^{a}12–14).

[11] See Hardie (1980), 194–5. Plato recommends such a penalty in *Laws*, XI 933^{e}10–934^{a}1.

[12] See Barnett (1977 and 1980) for a recent defence of a similar theory of corrective justice.

concept of injustice: corrective justice is called for 'if one person does injustice and another suffers injustice, and if one has harmed and the other has been harmed. Thus the judge tries to equalize this unequal result because it is unequal' (1132^a5-7). Here Aristotle is using a commonplace conception of injustice as harming others through force or deception or unfair exchange.[13] The harms in question may be due to vices other than excessive possessiveness (*pleonexia*): e.g. adultery often results from intemperance though it may result from possessiveness (2 1130^a24-8). Moreover, injustices frequently include bodily injuries such as wounds (4 1132^a7-9), which are often the result of insolence (*hubris*). 'Insolence' implies not merely pride or arrogance, but also a tendency to wanton and abusive behaviour. The verb *hubrizein* is frequently used for violent acts such as beatings or rapes (III 6 1115^a22-3, VII 6 1148^b30-1) typically due to false pride (IV 3 1124^a29).

Reciprocal justice, which Aristotle calls 'proportional reciprocity' (*to antipeponthos kat' analogian*), is concerned with communities of exchange (*EN* V 5 1132^b31-3). Although his discussion of this type of justice raises difficulties,[14] his main point is clear: individuals will form a community of exchange only if the exchange is just, and an exchange is just only if the things exchanged are in some way equal (see 1133^a12, 24). Hence, as he sees it, reciprocal justice requires that the things exchanged be in some way 'equalized' (*isasthēnai*). The basic idea is as follows:

$$\frac{\text{Value of } A}{\text{Value of } B} = \frac{\text{Units of } B}{\text{Units of } A}$$

[13] This commonplace notion of justice invites comparison with the vulgar (*phortikon*) conception which Socrates employs in *Rep.* IV $442^d10-443^a11$. A just person in this sense abstains from embezzlement, perjury, adultery, etc. This sort of justice lies in a person's 'external actions' regarding property, other persons, contracts, and political affairs (443^c10, 443^c3-4).

[14] The place of reciprocal justice in Aristotle's theory is obscure. At *EN* V 2 1130^b30- 1131^a9, he expressly distinguishes between *two* types of particular justice: distributive justice and corrective justice (cf. *to loipon hen*, 'the remaining one', at 4 1131^b25). But at 5 1132^b31-3 he recognizes reciprocal justice as a distinct type involved in communities of exchange and emphasizes that it holds the polis together (cf. *Pol.* II 2 1261^a30-1). This discrepancy may be due to the fact that *EN* V 2 and V 5 were written at different times. Jackson (1879), 87, is probably correct to take Aristotle to be introducing a third form of justice. Similarly, Ross (1949), 213, followed by Hardie (1980), 194, views *EN* V 5 as an 'afterthought' or appendix. See also Harrison (1957), 44–5. Aquinas uses the term 'commutative justice' for both corrective justice and reciprocal justice in his *Commentary to Aristotle's Nicomachean Ethics*, sect. 947–99. Strictly speaking, however, commutative justice is what makes an exchange just and is distinct from corrective justice (which corrects a previous unjust exchange).

Thus, if a housebuilder and a bedmaker exchange their products, and a house is five times as valuable as a bed, then five beds will be an equal exchange for one house. This analysis presupposes that there is some way of equalizing houses and beds. Aristotle proposes obscurely that the measure (*metron*) by which things can be equalized is need (*chreia*), since need holds people together in a community and there would be no exchange without need (1133^a25-^b10). Unfortunately, he does not explain what 'need' is or how it performs its measuring and equalizing function. He also claims that money has the effect of measuring and equalizing things exchanged at different times (1133^b10-26; cf. *Pol.* I 9 1257^a28-41). If a house is equal to five minas and a bed to one mina, then five beds are equal to one house. 'It is clear that this is how exchange preceded money, for it does not matter whether five beds were exchanged for a house or for the amount that the five beds cost' (1133^b26-8). Each party to the exchange, then, should get something 'equal'. In effect, parties to an exchange have a right to the value of their commodity. If either party gets less than this, he has been done an injustice and gets less than he has a right to (cf. *Pol.* I 10 1258^a40-^b2).[15]

3.3. NATURAL AND LEGAL JUSTICE

Aristotle's analysis of universal and particular justice is followed by a discussion of political justice, as distinguished from justice without qualification (*EN* V 6 1134^a24-6). The latter is presumably present in any sort of community, whereas political justice is found only in a *political* community, that is, among free and equal persons living together in order to establish a self-sufficient community (1134^a26-8). The other forms of justice (e.g. the form that holds within a household) resemble political justice, but the latter holds between individuals separate from one another. Political justice applies to those who are naturally suited (*epephukei*) for law, and those who have equality in ruling and being ruled (1134^b8-15).

According to Aristotle, political justice is in part natural (*phusikon*) and in part legal (*nomikon*) (7 1134^b18-19). Although this distinction is loosely related to what is traditionally called the 'nature–convention' distinction, Aristotle's formulation differs in that instead of distinguishing between

---

[15] For further discussion of commutative justice in the *Politics*, see Sect. 9.5 below.

natural and political (or civil) justice,[16] he makes the distinction *within* political justice itself. He seems to mean that certain features of a constitution and legal system are based on nature, whereas others are due simply to human contrivance. For he characterizes the natural part as having everywhere the same power and not depending on opinion, and the legal part as being a matter of indifference until legislated. Of the latter examples are the amount of a prisoner's ransom, the sacrifice for a particular religious cult, and various decrees (7 1134^{b}18–24). The legal (*nomikon, nomōi, kata nomon*) is also referred to as the contractual (*sunthēkēi, kata sunthēkēn*),[17] indicating that it is the result of agreement in some sense. It remains to be seen how Aristotle thinks the distinction between the natural and the legal can be justified, but it is noteworthy that the distinction is applied directly to constitutions:

The things that are just according to contract and advantage are similar to measures; for the measures of wine and corn are not equal everywhere, but they are bigger for wholesale and smaller for retail. Similarly, things that are just which are not natural but human [products] are not the same everywhere, since constitutions are also not [the same], but one [constitution] only is everywhere according to nature the best. (1134^{b}35–1135^{a}5)

Aristotle thus maintains that nature rather than law provides the standard for determining which constitution is the best.

Aristotle addresses the objection that there is no natural justice because the natural is unchangeable and has everywhere the same power, whereas we observe that just things change (from place to place and from time to time). He responds that although just things in the human realm may change, this does not prevent them from being by nature. He suggests an analogy with right-handedness: 'the right is superior (*kreittōn*) by nature, but it is possible for everybody to become ambidextrous' (1134^{b}33–5). Unfortunately he does not make clear the point of this analogy. Indeed, his discussion as a whole suffers from a high degree of abstractness. The *Magna Moralia* discussion of natural justice, which largely agrees with the *Nicomachean Ethics*, adds that the natural is that which holds for the most part and the greater time (I 33 1194^{b}37–9, 1195^{a}3–4). This suggests that the use of 'natural' in connection with justice is on a par with its use

---

[16] The sophists generally treated nature as *opposed* to convention: see especially Antiphon, *On Truth, DK* 87 B 44, Hippias in Plato, *Prot.* 337^{c}6–^{e}2, Callicles in *Gorg.* 482^{c}4–486^{d}1, Thrasymachus in *Rep.* I 343^{b}1–344^{c}8 (cf. Glaucon in *Rep.* II 358^{c}3–360^{d}7).

[17] See 1134^{b}32, 35. Although the word *nomos* is also translated as 'convention', I generally avoid this translation because the English term is vague, leaving it unclear as to whether it translates *nomos* or some term for agreement (e.g. *sunthēkē, homologia*, or *sumbola*).

in the physical sciences.[18] However, the analogy remains rather obscure, because the constitution which he regards as the best exists hardly ever if at all (see *Pol.* IV 11 1295ᵃ25–31).

In an attempt to understand the analogy with right-handedness, it is instructive to review the treatment of right-handedness in Aristotle's biological writings in connection with the claims about justice in *Politics*, I 2.[19] Regarding right-handedness, *De Incessu Animalium* states that the right is the same in all animals and that all animals alike are necessarily right-handed. Moreover, in human beings the left is disconnected from the right (that is, the limbs on the right side are capable of independent movement) to a greater extent than in other animals, so that the right is 'most right', i.e. dexterous (4 706ᵃ19–22). Aristotle would reject the contention of Plato's *Laws* that there is no natural difference between right and left (VII 794ᵈ5–795ᵈ5). For the natural superiority of the right is due, on Aristotle's view, to the fact that 'the nature of the right is to initiate movement, that of the left is to be moved' (*IA* 4 705ᵇ33–706ᵃ1). Indeed, he argues that the right is more honourable (*timiōteron*) precisely because it is the origin of movement for animals (5 706ᵇ12–16). This pattern of inference from causal efficacy to evaluative superiority, found throughout his biology, is based on his teleological method. This method explains the presence, structure, and interrelationships of the parts and processes of living things in terms of their contributions to goal-directed systems. This is evident from the following argument regarding the value of sleep:

> Since we say that nature acts for the sake of something and that this is a good; and that to everything which by nature moves, but cannot with pleasure to itself move always and continuously, rest is necessary and beneficial; and since, taught by truth itself, men apply to sleep this metaphorical term, calling it 'rest': we conclude that it occurs for the sake of the preservation of animals. (*Somn.* 2 455ᵇ17–22)

---

[18] The natural is connected with 'always or for the most part' at *An. Pr.* I 3 25ᵇ14, 13 32ᵇ5–8; *Phys.* II 1 198ᵇ35–6; *PA* III 2 663ᵇ28–9; *GA* I 19 727ᵇ29–30; IV 4 770ᵇ11–13, 8 777ᵃ19–21; and *Rhet.* I 10 1369ᵃ35–ᵇ2 (cf. *Met.* V 12 1027ᵃ8–11). Cf. Michael of Ephesus, who describes unnatural cases as rare (*spanioi*), *In Ethica Nicomachea*, V (*CIAG*, xx. 3), 47.25.

[19] What follows is a condensed statement of an interpretation which is developed and documented more extensively in Miller (1991), which also discusses the relation of the discussions of natural law in the *Rhetoric* to the treatments of natural justice in Aristotle's ethical works. I argue that a qualified concept of natural law (excluding the implicit theism of the *Rhetoric*) can be imputed to Aristotle, but this is not essential to my interpretation in this section.

The presence of an attribute is explained by the fact that it is necessary or beneficial for the end or good of the organism. In regard to right-handedness, self-movement is an essential characteristic of all animals, and the part by which animals originate movement is consequently of value. Thus, the claim that the right side is better and more honourable than the left is based on Aristotle's teleology.

The concluding argument of *Politics*, I 2 (discussed in Section 2.5 above), suggests why Aristotle regards right-handedness as analogous to justice. Right-handedness is a superior trait because it is necessary for the perfection or self-realization of animals *qua* self-movers. Similarly, justice in his view is indispensable for the perfection of human beings. Without it they are like beasts fighting over sex, food, and material possessions. Justice differs from right-handedness because the latter is an innate trait, whereas the former is acquired by habituation. However, it might be objected that justice is not 'natural' in the same sense as right-handedness because justice does not, in fact, exist always or for the most part. As noted above, the constitution which Aristotle regards as best and fully just is exceedingly rare if not non-existent. However, Aristotle is not committed to the view that justice is 'natural' in this sense. He needs only to hold that if human beings act justly, they will (always or for the most part) realize their natural ends.[20] This is consistent with the observation that humans often fail to act justly if they are not habituated appropriately in a legal system (see *EN* X 9 $1179^b31-1180^a24$). The claim that political justice is partly natural thus implies that the lawgiver should fashion the constitution and laws so that they exhibit this feature and thus promote the perfection of the citizens.

However, nature does not provide complete guidance, so that the politician needs to exercise inventiveness and even arbitrariness in designing constitutions and laws. Moreover, politicians will confront widely different circumstances, different populations with different aptitudes and different resources and geographical settings. Consequently, in addition to the ransom and religious rules mentioned in the *Nicomachean Ethics*, the political institutions may exhibit great variability: particular offices and their functions; terms of office; numbers of persons on councils, juries, and other bodies; precise methods of selecting officials; and so forth.

None the less, on Aristotle's view, justice in so far as it is natural serves as a normative constraint on the politician. For Aristotle's teleological

---

[20] Cf. *An. Pr.* I 13 32^b5-10: a man turns grey naturally in the sense that *if* a man exists, he turns grey necessarily or for the most part.

explanations have evaluative implications. To illustrate, the explanation of sleep cited above proceeds from two claims: 'we say that nature acts for the sake of something and that this is a good' (*Somn.* 2 455^{b}17–18). The first claim is that what is according to nature is for the sake of an end (*PA* I 1 641^{b}12, 5 645^{a}23–6; *Phys.* II 8 199^{a}7–8; *Pol.* I 2 1252^{b}32), and the second is that the end is good (*Phys.* II 2 194^{a}32–3, 3 195^{a}23–5; *Met.* I 3 983^{a}31–2; *Pol.* I 2 1252^{b}34–1253^{a}1). According to Aristotle's political naturalism a polis can exist in a natural or an unnatural condition. But the good for a polis is justice or the common advantage (III 12 1282^{b}14–18). Hence, a political community in a natural condition is a just community.

Aristotle does not say how his distinction between natural and legal justice is related to the distinction between universal and particular justice which is discussed in the previous section. However, he provides some clues as to what he would say. In the case of universal justice, the just is the lawful and the laws aim either at the common advantage of all or of the best or of those in authority, as based on virtue or some other standard; hence, universal justice promotes and safeguards happiness for the political community (*EN* V 1 1129^{b}11–19). The laws do this by promoting virtues such as courage and temperance and discouraging vices such as cowardice and insolence. Such laws may be good or bad depending on whether they are correctly or carelessly framed (1129^{b}19–25). This implies that universal justice in the sense of the lawful is natural justice in so far as it requires actions which accord with virtues (and prohibits actions which accord with vices) of the sort mentioned in *Politics*, I 2—i.e. in so far as it instils the traits necessary for human perfection and eliminates traits detrimental to the human natural end.

A similar distinction can be made for the particular forms of justice. An action or law will be naturally just in the particular sense (distributive, corrective, or reciprocal) to the extent that it is necessary for human perfection. This is especially evident from Aristotle's treatment of exchange. He views barter as a natural form of exchange: it arises from the natural fact that human beings have more or less than enough to meet their needs and that the exchange of goods exists in order to promote natural self-sufficiency (*Pol.* I 9 1257^{a}15–17, 28–30). A reasonable extension of this is commerce, involving the use of money, which in turn is introduced as a medium of exchange by contract or mutual agreement. Aristotle suggests that money derived its Greek name *nomisma* from the fact that it exists not by nature but by law (*nomōi*), and that it is in our power to change it and make it useless (*EN* V 5 1133^{a}28–31; *Pol.* I 9

$1257^b 10-13$). Money thus involves the kind of arbitrariness associated with legal justice. There is no necessity in terms of nature that a good should have a certain monetary price, but, given that it does, it is legally unjust to sell it for any other price. Legal justice can also come into conflict with nature, e.g. if the law permits a merchant to extract an excessive profit or a lender to collect interest. Aristotle regards such transactions as against nature and obviously thinks the laws should prohibit them (*Pol.* I 10 $1258^a 40^{-b}8$). In general, the politicians should strive to bring the polis into a natural condition by framing the correct laws and constitution.

3.4. POLITICAL JUSTICE, CONSTITUTION, AND LAWS

The particular embodiment of political justice is the constitution (*EE* VII 9 $1241^b 14-15$).[21] The following passage contains Aristotle's most important statement regarding the constitution:

> The constitution (*politeia*) is an order (*taxis*) in polises concerning the manner in which offices are distributed, what the authority (*to kurion*) of the polis is, and what the end is of each community. But the laws are separate from the [principles] that indicate the constitution, and it is according to the laws that the officials ought to rule and guard against those who violate them. (*Pol.* IV 1 $1289^a 15-20$; cf. 3 $1290^a 7-10$ and Plato, *Laws*, VI $751^a 4^{-b}2$)

Aristotle regards the constitution as, in effect, the formal cause and the final cause of the polis. The statement that the constitution defines the end of the community may be compared with the claim that it is a certain way of life (*bios*) of the polis (IV 11 $1295^a 40^{-b}1$). As the order or structure (*taxis*) of the polis (cf. III 6 $1278^b 8-9$), the constitution is, in effect, the form which the lawgiver has provided for the polis (see III 3 $1276^b 7-8$). The order of the political community is also identified with justice (*dikē*)

---

[21] Following tradition, I translate *politeia* as 'constitution', except where the term refers to a specific type of constitution, in which case it is translated as 'polity'. It is unfortunate that there is no English equivalent which captures the close relation to 'politics'. (*Politēs*, 'citizen', presents the same problem.) Strauss (1953), 136, objects to the legalistic connotations of 'constitution' and proposes instead 'regime' as a translation of *politeia*, which is acceptable provided that 'regime' is taken in the sense of 'a form of government'. The English 'constitution' derives from the Latin verb *constituo*, 'set up, establish', which corresponds to the Greek verb *sunhistēmi* (which is also used for the framing of constitutions: see I 2 $1253^a 29-31$).

in the sense of 'the administration of justice' in I 2 1253ª37–8 (see Section 2.5 above). The close connection between justice and the constitution is a central theme in Book III, and indeed throughout the *Politics*.

The constitution organizes the polis by assigning political authority or rule within it (cf. IV 2 1290ª7–11). *Politics*, III 6, distinguishes constitutions accordingly: 'those constitutions which look to the common advantage are correct according to justice without qualification, and those which look only to the advantage of the rulers are all mistaken and deviations from the correct constitutions; for they are despotic, but the polis is a community of free persons' (1279ª17–21).[22]

The constitution incorporates justice in the various forms discussed in Section 3.2 above. The distinction of constitutions in *Politics*, III 6–7, into correct (promoting the common advantage) and deviant (promoting the advantage of the rulers) parallels the distinction within universal justice between the laws aiming at the common advantage of all and the advantage of those in authority (*EN* V 1 1129ᵇ14–19). The constitution will also exemplify particular forms of justice. Distributive justice will guide the lawgivers and other politicians who are concerned with distributing offices and property among the citizens, as well as assigning burdens (taxes, military obligations, and public services). Corrective justice is to be exercised by the jurors and by those magistrates charged with rectifying past injustices. Reciprocal justice is to guide magistrates in regulating market exchanges and also the citizens as they take turns in holding office (*Pol.* II 2 1261ª30–7).

The concept of nature also underlies Aristotle's account of the justice of constitutions. He remarks that different groups are suited by nature for different types of rule, e.g. despotic rule for natural slaves and kingly or political rule for others—and that each of these is just and advantageous. But there is not a group which is suited according to nature for tyranny or any of the other deviant constitutions, because these come to be against nature (III 17 1287ᵇ37–41). Thus Aristotle holds the principle that the polis is in a natural condition (*kata phusin*) when it has a correct or just constitution and in an unnatural condition (*para phusin*) when it has a deviant or unjust constitution.[23] He thereby explicitly extends the teleological account of justice discussed in the previous section to his theory of constitutions. What is natural for an organism is good for it on Aristotle's

---

[22] Aristotle's classification of constitutions is discussed more fully in Sect. 5.2 below.

[23] The idea of natural and unnatural rule is found in Plato, *Rep.* IV 444ᵈ3–11. Cf. III 415ᶜ1–2 where honour is to be given in a manner appropriate to the recipient's nature; see also V 454ᵇ4–9.

view, and when a community of human beings is in a natural condition it achieves the common good—it is in a condition of justice.

In addition to framing the constitution the lawgivers (as their name implies) have the task of legislation: 'the laws ought to be laid down relative to the constitutions and all are so laid down, but the constitutions ought not to be laid down relative to the laws' (IV 1 1289ª13–15).[24] In general, the laws belonging to a just constitution are just, whereas those belonging to a deviant constitution are unjust (III 11 1282ᵇ6–13). However, particular laws may be poorly designed so that they defeat the end of the constitution. For example, the laws governing property rights may hinder the citizens from exercising their political rights effectively (see II 9 1270ª16–22).

The laws properly serve the constitution by defining the rights and duties of citizens. They determine who has the right to serve in which offices and what authority each office has, who has the right to possess arms and perform military service, who has the right to acquire or transfer property under what circumstances, who has the right to be educated and in what manner, and what duties are associated with the foregoing rights. Further, when such rights and duties are violated, the laws determine what compensation or punishment is due. Particular laws are able to perform their function because they possess three distinctive properties. First, the laws are universal or general rules (*EN* V 7 1135ª5–8, 10 1137ᵇ13; cf. *Pol.* III 11 1282ᵇ4–6, 15 1286ª9–11; II 8 1269ª9–12; and *Rhet.* I 13 1374ª28–ᵇ1). In this respect a law (*nomos*) differs from a decree (*psēphisma*), which is concerned with a particular circumstance or action such as the granting of citizenship or immunity (V 7 1134ᵇ23–4, 10 1137ᵇ27–32, VI 8 1141ᵇ24–8; cf. *Pol.* IV 4 1292ª36–7).[25] Second, the written laws are (or should be) as clear, unambiguous, and definite as possible (cf. *EN* VIII 13 1162ᵇ21–1163ª1, and *Rhet.* I 13 1374ª29–30, 34). A law might state that all citizens are at liberty to attend the assembly, but impose a specified fine upon citizens who fail to attend if they meet a certain property assessment (*Pol.* IV 13 1297ª17–19). Third, the laws have a compelling power (*anagkastikē dunamis*, *EN* X 9 1180ª21). They involve sanctions and are enforceable by the appropriate officials in the polis. In the most favourable circumstances, the laws will also exhibit stability over time (II 8 1269ª9–27). Because of all these features, the laws

---

[24] See the opening lines of *Pol.* III, which imply that the study of the constitution is the primary concern. Elsewhere, Plato's *Laws* is criticized for talking about the laws and neglecting the constitution (*Pol.* II 6 1265ª1–2).

[25] See MacDowell (1978), 45, on the difference between *psēphisma* and *nomos*.

are able to perform the function of organizing or structuring the polis (III 16 1287ᵃ18; cf. II 10 1271ᵇ32) and of instructing and habituating the citizens (*Pol.* III 16 1287ᵇ25–6; *EN* V 1 1129ᵇ19–25, X 9 1179ᵇ34–5).

These features of the laws support Aristotle's claim that 'where the laws do not rule, there is no constitution' (IV 4 1292ᵃ30–2).²⁶ The rule of law is present even in the deviant constitutions, except for the most extreme forms which do not deserve the name 'constitution': tyranny, dynasty (extreme oligarchy), and extreme democracy (5 1292ᵇ5–10). The rule of law is contrasted with the rule according to the wish or will (*kata boulēsin*) of the individual or multitude. Rule according to wish is exemplified by the monarch who rules by edict (*epitagma*) or the assembly which rules by decree (*psēphisma*). The rule of law is especially characteristic of systems where the citizens share in ruling, alternating or taking turns in ruling and being ruled. Each person must be willing to rule with a view to the advantage of others and to yield up authority when it is another person's turn to rule (cf. III 6 1279ᵃ8–13).

Aristotle considers a number of arguments for the rule of law from Plato and others: the law, in contrast to a human being, is impartial (III 16 1287ᵃ41–ᵇ5). If all political activity were left up to decisions by individuals on a case-by-case basis, there is a danger that they would be influenced by particular factors such as friendship or animosity, and by self-interest rather than justice. The process of framing the laws involves considerable deliberation, and the politician can take a broader view of the issues (see *Rhet.* I 1 1354ᵃ34–ᵇ11; cf. *Pol.* III 9 1280ᵃ14–16). Moreover, the law is the embodiment of 'intellect without desire'. Law as such is not subject to the influence of desire or spirit which subverts human decision makers, e.g. through spite or favouritism (III 16 1287ᵃ32).²⁷ Aristotle would presumably accept the equation of law with reason if it meant that the politician uses the science of politics and his practical wisdom to identify the best constitution and to fashion the laws best suited to this constitution (cf. *EN* X 9 1180ᵃ21–2; *Pol.* IV 1 1289ᵃ11–13). Reason and the law are impartial. Judges may err when deciding on their own case, and for similar reasons doctors when they are ill consult with other doctors (III 16 1287ᵃ41–ᵇ5). Impartiality is also essential to the political aim of promoting justice and the common good (cf. *EN* V 6 1134ᵃ35–ᵇ2).

Aristotle's endorsement of the rule of law is qualified. He holds that it

²⁶ On the development of the principle of rule of law in 5th-cent. Athens see Ostwald (1986).

²⁷ Plato also connects law (*nomos*) with reason (*logos*) at *Laws*, IV 714ᵃ1–2; cf. I 644ᵈ1–3, 645ᵃ1–2; VIII 835ᶜ4–5.

is not enough for the citizens to have good laws and institutions; they must also be morally habituated to abide by them (*Pol.* V 9 1310ᵃ14–17). This is necessary if they are to be committed to their constitution and if it is to become their 'way of life' (IV 11 1295ᵃ40–ᵇ1). Hence, a major task of the politician is to design and maintain a sound educational system.

An important qualification of the principle of the rule of law involves Aristotle's notion of equity (*epieikeia*). Although the universality of the laws is a source of their strength, it can sometimes be a cause of weakness. The lawgiver tries to frame laws which are almost always correct, but recognizes that in some cases they may yield unjust results. Equity is the correction of a law in so far as it is defective due to its universality. In such a case the equitable decision is just, because it is what the lawgiver would have decided in these particular circumstances if he had been present. Not all things can be decided according to the laws; in some cases a decree is needed. There is an indefiniteness in particulars which can sometimes only be handled in an *ad hoc* way. Aristotle compares the use of decrees to the use of a Lesbian rule (straight-edge) made of soft lead: just as the rule is not rigid but adapts itself to the shape of the stone, the decree is adapted to particular circumstances (*EN* V 10 1137ᵇ26–32; cf. *Pol.* III 11 1282ᵇ1–6 and *Rhet.* I 13 1374ᵃ25–ᵇ23).

A more serious difficulty arises for the principle of the rule of law in connection with absolute kingship. When an individual or small number of individuals so exceeds the other citizens in virtue and political ability that the others are not even commensurable with them, then Aristotle's theory of justice would seem to require that the superior person or persons have the right to rule over the others (III 13 1284ᵃ3–11, 17 1288ᵃ24–9). Aristotle describes the absolute kings as a law unto themselves (13 1284ᵃ13–14, 17 1288ᵃ3). This implies that the absolute king rules over the polis in a manner which is virtuous, practically rational, and impartial to the same degree and as consistently as the rule of law. Nevertheless, absolute kingship is not an instance of the rule of law in the strict Aristotelian sense.²⁸ Aristotle also speaks of kingship as the 'first and most divine' constitution (IV 2 1289ᵃ39–ᵇ1), which implies that the rule of law is only found in the 'second-best' constitution.²⁹ However, Aristotle's best constitution in *Politics*, VII–VIII, is not absolute kingship but a

---

²⁸ See Miller (1979).

²⁹ The Eleatic Stranger in Plato's *Statesman* argues that absolute kingship exercised by the enlightened individual with wisdom (*sophia*) is superior in principle to the rule of law (294ᵃ7–8, 297ᵇ7–ᶜ4, 300ᶜ9–ᵈ2), but remarks that such individuals do not commonly arise (301ᵈ8–ᶜ4; cf. *Pol.* VII 14 1332ᵇ23–5). Similarly, the Athenian Stranger in *Laws*, IX 875ᶜ3–ᵈ5, advocates the rule of law as the second-best solution. Cf. Morrow (1960), ch. 11.

system of shared authority implicitly involving the rule of law (although the term 'rule of law' is not explicitly used in Books VII–VIII).[30]

3.5. JUSTICE OUTSIDE THE POLIS

For Aristotle the virtue of justice in all its forms is essentially concerned with the community (see Section 3.2 above). However, he distinguishes between political justice and justice without qualification, which prompts the question whether he regards the scope of justice as confined to members of one's own political community. Would he acknowledge any appeals of justice concerning the treatment of individuals who fall outside the polis? There is, in fact, evidence that he recognizes non-political forms of justice. One passage which explicitly admits a non-political form of justice is in the *Eudemian Ethics*:

To seek, then, into how one ought to behave towards a friend is to seek into a sort of justice (*dikaion ti*). For generally all justice is in fact in relation to a friend. For justice belongs to persons who have [something] in common (*koinōnois*), and the friend is a person who has [something] in common, whether a family or a way of life. For a human being is not only a political but also a householding animal, and he does not form unions like other animals with any chance person, whether male or female;[31] . . . but a human being is an animal that is capable of having [something] in common (*koinōnikon*) with those with whom he is by nature akin; and therefore there would be a community (*koinōnia*) and a sort of justice (*dikaion ti*) even if there were no polis; for a household is a sort of friendship. (VII 10 1242ᵃ19–28)

We might, however, regard this as a type of 'proto-justice', in view of the subsequent statement: 'In the household first are the sources and springs of friendship, the constitution, and justice' (1242ᵃ40–ᵇ1; cf. *EN* V 7 1134ᵇ8–11, *MM* I 33 1194ᵇ5–13).

Another passage in the *Nicomachean Ethics* seems to allow for the possibility of justice and friendship even between a master and a slave:

For in cases where the ruler and ruled have nothing in common, there is no friendship; for there is no justice either; for example, in the case of the artisan in relation to his tool, the soul in relation to the body, and the master in relation to the slave; for in all these cases one is benefited by what he uses, but there is no friendship or justice in relation to soulless things. Nor is there any friendship or justice in relation to a horse or a cow, or in relation to a slave in so far as he is a slave. For they have nothing in common; for the slave is an ensouled tool, and a

---

[30] The problems raised by absolute kingship are discussed more fully in Sect. 4.8 below.

[31] Omitting *all' hai dia dumon aulikon*.

tool is a soulless slave. Therefore in so far as he is a slave, there is no friendship in relation to him; but in so far as he is a human being, there is; for every human being seems to have some justice in relation to everyone who is capable of having law and contract in common. There is friendship, then, to the extent that he is a human being. (VIII 11 1161ª32–ᵇ8)

This passage has attracted some attention from commentators, since it seems to palliate, if ever so slightly, Aristotle's advocacy of natural slavery in *Politics*, I (see also Section 6.9 below). However, what is relevant here is the statement that there is justice between individuals whenever they are capable of having law and contract in common. This provides a general criterion for justice which seems to transcend the bounds of the polis. However, as the example before us illustrates, the resulting principle of justice is too weak, in Aristotle's view, to serve as a barrier to natural slavery.

An evidently stronger principle of justice emerges, however, from a passage in the *Politics* where Aristotle is considering different views concerning the end of the polis, namely, whether it should promote the political or the philosophic way of life. He remarks: 'Some people believe that ruling over one's neighbours despotically involves very great injustice, whereas doing so politically is not unjust but an impediment to one's own cheerfulness' (VII 2 1324ª35–8). Others have opposing views, defending the practical and political life as the only way of life for a man.

Others, again, say that the despotic and tyrannical mode of constitution is the only happy one; indeed, among some people this is the standard of the constitution and the laws, to treat their neighbours despotically. . . . [T]hus in Lacedaemon and Crete education and the majority of the laws are mainly framed with a view to war. Further, among all those nations which are capable of excessive taking (*pleonektein*) this power has been honoured, for example among the Scythians, Persians, Thracians, and Celts. (1324ᵇ1–5, 7–12)

Aristotle goes on to criticize this view as follows:

Yet it might perhaps seem overly strange (*atopon*) to those who wish to consider it, if it is the function of the politician to be able to study how he can rule and treat his neighbors despotically whether they wish it or not. How can that which is not even lawful be the characteristic of the politician or the lawgiver? And it is not lawful to rule not only justly[32] but unjustly, and it is possible to conquer unjustly also. . . . Yet the many seem to believe that despotic rule is politics, and

---

[32] Following Ross (1957), I omit the comma after *dikaiōs*. The point of this rather difficult sentence seems to be that it is against the laws of a polis to exercise rule in a manner which is indiscriminately just and unjust. The following clause is generally taken as a repudiation of the doctrine that 'might makes right'; see Newman (1887), iii. 330.

what they say is not just or advantageous in their own case they are not ashamed of training [themselves to do] to others; they seek just rule for themselves, but where other men are concerned they care nothing about just actions. (1324^b22–8, 32–6)

The point here is that it is strange for the citizens of polises such as Sparta and Crete to expect to be treated justly themselves while they are ready to act unjustly towards their neighbours, that is, those outside the polis, against whom they make war. This argument clearly presupposes that the conduct of the citizens of one polis towards foreigners who are not citizens of the polis falls under a general principle of justice. Military training should not be for the purpose of enslaving those who do not merit it, but for the purposes of preventing enslavement by others, seeking leadership in order to benefit those who are ruled, and of mastering those who merit slavery (14 1333^b38–1334^a2).[33] Extrapolating from Aristotle's other remarks about justice, his grounds are probably that foreigners are capable of some limited forms of co-operation or community—such as the mutual respect for rights and the exchange of goods—and that justice of a sort applies wherever such co-operation is possible. Therefore, Aristotle, in this passage at any rate, is anticipating the more explicit efforts of later moral theorists such as the Stoics to develop a moral point of view which includes all of humanity in its scope. It also seems plausible to understand this passage as an important early step in the just-war tradition which was developed more systematically by medieval philosophers.

However, Aristotle does not think that political justice derives from, or depends on, a pre-political form of justice. Justice applies wherever human beings have something in common, i.e. where it is possible for them to co-operate and form a community. The most perfect form of community is the political community, and the justice which it embodies is the most perfect form of justice. Other forms of justice are so called by similarity (*kath' homoiotēta*), because they resemble the primary case of political justice (see *EN* V 6 1134^a29–30), but none of them is prior to political justice.

[33] Some 19th-cent. interpreters viewed this passage as advocating for the best polis an aggressively hegemonic role like that of the British Empire or Bismarck's Prussia: see Susemihl and Hicks (1894), 55, and Newman (1887), i. 328. However, Keyt (1993), 149–50, objects that Aristotle's insistence that leadership over other naturally free peoples be exercised, not despotically, but 'for the benefit of those who are ruled' makes imperialism an improbable outgrowth of the best constitution. Keyt remarks that for Aristotle, 'A city in a position of leadership that looks to the advantage of the cities under its sway would seem to be even rarer than a city with a correct constitution.'

4

Rights

4.1. ARE THERE ANY 'RIGHTS' IN ARISTOTLE?

The notion that Aristotle, in some sense, recognizes the rights of individuals is not new. Ernest Barker offered such an interpretation: 'The life-breath of the State . . . is a justice which assures to each his rights, enforces on all their duties, and so gives to each and all their own.' He also sees this as a noteworthy departure from Plato: 'Plato thinks of the individual as bound to do the *duty* to which he is called as an organ of the State: Aristotle thinks of the individual as deserving the right which he *ought* to enjoy in a society based on (proportionate) equality.'[1] Further, A. C. Bradley called attention to the parallel between the debate over suffrage in nineteenth-century England and the discussion of constitutional justice in Aristotle's *Politics*. Like Aristotle, the English used the word 'right', as well as 'justice', in a double sense. Bradley distinguished these senses as follows:

When we say that a man has a right to the franchise, what do we mean? We may mean that according to the constitution, the English political *dikaion*, he can claim it, because he satisfies the conditions laid down by the law as necessary to the possession of it. But when the franchise is claimed as a right by those who do not satisfy these conditions, this cannot be the meaning. They really affirm that the actual law, the English *dikaion*, is not properly or absolutely just and does not express 'natural right', that, according to real justice, they ought to have the suffrage, and that, if they had it, the state would be less of a *parekbasis* [deviation] and nearer to the ideal.[2]

H. H. Joachim also saw a distinction between 'natural and legal right' in the discussions of natural law and justice in *Rhetoric*, I, and *Nicomachean Ethics*, V. He found there

rights which all men recognize as obtaining between man and man, no matter of what special form of community they may be members: rights founded on the

---

[1] Barker (1959), 235, on *Pol.* II 2 1261ᵃ30; also p. 340 n.
[2] Bradley (1991), 49–50. This essay was originally published in 1880.

nature of things, on the nature of man, rights of 'humanity'. Thus, for example, Antigone claims the right to bury her brother, in defiance of Creon who represents the State, on the ground that this is an inalienable natural right which no special legislation in a given state can affect.[3]

Joachim's interpretation was overstated, however, because there is no evidence that Aristotle (or Sophocles' Antigone) thought that individuals possessed a set of 'inalienable' rights in the sense advanced, for example, in the American Declaration of Independence. Moreover, it is doubtful whether Aristotle would speak of justice and rights without reference to some sort of community (see Section 3.5 above). None the less, Joachim evidently agreed with Bradley's claim that Aristotle's theory of natural justice provides a basis for rights 'founded on the nature of man', in distinction from merely conventional rights (i.e. rights which are merely conferred upon individuals by a particular constitution and set of laws).

On the other hand, the natural-rights interpretation of Aristotle has been assailed by a host of adversaries, led by the venerable W. L. Newman:

> The State does not come into being, in Aristotle's view, in derogation from, or limitation of, man's natural rights: on the contrary, it calls them into existence. It enunciates what is just (1253[a]37): it is in the State, and with reference to its end, that men's rights are to be determined (1282[b]14).[4]

The disagreement of Newman with Bradley and Joachim is partly verbal, stemming from their different uses of 'natural' as applied to 'rights'. The uses can be distinguished as follows: a natural$_1$ right is *based on natural justice*; a natural$_2$ right is possessed *in a state of nature*, i.e. in a prepolitical state. The senses are not equivalent, because the political rights which a citizen possesses in a just polis may be natural$_1$ without being natural$_2$. Moreover, modern theories of natural$_2$ rights typically treat rights as universal and inhering in human beings as such apart from any social or political relations. Natural$_1$ rights have no such implications. In the passages above Bradley ascribes to Aristotle a theory of natural$_1$ rights, whereas Newman denies that Aristotle has a theory of natural$_2$ rights. So far, they do not disagree on any substantive issue of interpretation. On the other hand, Newman rejects Joachim's interpretation that Aristotle (like Locke) has a theory of natural$_2$ rights, and Bradley would probably disagree with Joachim as well. This chapter defends an interpretation that combines Bradley's positive thesis with Newman's negative thesis: Aristotle has a theory of natural$_1$—but not of natural$_2$—rights.

---

[3] Joachim (1951), 154–5.   [4] Newman (1887), i. 32.

The rights interpretation of Aristotle even thus qualified is controversial. It is defended by a few, including Alan Gewirth.[5] In contrast, interpreters influenced by Hegel, such as T. H. Green, acknowledge the presence of rights in Aristotle only in a very weak, instrumental sense:

[Aristotle] regards the State as a society of which the life is maintained by what its members do for the sake of maintaining it, by functions consciously fulfilled with reference to that *end*, and which in that sense imposes duties; and at the same time as a society from which its members derive the ability through education and protection to fulfill their several functions, and which in this sense confers rights.[6]

On this view, evidently, individuals have 'rights' only in the attenuated sense that they should be permitted to perform their political functions. Other commentators such as R. G. Mulgan argue that the notion of individual rights is scarcely, if at all, present in Aristotle:

Like all ancient Greeks, [Aristotle] has little conception of individual or human rights, of obligations which are due to individuals because they are individual human beings. . . . Because the individuals had no inherent rights, there was less sense of conflict between competing claims of individual and state and therefore less sense of sacrifice in depriving individuals of their property or liberties.[7]

And among more recent political theorists, it has become almost a truism that there is no trace of rights (natural or otherwise) in Aristotle or other Greek or Roman political philosophers. This dictum is often coupled with the claim that the very notion of 'a right' is so alien to the ancients that any interpretation of Aristotle, which imputes rights to him must be guilty of anachronism.[8] These objections are noted in the following section. Against this, Section 4.3 submits evidence of 'rights' locutions in the writings of Aristotle and his contemporaries and makes the case that these have a logical force comparable to that of modern 'rights' locutions and that they can be used for 'natural' as well as 'conventional' rights claims.

[5] Gewirth (1978), 98–102, offers a brief survey of the evidence for and against the imputation of rights to pre-modern legal systems. He understands rights as 'rightful claims or powers had by individuals as subjects of rights', and contends that the concept is found in medieval European, ancient Roman and Greek, and even primitive cultures. Among other sources, Gewirth cites Vlastos (1981). Vlastos (1977; 1978) also argues that Plato has a concept of rights. See also Hansen (1989) for an argument that the ancient Athenian democracy recognized individual rights, including personal liberty, political equality, and private property.

[6] Green (1937), sect. 39. Green also denies that there are 'rights' locutions in Aristotle.

[7] Mulgan (1977), 33.

[8] This claim is made by Golding (1978 and 1981), Holmes (1979), Irwin (1977), MacIntyre (1981), Roshwald (1959), Strauss (1953), and Tuck (1979).

Following this review, Section 4.4 rebuts the arguments that it is anachronistic to impute rights claims to Aristotle. The remainder of this
chapter argues that Aristotle recognizes rights claims 'based on nature' as
opposed to rights merely 'based on law'. As a preliminary to this, Section
4.5 sketches, for purposes of comparison and contrast, the two principal
modern variants of natural-rights theory, those of Hobbes and Locke.
Section 4.6 sets forth Aristotle's theory of rights in the context of his
political theory. Section 4.7 discusses Aristotle's reasons for holding that
the respect for rights is in accord with individual practical rationality.

To avoid confusion, however, some caveats are needed. First, there is
admittedly an important sense in which Aristotle does not have a 'theory'
of rights. As Newman remarks, Aristotle has not 'realized the importance of such questions as "what is a right?" or "how do rights come into
existence, and why?" '.[9] Within his scientific enquiries, practical as well
as contemplative, Aristotle develops theories about many phenomena,
such as substance, motion, place, time, infinity, soul, and so forth, which
typically seek to answer questions such as 'What is it? In what manner
does it exist? Is there only one type of it or many?' and so forth. It is correct that Aristotle does not try to answer these sorts of questions about
rights in an explicit and systematic way. However, it is consistent with
this admission to impute to Aristotle a 'theory of rights' in another
important sense, namely, that he advances a set of recognizable rights
claims which have a firm basis in his theory of justice and which explain
other significant features of his political theory. In this latter sense, I
argue, Aristotle does have a theory of rights.

Second, as noted above, the phrase 'natural rights' is misleading because
it has two different senses: (1) based on natural justice, and (2) possessed
in a pre-political state of nature. A theory of natural$_2$ rights would typically
hold that individuals possess certain rights solely on account of their
natures as individuals and apart from any social or political considerations.
Given that Aristotle also holds that it is a part of *human* nature to be a
political animal, it is highly unlikely that he would recognize any rights
inhering in humans *qua* individuals. However, I am arguing that Aristotle
has a theory of natural$_1$ rights but not a theory of natural$_2$ rights, so that
theory belongs to the family of political theories (along with Locke's

---

[9] Newman (1887), i. 93. Newman, however, also complains that 'Aristotle seldom, if
ever, goes behind the services, the exchange of which constitutes society, to the rights which
are implied in that exchange'. I think that this criticism goes too far, and, indeed, Newman's
own detailed commentary to the *Politics* provides ample evidence for a more central role for
rights in Aristotle.

theory) which denies that individuals possess rights merely by convention.[10] However, 'natural rights' is very commonly confined to natural$_2$ rights. Therefore, to avoid confusion I shall not impute 'natural rights' *simpliciter* to Aristotle, but instead shall speak of 'rights based on nature'.

Finally, it is necessary to distinguish between theories of rights 'based on nature' and the family of theories belonging to the modern liberal tradition. Historically, there is an overlap between the two groups, because many modern proponents of liberalism have invoked rights based on nature. However, other liberals, especially in the twentieth century, have appealed instead to utilitarianism, contractarianism, or other ethical doctrines for theoretical underpinnings. It is, on the other hand, possible for a rights theorist to advocate a more expansive and intrusive state than modern liberals would find acceptable, e.g. a perfectionist might argue that the state should secure the rights of individuals to be virtuous by habituating them coercively. Hence, to attribute a theory of rights based on nature to Aristotle is not *per se* to locate him in the liberal tradition.[11] Nor is it to ascribe to him the Enlightenment doctrines 'that all men are created equal' or 'that they are endowed by their Creator with certain unalienable rights'.

4.2. OBJECTIONS TO 'RIGHTS' IN ARISTOTLE

It has recently become fashionable to hold that it is anachronistic to impute any concept of rights to Aristotle or indeed to any ancient thinker. Some writers argue that modern locutions for rights are altogether alien to ancient languages such as Aristotle's Greek. This is ostensibly the position of Alasdair MacIntyre, who makes the sweeping declaration that 'there is no expression in any ancient or medieval language correctly translated by our expression "a right" until near the close of the Middle Ages: the concept lacks any means of expression in Hebrew, Greek, Latin or Arabic, classical or medieval, before about 1400, let alone in Old English, or in Japanese even as late as the mid-nineteenth century.'[12] G. H. Sabine also denies that the Greeks had any conception of rights:

[10] Thus, although Hegel is correct that 'Aristotle could not have had any thought of a so-called natural right (if a natural right be wanted), that is, the idea of the abstract man outside of any actual relation to others' (*Lectures on the History of Philosophy* (1955), iii. 208), it does not follow that Aristotle had no idea of rights possessed according to nature in a political context. From the fact that Aristotle did not recognize natural$_2$ rights, it does not follow that he rejected natural$_1$ rights (rights 'based on nature').

[11] Cf. Gray (1986), ch. 6, on the distinction between the natural-rights tradition and liberalism. See also Sects. 6.9 and 10.5 below.   [12] MacIntyre (1981), 67.

The modern notion of a citizen as a man to whom certain rights are legally guaranteed would have been better understood by the Roman than by the Greek, for the Latin *ius* does partly imply this possession of private right. The Greek, however, thought of his citizenship not as a possession but as something shared, much like membership in a family. This fact had a profound influence upon Greek political philosophy. It meant that the problem as they conceived it was not to gain a man his rights but to ensure him the place to which he was entitled.[13]

Some writers allow that the Greek term *dikaion* may be translated as 'right', but they contend that in such cases it has an 'objective' as opposed to a 'subjective' sense. For example, Michel Villey argues that in Roman law *ius* refers to a right or just thing in itself, or to a correct assignment of things to persons, rather than to a right that inheres in the individual right-holder as such.[14] A similar claim might be made about *dikaion*, the Greek counterpart to *ius*. Similarly, Leo Strauss uses 'right' in the adjectival sense in the expression 'classic natural *right*', which he distinguishes from modern theories of natural *rights*.[15] This use is also found in Harry Jaffa, who takes classic 'natural *right*' to refer to 'the objective rightness of things', whereas modern natural rights are the rights that all men possess.[16] Mordecai Roshwald also treats this as the distinction between 'the use of "right" as an adjective and as a noun'. He maintains that the ancients used 'right' only as an adjective, whereas moderns have attempted to derive the nounal use—e.g. 'the *rights* of man'—from 'natural right' (the adjectival use).[17]

Frequently combined with such linguistic points are theoretical arguments that it is a mistake to attribute a concept of rights to ancient philosophers such as Aristotle. The point is not simply that Aristotle does not share the concern of modern political theorists like Locke with advancing the rights of individuals against the state. Rather, it is, in effect, that there is no 'conceptual space' for the notion of rights in pre-modern theorists like Aristotle. Strauss contends, 'One could not assert the primacy of natural rights without asserting that the individual is in every respect prior to civil society: all rights of civil society or of the

---

[13] Sabine (1973), 5, does not explain how having a right to a place differs from being entitled to it.

[14] Villey (1946), 201–27, and (1962), 29–30, 183–6, 229–40. Tuck (1979), 7–13, is in substantial agreement with Villey.   [15] Strauss (1953), 182–3, and elsewhere.

[16] Jaffa (1968), 86.

[17] Roshwald (1959), 360. Golding (1981), 27, 31, also distinguishes between two senses of 'right': 'what is right' (objective right) and 'a right' of the sort that someone can have (subjective right). He finds in the ancients and the medievals 'a "no rights" theory of justice'. See also Golding (1984).

sovereign are derivative from rights which originally belonged to the individual.' This is diametrically opposed to the Aristotelian assumption 'that man cannot reach the perfection of his nature except in and through civil society and, therefore, that civil society is prior to the individual. It was this assumption which led to the view that the primary moral fact is duty and not rights.'[18] Jaffa also claims that the theory of natural rights is essentially Hobbesian: it assumes that 'in the state of nature, men's rights are perfect, and they have no duties', and that any obligation requires consent.[19]

Others have also argued for the dichotomy of rights and duties, but on the grounds that a theory of rights is conceivable only given certain social conditions. Stephen Holmes, for example, contends that 'Plato's and Aristotle's emphasis on duties instead of rights . . . depended on the relatively undifferentiated character of Greek social order'. The classical view presupposed a society which resembled an organism or a beehive, a view which became less relevant with the increasing differentiation of society in modern times, the conflict of church and state, the rise of capitalism, and so forth. Holmes argues accordingly that it is anachronistic to ascribe a conception of 'bourgeois rights of man' to any of the ancients.[20]

The foregoing objections may be viewed as variations on a common *modus tollens* theme: concepts of rights carry theoretical baggage incompatible with central features of Aristotle's political theory. However, I shall argue that these objections are all mistaken. The following section offers textual evidence that Aristotle did in fact have locutions for rights, including rights based on nature. Next, Section 4.4 returns to the arguments mentioned here and seeks to show where they have gone wrong.

4.3. EVIDENCE OF 'RIGHTS' LOCUTIONS IN ARISTOTLE

In making a fresh start on the question of whether there are any rights claims in Aristotle, this section begins with a provisional account of what would constitute such rights claims, which is based upon the analysis in W. N. Hohfeld's *Fundamental Legal Conceptions*. This analysis has special advantages for the purposes of our enquiry into Aristotle. First, although it was initially offered for legal rights, it has been adapted by many recent moral and political philosophers as an account of moral rights as well.[21] It

---

[18] Strauss (1953), 183.   [19] Jaffa (1968), 86.   [20] Holmes (1979), 115, 126.
[21] See Martin and Nickel (1980).

can thus provide a general basis for comparing recent theories of rights to other moral conceptions. Second, Hohfeld's analysis proceeds from the valuable insight that the term 'rights' is systematically ambiguous as it is used in modern legal and political discourse. His analysis enables us to distinguish among the different but logically interrelated senses of 'rights', and this part of his account has been especially influential. Third, and of central importance, his analysis provides a theoretically neutral way of framing the question, 'Are there any rights in Aristotle?', at least to the extent that it permits the separation of this question from the questions, 'What sort of theoretical justification is required for rights claims?' and 'Does Aristotle provide the required sort of justification?'. It seems reasonable to separate these latter questions involving justification, in view of the fact that contemporary philosophers differ fundamentally about the foundations of rights claims. They disagree on the scope of rights, how rights claims are to be justified, and whether the concept of rights can be reduced to more basic ethical notions. This section investigates only whether Aristotle's politics has affinities with this spectrum of modern theories, at least to the extent that it considers political issues in terms of 'rights' claims, and, if so, whether it is possible to construe these as, in some sense, 'natural rights' claims.

Hohfeld's analysis of rights

Hohfeld's analysis rests upon two fundamental theses: first, a right is a three-term relation involving an individual who is the right-holder, a specific type of action, and one or more other individuals against whom the right is asserted. Second, although 'right' as it is used in the law is not a univocal term (no single definition can capture its diverse uses), most assertions of rights can be analysed into, or reduced to, conjunctions of four distinct types of assertions: claim rights (rights *stricto sensu*), privileges (or liberties), powers, and immunities. On this analysis, then, there are four senses of 'right'. In each case, X and Y stand for individuals and A stands for an action or a forbearance from an action:

(1) X has a *claim right* to Y's Aing if, and only if, Y has a *duty* to X to do A.

(2) X has a *liberty right* to A relative to Y if, and only if, it is not the case that X has a *duty* to Y not to A.

(3) X has a *power right* to A relative to Y if, and only if, Y has a *liability* to a change in Y's legal position through X's Aing.

(4) X has an *immunity right* relative to Y's Aing if, and only if, Y does *not* have a *power right* to A with respect to X.[22]

In a legal context, the duties and liabilities referred to here carry the implication of legal enforceability: persons with the rights in question can appeal to courts and enforcement agencies to have their rights enforced. What are commonly referred to as particular 'rights' in the law, such as property rights, typically involve complex combinations of the above four sorts of rights relationships. For example, Coriscus' right to a certain jar of olive oil includes the claim right against Callicles' taking it without his permission, the liberty right to use or dispose of it himself, the power right to offer it for sale or enter into a contract promising its future sale, and the immunity right from Callicles' selling it without Coriscus' permission. Hohfeld's analysis is especially important in pointing out the distinction between a claim right and a liberty right. For Coriscus' claim right against Callicles entails that Callicles has a correlative duty to Coriscus—e.g. not to take the olive oil without permission. But Coriscus' liberty right does not entail any correlative duty on the part of another; it entails rather that Coriscus himself does *not* have a duty to Callicles not to use or dispose of it. Thus, some rights (viz., liberty rights) do not entail correlative duties.

The thesis that there are distinguishable uses of 'rights' corresponding to Hohfeld's four categories—claims, liberties, powers, immunities—is very plausible, but the foregoing Hohfeldian analysis is not free from controversy. It is necessary to make at least three qualifications. First, it should not be thought that a claim right can be 'analysed' as a mere correlative of an other-regarding duty. If, as in the Mosaic code, I have a duty not to covet my neighbour's ox, it does not follow from this alone that my neighbour has a right against me not to covet his ox. For my duty may stem from a commandment from God and be a duty to God to perform or refrain from an act involving my neighbour. (For example, I might have a duty not to interfere with my neighbour's performance of *his* duties.) In addition to entailing a correlative duty, on the part of another, a right, at the very least, justifies the right-holder in making a claim against the duty-holder. Further, failing to perform a duty of charity does

---

[22] The latter three senses of 'right' are often rendered by abbreviated forms: 'liberty', 'power', and 'immunity'. For sense (2) Hohfeld (1919), 25 n. 15, uses 'privilege' in a wide sense, which he regards as meaning the same thing as 'liberty', but the latter is the preferred term in the philosophical literature. 'Liability' in (3) means the possibility of undergoing a change (not necessarily adverse) in one's legal position due to the act of another.

not as such violate anyone's rights. From the fact that one has a duty to give alms to the poor, it does not follow that any particular indigent has a right to a contribution, even if, on some occasion, he has a duty of charity to that particular person. Also, on many accounts, the right is in some sense more basic than, and helps to ground, the correlative duty. Hence, it is better to say that Hohfeld gives a necessary condition of a claim right; i.e. *X* has a claim right to *Y*'s *A*ing *only if Y* has a duty to *X* to do *A*. The 'if, and only if' should be weakened to 'only if' in the other three types for similar reasons.

Second, Hohfeld's analysis of a liberty or privilege seems too weak. To be sure, the analysis captures a feature of liberty: the agent must be free of the obligation to refrain from doing the act in question. However, familiar liberties such as freedom of religion entail duties of non-interference by others, and it may be objected that Hohfeld has eviscerated liberties by omitting such obligations. However, this objection may be met by distinguishing between protected and unprotected liberty rights: *X* has a protected liberty right against *Y* to *A* only if *X* has in addition to the liberty right a claim right to *Y*'s non-interference; otherwise *X* has an unprotected liberty right.[23]

Third, the four Hohfeldian rights should be viewed as abstractions rather than rights in the ordinary sense, in that in a normal case a person has not merely one Hohfeldian right in isolation (for example, the liberty right to speak) but also associated rights (for example, a claim right against others interfering with one's speaking). We do not encounter free-floating rights of the sort Hohfeld distinguished. In contrast, we may regard a right, such as Coriscus' right to the jar of olive oil, as *robust* if it includes a full complement of Hohfeldian rights. Robust rights are often spoken of as 'bundles' composed of Hohfeldian elements; or, alternatively, the Hohfeldian relations may be viewed as 'aspects' of robust rights. On either approach, the value of the Hohfeldian analysis lies in its clarification of the detailed implications of ordinary robust rights claims.

A number of passages follow in which Aristotle evidently employs terms which closely parallel the 'rights' locutions as analysed by Hohfeld. As we shall see, Aristotle's translators and commentators have frequently translated these terms by 'rights' locutions. This does not by itself prove that they were correct to do so, but it is of interest that they so often arrived at similar solutions, and I shall argue that they were not guilty of anachronism in doing so.

[23] See Simmons (1992), 71 n. 15.

Just-claim rights

Of special importance are expressions comparable to Hohfeldian claim rights. A claim right is at the core of the concept of a right, because its correlative duty functions as a moral sanction or 'side constraint' upon the actions of others. The most important locution which Aristotle uses in the sense of a claim right is *to dikaion*, the noun phrase formed from the neuter definite article,[24] with the neuter form of the adjective meaning 'just'. In Greek the attributive adjective and definite article may be used as a substantive: thus *to leukon* means 'the white thing'. Similarly, the expression *to dikaion* means 'the just thing', and refers to a particular application of a virtue of justice, for example a just act or what is required by justice. One important use of *to dikaion* is to refer to a right in the sense of a just claim,[25] as the following examples illustrate.

Aristotle uses the expression *to dikaion* in connection with legal disputes in which opposing parties advance conflicting claims about what is theirs by right. The following passage is from his discussion of corrective justice in the *Nicomachean Ethics*:

... when people dispute [*amphisbētōsin*], they have recourse to a judge [or juror, *dikastēn*], and to go to a judge is to go to justice [*to dikaion*]; for the judge is meant to be a sort of ensouled justice [*empsuchon dikaion*]. And they seek the judge as an intermediary, and in some places they call judges mediators, assuming that if they get an intermediate amount, they will get justice [*tou dikaiou*]. The just [*to dikaion*] is therefore in some way intermediate, if the judge is also. (*EN* V 4 1132ᵃ19–24)

According to this passage, disputing claimants assume they will get justice (*to dikaion*) from the judge who is settling the dispute; and if they think the judge has correctly resolved the dispute, the disputants 'say that they have their own' (1132ᵃ27–9).[26] In this context, then, *to dikaion* means that which one receives in a just settlement of a dispute—i.e. to get that which is 'one's own'.[27] This is clearly what the claimant has a right to

[24] The Medieval Latin translators could not fully translate this Greek expression due to the absence of a definite article in Latin; e.g. William of Moerbeke typically translates *to dikaion* as *ius* or *iustum*.

[25] This particular use of *dikaion* is recognized by Bradley (1991), 49–50 (see Sect. 4.1 above); Susemihl and Hicks (1894), 405; Rackham (1932), 252–3; and Gewirth (1978), 100–1.   [26] Reading *to hautou* with manuscript Kᵇ.

[27] See *Rhet.* I 9 1366ᵇ9–10: 'justice is the virtue through which individuals have their own things [*ta hautōn hekastōi echousi*]'. Cf. Plato, *Rep.* IV 433ᶜ6–434ᵃ1: the assertion that the sole aim of judges is 'that individuals shall neither have what is of others nor be deprived of their

or is entitled to (cf. *Pol.* IV 4 1291ᵃ39–40). It is the task of the judge to determine what each party has a just claim to, i.e. what each owes to the other. Hence, *to dikaion* has a use which anticipates Hohfeld's notion of a claim right. I translate this use of *to dikaion* as 'right' or 'just claim' or more fully 'just-claim right' (i.e. a right based on a claim of justice).[28]

It might be objected that assigning to individuals what is 'their own' is different from deciding what they have a 'right' to receive. For 'having' or 'getting one's own' is a broader notion than having or getting what one's entitled to. This is, generally speaking, true. Someone can deserve a job, in the sense of being the best qualified for it, without having a 'right' to it.[29] Defendants can deserve punishment as 'what they have coming to them' without having a 'right' to the penalty. However, in the present context 'having one's own' has a narrower sense. The disputing parties are making opposing claims to the same piece of property. Each claims that it is just for him to possess the object and for the other party not to interfere with his possession. To 'have one's own' in this case is clearly to have one's claim legally enforced.

The expression *to dikaion* also evidently has this force in *Politics*, Book III, where Aristotle is concerned with claims to citizenship and political office. The first such passage is in III 1 where Aristotle is discussing the questions of what a citizen is and who ought to be called a citizen.

Nor is one a citizen because he dwells in a particular place, for metics [that is, resident aliens] and slaves have a community in the dwelling-place; nor are those persons [citizens] who partake of just-claim rights [*hoi tōn dikaiōn metechontes*] to the extent of undergoing and bringing lawsuits, for this [*touto*] also belongs to those who have a community as a result of treaties (for these [rights] also belong

own' is a premiss for the conclusion that justice is 'the having and doing of what belongs to one and is one's own' (*hē tou oikeiou te kai heautou hexis te kai praxis*). This idea is also attributed to Simonides at Plato, *Rep.* I 331ᶜ3–4: 'it is just to give to each person what is owed to him' (*to ta opheilomena hekastōi apodidonai dikaion esti*), an adage which is echoed in Ulpian's *Digest of the Institutes of Justinian*, I 1 1: *iustitia suam cuique tribuere*.

[28] Similar uses of *to dikaion* are found in other authors. Cf. Xenophon, *Anab.* VII 7 14, 17: *ta dikaia echein, lambanein*, 'have' or 'receive one's rights'; Thucydides, III 54: *to dikaion echomen pros*, 'have a right against'; Aeschylus, *Agamemnon*, 812: *ta dikaia prattesthai polin*, 'give a city the things it claims by right'; and other citations in Liddell, Scott, and Jones (1976): e.g. Aristophanes, *Birds*, 1435; Demosthenes, XI 179 and 177 (cf. XV 29); Lysias, II 12; Plutarch, *Lives*, Lucullus, 3; Thucydides, II 89; inscriptions from second and third century BC Priene, etc.

[29] However, a disagreement over a contest can easily develop into a dispute over who has the right to the prize, a dispute calling for a legal judgment. See, for example, Homer's account of the dispute arising from the chariot race in *Iliad*, XXIII 539–611.

to these persons).[30] In many places, moreover, the metics do not even partake completely in these rights [*toutōn*], but must be assigned a patron, so that they partake in such a community in an incomplete manner . . . (III 1 1275ᵃ7–14)

That the genitive plural *tōn dikaiōn* has the sense of 'rights' has been accepted by a number of commentators and translators.[31] This refers to the rights of 'undergoing and bringing lawsuits', i.e. the right to act as a defendant or prosecutor in a court of law. The right to participate in legal proceedings was, Aristotle notes, possessed by some non-citizens in some city-states, but often denied to many inhabitants: including metics in some places, women and children (who had to be represented by an authority or *kurios*), slaves, of course, and even alleged slaves (who had to be represented by a citizen friend until vindicated).[32] In contrast to such persons, a citizen could not be prevented from taking legal actions and other citizens were obligated to respond to such actions appropriately. Hence, this legal right has the character of a Hohfeldian claim right.

Another use of *to dikaion* occurs in *Politics*, III 9, where Aristotle criticizes Lycophron's theory of the polis as an alliance, in which the law is a contract (*sunthēkē*) and 'a guarantor of men's rights against one another' (*egguētē allēlois tōn dikaiōn*, 1280ᵇ11).[33] The implication is that individuals have just claims against others that impose duties on them, and that the polis should protect these claims. Aristotle's own view is that the protection of such rights is a necessary condition for the existence of the polis, but denies that it constitutes its true aim (1280ᵇ29–36).

---

[30] Following Dreizehnter (1970), I retain *kai gar tauta toutois huparchei* in 1275ᵃ11, which is omitted in the π¹ family of manuscripts and in Ross (1957). I take *toutois* to refer back to *hoi . . . metechontes* and *tauta* to *tōn dikaiōn*.

[31] Newman (1887) construes the clause at 1275ᵃ8–10, 'nor are those citizens who [as metics usually do] share in political rights to the extent of undergoing trial and suing . . .' Similarly, Jowett in Barnes (1984) translates *tōn dikaiōn* as 'legal rights', Barker (1946) as 'civic rights', and Robinson (1962) as 'the rights of citizens'. Schütrumpf (1991), ii. 386–7, translates as 'Rechte' and takes Aristotle to be trying to define rights possessed only by citizens. Susemihl and Hicks (1894) take the term to be equivalent to the Latin '*iura*', and although they here render *tōn dikaiōn* very loosely as 'the advantages of common jurisdiction, in the sense of the capacity to bring or defend a civil action', they construe *touto* at 1275ᵃ10 as 'these civil rights'. Rackham (1932) offers a more expansive translation conveying the same point: 'nor are those citizens who participate in a common system of justice, conferring the right to defend an action and to bring one in the law-courts.'

[32] See MacDowell (1978), 80–4. See also Harrison (1971), i. 78–81 on children, (108–9) on women; (178–80) on accused slaves; (189–99) on metics; and ii. 83–5 on women.

[33] Barker (1946) translation. Rackham (1932) translates 'men's just claims on one another', which implies duties of individuals towards one another. Schütrumpf (1991), ii. 485, translates *tōn dikaiōn* as 'ihrer Rechte' and notes a parallel in Xenophon, *Mem.* IV 4 8. Polybius uses a similar locution, *ta pros allēlous dikaia* (III 21 10).

Another important use of *to dikaion* occurs in *Politics*, III 12 1282ᵇ18–
30, where Aristotle is reviewing rival claims to political office on the basis
of justice:

> ... everyone believes that justice (*to dikaion*) is a kind of equality, and up to a
> certain point they agree with the philosophical discussions containing determina-
> tions about ethics. For they say that justice is a certain thing and it is for certain
> persons, and it must be equal for equal persons. But we ought not to overlook
> what sort of persons have equality or inequality. This is puzzling and involves
> political philosophy. For perhaps someone would say that the offices ought to be
> distributed unequally according to prominence in any good characteristic, although
> [or even if] in any remaining respects they do not differ at all but happen to be
> similar, because those who differ have a different just-claim right [*to dikaion*] and
> merit-based claim [*to kat' axian*]. But if this is true, those who are prominent in
> virtue of complexion, size, or any other good will have an excess possession
> [*pleonexia*] of political rights [*tōn politikōn dikaiōn*].³⁴

Many translators and commentators translate *to dikaion* here as 'right',
and they are nearly unanimous in taking 'political rights' to be the correct
rendering of *tōn politikōn dikaiōn*.³⁵ For Aristotle is considering a context
in which individuals are disputing (*amphisbētousi*) over political offices
(1283ᵃ11). Each of the parties is claiming that *he* should occupy the offices
on the grounds of alleged superiority, and the resolution of the dispute
will involve determining which members of society have a just claim to
political offices. The presumption is that people who are superior in some
respect and thus are more deserving have certain rights against others
who are inferior in that respect and have, accordingly, a duty to yield.
The right to hold office thus resembles a Hohfeldian claim right. Towards
the end of this discussion (1283ᵃ14–15) there is the suggestion that such
claims should be based upon attributes that go into the establishment of
the polis.

Aristotle also uses the phrase *kata to dikaion*, 'based on the just-claim
right', when he alleges a common difficulty for those who base their
claims to political honours on the basis of attributes such as wealth or
good birth.³⁶ It follows from their views that the one person who exceeds

³⁴ Cf. *to auto dikaion ... kai tēn autēn axian* at III 16 1287ᵃ12–13, and *to ison*, 'claim of
equality', at VII 14 1332ᵇ27.
³⁵ Susemihl and Hicks (1894) render 1282ᵇ26–7 as 'For people who differ have different
rights and their relative merits are different.' For 'political rights' see Jowett in Barnes
(1984), Barker (1946), and Robinson (1962). Braun (1965) interprets this passage along
similar lines, as concerned with having a greater share 'an staatlichen Gerechtsamen'. Lord
(1984), who systematically eschews 'rights' locutions, renders *tōn politikōn dikaiōn* as '[claims
to] political justice'.   ³⁶ Cf. Plato, *Gorg.* 471ᶜ2 for *kata to dikaion*.

all others in the relevant attribute 'ought to rule over all the others based on the same just-claim right [*kata to auto dikaion*]' (*Pol.* III 13 1283ᵇ17–18).³⁷ And 'if some man is better than the other excellent persons in the government, this person ought to have authority [*kurion*] based on the same just-claim right [*kata t' auto dikaion*]' (ᵇ21–3). These expressions are used to assert a right—i.e. to make a just claim against other individuals.

Aristotle also uses the predicate adjective *dikaios* with the infinitive verb to assert that the subject has a right to do something: 'if indeed, as was said earlier, the excellent man has a right to rule [*archein dikaios*] because he is better, two good men are better than one' (16 1287ᵇ11–13). The predicate adjective is also combined with the prepositional phrase: 'for if anyone has more wealth than the other wealthy persons, based on the oligarchic just-claim right [*kata to oligarchikon dikaion*] he alone has a just-claim right to rule [*dikaios archein*]' (*Pol.* VI 3 1318ᵃ23–4).³⁸

Because a right is a claim against other individuals, it imposes correlative duties upon these individuals. If Erastus has made a contract with Coriscus, then Coriscus has a right against Erastus and Erastus has a correlative duty towards Coriscus. Hence, we find that *to dikaion* (like *ius* in Latin) is also used to refer to the correlative duty. For example, *Rhetoric*, I 14 1375ᵃ9–10 mentions accusations that someone has disregarded or violated *dikaia*, such as oaths, promises, pledges, and rights of intermarriage. This is evidently a reference to the failure to obey duties associated with social conventions and institutions, which are correlatives of just-claim rights. In the political context, if *X* has a just-claim right to rule over *Y*, then it is just for *Y* to obey *X* (see *Pol.* VII 3 1325ᵇ10–12). *Y* does an injustice (*adikein*) to *X* when *Y* fails to respect *X*'s just-claim right, whether this is to property, to an office, or something else. *Pol.* V 8 1308ᵃ9 uses the phrase *adikein eis atimian* in the sense of 'unjustly depriving [someone] of honour' (e.g. of the right to hold political office).

Liberty rights

There are also locutions which correspond to the Hohfeldian notion of liberty or privilege. They concern actions which an individual *may* perform, in that the individual is not obligated to refrain from performing them.

---

³⁷ Cf. Lord (1984) 'in accordance with the same [claims of] justice'.

³⁸ Cf. Aristophanes, *Clouds*, 1434, and Sophocles, *Antigone*, 400. See also passages cited in Liddell, Scott, and Jones (1976): e.g. Antiphon, III 3 7, Thucydides, IV 17, Lysias, XX 12, Demosthenes, VI 37. For *eimi dikaios* with the infinitive in the sense, 'I have a duty to do *X*'; see Herodotus, IX 27, 60.

This notion is essential for a complete understanding of rights, because the set of such rights defines a sphere within which the agent is able to choose among alternatives. It is expressed by two Greek words, *eleutheria* and *exousia*, which I translate, respectively, as 'freedom' and 'liberty'.

Freedom (*eleutheria*) was, of course, an important concept in Greek politics, and it was especially prominent within the ideology of ancient Greek democracy, as is evident in the funeral oration delivered by Pericles.[39] Aristotle states in the *Metaphysics* that 'the free human being exists for his own sake and not for the sake of another' (I 2 982ᵇ26). To the ancient Greek a free man (*eleutheros*) or free woman (*eleuthera*) was fundamentally contrasted with a slave who belongs wholly to another person (*Pol.* I 4 1254ᵃ10; 6 1255ᵇ11). Slavery is commonly viewed as the rule of one human being over another through the use of force or coercion (*bia*, see *Pol.* I 3 1253ᵇ22 and 6 1255ᵃ14–16). Slaves differ from free persons, in that they do not live as they wish. Hence, living as one wishes is viewed by democrats as 'the function of freedom' and it serves as a political standard. Pushed to the extreme it implies the anarchistic ideal of being ruled by nobody, but if this is unattainable, the principle of political rule, i.e. ruling and being ruled in turn (cf. VI 2 1317ᵃ40–ᵇ17). Aristotle, like Plato, believes that the ideal of freedom is easily corrupted. In the opinion of the many, to be free is merely to be able to do whatever one wishes.[40] As interpreted by Callicles, individual freedom degenerates into licence (see Plato, *Gorg.* 492ᶜ5, and cf. *Rep.* I 344ᶜ5 and *Laws*, III 701ᵃ7). Nevertheless, freedom remains an important political ideal for Plato (see *Laws*, III 693ᵇ2–5) and for Aristotle, who contrasts slavery with *political* rule on the grounds that the subjects of the latter are free and equal (*Pol.* I 7 1255ᵇ20; cf. *EN* V 6 1134ᵃ26–8).

The term *exousia* is closely associated with freedom,[41] and denotes the unobstructed ability to perform a particular action. *Exousia* is an abstract noun connected with the verb *exesti* (infinitive *exeinai*) which is used in the impersonal form with a dative noun or pronoun and an infinitival verb. An important example of this use is found in Plato's *Crito*, when the

---

[39] Thucydides, II 37 1–3; cf. Plato, *Rep.* VIII 557ᵇ4–558ᶜ6; Aristotle, *Pol.* V 9 1310ᵃ28–30 and VI 2 1317ᵃ40–ᵇ16.

[40] *Pol.* VI 2 1317ᵇ11–13; cf. V 9 1310ᵃ31–2 and *Met.* XII 10 1075ᵃ19–22. Cf. also Herodotus, III 38 2–3, and Thucydides, II 37 2. See Barnes (1990a), 253–6, on the political implications of this democratic ideal.

[41] See especially Plato, *Rep.* VIII 557ᵇ4–6 where freedom (*eleutheria*) in democracy is associated with free speech (*parrēsia*) and the liberty (*exousia*) to do whatever one wants. On *exousia* in connection with free speech, cf. *Statesman*, 298ᶜ4, and Aristotle, *Ath. Pol.* XXXIX 3. Cf. also *Gorg.* 491ᵉ5–492ᵉ8.

Laws of Athens argue that Socrates has made a voluntary agreement to obey them:

We [the Laws] proclaim publicly that any Athenian who has been enrolled as a citizen and has observed the actions of the polis and of us the Laws, has the liberty [*exeinai*] to take his things and go away wherever he wants. And none of us Laws hinders or forbids you from going wherever you wish, keeping your belongings, whether you wish to go to a colony, if we or the polis do not satisfy you, or to go somewhere else as a metic. (51ᶜ8–ᶜ1)

Here the argument depends upon the fact that the verb *exeinai* implies that Socrates has the liberty to leave, in that he is not prohibited by the Laws from leaving.

Aristotle uses the *exesti* locution frequently to indicate that certain individuals have the right to participate in political institutions.[42] For example, in *Politics*, IV, he describes a moderate type of democratic constitution in which individuals must meet a low property assessment in order to be eligible for political office: 'a person who possesses [sufficient property] must have the liberty [*exousian*] to partake [in offices] and those who lose it ought not to have it' (IV 4 1291ᵇ40–1; cf. 6 1292ᵇ35–7). In the moderate type of oligarchy, the assessment is set so high that the majority, who are poor, cannot meet it, but 'a person who possesses [sufficient property] has the liberty [*exeinai*] to partake in the constitution' (5 1292ᵃ41). This notion of a liberty right also has an important place in Aristotle's definition of a citizen: a citizen is 'one who has the liberty to have in common [*exousia koinōnein*] deliberative or judicial office' (III 1 1275ᵇ18–19; cf. Plato, *Laws*, VI 768ᵇ2).[43] In this use, *exousia* is equivalent to political power or authority (*Pol.* V 11 1315ᵃ14).

Further, it may be denied that a person has the liberty to do something. e.g. 'in many oligarchies one does not have the liberty (*ouk exesti*) to make [commercial] acquisitions, but the laws prevent it' (V 12 1316ᵇ3–5). In general, if *X* is prohibited from doing *A*, then *X* does not have the liberty to do *A*.

A liberty right is not the same as a just-claim right. Instead, the liberty of *X* implies the absence of claim rights against *X*. For if *X* has the liberty to do *A*, it follows that *X* is not impeded, by legal obligations or the claim rights of others, from doing *A*. Ordinarily for the Greeks, as for

---

[42] He also uses it in connection with non-political acts—e.g. forming marriage alliances (*Pol.* V 7 1307ᵃ36–8). *Ath. Pol.* IX 1 mentions among Solon's reforms 'the liberty (*exeinai*) of every person who wished to claim redress on behalf of anyone to whom injustice had been done'.

[43] Barker (1946) translates *exousia* as 'right' here, and Schütrumpf (1991) as 'Recht'.

us, a liberty is a legally protected right, i.e. conjoined with a claim right against interference. But the essential meaning of 'liberty' (*exousia*) is that it is *open to* the agent to act. Further, *X* may have the liberty to do *A* without actually doing *A*. Indeed, as Aristotle observes, citizens often have political liberties which they are not obliged to exercise and which they in fact do not exercise.[44] Further, a deviant constitution may grant someone the *exousia* to engage in unjust acts of insolence and excessive possession (V 3 1302^{b}9). In this pejorative sense *exousia* may be rendered as 'licence' (cf. V 11 1315^{a}14, 23; VI 4 1318^{b}39).[45] Plato also uses *exousia* in this sense in the example of Gyges' ring (*Rep.* II 359^{c}7). In the same vein, Aristotle notes that Socrates characterizes the extreme freedom (*eleutheria*) of democracy as the liberty (*exeinai*) to do whatever one wants (*Pol.* V 12 1316^{b}21–5; cf. *Rep.* VIII 557^{d}4).

Authority rights

The term *kurios* is applied to persons, groups of persons, offices, political groups, and the law itself. Literally but awkwardly, *esti kurios* might be rendered 'is authoritative'; but 'has the authority' is a reasonably close translation. This use of *kurios* corresponds to Hohfeldian power rights. By exercising authority, *X* can create specific rights, duties, powers, etc., on the part of *Y*. *Kurios* can be used with the infinitive to indicate that a person has the authority to carry out a certain action—e.g. to execute someone (*kurios kteinai*).[46] The adjective can also take a genitive to indicate the things or affairs over which the person or office has authority—e.g. over sacrifices (*kurioi tōn thusiōn*).[47] The genitive plural may also indicate the persons over whom one exercises the authority right.[48]

Aristotle sometimes uses the term 'power' (*dunamis*) in a sense which seems to be equivalent to 'authority' (*kurios*), e.g.: 'Solon seems at any rate to grant the most necessary power [*dunamin*] to the people, namely to

[44] e.g. a citizen may have the liberty to attend the assembly but not be required to exercise it (*Pol.* IV 12 1297^{a}17–19). In Athens a citizen could abstain with impunity from the assembly, jury courts, and magistracies: see Hansen (1991), 99.

[45] Cf. Isocrates, *Areopagiticus*, 20.

[46] *Pol.* III 14 1285^{a}8; cf. *Ath. Pol.* III 5, XXIX 5; and Plato, *Laws*, XII 968^{c}5. For the same force with the genitive *thanatou* see IV 9 1294^{b}33–4; and for this sense with a participle *thanatountas* see *Ath. Pol.* XXXVII 1 and cf. Plato, *Laws*, VI 764^{b}7.

[47] *Pol.* III 14 1285^{b}9–10; cf. 16 1287^{a}6. See also *Ath. Pol.* IX 1 and Plato, *Laws*, VI 759^{c}5.

[48] See *Pol.* VII 3 1325^{a}35, which concerns the desire to have authority over all persons (*kurios pantōn*). But it is sometimes ambiguous as to whether this expression means 'over all persons' or 'over all things': see III 16 1287^{a}11; 17 1288^{a}2. The superlative, *kuriōtatos*, corresponds to the modern term 'sovereign': see 1 1275^{b}28 and cf. Sect. 5.1 below.

elect and audit the offices, for if they did not have the authority [*kurios*] over this, the people would be a slave and an enemy [of the constitution]' (II 12 1274ᵃ15–18; cf. 10 1272ᵃ5). However, Aristotle also contrasts *dunamis* with *kurios* in order to make the point that an official might have authority in accordance with the constitution and laws and yet not have the power to enforce obedience.

There is also a puzzle concerning [the king's] power (*dunameōs*): ought one who is going to be king to have some strength about him, by which he has the power to force those who do not wish to obey, or how else can he conduct his office? For even if he had the authority (*kurios*) according to law and acted in nothing according to his own wish contrary to the law, nevertheless he must possess power (*dunamin*) by which to guard the laws. (III 15 1286ᵇ27–33)

This passage indicates that *kurios* is a legal concept, defined by the constitution and laws of the polis. It leaves open the possibility that an official may possess *de jure* authority but lack the power of enforcement. It also implies that one may exercise power (*dunamis*) without legal authority.

Immunity rights

The idea of a legal immunity is expressed by different terms—e.g. by the noun *adeia* which applies to cases such as safe conduct, amnesty, and indemnity. In *EN* V 4 1132ᵇ15–16, Aristotle refers to the activities of buying and selling among those to which the law gives immunity (*adeia*). Grant interprets this passage as follows: 'In commerce of all kinds the law allows one to gain as much as one can. In involuntary transactions the law allows no gain to be made, but brings things always back to their level. This non-interference of the law with bargains becomes, if carried out, the principle of free-trade.'[49] This suggests that merchants were not generally subject to the authority of officials who could impose prices or limit profits. In a political context the term *adeia* may have the sense of 'impunity'. For example, Aristotle says that in the constitution which he calls a polity, the wealthy should be fined if they do not attend the jury court, but either the poor should have impunity (*adeia*) or there should be smaller penalties for the poor as in the law of Charondas (*Pol.* IV 13 1297ᵃ21–4).[50]

---

[49] Grant (1885), ii. 116. However, Aristotle would not endorse *laissez-faire* capitalism (see Sect. 9.8 below).

[50] Cf. Plato, *Laws*, III 701ᵃ8. See also the adverb *adeōs* at *Rep.* II 360ᵇ7.

TABLE 4.1. *Locutions for 'Rights'*

Hohfeld	Aristotle
claim	*to dikaion*
liberty, privilege	*exousia*
authority, power	*kurios*
immunity	*akuros, adeia*

The idea of immunity is also expressed by the correlative term *akuros*, 'without authority', corresponding to the modern concept of disability. *X* has an immunity right against *Y* if, and only if, *Y* is without authority against *X*, i.e. if, and only if, it is not the case that *Y* has authority against *X*. For example, *The Constitution of Athens*, XLV 3–4, states that the Athenian Council formerly had the authority to reject candidates as disqualified to be councillors or archons, but later the candidates could appeal to a jury. Hence, although the Council could challenge a candidate, it was without authority (*akuros*) over the outcome (cf. *EN* VII 10 1151^{b}15 and Plato, *Laws*, XII 954^{c}6).

Aristotle also implies that a creditor has the immunity not to have an obligation cancelled by a debtor. He remarks that the son does not seem to have the liberty to disown his father, but it is possible for a father to disown his son, because the liberty (*exousia*) to dissolve a debt belongs to the creditor, and the father is the creditor. In this case the liberty right is to annul legal or moral relations involving another, which is characteristic of authority. To deny such a right, then, is to assert an immunity (*EN* VIII 14 1163^{b}18–22; cf. Plato, *Laws*, VI 928^{d}5–^{e}6). The example also makes it clear that the liberty is relative: the some person may have a liberty towards one person (his son or a debtor) but not towards another person (his father or a creditor).

Aristotle's concept of rights

In summary, Aristotle and his contemporaries employ locutions which parallel the different concepts of rights distinguished by Hohfeld, as shown in Table 4.1. In spite of this correspondence there still may be reluctance to concede a concept of rights to Aristotle on the grounds that no *single* Greek word corresponds to the single modern term 'right'.[51]

---

[51] Cf. Vlastos (1978), 193, who recognizes that in ancient Greek 'there is no special word for "rights"; . . . no word which corresponds exactly to ours, behaving as it does in all the

The point is well taken, and it is true that modern languages do have a great advantage in possessing a single term for the ordinary, robust sense of rights. On the other hand, as Hohfeld has demonstrated, the modern term 'rights' is misleading in that it is used to make claims with quite different logical implications.[52] Ancient Greek has distinct locutions corresponding to the senses distinguished by Hohfeld, and the expression *to dikaion* closely parallels a claim right, which Hohfeld thought it most accurate to call a 'right'. In addition, the Aristotelian locutions, like the Hohfeldian senses, form a family. Both families have an analogous logical structure, involving claims made against other individuals regarding specifiable actions; and just as there are important logical interrelationships among the various senses of 'right' distinguished by Hohfeld,[53] there are similar relations among the Aristotelian concepts, as noted above.

Aristotle gives clear indications that he regards these concepts as closely related. For example, the concept of authority is connected with that of a just-claim right, in an argument which defends absolute kingship on the basis of the aristocratic principle of justice that persons should receive political authority in accordance with their virtue: 'if one man is better than the other excellent persons in the government, this person ought to have authority based on the same just-claim right' (*Pol.* III 13 1283ᵇ21–3, cited earlier). Regardless of Aristotle's final verdict on this argument, it conforms to his general view throughout *Politics*, III, that the right to authority ought to be based upon a claim of justice. Indeed, the context of Book III is the dispute among inhabitants of the polis over who has the right to be a citizen and to hold office (see 2 1275ᵇ37–9). The just claim to be a citizen is also closely related to claims of authority and liberty. The citizen has the liberty to participate in deliberative and judicial office (1 1275ᵇ18–19). Hence, he may not be hindered by other citizens or officials from participating in such offices. The individuals with this liberty are said to have the greatest authority (*kuriōtatoi*) in the polis (1275ᵃ28). In general, authority consists in a special type of liberty—viz., the ability to create (or to annul) relations of right or obligation involving other members of the polis, for example by issuing commands, prohibitions, promises, or taking various direct actions (such as the confiscation of property). On the other hand, Aristotle indicates that one may opt not

contexts in which we speak of rights', but does not regard this as an insurmountable impediment to a rights interpretation of Plato. Finnis (1980), 207–9, makes a similar point about the term *ius* in Roman law; see also Zuckert (1989).   [52] Cf. Milne (1986), 6.

[53] Kanger and Kanger (1966) offer a formal system exhibiting some of these interrelationships. Jon Elster called this article to my attention.

to perform an act which one has the authority to do (see 15 1286^{b}25–6). Finally, the authority of one person or office may constrain the liberty of another. For example, the authority to audit an office limits the liberty of the office-holder (see VI 4 1318^{b}36–1319^{a}1).

The family of concepts expressed by the Aristotelian locutions *to dikaion*, *exousia*, *kurios*, and *akuros* are thus tightly intertwined and have the common purpose of resolving disputes between rival claimants. These include disagreements over private matters such as the ownership of property and also political controversies, e.g. as to who should be a full-fledged citizen of the polis and as to who should play what role in the constitution of the polis. These are functions clearly assigned to the modern robust concept of rights. For these reasons, it is legitimate to speak of Aristotle's 'concept of rights' without qualification in spite of the fact that he has no single word which corresponds to the English term 'rights'.

Rights based on nature

There is, also, evidence that Aristotle has the conceptual resources to distinguish between rights based on nature and rights which exist merely according to law or convention. This distinction is implied, ironically, in the course of his discussion of slavery in *Politics*, I. After completing his argument that some people are free by nature (*phusei*) and others are slaves by nature, and that for the latter being a slave is both advantageous and just (*sumpherei . . . kai dikaion esti*), Aristotle makes the following concession:

But it is also not hard to see that those who say the opposite also speak correctly in some manner. For being enslaved and a slave are said in two ways. For someone can be a slave or be enslaved according to law [*kata nomon*]. For the law is a kind of agreement [*homologia*] by which things that are conquered in war are said to belong to the conquerors. This just-claim right [*touto to dikaion*] is indicted by many legal experts, just as they indict an orator for unlawfulness [*graphontai paranomōn*], on the grounds that it is terrible if that which is forced will be a slave and ruled by that which has the power to use force and is stronger in power. And among wise persons, some believe this, although others believe otherwise. (I 6 1255^{a}3–12)

The legal experts mentioned in this passage are explicitly repudiating the view that the convention (*homologia*) that captives of war are slaves is a genuine law.[54] According to Susemihl and Hicks, the expression *touto to*

---

[54] As asserted in Xenophon, *Cyrop.* VII 5 73; see Newman (1887), ii. 152.

dikaion has in this context the sense 'this conventional right'. The defenders of this right are said, later on, to think they are clinging to a kind of justice, since the law is a kind of justice (1255ᵃ21–3). The analogy with the indictment for unlawfulness (*graphē paranomōn*) is reminiscent of the claim of the *Rhetoric* that particular laws of a polis can conflict with natural law (I 13 1373ᵇ9–13, 15 1375ᵃ27–ᵇ8). Just as an orator who proposes a decree which contravenes laws in force at the time can be indicted for violating the constitution or fundamental laws of the polis, similarly a right based upon conventional laws may be indicted if it violates natural law or justice.⁵⁵ The present passage thus calls into question the merely conventional right (designated as *touto to dikaion*) to own a slave. Aristotle can therefore distinguish a right to own a slave which is natural and just (cf. I 5 1254ᵃ18–19) from a right which is merely conventional. From the fact that one has a right to own a slave, it does not follow that this is a right according to nature. It is unfortunate that Aristotle does not go further and concur with ancient Greek thinkers such as Alcidamus and Philemon who seem to imply that there could be no right by nature to own a slave.⁵⁶ But the relevant point here is that Aristotle is able to distinguish between rights based on nature and rights based on law.

Political rights based on nature

There is, further, evidence that Aristotle has the linguistic resources to distinguish between political rights which exist by nature and those which exist merely by convention or law. In *Politics*, III, Aristotle paraphrases an argument which assumes the existence of a right based on nature:

Some people think that it is not at all according to nature [*kata phusin*] for one individual to be the authority [*to kurion*] over all the citizens where the polis consists of similar individuals. For it is necessary that individuals similar by nature [*phusei*] have the same just-claim right and the same merit based on nature [*to auto dikaion . . . kai tēn autēn axian kata phusin*]. Thus, if for unequal individuals it is harmful for their bodies to have equal food or clothing, so the case is also in

---

⁵⁵ Cf. Susemihl and Hicks (1894), 163–4.

⁵⁶ Alcidamus, *c.*360 BC, says, 'God has set all men free; nature has made no man a slave' (Messenian Speech, cited by a scholiast on Aristotle, *Rhet.* I 12 1373ᵇ9–18). Philemon (*c.*368–*c.*267 BC) says, 'No one was ever a slave by nature, though chance enslaves the body' (fr. 95 Kock). However, the evidence for early criticism of slavery is admittedly scarce and tentative. See Schlaifer (1936), Guthrie (1962–81), iii. 155–60, (from which the foregoing translations were taken), and Kerferd (1981), 156. Regarding Aristotle's views on slavery, see Sects. 3.5 above and 6.9 below.

regard to honours. It is similar, then, when equal individuals have the unequal. Therefore, it is just not to rule any more than being ruled, and hence, [it is just] to rule and be ruled in turns. (III 16 1287ᵃ10–18)[57]

This argument relies upon the principle that those who are similar by nature have the same right (*to auto dikaion*) according to nature to rule or be ruled. Moreover, where there is such a body of citizens, total kingship is contrary to nature and unjust: '. . . there must be some offices, but it is not just, they say, for this [ruler] to be one person, when all persons are similar' (1287ᵃ22–3)—i.e. all the citizens have the same right based on nature to share in ruling. Because the argument concludes that all the individuals who are members of the polis have a right to participate in political rule, it is not at all implausible to regard this as an ancient Greek prototype of the ideal of universal suffrage. Indeed, the argument has revolutionary implications.

Nevertheless, it must be noted that the argument relies upon the premiss that all the citizens are in fact naturally equal. Under ideal circumstances all the members of the polis are naturally similar and equal, but in a particular actual polis there might be great natural inequalities and dissimilarities among the population. Hence, the argument that all the members of the polis have equal natural political rights might turn out to be sound for one polis but not for another. Further, the expression 'individuals who are similar and equal by nature' needs to be qualified. Aristotle will argue that individuals must be similar or equal in some respect which is relevant to the political life.[58]

Of greater importance here, however, is the other premiss: individuals who are similar and equal by nature have the same right to share in ruling. This premiss sets forth a norm by which different distributions of constitutional rights may be justified or criticized, and it is part of a more extended argument in support of the rule of law and against absolute kingship. Aristotle mentions it here without endorsing it, for this argument is qualified with 'some persons think' and 'they say', just as the objection to the conventional right to slavery was ascribed to 'legal experts'. Section 4.6 below takes up again the question of whether Aristotle himself would accept this principle. But, for now, there is no doubt that he possesses the linguistic and conceptual resources to distinguish between political rights

---

[57] Following Dreizehnter (1970), I retain *de* in 1287ᵃ10 and relocate *hena* after *kurion* (rather than after *politōn* with manuscripts M and S). I also understand *pantōn* to modify *tōn politōn* (cf. the note at 1281ᵃ3 in Newman (1887) for parallel constructions). In 1287ᵃ13 I take *auto* and *autēn* as attributive rather than predicate adjectives, *contra* Lord (1984).

[58] Cf. Plato, *Rep.* V 454ᶜ6–455ᵃ3.

which are based on nature and those which are merely conventional or
based on law.

4.4. REPLIES TO OBJECTIONS AGAINST 'RIGHTS' IN ARISTOTLE

The failure to recognize that Aristotle uses 'rights' locutions has resulted,
at least in part, from the conviction that the concept of rights is a peculiarly
modern European development. Consider, again, MacIntyre's claim that
'there is no expression in any ancient or medieval language correctly
translated by our expression "a right" until near the close of the middle
ages'. The passages collected in the previous section provide compelling prima-facie evidence that MacIntyre's claim is mistaken, as far as
Aristotle and other ancient Greek writers are concerned. However,
MacIntyre goes on to qualify his apparently sweeping claim:

By 'rights' I do not mean those rights conferred by positive law or custom on
specified classes of persons; I mean those rights which are alleged to belong to
human beings as such and which are cited as a reason for holding that people
ought not to be interfered with in their pursuit of life, liberty and happiness.
They are the rights which were spoken of in the eighteenth century as natural
rights or as the rights of man.[59]

MacIntyre does not make clear whether he concedes that ancient and
medieval languages do, after all, contain 'rights' locutions in some sense;
but he does clearly allege that there is no sense in which they could refer
to 'natural' rights. It appears that MacIntyre is offering the following sort
of *modus tollens* argument:

(1) Pre-modern speakers used a locution equivalent to 'natural rights',
    only if they held the equivalent of the Enlightenment theory of
    natural rights.
(2) Pre-modern speakers did not hold the equivalent of the Enlighten-
    ment theory of natural rights.
(3) Therefore, pre-modern speakers did not use a locution equivalent
    to 'natural rights'.

But premiss (1) is highly dubious, since there are different ways in which
one can speak of 'natural rights': e.g. as rights based on natural justice (as
opposed to convention) *or* as rights possessed in a pre-political state of

---

[59] MacIntyre (1981), 66. Cf. Berlin (1969), 129, who cites Villey (1962).

nature. To rule out the latter (asserted by Enlightenment theories) is not necessarily to rule out the former (see Section 4.1 above). In view of the plethora of theories of rights in currency today, it is tendentious to assume that a theory of non-conventional rights must be equivalent to an eighteenth-century Enlightenment theory.

MacIntyre here employs a common, but none the less faulty mode of reasoning, which relies on the objectionable premiss that if particular writers (e.g. Aristotle) do not subscribe to one peculiar theory of rights, they can not speak or think in terms of 'rights' at all. Similarly, although it certainly *would* be anachronistic to impute to Aristotle the modern liberal doctrine of the 'bourgeois rights of man',[60] since such a conception presupposes social classes and political relationships which Aristotle could scarcely be expected to have foreseen, it is a *non sequitur* to infer from this that Aristotle could not have had an alternative conception of rights framed in terms of his own social and political context.

A similar reply can be made to the argument, extrapolated from Michel Villey's analysis of pre-modern uses of the Latin term *ius*, that *dikaion* in Greek could only refer to an objective condition of justice, viz., the correct assignment or relation of things to persons, and thus could not be used for 'subjective' rights.[61] Whether this is a defensible analysis of the employment of *ius* in ancient Roman law and medieval canon law has been questioned, but this is beyond the scope of my study.[62] However, there is clear evidence, compiled in the previous section, that *to dikaion* is used in classical Greece by individuals to assert that they have a just claim to something, and that other citizens, jurors, and officials are expected to respond to this claim in regular legal and political proceedings. Even granting that the Greeks (including Aristotle) did not have Villey's peculiar notion of 'subjective right', it is undeniable that the Greeks described themselves as having numerous rights, including the right to hold and discharge political offices and to possess, use, and dispose of private property.

Villey also objects that there are fundamental differences between modern notions of rights and the ancient Roman concept of *ius*. On his view, theories of subjective rights are an outgrowth of a modern, 'very individualistic civilization'.[63] He emphasizes the central place of the ideal

---

[60] See Holmes (1979), cited in Sect. 4.1.
[61] Villey (1946, 1962, and 1969). Tierney (1988) provides a critical overview of Villey's arguments.
[62] See Tierney (1988) and Zuckert (1989) for criticisms of Villey's arguments.
[63] Villey (1946), 201.

of individual freedom of choice in most modern theories of rights. He traces these theories back to William of Occam (*c*.1285–*c*.1349), who brought about a veritable 'Copernican semantic revolution' through which the Occamist nominalist philosophy became 'the mother of subjective right'.[64] For Occam first equated right (*ius*) with a power (*potestas*) of the individual, e.g. the right of use as a licit power to use an external object of which one ought not to be deprived against one's will, and such that if one is deprived without warrant one can take legal action against the depriver.[65] Villey's historical claims regarding the confluence of individual rights and freedom (*libertas*) are controversial, for others trace the original connection back to Jean de Gerson (1363–1429),[66] or even earlier to medieval canon lawyers in the twelfth century.[67] However, the gist of Villey's argument is that a theory of individual subjective rights presupposes a deep commitment to the individual freedom of choice which is found only in relatively modern thinkers.

In response to this argument, we should observe first that Aristotle and his contemporaries did have a notion of voluntariness and free choice, and we should reiterate that they also used terms comparable to modern locutions which recognize individual autonomy, e.g. of 'liberty' (*exousia*), 'authority' (*kurios*), and 'immunity' (*adeia* and *akuron*). Further, even if modern theorists do place greater weight on freedom or autonomy than Aristotle, it does not follow that Aristotle lacked the concept of rights.[68]

[64] Villey (1975), 253–5, 261. Golding (1978) follows Villey in regarding Occam as the inaugurator of individual rights.

[65] Occam, *Opus nonaginta dierum*, ch. 2, in Villey (1964), 100–2; (1969), 166. Cf. McGrade (1980; 1982).

[66] Tuck (1979), 25–6, who agrees with Villey to a great extent, favours Gerson as the source of rights theory because 'by claiming that *ius* was a *facultas* [ability], Gerson was able to assimilate *ius* and *libertas*'.

[67] Tierney (1988 and 1989) argues that *ius* is tied to *potestas* and *facultas* as early as the 12th cent. He also notes that the Decretum of Gratian (*c*.1140) speaks of rights of liberty (*iura libertatis*) that could not be lost however long a man was in bondage. On Occam's antecedents see also McGrade (1980 and 1982). It should also be noted that much earlier the Latin terms *potestas* and *facultas*, with *libertas*, are used in Constantine's 'Edict of Milan' (313 AD) to grant freedom of religion to all Romans (in Lactantius, *De mortibus persecutorum*, 48). Both terms are translated into Greek as *exousia* and *eleutheria* (Eusebius, *Ecclesiastical History*, X 5). The edict also affirms the property right (*ius, to dikaion*) of Christian congregations. These were, however, rights conferred by the Roman Emperor and in no sense natural rights against the state.

[68] As Tierney (1988) remarks, Villey's thesis is difficult to evaluate because his phrase 'subjective rights' is a bit of a moving target, sometimes referring to rights belonging to the individual subject, sometimes to rights inhering in the individual as such, and sometimes to rights ultimately based on the individual will or even subjective whim. I maintain that Aristotle recognizes 'subjective' rights in the sense of rights belonging to individual subjects which can be claimed by them against other individuals.

For he could still have a concept of individual rights if, as I argue, he has a theory of justice which is sufficiently 'individualistic' to guarantee protection for each and every individual citizen. Aristotle's conception of rights could thus be viewed as an ancestor of modern conceptions which assign a more central role for liberty and autonomy.

Strauss also claims that the theory of natural rights is alien to ancient thinkers like Aristotle, but he emphasizes the divergence of Hobbes from Aristotle. On Hobbes's view,

One could not assert the primacy of natural rights without asserting that the individual is in every respect prior to civil society: all rights of civil society or of the sovereign are derivative from rights which originally belonged to the individual. The individual as such, the individual regardless of his qualities—and not merely, as Aristotle had contended, the man who surpasses humanity—had to be conceived of as essentially complete independently of civil society. This conception is implied in the contention that there is a state of nature which antedates civil society.[69]

Hobbes's theory of natural rights leads, on Strauss's interpretation, to a contractarian concept of justice:

If the only unconditional moral fact is the natural right of each to his self-preservation, and therefore all obligations to others arise from contract, justice becomes identical with the habit of fulfilling one's contracts. Justice no longer consists in complying with standards that are independent of human will.[70]

Strauss finds in Locke a similar abandonment of natural duties: 'Through the shift of emphasis from natural duties or obligations to natural rights, the individual, the ego, had become the center and origin of the moral world, since man—as distinguished from man's end—had become that center or origin.'[71]

Strauss is correct that there are important differences between the ancient and modern theories of 'natural right'. When he argues that Aristotle would have rejected a Hobbesian theory of pre-political natural rights, he is persuasive. However, it does not follow from this that Aristotle did not acknowledge individual rights based on nature in some other sense. Strauss also argues,

The tradition which Hobbes opposed had assumed that man cannot reach the perfection of his nature except in and through civil society and, therefore, that civil society is prior to the individual. It was this assumption which led to the view that the primary moral fact is duty and not rights. One could not assert the

---

[69] Strauss (1953), 183.   [70] Ibid. 187.   [71] Ibid. 248; cf. 227.

primacy of natural rights without asserting that the individual is in every respect prior to civil society . . .

This seemingly includes Aristotle as well as the 'pre-modern natural law' theorists Strauss is discussing.[72] However, Aristotle does not hold that duties are in general prior to rights. For example, from the fact that a creditor has the right to prosecute a debtor for non-payment of a debt, it does not follow that the creditor is obligated to do so; for the creditor generally also has the liberty to cancel the debt (cf. *EN* VIII 14 1163^{b}18–22). We may distinguish between two different sorts of just-claim rights: X has a *mandatory* right to do A if, and only if, in addition to having a claim right, X also has a *duty* to do A; but X has an *optional* right to do A if, and only if, in addition to having a claim right, X also has the liberty right not to do A.[73] But there is no evidence that Aristotle held that all rights are mandatory rights. The creditor example shows he recognized optional rights. It would thus seem a mistake to attribute to Aristotle 'the view that the primary moral fact is duty'.

In general, Aristotle's view of the relationship between the rights and duties of individuals is more complicated than Strauss suggests. A just-claim right (*to dikaion*) of individual X against individual Y entails that Y has a duty to act in the appropriate manner towards X. However, a liberty (*exousia*) to act in a certain way entails the absence of a duty by the agent to forbear from acting in this manner. Authority (*kurios*) implies the liability of other persons to be placed in new relations of rights or duties. 'The right to rule' and 'the duty to obey' will be analysable into such authority relationships between the ruler and the ruled. An immunity consists in a disability (*akuron*) or absence of authority, in which case there is not a 'duty to obey'. From the foregoing it should be concluded that, rather than giving primacy to duties over rights, Aristotle (like Hohfeld) has a theory which yields a system of logically interconnected rights and duties.

Finally, T. H. Irwin has argued that the 'teleological eudaimonism' of Aristotle (as well as Plato) is inconsistent with two deontological principles that are necessary conditions for a theory of rights:

(1)   If X has a right to A, then A is due to X, or X is morally entitled to A, whether or not we regard A's having X as morally best over all; and

(2)   in particular, some of X's rights give him freedom to claim or not

---

[72] Ibid. 183; Aristotle is mentioned in the same paragraph.   [73] Simmons (1992), 74.

to claim *A*, as he prefers, and to have his claim granted or his
failure to claim respected, whether or not the overall moral results
are best.[74]

According to Irwin, Aristotle (like Plato) holds that justice should promote
others' *interests*, and this 'allows no concern for rights apart from interest'.
Because individuals are valued on the basis of their virtuous character,
there is no 'respect for persons' in the modern Kantian sense of respecting
others as autonomous beings capable of choosing their own ends.

However, Irwin himself qualifies this argument by remarking that his
two conditions need not be understood to describe rights *simpliciter*, but
can instead be taken to describe 'morally distinctive rights', that is, 'the
kind of rights which are morally distinctive in that their possession and
exercise cannot be replaced by other people's benevolence or sense of
duty to the right-holder'.[75] Such 'morally distinctive' rights can prohibit
paternalistic interference by *X* with particular choices of *Y* based on *X*'s
conviction that the choices are not in *Y*'s best interests. The fact that
Aristotle assigns to the laws the role of inculcating virtue even in adults
(see *EN* X 9 1180^{a}1–5) may be taken as evidence that Aristotle does not
recognize 'morally distinctive' rights.

None the less, this objection resembles the objections considered earlier
in that it assumes without argument that a theory of 'morally distinctive
rights' must have a peculiar character, viz., to protect autonomy or liberty.
This is, to be sure, a widely held view,[76] but it is far from being universally
accepted. Joseph Raz, on the contrary, defines '*X* has a right' in terms of
whether 'other things being equal, an aspect of *X*'s well being (his interest)
is a sufficient reason for holding some other person(s) to be under a duty'.
He thus propounds an interest-based theory of rights: 'To assert that an
individual has a right is to indicate a ground for a requirement for action
of a certain kind, i.e. that an aspect of his well-being is a ground for a
duty on another person. The specific role of rights in practical thinking
is, therefore, the grounding of duties in the interests of other human
beings.' An interest-based theory of rights such as Raz's will place importance on the autonomy and freedom of right-holders, *provided* that the
value of personal autonomy can be demonstrated. That is, it must be
established that 'it is in their interest not to be subjected to the kind of
oppressive paternalism which consists in running their lives for them

---

[74] Irwin (1977), 273.   [75] Ibid. 344 n. 29.
[76] It is espoused, for example, by Hart (1984), Mackie (1984), and Nozick (1974). See
Sect. 10.6 for further discussion.

allegedly in their own best interest'. Raz's theory (which exhibits a number of parallels to Aristotle's, including a qualified endorsement of perfectionism) shows that a theory of rights may be essentially interest based, so that a candidate such as Aristotle's theory of rights should not be disqualified on the basis of Irwin's principles.[77]

In conclusion, although the arguments considered in this section point out important differences between Aristotle and modern rights theorists, none of them shows that Aristotle could not have had a theory of rights. The remainder of this chapter argues that he did have a theory of rights based on nature, proceeding from a comparison with the theories of Hobbes and Locke.

4.5. NATURAL RIGHTS IN HOBBES AND LOCKE

As a preliminary to discussing Aristotle's theory of rights, it will be helpful to use as foils two of the most influential modern theories of natural rights: the Hobbesian and the Lockian.

The Hobbesian theory

For Thomas Hobbes (1588–1679), 'The Right of Nature . . . is the Liberty each man hath, to use his own power, as he will him-selfe, for the preservation of his own Nature; that is to say, of his own Life; and consequently, of doing any thing which in his own Judgement, and Reason, hee shall conceive to be the aptest means thereunto.'[78] This natural right is contrasted with 'a Law of Nature', which is 'a Precept, or generall Rule, found out by Reason, by which a man is forbidden to do, that, which is destructive of his life, or taketh away the means of preserving the same; and to omit, that, by which he thinketh it may be best preserved.' More precisely, 'RIGHT consisteth in liberty to do, or to forbeare; Whereas LAW, determineth, and bindeth to one of them; so that Law, and Right, differ as much, as Obligation, and Liberty; which in one and the same matter are inconsistent.' Hobbes maintains that 'naturally every man has Right to every thing' by the following argument:

(1) 'The condition of Man is a condition of Warre of every one against every one; in which case everyone is governed by his own Reason.'

---

[77] Raz (1986), 166, 180, 191, 420–4.
[78] Hobbes, *Leviathan*, 1 14 (1968: 64); cf. *De Cive*, I 1 7.

(2) 'There is nothing he can make use of, that may not be a help unto him, in preserving his life against his enemyes.'

(3) 'It followeth, that in such a condition, every man has a Right to every thing; even to one another's body.'

It is evident from Hobbes's distinction between the notions of right and law, and from conclusion (3) above, that his understanding of a right is equivalent to a bare Hohfeldian liberty. Because there are no duties between individuals in the Hobbesian state of nature, individuals have no claim rights which impose correlative duties upon other individuals; rather, they possess only those rights which entail the absence of duties to other individuals. For example, two persons in the state of nature have the liberty to enslave each other, but neither has the claim right against the other not to be enslaved. Hobbes further reasons that 'as long as this naturall Right of every man to everything endureth, there can be no security to any man, (how strong or wise soever he be,) of living out the time, which Nature ordinarily alloweth men to live'. Hence, Hobbes derives his first two 'Laws of Nature', which are understood as 'precepts, or generall rules of reason'.[79] First, 'that every man, ought to endeavour Peace, as farre as he has hope of obtaining it; and when he cannot obtain it, that he may seek, and use, all helps, and advantages of Warre'; and second 'that a man be willing, when others are so too, as farre-forth, as for Peace, and defense of himselfe he shall think it necessary, to lay down this right to all things; and be contented with so much liberty against other men, as he would allow other men against himselfe'. According to Hobbes, when one lays down one's rights by transferring them to another, 'then is he said to be OBLIGED or BOUND, not to hinder those, to whom such a Right is granted, or abandoned, from the benefit of it . . .' Consequently, from the second law, argues Hobbes, 'there followeth a Third; which is this, that men performe their Covenants made: without which, Covenants are in vain, and but Empty words; and the Right of all men to all things remaining, wee are still in the condition of Warre.'

Hobbes's theory thus has the following features: in the state of nature, individuals are governed by laws of nature, which are rules of conduct imposing obligations upon them, and individuals there also possess natural rights. These natural rights, however, are unrestricted liberty rights, and the obligations are purely self-regarding. The obligations are rules discoverable by reason which assert a causal connection between the ends of

[79] Hobbes, *Leviathan*, I 14 (1968: 64–5); cf. *De Cive*, I II.

an agent and the forms of behaviour necessary to attain that end.[80] These must be obligations which will motivate a human being, and Hobbes's theory of motivation is materialistic, deterministic, and egoistic. Human beings are motivated purely by the passions, and human practical reason is solely concerned with satisfying these passions. For Hobbes, ethical theory is fundamentally subjectivistic and relativistic: 'good' and 'evil' are defined in terms of one's desires (or, in current parlance, subjective preferences).[81] However, Hobbes also claims that 'all men agree on this, that Peace is Good'.[82] He further holds that certain forms of co-operative behaviour are causally necessary for the attainment of peace. Thus, reason may derive hypothetical obligations or 'oughts' of the following form:

If X wants G, then X ought to do M.

In this case the substitution-instance for G is peace, which Hobbes takes to be an instrumental good for all individual agents, whatever their ultimate values may be, and desirable in so far as it is necessary for self-preservation; and M is co-operative behaviour, given the Hobbesian laws of nature. For transferring rights and keeping covenants, when performed in conjunction with others' performance of the same, are necessary means for the achievement of peace. Hobbes thus offers a contractarian theory of claim rights, since the interpersonal obligations entailed by such rights result from contracts, and the obligations to keep these contracts are derived by means of hypothetical imperatives.[83] Therefore, there are no natural claim rights for Hobbes, only natural liberty rights; however, natural law instructs us that it is rational to cede natural liberties and thus create claim rights.

The Lockian theory

John Locke (1632–1704) argues that the natural rights of individuals can be derived from the law of nature:

The State of Nature has a Law of Nature to govern it, which obliges every one: And Reason, which is that Law, teaches all Mankind, who will but consult it, that being all equal and independent, no one ought to harm another in his Life, Health, Liberty, or Possessions.[84]

The natural rights of individuals consist primarily in self-ownership, and by extension in property rights:

---

[80] Hampton (1986), 42–57. [81] Hobbes, *Leviathan*, 1 6 (1968: 24).
[82] Ibid., 1 15 (1968: 80); cf. *De Cive*, I 1 15–I II 2. [83] Ibid., cf. II 21 (1968: 111).
[84] Locke, *Second Treatise*, II 6.

Though the Earth, and all inferior Creatures be common to all Men, yet every
man has a *Property* in his own *Person*. This no Body has any Right to but himself.
The *Labour* of his Body, and the *Work* of his Hands, we may say, are properly his.
Whatsoever then he removes out of the State that Nature hath provided, and left
it in, he hath mixed his *Labour* with, and joyned to it something that is his own,
and thereby makes it his Property.[85]

The natural rights of individuals are derived from the law of nature, and
also the rights to enforce any violations of these rights:

And that all Men may be restrained from invading others Rights, and from doing
hurt to one another, and the Law of Nature be observed, which willeth the Peace
and *Preservation of all Mankind*, the *Execution* of the Law of Nature is in that
State, put into every Mans hands, whereby every one has a right to punish the
transgressors of that Law to such a Degree, as may hinder its violation.[86]

Locke rejects Hobbes's identification of 'the State of Nature' and 'the
State of War', and asserts that 'Men living together according to reason,
without a common Superior on Earth, with Authority to judge between
them, is properly the State of Nature. But force, or a declared design of
force upon the Person of another, where there is no common Superior on
Earth to appeal to for relief, is the State of War.' None the less, Locke
agrees that the state of nature is

a condition, which however free, is full of fears and continual dangers: And 'tis
not without reason, that he seeks out, and is willing to joyn in Society with others
who are already united, or have a mind to unite for mutual *Preservation* of their
Lives, Liberties and Estates, which I call by the general Name, *Property*. The
great and *chief end* therefore, of Mens uniting into commonwealths, and putting
themselves under Government, *is the Preservation of their Property*.[87]

In political society, the law of nature continues to serve a moral side
constraint upon positive, written laws, 'which are only so far right as they
are founded on the Law of Nature, by which they are to be regulated and
interpreted'.[88]

    Here Locke identifies 'the Law of Nature' with 'the Law of Reason',
contending that 'it is certain that there is such a Law, and that too, as
intelligible and plain to a rational Creature, and Studier of that Law, as
the positive Laws of Common-wealths, nay possibly plainer . . .'[89] However,
Locke's actual appeal to Reason explicitly relies upon a theistic premiss:

    [85] Locke, *Second Treatise*, v 27; cf. 44.   [86] Ibid., II 7; cf. III 16.
    [87] Ibid., IX 123–4. Cf. Pufendorf, *De jure naturae et gentium*, II 2 9, 12.
    [88] Locke, *Second Treatise*, III 19, IX 123, II 12.
    [89] Ibid., II 12; cf. *First Treatise*, IX 101. This confident statement is qualified in *Second
Treatise*, IX 124.

For Men being all the Workmanship of one Omnipotent, and infinitely wise Maker; All the Servants of one Sovereign Master, sent into the World by his order and about his business, they are his Property, whose Workmanship they are, made to last during his, not anothers Pleasure.[90]

From this premiss he derives several conclusions. First, since God furnished humans with like faculties and made them to share 'all in one Community of Nature', he did not establish any such subordination among humans which would authorize some to destroy or consume others (in contrast, God did make the lower animals for the use of human beings). Second, every human being 'is bound to preserve himself, and not to quit his Station wilfully'. Third, by the same reasoning, 'when his own Preservation comes not to competition, ought he, as much as he can, to preserve the rest of Mankind, and may not unless it be to do Justice on an Offender, take away, or impair the life, or what tends to the Preservation of the Life, Liberty, Health, Limb or Goods of another'. In conclusion, Locke derives a more robust set of natural rights than Hobbes; they are not merely Hohfeldian liberty rights but are also claim rights entailing interpersonal obligations to respect the exercise of these rights.[91] But, as noted above, this derivation relies upon the controversial theistic assumption that human beings are the creatures and property of a divine craftsman, who has assigned them certain functions.[92]

4.6. POLITICAL RIGHTS BASED ON NATURE

Locke's theory of 'the Law of Nature' is a direct descendant of Aristotle's theory of natural justice. In his early work, *Questions concerning the Law of Nature* (untitled and unpublished, written in Latin *c*.1664), Locke's first argument for the existence of natural law appeals explicitly to Aristotle's claim in *Nicomachean Ethics*, I 7, that 'the proper function of man is the activity of the soul according to reason'.[93] Locke also notes a

---

[90] Ibid., ii 6.

[91] See Simmons (1992) for an overview of the secondary literature. Simmons criticizes interpreters like Strauss (1953) who view Lockian natural rights as tantamount to Hobbesian rights with no correlative duties, and also commentators like Tully (1980) who see Lockian rights as entirely derivative from duties to God.

[92] Tully (1980), 35–43, emphasizes the dependence of Locke's theory on his theism. However, Simmons (1992) argues that Locke's theory of rights is detachable from his theology.

[93] *Questions*, i 13. As noted by the editors, Locke's Greek citation is likely from memory (1990), 103 n. 12.

similarity with the notion of natural justice in *Nicomachean Ethics*, V 7, as 'that law which has everywhere the same force'.[94] Locke defends Aristotle's distinction between natural and positive law at some length (*Questions*, I. 13–17). The *Two Treatises of Government* (published in 1690) also implicitly places Locke's theory in the Aristotelian tradition, since he appeals a number of times[95] to the writings of the 'judicious' Richard Hooker (1554–1600), whose views on natural law derive from Thomas Aquinas (1225–74) and ultimately from Aristotle. Both Aristotle and Locke view nature as a standard by which legal systems and laws may be compared and evaluated. For Aristotle states that 'only one constitution is everywhere according to nature the best' (*EN* V 7 1135^{a}4–5), and Locke maintains that 'the *Municipal Laws* of Countries . . . are only so far right, as they are founded on the Law of Nature, by which they are to be regulated and interpreted' (*Second Treatise*, II. 12).

This section will consider another possible similarity: Does Aristotle hold that individuals possess natural rights in some sense? First, however, it is necessary to recall the two senses of 'natural rights' distinguished earlier: natural$_1$ rights based on natural justice, and natural$_2$ rights possessed in a pre-political state of nature. Lockian natural rights are 'natural' in both senses. Hobbesian natural rights are natural in the second but not the first sense. Aristotle, as I shall now argue, endorses natural rights in the first (which I am calling 'rights based on nature') but not the second sense.

That Aristotle would not derive political rights from pre-existing pre-political natural rights seems clear. Unlike Locke, who regards the natural law which governs the state of nature[96] as prior to political justice, Aristotle treats natural justice as part of, rather than prior to, political justice (*EN* V 7 1134^{b}18–19; see Section 3.3 above). Political justice is found in a polis, a community concerned with a self-sufficient life (6 1134^{a}26–7). Thus Aristotle's natural justice presupposes a political context.[97] Because natural justice is understood as inherently political, it

[94] Locke misquotes and misinterprets *EN* V 7. He erroneously understands Aristotle to be dividing law into civil and natural parts, rather than to be dividing political justice into natural and legal (or conventional) parts (1990: 103 n. 14). The misinterpretation is understandable since Locke himself views natural law as distinct from and prior to the political state.

[95] See, e.g. Locke's *Second Treatise*, II 15. On the parallels between Locke and Aristotle, see Rasmussen (1984).

[96] Locke, *Second Treatise*, II 15: 'The *State of Nature* has a Law of Nature to govern it.'

[97] Although Aristotle recognizes non-political forms of justice, he does not treat them as prior to political justice. Rather they are called just due to their similarity to political justice, which is the most perfect form of justice. See Sect. 3.5 above.

obviously cannot support pre-political natural rights possessed by individuals in a pre-political state of nature.

But this does not rule out rights based on natural justice. Indeed, as I shall now argue, the central thesis of *Politics*, III, is that Aristotle's theory of distributive justice yields a theory of political rights which can be evaluated as natural or unnatural (and hence correct or deviant). The underlying ideas are that a polis in a natural condition has a constitution which promotes universal justice (i.e. the common advantage of the citizens), and that a correct theory of distributive justice will yield the assignment of political rights that promotes universal justice.[98] *Politics*, III, contains two important references to the discussions of distributive justice in the treatise on justice.[99] The context in which these references occur is a dispute over the constitution,[100] concerning which inhabitants will hold offices, comprise the government, and possess authority over the polis (cf. III 6 1278^{b}8–11, 7 1279^{a}25–7). The verb *amphisbēteō*, 'to dispute', is also used in connection with legal disputes, e.g. over the ownership of property or over an inheritance.[101] The dispute over the constitution is thus modelled after a lawsuit in which individuals dispute over their rights. The task of the theory of justice in *Politics*, III, is to settle constitutional disputation by determining how political rights are to be distributed and how authority is to be assigned.[102]

A central and pressing question of political philosophy as a practical science is how to assess competing appeals to distributive justice (see III 12 1282^{b}23). In a business venture one would expect this to be determined by agreement or contract, e.g. whether the worth of the contribution is

---

[98] Cf. Rawls (1971), 4: '. . . the principles of social justice . . . provide a way of assigning rights and duties in the basic institutions of society and they define the appropriate distribution of the benefits and burdens of social co-operation.'

[99] The references are to the opening lines of this discussion: *Pol.* III 12 1282^{b}20 refers to the claim that justice is a sort of equality (*EN* V 3 1131^{a}11–14), and *Pol.* III 9 1280^{a}18 alludes to the claim that justice involves an equal relation between persons and objects to be divided among them (1131^{a}14–24).

[100] This is introduced by the concluding words of *Pol.* III 8: 'they both dispute over the constitution' (*amphisbētousin amphoteroi tēs politeias*) (1280^{b}6). Cf. *amphisbētousi tōn archōn* at 12 1283^{a}11, cited in Sect. 4.3 above. Similar uses of the verb with the genitive are found in Isocrates, IV 20 (with *tēs hēgemonias*), Demosthenes, XXXIX 19 (with *tēs archēs*), and Plato, *Statesman*, 290^{a}2 (*tēs politikēs*).

[101] See *EN* V 4 1132^{a}19, cited in Sect. 4.3 above, and *Rhet.* I 1 1354^{a}31. The use for legal disputation is common in other authors: see Isocrates, III 1, 61; VI 3; XIX 1, 3; Demosthenes, III 5, and XLIV 38; Plato, *Laws*, VI 766^{d}3–767^{a}4 and XII 948^{b}3–^{c}1. In Plato the jurist settles the dispute by making a decision concerning just-claim rights (*tēn tōn dikaiōn krisin*).

[102] As Schütrumpf (1991), ii. 110–11, remarks, *Pol.* III resembles a Platonic dialogue and many passages are 'aporetic', i.e. considering different solutions to difficulties (*aporiai*). Hence, the context in which passages occur must be taken into account.

based on time devoted to the project, capital invested, or some other criterion. But the problem is more contestable in the political context:

> For everyone agrees that the just in distributions ought to be according to some merit, yet everyone does not say that merit is the same thing; advocates of democracy say it is freedom, some advocates of oligarchy say it is wealth, and others good birth, and advocates of aristocracy say it is virtue. (*EN* V 3 1131^{a}25–9; cf. Plato, *Laws*, XII 962^{d}7–^{e}9)

Politics, III, contains similar remarks:

> Hence, since the just is for some persons and is divided in the same manner in respect of things and for the recipients, as has been said before in the *Ethics*, they agree about the equality of the things, but dispute about [equality] for the recipients . . . (III 9 1280^{a}16–19; cf. 12 1282^{b}18–22)

This is a dispute among different theories of justice: oligarchic justice, democratic justice, and aristocratic justice. At issue are rights within the political community.[103] The formal principle of distributive justice generates political rights by means of the following general formula (cf. Section 3.2 above):

$$\text{(PR)} \quad \frac{\text{Merit of } X}{\text{Merit of } Y} = \frac{\text{The political rights of } X}{\text{The political rights of } Y}$$

(PR) is an abstract or formal principle on which all sides agree, but the formula will not have substantive, political implications until a standard of merit is proposed.

Aristotle mentions four competing standards of merit—freedom, wealth, good birth, and virtue—each of which then yields a material principle of political rights. The democratic theory takes the standard of merit to be freedom:

$$\text{(DR)} \quad \frac{\text{The freedom of } X}{\text{The freedom of } Y} = \frac{\text{The political rights of } X}{\text{The political rights of } Y}$$

Since all free-born citizens[104] are equal in being free-born, they will all have equal political rights (*Pol.* III 9 1280^{a}24–5).[105] Equality is thus a corollary of freedom in the democratic theory. Given that each citizen has

---

[103] This interpretation is found in other commentators. The issue is one of 'just claims' in Newman (1887), iii. 199, and one of 'rights' in Susemihl and Hicks (1894), 390, and in Barker (1946), 116.

[104] Slaves, of course, being unfree, have no political rights. Women are also left out of the equation, in spite of I 12 1260^{b}18–19. See Sect. 6.9 below.

[105] Cf. Plato, *Rep.* VIII 557^{a}4–5.

equal political rights and that the majority of right-holders has authority (IV 8 1294^{a}11–14), it will also follow that the majority of citizens has authority (*kurios*) within the constitution (see V 9 1310^{a}28–32). For example, the majority voting in the assembly has the authority to make deliberative and judicial decisions for the entire polis.

There are two versions of oligarchic theory, one of which may be called 'propertarian', because it takes the standard of merit to be one's personal wealth:

$$\text{(OPR)} \quad \frac{\text{The wealth of } X}{\text{The wealth of } Y} = \frac{\text{The political rights of } X}{\text{The political rights of } Y}$$

Equally wealthy citizens will have the same political rights, but wealthier citizens will have more political rights than poor citizens (*Pol.* III 9 1280^{a}25–31). In other words, a wealthy person will have all the rights of a poor person as well as other rights. The other version of oligarchic theory may be called 'hereditary', since it takes the standard of merit to be quality of birth, family, and descent:[106]

$$\text{(OHR)} \quad \frac{\text{The pedigree of } X}{\text{The pedigree of } Y} = \frac{\text{The political rights of } X}{\text{The political rights of } Y}$$

Better-born citizens will have more political rights than low-born citizens, although citizens with equal pedigrees will have equal rights. Aristotle tends to ignore the second variant of oligarchy, or lump it together with the propertarian version (cf. V 1 1301^{b}1–4). On both versions, the reins of authority tend to be in a few hands.

Finally, the aristocratic theory is interpreted in terms of virtue:

$$\text{(AR)} \quad \frac{\text{The virtue of } X}{\text{The virtue of } Y} = \frac{\text{The political rights of } X}{\text{The political rights of } Y}$$

Equally virtuous individuals have equal political rights on the aristocratic theory, but more virtuous persons have more political rights than do less virtuous persons (*Pol.* III 9 1281^{a}4–8). Each theory—the democratic, the two oligarchic (propertarian and hereditary), and the aristocratic—provides a standard (*horos*) by which constitutions can be compared, evaluated, and, if necessary, changed or reformed. *Politics*, III, is concerned with

---

[106] Good birth (*eugeneia*) generally involved descent from an ancient noble family, especially from a hero or a god. Newman (1887), iii. 234, remarks that in practice, 'The well-born were citizens in a higher degree than the low-born, for they could reckon more generations of citizen descent, and this was with many a test of citizenship.'

adjudicating the dispute among these competing political theories and their standards of justice and rights.

In *Politics*, III 12, Aristotle considers the argument that because people with different characteristics have different rights based on justice and merit, those who are superior in any respect should have a greater share in offices. It will follow that those who are superior in complexion, size, or any other good will have an excessive possession of political rights (*pleonexia tōn politikōn dikaiōn*) (1282^{b}26–30). Aristotle objects, however, that the dispute over political offices necessarily involves 'the things out of which the polis is established' (1283^{a}14–15). He supports this conclusion by an analogy with other sciences and crafts, in particular flute playing. Flute players should not have an excessive possession of flutes on the grounds that they are better born or more handsome; rather, the criterion should be whether their trait 'contributes to the function' of flute playing (1283^{a}1–3).[107] Hence, flute players who are equal in flute-playing excellence should receive equal flutes, and superior players should receive superior flutes.

The distribution of political rights should be based upon similar considerations:

> But the dispute [over offices] necessarily involves the things out of which the polis is established. Therefore, it is with good reason that the well-born, the free and the wealthy make contending claims to honour [i.e. political office]. For there must be both free persons and persons bearing the assessment, for there could not be a polis consisting entirely of poor persons, nor of slaves; yet truly if these things are needed, it is clear that justice and military virtue are also needed. For a polis cannot be managed without these things. However, without the former things the polis cannot exist, but without the latter it cannot be nobly managed. (1283^{a}14–22; cf. IV 12 1296^{b}17–19)

Aristotle thus allows that in so far as the *existence* of the polis is concerned, there is some basis for the democratic theory of political rights and for the propertarian and hereditary versions of the oligarchic theory of political rights.

Nevertheless, the aristocratic theory has the best case. 'But in relation to the good life education and virtue dispute justly above all, as was also said before' (13 1283^{a}24–6; cf. ^{a}37–8). This is evidently an allusion to an earlier passage in *Politics*, III:

---

[107] At 1282^{b}33–4 he mentions a closely related criterion, whether a person is 'outstanding at the function [*ergon*]' in question. See Keyt (1991a), 247–9, for discussion of these criteria.

A polis is a community of families and villages in a complete and self-sufficient life. This is, as we say, living happily and nobly. Therefore, one should suppose that the political community is for the sake of noble actions, but not the sake of [merely] living together. Therefore those who contribute the most to such a community participate more in the polis than those who are equal or greater according to freedom or family but unequal according to political virtue, or than those who are prominent according to wealth but inferior according to virtue. (9 $1280^b40-1281^a8$)

The argument proceeds from the premiss that the polis is a self-sufficient co-operative endeavour aiming at the good life of its members. According to the principle of distributive justice, an individual has a right to political offices in proportion to his contribution to the polis. If the hypothesis were that the end of the polis is the accumulation of wealth or property, the propertarian-oligarchic theory would provide the appropriate theory for distributing political rights, and if the hypothesis were that freedom is the end, the democratic theory of justice would be most apt. But the correct hypothesis on Aristotle's view is that the end is a noble, virtuous life. In so far as the citizens are free, well-born, or wealthy, they can help to keep the polis in existence; but only in so far as they possess virtue can they directly contribute to its natural end. Therefore, the aristocratic theory is correct, and the virtuous[108] have a just claim to political authority which is superior to that of other members of the polis. Furthermore, the aristocratic constitution is best because it is just without qualification (6 1279^a18-19) and based on nature (cf. 17 1287^b37-41; VII 3 1325^b7-10); i.e. it exemplifies natural justice (cf. *EN* V 7 1135^a5). Those who are virtuous therefore have a right to authority in such a constitution. These political rights based on nature belong to 'those persons who are capable and who choose to rule and be ruled for the sake of a virtuous life' (see *Pol.* III 13 $1283^b42-1284^a3$). Thus the aristocratic theory of political rights is the authoritative theory of rights (*to kuriōs dikaion*, 9 1280^a10-11).

Although Aristotle makes clear the superiority of the aristocratic theory, he leaves important issues unresolved. One set of issues concerns the interpretation and application of the aristocratic theory itself. Does it

---

[108] This account is incomplete. Aristotle elsewhere remarks that virtue must be equipped (*kechorēgēmenē*), i.e. complemented by the external means needed to carry out virtuous actions (see VII 1 $1323^b41-1324^a1$; IV 2 1289^a31-3). The implications of this are discussed in Ch. 9 below. He also takes it for granted that the citizens must be naturally free and equal (cf. I 7 1255^b20). Further, Aristotle speaks of this virtue as *political* virtue (III 9 1280^b5, 1281^a7).

imply that only one or a few persons ought to possess political rights, or should these rights be shared equally by a multitude of citizens? Suppose that there is one person or a few persons who are so superior to the others that the latters' virtue and political capacity are not commensurable with the formers'? Do such 'godlike' persons have the natural right to become absolute kings with unlimited authority over the others? Aristotle considers, without fully resolving, such questions in *Politics*, III 13–17. They are examined further in Chapter 6 below. Another set of issues concerns the practical application of his theory. Should the lawgiver ignore claims based on democratic or oligarchic standards? Since the virtuous are few in number, a constitution based on the aristocratic theory would resemble the ideal polis of Plato's *Republic*, with a virtuous minority monopolizing authority. Would the disenfranchised members of the polis accept the role of 'slaves and friends' of the guardian class (cf. *Rep.* X 590^{c}8–^{d}6)? Would they not be alienated, since 'when many dishonoured [i.e. disenfranchised] and poor persons are present, the polis is necessarily filled with enemies' (*Pol.* III 11 1281^{b}29–30)? But how can the lawgiver admit unqualified citizens without fatally compromising the true purpose of the polis? These vexing issues are examined more fully in Chapters 7–8 below.

4.7. PRACTICAL WISDOM AND RESPECT FOR RIGHTS

This section takes up a problem which Aristotle himself considers only obliquely, but which cannot be evaded: Is it rational for individuals to participate in and conform their conduct to a political community in which they possess rights and respect the rights of others? In Aristotle's terms, would their practical wisdom guide them to follow such a course of action? I understand 'practical wisdom' here in the sense of *individual* practical wisdom or prudence. In this sense, 'the prudent person [*phronimos*] seems to be able to deliberate nobly concerning the things that are good or advantageous for himself [*hautōi*], not in a particular area, for example, for what sort of thing promotes health or strength, but what sort of thing promotes the good life as a whole' (*EN* VI 5 1140^{a}25–8).[109] *Politics*, III 6 1278^{b}15–30 (discussed in Section 2.2 above), mentions three motivations

---

[109] Aristotle distinguishes species of practical wisdom: 'that [species] which is concerned with the individual himself, seems most of all to be practical wisdom, and it has the common name of practical wisdom'; but there are other species, most importantly, household science and politics (8 1141^{b}29–32). See also Sect. 1.2 above.

for entering a political community. The first involves a pre-reflective innate impulse for communal living: 'even if they had no need of mutual help, they would strive to live together' (^{b}20–1). The two other motivations involve putatively rational justifications for political co-operation. The former justification is that 'the common advantage also brings them together in so far as there falls to each of them a part of the good life' (^{b}21–3). The latter is that 'also for the sake of living itself they come together and keep together the political community. For perhaps there is some noble portion even in life alone by itself, if there are not too many hardships in life' (^{b}24–7). Before returning to the former justification, which Aristotle regards as the most important, let us consider the latter.

The justification from life

The claim that political co-operation is justified as a means for self-preservation anticipates Hobbes's contractarian argument (see Section 4.5). Aristotle suggests in *Politics*, III 9, a line of argument offered by several theorists including Lycophron. On this theory, in order to preserve their lives individuals form an alliance to ensure that they are not treated unjustly by anyone and that they can carry out exchange and co-operation with each other (1280^a31–6, cf. ^{b}30–1). Lycophron views law as a contract (*sunthēkē*) and a guarantee of mutual just-claim rights (1280^b10–11).

Plato provides an account of this type of justification in the *Republic*, when Glaucon offers an explanation of the origin of justice on behalf of Thrasymachus:

They say that to do injustice is naturally good, to suffer injustice is bad, but the suffering of injustice so far exceeds in badness the good of doing injustice, that when they do injustice to each other and suffer it, and taste both, those who are unable to avoid the latter and choose the former decide that it is profitable to make an agreement with each other neither to do nor to suffer injustice. Henceforth, they begin to lay down laws and contracts, and they name what the law enjoins 'lawful' and 'just'. This, they say, is the origin and being of justice: it is between the best and the worst, the best being to do injustice without paying the penalty and the worst to be done an injustice without being able to exact vengeance. The just then is a mean between two extremes; and it is valued not as good but because people are unable to do injustice. (II 358^e3–359^b1)

This explanation assumes that rational individuals follow the course of action which they think will bring about the best consequences for themselves, all things considered. In the present instance, they determine that they will be best off if they agree not to inflict injury upon one another and if they make appropriate laws and contracts. They also conclude that they will be best off if they comply with these agreements and respect one another's rights (the just claims arising from their laws and contracts).

However, Glaucon himself points out two difficulties with this reasoning. First, if an individual is strong enough to advance his ends through coercion rather than co-operation, he will have no reason, even at the outset, to agree with others to refrain from attacking and exploiting them (*Rep.* II 359ᵇ1–3). Second, even if an individual finds it advantageous to enter into such agreements with others, there is no reason for him to continue to comply with such agreements if he can successfully violate them, without detection or otherwise with impunity. Glaucon illustrates the latter difficulty with the example of the legendary ring which rendered its bearer invisible and which an ancestor of Gyges used to kill and replace the king of Lydia. This is supposed to show that anyone will act unjustly who has the liberty to do whatever he wishes (359ᵇ6–360ᵈ7). In addition, there is a difficulty mentioned by Aristotle. Some people see participation in politics as contrary to their own self-interest, along lines stated by Euripides: 'But how could I be prudent, who might have been at ease, numbered among the many in the army, and have had an equal share?' (*EN* VI 8 1142ᵃ3–5). Individual members of the polis have no reason to go out of their way in order to support its constitution and legal systems if they can enjoy the protection of these institutions without making a personal sacrifice. Therefore, even if it is to one's advantage to have a political system which protects one's rights, it may still be in one's interest to violate the rights of others or to shirk the personal costs of maintaining the system of protections.[110]

Even if all these difficulties could be surmounted, Aristotle would find the justification from life wanting. For he maintains that it is founded upon an erroneous view of the natural end of human beings and the polis. It takes the end to be life alone rather than the good life (*Pol.* III 9 1280ᵃ31–2; cf. Plato, *Laws*, IV 707ᵈ1–6). However, although the polis comes to be for the sake of life, it exists for the sake of the good life or

---

[110] This is a form of the free-rider problem, which arises in the case of public goods. A public good has two characteristics: it is equally available to everyone, and it is impossible to exclude non-contributors from the consumption of the good. Public goods might include such things as good government, defence of the polis, and provision of a pure water supply. The problem arises if individuals decide that it is not rational to make a personal contribution to a co-operative endeavour, because they can derive the benefits of co-operation without paying.

living well (*Pol.* I 2 1252^{b}29–30). Hence, Aristotle rejects Lycophron's conception of political co-operation which is derived from this view:

> It is clear therefore that the polis is not a community in a place for the sake of not doing injustice to each other and of making transactions; but it is necessary for these things to be present if there is to be a polis; yet even when all of them are present there is not yet a polis, but it is the community in living well [*hē tou eu zēn koinōnia*] for households and families, for the sake of a complete and self-sufficient life . . . This is, as we say, living happily and nobly. We should, then, suppose that the political community exists for the sake of noble actions and not of [mere] living together. (III 9 1280^{b}29–35, 1281^{a}1–4)

Thus, the end of the polis should be not mere life, but life as a human being, a life of happiness and nobility.

The justification from the good life

Aristotle does believe that the justification from life is partially correct. Just as life as such is a necessary condition for the good life, the political arrangements which sustain and protect life—viz., protection of individual rights and enforcement of contracts—are necessary if the polis is to attain its end. Nevertheless, Aristotle favours the justification from the good life: 'the common advantage brings them together in so far as there falls to each of them a part of the good life. This is most of all the end, for all in common and separately' (6 1278^{b}21–4).

This compressed passage contains part of an Aristotelian solution to the problem we are considering: does prudence guide individuals to participate in a polis where they respect each other's rights? The following reconstruction seeks to make explicit the main premisses supporting an affirmative answer to this question.

(1) Prudence (individual practical wisdom) is for Aristotle an action-guiding excellence concerning what is good or advantageous for the agent in the sense of promoting the good life (*EN* VI 5 1140^{a}25–8). Hence it involves a type of reasoning which is 'agent-relative' or 'agent-centred'.[111] Prudence has a prescriptive function: i.e. it produces judgements of obligation of the form, 'I ought to do *X*' or 'I ought not to do *X*' (see

---

[111] As the terms are now used, a value or reason is *agent-relative* if its description includes essential references to an agent who has that value or reason, and *agent-neutral* if its description does not include an essential reference to a person who has the value or reason. See e.g. Parfit (1986), 104, Scheffler (1982), Mack (1989), and Den Uyl (1991). The latter two argue that agent-relativity is compatible with an objectivist account of values and reasons.

EN VI 10 1143ᵃ8–9). These Aristotelian obligations are hypothetical in character,[112] i.e. they have the general form: 'If *E* is *A*'s end, then *A* ought to do *M* [as a means to *E*]'. Aristotle provides examples of these hypothetical 'oughts' and their enactments: e.g. 'A covering is what I need. A coat is a covering. Therefore, a coat is what I need. What I need I ought to make. Therefore, a coat is what I ought to make' (cf. *MA* 7 701ᵃ17–19).[113] These hypothetical obligations are objective—i.e. they are true independent of the opinions or desires of the agent, who could be mistaken about what natural ends are or about how to attain them.

Aristotle's teleology includes a notion of hypothetical necessity. When Aristotle says that 'nature does nothing in vain', he means that when nature provides living things with something (e.g. hair on the human head), it is providing them with something which is hypothetically necessary (hair is needed to protect the head from an excess of heat or cold). But nature does not always provide human beings with what they need in order to realize their natural ends. In such cases, human beings must employ reason in order to find out what they need to attain their natural ends, as is illustrated by the examples of making a coat or building a house (cf. *Pol.* VII 17 1337ᵃ1–3). This provides the ground for obligation in practical reasoning. When doing *M* is necessary for individuals to achieve their natural ends and it is open to their decision, they have an objective hypothetical obligation to do *M*. It is through deliberation that rational agents identify the actions which will serve as the most effective means to their ends (*EN* III 3 1112ᵃ30–1, ᵇ11–12). Practical wisdom (including prudence) is excellence in deliberating about the means necessary to living well (VI 7 1141ᵇ9–10; cf. 5 1140ᵃ25–8, 9 1142ᵇ32–3). In aiming at a good life or happiness for human beings, prudence seeks to realize their natural end.[114]

Aristotle identifies the human end with happiness, i.e. the actualization of the soul according to complete (or perfect) virtue (*Pol.* VII 13 1332ᵃ9; *EE* II 1 1219ᵃ38–9; *EN* I 7 1098ᵃ16–18). However, his understanding of 'complete (or perfect) virtue' is not altogether clear from his various writings. He implies that happiness includes the actualization of ethical virtue as well as intellectual virtue (*EE* II 1 1219ᵃ23–39, 1220ᵃ2–12). On

---

[112] In this they resemble the Hobbesian hypothetical obligations discussed in Sect. 4.5. However, Aristotelian obligations or 'oughts' differ from Hobbesian ones in that they are conditional upon the individuals' objective natural ends rather than their subjective preferences.

[113] The claim 'what I need I ought to make' thus provides the bridge from 'need' to 'ought'. For further discussion see Miller (1984).

[114] On happiness as the natural end see Sect. 2.3 above.

the other hand, he defends the intellectualist thesis that the contemplative or philosophic life is the happiest: 'the life involving intellect [*nous*] is best and most pleasant' (*EN* X 7 1178^{a}4–8). Yet he also maintains the ethically virtuous acts are chosen for their own sakes (II 4 1105^{a}32). This suggests that happiness is, for Aristotle, a 'mixed' life, of which contemplation is the most valued component but noble, virtuous activity is also an essential constituent. On this moderate-intellectualist interpretation, which I think is most plausible, practical wisdom and prudence will direct human beings not only to pursue contemplative wisdom as far as they are able (X 7 1177^{b}33–4) but also to choose to act virtuously in so far as they are human beings and live in groups (8 1178^{b}5–6).[115] Aristotle thus understands 'living well' as including an ethical life rather than pursuing crassly selfish goals such as the greatest share of wealth, honours, and bodily pleasures for oneself, which Aristotle describes as the life of 'the many' (cf. IX 8 1168^{b}15–23). Nevertheless, prudence is on his view concerned with the good life *for the individual agent* (see VII 5 1140^{a}25–8, cited above; cf. IX 8 1168^{b}28–34).

(2) According to Aristotle, human beings attain perfection only by participating in a polis which is itself in a natural condition. He describes the polis as a 'complete' community which reaches the 'goal of self-sufficiency', so that it can exist for the sake of the good life. Self-sufficiency is the end and hence the nature of the community (*Pol.* I 2 1252^{b}27–1253^{a}1; cf. II 2 1261^{b}11–15, VII 4 1326^{b}7–9). Thus, the polis may be said to be self-sufficient by nature (cf. *Pol.* IV 4 1291^{a}8–10). Lycophron's vision of the polis as a mutual-protection association is rejected because he fails to recognize its natural end: a polis is a community 'for the sake of a complete and self-sufficient life' (III 9 1280^{b}34–5; cf. 1 1275^{b}20–1, VII 4 1326^{b}22–4).

Self-sufficiency implies an adequate level of property—i.e. land and other material equipment needed for the exercise of virtue (see I 8 1256^{b}26–34, VII 8 1321^{b}14–18; cf. 1 1323^{b}40–1324^{a}2). But even more importantly, Aristotle regards it as part of the natural end of the polis that it provide

---

[115] There is a scholarly controversy over how Aristotle understands happiness and whether his various discussions of happiness are even consistent with each other. Against the inclusivist, 'moderate-intellectualist' line of interpretation offered above, some scholars defend a 'strict-intellectualist' reading, according to which contemplation is the sole constituent of true happiness. This difficult issue is discussed in Sect. 10.3 below, where reasons are offered for favouring the inclusivist view (see also Sects. 6.2 and 8). For purposes of the present discussion, however, it seems safe to say that most commentators would agree that for Aristotle, in so far as they are human beings and thus political animals, moral agents should choose ethically virtuous activities.

for the care and education of its members (VIII 1 1337ᵃ21–30). Thus the polis will be in a natural condition only if it contains the institutions necessary for the moral habituation of the citizens. The constitution or structure of the polis is the way of life for the citizens, and this must be the best life if the polis is to be in a natural condition (see IV 11 1295ᵃ40– ᵇ1). Consequently, individuals must participate in such a constitution if they are to realize their natural ends.

(3) If a polis is in a natural condition, then it must have a constitution which embodies justice and the common advantage. Justice has two necessary functions: first, mutual deference and respect for the rights of others; and, second, the facilitation of co-operation and exchange between the members of the community. Aristotle recognizes the necessity of both functions (III 9 1280ᵇ29–32), but he maintains that justice serves a higher end, viz., the pursuit of a life which is self-sufficient or lacking nothing (see *EN* V 6 1134ᵃ26–7).

Aristotle argues that human perfection requires the acquisition of practical wisdom and virtue in a system of justice and laws (*Pol.* I 2 1253ᵃ31–9; see Section 2.5 above). A primary concern of political science is the development and exercise of virtue (*EN* X 9 1179ᵃ35–ᵇ4; see also Section 1.2 above). Within the political context this is the problem of producing citizens who are reasonable (*epieikeis*)[116]—i.e. who are disposed to act in a virtuous manner. Aristotle believes that moral education requires a legal system, because young persons generally are numbered among 'the many' who do not enjoy living in a virtuous and moderate manner; they are instead inclined to live by passions and pursue bodily pleasures. Therefore, the law should prescribe the rearing and conduct of the young. Once they have been habituated to live in a virtuous and noble manner, they will find such a life truly enjoyable. 'The soul of the student

---

[116] The word derives from the verb **eikein*, 'to be like'. (The present tense is not used, but the perfect *eoike* is used in the present sense.) Aristotle notes that *epieikēs* (pl. *epieikeis*) is used in a very general sense as a substitute for 'good' (V 10 1137ᵇ1–2), encompassing the diverse virtues. It is used in this sense in *EN* at X 9 1179ᵇ5 and throughout the *Politics*, e.g. at III 11 1282ᵃ26 for persons who act virtuously. At *EN* X 9 1180ᵃ10–11 the reasonable person follows reason when he lives for the noble. This best sums up Aristotle's notion of *epieikēs*. In the political context it refers to the group of persons who possess the virtues, as distinct from other social groupings such as the masses, the wealthy, etc. (see *Pol.* III 10 1281ᵃ12, 28; 11 1282ᵃ26). The word also has a connotation of 'reasonable' or 'plausible' when applied e.g. to arguments (see references in Liddell, Scott, and Jones (1976), s.v.). Sometimes the word is equivalent to justice (*Rhet.* I 15 1375ᵃ31–2), but Aristotle also treats *to epieikes* as a special virtue, contrasted with justice (e.g. in *EN* V 10 and VI 11 and *Rhet.* I 13), in which sense it is rendered 'equity'. Even when the term has a wider sense of 'good' or 'reasonable', there is a connotation of 'just': see Stewart (1892), ii. 369–70.

must have been prepared by habits for enjoying and hating nobly, as earth that is to nourish seed' (see 1179^{b}23–1180^{a}5). Although parents make an important contribution to their children's upbringing, they lack the compulsory force of the laws which is indispensable for habituation (1180^{a}18–22). In conclusion, individuals require the structure of legal justice in order to realize their natural ends as excellent and reasonable beings.

Aristotle further defends the idea that justice presupposes the community in his claim that 'all justice is in relation to a friend' (*EE* VII 10 1242^{a}20–1).[117] In the *Nicomachean Ethics* he says:

In every community there seems to be a sort of justice, and a sort of friendship also. At any rate, shipmates and fellow soldiers are called friends, and similarly members of other communities. And to the extent that they have [something] in common there is friendship. For there is also justice. The proverb 'What friends have is common' is correct. For there is friendship in community (*EN* VIII 9 1159^{b}26–32)

The *Eudemian Ethics* further emphasizes the connection between friendship and justice within the political context:

All constitutions are a particular form of justice; for [a constitution] is a community, and everything common is established through justice, so that however many forms of friendship there are, there are as many of justice and community; these all border on one another, and the forms of one have differences akin to those of the other. (*EE* VII 9 1241^{b}13–17; cf. *EN* VIII 11 1161^{a}10–11)

It is true that Aristotle believes that the highest form of friendship involves befriending another on account of his virtue, loving him for his sake, and regarding him as 'another self' (see *EN* VII 3 1156^{b}7–12, IX 9 1170^{b}6–7; cf. *EE* VII 2 1236^{b}2–5, 6 1240^{a}23–8), and he believes that political friendship cannot attain this ideal:

It is possible to be a friend of many persons in a political way, and to be not an obsequious but a truly reasonable person [*epieikē*]; but it is not possible [to be a friend] to many persons for their virtue and for themselves, but one should be satisfied to find even a few such [friends]. (*EN* IX 10 1171^{a}17–20; cf. *EE* VII 1245^{b}20–5)

Political or civic friendship is a form of friendship based on utility rather than based on virtue (*EE* VII 10 1242^{a}6–7). However, one very important characteristic of virtue-friends does belong to political friends: this

---

[117] See Yack (1993), 33–43, and Sect. 3.5 above. See also Badhwar (1985) for a defence of Aristotle's thesis that friendship and justice are interconnected virtues.

is unanimity (*homonoia*). Unanimity consists not in agreement about everything—e.g. on whether or not the sun revolves around the earth—but about practical issues fundamental for politics.[118] There is unanimity in a polis when all the citizens agree about what is advantageous, make their choices (law or decree), and act on their common resolution. They all agree on the proper end of the polis and on other basic constitutional issues such as the mode of selecting officials or the making of alliances (*EN* IX 6 1167ᵃ26–32).[119] Because such agreement is basic to political co-operation, unanimity appears to be political friendship, 'for it is concerned with the things that are advantageous and things that promote life' (1167ᵇ2–4).[120] Unanimity binds the citizens together and provides the psychological basis for political co-operation and mutual respect (cf. *Pol.* IV 11 1295ᵇ23–5):

This sort of unanimity is found in reasonable persons. For these have a unanimity with themselves and with each other, since they are, so to speak, of the same mind (for their wishes remain, not flowing back and forth like a tidal strait). They wish for just and advantageous things, and also seek them in common. Base persons, on the other hand, cannot have unanimity, except to a small extent, just as they can be friends only to a small extent; for they strive for excessive possession of benefits, and fall short in toil and public services. And since each wishes these things for himself, he scrutinizes and obstructs his neighbour; for when people do not watch out for the common [good], it is destroyed. The result is that they are in faction, compelling each other to do just things, but not wishing to do it themselves. (*EN* IX 6 1167ᵇ4–16)

Because base persons do not share a common commitment to a life of virtue but instead are motivated by excessive possessiveness, they are consequently locked in faction with each other (1167ᵃ32–4). Justice does not serve as a bond between such persons. Rather, they are in the position described by Glaucon: they each try to compel the others to comply with justice, yet they each also wish to evade it for themselves.

In contrast, reasonable persons will recognize that in order successfully to pursue the good life, they should strive for it in co-operation with others. This is fully in accord with individual prudence, for they can

---

[118] The ideal of unanimity is expressed in a political maxim which is discussed in Sect. 7.4 below.

[119] Aristotle gives as an example that all decide that Pittacus should rule when he himself is willing. Pittacus, having ruled Mitylene for ten years in the early sixth century BC, resigned although the Mitylenaeans wished him to continue. Aristotle's point is that everyone must agree if there is to be unanimity. See Stewart (1892), ii. 368–9.

[120] Cf. Plato, *Rep.* I 351ᵈ5–6, on the connection between justice, unanimity, and friendship.

most successfully pursue the good life when they co-operate with others and when they maintain control over their own wishes. By maintaining inner motivational stability, they both agree within themselves (i.e. they keep the parts of their own souls in concord) and with other persons (i.e. they continue to co-operate with others).[121] This form of unanimity forms the basis for mutual trust: the different parties can rely upon each other to abide by the system of political justice. But the mutual reinforcement is also indispensable for the ethical education and full self-realization of each of the citizens. It is noteworthy that this argument is applicable only to individuals who are 'reasonable' (*epieikeis*) in Aristotle's sense. Those who are inferior or 'base' (*phauloi*) will have to be persuaded to comply with justice by different sorts of arguments (see Chapter 8).

(4) Finally, Aristotle states in *Politics*, III 6, that 'the common advantage also brings [human beings] together in so far as there falls to each of them a part of the good life' (1278^b21-3), and he also says later in this chapter that constitutions which aim at the common advantage are correct constitutions 'according to the just without qualification' (1279^a17-19). Aristotle also connects the concepts of justice and the common advantage at 12 1282^b16-18: 'the just, i.e. the common advantage, is a political good' (cf. *EN* VIII 9 1160^a8-14, *Rhet.* I 6 1362^b27-8). But it is especially significant that in *Politics*, III 6, 'the common advantage' (*to koinēi sumpheron*) implies that a part or share of the good life falls to *each* (*hekastōi*) of the participants in the polis. Hence, justice should be understood as consisting in the mutual advantage. This entails a moral constraint upon legislation: the interests of some citizens should *not* be compromised in order to promote those of other citizens.[122] Therefore, his conception of justice implies a respect for the rights of each member of the political community, and each individual has a reason to support such a system.

To sum up, the foregoing reconstructed derivation of the respect for rights involves four main premises:

(1) Prudence directs human beings to form and act on habits which are necessary for their natural ends—namely, the good life and happiness.

(2) Human beings are political animals; i.e. they can realize their

---

[121] Cf. Plato, *Rep.* I 352^a5-8. See also Stewart (1892), ii. 68: the individual needs the polis not only for its resources but also to carry on the deliberation necessary to secure his own good. On the place of psychological stability in Aristotle's theory of nobility and virtue, see Rogers (1993).

[122] Chapter 6 below defends this 'individualistic' interpretation of Aristotle's correct constitution.

natural ends only by participating in a polis which is in a natural condition.

(3) A polis is in a natural condition only if it has a constitution through which it is organized in accordance with justice or the common advantage.

(4) A polis which is organized in accordance with justice or the common advantage protects the rights of each of the participants.

Therefore, individual human beings, in order to realize their natural ends, ought to form the virtues (especially justice) necessary to maintain a community that respects the rights of each and every citizen.[123]

As individuals, citizens ought to treat each other justly, and those in authority ought to govern the polis with a view to the advantage of the ruled and of themselves only incidentally (i.e. in so far as they are citizens). Thus mutual respect for rights is justified on the basis of practical wisdom and a correct understanding of the good life.

The rights of greatest importance for Aristotle are *political* rights, although he does recognize other rights including property rights and commercial rights (see Chapter 9 below). The emphasis on political rights is due to the centrality of the polis in Aristotle's ethical and political theory. As a consequence, his view of individual rights is very different from the modern views of Hobbes or Locke, who hold that individuals possess their most important natural rights independently of any political community. Aristotle's theory also differs from the modern libertarian view that the state should be confined to being a 'night-watchman' protecting individual liberties and property. However, his theory of justice does require that the happiness and virtue of each and every member of the polis be protected by the constitution, and in this sense entails a respect for individual rights (see also Chapter 6 below). After Aristotle the concept of individual rights was to evolve in fundamental ways. In the Middle Ages, at least as early as the twelfth century, canon lawyers were beginning to explicate the concept of a right (*ius*) in terms of power or liberty.[124] The link between liberty and rights and the distinctness of individuals from communities became more pronounced in late medieval thinkers such as Occam and Francisco Suárez (1548–1617), who in turn set the stage for early modern theorists such as Samuel Pufendorf (1632–

---

[123] For the argument that prudent individuals will voluntarily support a just constitution see also Sect. 7.4 below. The case for mutual deference and respect for the rights of others takes a different form in deviant constitutions, relying upon arguments of expedience; see Sect. 8.4 below.   [124] See Tierny (1988, 1989, 1991, 1992).

94).[125] This led in turn to the revolutionary theories of rights promulgated by Locke and many others. But, as the following chapters argue, Aristotle's own constitutional theory was already influenced by his own early concept of individual rights.

[125] Pufendorf, *De jure naturae et gentium*, appeals to Aristotle's concepts of practical wisdom (I 2 4) and natural law (II 3 7). Pufendorf's reliance on Aristotle is discussed by Buckle (1991), ch. 2. See also Sect. 2.6 above.

PART II

Constitutional Applications

5

Constitutions and Political Rights

5.1. THE CITIZEN AND THE CONSTITUTION

Aristotle's constitutional theory applies his theory of justice and rights to the unifying institutions of the polis. 'All constitutions', he says, 'are a form of justice; for [a constitution] is a community, and everything common is established by the just' (*EE* VII 9 1241^{b}13–15). *Politics*, III 1 1274^{b}32–41, begins the investigation of the constitution by characterizing its genus as a certain order (*taxis*) of the inhabitants of the polis.[1] Because the polis is a whole established out of many parts,[2] we must first investigate the parts of the polis, and hence the citizens, since the polis is a multitude of citizens.[3]

The sense in which the citizens are parts of the polis will be clearer if we consider how Aristotle speaks of a part (*meros*) or portion (*morion*)[4] in a political context. The general meaning of *meros* is given in the *Metaphysics*: 'The part is that into which a quantity can be divided in any way, for that which is taken from a quantity in so far as it is a quantity is always called a part of it, for example, two is called in a way a part of three' (V 25 1023^{b}12–15). This broad sense admits of further distinctions. In the first place, it is necessary to distinguish between parts (such as subcommunities or cross-sections of the polis) which are further divisible into parts, and those which are the 'smallest parts' (*elachista merē*), i.e. parts which cannot

---

[1] The constitution is called a *taxis* of the polis itself at III 6 1278^{b}8–10 and IV 1 1289^{a}15–18. See also IV 3 1290^{a}7–11; and cf. III 3 1276^{b}7–8 where the constitution is 'the form of the compound' (*eidos . . . tēs suntheseōs*).

[2] On the polis as a *holon* see also I 2 1253^{a}20 and VII 8 1328^{a}21–5.

[3] The polis is also described as a *plēthos*, 'multitude' or 'plurality', at 1275^{b}20 and at II 2 1261^{a}18. However, it is made clear in other passages that the polis is not a chance multitude (VII 4 1326^{a}18, 7 1328^{a}16), but a multitude which forms a community (*tēn koinōnian . . . tou plēthous*) (II 2 1261^{b}13; see also VII 4 1326^{b}8–9). Thus, the genus of the polis is a multitude of individuals who form a community (cf. I 1 1252^{a}1–6; III 3 1276^{b}1, 6 1279^{a}21; VII 8 1328^{a}35–6).

[4] *Meros* and *morion* are often closely linked. See e.g. VII 4 1326^{a}20–1.

themselves be subdivided into parts of the polis.[5] For example, in *Politics*,
I 3, he says that the polis is composed of households (1253^b2-3; see also
IV 3 1289^b28-9, and cf. III 9 1280^b33-4), which themselves have as their
smallest parts: master, slave, husband, wife, father, and children (1253^b5-
7). The implication is that these are also the smallest—i.e. indivisible—
parts of the polis. Again, in *Politics*, I 13, he infers from the observation
that the household is a part of the polis, that men, women, and children
are all part of the polis (1260^b13-18; cf. III 4 1277^a5-10). In these cases
the divisible part is the household, a subcommunity of the polis. In other
contexts the divisible parts are subsets or cross-sections of the multitude
of individuals who belong to the polis. For example, in *Politics*, IV 3–4,
he says that the polis is composed of many parts, each dedicated to a
certain function or profession. He also divides the inhabitants on the basis
of economic level: rich, poor, and middle.

The individual inhabitants of the polis are also distinguished into
two kinds: citizens and those who perform some necessary function for
the polis but do not qualify as citizens, e.g. slaves and metics. However,
Aristotle regards only the citizens as genuine parts or members of the
polis.[6] Those who perform necessary functions but are not citizens should
be regarded instead as adjuncts or accessories (*Pol.* VII 8–9).[7]

The burden of *Politics*, III 1, is to define the citizens as holders of
distinctive political rights.[8] After ruling out merely nominal or honorary
citizens (who are often not even residents), Aristotle considers and rejects
several candidates for the definition of citizens:

Df. 1. those who have a dwelling-place in common (1275^a7-8),

but this is true of metics (resident aliens) and slaves as well. Again,

---

[5] A different use of 'smallest portion' (*tōn moriōn tōn elachistōn*) is found at IV 14 1298^a16
which refers to a political division such as a deme (*dēmos*). The citizen population of Athens
was partitioned into 139 demes, which were combined into 10 tribes (*phulai*). In Athens
eligibility for office generally depended on deme and tribe membership as well as on
property assessments. The deme is the 'smallest part' of the polis in the sense that it
contains no smaller political parts.

[6] III 1 1274^b38-41 implies that the portions (*moria*) of the polis are citizens. Cf. 1275^b20
where 'the polis is the multitude of such persons [*toioutōn*]' is to be understood as 'the polis
is the multitude of citizens as defined in lines 18–20'.

[7] The distinction between genuine parts and mere necessary adjuncts is made at VII 8
1328^a33-5; cf. VII 4 1326^a16-21; IV 4 1291^a24-8; and III 5 1278^a3.

[8] Schütrumpf (1990), ii. 388, remarks that Aristotle departs fundamentally from the
ideal constitution of Plato's *Republic* where citizens, apart from guardians, possess no political rights (III 416^d1, V 463^a4).

Df. 2. those who partake in just-claim rights (*ta dikaia*) to the extent of undergoing suits and bringing suit (1275ᵃ8–10),

but this applies also to those who have contracts with the polis or its members, as well as metics in some cases.[9] But metics are not the unqualified citizens Aristotle is seeking to define. In Athens the process of registration (*dokimasia*) involved confirmation by the candidate's deme that he was of free birth, 18 years old, and after 451 BC, that both his parents were citizens (*Ath. Pol.* XLII 1–2).[10] Aristotle also mentions those who have been removed from the rolls due to extreme age. The young and very old are citizens in a qualified sense: immature or superannuated.

A tentative definition of unqualified citizens follows:

Df. 3. those who partake of judgement and office (1275ᵃ22–3).

'Judgement' (*krisis*) is associated with the administration of justice (*dikē*) (see I 2 1253ᵃ38) and is especially connected with the role of a judge or jurist (*dikastēs*) (see III 16 1287ᵇ16; cf. *Laws* VI 767ᵃ5–9). Aristotle calls attention to the vagueness of the term 'office' (*archē*) (cf. *Laws* VI 768ᶜ3–5). Some offices may be occupied only for limited terms, and a person may not have the right (*ouk exestin*) to hold the same office twice, or twice in immediate succession. Other offices are indefinite, in the sense of having unlimited terms as in the case of a jurist or a member of the assembly (*ekklēsiastēs*) in a democracy. Presumably because the latter sorts of offices appear less exalted, some might deny that the latter sort of office-holder really partakes of office or rule (the word *archē* has both senses); but Aristotle retorts that it would be ridiculous to suggest that those people who have the greatest authority (*kuriōtatoi*) do not have offices. He therefore introduces the expression 'indefinite office' (*aoristos archē*) to cover cases such as belonging to a jury or assembly and revises the definition of citizens accordingly:

Df. 4. those who partake of indefinite office (1275ᵃ32–3).

[9] A metic (*metoikos*) is defined as 'any one who comes from a foreign place to live in the polis, paying taxes towards certain fixed needs of the polis. For a number of days he is called a visitor and is free from taxes, but if he exceeds the time laid down he then becomes a metic and is liable to taxation', by Aristophanes of Byzantium, fr. 38 (2nd cent. BC) (trans. in Rhodes (1986), 101. On the status of metics generally see Harrison (1971), i. 187–99, MacDowell (1978), 76–8, and Hansen (1991), 116–20.

[10] A candidate who was denied could sue his deme in a jury court. If it was found that he had a right (*dikaiōs*) to be registered, the deme was compelled (*epanagkes*) to do so. But if he lost, he could be sold by the polis into slavery (*Ath. Pol.* XLII 1).

Now there arises the further difficulty that indefinite offices do not exist in all constitutions. There are different kinds of constitutions—primary and posterior, correct and mistaken[11]—and these will not contain the same institutions. Df. 4 applies above all to the citizens in a democracy like Athens, which has an assembly and juries selected by lot. However, oligarchies like Sparta and Carthage do not contain such institutions, but instead assign the tasks of deliberation and trials of murder and other crimes to offices with definite terms. Hence, in these constitutions the citizens are:

> Df. 5. those who are definite (in regard to time) in respect of their office ($1275^{b}13$–15).[12]

Aristotle concludes his discussion with a general definition of citizens, which is evidently intended to cover both Df. 4 and Df. 5:

> Df. 6. those who have the right to have in common (*exousia koinōnein*) deliberative or[13] judicial office ($1275^{b}18$–19).

Referring to this right with the term *exousia* entails that one has the liberty to hold office; i.e. one is not legally excluded from doing so. What else is entailed by this right? Clearly it would include a claim against interference by others in the exercise of such a right. But the further implications vary in different constitutions. In some places (typically more extreme democracies) the citizens have a claim to compensation for serving in office; in some places some citizens (e.g. wealthy citizens in some oligarchies) are fined for not serving, but generally citizens are not required to do so (see *Politics*, IV 9). As noted earlier those who hold indefinite offices in a democracy are described as the most authoritative (*kuriōtatoi*) persons in the polis (see $1275^{a}28$), presumably because these offices involve the authority to select or oversee others. In conclusion, the rights associated with citizenship vary considerably from one constitution to another, but the definition in Df. 6 is intended to be as

---

[11] This distinction is discussed in the following section. See also Fortenbaugh (1991).

[12] See Newman (1887), iii. 140. Johnson (1990), 119–20, contends that Df. 5 is intended as a comprehensive definition covering all the constitutions, because 'what counts for citizenship is the sphere of authority occupied by office-holders'. This interpretation is open to two objections: first, Aristotle explicitly applies this definition to the other constitutions (i.e. other than democracy; see Newman (1887), iii. 139); and second, it requires that *archē* abruptly shift in meaning from 'office' to 'authority' without explanation.

[13] I read *ē* with the manuscripts, rather than *kai* ('and'), which is substituted by some editors including Ross (1957) and Schütrumpf (1991). The manuscript reading is more inclusive: a citizen might have only the right to serve on juries.

comprehensive and illuminating as possible, revealing the core rights that define citizenship.[14]

Among the inhabitants who do not satisfy the definition of 'citizen' Aristotle distinguishes several types: slaves, who are treated as property and have virtually no rights;[15] metics or resident aliens, who were citizens of other polises and possessed limited rights within the host polis (e.g. rights to movable property and limited civil rights); and other foreigners who are merely temporary visitors. Citizens are also divided into different types: boys who are not yet old enough to be enrolled as citizens (potential citizens); old men who have been removed from the rolls due to senility (superannuated citizens); and men in their prime who possess the full rights of citizenship (genuine citizens). One group which Aristotle overlooks in *Politics*, III 1, is the female citizen (*politis*), who is elsewhere treated as an inferior citizen. Greek women were nominally citizens and descent from them was often necessary and sometimes sufficient for citizenship (III 2 1275^{b}22–3, 5 1278^{a}28; cf. *Ath. Pol.* XXVI 3). Although Aristotle thinks that the constitution should be concerned with their virtue and education because they are half of the free persons (I 13 1260^{b}13–20; *Rhet.* I 5 1361^{a}8–12), he takes for granted throughout the *Politics* that women have no political rights.[16] In conclusion, the only genuine citizens are males in their prime possessing political rights.

There is another group which has an ambiguous status: free, native-born individuals who fail to qualify for citizenship but do possess certain limited civil rights and legal protections. These would often include the descendants of metics, foreigners, or freed slaves, along with manual labourers and dispossessed persons who could not meet the minimal qualifications for citizenship. Among the constitutions which Aristotle surveys, only the most extreme form of democracy grants citizenship to all the free inhabitants. In the main Aristotle conforms to the strict

[14] Cf. Newman (1887), i. 229, and most commentators. However, Irwin (1990), 82, argues that Df. 3 is in fact Aristotle's preferred definition which 'admits of correction' only in the sense that it can be qualified so as to cover less complete citizens. However, this seems implausible in view of the fact that Aristotle concludes the chapter with the statement that the polis is composed of citizens as defined by Df. 6, and adds that he is speaking without qualification (1275^{b}20–1). In addition, Df. 6 is repeated at 5 1277^{b}34–5. Cf. also Plato, *Laws*, VI 768^{b}1–3.

[15] On slaves generally, including the legal status of alleged slaves, see Harrison (1971), i. 163–80, and MacDowell (1978), 79–83. Also, in Sparta and other polises there were helots and others in conditions of servitude or repression. Aristotle's own views on slavery are discussed in Sect. 6.9 below.

[16] On the actual legal rights of female citizens in Athens, see Harrison (1971), i. 1–60, 108–15, and 132–8, and MacDowell (1978), 84–108.

definition of 'citizen' of *Politics* III 1, but occasionally he uses the term in a wider sense covering all free natives. For example, he speaks of a king (who possesses all of the political rights) as defended by citizens (rather than by foreigners as in the case of a tyrant) (III 14 1285^{a}25–7; V 10 1311^{a}7–8). Also, he speaks of citizens who partake of the constitution (VII 13 1332^{a}32–4), which may imply that other citizens do not share in the constitution. On this basis some commentators[17] attribute to him a broader notion of a citizen. Aristotle's polis thus contains the following groups:[18]

A Citizens
   1. Enrolled citizens with political rights
   2. Children who will become enrolled citizens
   3. Superannuated citizens removed from the rolls
   4. Female citizens
B Non-citizens (necessary adjuncts)
   5. Free native inhabitants without political rights ('second-class citizens')
   6. Metics (resident aliens)
   7. Foreigners
   8. Slaves, helots, etc.

The absolute size of the citizen body as well as the ratio of citizens to the total population varied widely from polis to polis and fluctuated dramatically within the same polis over time. Sparta and many other polises suffered from a chronic shortage of citizens (*oliganthrōpia*). In Athens, the adult-male citizen population peaked at about 60,000 in the mid-fifth century BC, partly as a result of Cleisthenes' reform of 507 BC granting citizenship to many metics and foreigners (*Pol.* III 2 1275^{b}35–7; *Ath. Pol.* XXI 4). After the citizenship law of Pericles (451 BC), requiring that both parents be citizens, the citizens declined to about 40,000, which amounted to about a fifth of the adult population and about one-tenth of the total population. The disasters befalling Athens in the late fifth century—war, plague, and famine—took a great toll, from which the city never fully recovered. Throughout most of the fourth century the citizen population was about 30,000. A census of Athens shortly after Aristotle's death showed only 21,000 citizens and 10,000 metics prepared for military service.[19]

---

[17] Newman (1887), i. 229, 324, 569–79, Cooper (1990), 228 n. 11, and Keyt (1993), 21–4.   [18] Cf. Keyt (1993), 24. Keyt calls group 5 'second-class citizens'.
[19] The demographic evidence is sketchy for Athens and nearly non-existent for most other polises. See Gomme (1993), Hansen (1991), 52–4, 86–94, and Stockton (1991), 15–17.

Historically the term *politeia* (constitution) derived from *politēs* (citizen) and originally had the meaning of 'citizenship',[20] a connotation which it also has in Aristotle (VII 9 1329ᵃ14). In his definition of constitution, the genus is a certain order (*taxis*) of the citizens; IV 1 1289ᵃ15–18 states three differentiae of the constitution:

   i. concerned with offices, (determining) in what manner they are distributed (cf. III 6 1278ᵇ8–10, IV 3 1290ᵃ7–11);
  ii. (determining) what is the authority (*to kurion*) of the constitution (at III 6 1278ᵇ8–10 it is the order of the different offices and of the office which has authority over all (things)); and
 iii. (determining) what is the end of the community.

This definition has several important implications. First, since the constitution determines how offices are distributed within the polis (differentia i) and since citizenship is defined by the right of office (Df. 6), the constitution determines who are the citizens and how citizenship is exercised. Each constitution has specific laws for this purpose. For example, oligarchies typically make office-holding and citizenship conditional on meeting large property assessments; whereas in democracies vulgar craftsmen and common labourers will qualify, and in more extreme cases the offspring of a female citizen, even if the father is a slave or foreigner (III 5 1278ᵃ21–34).

The second implication concerns the concept of political authority. Since each office is vested with specific authority rights, the distribution of offices (differentia i) determines how authority is assigned within the polis (differentia ii). In particular, the constitution is said to assign the office which is authoritative over everything. By this Aristotle means deliberative office (IV 14 1299ᵃ1; VI 1 1316ᵇ31–2; see Section 5.3 below). The expression *to kurion* is often translated as 'sovereign' when it refers to the element which has the supreme authority (*to kuriōtaton*), i.e. the element which is superior to all others in a political system.[21] However, it should be emphasized that Aristotle uses *kurios* more generally for the authority exercised by individuals in specific contexts. In this sense, authority is dispersed throughout the citizen body in various and sundry offices, each of which is vested with quite specific rights and all of which are exercised according to the laws of the polis. An important instance is

[20] See Herodotus, IX 34 1; cf. Meier (1990), 170–3, on the term *politeia* and its connection with citizenship and political rights.

[21] Cf. White (1992: 6 n. 7, 103 n. 22, 122 n. 19) who translates *kurios* generally as 'sovereign'.

the authority to pass laws defining the basic legal structure of the polis, or decrees prescribing particular actions for citizens and officials. In Athens this authority was divided as follows. Any citizen had the right to propose a new law. The measure had first to be considered by the Council (*boulē*), composed of 500 members, a process called 'advance deliberation' (*probouleusis*). Then the measure was published by the president (*prutanis*) and forwarded to the Assembly (*ekklēsia*) in which every citizen had the right to participate (hence it was also called *dēmos* or 'the people'). The Assembly met in an auditorium on a hill called the Pnyx, which could accommodate 6,000 assemblymen. After discussion, during which the measure could be amended, it was either approved or defeated by a majority vote of those present.[22] After 403/2 BC a new check was placed on the authority of the assembly, requiring that the law also be approved by a small body of officials called lawgivers (*nomothetai*).[23] Aristotle would regard this latter sort of constraint as typical of a polity (see IV 14 1298^{b}38–1299^{a}1). Sparta had a more stringent requirement of advance deliberation: a measure had to be approved by the Senate (*gerousia*) before it could even be considered by the assembly (which was itself composed of a relatively small body of citizens).[24] Aristotle regards this as a feature suitable for oligarchies (IV 14 1298^{b}32–8). This provides some indication of how authority is dispersed throughout the citizenry by the constitution.[25]

The foregoing explains the connection between the constitution and the government or governing body (*politeuma*), which Aristotle identifies with the authority (*to kurion*). In this same passage he says that *politeia* (constitution) signifies the same thing as *politeuma* (government) (III 7 1279^{a}25–7, cf. 6 1278^{b}11). The government comprises all of the offices of the polis and thus the collective authority of the polis, so that it may be viewed as the embodiment of the constitution.

Further, differentia iii of the constitution indicates that it functions as a final cause, determining the end of the polis. The assignment of political rights and authority to the citizens is premised upon a particular conception of the good, expressed in the hypothesis of the constitution (a notion which is discussed more fully in the following section). In so far as this end is realized in the citizens, the constitution, understood as a

---

[22] *Ath. Pol.* XLIII 3–6. See Hansen (1991), ch. 6.

[23] See MacDowell (1978), 44–9, and Hansen (1991), ch. 7.

[24] See Rhodes (1986), 76. The Senate also evidently had a veto power over decisions of the assembly; see Forrest (1968), 47–50, who makes use of Plutarch's *Lives*, Lycurgus.

[25] Sects. 5.3–5 below provide a more detailed account of how political authority is divided among the citizens in the various constitutions.

system of political rights, becomes the way of life (*bios*) of the polis (IV 11 1295ᵃ40–ᵇ1, VII 8 1328ᵇ1–2).

The constitution is thus viewed from several related perspectives by Aristotle. Considered as a final cause it defines the end of the polis. Considered as a system of political rights it is the form of the polis. From this point of view the constitution may serve as its principle of identity (III 3 1276ᵇ1–11). When a polis undergoes a change of constitution, as in a revolution, it may be regarded as a different polis, even though it has the same population. Finally, considered as a government, the constitution may be viewed as the embodiment of a system of rights in the citizenry.

In playing these different roles, the constitution, as described in *Politics*, III 3, displays important similarities with substance (*ousia*) in Aristotle's metaphysics. The term 'substance' is used in two closely interconnected senses: first, it designates entities which are primary beings, especially animals, plants, and simple material bodies; but second, it refers to that which makes something a substance in the first sense, i.e. its form or essence.[26] In the case of a living thing, its substance in the second sense is its soul. It performs the roles of formal, efficient, and final cause for the living organism, as it directs its performance of its distinctive functions.

The constitution plays a comparable role for the polis, organizing it, guiding it to its end, and defining its essential identity. The concept of authority helps to illuminate this parallel. In Aristotle's metaphysics the source of the unity (*to henopoioun*) of a thing is by nature its authoritative (*kata phusin kurion*) and ruling principle (*archon*), and this is the formal cause rather than the material cause (*DA* I 5 410ᵇ10–15; cf. *Pol.* I 5 1254ᵃ34–6). The constitution performs a similar function in Aristotle's politics. By assigning political rights the constitution defines the government (*politeuma*) which is the authority (*to kurion*) for the polis. The constitution thereby serves as the unifying principle of the polis, transforming it from a mere multitude or collection of unintegrated communities, into an orderly, goal-directed community.

Finally, the definition of the constitution explains the unity of Book III of the *Politics*, which otherwise appears to be broken into two separate discussions: Chapters 1–5 concerned with citizenship and Chapters 6–18 with constitutions. The first part poses a series of questions regarding

---

[26] The word 'substance' (*ousia*) is used in both senses in the *Metaphysics*: e.g. 'This [the formal cause] is the substance of each thing, for this is the primary cause of its being; and since, while some things are not substances, as many as are substances are formed naturally and by nature, their substance would seem to be this nature, which is not an element but a principle' (VII 17 1041ᵇ27–31; trans. in Barnes (1984)).

citizenship: Who is the citizen? (III 1 1275ª1); more importantly, Who should be called a citizen, or who is justly a citizen? (1275ª1, 2 1275ᵇ37–8). The latter issue is connected with two others: When may an act be ascribed to the polis as a whole? (III 3 1276ª6–16); and Is the virtue of the good human being identical with the virtue of the excellent citizen? (III 4 1276ᵇ16–18).

The definition of the constitution explains why the discussion of the rights of citizenship leads directly to the discussion of different types of constitutions (III 6 1278ᵇ6–8). For the constitution determines how offices are to be distributed among the inhabitants and who possesses what authority on the basis of a hypothesis concerning the end of the polis. A correct constitution is one which assigns the rights of citizenship and hence the rights of political rule to those who are able and willing to exercise these rights in the proper manner:

It is evident therefore that such constitutions as aim at the common advantage are correct according to justice without qualification, whereas such constitutions as aim only at the advantage of the rulers are all mistaken and deviations from the correct constitutions; for they are despotic, but the polis is a community of free persons. (6 1279ª17–21)

The concept of the constitution provides a bridge between the final-cause account of the polis (as a community of human beings co-operating for the common advantage) and the formal-cause account (as a community ordered by means of a system of rights), and the main theoretical support for this bridge is the theory of justice. The dispute concerning constitutions in *Politics*, III, ultimately turns on the question of what the theory of the good life implies concerning the rights of the citizens of the polis. This is ultimately a dispute over what standard of merit should serve as a basis for the theory of political rights, and on Aristotle's view this standard is aristocratic supporting a virtue-based theory of rights (see Section 4.6 above).

The problems concerning citizenship in *Politics*, III 1–6, are solved by reference to the constitutions. The constitution, by distributing political rights, determines who is a citizen and full member of the polis and who is not. By defining the government or authority of the polis the constitution answers the question of which actions belong to the polis: viz., those actions which are performed by citizens in their official capacity. The constitution also determines the identity of the polis by defining its government or sovereign, for, as he also notes in the *Nicomachean Ethics*, 'the polis and every other composite thing [*sustēma*] seems to be most of all

TABLE 5.1. *Sixfold Classification of Constitutions*

Number	Quality	
	Correct	Deviant
One	Kingship	Tyranny
Few	Aristocracy	Oligarchy
Many	Polity	Democracy

[identical with] the thing that has the greatest authority [*to kuriōtaton*]'
(IX 8 1168^{b}31–2). The theory of the correct constitution also provides
the answer to the question of who has a right to be a citizen. Aristotle
acknowledges claims based upon freedom, good birth, and wealth as just
in a way, viz., in so far as they presuppose a particular theory of justice;
but he regards claims based upon education and virtue as most of all just
(III 9 1281^{a}4–8, 12 1283^{a}3–13, 1283^{a}42). In addition, this gives an answer
to the question whether the good man and the good citizen—or the virtue
of a human being and the virtue of a citizen—are the same. For in the
best constitution those with ethical virtue and practical wisdom *are* the
citizens, since it uses ethical virtue as its ultimate standard of merit (see
III 18 1288^{a}37–9).

5.2. THE DIVERSITY OF CONSTITUTIONS

Aristotle's theory of constitutions is supposed to determine how many
constitutions there are (III 6 1278^{b}7–8; IV 1 1289^{a}7–8, 2 1289^{b}12–13). His
most familiar classification distinguishes six different constitutions (*Politics*,
III 7).[27] This classification has two dimensions: first, how widely political
rights are distributed among the inhabitants, viz., to one, few, or many;
second, whether the constitution is correct (unqualifiedly just) or deviant,
i.e. whether or not it aims at the common advantage. This classification
is depicted in Table 5.1. Aristotle describes each deviant constitution as

---

[27] The sixfold classification is also used in *EN* VIII 10 1160^{a}31–^{b}22. It first occurs in
Plato's *Statesman*, 302^{c}8–^{e}8, although in Plato all six are inferior to a seventh, best form in
which the ruler is the real politician or statesman possessing genuine knowledge (see 294^{a}6–
8, 300^{c}9–10). Further, Plato distinguishes the better three constitutions from the worse
three on the basis of whether they are lawful or unlawful. In contrast, only the most extreme
of Aristotle's deviant constitutions are unlawful. Plato's *Laws*, IV 715^{b}2–6, distinguishes
correct constitutions which are for the common interest of the whole polis (*sumpasēs tēs
poleōs heneka tou koinou*) from those which serve the interests of only some persons.

a deviation from the correct constitution of the same number: tyranny is a deviation from kingship, oligarchy from aristocracy, and democracy from polity.

Even in his initial discussion, Aristotle implies that a distinction based on the mere number in authority does not capture what is essential to the constitutions being classified. He initially describes polity as rule by the multitude (*plēthos*), but adds that the military or hoplites (those possessing heavy arms) have the most authority in this constitution (1279^{b}2–4; IV 13 1297^{b}1–2). A corresponding discussion in *Nicomachean Ethics* calls polity a 'timocracy', from the moderate property-assessment (*timēma*) that each citizen was required to have (VIII 10 1160^{a}33–5, ^{b}18–19).

Aristotle frequently mentions the use of the property assessment to assign different political rights to different groups within the polis. This device is illustrated by the constitution of Solon (probably instituted during his eponymous archonship, *c.*594/3 BC):

[Solon] divided [the citizens] by assessment into four ranks, as they had been divided before: the 500-measure men, the horsemen, the teamsters, and the workers. And he distributed the various offices (namely, the nine archons, the treasurers, the commissioners of public contracts, the Eleven, and the bursars) to the 500-measure men, the knights, and the teamsters, assigning offices to each class in proportion to the amount of their assessment; but to those who ranked in the workers he only gave a place in the Assembly and juries. A man was ranked as a 500-measure man if he produced from his household 500 measures whether dry or wet [that is, measures of grain, or of wine and oil]. Those were ranked as knights who produced 300 measures or, some say, those who could keep a horse [and serve in the cavalry] . . . Those were ranked as teamsters [those who had a plough and team of oxen] who produced 200 measures, wet or dry; and the rest were ranked as workers and did not partake of any office. (*Ath. Pol.* VII 3–4; cf. Plutarch, *Lives*, Solon, 18 1–2)

The assessment is based upon a measure (*medimnos*, about 1.5 bushel) of grain produced by a piece of property. A 500-measure estate of perhaps 70 acres could support up to twenty families. The amount of the assessment was probably given by the property-owners themselves, subject to some sort of review by other citizens. The rationale for the use of assessment was that a citizen required a certain level of agricultural income in order to hold an office effectively and to serve in a designated military post. For example, teamsters could afford the heavy arms required for service as hoplite soldiers. The citizens were also taxed on the basis of their annual production. During the tyranny of Peisistratus (*c.*561–527 BC) the tax was

apparently one-tenth of a citizen's production (*Ath. Pol.* XVI 4).[28] In 428
BC a tax on property or wealth itself (the *eisphora*) was also introduced
(Thucydides, III 19 1).[29] The top two classes were regarded as the rich,
the teamster or hoplite class as moderately wealthy, and the worker class
as the poor or the many (*hoi polloi*). With the rise of democracy in the
fifth and fourth centuries BC, Solon's property classes became increasingly irrelevant to the assignment of political rights and duties to the
citizens.[30]

Politics, III 8, distinguishes oligarchy from democracy on the basis of
property ownership: in oligarchy those who possess property (*ousia*) have
authority over the constitution, and in democracy the multitude which
does not have property but is poor has authority ($1279^{b}17-19$). Here
oligarchy and democracy essentially differ in terms of the comparative
wealth of the governing body, and the difference in number is accidental
($1279^{b}39-1280^{a}5$; cf. IV 4 $1290^{b}17-20$). This is, however, not Aristotle's
only view on this subject (see Chapter 8 below).

Politics, IV 2, recalls the sixfold scheme from 'the first inquiry' ($1289^{a}26-$
38) and then ($1289^{a}38-^{b}11$) offers, in effect, an ordinal ranking of the six
constitutions from best to worse.[31] The idea that the constitutions can be

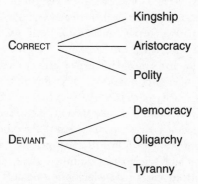

Fɪɢ. 5.1. Hierarchy of Constitutions

[28] This is a controversial passage; see Rhodes (1984), 215.

[29] After Solon's time agricultural production was given a cash equivalent, and over time
these property requirements were in effect lowered due to inflation. However, the Athenians
did not have an income tax in the modern sense, including wages, intangible income, etc.
See Stockton (1991), 6–14, and Hansen (1991), 43–6, for further details.

[30] See Hansen (1991), 106–9. Plato's *Laws*, V $744^{a}8-^{d}1$, contains a similar four-class
division of citizens which is probably also modelled after Solon: cf. Morrow (1960), 131–8.

[31] The ranking again follows for the most part that of Plato in *Statesman*, $302^{e}10-303^{b}5$,
evidently alluded to at $1289^{b}5-11$. Cf. also *Laws*, IV $710^{e}3-711^{a}3$. Newman (1887), iv. 147,
objects that Aristotle's interpretation of Plato is not altogether accurate.

ranked is based on the normative principle of proximity, that it is best to attain perfection, but, failing that, a thing is better in proportion as it is nearer to the end (cf. IV 11 1296^{b}7–9, *DC* II 12 292^{b}17–19). The corresponding discussion in the *Nicomachean Ethics* reveals the two main ideas underlying this ranking: that among the correct constitutions, those in which political authority is relatively more concentrated are relatively better (VIII 10 1160^{a}32–6); and that if C_1 is a better correct constitution than C_2, then the deviation from C_1 is worse than the deviation from C_2 (1160^{b}9; cf. *Pol.* IV 2 1289^{a}39–41). The basis for the first idea seems to be that complete political virtue tends to be found only in relatively few persons: '. . . it is possible for one or a few to excel in virtue, but it is difficult for more persons to become exacting with regard to all of virtue' (*Pol.* III 7 1279^{a}39–^{b}1). Accordingly, the best constitutions are kingship and aristocracy, and of these kingship is the most divine, owing to the great superiority of the individual ruler.[32] Polity, on the other hand, bases the distribution of political rights upon an inferior or incomplete form of virtue called 'military virtue' (*polemikē aretē*) which is exemplified by the multitude of hoplite soldiers in a polis such as Sparta (*Pol.* III 7 1279^{b}1–4; cf. II 9 1271^{b}3). The basis for the second idea is evidently that, conversely, political vice will be increasingly potent to the extent that political rights are concentrated. Aristotle here may be influenced by the series of vivid and persuasive portraits in *Republic*, VIII–IX, of the souls corresponding to the oligarchic, the democratic, and the tyrannical person. Plato's rationale for his similar ranking of constitutions is that rule by the multitude is inherently inferior because the multitude is unable to acquire political science (*Statesman*, 292^{c}1–2, 297^{b}7–^{c}4; *Rep.* VI 494^{a}4–6). Moreover, rule by the multitude is weak and able to accomplish nothing great, whether good or bad, when compared to the other forms, because offices are distributed in small lots to many persons (*Statesman*, 303^{a}4–7). The rankings among the good constitutions, and among the bad, are thus due to the effectiveness with which office-holders are able to wield authority.

Aristotle also employs the method of hypothesis to distinguish and evaluate constitutions. This method enables him to consider any given constitution both from the standpoint of the hypothesis appropriate to the best constitution and from that of the hypothesis of its own citizens (cf. II 6 1269^{a}31–4). Thus, the method provides both external and internal

---

[32] For further discussion of the arguments for and against kingship in *Pol.* III 13–18 see Sect. 6.8 below.

criteria of analysis and evaluation. The term *hupothesis*[33] suggests a principle which supports a constitution, much as a premiss supports the conclusion of an argument (see *Met.* V 1 1013^{a}16, 2 1013^{b}20).[34] The hypothesis is related to the third defining function of the constitution, that of determining the end of the political community. Hence, a hypothesis has the form, 'The end of the polis should be *E*'.[35] Thus, the discussion of constitutions begins with the remark that one must first make a hypothesis (*hupotheteon*) about the end of the polis (III 6 1278^{b}15–17).

Each constitution in the classificatory scheme of *Politics*, III 7, has a hypothesis, including aristocracy and polity (II 11 1273^{a}4–5). The end of the constitution is happiness, defined as 'the perfect [or complete] activity and employment of virtue' (VII 13 1332^{a}7–10). (Presumably kingship has the same hypothesis; cf. III 18 1288^{a}39–^{b}2.) The end of the second-best constitution is a 'happy life unimpeded according to virtue', but the level of happiness is of a more modest sort attainable by ordinary persons in ordinary circumstances (IV 11 1295^{a}25–40). The virtue referred to here presumably includes the military virtue associated with polity (III 7 1279^{b}1–3; cf. II 9 1271^{a}41–^{b}2). The incorrect constitutions also have hypotheses. For example, 'the hypothesis of the democratic constitution is freedom' (VI 2 1317^{a}40–1).[36] It is also implied that the hypothesis of oligarchy is that wealth is the end (III 9 1280^{a}25–8; *Rhet.* I 6 1366^{a}5). The hypothesis of tyranny is less definite: in one passage it is power (V 11 1314^{a}38–9), although elsewhere we are told that it has the same end as oligarchy, namely wealth (10 1311^{a}10); and the *Rhetoric* says that its end is the ruler's [self-]protection (I 8 1366^{a}6). It would seem, however, that it is the pursuit of power which distinguishes tyranny from other regimes. Also, Aristotle criticizes what he calls Socrates' 'incorrect hypothesis', viz., that it is best for the polis to be entirely one as far as possible (*Pol.*

---

[33] *Hupothesis* is also translated as 'presupposition', 'assumption', 'postulate', etc. Note that the term is used in this sense by Plato, e.g. at *Laws*, V 743^{c}5.

[34] In the *Posterior Analytics* a hypothesis is a proposition which asserts that something is or is not the case and which is used as a premiss of an argument (I 2 72^{a}18–20). Although a hypothesis is a premiss, it differs from a first principle of demonstration which is intrinsically necessary (*anagkē kath' hauto*), because a hypothesis is susceptible of proof. A hypothesis is accepted because it agrees with the beliefs of an individual, e.g. someone learning, so that it is necessary to speak of a hypothesis relative to that individual (10 76^{b}23–34). The fundamentality of a hypothesis is thus relative to a particular system of beliefs.

[35] The term 'hypothesis' is also used for other assumptions on which the constitution rests, e.g. regarding the material available for the formation of the polis (VII 4 1325^{b}35–6) or opinions which can be used to sustain the constitution (V 11 1314^{a}28). But these may be regarded as corollary theses, and the teleological hypothesis is the most fundamental.

[36] Cf. *Rhet.* I 6 1366^{a}4 and Pericles' funeral oration (Thucydides, II 37 1–3).

II 2 1261ᵃ15–16, 5 1263ᵇ29–31). With the exception of the best, these constitutions all have mistaken or only partially correct hypotheses concerning the end of the polis. It is noteworthy that each of the three deviant constitutions—democracy, oligarchy, and tyranny—has as its hypothetical end some type of external equipment which is necessary for the attainment of moral virtue—respectively, liberty, wealth, and power (cf. *EN* X 8 1178ᵃ23–34). Even polity, a correct but inferior constitution, has as its hypothetical end a part of virtue (II 9 1271ᵇ1–3; III 7 1279ᵃ39–ᵇ2). Socrates' hypothesis might be faulted for exaggerating one necessary ingredient of the good life: co-operation with others in the polis. It would seem, then, that each of the inferior constitutions has a partially correct but overall mistaken hypothesis about the human good. Either it mistakenly identifies an external good with the ultimate end, or it grasps the end only in part.

Although, as just remarked, the correct constitution has a correct hypothesis, Aristotle often contrasts the correct constitution with one based on (or relative to) a hypothesis. The point of this is to emphasize the questionable character of the hypothesis underlying the inferior constitution.[37] Thus, he says that a democracy or oligarchy which more nearly approximates polity will be comparatively better, 'unless one is judging relative to a hypothesis'. He adds the qualification 'because although one constitution is more choiceworthy, often nothing prevents another [constitution] from being advantageous for some persons' (IV 11 1296ᵇ7–12). If the hypothesis of a given polis is freedom (or wealth) it may be more advantageous, relative to that hypothesis, for the constitution to be an extreme democracy (or oligarchy). However, as we shall see, lawgivers make a serious mistake if they try to frame all institutions with a view to their imperfect hypothesis (VI 1 1317ᵃ35–7).

Closely related to the concept of a hypothesis is that of a standard (*horos*),[38] e.g. freedom is characterized as both the hypothesis and the standard of democracy (VI 2 1317ᵃ40–1, ᵇ11; see also V 11 1314ᵃ25, 28). The standard of a constitution governs the application of justice in the distribution of political rights among the members of the polis (see III 9

---

[37] Similarly, Aristotle contrasts virtue 'on the basis of a hypothesis' (*ex hupotheseōs*) or 'relative to a hypothesis' (*pros hupothesin*), with virtue without qualification (*haplōs*) (IV 7 1293ᵇ3–5; VII 9 1328ᵇ37–9, 13 1332ᵃ10). This indicates that virtue and justice may be defined relative to the hypothesis peculiar to a constitution. Accordingly, Aristotle also speaks of virtue and justice 'relative to the constitution', in the same sense as 'relative to the hypothesis' (V 9 1309ᵃ36–7).

[38] The term *horos* also has the sense, 'distinguishing principle' or 'mark', e.g. in connection with constitutions at II 9 1271ᵃ35 and IV 9 1294ᵃ35, ᵇ15.

1280ᵃ7–8). Hence, it determines the type and extent of equality among the inhabitants. Thus, 'aristocracy seems to be most of all the distribution of honours according to virtue; for virtue is the standard of aristocracy, whereas wealth is that of oligarchy, and freedom [i.e. free birth] that of the people [that is, democracy] . . .' (IV 8 1294ᵃ9–11). The standard governing the distribution of rights is based upon the teleological hypothesis concerning the end of the polis. Since the polis is a community organized for the sake of a particular end, justice requires that rights be distributed on the basis of one's contribution to this end (see Section 4.6 above).

Aristotle was plainly fascinated by the rich diversity of Greek constitutions, and he tries to explain this phenomenon repeatedly. These explanations seem to be of three distinct types. First, in *Politics*, VII, he traces the diversity of constitutions to the fact that not all human beings are so fortunate as to be capable of or inclined to the best way of life:

And the polis is a certain community of similar persons, for the sake of the best life possible. And since the best thing is happiness and this is a certain perfect [or complete] activity or employment of virtue, and since it happens that it is possible for some to partake of it, but for others only a little or not at all, it is clear that this is the cause of there being several kinds and varieties of polises and constitutions . . . (VII 8 1328ᵃ35–41; cf. IV 11 1295ᵃ25–ᵇ1)

This explanation seems closely connected with the classificatory scheme discussed so far in this section: which constitution tends to emerge in a given polis will depend upon the hypothesis concerning the end of political life and the standard governing the distribution of political rights which prevail in that polis.

The second and third explanations of constitutional diversity appear in *Politics*, IV 3–4. They are variants of the idea that the polis contains a diversity of parts or groups of inhabitants. The second explanation generally emphasizes that groups have different levels of wealth or income. In some cases three groups are mentioned: the wealthy, the poor, and the middle group (IV 3 1289ᵇ29–31, 11 1295ᵇ1–3); in other cases only two: the rich and the poor (IV 4 1291ᵇ7–8; V 11 1315ᵃ31–3; VI 3 1318ᵃ30–1).[39] It

---

[39] The rich and poor are also distinguished respectively as the notables (*gnōrimoi*) and the people (*dēmos*); see IV 3 1289ᵇ32, 33–4. However, 'notables', as Aristotle ordinarily uses it, can imply a number of attributes: wealth, good birth, virtue, education, and so forth (4 1291ᵇ28–30). Aristotle's identification of the *dēmos* with the many or the poor may be tendentious. Hansen (1991), 303, contends that the Athenians of Aristotle's day used *dēmos* to refer to the entire citizenry and not just the commoners. Aristotle also refers to the poor as 'the multitude' (*to plēthos*) (e.g. III 10 1281ᵃ24) although *plēthos* is also used for any group including the entire citizenry (1 1274ᵇ41).

should be emphasized that this is not exclusively an economic analysis, because he adds that in addition to differences based on wealth there are also differences based on good birth and virtue, since these groups also partake of the constitution in many cases (3 1289^{b}40–1290^{a}3). Nevertheless, economic factors are dominant even in the lines which immediately follow:

It is evident, therefore, that there are necessarily many constitutions different from one another in kind, for these parts also differ from one another in kind. For a constitution is an order (*taxis*) of offices, and everyone distributes this either according to the power of those who partake of it or according to some equality common to them—I mean, for example, the power of the poor or the well-off, or some equality common to both. (3 1290^{a}5–11)

The third explanation refers to parts or groups which perform functions necessary if the polis is to attain its ends. This appears in the middle of *Politics*, IV 4, as a supplemental account of constitutional diversity. Aristotle first offers a biological analogy (1290^{b}21–39): we could arrive at a classification of animals if we were to enumerate every kind of part which every animal must have—e.g. sense organs, mouth, stomach, limbs for locomotion—and to enumerate specific types of organs falling under each necessary kind, we could by taking all possible combinations of all of these types enumerate all possible animals. Aristotle then suggests that we could enumerate all the possible constitutions, because polises are also composed of parts with distinct capacities. These are farmers, vulgar artisans, merchants, menial labourers, soldiers, those capable of adjudication (*to dikastikon*), those who use their property to perform public (including religious) services, those who hold offices, and those who deliberate about public affairs (1290^{b}39–1291^{b}2). This list invites comparison with the list of functions associated with the ostensible parts of the polis in VII 8 1328^{b}5–15. Aristotle adds in the latter passage that these are the functions which the polis needs in order to be self-sufficient for life (1328^{b}15–23).

The fact that Aristotle does not attempt to reconcile these apparently incompatible explanations of constitutional diversity has provoked much scholarly discussion, although Newman seems correct in saying that they are ultimately reconcilable.[40] The third explanation distinguishes between groups within the polis on the basis of the function they perform. He recognizes that the functions may be performed by the same groups, that

---

[40] Newman's discussion (1887), i. 220–2, 565–9, remains among the best. However, Schütrumpf may be right that these accounts belong to different periods; see (1980), 127 ff.; (1991), i. 51–2.

the three groups of farmers, soldiers, and artisans might all coincide (IV 4 1291ᵇ2–4). But they are all necessary for the polis to attain its self-sufficiency, and the functions are often carried out by disparate groups. Moreover, these groups typically divide up into the incompatible groups of the poor and the rich, which explains why democracy and oligarchy seem to be most prevalent (1291ᵇ7–13). Thus the second explanation is connected with the third. Further, Aristotle indicates connections between the latter two explanations and the first. He states that those in the vulgar artisan or merchant groups are incapable of pursuing genuine happiness or possessing unqualified justice and virtue, and that farmers lack the leisure to do so (VII 9 1328ᵇ33–1329ᵃ2; cf. VI 4 1319ᵃ26–8). It is his view that those who occupy the wealthier groups are disposed to value wealth most highly (cf. III 9 1280ᵃ25–8), and those who ply the baser professions desire freedom most highly, where freedom is understood as the liberty to live as one wishes in a disorderly fashion (VI 2 1317ᵇ11–13, 4 1319ᵇ30–2).

Aristotle can thus explain the constitutional diversity described in his original scheme. In the best constitution the citizens have the innate capacity and the resources to act on the correct hypothesis concerning the end of human life, but in actual polises the citizens can at best attain a second-best form of happiness. Further, a deviant or mistaken constitution will result when a group such as the rich or the poor is in a dominant position pursuing a mistaken aim. However, this explanation has the important consequence that the diversity of constitutions is more far-reaching than is implied by the initial sixfold classification of *Politics*, III 7. Hence, a much more elaborate classificatory scheme is set forth in Books IV–VI. In the first place, it transpires that both democracy and oligarchy admit of subtypes on a spectrum from moderate to extreme, depending on which groups of inhabitants are admitted as citizens. Moreover, it becomes evident in the middle books that the character of the constitution determines the kind of constitution suitable for it, and that a 'good' constitution must agree with its character (rich, poor, agricultural, etc.) and must aim at the form of 'justice' appropriate for it.

In the case of democracy there are at least four main types.[41]

---

[41] See IV 4 1291ᵇ30–1292ᵃ38, 6 1292ᵇ22–1293ᵃ10, VI 4 1318ᵇ6–1319ᵇ32. There are five types enumerated in IV 4, but the first appears to be an 'ideal' type of democracy not discussed elsewhere. Newman may be right that the first two 'are perhaps treated as virtually one' (1887: iv, p. xxxvi). Alternatively, the ideal type in IV 4 closely resembles democratic polity, since neither the wealthy nor the poor have authority over the other. Democratic polity is described below.

(1) *Most moderate democracy* There is a moderate property requirement (*timēma*). Those who have it have the right (*exousia*) to hold office but those who lose their property also lack this right. These include mainly farmers and any others who possess the qualification defined by the laws (IV 4 1291^{b}39–41, 6 1292^{b}25–34).[42] Typically, the multitude of agrarian citizens generally elect others to offices on the basis of property requirements or ability, and mainly occupy themselves with auditing offices and serving on juries (VI 4 1318^{b}18–1319^{a}38).

(2) *Less moderate democracy* All those who are legitimate, i.e. descended from citizens, have the right to hold office, but only those who can afford to actually do so, because there are not revenues to support them (IV 4 1292^{a}1–2, 6 1292^{b}34–8). As a result, baser elements are admitted to the citizen body, e.g. herdsmen, artisans, merchants, and so forth (VI 4 1319^{a}39–^{b}1).

(3) *Least moderate democracy* All inhabitants of the polis have the right to participate, provided they are free born, but again not all do so for lack of funds (IV 4 1292^{a}2–4, 6 1292^{b}38–41). Types (1)–(3) are all instances of the rule of law, because the many are constrained by their limited resources from gaining complete authority over political institutions.

(4) *Extreme democracy* All the free-born members of the polis have the right to participate in government and they are able to exercise this right, no matter how poor they are, because they receive a fee for holding offices. The result is that they are unconstrained, ruling by arbitrary decree rather than by established law. This is a case of rule by humans rather than by law, and resembles tyranny (IV 4 1292^{a}4–38, 6 1292^{b}41–1293^{a}10; VI 4 1319^{b}1–11; cf. *Ath. Pol.* XXVII–XXVIII). The democratic theory of rights thus has in Aristotle's view two radically egalitarian corollaries. Because democratic justice requires that individuals have rights according to their freedom and all free-born members of the polis are equal, (i) all free persons should have equal rights to the greatest extent possible and (ii) all free persons should exercise their rights to an equal degree to the greatest extent possible. Extreme democracy most fully satisfies these corollaries. Fees are paid to citizens for holding office to ensure that they all have the leisure to exercise equally their equal rights.

---

[42] The second passage includes a difficult sentence at 1292^{b}30–3 which seems to have a lacuna. The most plausible construal is along the lines suggested by Newman: It is characteristic of oligarchy that not everyone has the right (*mē exeinai pasin*) to partake of office, but it is characteristic of democracy that they all have the right (cf. V 9 1309^{a}2–3). In the constitution under discussion they have the right, but they cannot have the leisure to exercise it unless there are public funds to pay them (*scholazein <d'> adunaton mē prosodōn ousōn*). A similar point is made at 1292^{b}35–7.

There are also four main types of oligarchy.[43]

(1) *Most moderate oligarchy* There is a property requirement, higher than in the first type of democracy, but low enough so that numerous citizens, a multitude, can meet it. Those who possess the required property have the right (*exeinai*) to participate in government,[44] but the poor do not (IV 5 1292^{a}39–41, 6 1293^{a}12–20). These constitutions typically have two sorts of assessment, a lower one for eligibility to necessary offices, a higher one for more authoritative offices (VI 6 1320^{b}21–9; on offices see Section 5.4 below).

(2) *Less moderate oligarchy* The property requirement is high, and those who have the required property are fewer. Those who have political rights also have the right to elect new members to replace vacancies (IV 5 1292^{a}41–^{b}4, 6 1293^{a}21–6; VI 6 1320^{b}29–30).

(3) *Least moderate oligarchy* The requirements for office-holders are tightened further, with even more stringent property qualifications and the additional law that only descendants from previous office-holders are eligible for office (IV 5 1292^{b}4–5, 6 1293^{a}26–30). Again, types (1)–(3) all involve the rule of law, because the office-holders are subject to constraints in exercising their political rights.

(4) *Extreme oligarchy* This form resembles (3), but the office-holders are so powerful that they can do as they please without legal impediment. This is the extreme form called 'dynasty', which resembles tyranny, the rule of men rather than of law (IV 5 1292^{b}5–10, 6 1293^{a}30–4; VI 6 1320^{b}30–1321^{a}1).

The foregoing descriptions of the four types of oligarchy reveal the radically inegalitarian implications of the oligarchic theory of rights. This is made explicit in one description of the second type of oligarchy, when Aristotle says that because the oligarchs are stronger due to their wealth they claim on the basis of merit that they should possess an excess of political rights (IV 6 1293^{a}23; cf. III 12 1282^{b}29). Because oligarchic justice requires that individuals have rights according to their wealth and the members of the polis are quite unequal in terms of the property they possess, (i) wealthy individuals should have greater political rights, in accordance with their wealth, than poor persons, and (ii) wealthy individuals should exercise their political rights more than poor persons are

---

[43] See IV 5 1292^{a}39–^{b}21, 6 1293^{a}12–34; VI 6 1320^{b}18–1321^{b}1.

[44] In these descriptions and elsewhere Aristotle either uses an incomplete form of *metechein*, 'partake', or else provides a very vague object, e.g. 'in offices' (*tōn archōn*) or 'in the constitution' (*tēs politeias*). Aristotle elsewhere provides a more precise characterization of these political rights, especially in *Politics*, IV 14–16, discussed in Sects. 5.3–5 below.

able to. These corollaries are realized most fully in extreme oligarchy, where the wealthiest few exercise their political rights without constraint because no other citizens have any rights to restrain them.

In addition to supporting a more fine-grained classification of democracy and oligarchy, *Politics*, IV, also reveals a set of constitutions which are evidently omitted in Book III, constitutions which are described in terms of the metaphor of mixture (*mixis*). If the polis contains more than one powerful group, these groups may share power within a single constitution. Indeed, this may be the only way to avoid conflict and revolution. Aristotle describes this phenomenon as a 'mixed' constitution. This is found, for example, when there is, in addition to the rich and the poor, a group of individuals who are educated and capable of moral virtue. An example of this is a 'so-called aristocracy' such as Sparta or Carthage: 'whenever they elect offices not only on the basis of wealth but also on the basis of merit, this constitution is different from both [oligarchy and polity] and is called aristocratic' (IV 7 1293^{b}10–12). So-called aristocracy differs from true aristocracy, because in the latter the government is composed solely of those who possess true virtue equipped with the necessary resources, but in so-called aristocracy the government is composed only partially of virtuous persons. Indeed, we may distinguish between three different types of so-called aristocracy,[45] on the basis of the standards used to assign political rights:

TABLE 5.2. *The So-Called Aristocracies*

Aristocratic Democracy	Aristocratic Polity	Aristocratic Oligarchy
Virtuous Free	Virtuous Free Wealthy	Virtuous Wealthy

Aristotle also indicates that polity itself may be viewed as a mixed constitution, i.e. a mixture of democracy and oligarchy (8 1293^{b}33–4). When the democratic standard, basing political rights exclusively on freedom, is tempered by using wealth as a standard of merit, the result is a demo-

---

[45] Aristocratic polity is mentioned at IV 15 1300^{a}41–^{b}1 and described at 8 1294^{a}23–4 (cf. 11 1295^{a}31–4). Aristocratic oligarchy is described at 7 1293^{b}10–12 and aristocratic democracy (e.g. Carthage) at 7 1293^{b}16–18.

cratic polity;[46] and similarly, when the oligarchic standard of wealth is tempered by the use of free birth as a standard, the result is an oligarchic polity.[47] Closely related to these is the 'middle' constitution dominated by a moderately wealthy middle class (*Pol.* IV 11; see Section 7.3 below). The mixed constitutions greatly complicate Aristotle's analysis because they do not have a single hypothesis or standard like the constitutions in the original sixfold classification.[48]

In summary, we can distinguish several new constitutions, including subtypes of democracy and oligarchy and the mixed constitutions. These may be represented in the following:

Extreme Democracy	Aristocratic Democracy	Moderate Democracy
Democratic Polity	Aristocratic Polity	Oligarchic Polity
Moderate Oligarchy	Aristocratic Oligarchy	Extreme Oligarchy

FIG. 5.2. Revised Classification of Inferior Constitutions

Generally the leftmost and upward boxes on each row indicate a greater representation of the free, the rightward and downward boxes a greater representation of the wealthy. The upper left and lower right boxes represent the extreme forms where there is no rule of law. The mixed constitutions are represented by the central cross which is the union of the middle row and the middle column. The diagonal from bottom left to top right represents the best type of each kind of constitution. The table is overly simplified, because Aristotle recognizes that democracies and oligarchies can be more or less moderate, and that polities can be more or less democratic or oligarchic with a perfect blend of the two as an ideal limiting case. But it will provide a useful point of reference for understanding Aristotle's analysis of political institutions and his comparative evaluation of these diverse constitutional types.

[46] The 'ideal' form of democracy, in which the rich and the poor have equal rights and neither has authority over the other, looks like a form of democratic polity (IV 4 1291^{b}30–8; cf. 8 1293^{b}34–6).

[47] It is customary, however, to call these aristocracies, because the well-to-do usually are educated and of good birth (8 1293^{b}36–8).

[48] Yet another complication is that the moderate forms of oligarchy and democracy are also mixed in that they make concessions to a greater or lesser extent to the opposite standard of justice. Strictly speaking, only the extreme forms are 'unmixed' (V 10 1312^{b}35). However, for simplicity, I shall reserve 'mixed constitution' for the forms which Aristotle regards as just or noble mixtures.

5.3. RIGHTS OF DELIBERATION

Aristotle distinguishes three institutional parts of the constitution, each involving a distinctive set of rights and obligations (IV 14 1297^{b}38–1298^{a}3). He remarks that 'if these portions are in a noble condition, then necessarily the constitution is in a noble condition and constitutions differ from each other because of each of these parts differing'. The three components are:

(1) The part which deliberates (*to bouleuomenon*) about common affairs.
(2) The part concerned with offices or magistracies (*archai*), namely,
     (*a*) which offices there are;
     (*b*) what things the offices have authority over;
     (*c*) how selection is made to offices.
(3) The judicial or adjudicative part (*to dikazon*).

A couple of remarks should precede the detailed examination of Aristotle's constitutional analysis. First, Aristotle is offering a generic analysis arrived at by comparing different types of constitutions in a number of different respects. Some constitutions are accommodated by his framework more easily than others, and some of his schemata are logical possibilities exemplified by no ancient Greek constitutions. Nevertheless, as we shall see the analysis is both comprehensive and illuminating. Second, Aristotle's tripartite distinction is obviously suggestive of the modern distinction among the legislative, executive, and judicial branches of government, a distinction defended by Montesquieu (1689–1755) and embodied deliberately in the constitutions of the United States and other modern states. Of particular interest is the presence of a separate judiciary in Aristotle's scheme. However, Aristotle's tripartite distinction differs from the modern one in important respects. Most importantly, his deliberative part typically has considerable 'executive' authority. Moreover, the offices or magistracies[49] do not collectively form a single executive branch which is balanced against a single legislative branch. Further, the judicial part is composed of individuals who serve as jury members in courts; in so far as there is a counterpart to a 'supreme court' in some constitutions, it is an office, that of the law-guardians (*nomophulakeis*).

Politics, IV 14, considers the part of the constitution that deliberates about common affairs. The deliberative part is called the 'authoritative' part of the constitution (1299^{a}1–2; VI 1 1316^{b}31–2), because it has the

---

[49] 'Office' (*archē*) in this context is used more narrowly than in *Pol.* III 1 where membership in an assembly or jury counts as an office (at least in the 'indefinite' sense). 'Magistracy' is also used to translate this narrower sense of 'office'.

authority to declare war and peace, make alliances and dissolve them, pass laws, impose penalties of death, exile, confiscate property, and elect and audit officials (1298^a3–7). A very important area of authority is the enacting, amending, and rescinding of laws, since the laws fundamentally determine all the political rights of the citizens (including who is qualified to be a citizen) and the manner in which decisions are made in every department of the constitution.[50] In addition, the deliberative part could make changes in the constitution itself (1298^a18). The Greeks also placed great weight upon the selection and auditing of officials or magistrates. The selection of officials is discussed in the following section. The officials were subject to scrutiny and could be investigated and impeached for misfeasance or malfeasance. After the completion of their term of office they underwent an audit (*euthuna*) to determine whether they had misappropriated funds, accepted bribes, or committed any other misdeeds while in office. In Athens the auditors were chosen from the citizen body by lot and if they found any irregularities the case would take place in the court appropriate for the alleged offence (see Section 5.5 below).[51] The other decisions, viz., regarding execution, exile, and confiscation of property, were made by law courts or officials in most constitutions, but could fall to the assembly in extreme democracies.[52] Aristotle's list includes most important areas of authority, although there are others, such as the authority to confer or remove citizenship by decree and to impose taxes. Also omitted is the authority to suspend or dismiss an official, but Aristotle may have assumed that this accompanied selecting and auditing officials. The Athenian Assembly also had the authority to ostracize citizens (see Section 6.9 below).

The citizens who have rights to deliberate and decide about common affairs 'have authority over deliberation' (1298^b3). Aristotle distinguishes three patterns by which these rights might be distributed among the citizens:

(1.1) All the citizens have the right to deliberate about all common affairs (1298^a7–8).

(1.2) Some of the citizens have the right to deliberate about all common affairs (1298^a8–9).

---

[50] On the laws generally see Sect. 3.4 above.

[51] Modern representative democracies might benefit from regular audits of public officials. For a detailed discussion of auditing, see MacDowell (1978), 170–2.

[52] As in the trial of the Athenian generals following the naval battle at Arginousai (406 BC). See Xenophon, *Hell.* I. 7, Plato, *Apol.* 32^b2–3, and Aristotle, *Ath. Pol.* XXXIV 1. See also Kagan (1987), 362–75, for further references.

(1.3)   All of the citizens have the right to deliberate about some com-
         mon affairs, and some of the citizens have the right to deliberate
         about the others (1298ᵃ9).

Pattern (1.1) is characteristic of democracy, (1.2) is oligarchic, and (1.3)
typifies the mixed constitutions, polity and so-called aristocracy.[53]

(1.1) The Democratic Pattern

This pattern embodies the egalitarian ideal of democratic justice (1298ᵃ9–
11, 33–4). It satisfies two corollaries of the democratic theory of justice:
(i) that every free citizen should possess *equal* political rights, and (ii) all
free citizens should exercise their political rights equally. An institution
which embodied this ideal was the Assembly (*ekklēsia* or *dēmos*) of Athens
since every citizen had the right to be an assemblyman (*ekklēsiastēs*). The
Assembly met frequently, with at least forty regularly scheduled sessions
a year. Aristotle distinguishes four deliberative 'modes' (*tropoi*)[54] which
fall under pattern (1.1).[55]

(1.1.1)   All the citizens have the right to deliberate but they exercise
           this right by turns rather than collectively (1298ᵃ12–19).[56]

(1.1.2)   All the citizens have the right to deliberate collectively about
           the laws, war and peace, and election and auditing of officials;
           and officials (selected by election or lot) are assigned to deal
           with the rest on an individual basis (1298ᵃ19–24).

(1.1.3)   All the citizens have the right to deliberate collectively about
           the laws(?),[57] war and peace, alliances, and election and auditing

---

[53] The remainder of this section is devoted to Aristotle's detailed analysis of modes of
deliberation exemplifying these three patterns. In view of the technical character of this
discussion the reader may wish to skip the remainder of this section and proceed to Sect.
5.4.   [54] He also uses the term *taxis* (order) in the same sense as *tropos* (see 1298ᵇ5).
[55] To simplify reference to these deliberative modes I shall refer to each by a sequence
of digits, e.g. '(1.2.3)'. The order of these digits is determined as follows: in the case of the
first digit, '1' indicates it belongs to the deliberative part, '2' to that of offices, and '3' to the
adjudicative part. In the case of the *second* digit, '1' indicates it falls under the democratic
pattern, '2' the oligarchic pattern, and '3' the mixed pattern. The *third* digit indicates the
order in which it is listed by Aristotle. Thus, in the example, '(1.2.3)', the '1' indicates that
it is a deliberative mode, the '2' that it is oligarchic, and the '3' that it is the third such mode
listed by Aristotle. A system of four digits is needed to designate modes of office in the
following section.
[56] He also mentions a variant in which all the citizens take turns as joint office-holders
(*sunarchiai*) having authority over deliberation, although all citizens deliberate collectively
concerning the laws and constitution.
[57] Newman (1887), iv. 245, remarks that the omission of a reference to the making of laws
here is 'probably accidental'.

of officials; and officials, who deliberate about the remaining matters, are selected by election to the greatest extent possible where they require knowledge to carry out their offices (1298ᵃ24–8).

(1.1.4) All the citizens have the right to deliberate collectively about all common affairs, and officials merely make preliminary decisions (1298ᵃ28–33).

There is no indication that this list is intended to be exhaustive, but it does represent the variety possible under pattern (1.1). Each of the modes may be viewed as satisfying this pattern more or less fully. Mode (1.1.1) with its relatively inactive citizenry does so the least, whereas mode (1.1.4) does so most completely. These modes also correspond roughly with the different types of democracy discussed in Section 5.2 above. Mode (1.1.4) is explicitly connected with the extreme type of democracy, and compared to tyranny and dynastic oligarchy.

(1.2) The Oligarchic Pattern

Pattern (1.2) is oligarchic (1298ᵃ34–5), confining the right to deliberate on all common affairs to only some of the citizens. This pattern satisfies the two inegalitarian corollaries of the oligarchic theory of justice: (i) members of the polis should possess greater political rights than other individuals in proportion to their wealth, and (ii) they should exercise these rights more than other individuals in proportion to their wealth.

Aristotle distinguishes three modes or types of order (*taxis*) under pattern (1.2). Again, there is no effort at completeness. He is mainly interested in the criterion by which only 'some' of the citizens have the right to deliberate. The types range from moderate to extreme:

(1.2.1) [Those who deliberate] are elected on the basis of moderate property qualifications, and anyone who possesses the qualification has the right (*exēi*) to partake [in deliberation].⁵⁸ (This group is numerous because of the moderate assessment, and they make no changes which the laws prohibit but follow the laws.) (1298ᵃ35–40)

(1.2.2) Not all citizens who possess the property qualification have the right to deliberate but only those elected have the right. (They rule according to law.) (1298ᵃ40–ᵇ2)

---

⁵⁸ The verb *metechein* has no object, but 'in deliberation' seems intended (cf. 1298ᵃ40–ᵇ1).

(1.2.3)   Only those citizens have the authority to deliberate who have
          been elected by other citizens having this right, and only
          they have the right to elect other citizens with this right.[59]
          (Sons succeed fathers, and they are in authority over the
          laws.) ($1298^{b}2-5$)

These deliberative modes correspond roughly with the different types
of oligarchy enumerated in *Politics*, IV 5–6. Mode (1.2.1), described here
as characteristic of oligarchic polity, corresponds to the most moderate
form of oligarchy, in which numerous small-property holders are enfranchised and which has two tiers of officeholders. The description of mode
(1.2.1) is, however, somewhat indefinite, allowing for different possible
arrangements: e.g. all moderate property owners might have the right to
participate in an assembly (an oligarchic assembly is alluded to at IV 9
$1294^{b}4$) and to elect individuals to higher offices; or there might be an
assembly including all those who meet the minimum, and other more
selective deliberative bodies to which some individuals are elected (the
possibility of a plurality of deliberative bodies is mentioned at $1298^{a}8-9$).
Mode (1.2.2) corresponds to the second type of oligarchy in that the right
to deliberate is confined to those who are elected. Aristotle notes that
modes (1.2.1) and (1.2.2) both involve the rule of law. This is not the case
with mode (1.2.3) which is 'necessarily oligarchic'. Indeed, it fully realizes
oligarchic justice, because a small group of the wealthiest citizens will
possess and exercise all of the deliberative rights. Since there are no institutional constraints on the decisions of these supreme individuals, they
will have supreme authority, rather than ruling according to law.[60] The
greater the scope of their authority, the more far-reaching and potentially dangerous will be this mode. Mode (1.2.3) is thus characteristic of
the extreme type of oligarchy called 'dynastic'; and it is the oligarchic
counterpart of (1.1.4), the deliberative mode characteristic of extreme
democracy.

(1.3) The Mixed Pattern

According to this pattern some of the citizens have the right to deliberate about some of the common affairs, and all of the citizens have the

---

[59] This seems to be the upshot of 'those with the authority to deliberate elect themselves'
(*hairōntai autoi hautous hoi kurioi tou bouleuesthai*).

[60] In *Pol.* IV 5 and 6 the third type of oligarchy resembles the fourth except that in the
former there is still rule of law.

right to deliberate about others. It characterizes the mixed constitutions: 'for example, when everyone [has authority] concerning war and peace and audits [of officials], and officials [have authority] concerning other affairs, and these are selected by election or lot, there is aristocracy or[61] polity' ($1298^{b}5$–8). It is essential to this pattern that authority is divided: no single group of citizens has the right to deliberate collectively about all common affairs. In contrast to even the more moderate democratic modes, (1.3) assigns a less important sphere of authority to the collectively deliberating citizens. Most importantly, it evidently does not grant to them the authority to pass or rescind laws or to change the constitution. Aristotle distinguishes ($1298^{b}8$–11) three mixed modes of (1.3):

(1.3.1)   Some citizens chosen by election have the right to deliberate about some affairs; some citizens chosen by lot from the total citizen body[62] have the right to deliberate about other affairs; and all the citizens have the right to deliberate collectively about the remaining affairs.

(1.3.2)   Some citizens chosen by election have the right to deliberate about some affairs; some citizens chosen by lot from a group of citizens previously selected have the right to deliberate about other affairs; and all the citizens have the right to deliberate collectively about the remaining affairs.

(1.3.3)   Some citizens chosen by election or by lot [from the total citizen body?] have the right to deliberate about some affairs, and they exercise this right together; and all the citizens have the right to deliberate collectively about the remaining affairs.

The first two modes are characteristic of aristocracy, the second imposing a more exacting requirement upon membership. The third mode characterizes polity.[63] If it may be presumed that the method of electing officials is more likely to pick out candidates who are superior in terms of virtue (at any rate, the ordinary virtue attainable by ordinary people), then (1.3.1) and (1.3.2) are supported by the aristocratic theory of rights, according to which virtue is a criterion of merit appropriate for the distribution of political rights. If in mode (1.3.2) the second group is selected

[61] Reading *ē* with the π^{2} family of manuscripts and with Dreizehnter (1970).

[62] This is the force of *haplōs* as contrasted with *ek prokritōn*. The latter expression is explained more fully by Morrow (1960), 233–8, in connection with Plato's *Laws*, XII $945^{b}5$ (cf. VI $759^{b}4$–5).

[63] I understand *politeias* in the phrase *politeias aristokratikēs* ($1298^{b}10$) in the generic sense of 'constitution', and in the phrase *politeias autēs* ($1298^{b}11$) in the specific sense of 'polity'.

from a group screened on the basis of criteria including virtue,[64] this outcome is even more likely. Mode (1.3.3) suggests less confidence that we
can single out such a virtuous group, since it includes both the elected
and those selected by lot.

In the course of discussing a number of suggested reforms to democracy and oligarchy (which are examined in Chapter 8 below), Aristotle
mentions some related institutions of importance. Some oligarchies have
officials called 'preliminary counsellors' (*probouloi*) who must deliberate on and approve proposals before they are taken up by an assembly
(1298^b29; cf. 15 1299^b31). The 'guardians of the law' (*nomophulakeis*) are
said to have a similar function, although they are later said to be found
in aristocracies (1298^b29, VI 8 1323^a8). By controlling the agenda which
is considered by the assembly, these offices greatly limit the rights of the
general citizenry to deliberate collectively. Further, he mentions that in
polities the few, i.e. a small group of officials, have the authority to veto
measures (*apopsēphisamenoi*) but not to approve them (*katapsēphisamenoi*),
since the latter right belongs to the many, i.e. the citizens in the assembly
($1298^b39–1299^a1$). These are examples of the internal checks and balances
characteristic of moderate constitutions.

5.4. RIGHTS OF OFFICE

Politics, IV 15 (cf. VI 8), provides an overview of the offices or magistracies which each constitution distributes among the citizenry. The norm is
that an office (*archē*) is filled by an individual official (*archōn*) who is
selected by a prescribed process (generally involving lot or election),
holds office for a fixed term, and has authority (*kurios*) over a fairly well-
defined sphere. Holding an office often consists of belonging to a board
or committee, and exercising political rights collectively; e.g. in Athens
a councillor (*bouleutēs*) is a member of the Council (*boulē*), and in Sparta
a senator (*gerōn*) belongs to the Senate (*gerousia*). Aristotle states what
he regards as the proper use of the term 'office': 'One should especially
designate as "offices" without qualification those things which are assigned
[the functions of] deliberation, judgement, and giving orders in particular affairs, and especially the latter, since giving orders is more characteristic of official work' ($1299^a25–8$). An office thus typically endows its

---

[64] Cf. 15 $1300^a16–19$ where requirements for eligibility for office include property
qualification, family membership, virtue, or some past meritorious deed.

possessor with authority to give orders (*epitattein*) to other citizens and thereby to create new relations of duties and rights among them.[65]

Aristotle distinguishes a number of questions which each constitution must answer: (1) How many offices are there? (2) Concerning what affairs does each office have authority? (3) What are the temporal limitations on holding office? For example, what is the term of each office? Can an official continue for successive terms or in perpetuity? Can the same citizen hold an office for repeated, non-consecutive terms? (4) How are the citizens selected for offices? For example, who is eligible, who has the right to select them, and by what means? As with the deliberative part, Aristotle claims that on each of these topics one should be able to distinguish a number of modes (*tropoi*) and determine which are appropriate to which types of constitution. He takes up the first two questions together in an unsystematic and cursory manner, and he neglects the third except in passing; so I will only offer a summary of his views on these topics. But in regard to question (4) he is more orderly in trying to lay out different modes of organization.

Regarding the array of possible offices, he first distinguishes between necessary and useful offices (1299ᵃ31–3). 'Without necessary offices a polis cannot exist, but without the offices related to good order and regularity it cannot be nobly managed' (VI 8 1321ᵇ6–8). He says this distinction provides guidance for all polises but especially for small ones. In a larger polis 'it is both possible and necessary [for offices] to be ordered [*tetachthai*] so that there is one for each function' (IV 15 1299ᵃ34–6). This is a principle of functional organization which Aristotle regards as natural, since a polis, like a biological organism, can better achieve its end to the extent that the functions which promote this end are performed by specialized members (see *Pol.* I 2 1252ᵇ1–5).[66] But smaller polises are constrained to consolidate the offices, although this is offset by the fact that the specific

---

[65] He adds (1299ᵃ28–30) that this technical analysis does not reflect the vagaries of ordinary use. The terms *archē* and *archōn* have a wide range of uses. The specific office of archon is one of the most ancient in Athens and other polises, but *archōn* more generally means 'ruler'. The caveat is prompted by his mentioning that some offices are so subordinate that polises tend to assign their duties to slaves when they can afford to do so (1299ᵃ24). These might be clerks, aids, or supervisors of other slaves. His remark may also be intended to exclude priests, equippers of choruses, heralds, envoys, and others even when these are elected to serve in an official capacity, on the grounds that the office does not carry the authority to give orders to other citizens. Moreover, the use of 'office' in *Pol.* IV 15 is narrower than the 'indefinite' sense in III 1 1275ᵃ26, which also includes assemblymen and jury members.

[66] The Carthaginian constitution is praised for not assigning different offices to the same person (II 11 1273ᵇ8–12).

functions need to be discharged less frequently in a small polis (IV 15 1299^{b}1–10; VI 8 1321^{b}8–10). The implication is that the necessary offices should be filled before the offices which will enable the polis to reach a condition of flourishing. Elsewhere (II 11 1273^{b}12–15) he remarks that except for small polises, it is more characteristic of political rule[67] and of democracies to have more offices, because it is 'more common' (hence, more just) for more persons to share in political rights as well as because this provides nobler and more expeditious performance.

Each office is distinguished by the power (*dunamis*) or authority (*kuria*) vested in it (1300^{b}9). *Politics*, VI 8, contains a list of different types of offices and their spheres of authority (parallel discussions in the *Constitution of Athens* are also noted). First are necessary offices: the market magistrate (usually called *agoranomos*) regulates buying and selling and contracts (1321^{b}12–18; VII 12 1331^{b}9; *Ath. Pol.* LI 1–3; cf. Plato, *Laws*, VI 759^{a}8, 763^{e}4–764^{c}4); the urban magistrate (*astunomos*) maintains order in the town outside the market especially pertaining to the maintenance of walls, water sources, harbours, and public buildings and to the orderly use of private property, for example by preventing encroachments into public fairways and regulating the location of drainpipes (1321^{b}18–27; VII 12 1331^{b}10; *Ath. Pol.* L 2, LIV 1; cf. *Laws*, VI 759^{a}7, 763^{c}3–^{e}3); the rural magistrate (*agronomos* or *hulōros*) has comparable authority in rural areas (1321^{b}27–30; VII 12 1331^{b}15; cf. *Laws*, VI 760^{b}6, 761^{d}4–763^{c}2). The foregoing officials have the authority to preside over lawsuits, assign blame, and impose penalties (1322^{a}10–15; cf. VI 12 1331^{b}6–9). Other necessary offices are the receiver (*apodektēs*) or treasurer (*tamias*) who receives tributes, taxes, tolls, and other public income and dispenses funds to other officials (1321^{b}31–3; *Ath. Pol.* XLVII 5, XLVIII 1–2; cf. *Laws*, VI 759^{c}3–760^{a}5); the recorder (*hieromnēmōn, mnēmōn,* or *epistatēs*) who keeps records of private contracts, decisions by jury courts, indictments, and suits (1321^{b}34–40; *Ath. Pol.* XLIV 1); and the official who enforces legal judgement (*praktōr* or one of 'the Eleven' in Athens), exacts fines for offences against the polis, collects debts to the polis, guards prisoners, and imposes capital punishment (1321^{b}40–1322^{a}29; *Ath. Pol.* LII).[68]

---

[67] *Politikōteron* here could, however, mean 'more characteristic of polities'.

[68] Aristotle notes that the latter office, though very necessary, is held to be odious and is also easily abused by depraved persons. He recommends that the authorities associated with enforcement be divided and separated from judgement. In Athens, however, these officials also presided over some criminal trials. It should also be kept in mind that enforcement by public officials was much more limited in ancient Greece than in modern legal systems. In private lawsuits successful plaintiffs were generally responsible for enforcing verdicts and for recovering what was due to them. See MacDowell (1978), 53–66.

Next is the higher grade of offices requiring more experience and reliability: military officers responsible for the defence of the polis and for carrying out war, including the general (*stratēgos*, or *polemarchos*) as well as more specialized positions such as admiral (*nauarchos*), cavalry commander (*hipparchos*), and infantry commander (*taxiarchos*), and many other lower posts (1322^a 29–^{b}6; *Ath. Pol.* LXI; cf. *Laws*, VI 755^{b}7–756^{b}6); the auditor or accountant (*euthunos, logistēs, exetastēs, sunēgoros*) who scrutinizes the accounts of other officials who have authority over public funds (1322^{b}6–12; *Ath. Pol.* XLVIII 3–5, LIV 2; cf. *Laws*, XII 945^{b}3–948^{b}2); and the members of the body which controls the introduction and final disposition of measures in the deliberative body. These last were called councillors (*bouleutai*) in Athens and the preliminary councillors (*probouloi*) elsewhere (1322^{b}12–17). The Athenian Council (*boulē*) consisted of 500 members, with fifty men from each of the ten tribes. The fifty representatives of each tribe served as presidents (*prutaneis*) for one-tenth of a year. (Socrates' role as a president is described in Plato, *Apol.* 32^{a}8–^{c}3.) The duties of the presidents included convening and presiding over the Council and Assembly. (The Assembly held four regular sessions in a presidential term, as well as special sessions as necessary.) Each day one of them was chosen by lot to serve as chairman (*epistatēs*) of the Council and Assembly (*Ath. Pol.* XLIII–XLIV). The latter offices are called 'the most authoritative over all things' because they convene the deliberative body. Finally, there are non-political officials, priests (*hiereis*), and others who manage religious cults and maintain sacred property. In addition, some public officials (e.g. the *basileus* and the *prutanis*) are authorized to carry out public sacrifices and rituals (1322^{b}17–29; *Ath. Pol.* XLVII 1, LIV 6–8, LVII).

Aristotle also briefly notes possible criteria for delimiting the jurisdictions of different offices: viz., location (e.g. a particular market), activity (e.g. keeping order), or human beings subject to them (e.g. women or children) (1299^{b}14–20). Next, he demonstrates that different offices are peculiar to specific types of constitutions, and that different offices can be advantageous to these constitutions (1299^{b}20–1300^{a}8; VI 8 1322^{b}37–1323^{a}9). Oligarchies typically have fewer and more powerful officials. For example, some moderate oligarchies have the office of the preliminary councillors, which is contrasted with the council, a larger body typical of democracies including Athens. The preliminary councillors, who are drawn from the wealthy class, effectively control the agenda of the citizens when they collectively deliberate and are thus able to constrain their exercise of political authority. In a (moderate) democracy the council carries out the function of preliminary deliberation (*probouleuein*) for the people in the assembly 'so that they can be without leisure' (1299^{b}32–3)—i.e. so that they can keep busy at their occupations rather than engaging in political activity. Aristotle mentions that in some constitutions (Newman cites Corinth) the council and the preliminary councillors coexist, the latter having been established in opposition to (*epi*) the former, another example of the checks and balances of 'mixed' political institutions (1299^{b}36–7). A more extreme oligarchy has no need for preliminary councillors because there is no popular deliberative body. The more extreme democracies also dispense with the office of councillor because the popular assembly has assumed authority concerning everything. The latter becomes possible when the citizens receive a fee for attending the assembly and are thereby prosperous and have the leisure to exercise their deliberative rights collectively, as in mode (1.1.4).

In regard to problem (3) about the temporal limits on offices, he elsewhere indicates that democratic constitutions typically have offices with short terms and either prohibitions on repeated terms in the same office or a long interval between terms (see VI 2 1317^{b}23–5). On the other hand, oligarchies have a propensity for longer terms (e.g. the ninety elders with perpetual terms in Elis, V 6 1306^{a}14–16). These differences are easily understood in terms of their respective theories of political rights. On the democratic theory the citizens should have equal rights of office and should exercise them equally, and this is facilitated by keeping terms short and prohibiting or limiting repeated terms. This will increase the probability that each free citizen will be able to hold office at some time in his lifetime. On the oligarchic theory the rights of office should be confined to the wealthy few, and this is promoted by making terms longer and continuous.[69]

Aristotle's account of how citizens are selected for offices is very systematic. There are three defining standards (*horoi*): who selects officials, from whom they select, and how they select (IV 15 1300^{a}10–14). Each of these admits of three[70] patterns of distribution, analogous to the three patterns for distributing deliberative rights: viz., a democratic, an oligarchic, and a 'combined' (*sunduazomena*) or mixed pattern (1300^{a}19–20).[71] The combinations of these different principles and patterns result in a number

---

[69] Cf. Keyt (1991*a*), 244–7.

[70] The manuscripts state that each of them has three (*treis*) types. Dreizehnter (1970) implausibly replaces *treis* with *duo*, 'two'.

[71] The following discussion is rather technical and the reader may want to skip to the final two paragraphs of this section.

of different modes.[72] The general layout is as follows (where each pattern is briefly described and referred to by a symbol composed of a series of digits):

The patterns for distributing the rights to select officers:[73]

All the citizens have the right to select all the officers: modes of type $(2.1.Y.Z)$.

Only some of the citizens have the right to select all the officers: modes of type $(2.2.Y.Z)$.

All the citizens have the right to select some officers, only some of them have the right to select others: modes of type $(2.3.Y.Z)$.

The patterns for eligibility to fill offices:

All the citizens are eligible to hold all the offices: modes of type $(2.X.1.Z)$.

Only some of the citizens are eligible to hold all the offices: modes of type $(2.X.2.Z)$.

All the citizens are eligible to hold some of the offices, and only some of them are eligible to hold some other offices: modes of type $(2.X.3.Z)$.

The patterns for selection of officers:

All officers are selected by lot: modes of type $(2.X.Y.1)$.

All officers are selected by election: modes of type $(2.X.Y.2)$.

Some officers are selected by lot and others by election: modes of type $(2.X.Y.3)$.

Aristotle remarks (1300^a16-19) in connection with the $(2.X.2.Z)$ type modes for eligibility that this right may be restricted by various criteria: property requirements, family (e.g. in the strict type of oligarchy called 'dynasty'), or virtue. (He also mentions Megara, where only those who fought against the democracy to restore an oligarchic constitution had this right.) Undoubtedly, the restriction of the right to select officers in modes of type $(2.2.Y.Z)$ will be based upon similar criteria. Both types of modes are oligarchic, including aristocratic oligarchy.[74] Regarding methods

[72] To standardize reference to these modes I shall again refer to each by a sequence of digits such as the following: '$(2.2.1.3)$'. The first digit '2' indicates it is a mode for offices. (Recall that an initial '1' indicates a mode for deliberative rights.) The second digit '2' indicates a pattern of distributing the right to select citizens to office; the third digit '1' a pattern of distributing eligibility or the right to be selected for office; and the final digit '3' a pattern exemplified in the method of selection. I also use 'X', 'Y', and 'Z' as variables for the latter three digits in order to refer to all the modes which share a given pattern in common. [73] For the first two patterns, see also IV 5 1292^b2-4.

[74] He adds, rather obscurely, 'and there will be four modes of each type of these [*toutōn*]' (1300^a22-3). However, it is not necessary to change the text with Ross (1957). Assuming

of selection, the *klēros* or lot was named after twigs or potsherds which were drawn out of a helmet to determine a winner. A bean (*kuamos*) could also be used as a lot. The *Constitution of Athens*, LXIII–LXVI, describes in detail the machines and procedures used to select jurors and officials by lot. The process of election (*hairesis*) involved casting votes for candidates. The term for 'voting', *psēphisthai*, derived from *psēphos* or 'pebble', since voting was originally by throwing stones into an urn. Also, voting by show of hands (*cheirotonia*) was a common method in Aristotle's Athens. Aristotle regards the lot as democratic, and voting as aristocratic (cf. Plato, *Laws*, VI 759^{b}4–7).

Aristotle[75] enumerates twelve modes of distribution of rights:

(2.1.1.1)   All select from all by lot.

(2.1.1.2)   All select from all by election.

(2.1.1.3)   All select from all by the combined method.

(2.1.2.1)   All select from some by lot.

(2.1.2.2)   All select from some by election.

(2.1.2.3)   All select from some by the combined method.

(2.2.1.1)   Some select from all by lot.

(2.2.1.2)   Some select from all by election.

(2.2.1.3)   Some select from all by the combined method.

(2.2.2.1)   Some select from some by lot.

(2.2.2.2)   Some select from some by election.

(2.2.2.3)   Some select from some by the combined method.

These total twelve modes so far; but they include only the combined pattern for the method of selection and not, he notes, the other two

toutōn refers back to the three combined patterns just mentioned, he may mean there are four ways of conjoining the combined patterns with the uncombined patterns; e.g. if there is a mixed pattern (3) for assigning rights to select, this can be conjoined in four ways with the uncombined patterns (1 and 2): viz., all are eligible by lot: mode (2.3.1.1); all are eligible by election: mode (2.3.1.2); some are eligible by lot: mode (2.3.2.1); and some are eligible by election: mode (2.3.2.2).

[75] The passage (1300^{a}23–30) raises difficulties, but they were mainly resolved by the time of Newman (1887). The text certainly does not deserve the drastic treatment it has received from Dreizehnter (1970). The evidence for the twelve modes is as follows: (2.1.1.2) and (2.1.1.1) at 1300^{a}23–4. Incidentally, the clause *kai . . . hapantōn* (^{a}24–6) which follows *klērōi* in the manuscripts should be left in parentheses at ^{a}24–6; there is no need to move it to after l. ^{a}28 with Dreizehnter. (2.1.2.2) and (2.1.2.1) understood at 1300^{a}26. Newman and other editors insert *ē pantes ek tinōn hairesei ē pantes ek tinōn klērōi* in order to give a parallel with *ē ek tinōn hairesei ē ek tinōn klērōi* at ^{a}28–9. (2.1.1.3) and (2.1.2.3) at 1300^{a}27. Dreizehnter deletes *ē ta men houtōs ta de ekeinōs*, which destroys the parallel with ^{a}29–30. (2.2.1.2) and (2.2.1.1) at 1300^{a}28. (2.2.2.2) and (2.2.2.1) at 1300^{a}28–9. (2.2.1.3) and (2.2.2.3) at 1300^{a}29–30. Newman inserts *kai ta men ek tinōn hairesei ta de klerōi*. This is clearly the sense, but the *legō* clause of ^{a}29–30 may be a gloss, and the addition unnecessary.

combined patterns (for rights to select and eligibility) (1300^a30-1). If these were included there would be a total of 27 modes ($3 \times 3 \times 3$).

Aristotle then relates the various modes of office to his classification of constitutions. Although the passage (1300^a31-^b5) is difficult, it yields some valuable insights into the purpose of his institutional analysis. Two types[76] of selection are democratic. The first (1300^a32-4) combines a universal right to select officials with universal eligibility, and has three modes for the three patterns of selection: modes (2.1.1.1), (2.1.1.2), and (2.1.1.3). These embody the pure form of democracy. The second democratic type (1300^a34-8) is a democratic form of polity, involving a universal right to select officials, but constrained in that the citizens do not all exercise it simultaneously but by turns. This includes a number of modes, involving universal, restricted, and mixed eligibility, in all three patterns of selection: hence the nine modes of type (2.1.Y.Z.).[77]

There follows (1300^a38-^b1)[78] an apparent description of oligarchic and aristocratic forms of polity. Oligarchic polity (1300^a38-40) has as its distinctive feature a combination of the restricted right to select officials with universal eligibility, with all three patterns of selection: modes (2.2.1.1), (2.2.1.2), and (2.2.1.3).[79] Aristocratic polity (1300^a41-^b1) involves mixed eligibility. This is presumably combined with a qualified universal right to elect (cf. 1300^a34-8); hence, modes of type (2.1.3.3) and perhaps (2.1.3.2).[80] It is characteristic of oligarchy (1300^b1-3) for some to select from some, i.e. to combine the second pattern for rights to select officials with the second pattern for eligibility, hence the three modes of type (2.2.2.Z), although he notes that (2.2.2.1) involving selection by lot does not in fact occur. Finally, it is characteristic of aristocracy (1300^b4-5) to employ election, the second pattern of selection. Most commonly, some select from all (2.2.1.2), and occasionally all select from some (2.1.2.2).

---

[76] As Newman (1887) remarks, the two types mentioned in the text (*duo*, 1300^a32) are most probably pure democracy and democratic polity. Ross (1957) replaces *duo* with *treis*, understanding it to refer to three patterns of selection.

[77] This corresponds to the first democratic mode of deliberative rights (1.1.1) in which the citizens also take turns. However, the universal right to deliberate is peculiar to democracy, whereas the universal right to select officials is also found in polity (as well as aristocracy in some cases, as noted below). Because democratic polity involves a qualified form of the universal right to elect, we could also expect it to include the various modes involved in a mixed right to elect (2.3.Y.Z.) which are not discussed by Aristotle.

[78] The manuscripts vary widely and the text seems at times inconsistent, but it is unnecessary to bracket the entire passage with Dreizehnter (1970).

[79] I follow the π^1 manuscripts which omit *oligarchikon* at 1300^a40 and *to de* at $^a41$.

[80] Newman (1887) suggests *ē hairesei ē klērōi* in 1300^b1, which makes it easier to understand the following *ē tas men hairesei tas de klērōi*, but it is hard to believe that an aristocratic polity could rely exclusively on the lot.

We may regard the former as aristocratic oligarchy, and the latter as aristocratic democracy.

In general, democratic modes feature universal rights to select individuals for office and universal eligibility, and oligarchic modes feature restricted rights to select and restricted eligibility. Democratic modes incorporate the lot in order to equalize the chances of holding office, whereas oligarchic and aristocratic modes favour election as more selective.[81] The modes characteristic of polity and aristocracy typically balance these universal and restricted patterns. These features can be plausibly connected with the competing theories of rights: democratic theory requires that the rights of office be distributed equally among the citizens; oligarchic theory requires that these rights be restricted to the wealthy; and aristocratic theory requires that they be restricted to the virtuous. The modes characteristic of the three varieties of polity can also be viewed as reflecting these theories: democratic polity reflects the universal right to select in accord with democratic theory although this is tempered in various ways (e.g. in Tarentum by a mixed mode of selection; cf. VI 5 $1320^{b}11-16$); oligarchic polity adds a restricted right to select in accord with oligarchic theory; and aristocratic polity incorporates a mixed eligibility, permitting some selections to be based on virtue. Sometimes different types of constitutions may use the same mode, for example, both oligarchic polity and oligarchic aristocracy might use mode (2.2.1.3). This mode is an abstract description indicating that the right to select officials is restricted by some standard, without specifying what the criterion is. Presumably, oligarchic polity would appeal to wealth and oligarchic aristocracy to virtue.

The technique of balancing certain patterns against each other, the universal pattern of democracy and the restricted pattern of oligarchy, typifies the Aristotelian mixed constitution. In the case of rights to office, the technique produces a rich variety of mixed modes appropriate to different political circumstances.

5.5. JUDICIAL RIGHTS

The judicial part of the constitution involves the right of citizens to serve on jury courts. In Athens the jury court was called *dikastērion*, and the

---

[81] On the democratic character of the lot, see *Pol.* VI 2 $1317^{b}20-1$ and *Rhet.* I 8 $1365^{b}31-$ 2; cf. Herodotus, III 80. On election by lot in Athens see Headlam (1933).

jury member *dikastēs*. More specific titles were sometimes associated with specific courts. The ancient Greek courts operated in a different manner from modern courts because an individual served on a jury for an extended period of time. The function of judge and jury were for the most part combined in the *dikastēs*, although an official might preside over certain proceedings. In spite of the notorious litigiousness of Athenians, there were no lawyers. Plaintiffs and defendants spoke for themselves if they were full citizens, or were represented by citizens (in the case of minors, women, foreigners, dishonoured citizens, and slaves). Even in most cases of alleged crimes against the polis, such as the trial of Socrates, private citizens acted as prosecutors. In some circumstances, however, an official would be selected *ad hoc*, for example to prosecute an official for malfeasance.

Politics, IV 16 1300^{b}18–35, distinguishes eight general types of court on the basis of their spheres of authority: (i) auditing officials, (ii) injustices regarding common affairs, (iii) constitutional affairs, (iv) disputes over fines concerning officials and private persons, (v) private transactions involving larger amounts, (vi) homicide, with several subdivisions (*a*) homicide with foreknowledge, (*b*) involuntary homicide, (*c*) justified homicide, and (*d*) returning persons exiled for homicide; (vii) cases involving aliens, of two types (*a*) aliens versus aliens and (*b*) aliens versus citizens, and (viii) transactions involving small amounts.[82] Aristotle distinguishes the first five in this list as 'political courts' and remarks that when things do not proceed nobly on these affairs, conflict and revolution often follow (1300^{b}35–8). This underscores the importance of assigning judicial rights in a correct manner.

Aristotle uses the same technique here as with the two previous kinds of political rights. He distinguishes three main patterns for distributing adjudicative rights—universal, restricted, and mixed—and then shows how modes involving these patterns exemplify certain types of constitution.[83] Since the method is by now familiar, I present it here in a more cursory fashion.

First are modes involving the universal pattern (1300^{b}38–1301^{a}2): (3.1) All citizens have the right to adjudicate on all affairs. This is subdivided into four modes depending on how they are selected: (3.1.1) they are selected by lot, (3.1.2) they are elected, (3.1.3) they are selected by lot for some juries and by election for others, and, an apparent variant of the

---

[82] Newman (1887), iv. 269, complains that Aristotle ignores various sorts of cases dealt with by jury courts. See MacDowell (1978), 57–61, for an overview.

[83] Once again, the reader may wish to skip to Sect. 5.6.

latter, (3.1.4) they are selected by lot and by election for some of the same juries.[84] The first of the modes was exemplified in Athens where every citizen over 30 years old who was not in debt or disenfranchised (*atimos*) had the liberty to serve on a jury (*dikazein exestin*) (*Ath. Pol.* LXIII 3).

Next are the modes involving the restricted pattern (1301ª2–7): (3.2) (Only) some of the citizens have the right to adjudicate on all affairs. This is divided into four modes along the same lines: (3.2.1) by lot, (3.2.2) by election, (3.2.3) some by lot and some by election, and the variant (3.2.4) by lot and by election for some of the same juries.

Third are the ones which are mixed or combined (*sunduazomena*) (1301ª7–10): (3.3) All of the citizens have the right to adjudicate in some courts, only some have the right to adjudicate in others, and both groups of citizens have the right in a third group of courts ('for example, if some from all and some from some were members of the same jury court', 1301ª8–9). There is the familiar array of modes: (3.3.1) by lot, (3.3.2) by election, and 'by both'; the latter in this context presumably refers to the same two variants as above, (3.3.3) and (3.3.4).

Again, Aristotle remarks that modes of type (3.1.*X*) are democratic, because they distribute the right to adjudicate as equally as possible among the free citizens.[85] Those of type (3.2.*X*) are oligarchic, because they restrict this right to a select group, those who have the property-assessment. And modes of type (3.3.*X*) are aristocratic or characteristic of polity, because they balance the criteria of freedom and wealth against each other and, in favourable circumstances, facilitate the appointment of virtuous citizens to jury courts.

Addendum on complex constitutions

In *Politics*, IV 14–16, Aristotle discusses the three parts of the constitution in isolation from each other. In VI 1 1316ᵇ39–1317ª10 he adds that it is also possible to form aggregates (*sunagōgai*) or conjunctive modes (*sunduasmoi tropoi*). The result will be, for example, oligarchic aristocracies or more democratic polities. Aristotle gives two examples of oligarchic aristocracies (I have added illustrative modes):

---

[84] Literally, 'concerning some of the same affairs', *peri eniōn tōn autōn* (1300ᵇ41).

[85] He might also have noted that democracies like the Athenian tend to have very large juries, in order to ensure that the right to adjudicate is distributed equally and to the greatest possible extent. Paying jurors to attend would also promote this end. Newman (1887), iv. 274, objects that mode (3.1.2) in which jury members are elected would *not* have been regarded as democratic by the ancient Greeks.

Deliberative	+	Official	+	Judicial
Oligarchy		Oligarchy		Aristocracy
(1.2.2)		(2.2.2.2)		(3.3.3)

Deliberative	+	Official	+	Judicial
Oligarchy		Aristocracy		Oligarchy
(1.2.2)		(2.2.1.2)		(3.2.3)

The study of conjunctive modes could help politicians and lawgivers make fine-tuned adjustments in a constitution without altering its dominant character. For example, an oligarchy could be corrected and moved in the direction of an oligarchic aristocracy through some barely perceptible changes in its modes. Even if there was resistance against any tinkering with the deliberative part, a tincture of aristocracy could be introduced by changing the judicial and official parts along the lines suggested above. Unfortunately, however, Aristotle does not elaborate on this technique, perhaps because *Politics*, VI, was not completed.

5.6. THE FUNCTIONS OF POLITICS

Politics, IV 1–2, contains Aristotle's most extensive discussion of the functions of politics and political practitioners: lawgivers and politicians. Although it offers a synoptic account of the Aristotelian politics, its primary purpose is to argue that a *complete* science of politics must include not only the study of the best constitution but also detailed knowledge of the inferior and even deviant constitutions. Although the discussion sheds valuable light on how the different parts of this science are supposed to cohere, there remain questions as to its ultimate consistency.

He begins with a general thesis: 'In all crafts or sciences which do not come to be partially but are complete concerning one subject-matter, it belongs to one science or craft to study[86] what is suited for each subject-matter' (1288[b]10–12). For example, gymnastics, which is concerned with the training of the body, considers the questions

[1] what sort of training is advantageous for what sort of body? [2] what sort of training is best? (for the best training is suited for the body which is in nature and equipment in the noblest [finest] condition); [3] what one sort of training is best for most bodies? and [4] if [a pupil] desires neither the condition nor the knowledge

---

[86] In this discussion *theōrein* is used in the wide sense, including practical enquiry, and is translated as 'study' (the wider sense of 'theorize').

which suffices for athletic contests, it is no less the task of the athletic trainer and gymnastic expert to provide this [inferior] capacity.

There is a similar range of concerns in medicine, shipbuilding, clothes-making, and every other craft ($1288^b13–21$).

Analogously, politics, 'the same science', and its practitioners, 'the good lawgiver and the true politician', will study a range of constitutions:

(1)   The constitution which is best without qualification; i.e. the constitution most of all of our prayers with no external impediment ($1288^b21–4$).

(2)   The constitution which is suited to a particular polis, i.e. the polis which is best under the given circumstances as well as the best without qualification ($1288^b24–7$).

(3)   'The constitution based on a hypothesis: for [the good lawgiver and the true politician] ought to be able to study a given constitution, both how it might originally come to be, and, when it has come to be, in what manner it might be preserved for the longest time; I mean, for example, if a particular polis happens neither to be governed by the best constitution, nor to be equipped even with necessary things, nor to be the [best] possible under existing circumstances, but to be a baser sort' ($1288^b28–33$).

(4)   The constitution that is most suitable for all polises ($1288^b34–5$).

The implication is that, like the gymnastics trainer, the politician has as his business the provision of each of these in appropriate circumstances.[87]

In the following passage ($1288^b35–1289^a7$), Aristotle complains that most preceding political theorists have failed to offer useful results. 'For one ought to study not only the best constitution, but also the [best] possible, and similarly the constitution which is easier and more common [i.e. attainable] to all [polises].' He faults those who seek only the ideal constitution and also those who talk about the common constitution but then ignore the existing constitutions and praise the Spartan constitution or the like.

---

[87]   See Pellegrin (1987), who sees an exact parallel between the lists of tasks for gymnastics and political science. Mayhew and Smith (1994) point out discrepancies between the two lists (e.g. the lists are incomplete and do not correspond exactly), and deny that Aristotle intends at $1288^b21–35$ to prescribe from tasks for the political scientist. However, their objection that general task [2] for politics is more exclusive than general task [1] for gymnastics can be met if the former is understood to cover the best constitution without qualification as well as the best feasible. Their other objection, that politics item [3] would be too 'Machiavellian' a task is discussed below.

But one ought to introduce an order such that under existing circumstances they [the leaders of existing constitutions] will easily be persuaded and will be able to participate, since to reform (*epanorthōsai*) a constitution is no less a task [of politics] than it is to establish one from the beginning, just as relearning [something is no less a task than is] learning from the beginning. Therefore, in addition to what was just said, the politician ought also to help the existing constitutions, as was said before [at 1280ᵃ1–7].[88]

Politicians as practical scientists should aspire to bring the polis to perfection by implementing the best constitution. Failing this, they should aim at the best feasible constitution given the available resources. In the ancient Greek world there were opportunities to frame new constitutions, for example, when new colonies were being established (the dramatic background for Plato's *Laws*). However, more commonly, politicians had to consider the practical relevance of this science to the conduct of politics in the polises as they actually existed. They had to understand the population, and take into account their capacities and dispositions for particular forms of political life. They needed to accept as a starting-point the constitutions as they actually existed and to improve them where conditions permitted. The study of politics would enable politicians to make valuable contributions in the ongoing practice of politics. For this science includes knowledge which can be applied to a wide range of circumstances, including the following: the different kinds of constitutions as well as their more specific types; the laws and political institutions which are appropriate for various constitutions; the populations and natural resources which are suited for different types of conditions; and the sources of the destruction and preservation of constitutions (1 1289ᵃ7–25, 2 1289ᵇ11–26).

However, in II 8 1268ᵇ22–1269ᵃ28 Aristotle considers the hazards of constitutional reform in connection with the proposal of Hippodamus of Miletus (who planned the Piraeus *c.*450 BC). Aristotle considers arguments for and against political change. On the one hand, change has been advantageous in sciences and arts such as medicine and gymnastics, and politics has also changed for the good. 'Ancient laws were too simple and barbaric.' They included primitive practices such as wife-buying which have become obsolete. 'Everyone in general seeks not the ways of forefathers but the good.' It would seem strange to follow the opinions of our primitive forebears who were undistinguished or foolish. Further, the

---

[88] Following the translation of Curren (forthcoming: n. 19) and reading *koinōnein* and *hōs* with the manuscripts at 1289ᵃ3.

written laws may require revision, for just as with medical treatments, it is impossible to write everything precisely regarding the political order. For the laws must be written in universal form, but actions are concerned with particulars.[89] These arguments support the conclusion that 'some laws should be changed some times'. On the other hand, however, Aristotle notes the case for caution. Slight benefits from change may be offset by a diminution in respect for the laws: 'it is evident that some mistakes of the lawgivers and officials should be let go; for [the polis] will not be benefited by changing as much as it will be harmed by being habituated to disobey the officials.' He then criticizes the analogy of the crafts: 'for change of a craft is not similar to change of a law; for the law has no strength regarding obedience apart from habit, but this does not occur unless there is an extent of time, so that the easy change from existing laws to other new laws weakens the power of the law.'

The upshot of this discussion is that political change is sometimes justified, but the practitioner of politics must exercise the greatest care in recommending and implementing any change. Even minor changes can tend to erode the psychological foundations of the constitution. Aristotle's concluding remarks suggest that this argument could be pressed further: the more radical the change the greater the hazards. Indeed, when revolutions occur the restraints of law may lose their grip altogether and result in a reversion of human beings to the apolitical condition of being the most savage of all animals. Radical Utopian change in which the established constitutional and legal order is torn out root and branch may also destroy the traditional bonds of habit and morality. These implications of Aristotle's remarks have undeniably been borne out in many misguided political experiments of the twentieth century, which have resulted in the dissolution of moral inhibitions leading to widespread death, destruction, and terror. In contrast, Aristotle's attitude towards political change is, on the whole, very conservative.

Nevertheless, it has been questioned whether Aristotle gives a coherent account of the practical applications of the science of politics. Aristotelian politics has two poles: one is 'ideal' or 'Utopian', concerned with identifying the best constitution consistent with human nature and with the resources that can be expected to be available under the most favourable circumstances or, failing that, the best constitution attainable by a Greek polis; the other pole is 'mundane' or 'empirical', concerned with main-

---

[89] On the universal character of laws and the need for variability see Sect. 3.4 above.

taining and preserving actually existing political systems. There are obvious tensions between these poles: for example, as noted above, Aristotle
recommends letting go some mistakes of lawgivers and officials in order
to preserve the constitution. Some critics have maintained that these
opposed poles are in fact incompatible programmes. In fact, this alleged
incoherence is the linchpin for Werner Jaeger's thesis that the *Politics* as
we have it contains strata written at different times. On his view Books
II–III and VII–VIII belong to Aristotle's earlier age and reflect 'the old
Platonic spirit' of idealism and Utopianism, whereas Books IV–VI reflect
Aristotle's later empirical and pragmatic interests.[90] On this interpretation politics is in part an empirical science which can be employed in the
pursuit of whatever ends, good or bad, the political expert may have.
This view of politics as a type of 'value-free' technical expertise clearly
conflicts with the view of politics as an exercise of the intellectual virtue
of practical rationalists which aims at the perfection of the polis and its
citizens. But are the aims of Books IV–VI radically discordant with those
of the rest of the *Politics*?

The principal evidence for the intrusion of a pragmatic conception of
politics is the third function assigned to politics in the passage of *Politics*,
IV 1, discussed above.[91] For this involves studying how any given constitution might originally come to be, and, when it has come to be, in
what manner it might be preserved as long as possible.[92] This includes
not only a constitution which is the best or best possible in the given
circumstances, but also a baser one (1288^b28–33). This interpretation is
also suggested by the fourth function of gymnastics, for example, if a
person is not capable or desirous of competing in athletic contests, the
trainer could help him to maintain his present condition or to improve
it slightly but to a level inferior to that of the fully conditioned athlete
(IV 1 1288^b16–19).[93] This implies that the politicians may have a legitimate aim that falls short of the perfection which a given polis is capable of
attaining. This interpretation gains further support from the unstint-
ing advice in *Politics*, IV–VI, on techniques to preserve corrupt regimes.
The most notorious example is the extended discussion in *Politics*, V 11,
of techniques for maintaining tyranny, which seem to be 'marked by a

---

[90] Jaeger (1948), ch. 10, following Wilamowitz (1893), i. 355–6. Similarly, Sabine (1973),
91, sees a new vision of political science emerging in *Pol.* IV–VI.

[91] See Rowe (1991).

[92] Mulgan (1977), 130–8, ascribes to Aristotle 'the attempt to preserve every type of
constitution whatsoever'.   [93] Cf. Rowe (1991), 64 n. 27.

sort of Machiavellian realism'. Aristotle appears like a 'hired consultant' equipped with 'political mechanics employed perhaps for an inferior or even a bad end'.[94]

Against this, however, it may be objected that the third function of politics and the fourth function of gymnastics must be interpreted in context. For, as noted above, Aristotle *also* states that the political scientist should study existing constitutions with a view to *reforming* them (1289ᵃ1–7).[95] The description of the third task of political science (1288ᵇ28–33) does not say that the politician should try to preserve a base constitution *without* trying to correct it. The description is consistent with a reformist agenda. His language also implies that to reform (*epanorthoun*) a constitution is to make an inferior constitution more like a correct (*orthē*) one. The best constitution provides the standard of justice by which inferior constitutions can be evaluated and improved. The assumption throughout *Politics*, IV–VI, is that lawgivers and politicians are severely constrained by the recalcitrant populations with which they must deal. Nevertheless, it is suggested, they should be guided by the ideal of the best constitution. This idea is also suggested by the ranking of constitutions from best to worst at *Politics*, IV 2 1289ᵃ38–ᵇ11 (see Section 5.2 above). In addition, *Politics*, IV 2, ends with an enumeration of the tasks of political science which implies that it is to be guided by normative considerations:

. . . we must first [1] distinguish how many sorts of constitutions there are, whether there are numerous forms of democracy and oligarchy, and next [2] which [constitution] is the most common and choiceworthy after the best constitution, and which it is, if there is any other that happens to be aristocratic and established nobly, and at the same time suitable for most polises; and next [3] which among the other constitutions is choiceworthy for which [polises] (for perhaps democracy is more necessary for some than oligarchy, and the latter is more so than the former for others); and after these [4] in what manner one who wishes, ought to establish these constitutions, I mean the particular form of democracy and again of oligarchy; and finally [5] when we have made concise mention of all these things to the best of our ability, we must try to discuss the things that destroy and preserve constitutions for all together and for each separately, and the causes by which these things most naturally come to be. (1289ᵇ12–26)

---

[94] See Barker (1931), 164; Irwin (1985*a*), 155; and Sabine (1973), 91.

[95] This passage contains a reference at 1289ᵃ7 which seems almost certainly to be back to 1288ᵇ24–39, which includes the description of the problematic third function of politics. On the connection between preserving constitutions and reforming them see Newman (1887), iv. 140.

This passage does not suggest that it is proper to establish or preserve any and every constitution. On the contrary, it clearly implies that the practical functions (4) and (5) of establishing and preserving constitutions should be based on (3) an understanding of which forms of constitutions are choiceworthy.[96]

However, this presents the problem of how the concept of the best constitution is supposed to guide the politician attempting to cope with adverse circumstances. This problem involves two more specific difficulties.[97] The first concerns the teleological hypothesis of the constitution. The best constitution has the correct hypothesis that the end of the polis is perfect happiness or morally virtuous activity, whereas the deviant constitutions have incorrect hypotheses: oligarchy holding that the end is wealth and democracy that it is freedom or the liberty to do whatever one wishes (see Section 5.2 above). According to what hypothesis should the Aristotelian politician reform a deviant constitution? Aristotle proposes to reform deviant constitutions by 'combining features from each so as to produce a "just mixture" ' (IV 13 1297ᵃ38–ᵇ1). This suggests that reform consists in 'mixing' incorrect hypotheses together. But how is this type of reform supposed to be guided by, or justified on the basis of, the correct hypothesis?

A parallel difficulty concerns the standard (*horos*) of justice embodied by the constitution. The best constitution is based upon justice without qualification: it correctly recognizes moral virtue as the standard of merit. The deviant constitutions are based on mistaken standards of justice: they erroneously use personal wealth or free birth as measures of merit. Hence, the deviant constitutions are unnatural and unjust, and their laws will also be unjust (see III 11 1282ᵇ10–13). But this presents the same problem as with the hypothesis: how can the standard of justice guide the prescription of incorrect standards? Aristotle goes so far as to say that even the more moderate of the deviant constitutions should be described not as 'better' but as 'less base' (IV 2 1289ᵇ10–11). The problem is compounded by the

---

[96] Rowe accepts this interpretation in (1977) but rejects it in (1991) and (1989). The basis for this rejection is that 'these constitutions' in (4) refers back to item (1) rather than to the immediately preceding (3), because in (4) Aristotle adds the clause 'I mean the particular forms of democracy and again of oligarchy'. Against Rowe's later interpretation, we should note that Aristotle carefully orders this list of topics: first (*prōton*) (1), then (*epeita*) (2), then (*epeita*) (3), and after these (*meta tauta*) (4), and finally (*telos*) (5), 'when we have made concise mention of all these things, to the best of our ability'. This is evidence that he thinks that topics (1)–(3) should all be mastered before (4), and (1)–(4) before (5).

[97] Both are set forth in Rowe (1991), 66–8.

fact that, in his actual discussions of mixed constitutions, Aristotle seems at times to be more concerned with whether the mixture is stable than whether it is just (see VI 5 $1319^{b}33-1320^{a}4$).

These are indeed serious difficulties, but comparable problems arise for any political theory which attempts to proceed from an ideal political model, based on assumptions which are not in fact true of actually existing communities. The problem seems especially acute for Aristotle, in view of the disparity between his ideal—a community composed of individuals qualified for and disposed to a life of complete ethical virtue, in basic agreement as to what such a life entails, and fortunate enough to possess all the resources needed to lead such a life—and the stark reality of his day—polises composed of persons unqualified for Aristotelian virtue, who suffer from many deficits of education and property, and who disagree in a fundamental way about their ultimate ends and standards of justice. Nevertheless, I shall argue, there are important connections in Aristotle's view among the different roles of the politician in that the study of the best constitution will provide guidance to the practical politician concerned with establishing or reforming a constitution in less fortunate or diverse circumstances. These connections will become evident only by examining in some detail the three main applications of politics: the best possible constitution given optimistic assumptions about the population and the resources at its disposal; the second-best constitution, i.e. the best constitution which was realistically attainable by the Greek polis of Aristotle's day; and the inferior constitutions which in fact prevailed in classical Greece. These applications are examined in turn in the following three chapters.

6

The Best Constitution

6.1. THE POLIS OF OUR PRAYERS

Aristotle states in the *Nicomachean Ethics* that 'there is only one constitution which is everywhere according to nature the best' (V 7 1135^{a}5). The study of this best constitution is the primary task of the 'philosophy of human affairs' (X 9 1181^{b}12–22). In the *Politics*, also, it is the first function of the lawgiver and true politician to establish and maintain the best constitution, which is also characterized as 'according to our prayers impeded by no external thing' (IV 1 1288^{b}23–4). Much of the *Politics* is a quest for this best constitution: Book II criticizes the candidates offered by Plato and other theoreticians, and then assesses some of the best actual constitutions, viz., those of Sparta, Crete, and Carthage. Book III sets forth theoretical prerequisites for the best constitution and canvasses the candidates in broad theoretical terms. Books VII–VIII give a more detailed (albeit still sketchy) portrait of the best constitution.

The best constitution is the 'most correct' of those constitutions which are called 'correct', 'just without qualification', and 'according to nature' (III 6 1279^{a}17–21, 17 1287^{b}37–41; IV 8 1293^{b}25). The best constitution most fully satisfies the two criteria of the correct constitution: (i) it assigns political rights on the basis of merit, viz., unqualified moral virtue (III 13 1283^{a}23–40); and (ii) those who are in political authority rule for the common advantage rather than for their own private advantage (7 1279^{a}28–31). These criteria derive from particular (distributive) and universal justice respectively. Each of them raises a problem of interpretation.

The first problem concerns criterion (i), which requires that the best constitution assign political authority to the best persons, those who are pre-eminent in moral virtue over everyone else (see III 18 1288^{a}32–6). The declaration that 'only one' constitution is 'the best' seems to imply that one and only one such assignment of political authority is best. However, Aristotle in fact allows that more than one may be the best, for example, when he says that the best constitution is that 'in which there happens to be either some one person or a whole family or a multitude that is superior in virtue to everyone' (1288^a34-6). Further, Aristotle seems to award the first prize to different constitutional forms in different parts of the *Politics*.[1] In Book III absolute kingship (*pambasileia*) is the best constitution, provided 'there is one person so distinguished by superiority in virtue . . . that the virtue and political capacity of all the others are not commensurable . . . with his own' (III 13 1284^a3-8). If there is such a superior person, 'it only remains that one is to obey such a person and he is to have authority [ruling] not by turns but without qualification' (17 1288^a28-9). The absolute king rules like a god among human beings; he is not subject to the laws; rather, he is a law unto himself (13 1284^a13-14, 14 1285^b29-33). This is called the 'first and most divine' when the six constitutions are rank ordered (IV 2 1289^a40). However, in Book VII Aristotle dismisses kingship as highly unlikely, and describes the best constitution as involving the rule of an entire citizen body sufficient to constitute a polis (13 1332^a34-5, 14 1332^b23-7). The latter is an aristocracy, where a number of good persons share in governance according to law (III 15 1286^b3-7; cf. IV 7 1293^b1-7). Hence, not one, but at least two distinct constitutions—kingship and aristocracy —can be 'the best' according to Aristotle (see IV 2 1289^a30-2).[2]

A plausible solution[3] is suggested by Newman:

The answer is that the best constitution will assume the form of an Absolute Kingship or the more equal form of an Aristocracy of *spoudaioi* [excellent persons], according to circumstances. It will be the former, if an individual or a family of surpassing excellence exists in the State; it will be the latter, if this surpassing excellence is possessed by a body of citizens capable of ruling or being ruled with a view to the most desirable life.[4]

---

[1] Schütrumpf (1991), i. 50, sees this as evidence that different books of the *Politics* reflect different chronological stages of Aristotle's thought.

[2] Evidence can be offered for two other candidates: *Pol*. III 11 for democracy and IV 11 for polity. However, it is evident that Aristotle would regard these as 'the best' only in a very qualified sense (see Chs. 7–8 below).

[3] An alternative, less flattering solution is to see Aristotle as not following his argument wherever it might lead, but as yielding at different times to different pressures: Plato's lingering influence, a desire for Macedonian patronage, and intimidation by the Athenian democracy. See Kahn (1990), 373–4, and Keyt (1991*a*), 239–40. Both Kahn and Keyt reject the 'biographical explanation'. It is, however, endorsed in part by Kelsen (1937), 37: Aristotle's 'apology for royalty was intended to be the ideology of one definite hereditary monarchy', viz., that of his patron, Alexander the Great. Cf. Popper (1962), 200–2. However, Aristotle does not explicitly endorse the Macedonian monarchy, and *Pol*. V 10 1313^a3-5 states that the monarchies of his time are tyrannies; cf. the unflattering reference to King Philip at 1311^b1-3.   [4] Newman (1887), i. 291.

Keyt makes an advance on this suggestion, arguing 'that "the one constitution that is best" is a genus whose species are absolute kingship and
true aristocracy (*Pol.* IV 2 1289ª31–3)'.[5] This genus is a constitution
which embodies Aristotle's aristocratic theory of justice and rights. How
the Aristotelian lawgiver applies this theory will, as Newman remarks,
depend upon circumstances, i.e. upon the moral capacities and the resources of the inhabitants.[6]

The second problem of interpretation concerns criterion (ii), which
requires that the best constitution promote the common good. What
exactly does this imply about political justice? How is the good of the
polis as a whole related to the good of its individual members? This
question pertains to the passage in the *Nicomachean Ethics* clarifying the
statement that political science is concerned with the human good: 'For
even if [the good] is the same for one person and for a polis, that of the
polis appears to be greater and more complete [or perfect] to attain and
preserve; for although it is valuable to attain and preserve it for even one
person alone, it is nobler and more divine to do so for a nation and for
polises' (I 2 1094ᵇ7–10). This passage does not strictly say that the good
of the polis exceeds that of a single individual, but that it is better *to
attain and preserve* the good of the polis.[7] Is the point that politics should
aim at the good of the polis in the sense of the good of *all* the citizens (in
contrast to merely promoting the interests of merely *some* of them)? Or is
the passage meant to assert that the polis has a higher end, which transcends
and may even be detrimental to the good of its citizens?

This question is crucial for determining whether Aristotle's theory of
justice supports strong individual rights. A right is a claim of an individual
against other individuals. Such a claim is *strong* when it implies that the
interests of the individual may not be sacrificed in order to advance the
interests of others. Hence, if a theory of political justice requires that
the interests of *each* individual be protected, then the theory supports
individuals' rights in a strong sense; but if a theory of political justice
permits (or requires) individuals to be sacrificed in order to promote the
common good, then individuals will not possess rights in a strong sense.
This chapter addresses the second problem: whether Aristotle's best

---

[5] Keyt (1991a), 257 n. 43. This interpretation is also supported by *Pol.* V 10 1310ᵇ32–3:
'. . . kingship has been ranked with aristocracy, for it is based on merit [i.e. virtue] . . .' (cf.
ᵇ2–3).

[6] While satisfactory as a formal solution, this treatment leaves out of consideration the
paradoxical character of kingship, a problem taken up in Sect. 6.8 below.

[7] Cf. Schütrumpf (1991), i. 81 n. 4.

constitution is committed to the protection of individual rights in a strong
sense.

6.2. INTERPRETATIONS OF THE COMMON ADVANTAGE

The best constitution is the 'most correct' constitution (*Pol.* IV 8 1293^{b}25),
and in correct constitutions the political authorities rule for the common
advantage rather than for their own private advantage (III 7 1279^{a}28–31).
The common advantage is equated with justice (*Pol.* III 12 1282^{b}16–18;
EN V 1 1129^{b}14–19, VIII 9 1160^{a}13–14).[8] The best constitution therefore
most fully embodies this standard. However, the concept of 'the common
advantage' (*to koinēi sumpheron*) is open to different interpretations.[9] One
line of interpretation is *individualistic*: to promote the common advantage
is to promote the ends of its individual members. The polis is happy or
flourishing provided that its individual citizens are happy. Hence, the best
constitution must take seriously the fact that its members are distinct
individuals and must respect the interests of each of them. Another line
of interpretation is *holistic*: the polis resembles an organism in that it has
an end which is distinct from, and superior to, the ends of its individual
members. Just as the end of Socrates' eyelashes (protecting his eyes from
foreign material) is subordinate to the end of Socrates (rational activity),
Socrates' own end is subordinate to the end of the polis as a whole.

The individualistic and holistic interpretations[10] of the common ad-

---

[8] In this context 'just' refers to universal (or general) justice, as described in Sect. 3.2,
unless otherwise noted. Distributive justice and other particular forms of justice promote
the end of universal justice, i.e. the common advantage.

[9] The verb *sumpherein* (participle, *sumpheron*) means 'to promote an end or confer a
good'. The impersonal sense is 'to be advantageous or expedient'. (Closely related is *chrēsimon*,
'useful'). Like the English term 'expedient', *sumpheron* can have a negative connotation,
since it can refer to an object of choice contrasting with the noble and the pleasant (*EN* II
4 1104^{b}31, IX 8 1168^{a}12). However, it can also refer to the means to a noble end, and is as
such an object of practical wisdom (VI 10 1142^{b}31–3). When the common advantage is
equated with justice, 'advantage' of course has this positive connotation.

[10] These two interpretations correspond to the two sorts of political theories distinguished
by Popper (1962), i. 79–80, 100. As noted below, Popper understands by 'holistic' the view
that the whole has a higher reality than its individual members and has interests which the
individual should subserve. He understands by 'individualistic' the view that individuals are
what fundamentally exist and that they should be the fundamental concern of normative
theory. Individualism for Popper is compatible with altruism as well as egoism. 'Individualism'
is, of course, used in other senses. For example, Nussbaum (1980), 422–3, denies that
Aristotle's view is 'individualistic', but she understands by this 'a view that supports diversity
in the choice of goods'. I shall refer to the latter sort of view as 'pluralism' rather than
'individualism', and the opposed view as 'monism' which holds 'that the good life is the
same for us all—or at least that all rational agents, after sufficient reflection and consideration of the alternatives, could agree about the plan of the best life'.

vantage have profoundly different implications concerning justice and individual rights. On the holistic view, the sacrifice of Socrates would be justified if this would make the polis as a whole better off, just as a doctor would be justified in amputating an arm or leg in order to benefit Socrates. The holistic interpretation has affinities with modern consequentialist theories which take the end of the individual to be the promotion of the collective interest.[11] As a holistic theorist, Hegel views the state as the ultimate end of the individual: individuals should 'knowingly and willingly acknowledge this universal interest even as their own substantial spirit, and actively pursue it as their ultimate end'.[12] In contrast, on the individualistic view, a constitution which aims at the common advantage will protect the interests of each individual citizen.[13] To the extent that it regards the interests of individuals as a matter of basic concern, the individualistic view must support a strong theory of individual rights which prohibits the sacrifice of individual ends. The distinction between holism and individualism is, however, oversimplified and misleading, because holism and individualism can take different forms, depending upon how they understand the common advantage and individual advantage as interrelated. The rest of this section canvasses the possible positions, ranging from extreme holism to extreme individualism.

Extreme holism

The extreme version of holism is ascribed by Karl Popper to Plato, who allegedly regards the state (polis) 'as a kind of superorganism', which is a higher form of reality than its individual members, and which 'should, by

---

[11] Mulgan (1977), 33, states that for Aristotle 'the good of any individual member is less important than the good of the whole'. Because 'the individual had no inherent rights', Aristotle follows other ancient Greeks who 'were much more willing to sacrifice the status, property, or lives of individuals for the sake of the common good'. Mulgan takes the institution of ostracism to be 'a good example of the general Greek view of the legitimate power of the group over the individual'. The problem of ostracism is discussed in Sect. 6.9 below.

[12] Hegel, *Philosophy of Right*, sect. 261. A corollary for Hegel is that the 'rights' of individuals are identical with their duties to the state, which should be freely performed: 'what the state requires as a duty should also in an immediate sense be the right of individuals.'

[13] e.g. Locke argues that the magistrate should use his sword 'to enforce Men to observe the positive Laws of the Society, made conformable to the Laws of Nature, for the public good, i.e. the good of every particular Member of that Society, as far as by common Rules, it can be provided for; the Sword is not given the Magistrate for his own good alone' (*First Treatise*, IX. 92; cf. *Second Treatise*, XI. 135, XV. 171). Cf. Tulley (1980), 162–3, and Simmons (1992), 57.

its nature, be one, and not many. . . . Only a stable whole, the permanent collective, has reality, not the passing individuals. It is "natural" for the individual to subserve the whole, which is no mere assembly of individuals, but a "natural" unit of a higher order.' The whole has an end or good which supersedes that of its individual members, with implications for moral or political theory: 'the individual should subserve the interests of the whole, whether this be the universe, the city, the tribe, the race, or any other collective body.' Popper finds this view stated baldly in Plato's *Laws*: 'The part exists for the sake of the whole, but the whole does not exist for the sake of the part. . . . You are created for the sake of the whole and not the whole for the sake of you' (903^c, Popper's translation). He contends that Plato's holism perpetuates primitive 'tribal collectivism' and prefigures Hegel and twentieth-century totalitarianism (National Socialism, Fascism, and Marxism-Leninism).[14]

Few commentators venture to ascribe to Aristotle such an extreme form of holism as Popper finds in Plato.[15] However, Jonathan Barnes does argue that Aristotle 'had a tendency towards totalitarianism' and that he treated the individual as an organic part of the state.[16] Barnes detects in Aristotle the following reasoning:

(1) If X is essentially (or naturally) a part of some natural whole Y, then it is good for X that X is F if, and only if, it is good for Y that X is F.[17]

(2) The individual human being is essentially (or naturally) a part of the polis which is a natural whole.

(3) Therefore, it is good for the individual to be F if, and only if, it is good for the polis that the individual be F.

[14] Popper (1962), i. 79–80, 100. In support Popper cites *Rep*. IV 420^b–421^c, 424^a, 449^c, 462^a; VII 519^c; and *Laws*, IV 715^b, V 739^c, IX 875^a, especially X 903^{b-c}, XI 923^b, XII 942^a. (See, however, *Laws*, IX 875^{a}5–^{b}1.)

[15] Popper does not explicitly ascribe holism to Aristotle, although he finds the latter's thoughts, in politics as elsewhere, to be 'entirely dominated by Plato' (1962: ii. 2) with notes favourably quoting Zeller and Grote, who suggest the *Politics* is closely modelled after the *Laws*, with only fairly trifling alterations. Popper does not, however, take note of Zeller's sharp distinction between Aristotle and Plato, discussed below.

[16] Barnes (1990*a*), 259–63; (1990*b*), 16–22; (1982), 82–3. Stewart (1892), ii. 464, also seems to favour a 'social organism' interpretation.

[17] Barnes takes this premiss, which he calls 'Aristotle's axiom', to be explicitly asserted at *Pol*. I 13 1260^{b}13–18 and VIII 1 1337^{a}27–30, and to be foreshadowed in Plato's *Laws*, X 903^b, and *Charm*. 156^c. Barnes (1990*b*) formulates it in different, more technical language, but his refinements do not need to be considered here, since they are designed to exclude trivial counter-examples. Barnes also gives a version of the axiom concerned with duties: this differs from (1) in having as its consequent: 'X ought to do A in so far as it is best for Y that X do A.'

Barnes distinguishes (1) from another principle,

(1_H) If X is essentially (or naturally) a part of some natural whole Y, then it is good for X that X is F in so far as it is good for Y that X is F.

(1_H), he notes, is stronger than (1), because the 'in so far as' in (1_H) implies that 'individual interests are *determined by* and *depend upon* the interests of the whole', but this asymmetrical dependence is not captured by the 'if, and only if' in (1). This stronger premiss is necessary to derive the thesis of extreme political holism,

(3_H) Therefore, it is good for the individual to be F in so far as it is good for the polis that the individual be F.

Barnes's observation is correct, but it also reveals that (1) and (3) admit also of individualist readings, namely,

(1_I) If X is essentially (or naturally) a part of some natural whole Y, then it is good for Y that X is F in so far as it is good for X that X is F.

(3_I) It is good for the polis that the individual be F in so far as it is good for the individual to be F.

(3_I) takes political goodness to depend ultimately upon what is good for the individual members of the polis. A polis can attain happiness and the good life only because, and to the extent that, its individual members are happy and live well. However, (3_H), which describes extreme holism, is not the only alternative to individualism. Aristotle could instead be understood as offering a moderate version of holism, which will now be described.

Moderate holism

Moderate holism rejects the extreme holistic view that the end of the individual is a mere means to the higher end of the polis. It is closer to individualism in that it regards the good of the polis as including the good of its individual members, so that the aim of the lawgiver and politician includes the promotion of the perfection or happiness of the individual members of the polis. However, moderate holism rejects the strict requirement of individualism that the common advantage must promote the perfection of each member of the polis. Rather, moderate holism still maintains that the political good is a collective good distinct from the good of all the members: for example, that it is an indivisible 'communal' good which cannot be reduced without remainder to a sum of individual goods, or that (as with modern utilitarianism) it is some sort of aggregation of individual interests.[18]

Such a moderate-holistic interpretation is evidently offered by Alasdair MacIntyre.[19] He takes Aristotle's thesis that a human being is a political animal to imply that individuals can achieve their end only within a polis, which is 'a community whose shared aim is the realisation of the human good', presupposing 'a wide range of agreement in that community on goods and virtues'. This necessitates political or civic friendship, 'the sharing of all in the common project of creating and sustaining the life of the city, a sharing incorporated in the immediacy of an individual's particular friendships'. It is 'this notion of political community as a common project' which MacIntyre finds 'alien to the modern liberal individualist world'. Aristotle, he says, would regard the modern liberal individualist state as not a genuine polis at all, but 'only as a collection of citizens of nowhere who have banded together for their common protection'. For Aristotle conceives the polis as a community 'in which men in company pursue *the* human good and not merely as—what the modern liberal state takes itself to be—providing the arena in which each individual seeks his or her own private good'. On this interpretation, the good is *essentially* collective or political. The modern problem of egoism and altruism does not arise, because 'my good as a man is one and the same as the good of those others with whom I am bound up in the human community. There is no way of my pursuing my good which is necessarily antagonistic to you pursuing yours because *the* good is neither mine peculiarly nor yours peculiarly—goods are not private property.' MacIntyre believes that the concept of rights is quite alien to this Aristotelian framework. This seems plausible, if the end of the polis as a whole is indeed a greater good than the ends of its members considered as separate individuals. For it could then be expected to override any claims on behalf of the ends of the citizens considered as separate individuals.

Individualism

In contrast to the foregoing, the individualist interpretation requires that the advantages of individuals considered separately must be protected. It

[18] Miller (1981) argues that Aristotle is a 'consequentialist' like Marx, unpersuasively because he disregards the central role of justice in Aristotle's politics.

[19] MacIntyre (1981), 141, 146–7, 160, 213; cf. 67. Cf. Madigan (1991).

assumes that the good of the polis consists of the set of activities involving the perfection or flourishing of its members, and that this set of activities can be partitioned into disjoint subsets of activities such that each subset belongs to one and only one individual in the polis. It contends that the best constitution must take seriously the fact that its members are distinct individuals and, therefore, must recognize the interests of each of them.[20] The individualistic view presupposes that the ends of individuals are compossibly realizable, i.e. that it is possible for every member to attain perfection without impeding anyone else from doing the same. What makes the best constitution *best* on this view is that it facilitates the compossible realization of individual ends. As in the case of holism, there are extreme and moderate versions of individualism.

Extreme individualism

Extreme individualism holds that the activities which constitute the good for an individual are done solely for the sake of the agent and not for the sake of anyone else. A version of extreme individualism is advanced in Plato's *Republic*, when Glaucon claims that it is only because the bad of being a victim exceeds the benefits of wrongdoing that individuals form contracts and agree to treat each other justly (II 358ᵉ3–359ᵃ2; see Section 4.7 above). Glaucon assumes that justice is only instrumentally valuable and that everyone naturally pursues excessive possession as a good (359ᶜ2–6). He anticipates the case for political co-operation offered by Hobbesian contractarian theorists, who assume that individuals are motivated exclusively by self-interest and are willing to co-operate with each other only when they believe this will be to their own advantage.[21]

Not surprisingly, no scholar (at least none known to me) has ascribed the extreme-individualist view to Aristotle. However, such an interpretation *is* conceivable, if, for example, the human good is understood along strictly intellectualist lines as consisting exclusively of contemplation. For contemplation is a self-sufficient activity not essentially involving other

---

[20] This theme is stressed by Nussbaum (1980, 1990); see also Khawaja (1991), e.g. 75. The separateness of persons is also a central feature of modern liberal theory. Rawls (1971), 27, objects against utilitarianism that it 'does not take seriously the distinction between persons'. Similarly, Nozick (1974), 33, emphasizes, 'There are only individual people, different individual people with their own individual lives.'

[21] For the self-interest (or non-tuistic) assumption see Gauthier (1986), 87; Hampton (1986), 6–11; and Kavka (1986), ch. 2. However, some contractarian theorists reject the self-interest assumption, e.g. Morris (1988).

persons (*EN* X 7 1177ᵃ32–ᵇ1; *Pol.* VII 3 1325ᵇ16–27).[22] The good for each individual is therefore a purely self-regarding activity. The common advantage could then be understood as what promotes the highest good for each individual.[23] The common advantage would promote the purely self-confined advantages of individuals so understood.

Moderate individualism

However, there is also a moderate version of individualism which holds that other-regarding virtuous activity is an essential part of individual perfection.[24] The good life of the individual would be a mixed life, including not only contemplation but also the exercise of other-regarding virtues such as friendship, justice, and generosity.[25] On this interpretation there is no strict dichotomy between egoism and altruism, for individuals would correctly regard it as in their own self-interest to act for the sake of others. This interpretation is suggested by Aristotle's theory of friendship, for example in his distinction between base and noble self-love in *Nicomachean Ethics*, IX 9. Base self-love aims at the gratification of the agent's desires for pleasure, wealth, or honour, whereas noble self-love seeks the gratification of the agent's rationality or intellect. A true self-lover is willing to labour for his friends and fellow citizens, to give up external goods for their sake, and even to die for them; in this 'he gains the noble, and so awards himself the greater good' (1169ᵃ28–9). Even death in battle need not be a self-sacrificial act (cf. III 7 1115ᵇ17–24). On the moderate-individualist interpretation, the individual advantage promotes the good life, in this wider sense, of the individual, and the common advantage promotes the good life, in this wider sense, for each individual in the polis. A fine statement of the moderate-individualist interpretation is offered by Eduard Zeller:

Plato had demanded the abolition of all private possession and the suppression of all individual interests, because it is only in the Idea or Universal that he acknowledges any title to true reality. Aristotle refuses to follow him here. To him the Individual is the primary reality, and has the first claim to recognition. In his

---

[22] Note especially 1325ᵇ16–17: 'It is not necessary that the active [life] be in relation to other persons.' See Khawaja (1991), 74.

[23] Cf. Nozick (1974), 298: 'Utopia . . . must be, in some restricted sense, the best for all of us; the best world imaginable for each of us.'

[24] Bodéüs (1993), 42–3, correctly argues against an extreme individualist interpretation, but fails to consider whether Aristotle can be regarded as an individualist in the moderate sense.

[25] This involves an 'inclusivist' interpretation, viz. moderate intellectualism. See also Sects. 4.7, 6.8, and 10.3.

metaphysics individual things are regarded, not as the mere shadows of the idea, but as independent realities; universal conceptions not as independent substances, but as the expression for the common peculiarity of a number of individuals. Similarly in his moral philosophy he transfers the ultimate end of human action and social institutions from the State to the individual, and looks for its attainment in his free self-development. The highest aim of the State consists in the happiness of its citizens. The good of the whole rests upon the good of the citizens who compose it. In like manner must the action by which it is to be attained proceed from the individual of his own free will. It is only from within through culture and education, and not by compulsory institutions, that the unity of the State can be secured. In politics as in metaphysics the central point with Plato is the Universal, with Aristotle the Individual. The former demands that the whole should realise its ends without regard to the interests of individuals: the latter that it should be reared upon the satisfaction of all individual interests that have a true title to be regarded.[26]

Some interpretations of Aristotle seem to combine features of individualism and holism. For example, T. H. Irwin notes that 'the common advantage' suggests a utilitarian conception of the public interest. According to Irwin, however, Aristotle is not a utilitarian because he uses the particular (or special) forms of justice—such as distributive and corrective justice—to protect the 'self-confined interests' of individuals. Particular justice, like the virtue of friendship, involves concern for others for their own sake and thus seems 'to prohibit the sacrifice of the individual person's interests for a collective interest'. Since the particular forms of justice subserve universal (or general) justice on Irwin's view, the protection of individual interests is included within Aristotle's concept of the common interest. However, Irwin's interpretation seems to be ultimately holistic, because he apparently sees the aim of universal justice as the promotion of the good of the polis as an aggregated whole as opposed to the 'self-confined interests' of individuals. (He does not, however, consider the alternative, discussed here, that its aim is the promotion of individual interests in the wider sense involving other-regarding virtues.)[27]

---

[26] Zeller (1897), ii. 224–6. Zeller's accompanying footnotes cite *Pol.* II 5 1263^{b}29–40, 1264^{b}17–19, and VII 9 1329^{a}22–4. Individualistic interpretations of Aristotle are also offered by Allan (1964), cf. (1952), 166–7, 183; Khawaja (1991); Lerner (1969), 147; and Nussbaum (1988; 1990).

[27] Irwin (1988), 425–6, 430–1; cf. (1990). Irwin (1985d; 1988: sect. 239) also argues that virtuous or noble action is altruistic for Aristotle, in the sense that it is essentially concerned with promoting the common good rather than that of the agent; cf. Engberg-Pedersen (1983), ch. 2. Against this, Rogers (1993) argues that virtue and nobility (*to kalon*) are concerned with both the good of the agent and of others for Aristotle (e.g. at *EN* IX 8 1169^{a}8–11).

Another subtle blend of holism and individualism is the interpretation of John M. Cooper:[28]

[t]he common advantage of a civic community conceived as Aristotle conceives it, like that of a family, does not consist wholly (though of course it might well consist partly) of something that can be broken down into a sum of separate advantages belonging individually to the citizens one by one. To the extent that each citizen participates in the good of the others, a good that may belong in the first instance to a single individual (whether a material possession or a good quality of mind or character) becomes a communal good shared in by all who are members in good standing of the community. Insofar as part of the common good of the citizens is thus a set of communal goods, it is not divisible into separate shares at all, but remains indissolubly an 'advantage' of the common enterprise itself in which the members of the community are associated. The citizens share equally in the whole of this part of their common good, just because they are associated in the civic enterprise and care about it.

The basis for the allegedly indissoluble collective good is, again, civic or political friendship, which is 'just an extension to a whole city of the kinds of psychological bonds that tied together a family and make possible this immediate participation by each family member for the good of others. In a city animated by civic friendship the citizens are engaged in a common enterprise, an enterprise aimed at a common good in two different senses.' First, the common advantage is 'the sum of the advantages of its citizens, separately considered', and second, the good attained in the first instance by other individuals becomes, and is conceived of by oneself as being, also, a part of one's own good. By means of civic friendship an individual's life becomes 'merged in the life of the whole city'. Although this has obvious affinities with holism, by holding that the common advantage is in a sense more than the totality of individual advantages, Cooper's interpretation differs from extreme holism, because he understands the individual good to depend ultimately not on the good of the polis as a whole, but on the good of other individuals. Moreover, it allows that individuals in part realize the good as separate individuals, so that the common advantage consists at least partly of the separate advantages of individuals. Yet, on the leading issues that divide holism and individualism, Cooper rejects the holistic theses that the polis has an end separate from, and superior to, that of the individual citizens, and that it can be just to

[28] Cooper (1990), 236–40. Cooper's interpretation contains an added complication regarding second-class citizens who are not able to attain as individuals the full share of virtue that happiness requires. This is discussed in Sect. 6.6 below.

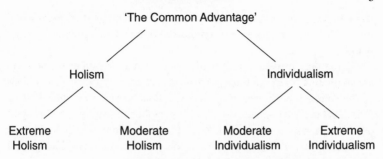

FIG. 6.1. Interpretations of 'The Common Advantage'

sacrifice or compromise the good of some individual citizens in pursuit of the end of the polis as a whole. For example, in an aristocracy the virtuous life of the ruling class cannot be 'bought at the price of limiting the moral development of the other citizens'. Rather, Cooper's view agrees with moderate individualism that in the best constitution political institutions must be arranged so that each and every citizen can achieve an active, perfected, self-sufficient life.

To summarize, the following interpretations of 'the common advantage' are possible, as shown in Fig. 6.1. Of these, the moderate views resemble each other closely. For both the good of the individual has an other-regarding dimension. They agree that the perfection of individuals includes morally virtuous acts performed for the sake of others, and thus they both reject the strict egoism–altruism dichotomy, albeit for somewhat different reasons. Moreover, the most moderate forms of holism (especially Irwin's) almost converge with moderate individualism in stressing the interests of individuals.[29] None the less, there is an important difference between them: moderate individualism understands the common advantage to promote the perfection or happiness of each individual in the more inclusive sense involving other-regarding virtue; whereas moderate holism does not regard the common advantage as necessarily promoting the good of its individual members even in this more capacious sense. The best

---

[29] Alexander of Aphrodisias *in Topicorum* (*CIAG* II. ii. 247, 4–10) states that 'the benefiting of the polis contains also the benefiting of those belonging to it, so that treating both [sc. the polis and its citizens] well is not more choiceworthy than treating the polis well'. He adds that in this case the good of the whole cannot be compared to or enumerated with the good of its members (referring to *EN* I 7 1097^{b}17), presumably because, if one achieves the good of the polis, one has thereby brought about the good of its individual members. Although this sounds individualistic, Alexander does not say whether the political good must contain the good of *each and every* individual, so that it is not clear whether he has a moderate-individualistic or moderate-holistic view.

constitution may forsake the ends of some of its individual members if this is deemed necessary to promote the good of the community as a whole.

On the present issue, as in many others of Aristotelian exegesis, there are conflicting interpretations for several reasons.[30] Aristotle's discussions of the common advantage and of the relation between the polis and the individual are incomplete, vague, and metaphorical, so that they suggest different views to different readers. His discussions occur in separate contexts which may also be understood in different ways. However, I shall argue in the following sections that the preponderance of evidence in the *Politics* indicates that Aristotle has a moderate-individualist position.

6.3. AGAINST EXTREME INDIVIDUALISM

The defence of political naturalism at the beginning of the *Politics* is widely viewed as supporting a holistic interpretation of Aristotle's political theory. However, an inspection of the relevant texts shows only that Aristotle rejects the extreme form of individualism. This is evident, first, in his argument for the naturalness of the polis at *Politics*, I 2 1252^{b}27–1253^{a}1, where he contends that the polis is the end, and hence the nature, of the more basic communities (households and villages), 'for we say that what each thing is when its coming to be is completed [or perfected] is the nature of each thing, for example of a human being, a horse, or a household'. This argument does not assume that the individual stands to the polis as a mere means to an end. For (as argued in Section 2.3 above) Aristotle only argues that the polis is natural in the sense that it provides the level of self-sufficiency which its individual members require in order to live well and fulfil their natures. Indeed, the passage concludes by saying that 'the final cause, that is, the end, is best, and self-sufficiency is an end and best'. This argument does not require that the polis has as its ultimate end anything other than the good life of its individual members.

However, the subsequent discussion at *Politics*, I 2 1253^{a}18–39, has

---

[30] Variations on and combinations of these are, of course, possible. Nussbaum (1990), 156–9, finds both holistic and individualistic conceptions of the functions of the polis in Aristotle, conceptions which are inconsistent with each other. The holistic interpretation, as allegedly evidenced at *Pol.* VII 1 1323^{b}33 ff., is opposed to more individualistic conceptions which 'think of the goodness of city members distributionally: that is, taking them one by one as separate units' (p. 156). She suggests the holistic conception may represent a 'more primitive stage', that is, more Platonic, stage in Aristotle's thought, and she argues that Aristotle's predominant and considered view is individualistic (in the sense I am using the term). I criticize this interpretation in n. 62 below.

been taken by many commentators[31] to provide strong, explicit support for a holistic interpretation, because it defends the claim that the polis is by nature prior to the individual and does so by a literal analogy with a living body and its organs. However, this literal interpretation encounters an insuperable difficulty: it saddles Aristotle with the claim that individuals cannot exist apart from the polis. This is transparently false, and Aristotle implicitly rejects it (1253^a3-4 allows that individuals may be without a polis due to chance). Aristotle clearly intends a looser analogy with an organism.[32]

As Section 2.4 above argues, the point of the analogy is that individuals (like body parts) cannot perform their defining function as human beings when they are separated from the polis. The conclusion of the analogy is that the polis is prior in completeness or perfection to the individual. For although individuals in isolation are not self-sufficient, the polis is a community which attains 'the limit of self-sufficiency'.

This argument is inconsistent only with extreme individualism, which denies the first premiss that the good of the individual essentially involves justice and the other-regarding virtues. Extreme individualists would also reject the claim that participation in a polis is necessary for individual perfection. They could accept at most an argument along the lines offered by Glaucon in *Republic*, II, that justice and the polis are an instrumental means for individuals to attain their self-confined ends. However, Aristotle's argument is compatible with moderate individualism which agrees that the individual good includes other-regarding virtuous activities and hence requires participation in a polis.

6.4. ARISTOTLE'S CRITIQUE OF EXTREME HOLISM

The extreme form of holism seems to be a view which Aristotle himself attributes to Socrates as depicted in Plato's *Republic* and rejects as untenable and even incoherent in *Politics*, II 1–5.[33] Aristotle sets the stage by

---

[31] See e.g. Hegel, *Lectures on the History of Philosophy* (1955), ii. 202; Newman (1887), i. 31–3; Barker (1906), 278–80; Mulgan (1977), 32–5; Keyt (1991*b*), 135–40; Barnes (1990*a*), 262; and Kraut (1989), 96. [32] Cf. Irwin (1988), sect. 217.

[33] I follow Aristotle in attributing the doctrines under attack to 'Socrates' in the *Republic*. My concern here is not with whether these doctrines form an integral part of Plato's own political philosophy, but with what Aristotle's response to them reveals about his own views. Although communism is attributed to Plato himself at II 12 1274^b9-11, the genuineness of *Pol.* II 12 has long been questioned: see Newman (1887), ii. 373, 376–7. On the issue of whether Aristotle's characterization of the communism of the *Republic* is fair, see Stalley (1991) and Mayhew (1993*b*).

remarking that since the polis is a community (*koinōnia*) its members must have something in common (*koinōnein*), but he questions whether they should have everything in common, as when Socrates allegedly recommends that the citizens ought to have families and property in common (II 1 1261ª2–8). Aristotle objects that Socrates has conflated the common and the private because he has misunderstood the nature of the *polis* and, by implication, that of the political good, when he makes 'the hypothesis that it is best for the entire polis to be one as far as possible' (*Pol.* II 2 1261ª15–16; cf. *Rep.* IV 422ᵈ1–423ᵈ6, V 462ª9–ᵇ2; also *Laws*, V 739ᶜ2–ᵈ5). Aristotle argues,

[I]t is evident that as it becomes progressively more one it will no longer be a polis; for the polis is with respect to its nature a sort of multitude, and if it becomes more one it will become a household instead of a polis, and a human being instead of a household; for we would say that a household is more one than a polis, and one human being is more one than a household; so that even if one could do this, it ought not to be done; for it would destroy the polis. (1261ª16–22)

Here Aristotle asserts unequivocally that the polis does not, and ought not to, possess the unity of a living, organic substance.[34] Some critics have defended Socrates by objecting that Aristotle has confused two senses in which the polis is 'one': possessing inner harmony and agreement (which is all that Socrates means), as opposed to being one in number like an individual organism (which Aristotle takes him to mean).[35] Regardless of whether Aristotle is fair to the *Republic*,[36] he clearly denies that the polis is by nature an organic unity like an individual human being.[37]

Aristotle also criticizes Socrates' contention (*Rep.* V 462ᶜ) that the end

[34] He supports this assertion with arguments that unity is a misplaced political ideal: the polis must be composed of persons who are different in kind and perform different functions (1261ª22–ᵇ9). Self-sufficiency takes precedence over unity, and less unity is preferable when this enhances self-sufficiency (1261ᵇ10–15).

[35] See e.g. Bornemann (1923), 128. If the former is Socrates' meaning, then Aristotle is open to the *ad hominem* criticism that he also emphasizes the importance of unanimity or *homonoia* (at 3 1261ᵇ31–2; cf. 5 1263ᵇ35; see also *EN* IX 6 1167ᵇ4–16).

[36] Stalley (1991), 187–91, offers a plausible defence: viz., Aristotle is justifiably objecting to Socrates' obliteration of individual differences in the ideal polis. Cf. Newman (1887), ii. 230, and Mayhew (forthcoming).

[37] This implication is noted by Irwin (1991*b*), 216 n. 20, who remarks that 'there is an apparent prima facie difficulty in making [Aristotle's own use of the organic analogy in I 2 1253ª15–29, VIII 1 1337ª27–30] consistent with his criticism of Plato's use of the analogy'; cf. Irwin (1988), ch. 21 n. 52. However, the passages referred to by Irwin can in fact be reconciled with the moderate individualism underlying the critique of Plato (as I argue in Sections 6.3, 7).

of political unity will be most fully realized if all say 'mine' and 'not mine' at the same time.

For 'all' [is said] in two ways. If it means 'each', perhaps this will be more like what Socrates wants to do; for each will say that the same [boy] is his son, and the same [woman] his wife and similarly concerning his property and indeed each thing that falls to him; but those who have wives and children in common will not now speak in this way, but [they will] say that *all* and not *each* of them [have the wives and children], and similarly that *all* but not *each* of them have the property. It is evident therefore that there is a fallacy in the expression 'all say' . . . Therefore, that all say the same thing [is mine or not mine] in one sense [that is, 'each'] is noble yet impossible, but in another sense is not even able to produce unanimity. (3 1261^{b}20–32)

The term 'all' may be understood in a holistic sense, referring to everyone collectively; or it may be understood in an individualistic sense, as applying to each person separately. For example, depending on how one interprets 'all', the statement made of four persons that 'They all weigh over four hundred pounds', will have quite different implications as to their individual weights. Aristotle finds Socrates again promoting the extreme-holistic form of unity which entails the obliteration of the separate identities of individuals.[38] But true unanimity involves agreement among distinct persons on a set of common virtues or common principles. Aristotle objects that if the citizens have their families or their property in common, this will lead not to consensus but to indifference and resentment.

Aristotle further argues that Socrates has misunderstood the true character of friendship, which 'we believe is the greatest of goods for polises' (4 1262^{b}7–8).

[I]n the polis friendship necessarily becomes watery through this sort of community [viz., having wives and children in common], and because the father least of all calls his son 'mine', or the son his father. Just as a little wine mixed in a lot of water makes the mixture imperceptible, so the relationship towards each other based on these words also turns out [to be imperceptible]; hence,[39] it is least of all necessary in this sort of constitution for the father to care about his son or the son about his father or brothers about each other. For there are two things which especially make human beings be concerned about or befriend [another]: [viz., that the other is] private (*idion*) or valued; but neither of these can belong to those who govern themselves in this way. (4 1262^{b}15–24)

---

[38] Cf. Nussbaum (1980), 417–18, and Stalley (1991), 191–2. As Woodruff (1982), 82, remarks, Aristotle's argument here is a striking parallel to Plato, *Hip. Maj.* 300^{b}6–302^{b}6.
[39] Reading *di' ha* with Dreizehnter (1970).

This passage also implies that Aristotle does not view the friendship which is 'the greatest of goods for polises' (because it holds the polis together) as a single relationship like a single chain linking all of the citizens together. Such a relationship would be too 'watery' or attenuated to bind them together, because the individuals could not regard themselves as connected in a personal or private way (*idion*) with one another. Rather, friendship consists of a multiplicity of personal relationships, which reinforce each other like pieces of straw which are woven together in a basket which can bear a heavy load.[40]

This passage presents a problem for moderate-holistic interpreters who see political friendship as linking the individual citizens together so tightly that their identities and their ends become merged together. For in this passage, Aristotle eschews just such a global friendship in favour of personal friendships, on the grounds that the former is too 'watery' to bind the citizens together. This is quite consistent with Aristotle's treatment of friendship in the ethical works, where he says that a person cannot have many friends in the primary sense, because friendship in the primary sense (virtue or character friendship) requires that friends spend their days together and be aware of one another's character, thoughts, and feelings.[41]

None the less, it can be argued that Aristotle recognizes political friendship as a specific type of friendship, distinct from family friendship, based on the fact that fellow citizens are related to one another in a common work, and that this mode of friendship does not compete with, but supplements, the links between family members.[42] The importance of political friendship is also indicated in the *Nicomachean Ethics*:

> Friendship seems also to hold polises together, and lawgivers seem to be more concerned with it than justice; for unanimity (*homonoia*) seems to be similar in a way to friendship, and they aim at this most of all and they try to expel faction, i.e. enmity . . . (VIII 1 1155ᵃ22–6)

Political friendship is the bond holding the polis together, and because human beings are by nature political animals, this form of friendship is indispensable for the perfection of human beings.[43] However, it does not follow that political friends find happiness by 'merging' their ends. For

---

[40] Cf. III 9 1280ᵇ35–9 which mentions in addition marital relations, religious cults, and convivial pastimes.

[41] See *EN* IX 10; cf. *EE* VII 2 1237ᵇ34–1238ᵃ10 and 12 1245ᵇ19–25.

[42] See Cooper (1990), 233 n. 15.

[43] As Sect. 4.7 above argues, political friendship and unanimity are indispensable for the moral habituation of human beings.

Aristotle views political friendship as an inferior sort of friendship.[44] This is apparent in the statement, quoted above, that friendship is found most of all (*malista*) where the friend is private or personal (*idion* as opposed to *koinon*, common) and beloved (*Pol.* II 4 1262^{b}15–24). This is consistent with the statements in the *Eudemian Ethics* that political friendship is based on utility (*kata to chrēsimon*) (VII 10 1242^{a}6–7, ^{b}31–2, 1243^{b}4) and is thus not the primary form based on virtue. The *Nicomachean Ethics* also denies that one can extend the primary form of friendship to all the citizens: 'It is possible to be a friend of many persons in a political way, and to be not an obsequious but a truly reasonable person; but it is not possible [to be a friend] to many persons for their virtue and for themselves, but one should be satisfied to find even a few such [friends]' (IX 10 1171^{a}17–20). This clearly implies that the citizens of Aristotle's best constitution could neither be friends of all of the other citizens in the primary, virtue-based sense nor value all of them for their own sakes. The passage thus raises very serious problems for any interpretation which attempts to treat political friendship as closely akin to virtue-based friendship.[45] In sum, Aristotle's reservations about polis-wide friendship (*Pol.* II 4 1262^{b}15–24) and his caveat about political friends at *EN* IX 10 1171^{a}17–20 make it doubtful that political friendship can support the moderate-holistic interpretation.

Finally, the critique of the *Republic* concludes (*Pol.* II 5 1264^{b}15–24) with a significant criticism of Socrates' conception of happiness (cf. *Rep.* IV 419^{a}1–421^{c}6; V 465^{c}4–466^{a}6):

Further, destroying even the happiness of the guardians, he says that the lawgiver ought to make the polis as a whole happy. But it is impossible for a whole to be happy unless most or all or some of its parts possess happiness. For being happy is not the same as [being] even; for the latter can belong to the whole, even if neither of its parts does, but being happy cannot. But if the guardians are not happy, what other persons are? For at any rate the artisans and the multitude of vulgar persons are surely [not happy].

[44] Annas (1990), 245, persuasively argues this.

[45] Irwin (relying on *EN* VIII 3 1156^{a}10–16, ^{b}7–12) challenges Cooper's (1977) more general claim that friends of utility value one another for themselves (1988: ch. 18 n. 2; cf. 1990: 87 n. 16). However, Irwin (1990), 94, tries to show that political friendship (in the best constitution) is a special case of virtue-based friendship: 'If I know another person is a virtuous fellow-citizen, I know, without knowing anything else about him, that I have reason to regard him as another self; for I know that I share with him the virtuous aim of maintaining the comprehensive association of the city.' *Contra* Irwin, Aristotle does not speak of political friends as other selves, and it is very doubtful that he would do so, for he assumes that the 'other self' is an object of direct awareness, with whom one can share thoughts, feelings, pleasures, and pains (see *EE* VII 12 1245^{a}34–^{b}4; *EN* IX 9 1170^{b}8–14).

Aristotle here objects against Socrates' alleged conception of happiness as belonging to the polis as a whole without belonging to its individual members.[46] Aristotle clearly holds that the happiness of the whole is in some manner analysable into the happiness of the individual members of the polis. He thus repudiates unequivocally the extreme-holistic view of the political good. It should also be emphasized, however, that this passage only states a very weak necessary condition: the polis is happy only if some members of the polis are happy. This obviously cannot provide a standard for the best constitution, because it is satisfied by deviant regimes which promote only the advantage of the rulers (see III 7 1279^{a}30–1).[47] But in this passage Aristotle does suggest two alternative standards for the best constitution, which correspond to the two interpretations of the common advantage:[48]

> *The overall advantage* The polis is happy only if most of the members are happy.
> *The mutual advantage* The polis is happy only if each of the members is happy.

The standard of overall advantage is aggregative and thus permits trade-offs, viz., sacrifices of the basic interests of some individuals in order to promote the advantage of others.[49] The overall advantage thus reflects a viewpoint which is not deeply committed to the rights of individuals. The *mutual* advantage on the other hand reflects the concern of individualism that the happiness of *each* of the participants must be protected by political institutions. *Politics*, II 5 1264^{b}15–24, does not say which of these standards should be applied in the best constitution.

In conclusion, just as *Politics*, Book I, clearly excludes extreme individualism, Book II rules out extreme holism as Aristotle's position. It remains to be seen whether moderate holism or moderate individualism best represents Aristotle's view of the common advantage and political justice.

---

[46] Socrates may be assuming that the polis must be happy in the same sense as the individual (cf. *Rep.* IV 435^{b}1–2). However, some scholars regard this particular criticism of the *Republic* as unfair or misguided; for references see Stalley (1991), 197 n. 29. The general logical point about applying predicates such as 'happy' to collectives should be compared to the point about 'all' at 3 1261^{b}20–32.   [47] See Seel (1990), 43–4.

[48] For a similar distinction in Hume's ethics see Gauthier (1990).

[49] It is questionable, however, as to whether there is any basis in Aristotle for modern utilitarian notions such as the maximization of individual or social well-being. On this see Wiggins (1975), 232–3; (1978), 260–1. When Aristotle says that 'what is choiceworthy for each person is the highest it is possible for him to achieve' (VII 14 1333^{a}29–30), he seems to understand this in terms of reaching a natural limit rather than of maximizing desire satisfaction.

6.5. THE COMMON ADVANTAGE AND CONSTITUTIONAL JUSTICE

There is some evidence in *Politics*, III, of the moderate-individualist, mutual-advantage interpretation (see also Sections 2.2, 4.7): '[T]he common advantage (*to koinēi sumpheron*) brings [human beings] together, in so far as a part of the noble life falls to each (*hekastōi*) [of them]. This is most of all the end, both in common (*koinōi*) and separately (*chōris*) . . .' (III 6 1278ᵇ21–4). This passage underscores three important features of the common advantage. First, it promotes the ultimate human good, which is the noble life or happiness. Second, it entails that *each* individual benefits from co-operating in the community.[50] It is clear from this that Aristotle understands the polis as a form of co-operation for the *mutual* advantage rather than merely the overall advantage. The common advantage or good is understood as providing *each* individual reason to accept it as good *for him*. On a holistic view, the individual's good is merged or aggregated together with the goods of other individuals. The resulting overall advantage is not necessarily, nor even normally, in a given individual's interest.[51] Third, it is the end for the members both in common and separately (cf. VII 1 1323ᵃ21, 3 1325ᵇ30–2), which clearly implies that the ultimate good can be separately and distinctly realized by each individual.[52] These three points provide strong support for the moderate-individualistic interpretation of the political end and against any version of the holistic interpretation.

The mutual-advantage interpretation also fits Aristotle's discussion of the types of rule (1278ᵇ30–1279ᵃ16). Despotic rule in the case of a natural master and a natural slave is for the sake of the master and only accidentally for the sake of the slave, although the same thing is (Aristotle alleges) in fact advantageous for both of them (1278ᵇ32–7; cf. I 6 1255ᵇ4–15). In contrast, household rule over one's children and wife is as such for the

---

[50] Bradley (1991), 47, notes that the common good is here understood as the good of each and every citizen.   [51] See Narveson (forthcoming), 3.

[52] Cf. Susemihl and Hicks (1894), 382. This passage casts doubt on Cooper's contention (1990), 240 n. 22, that the parallel use of 'in common and separately' at VII 1 1323ᵃ21 (cf. 3 1325ᵇ30–2) can be understood more broadly so that 'even someone who is not himself a virtuous person and so not constantly exercising virtues in his daily life is none the less in a secondary way leading a virtuous life, by having his life merged in the life of the whole city which itself *is* a virtuous one, by reason (primarily) of the virtues possessed, and exercised in its political and otherwise communal life, by its ruling class'. For the present passage clearly requires that *each* individual as an individual ('separately') have a share in the noble life. It does not suffice if one merely merges oneself into a greater, happy whole. Subsequent references in this section are to *Pol.* VII unless otherwise indicated.

sake of the ruled but is accidentally for the sake of the ruler, i.e. in so far as he is a member of the household ($1278^b37–1279^a8$). But political rule in its natural (and just) condition involves equal parties taking turns at holding office and performing public service for the advantage of the ruled ($1279^a8–13$).[53] Similarly, Aristotle in II 2 $1261^a30–4$ treats such rotational rule as an instance of proportional reciprocity or commutative justice, which is exchange for the mutual advantage.[54]

Aristotle then distinguishes between correct constitutions, which aim at the common advantage according to justice without qualification, and deviations from these, which aim only at the advantage of the rulers (III 6 $1279^a17–21$; cf. 7 $1279^a28–9$; VII 14 $1333^a3–6$; *EN* VIII 10 $1160^b2–3$). This way of making the distinction prompts the question: Whose interests are included in the common advantage? The domain is presumably the citizens, since the polis is a multitude of citizens (*Pol.* III 1 1274^b41).[55] However, this presents a difficulty:[56] Correct constitutions promote the common advantage whereas deviant constitutions promote the advantage of the rulers only. Citizens are defined as those who possess political rights and, hence, as the ruling class (1 $1275^b18–20$). But deviant constitutions would also seem to promote the common advantage. For example, oligarchy would promote the advantage of the few persons who qualify as citizens, and tyranny would promote the advantage of the one and only citizen, viz., the monarch. Thus the distinction between correct and deviant constitutions would collapse. One solution to this problem is to identify the common advantage with the advantage of the citizens in a wider sense of 'citizens', viz., encompassing all the ruled who are free, native-born inhabitants of the polis. Aristotle does occasionally speak of 'citizens' in this wider sense (see Section 5.1 above). Alternatively, he could understand the common advantage as including the advantage of all free native-born inhabitants, including non-citizens as well as citizens. The two solutions are practically equivalent.[57]

Because Aristotle viewed democracy as a deviant constitution, it is

[53] Cf. Isocrates, *Areopagiticus*, 24. On performing public service (*leitourgein*) as a burden see Susemihl and Hicks (1894), 384.

[54] There is an explicit reference to *EN* V 5 $1132^b31–4$; see also Sect. 3.2 above.

[55] See 7 $1279^a31–2$; 13 1283^b40; cf. Newman (1887), i. 119 n. 1.

[56] See Cooper (1990), 228–9, for the difficulty and the first proposed solution. For a similar treatment see Keyt (1993), 21–5.

[57] As we shall see, in Sect. 6.9, this problem is not supposed to arise for the ideal constitution as described in *Pol.* VII–VIII, where the two groups are assumed to coincide. For here the non-citizens engaged in productive labour are slaves, barbarians, or metics (see VII 10 $1330^a25–31$). But the problem cannot be avoided so easily by more feasible constitutions which contain a substantial number of disenfranchised free persons.

clear that he does not regard the common advantage as the 'overall advantage' consisting in the advantage of a mere majority of individuals in a utilitarian aggregative sense. However, this leaves open the possibility that the correct constitution might promote the common advantage in another collectivist sense, for example, by benefiting every class within the polis or every household[58] but not necessarily every individual.[59] To resolve this question, we need to consider the account of the best constitution in *Politics*, VII–VIII.

6.6. MODERATE INDIVIDUALISM IN THE BEST CONSTITUTION

The aim of the best constitution

Aristotle begins his study of the best constitution in *Politics*, VII, with two questions: What is the most choiceworthy way of life? and What is the best constitution, which embodies this way of life? (1 1323ᵃ14–16, 2 1324ᵃ13–23).[60] The answer to the first question is that 'the best way of life both separately for each person (*chōris hekastōi*) and in common (*koinēi*) for polises' is 'accompanied by virtue which is equipped to the extent that they can partake of virtuous actions' (1323ᵇ40–1324ᵃ2). This conforms to the principle of perfection: the end is variously called happiness and noble action (1323ᵇ30–1; cf. III 9 1281ᵃ2), living blessedly (2 1324ᵃ24–5), the good life (1325ᵃ9), and 'the actualization and perfect [or complete] employment of virtue' (8 1328ᵃ38, 13 1332ᵃ7–10). Moreover, this way of life is best in two ways: for each individual and for the entire polis. When Aristotle says that happiness is the same for a single human being and for the polis he means that it is the same *in kind*: i.e. the same standard

---

[58] Cooper (1990), 239, notes the reference to households and families at III 9 1280ᵇ33–4: 'The "living well" aimed at in cities is not, anyhow not immediately, the "living well" of the individual citizens residing in it. What is aimed at is rather the living well of the constituent households and village-communities. Individual citizens' lives are affected just insofar as, in one way or another, the good living of the communities to which they individually belong carries with it the individual citizens' living well too.' However, Cooper views this passage as compatible with the view that the good living of a family is the good living of *each* member of the family. It would be a mistake to view this passage as counting against individualism, since Aristotle would be open to the same objection that he himself brings against Plato at II 5 1264ᵇ15–24: the subcommunities are themselves wholes which cannot be happy unless their ultimate parts, viz., individuals, are happy.

[59] Aquinas, *Commentary on the Politics*, 393, interprets the common advantage here as promoting the greatest good of the polis and every citizen (*omnium civium*).

[60] All references in this section are to *Pol*. VII, unless otherwise indicated.

should be used in evaluating whether a single human being or a community of human beings is happy.[61] This does not mean that we need to view the polis as if it were an individual organism in evaluating whether or not it is happy.[62]

The second question, which is the central task for political theory,[63] is answered as follows: 'Now it is evident that the best constitution must be that order under which anyone whatsoever (*hostisoun*) might act in the best way and live blessedly' (2 1324ᵃ23–5). The term 'anyone whatsoever' (*hostisoun*) clearly refers to individual members of the polis. The criterion by which we evaluate a constitution as 'best' is thus whether it enables the members of the polis, considered as individuals, to attain the highest level of activity of which they are capable (cf. 14 1333ᵃ29–30).[64] The scope of 'anyone whatsoever' is not explicitly specified here but it evidently refers to the citizens, since only these are supposed to partake of the end of the polis.[65] This formulation thus supports an individualistic interpretation of the best constitution.

---

[61] The same aim should apply to each (*hekastōi*) human being and the constitution in common (*koinēi*) (2 1324ᵃ32–5; cf. 3 1325ᵇ15–16, 30–2). Similarly, 'there seems to be the same end for human beings both in common (*koinēi*) and privately (*idiai*), and there must be the same standard for the best man and the best constitution' (15 1334ᵃ11–3; cf. III 6 1278ᵇ23–4).

[62] Nussbaum (1988), 155–60, maintains that 1 1323ᵇ33–2 1324ᵃ13 introduces a 'holistic' conception of justice, viz., that a polis is good just in case it has the same structure found in an individual virtuous soul. She sees this as in tension with her own overall interpretation that the best constitution involves a 'distributive conception' of justice. She suggests that this apparent inconsistency may be part of a 'more primitive stage in Aristotle's thinking', due to the lingering influence of Plato's *Republic*. However, this passage does not in fact employ Plato's tripartite structural analogy between the individual soul and the polis, and it is open to the non-holistic interpretation I have suggested. Moreover, the supposedly 'holistic' passage concerns Aristotle's answer to his first question (What is the best life?) and not the second (What is the best constitution?). Hence, there need not be a conflict with an individualistic interpretation of Aristotle's answer to the second question.

[63] Thus 2 1324ᵃ19–20 begins, 'Since this (*touto*) is the function of political thought and theory . . .' The antecedent of 'this' is the second of Aristotle's two questions, viz. 'What constitution is best?', as Lord (1984) correctly translates. However, the Oxford translation in Barnes (1984)—'Since the good of the state and not of the individual is the proper subject of political thought . . .'—gives the misleading impression that Aristotle's point is that politics is concerned with the good of the state and *not* with the good of the individual. Lines 23–5, translated in the main text, show this is not his meaning.

[64] See Nussbaum (1988), 146–50, for an illuminating discussion of this passage, which exhibits what she calls 'the distributive conception': 'This conception urges us to assess political arrangements by looking to the functionings of individuals, taken one by one—as to whether they are enabled by that arrangement to function best.'

[65] See especially *Pol.* VII 8–9 discussed below and cf. III 13 1283ᵇ40–2 (where *kai* is explanatory). See also Newman (1887), i. 119. Nussbaum (1988), 147, contends that *hostisoun* has a broader scope in the light of VII 2 1325ᵃ7–10, which states that the lawgiver should be concerned with the happiness of 'a polis, a class of human beings [*genos anthrōpōn*], and

This sets the stage for the third issue of *Politics*, VII 2–3: Is the most choiceworthy way of life the political and active[66] way of life or is it the philosophical and contemplative way of life which eschews external goods? (1324^a25–9). Aristotle carefully considers the objections raised against each of these candidates: that the political life either involves despotic, coercive, and unjust rule over others, or is an impediment to one's own well-being; and that the philosophical life is inherently inactive and thus cannot be happiness. First, Aristotle sympathetically discusses the political way of life, distinguishing it from the tyrannical, which involves the performance of unjust acts of excessive possession towards one's neighbours. The political way of life involves the recognition that justice applies to the treatment of foreigners as well as to relations within the polis (1324^b1–1325^a5).[67] Moreover, the virtuous acts which make up the political way of life are inherently valuable, for the actions of just and moderate persons contain the perfect realization of many noble things (1325^a32–4).[68] However, he rejects the implication that politicians should strive for as much power as possible, so that they have authority to perform the greatest number of noble actions. Rather, they should observe the moral constraints of natural justice (1325^a34–$^b12$). If this is correct, the political life will conform to the same requirements as the individual moral life, so that 'the best way of life both in common [*koinēi*] for every polis and for the individual [*kath' hekaston*] will be the active way of life' (1325^b15–16).

In defence of the philosophical way of life, Aristotle observes that 'the active way of life is not necessarily relative to other persons, nor are those thoughts active which issue for the sake of their consequences, but much more [active] are the contemplations and thoughts which are ends in themselves and for their own sakes, for acting well, and therefore a kind of action, is the end'. Happiness consists of actions which are intrinsically valuable. Of these contemplation is a cardinal example, although practical

every other community'. However, as Charles (1988), 192, points out, the context of this passage 'shows that Aristotle's concern in these phrases is not with the lot of all individuals inside the lawgiver's community (slaves, workers, etc.) but rather with how he should behave towards neighbouring people in time of war', and these neighbours (presumably the citizens of other polises) constitute 'the classes of men and other communities' considered in 1325^a7–10. Similarly, Newman (1887) understands *genos* as equivalent here to *ethnos*, 'nation'.

[66] *Praktikos*, 'active', has a broader sense here than the sense (translated as 'practical') which is opposed to 'contemplative'. Aristotle will argue that the contemplative life is *praktikos* in this broader sense.

[67] Note the references to justice at 1324^b22–36 and the occurrences of *phusei* (by nature) at 2 1324^b37 and of *para phusin* (contrary to nature) at 3 1325^b10. See also Sect. 3.5 above.

[68] Cf. Newman (1887), iii. 334.

reasoning concerned with external actions is also active in this sense. Similarly, a polis need not be inactive even if it chooses to live in isolation from other polises, since it can be active on account of its parts which have many sorts of community with each other. In this the polis resembles an individual human being and also God and the cosmos, which are able to be in a noble condition even though they perform no external actions beyond those proper to themselves. Hence, Aristotle concludes, the same way of life must be the best for each (*hekastōi*) human being and in common (*koinēi*) for polises and human beings (1325^{b}16–32).

Aristotle's discussion is somewhat inconclusive because he does not explicitly answer the question he has posed as to whether the best life is political or philosophical. The parallel between 1325^{b}15–16 and ^{b}30–2 suggests that the best way of life may include both of them (with contemplative activity having priority).[69] However, it is very clear from this discussion that he holds that the same way of life is best both for each human being individually and for the polis, so that his account of the best way of life is compatible with the moderate-individualist interpretation.

The equipment of the best constitution

Politics, VII 4–7, considers the hypotheses regarding political equipment, i.e. the population and territory which must be present if the best polis is to be established. These should be such as one would pray for, but none of them should be impossible (4 1325^{b}38–9). The discussion presupposes Aristotle's political naturalism: the polis has a natural function or end, but the lawgiver has a necessary role in its fulfilment. Like a craftsman, the lawgiver must have a suitable 'proper material' if his product is to be noble. Such material must be provided by nature or fortune, and it is not available in most cases (see 12 1331^{b}21–2; IV 11 1295^{a}25–31). However, the excellence of the polis is due to the science and choice of the lawgiver (13 1332^{a}28–32).

Aristotle criticizes those who gauge the excellence of a polis by its size alone. Since a polis has a function, the one which is most able to realize its end (*apotelein*) should be regarded as the greatest. Similarly, one would say that Hippocrates is greater, not as a human being but as a doctor, than someone who was superior to him in bodily size. However, in evaluating the population we ought to consider not any chance multitude (including

---

[69] Cf. *Pol.* I 7 1255^{b}35–7; and also VII 14 1333^{a}16–^{b}3 and 15 1334^{a}11–40, which are discussed in Sect. 6.7 below.

slaves, metics, and foreigners) but the citizens who are proper parts of the polis ($1325^b33-1326^a25$). The function of the polis thus provides a teleological standard for evaluating its population and territory. An animal, plant, or tool that is too large or too small will be unable to fulfil its function and thus will fail to realize its nature. For example a ship that is a foot long will not be a ship at all, and a ship that is 1,200 feet long will (in Aristotle's day) be too unwieldy to carry out a voyage. Similarly, a polis that is too small will lack self-sufficiency regarding things necessary for the good life, whereas a polis which is too large cannot maintain a correct constitution or system of laws: 'For the law is a sort of order [*taxis*] and good law [*eunomia*] is necessarily good order [*eutaxia*], but an excessive number [of citizens] is not capable of partaking in order . . . Who will be a general of an excessively enlarged multitude? or who will be a herald unless he is like Stentor [the Homeric hero]?' (1326^a25-^b7; cf. III 3 1276^a27-30).

Aristotle's teleological standard thus defines a population range from the minimum level at which the polis is self-sufficient for the good life of the citizens (1326^b7-9; cf. I 2 1252^b27-30), up to the maximum level at which it is still possible for the polis to enforce justice and respect the rights of the citizens:

The actions of the polis are those of the rulers and the ruled, and the function of the ruler is command and judgement; regarding judgement concerning rights [*tōn dikaiōn*] and regarding the distribution of offices according to merit [*dianemein kat' axian*], the citizens must be knowledgeable of one another's qualities. Where this does not happen, matters involving offices and judgements occur in a base manner. Regarding both of these it is not just to act in an off-hand manner, which obviously occurs in an over-populated polis. (1326^b12-20; cf. Plato, *Laws*, V 738^c2-8)

Thus the requirements of self-sufficiency and of justice define a standard for the maximum size of the best polis: 'the greatest multitude self-sufficient for the good life that is easily within view' (1326^b23-4).[70]

Further, the population must have a specific psychological nature which Aristotle specifies in an argument replete with broad generalizations about different nationalities: the nations of cold locales, including Europe, are filled with spirit (*thumos*) but are deficient in thought and craft, so

---

[70] In *Pol.* VII 5 the standard for the territory is analogously a range: as a minimum, it should be self-sufficient in the sense of lacking nothing that the citizens need to live liberally and moderately in a condition of leisure; as a maximum, it should be no larger than can be easily defended against invaders and hence easily surveyable.

that they demand freedom but are unable to exercise political rights in a rational and co-ordinated manner. The Asian nations in contrast possess thought and craft but are spiritless, so that they remain ruled and enslaved. However, the race of the Greeks is a mean between these two extremes, since it 'is both spirited and intelligent; therefore, it continues to be free and to govern itself in the best way and to be capable of ruling over everyone if there happened to be one constitution.' The citizens of the best polis, whom the lawgiver can guide to a life of virtue, must be endowed by nature with both thought and spirit (7 1327^{b}23–38).[71] Spirit impels one to rule over others and to resist their rule over oneself; hence, it is the psychological basis for ruling and freedom. Aristotle adds that spirit reacts when one perceives that others are acting unjustly and especially when one is done an injustice by a friend (1327^{b}38–1328^{a}16). In summary, the population of the best polis must possess the natural aptitude for self-governance in the polis. They must be able to exercise political rights in a rational manner in co-operation with others and also to be prepared to insist on and defend their rights.

In conclusion, the 'political equipment' of the best constitution is evaluated by two standards: what is needed for the polis to be self-sufficient and what is required for a just constitution.

Citizens and their rights

Politics, VII 8–14, addresses the same issue as *Politics*, III, viz., which inhabitants of the polis have a just claim to be citizens. *Politics*, III, argues that the polis is a community of individuals co-operating for the happy and noble life, and that those who contribute most to this common endeavour have the greatest claim to be full members. *Politics*, VII, approaches this issue by asking which inhabitants truly belong to the polis. Because the polis is a natural whole, it is necessary to distinguish between its proper members (or parts) and those who are present of necessity but do not qualify as proper members (8 1328^{a}21–5; see Section 5.1 above). The members are the citizens, whereas possessions, including

---

[71] This is reminiscent of the theory in Plato, *Rep.* IV 435^{b}9–441^{c}8 that the soul is composed of three parts: reason, spirit, and appetite. *Pol.* VII 7 is filled with echoes and criticism of Plato's psychology. For details see Newman (1887), iii. 363–9. It should be noted that although Aristotle elsewhere rejects Plato's tripartite psychology (*DA* III 9 432^{b}4–7), he recognizes spirit (*thumos*), along with appetite (*epithumia*) and rational wish (*boulēsis*), as one of the three forms of desire (*orexis*) (*DA* II 3 414^{b}2). On the role of spirit in Aristotle's *Politics* generally, see Berns (1984).

slaves, are merely necessary adjuncts.[72] If these citizens also merely performed a necessary function, there would be no fundamental difference between them and the adjuncts. But the polis is not an *organism* whose members are merely instruments for its own higher end; instead it is a *community* whose members partake directly of the end (see 1328ᵃ25–33).[73] Aristotle implies that the best polis is a group of individuals co-operating for *mutual* advantage, when he characterizes it as 'a community of similar persons for the sake of the best possible life' (1328ᵃ35–7). It is implied that all[74] the members of the polis must take part in the good life, since the inhabitants who play a merely functional role in promoting the end without partaking are adjuncts rather than members (cf. IV 4 1291ᵃ24–8).

Members of the polis must, therefore, satisfy two criteria: performing an indispensable function (1328ᵇ4–5) and partaking of the end of the polis. Several groups of inhabitants—viz., those engaged in productive activities: farmers, merchants, artisans, sailors, and menial labourers—satisfy the former criterion but not the latter. This is supported by the following argument (9 1328ᵇ33–1329ᵃ2):

(1) The best polis, which has the best constitution and is most nobly governed, will be most happy (cf. 13 1331ᵇ25–6, 1332ᵃ5–6).

(2) Happiness cannot be separate from virtue and justice (cf. 1 1323ᵇ29–36, 8 1328ᵃ37–8; 13 1332ᵃ9–10; IV 7 1293ᵇ3–5).

(3) Therefore, the citizens ought not to live a way of life that is ignoble or contrary to virtue.

(4) Leisure is necessary for virtue and political activities.

(5) Therefore, the citizens must have leisure (cf. II 9 1269ᵃ34–6).

(6) Farmers do not have leisure (cf. VI 4 1318ᵇ11–12).

(7) The way of life of menial labourers and merchants is ignoble and contrary to leisure (cf. VIII 2 1337ᵇ8–15).

(8) Therefore, the citizens of the best polis cannot be farmers, menial labourers, or merchants, but must be persons with a leisurely way of life suitable for virtue and political activities (cf. III 5 1278ᵃ8–11, 17–20).

The argument so far has been that certain functionally defined groups do not qualify for citizenship in the best constitution because their way of

---

[72] See 8 1328ᵃ33–5 and cf. III 9 1280ᵃ31–4 which denies that a polis can be composed of slaves or beasts because they cannot partake of happiness (cf. *EN* X 6 1177ᵃ8) or choice (cf. *Pol.* I 13 1260ᵃ12; *Phys.* II 6 197ᵇ6–8).

[73] See Sect. 2.4 above. Cf. Kullmann (1991), 110–11.

[74] Lord's translation (1984) of 1328ᵃ25–6 has an 'all' corresponding to nothing in the Greek text, but the context and sequel indicate that 'all' accurately reflects Aristotle's view.

life impedes them from partaking of the happiness which characterizes such a constitution. Aristotle suggests that in the polis of our prayers the non-citizens engaged in productive labour will be slaves, barbarians, or foreign merchants (see VII 10 1330ª25–31).[75] The next stage of the argument relies on a tacit premiss:

[(9)   Soldiers and officials (i.e. those who exercise deliberation and judgement) lead a way of life that is noble and virtuous.]
(10)   Therefore, soldiers and officials qualify for citizenship.

The citizen body will accordingly consist of those individuals who possess the leisure, wealth, and moral character enabling them to serve as soldiers and officials. There is, however, a problem in assigning these functions. On the one hand, each function involves a different excellence: a soldier requires strength, and an office-holder practical wisdom. This presents a problem because those who exercise force will not tolerate being always ruled over, so that the right to bear arms and the right to hold offices cannot be assigned to different classes as in Plato's *Republic*. However, Aristotle observes that the same persons exhibit these excellences at difference primes in their lives: first strength and later practical rationality. 'It remains then to assign the rights of citizenship to both groups' in the following manner:[76]

(11)   A distribution based on merit is just and advantageous (i.e. for the mutual advantage).
(12)   A distribution according to nature is based on merit.
(13)   Therefore, a distribution according to nature is just and advantageous.
(14)   Strength is the criterion of merit for a soldier, and practical wisdom is that for an office-holder.
(15)   It is natural for strength to be found among younger persons, and practical wisdom among older persons (cf. *Rhet.* II 14).

[75] Aristotle's controversial claim that those engaged in productive or commercial occupations are incapable of virtue and happiness is taken up in Sect. 6.9 below.

[76] I read *amphoterois . . . tautēn* at 1329ª13–14 with the manuscripts and Dreizehnter (1970). On 'the rights of citizenship' for *tēn politeian tautēn*, cf. 'these constitutional rights' in Newman (1887), iii. 378. For similar uses of *politeia* see *Ath. Pol.* LIV 3 and Demosthenes, XXIII 89. An alternative reading *amphotera . . . tauta* is offered by Susemihl and Hicks (1894) and Ross (1957), and is translated by Keyt (1991a), 265: 'It remains then for the [best] constitution to assign both of these [occupations] to the same men . . .' The difference in reading does not affect the argument. The following reconstruction of the conclusion of Aristotle's argument is on the whole indebted to Keyt.

(16) Therefore, it is just and advantageous for younger persons to be soldiers, and for older persons to be office-holders.

Steps (11)–(13) are an expansion of 1329^{a}14–17. (11) makes a connection explicitly between distributive justice and universal justice, which aims at the common advantage. Among co-operating individuals it is to their common advantage for tasks to be assigned on the basis of merit, because they are then carried out in the best manner. (12) implies that individuals who are equal or similar in terms of merit or virtue should be regarded as naturally equal. As Aristotle earlier (3 1325^{b}7–10) remarks, treating equals or similar persons in an unequal or dissimilar manner is unnatural (*para phusin*), and 'nothing unnatural is noble'. (12) also implies that a standard based on natural superiority will assign a task to the most meritorious person (cf. 1325^{b}10–12). Hence, it is just to discriminate among the citizens on the basis of age, reserving more important offices for those with more experience.[77]

A holistic interpretation of this argument might try to construe the assignment of citizenship and political rights in merely instrumentalist terms, with premiss (1) positing as the end the happiness of the polis as a whole (overall advantage) and conclusion (16) conferring or denying rights of citizenship on the basis of whether or not a particular group furthers this objective. But this interpretation is excluded by the requirement already noted that the citizens (in contrast to necessary adjuncts) must themselves partake of the common end.

The individualist, mutual-advantage interpretation is confirmed by the argument for universal property rights which follows.[78] This argument may be expanded as follows:

(17) Happiness requires equipment (cf. 1 1323^{b}40–1324^{a}2).
(18) 'A polis should be called happy not by viewing a part of it but by viewing all the citizens' (9 1329^{a}23–4).
(19) Therefore, each citizen ought to have property (cf. 10 1330^{a}15–18).

This argument implies that the citizens of the best polis possess rights which may be ranked in terms of fundamentality. The most basic rights concern the natural ends of the citizens. The principle of universal justice or mutual advantage entails that each citizen has a right to happiness or

---

[77] Not surprisingly, this recommendation reflects the practice of Athens and other polises. See Hansen (1991), 88–90.
[78] The individualist import of this passage is noted by Zeller (1897), ii. 225 n. 1.

moral perfection. From this may be derived political rights and in turn property rights. Property rights may be regarded by Aristotle as less basic than political rights, since they are confined in this argument to office-holders and soldiers (see Section 9.7 below).

Moderate individualism preferable to moderate holism

This individualistic tendency is again evident in *Politics*, VII 13, where Aristotle restates the moral principle that is to guide the lawgiver of the best constitution. First, he reiterates the standard of value: the best constitution is 'that according to which the polis could be most happy' (1332^a4-6), and happiness again is defined as the 'actualization and perfect [or complete] employment of virtue'. Such virtue is not relative to the hypothesis of an inferior constitution (e.g. excellence at acquiring wealth as in an oligarchy, or military virtue as in Sparta) but is without qualifi-cation, i.e. complete virtue as defined in the *Eudemian* and *Nicomachean Ethics*.[79] Second, Aristotle indicates how happiness and virtue are to be realized:

But a polis is excellent due to the fact that the citizens who partake in the constitution are excellent; but in our case all the citizens partake in the constitution. We must therefore enquire as to how a man becomes excellent; for even if all the citizens could be excellent without each of the citizens [being excellent], the latter would be more choiceworthy; for 'all' follows from 'each'. (1332^a32-8)

There are two different principles which could guide the lawgiver:

(1) *All* the citizens (considered collectively) should be excellent.[80]
(2) *Each* citizen considered as an individual (*kath' hekaston*) should be excellent.

(2) is logically stronger than (1), because (2) entails, but is not entailed by, (1). For (1) is compatible with a state of affairs in which the interests of some (or all) citizens are sacrificed in order to advance the happiness of 'the polis as a whole', whereas (2) requires the mutual advantage, i.e. the promotion of the excellence of each and every citizen. It is noteworthy that (2), which Aristotle describes as 'more choiceworthy', rules out not only extreme holism but also, by implication, the more moderate forms of holism which would sacrifice the happiness of some individuals in order

---

[79] The reference to 'the *Ethics*' is probably to *EE* II 1 1219^a38-9, $^b1-2$, although similar points are made at *EN* I 7 1098^a16-18 and 10 1101^a14-16.

[80] Cf. the interpretation of 'all' attributed to Socrates in *Pol.* II 3 1261^b20-32.

to promote the well-being of others, which would promote the well-being of classes or groups rather than of individuals, or which regard it as sufficient if some individuals vicariously bask in the reflected happiness of others or 'merge' themselves in a greater happy collective. None of these meets the stringent requirement that each and every citizen should be excellent. Further, Aristotle's statement that 'in our case all the citizens partake in the constitution', seems meant to rule out a tiered arrangement in which only the top rung of citizens directly and fully share in happiness.[81]

In *Politics*, VII 14, Aristotle employs the principle of natural justice to justify political rule (i.e. the participation of all the citizens in ruling and being ruled) after he dismisses as infeasible its most serious competitor, kingly rule.[82]

[I]t is evident that for many reasons it is necessary that all [the citizens] alike partake in ruling and being ruled in turn. For equality is the same thing for those

---

[81] This also counts against the interpretation of Cooper (1990), 240 n. 22, who argues: 'If under such a constitution "everyone in common" leads the best life, then even someone who is not himself a virtuous person and so not constantly exercising virtues in his daily life is nonetheless in a secondary way leading a virtuous life, by having his life merged in the life of the whole city which itself *is* a virtuous one, by reason (primarily) of the virtues possessed, and exercised in its political and otherwise communal life, by its ruling class.' On Cooper's interpretation, the stronger principle (2) is fully satisfied only for the ruling class, because they alone are able to partake directly of virtue; but the principle is also realized in a secondary way for second-class citizens: '. . . even those who are less well endowed for the excellences of mind and character share in the exercise of the excellences of the better-endowed citizens. In this way all the citizens achieve . . . an active, perfected, self-sufficient life' (240). In written comments, Cooper adds, 'I meant: each and every individual citizen achieves this.' Thus, Cooper's interpretation resembles mine in insisting that the best constitution satisfies (2), but differs in holding that the principle is applied in very different ways to first-class and second-class citizens. Cooper thinks that the two-tier arrangement is necessary to explain how an aristocratic system can promote the good of second-class citizens who do not qualify as rulers. The explanation is that, in addition to having the opportunity to have as good a life as they are severally able to manage, they also partake of genuine excellence in a derivative or second-hand sense, as co-participants in a collective enterprise of which such excellence is one element.

I have two main doubts regarding Cooper's interpretation. First, I see no textual evidence for the interpretation that the citizens partake of a second-hand form of happiness or that justice is served by their doing so. Nor do I see any evidence that political or civic friendship involves this sort of merging of selves or derivative participation in a good. Second, I doubt whether the problem Cooper poses really does arise for *Pol.* VII–VIII, where there is no mention of second-class citizens. In fact, VII 9 and 13 imply that there are only first-class citizens, supported by slaves, serfs, and foreigners. One reason it is the polis 'of our prayers' is that there are enough excellent persons to compose a complete citizen body. As I shall argue in Ch. 7, something akin to Cooper's problem does arise in *so-called* aristocracy, which is a second-best constitution, although I think it has a different sort of solution from Cooper's.

[82] This perfunctory dismissal of the option of absolute kingship leaves unresolved some serious difficulties, which will be examined more fully in Sect. 6.8 below.

who are similar, and it is difficult for a constitution to endure which has been established contrary to justice. (1332^b21-9)

The principle of natural distributive justice thus requires that all members of the polis who are (naturally) similar, have the same political right: viz., the right to take turns in ruling and being ruled.[83]

Aristotle gives no indication in *Politics*, VII, of the specific manner in which political rights are to be distributed among the citizens of the best constitution, other than to mention a few officials: e.g. the market magistrate, urban magistrate, rural magistrate, military officers, and priests (12 1331^b4-18). Instead his concern lies with how the citizens become virtuous and just through the appropriate moral education (see Section 6.7 below). However, the statement that 'in our case all the citizens partake of the constitution' (13 1332^a34-5) implies that the constitution will exemplify modes in which all the citizens participate in deliberation, office, and adjudication. In an aristocratic constitution the entire citizenry would presumably be eligible for office and election would be used to select the most qualified (IV 15 1300^b4-5). It might be objected that election is not foolproof, so that a person could dispute the outcome of an election, claiming that he had the best claim based on nature to the office. However, Aristotle could reply that because the electorate is composed of virtuous and practically wise individuals, election is the most reliable procedure for selecting those who have a right based on nature to hold office. Hence, individuals should abide by elections even when they disagree with the outcome (especially since they tend to be more likely to err in judging their own merits).

Because all the citizens participate in the constitution, an aristocracy resembles democracy. However, the typical office in a democracy is assemblyman or juror, which have indefinite terms and wide-ranging authority. In a true aristocracy, in contrast, a much smaller body of citizens could be expected to hold more exalted magistracies with limited terms and sharply defined authority. When Aristotle says that all the citizens partake of his constitutions, he can be understood to mean that all of them are eligible to hold special elective offices and that each of them will spend fairly equal amounts of time holding such offices over the course of a lifetime.

---

[83] Cf. Newman (1887), iii. 435, who understands *to te gar ison t'auton tois homoiois*, 'for the equal is the same thing for similar persons', to assert: 'equality demands that each shall have the same share (i.e. an identity of political privilege).' See also Bradley (1991), 41: 'In virtue of the equality of the citizens [justice] demands that *all* share in civil rights.'

6.7. THE AIMS OF EDUCATION

Perfectionist standard of education

The aim of the best constitution is the happiness of each and every citizen (VII 2 1324ᵃ23–5, 9 1329ᵃ23–4), and happiness is an activity essentially involving ethical virtue and practical wisdom (1 1323ᵇ21–3; 8 1328ᵃ37–8; 9 1328ᵇ35–6, 1329ᵃ22–3; 13 1332ᵃ21–5; the latter referring to *EE* II 7 1219ᵃ38–9, ᵇ1–2; cf. *EN* I 10 1101ᵃ14–16). Therefore, the lawgiver of the best constitution must bring it about that every citizen is excellent or good (VII 13 1332ᵃ28–38; cf. *EN* I 13 1102ᵃ7–10, II 1 1103ᵇ3–6). The lawgiver must, therefore, be concerned with education (*paideia*), a process in which the younger are ruled for their own sakes, i.e. so that they may become virtuous and rulers themselves (VII 14 1332ᵇ41–1333ᵃ11; cf. Plato, *Laws*, I 643ᵉ3–6). This topic dominates the rest of Aristotle's discussion of the best constitution (from *Politics*, VII 14, to the end of Book VIII):

> Since we say that the citizen and the ruler [of the best constitution] have the same virtue as the good man, and the same person ought to be ruled over first and to rule later, the lawgiver should be concerned with how men become good and by what practices they do so and with what is the end of the good life. (VII 14 1333ᵃ11–16)

The discussion of education begins with some normative psychology (1333ᵃ16–30). First, Aristotle distinguishes parts or faculties of the soul: the rational faculty and the desiring faculty, which is able to obey reason. The rational faculty is further divided into contemplative and practical (i.e. calculative) reason. He alludes to the virtues belonging to these parts: contemplative wisdom (*sophia*), the virtue of contemplative reason; practical wisdom (*phronēsis*), that of practical reason; and ethical virtue, that of the part obeying reason.[84] He then claims that there is a natural hierarchy[85] among the parts or faculties of the soul, from better to worse:

CONTEMPLATIVE REASON > PRACTICAL REASON > RATIONAL DESIRE.

An item that is lower down on the hierarchy is teleologically subordinate to an item higher up: 'the worse is always for the sake of the better.' This yields a hierarchy of actions based on the following principle: if P_1 is a

---

[84] See Sect. 1.2 above regarding these distinctions.

[85] The alleged hierarchy is, of course, very controversial. *EN* X 7 argues for the superiority of contemplation. The superiority of practical reason over desire is due to the ubiquitous principle of rulership (*Pol.* I 2 1252ᵃ31–4, 5 1254ᵇ6–9).

naturally better part of the soul than is P_2, then any activity A_1 of part P_1 is higher than any activity A_2 of part P_2. This yields in turn a normative ranking of actions based on the principle of perfection: 'What is most choiceworthy for each individual is always the highest [activity] it is possible for him to attain' (1333^a29–30). If an individual has all three parts or faculties, his activities are ranked in terms of choiceworthiness as follows:

CONTEMPLATION > PRACTICAL REASONING > ETHICALLY VIRTUOUS ACTS.

However, if an individual has only the lower two parts,[86] his activities are ranked as follows:

PRACTICAL REASONING > ETHICALLY VIRTUOUS ACTS.

The next passage (1333^a30–$^b5$) examines the implications of this for the lawgiver. The citizens' way of life can be divided into two sorts of activities, characterized by leisure (*scholē*) or absence of leisure (*ascholia*, also translated as 'work' or 'occupation'). This is illustrated by the contrast between peace and war, and between action with noble objects and the pursuit of necessary or useful things. It is presupposed that higher activities of the soul are characterized by leisure, lower activities by absence of leisure (cf. *EN* X 7 1177^b4–26). Aristotle invokes the principle of perfection: 'the politician must legislate looking to all these things regarding the parts of the soul and its activities, but more so to those which are better and ends' (*Pol.* VII 14 1333^a37–9). Using Aristotle's normative psychology as a guide, therefore, the lawgiver should observe the following precepts in educating the citizens: the citizens ought to be able to make war but it is better for them to remain at peace; they ought to be able to be occupied or busy (*ascholein*), but it is better for them to be at leisure; and they ought to do necessary and useful things, but noble acts are better.

The highest aim of the lawgiver and the educator is to promote those actions which involve leisure, peace, and nobility. Leisure is understood as intrinsically valuable activity, and its opposite, absence of leisure, as 'for the sake of something not present' and 'not chosen for itself' (VIII 3 1338^a1–6; cf. *EN* X 7 1177^b16–26). The goal of the lawgiver is thus to promote activities of the citizens which are ends in themselves existing for their own sakes (cf. *Pol.* VII 3 1325^b20).

---

[86] At 1333^a29 *ē pasōn ē toin duoin* seems to cover two possibilities: that the individuals are able to use all three parts or only two, viz., the lower two parts.

Politics, VII 15, proceeds from principles defended earlier: human beings have the same end as individuals and in common, and the same standard applies to the best man and the best constitution. Therefore, the virtues concerned with leisure must be present in the best polis (1334ª13–14; cf. 34–6). The following passage (1334ª16–25) distinguishes three types of virtues which are useful in relation to leisure and pastime:[87] non-leisurely virtues (e.g. courage and fortitude), purely leisurely virtues (e.g. philosophy), and partially leisurely virtues (e.g. temperance and justice).[88] Non-leisurely virtues are exercised only in order to promote peace and the things necessary for a life of leisure and happiness.[89] On the need for the purely or partially leisurely virtues:

For war compels persons to be just and moderate, but good fortune and the state of leisure that accompanies peace tends to make them insolent. Therefore, those who are believed to do the best things and to enjoy every blessed thing (such as those, if there are such, in the Isles of the Blessed, as the poets say) need much justice and much moderation; for these will especially need philosophy, temperance, and justice, in so far as they are at leisure in an abundance of good things. (1334ª25–34)[90]

Aristotle infers that the best polis requires the cultivation of the (purely and partially) leisurely virtues:

Therefore, it is evident that the polis which is to be happy and excellent must partake in these virtues. For if it is disgraceful to be unable to use good things, it is still more [disgraceful] if one is not able to use them in a state of leisure, but one appears good while one is busy or at war but servile while one is at peace or at leisure. (1334ª34–40)

---

[87] 'Leisure' and 'pastime' translate, respectively, *scholē* and *diagōgē*. *Scholē* implies freedom from necessity in some significant area of one's life: Irwin (1985c), 414, notes that 'one need not devote all or most of his time and energy to securing the means to staying alive and satisfying his most immediate and basic desires'. However, *scholē* denotes not the cessation of all activity, but on the contrary a state in which one is doing something pleasurable and inherently satisfying (cf. VIII 3 1337ᵇ34–5). Newman (1887), iii. 449, remarks that *diagōgē* similarly refers to 'the use of leisure in occupations desirable for their own sake'.

[88] This differs from the distinction in *EN* X 7 1177ᵇ16–24 between non-leisurely and leisurely virtues because it introduces a third category of mixed virtues not relevant to the *EN* argument.

[89] Cf. *EN* X 7 1177ᵇ4–18. However, Aristotle elsewhere speaks of courage as also intrinsically valuable in that it has the noble as its end (see e.g. *EN* III 7 1115ᵇ11–13, 21–2; *EE* III 1 1229ª4, 1230ª29, 32; cf. VIII 3 1248ᵇ16–37). This suggests that the point in *Pol.* VII 15 is that although virtuous persons will perform courageous acts and view them as noble and intrinsically valuable, they will not go out of their way to perform such acts when they are not necessary to defend themselves, their friends, or the polis.

[90] Again, unlike *EN* X 7, *Pol.* VII 15 here distinguishes two tiers of ethical virtue.

Philosophy, the one purely leisurely virtue mentioned here, is clearly an intellectual virtue; whether it refers to, or at any rate includes, contemplative wisdom of the sort defended in *Nicomachean Ethics*, X 7, is a matter of controversy.[91] At any rate, this virtue enables the citizen to use his leisure to achieve 'the highest it is possible for him to attain' (14 1333^{a}30). The leisurely virtues enable individuals to achieve their own perfection rather than merely to serve as instruments.

Aristotle next turns to the factors contributing to moral education: viz., nature, habit, and reason (15 1334^{b}6–9; cf. 13 1332^{a}38–^{b}11 and *EN* X 9 1179^{b}20–1). These factors ought to be consonant with each other, so as to promote the natural ends of the persons who are being educated.[92] The highest human end is rationality: 'reason [*logos*] and intellect [*nous*] are the end of our nature, so that in relation to these things one ought to provide for birth and the training of habits' (1334^{b}14–17).[93] Aristotle again identifies a natural hierarchy of ends: the body is prior in generation to the soul and, within the soul, the desiring faculty is prior in generation to the rational faculty. The elements prior in generation are for the sake of those which are prior in perfection. Education ought to follow this natural hierarchy: 'Therefore, the care of the body is necessarily prior [in generation] to that of the soul, and next [occurs] that of desire; but [the care of] desire is for the sake of the intellect, and that of the body is for the sake of the soul' (1334^{b}25–8). The stages of education may be distinguished by reference to natural human development: 'one ought to follow the distinction of nature, for all craft and education wish to provide what is lacking in nature' (17 1337^{a}1–3).

Aristotle's discussion of child-bearing customs and early child-rearing practices follows these naturalistic guidelines. The aim is, first, that the bodies of the citizens are the best possible (16 1334^{b}29–30). Lawgivers and parents themselves are enjoined to study the findings of doctors and natural scientists concerning reproduction in order to produce the healthiest

---

[91] On intellectual virtue cf. Newman (1887), iii. 450. Solmsen (1964), 24–7, holds that 'philosophy' has a broad, popular sense encompassing a range of leisurely activities such as music and poetry. Cf. Lord (1982), 198–201. In contrast, Depew (1991), 348–61, 374, argues persuasively that Aristotle retains his attachment to the contemplative ideal in *Pol.* VII–VIII and intends for the best polis to accommodate this ideal (noting the parallel with divine contemplation at VII 3 1325^{b}16–30).

[92] Aristotle remarks at *EN* X 9 1179^{b}23–6, 'Reason [or argument] and teaching are not strong with everyone, but the soul of the pupil ought to have been cultivated through habits for enjoying and hating nobly, like earth that is going to nourish seed.'

[93] 'Nature' (*phusis*) is used here in the sense of a natural end. 'Naturally' (*pephuken*) at 1334^{b}24–5 also has this sense, which is compatible with habituation and instruction. See Sect. 2.3 above.

progeny. To this end Aristotle advocates regulations concerning the ages of parents, the conduct of pregnant mothers, and the numbers of children. Although these policies are authoritarian and paternalistic, severely limiting the discretion of individuals over their procreative practices, they are aimed at the proper development and perfection of the individual citizens. For example, although he advocates a law requiring the exposure of deformed infants, he evidently does not countenance the exposure of healthy infants in order to meet population limits.[94] There should be customs prescribing the number of children, but if any parents have offspring beyond the prescribed limits 'abortion ought to be induced before perception and life occur; for what is pious and impious will be defined with respect to perception and life' (1335^b19–26). The religious notion of the pious or holy (*to hosion*) is here analysed in terms of the natural. This is consistent with the general tendency in Aristotle's theory of natural justice to transform transcendent, religious notions into naturalistic, biologically based conceptions (see Section 3.3 above). It is significant here that Aristotle rejects infanticide and abortion of developed foetuses as methods of population control, and that his stated reason is that a human being possessing perception and life ought not to be killed. This implies that the lawgiver is concerned with the life of each individual.[95] In contrast, a holistic view would sanction the sacrifice of the individual in order to promote the overall advantage of the polis.

Aristotle's case for public education

The final lines of *Politics*, VII (17 1337^a3–7), pose three problems: (i) Should the lawgiver create some order (i.e. some set of laws or customs) concerned with children? (ii) Should the care of children be public or

---

[94] The text is disputed. The π^2 manuscripts have *ean*, 'if', with the subjunctive mood at 1335^b21–2, whereas the π^1 manuscripts have the indicative mood without *ean*. Newman (1887) and Dreizehnter (1970) follow the former; Ross (1957) the latter (also Immisch (1929) with an emendation). Barnes's revised Oxford translation (1984) follows π^2: 'if the established customs of the state forbid the exposure of any children who are born.' A translation based on π^1 would drop the 'if'. Although Newman accepts *ean*, he takes *mēthen apotithesthai* at $^b22$ to be parallel to *trephein* at $^b21$, so that on his view Aristotle does intend to prohibit the exposure of children for the purpose of population control; further, Newman places a comma after *kōluēi* at $^b22$, understanding by the *ean* clause, 'if the established customs forbid [an excessive number]'. Despite the textual uncertainty noted here, the fact that Aristotle goes on to condemn abortions of developed foetuses is evidence that he would also condemn the exposure of healthy infants.

[95] Assuming of course that the individual is a perfectible human being. Deformed human beings, like natural slaves, are largely beyond the pale of Aristotelian justice.

private? (the latter being the practice in most polises in Aristotle's day), and (iii) What sort of care should this be? Questions (i) and (ii) are taken up and answered in the brief chapter VIII 1, and the remainder of Book VIII (which breaks off at 7 1342^{b}34) pursues (iii).

Politics, VIII 1, answers (i) in the affirmative on the basis of two arguments. First (1337^{a}11–18), it is the function of the lawgiver to establish and safeguard the best constitution, the best (moral) character is the cause of the best constitution, and excellence of character is produced through education.[96] Second (1337^{a}18–21), just as education and habituation are needed to produce all capacities and crafts generally, they are also needed to produce virtuous actions, and it is the aim of the lawgiver to promote virtue.[97] Both of these arguments that the lawgiver ought to be concerned with education are neutral in regard to the individualism–holism issue. However, Aristotle's discussion of question (ii) concerning public versus private education is often cited in support of a holistic interpretation,[98] so it is necessary to examine it closely.

Two arguments are advanced for a public system of education over a private system in which individuals care for their own offspring privately and give them the private learning which they think is best. First (1337^{a}21–7), the polis has one end, and there ought to be common training for common things. Second (1337^{a}27–32) is the following argument:

(1)   Each citizen is a [natural] part of the polis.
(2)   Therefore, a citizen does not belong to himself, but all citizens belong to the polis.
(3)   Therefore, the care of each citizen naturally aims at the care of the polis as a whole.

Aristotle concludes by praising the Spartans for providing common or public education for their children. The Spartan system of *agōgē* or public training is described by Plutarch (*Lives*, Lycurgus, 14–25). Aristotle here follows Plato's endorsement of public education (cf. *Pol.* II 5 1263^{b}36–40 and 6 1265^{a}6–7, which refer to the *Republic* and *Laws*). Aristotle's *Politics* does not mention that the Athenians also instituted the *ephēbeia* to provide

---

[96] The claim that excellence of character (*ēthos*) is produced through education or habituation is a recurring theme: see *EN* II 1 1103^{a}23–6, 3 1104^{b}11–13; IV 1 1121^{a}23; X 9 1180^{a}1–4, 14–15; *EE* I 1 1214^{a}9–20; II 2 1220^{a}39–^{b}2; *Pol.* II 5 1263^{b}36–40; III 4 1277^{a}16–20, 13 1283^{a}24–6, 18 1288^{a}41–^{b}2; see also Sect. 2.5 above.

[97] Cf. *EN* II 2 1103^{b}3–6; X 9 1180^{a}5–24; *Pol.* II 6 1266^{b}29–38; III 9 1310^{a}12–25; VII 14 1333^{a}37–^{b}5.

[98] Susemihl and Hicks (1894), 370, see this passage as endorsing the sacrifice of the individual to the state. See also Barnes (1990a), 262, and Barker (1906), 280.

military training for all youths in the fourth century BC (but cf. *Ath. Pol.* XLII 2–5).

Aristotle's argument echoes the claim that the polis is prior to the individual (cf. I 2 1253ᵃ18–20). Inference (2) also invites comparison with the claim made on behalf of natural slavery that 'a part is not merely a part of another, but belongs wholly to another' (I 4 1254ᵃ9–10). Are we to infer from this that the individual stands to the polis in the way that a slave stands to its master, i.e. that the citizen is the property of the polis? This would support an extreme-holist interpretation, since despotic rule is exercised for the advantage of the master primarily and for that of the slave accidentally.[99] This can hardly be Aristotle's meaning, in view of his sharp distinction between despotic rule and political rule which is for the sake of the ruled (III 6 1278ᵇ32–1279ᵃ16).

Although Aristotle views the natural whole as prior to its parts, he distinguishes between two quite different sorts of natural wholes: an organism versus a community (see Sections 2.4 and 6.6 above). In an *organism* the part is a mere tool or instrument performing a function subordinate to the higher end of the whole, but in a *community* the part is a *member* partaking directly in the end of the whole. The latter relation is compatible with moderate individualism, according to which the final end of the whole polis includes the flourishing of all its individual members.[100] The force of his conclusion (3), on such an interpretation, is that because the citizens are by nature political animals their proper care is necessarily interconnected. It is in this sense that the care of each aims at the care of all. They cannot be nurtured or educated in isolation from each other, but instead need a system in which all the citizens are educated together.[101] Hence, parents should not be at liberty to educate their children as they wish. Instead, they must defer to the law and custom concerning the public education of their children (cf. Plato, *Laws*, VII 804ᵈ3–6).

The concluding chapter of the *Nicomachean Ethics* contains another argument that moral education ought to be public rather than private,

---

[99] Cf. Barnes (1990*a*), 262–3.

[100] Cf. Verbecke (1990) 77: according to Aristotle 'a republic does not possess an end in itself distinct from that of its individual members: it is established for the benefit of its members; individuals do not exist as a means for the development of the state. . . . there is no worship of the state as a subsistent entity. The state is important because the full development of individuals depends upon it.'

[101] A similar interpretation may be given of *Pol.* I 13 1260ᵇ8–20 which says that 'the virtue of the part must look to the virtue of the whole'. This does not require that the end is prior in a holistic sense, but only that the constitution defines a universal standard of virtue for the citizens. Cf. Mayhew (forthcoming).

which rests on two main claims (X 9 1180ᵃ14–24). First, someone who is going to be good must be nobly reared and habituated and then live in reasonable practices, and this will happen if intellect and correct order (*taxis*) have strength or force over his way of life. Second, the order or command of a parent or of any individual generally (except for a king) does not have the strength or compulsory force to yield this result, but the law does have compulsory force (*anagkastikēn dunamin*) while it is also reason proceeding from a sort of practical rationality and intellect. Aristotle here, as in the *Politics*, praises the Spartan lawgiver for attending to the rearing and training of children, remarking that 'in most other polises these things are neglected, each person lives as he wishes, laying down ordinances for his children and wife like the Cyclopes' (1180ᵃ24–9, quoting Homer, *Odyssey*, IX 114; cf. Plato, *Laws*, II 660ᵈ1–3, III 680ᵇ5–ᶜ1).

This argument presupposes two controversial Aristotelian doctrines: the principle of community, according to which the perfection of individuals requires their subordination to the political community; and the principle of rulership, according to which order must be imposed on the community by individuals possessing authority. Although these two doctrines may be antithetical to modern liberal theories, Aristotle's argument does not support a holistic doctrine which licences the sacrifice of individual interests for the overall good.

It is noteworthy, however, that Aristotle goes on in *Nicomachean Ethics*, X 9 1180ᵃ30–ᵇ28, to remark that if (as generally happens) the community does not provide public education, it would seem proper for individuals to contribute to the virtue of their children and friends. Indeed, Aristotle adds,

Education for the individual is even superior to common education, just as in the case of medicine; for although in general rest and fasting are advantageous for a person with fever, they are perhaps not for a particular person; and a boxer perhaps does not prescribe the same method of fighting for all his students. It would seem that the treatment for the individual is worked out with greater precision if there is private [or special] care; for the individual more likely obtains suitable treatment. (1180ᵇ7–13)

The concession that private education is superior to public comes as something of a surprise. For Aristotle implies that what is most important for educators (as for gymnastics instructors or a doctor) is that they possess a universal science and know what is good for all the individuals of the relevant kind, for every expert in a craft or theoretical science must know the universal as far as possible. In the case of education this will be the legislative science (1180^b13-28). None the less, this discussion underscores Aristotle's concern with the education of the individual citizen. His considered view seems to be that the individual citizens will be best educated if there is a public system of education, although attention should be paid to the individual characteristics of students. The second-best solution will rely on private education of children and friends by private individuals who have acquired the legislative science.

The moderate-individualist interpretation receives support from the fact that the leisurely virtues are assigned a higher value than the non-leisurely instrumental virtues in the best educational system. *Politics*, VIII 3, proceeds from the assumption that traditional Greek education with its curriculum of gymnastics, letters (i.e. reading and writing), drawing, and music is in accord with nature. It also assumes that the traditional curriculum has an order (*taxis*)[102] fashioned by ancient founders. Although gymnastics, letters, and drawing have obvious utilitarian value, there is a question about music. Most of Aristotle's contemporaries value music solely for the pleasure it yields, but the founders of education included music along with the other subjects on the grounds that nature aims not only at correct non-leisurely activity but also at noble leisurely activity, and the latter is more choiceworthy and is the end ($3 \ 1337^b30-5$).

Aristotle endorses this traditional view of the order of education, arguing that education should include preparation for a life of leisurely pursuits: 'these types of learning ought to be for their own sake, whereas those types of learning with a non-leisurely aim are necessary and for the sake of other things' (1338^a9-13). Each of the components of the traditional curriculum thus has a teleological explanation: the function of gymnastics is to contribute to health, strength, and, ultimately, courage (1337^b26-7, 1338^a19-20); of letters to facilitate property acquisition, household management, learning, and many political activities (1338^a15-17); and of drawing, to serve various purposes, e.g. enabling one to judge better the works of artisans for purposes of buying and selling (1338^a17-19, $1338^a41-{}^b1$). Music, however, serves none of these necessary or useful functions. It is noteworthy that music was not included for its contribution to political activity. Rather, the ancient founders of education included music because they believed that it belonged to the leisurely pastime of free persons, a view shared by Homer. 'It is evident, therefore, that there is a sort of education in which the sons [of citizens] should be educated, not because it is useful or necessary but because it is liberal [*eleutherion*] and noble'

---

[102] Note the uses of the verb *tattein* at 1337^b29, 1338^a14, $23-4$.

(1338^a21-32). This is most clear in the case of music, but other parts of the curriculum can serve a higher end. For example, drawing can also make one capable of contemplating the beauty of bodies (1338^b1-2). Aristotle is thus an exponent of liberal education, which aims at knowledge for its own sake rather than for its utility (or practical usefulness).

Aristotle disagrees, however, with those who would regard the end of music as merely play (*paidia*), i.e. relaxation, amusement, or diversion. For music has a more honourable nature than this, owing to its contribution to moral character and virtue (5 $1339^b42-1340^a6$; cf. 1339^a21-6).[103] Music on his view involves a type of imitation of moral characters through rhythms and melodies which leads one to experience certain passions. Music is thus able to contribute to the formation of ethical virtue and practical wisdom:

Since music happens to belong among the pleasant things, and virtue is concerned with enjoying correctly and loving and hating correctly, it is clear that one ought to learn and be habituated to nothing more than to judge correctly and enjoy reasonable characters and noble actions; and in rhythms and melodies there are likenesses closest to the true natures of anger and gentleness, and further of courage and temperance and of all their opposites and of the other states of character . . . (1340^a14-21)

Thus music contributes to the formation of political virtue which enables individuals to participate in the polis as first-class citizens ($1340^b40-1341^a3$). In sum, Aristotle assigns three functions to music: the moral education of the citizens, play or amusement, and pastime or leisurely pursuits (1339^b13-15). These are distinct but compatible functions, each of which contributes to the perfection and happiness of the citizens as individuals.

6.8. THE PARADOX OF KINGSHIP

The distribution of political rights poses a problem for Aristotle because the best constitution must satisfy two requirements: first, it must aim at the common advantage in the sense that it promotes the best life for each member of the polis; and, second, it assigns authority according to a

---

[103] For an illuminating discussion see Lord (1982), ch. 2. However, Lord (76–7) argues that Aristotle criticizes the ancient founders of education for reducing music to enjoyable play and neglecting its role in ethical habituation. Depew (1991), 367–8, plausibly disagrees with this part of Lord's interpretation. Depew is also correct to point out that music for Aristotle has distinct but compatible functions, including leisurely activity.

merit-based, aristocratic theory of distributive justice. The best constitution of *Politics*, VII–VIII, meets both requirements because all the citizens participate in ruling and moral virtue is identified with political virtue in the best constitution (see Sections 6.6–7 above). However, it seems that the common advantage and merit-based justice can pull in different directions, as in the case of absolute kingship.[104] Aristotle seemingly accepts the following three propositions:

(1) In the best constitution political virtue is the same as ethical virtue.

(2) A polis in which every citizen exercises ethical virtue is better than one in which only a single person exercises it.

(3) In a kingship only one person exercises political virtue.

But these three propositions entail the conclusion:

(4) Kingship is not the best constitution.

However, Aristotle seems not to agree that kingship can be dismissed so summarily.[105] On the contrary, *Politics*, III, holds that the best constitution may be a kingship. Provided that one person (or a few) is incomparably superior to all the rest in virtue, he has a natural right to rule over them (III 13 1284^{a}3–8, and 17 1288^{a}26–9; see Section 4.6 above). Kingship is even called 'the first and most divine' constitution (IV 2 1289^{a}40). This seems to lead to some bizarre consequences, for example, the king 'can no longer be held to be a part of the polis', implying either that he is outside it or, perhaps, identical with the whole of the polis (III 13 1284^{a}8, 17 1288^{a}26–8).[106] Either an absolute king will be the only citizen, or else the best constitution will contain no citizens in Aristotle's sense (but only second-class citizens ruled by a benevolent despot). Curiously, however, Aristotle does not recognize the paradoxical place of kingship in his theory. He sees no inconsistency when (1)–(3) are conjoined with the denial of (4). Book III concludes that, because (among other things) the virtue of a good man is necessarily the same as the virtue of the citizen of

---

[104] Kingship and true aristocracy represent opposed patterns of distributed political rights. Kingship is the extreme case of pattern 2, by which authority is confined to some citizens. True aristocracy is an ideal case of pattern 1, by which authority is distributed to every member of a small virtuous citizen body. So-called aristocracies seek to 'mix' in virtue with other standards by means of pattern 3 (see Sects. 5.3–5 above).

[105] Kahn (1990), 380–1, mentions this difficulty, and thinks it leads Aristotle to prefer an ideal form of polity over kingship. However, Aristotle gives no indication of offering this as an objection against kingship.

[106] Cf. Newman (1887), i. 230, Barker (1906), 336, Nichols (1992), 74–5, and Yack (1993), 85–7, for the problems posed by kingship.

the best polis, 'it is evident that in the same manner and because of the same things a man becomes excellent and one might establish a polis governed in an aristocratic or kingly way, so that the education and habits that make a man excellent are nearly the same as those that make him a political and kingly [man]' (18 1288ᵃ32–ᵇ2). Here Aristotle discerns no conflict between the identity of human virtue with political virtue and the constitution of kingship.

The paradox of kingship seems unavoidable if one adopts a particular interpretation of Aristotelian perfectionism: viz., that the human good requires political participation as an essential component, where 'political participation' refers to the exercise of political rule (cf. VII 2 1324ᵃ39–ᵇ1). Some commentators do maintain that this is Aristotle's view.[107] However, there are two other interpretations according to which the best way of life in the *Politics* does not essentially involve political participation. The first of these interpretations[108] assumes strict intellectualism: the best life consists solely in contemplation or philosophical activity. Aristotle rejects the political life in favour of the purely philosophical life: the aim of the best constitution would be to promote a contemplative life, and political activity is regarded as an impediment to such a life, because, among other things, it entails the absence of leisure (cf. *EN* X 7 1177ᵇ4–18). Absolute kingship is the best constitution precisely because the king relieves the citizens of the onerous task of ruling themselves so that they can devote themselves to a life of leisure and philosophy. Unfortunately, however, there are no candidates for absolute king, so that the citizens are obliged to rule themselves by turns (14 1332ᵇ23–7; cf. V 10 1313ᵃ3–5). Presumably, this is because the job description of absolute king requires unattainable qualifications: the king must be like a god among human beings (III 13 1284ᵃ10–11), because he is self-sufficient (*EN* VIII 10 1160ᵇ2–6) and thus resembles a god rather than a normal human being (cf. *Pol.* I 2 1253ᵃ27–9).

This strict-intellectualist interpretation has affinities with the strict-intellectualist interpretation of happiness in the *Nicomachean Ethics*. The latter holds that happiness in the *Ethics* consists exclusively of contemplative activity, and the life of moral virtue and political activity is only a second-best or inferior grade of happiness.[109] In support of a strict-intellectualist

---

[107] e.g. Irwin (1988), sect. 219; (1990), 78–9, and Adkins (1991), 90.

[108] See Vander Waerdt (1985) and Lord (1982), 196–202.

[109] See e.g. *EN* X 7 1178ᵃ4–8 1178ᵃ10. On the distinction between strict and moderate intellectualism see Sects. 4.7 above and 10.3 below. Depew (1991), 360–1, has an illuminating discussion of the relation between the intellectualist interpretations of the *Politics* and Aristotle's ethical works.

interpretation of *Politics*, VII–VIII, it may be noted that the term 'philosophy' is used at VII 15 1334ᵃ23, 32, for the highest aim of the best constitution. However, there may be a gap between this use of 'philosophy' and the use of the term for contemplative activity at *EN* X 7 1177ᵃ25.[110] *Politics*, VII–VIII, does not explicitly say that the citizens are to be prepared for a life devoted to first philosophy, natural science, and mathematics. Here 'philosophy' seems intended more broadly to include the leisurely enjoyment of music, poetry, and the arts (see VIII 7 1341ᵇ28, 33; 1342ᵃ31–2). Further, VII 14 1333ᵃ27–30 may even concede that not all citizens of the best constitution are capable of contemplation in the narrow sense.[111] Hence, on this interpretation the aim of the best constitution is leisurely enjoyment of culture which can include (but does not necessarily include) contemplation in the narrower sense.

Even thus qualified, however, the strict-intellectualist interpretation is vulnerable to objections similar to those levelled against the strict-intellectualistic interpretation of *Nicomachean Ethics*, X. As indicated in Section 4.7 above, Aristotle's view in the latter is more plausibly characterized as moderate intellectualism, which accords priority to contemplation without denying a place to ethical virtue in the best life. That the arguments of *Politics*, VII, require an analogous, moderate-intellectualist interpretation (keeping in view that 'philosophy' has a wider and less technical sense here) is evident from the previous section. For the good life promoted by the lawgiver involves both 'philosophy', a virtue solely concerned with leisure, together with the moral virtues of moderation and justice, which are concerned with leisure as well as with non-leisurely activities.[112]

There is, however, a second, more defensible solution[113] to the paradox of kingship, which is compatible with an 'inclusive-end' interpretation of the human good such as moderate intellectualism. This solution requires a distinction between ethical virtue and political participation. Such a distinction conflicts with the interpretation that for Aristotle 'the idea of complete *aretē* [virtue] is inseparable from that of defending the polis and

---

[110] Note that *Pol.* VII 1 1323ᵃ22–3, refers to 'exoteric' works on the best way of life, which evidently does not mean the *EN* or *EE*. See Newman (1887), iii. 308–9; cf. i. 299; Solmsen (1964), 25–7; Lord (1982), 199–200; Vander Waerdt (1985), 257–8; and Depew (1991), 371–2.

[111] The passage has this implication if *tois dunamenois* in l. 28 refers narrowly to citizens of the best polis rather than to human beings more generally, although this is not certain from the context. See Solmsen (1964), 25–7.

[112] See Depew (1991), 356, and Irwin (1990), 80–1.

[113] See Mulgan (1990), 207–8.

exercising political power in it'.[114] It is true that the paradigmatic exercises
of the practical virtues are political and military activities (see *EN* X 7
1177[b]6). None the less, it is possible to distinguish between two different
claims:

(1) Individuals can practise political virtue only if they practise ethical
virtue.

(2) Individuals can practise ethical virtue only if they practise political
virtue.

The passages which are cited[115] in this connection in fact support only (1),
e.g. 'the ruler must have complete ethical virtue' (I 13 1260[a]17–18); 'the
excellent ruler is good and practically wise' (III 4 1277[a]14–15); 'practical
wisdom is the only virtue peculiar to a ruler' (1277[b]25–6); 'the education
and the habits that make a man excellent are nearly the same as those that
make him a political or kingly [man]' (18 1288[b]1–2);[116] 'only in [aristocracy]
are the good man and citizen the same without qualification' (IV 7 1293[b]5–
7); 'no group partakes of the [best] polis which is not a craftsman of
virtue' (VII 9 1329[a]20–1); 'a citizen and ruler have the same virtue as
the good man' (14 1333[a]11–12). These texts do support claim (1), which
is necessary to support Aristotle's general argument for a virtue-based
assignment of political rights. Also, because political participation is an
exercise of moral virtue in the best polis, political activity is not an
impediment to the best life. But these passages do not entail claim (2).
They do not rule out the possibility that some individuals may possess
complete ethical virtue even if they do not have the opportunity to participate in political rule. Aristotle implies such a possibility:

Self-sufficiency and action do not depend on excess and one can do noble acts
without ruling earth and sea; for even with moderate assets one can act according
to virtue (this is plain to see, for private persons are thought to do worthy acts no
less than those with great power—indeed, even more) and it is enough if [moderate
assets] are present; for the way of life of the person who is active in accordance
with virtue will be happy. (*EN* X 8 1179[a]3–9)

This passage contrasts a private person (*idiōtēs*) with a person holding
great political power (*dunastēs*) (cf. *Pol.* V 8 1308[a]23). Those who lead private lives are also contrasted with those who engage in political actions

---

[114] Adkins (1991), 90.
[115] See Vander Waerdt (1985), 215; Kahn (1990), 380; and Irwin (1988), 410.
[116] Lord's (1984) translation of *schedon* as 'essentially' (rather than 'nearly') might mislead
one into taking this as an essential identity.

at II 12 1273^{b}27–9. The above passage thus implies that it is possible for a person to lead a happy virtuous life even if there is no occasion for political activity.[117] If so, Aristotle can consistently admit absolute kingship as a possible candidate for the best constitution. Such a constitution can still promote the common advantage through laws and education designed to promote moral virtue and the good life for all the citizens. Aristotle's concession to kingship is thus compatible with a moderate-individualist interpretation. Such citizens would thus be fully qualified to engage in political ruling if it were necessary—but it is not necessary if there is a god-like person available as a king.

6.9. OTHER PROBLEMS IN THE BEST CONSTITUTION

Aristotle asserts as we have seen that the best constitution should aim at the happiness of each and every citizen. This presupposes that the natural ends of the citizens are compossibly realizable: the fact that some of the citizens are happy does not bar other citizens from being happy. On this basis, Aristotle argues that each of the citizens should have full rights of citizenship and the right to own private property. Again, the implication is that the rights of the individuals are compossibly realizable in the best constitution.[118] This is the sense in which the best constitution promotes the mutual advantage.

Compossibility in this sense is a strong requirement and may be hard to satisfy—indeed, in Aristotle's view it is hardly ever satisfied. Where there are irresolvable conflicts of interest among the inhabitants or men who are incapable of a truly good life, the lawgiver must devise a second-best solution (*deuteros plous*) or even worse (see *Pol.* IV 11 1295^{a}25–34). However, Aristotle's best constitution itself has been criticized for containing serious imperfections such as the institution of slavery, the subordination of women, institutions such as ostracism, and pervasive authoritarian provisions. Some commentators suggest that Aristotle himself was cognizant of these as serious injustices. If so, he must have regarded the

---

[117] Schütrumpf (1991), i. 84, sees a connection between this passage and the concession to private, individualized instruction at *EN* X 9 1180^{b}7–38 (noted in Sect. 6.7 above). The latter passage seems to shift the focus from the need for coercive laws to the need for a legislative science providing universal principles for education.

[118] The principle of compossibility is formulated by Steiner (1977), 169: 'A possible set of rights is such that it is logically impossible for one individual's exercise of his rights within that set to constitute an interference with another individual's exercise of his rights within that same set.'

so-called 'constitution of our prayers' as seriously flawed, or he may not have intended to propose it as a serious political ideal at all.[119] In order to defend the interpretation that Aristotle did regard the best constitution of *Politics*, VII–VIII, as fully just, it is necessary to consider more fully his view of these problematic features.

Inequalities in the best constitution

For ancient democratic theory,[120] as for modern liberalism, equality was a central value. The term *ison*, 'equal', is contained in the democratic catchword *isonomia*, which implies an equal share of the 'fund of civil and political rights which makes up a constitution from the Greek point of view'.[121] Aristotle recognizes and endorses equality because political justice and political rule presuppose that the citizens are equal, either proportionately or numerically (*EN* V 6 1134ᵃ26–8; *Pol.* I 7 1255ᵇ20). In this he follows a view widely held by the Greeks: '. . . if the unjust is unequal, the just is equal, as everyone believes even without argument' (*EN* V 3 1131ᵃ13–14; cf. 1 1129ᵃ33–4 and 1130ᵇ9).[122]

Aristotle observes that everyone agrees that equality in a political context is not numerical equality but proportionate equality based on merit, although they do not agree on the standard of merit (*Pol.* V 1 1301ᵇ29–39; *EN* V 3 1131ᵃ14–29). The basis for this agreement, as we have seen, is the view of the polis as a co-operative association in which members are accorded offices, honours, and other rights in proportion to their contribution to the enterprise. This view that individuals should be rewarded in proportion to their contribution is in agreement with those versions of modern liberalism which incorporate a merit-based principle of justice as opposed to a need-based standard or strict egalitarianism.

None the less, Aristotle's best constitution places severe restrictions upon equality, for example in the partition of the polis into two groups:

[119] Zuckert (1983) argues for the former view. Nichols (1992), 145, maintains the latter, e.g.: 'The regime in Book VII is less an ideal model for politics than a lesson in its imperfection. Aristotle's designation of that regime as the "best" is surely ironic'; cf. Ambler (1985), 173–4.

[120] See Pericles' funeral oration in Thucydides, II 37 1–3; Plato, *Rep.* VIII 557ᵃ2–558ᶜ1; and Aristotle, *Pol.* IV 4 1291ᵇ34–9, V 9 1310ᵃ28–32. See also Sect. 4.6 above on equality as a corollary of freedom in the democratic theory.

[121] Vlastos (1981: 184) argues that even when this term is used occasionally in connection with non-democratic constitutions, it still refers to equality of political rights among a more limited governing body (e.g. in contrast with tyranny).

[122] Note that *ison* means 'fair' as well as 'equal' in these contexts. See also Vlastos (1977), 18 n. 61.

the citizens who partake directly in the end of the polis; and a large number of slaves, metics, and foreigners who are merely adjuncts necessary for its functioning (VII 4 1326ᵃ19–20). In excluding from citizenship altogether the classes involved in the production of goods and services for the best polis, the best constitution in effect disenfranchises the majority of the population. Furthermore, Aristotle dismisses the proposal of Socrates in *Republic*, V 456ᵃ10−ᵇ3, that women who are suitably qualified should be admitted to the ranks of the guardians, on the apparent ground that their natural function is confined to the household (II 5 1264ᵇ4–6). Such unequal treatment of individuals is condemned as unjust by the modern liberal, but it should be noted that the citizens were a minority of the total population even in the ostensibly egalitarian democratic constitution of ancient Athens.

In assessing Aristotle's inegalitarianism, it is necessary to emphasize that the theory of natural justice as such neither entails nor excludes the doctrine that individuals have equal rights according to nature. From the standpoint of natural justice, individuals possess equal rights according to nature if, and only if, they are in fact equal according to nature. Modern natural rights theorists, including Hobbes and Locke, argue, against Aristotle, that all human beings are equal in respect to the natural characteristic which justifies the recognition of their rights. Locke argues for the natural equality of all human beings in the state of nature along those very lines: 'there being nothing more evident than that Creatures of the same species and rank promiscuously born to all the same advantages of Nature, and the use of the same faculties, should also be equal one amongst another without Subordination and Subjection . . .' Locke expressly follows 'the judicious Hooker' who makes natural equality 'the Foundation of that obligation to meet and Love amongst Men, on which they Build the Duties they owe one another, and from whence he derives the great Maxims of *Justice* and *Charity*'. Contrary to Aristotle, Locke argues that the various ways in which humans are unequal (e.g. age, virtue, birth) are not relevant. The '*Equality*, which all Men are in, in respect of Jurisdiction of Dominion one over another', consists in 'that *equal right* that every Man hath, *to his Natural Freedom*, without being subjected to the Will or Authority of any other Man'.[123] Locke here follows Pufendorf who rebukes the Aristotelian theory of natural slavery as 'directly at odds with the natural equality of men'.[124] Similarly, Hobbes

---

[123] Locke, *Second Treatise*, II. 4, 5; VI. 54.
[124] Pufendorf, *De jure naturae et gentium*, III. 2. 8.

argues for the natural equality of human beings in the state of nature, arguing that all human beings possess equally the capacity of deliberation: 'For Prudence, is but Experience; which equal time, equally bestows on all men, in those things they equally apply themselves unto.'[125]

Aristotle's inegalitarianism is based on the alleged natural inferiority of whole classes of persons as defined by nationality, gender, and profession (cf. I 13 1260ᵃ2–7). Natural slavery is defended on the grounds that natural slaves lack practical wisdom and the capacity to deliberate (1260ᵃ12). The natural ruler exercises foresight through cognition and assigns tasks for natural slaves to carry out with their bodies (2 1252ᵃ31–4). Although natural slaves lack the full rational faculty, they possess the inferior rational part of the soul, i.e. the desiring part in so far as it perceives and obeys rational commands (5 1254ᵇ20–3). In addition to the absence of empirical support for these theories, critics have pointed out serious inconsistencies in Aristotle's defence of slavery.[126] For example, the defence of natural slavery in *Politics*, I, hinges on the claim that the despotic relation is mutually advantageous for master and slave (2 1252ᵃ34, 5 1254ᵇ4–9, 6 1255ᵇ4–15). Slaves are better off because they benefit from the master's rational rule which they are unable to exercise over themselves. However, he severely qualifies this in *Politics*, III 6, remarking that although despotic rule is advantageous to both master and slave, it is advantageous to the master primarily and to the slave only accidentally, because the continued existence of the slave is necessary for that of the master (1278ᵇ32–7; cf. Plato, *Laws*, VI 777ᵈ1–2). This qualification seems to undermine the argument of *Politics*, I, that despotism is a natural and even 'friendly' relation because it is genuinely advantageous for the slave as well as the master (6 1255ᵇ13).[127]

Aristotle's arguments for female inequality are sketchier and enigmatic. He maintains that wives like children should be ruled as free persons, but wives should be subject to political rule and children to kingly rule. The

---

[125] Hobbes, *Leviathan*, I. 13 (1968: 60–1).   [126] See especially N. D. Smith (1991).

[127] Aristotle has also been accused of inconsistency when he says that in the best constitution 'it is better to set out freedom as a prize for all slaves' (VII 10 1330ᵃ32–3). If these are natural slaves, how would they be better off by being free? But if they are not, it is unjust to have enslaved them in the first place. However, he does not explicitly claim that the *freedmen* are better off. He may only mean that it is better *for the citizens* to free them. See Schofield (1990), 22 n. 45. Also, Nichols (1992), 144–5, states that the presence of unnatural slaves in *Pol.* VII indicates that Aristotle is being 'ironic' when he calls this constitution 'the best' and 'according to our prayers'. However, there is no evidence that he was cognizant of any inconsistency regarding slavery or that he saw slavery in the 'best' constitution as unjust. Cf. also *Oec.* I 5 1344ᵇ14–17 which describes the promise of emancipation as 'just and beneficial'. (This work is perhaps by Theophrastus.)

reason is that 'the male is by nature more capable of leadership than the female, unless he is constituted in some way contrary to nature, and the elder and perfect [is by nature more capable of leadership] than the younger and imperfect'. In political rule individuals generally take turns in ruling and being ruled because they are inclined to be equal by nature, 'but the male is always related in this manner to the female' (12 1259ᵃ39–ᵇ10). He remarks further that the female (unlike the natural slave) has a deliberative faculty but it is without authority (*akuron*) (1260ᵃ13). By this he seems to mean that although women possess this capacity they are unable to control their passions fully and are thus unable to attain the practical wisdom and moral virtues exhibited by men.[128] The virtues of which women are capable will be relative to their inferior souls (1260ᵃ20–4; III 4 1277ᵇ21–3). None the less, women are by nature free and have a kind of equality with men, so that their relation with men should be 'political' (cf. I 7 1255ᵇ20). Further, the polis should be concerned with the education and virtue of female citizens (I 13 1260ᵇ13–20; *Rhet.* I 5 1361ᵃ8–12; cf. Plato, *Laws*, VI 781ᵃ2–ᵇ4, VII 805ᵃ7–ᵇ1). The fact that Aristotle assigns women a sphere of authority in the household implies that their deliberative capacity is partly functional.[129] But because this capacity is not fully functional, they are always ruled over.

Aristotle's evidence for these claims is very weak, even on his own grounds. He appears to think his distinctions between the souls of free men, free women, children, and slaves are supported by the observation that free persons rule slaves, males rule women, and men rule children in different ways (I 13 1260ᵃ9–12). This is open to the objection that these different modes of rule need not be explained in terms of innate psychological differences. If slaves are generally observed to be servile and incapable of self-direction, this may be due, on Aristotle's own psychological

---

[128] See Fortenbaugh (1977), 138, and Smith (1991), 475–6. Against this, Saxonhouse (1982), 208, contends that *akuron* is ambiguous, since Aristotle may mean that groups of men would scorn deliberation coming from a woman; cf. Swanson (1992), 56, Nichols (1992), 31–2, and Salkever (1990), 184. However, if this were Aristotle's meaning, the subordination of women (half the population) would represent a striking concession to brute necessity at the expense of natural justice in the so-called best constitution (as argued by Zuckert (1983), 195–6). At any rate, it is difficult to reconcile Saxonhouse's suggestion with the fact that Aristotle's *akuron* claim is a premiss for his conclusion that men are *by nature* rulers over women (1260ᵃ8–14; cf. 12 1259ᵇ1–2). If Aristotle does not mean to assert the *natural* superiority of men over women, his argument is a *non sequitur*.

[129] III 4 1277ᵇ24–5; cf. *Oec.* I 6 1345ᵃ5–7. At *EN* VII 10 1160ᵇ32–1161ᵃ1 the husband-wife relation is described as 'aristocratic'. Nichols (1992), 29–35, argues persuasively that Aristotle seeks to include women in governance as far as he thinks possible; cf. Saxonhouse (1992), Swanson (1992), ch. 3, and Salkever (1990), ch. 4.

theory, to their previous habituation. In fact, the practice of slavery is based on coercion (reinforced by habituation), as some of Aristotle's contemporaries recognized (3 1253^b20–3). Similarly, the dominance of men over women, although ubiquitous in Aristotle's day, could be explained by Aristotle himself as the result of deeply ingrained traditional customs, combined with the comparatively late development of technologies favourable to greater freedom for women.[130]

Aristotle also supports his thesis that the citizens of the best constitution should not engage in productive professions with the psychological claim that these occupations have morally debilitating effects on their practitioners which render them incapable of the perfection and flourishing which are the end of this constitution.[131] For example, he views menial workers and artisans as vulgar and slavish, with souls in an unnatural condition and hence incapable of virtue (I 13 1260^a36–$^b2$; III 4 1277^a37–$^b7$, 5 1278^a17–21; VII 9 1328^b39–41, 1329^a19–21; VIII 7 1342^a22–3); merchants as acquisitive and obsessed with bodily desires (I 9 1257^b23–1258^a14; VII 9 1328^b39); farmers as too busy for political virtue (1328^b41–1329^a2; cf. IV 6 1292^b25–9) and as tending to be conceited and troublesome (II 5 1264^a32–6). It is presumably for the latter reason that he says it would be best if farmers were without spirit so that they were not rebellious (VII 10 1330^a25–30).

In addition to these sweeping generalizations, Aristotle displays an unwarranted partiality for certain pursuits: he takes it for granted that providing goods and services for others is inferior to political activity and philosophizing (I 7 1255^b35–7). It is, however, an oversimplification to denigrate Aristotle as an unqualified apologist for the Greek aristocratic class, since he does view the contemplative way of life as superior to the traditional noble lifestyle. None the less, he does not take into account the extent to which his own theory of ethical virtue is capable of accommodating a wide diversity of circumstances and practices. Because virtue and practical rationality involve attaining the mean as grasped in particular circumstances, they are highly adaptable to the context of action, to a far greater extent than Aristotle himself is inclined to acknowledge. Although he recognizes that there are a number of competing ways of life even in the Greek world, he assumes that one uniquely specifiable lifestyle will be superior to all the others. His claim that the refined class of his day is

[130] Nussbaum (1988), 165–6, and Yack (1993), 66–8, argue persuasively that given that women *do* have the same deliberative capacities as men, they should by Aristotle's argument be full members of the political community.

[131] Cf. Plato, *Laws*, VII 846^d1–$^e2$, XI 919^d2–920^c8; Xenophon, *Oec.* IV 2–3.

morally superior to the productive classes is not adequately defended. He does not make plausible the claim that productive activities, which aim at goods and services intended to be consumed by others, are inherently inferior. He does not consider seriously the objection that the creative achievements of artists, musicians, inventors, and producers of goods and services are expressions of human intelligence, which rival the discoveries of scientists and philosophers. Nor does he show that the life of a person engaged in production, even manual labour, cannot be on the whole intrinsically valuable. The presumption that physical labour as such is detrimental to the soul seems to rely on a dualistic view pitting the body against the mind which is in conflict with his own hylomorphic psychology. He does not consider that productive activity might actually be conducive to the formation of the virtues. He does recognize that a virtuous person may perform menial services (as when a soldier digs a ditch or nurses a wounded comrade) (VII 14 1333^{a}6–11; VIII 2 1337^{b}17–21). But he does not envision the possibility that all the citizens of the best polis could spend part of their time engaged in necessary productive activities rather than relying upon a subservient class of non-citizens.[132] It would seem to be more consistent for Aristotle to rely upon moral education to ensure that the citizens pursue noble activities rather than to exclude them from productive labour due to its alleged corrupting influence.

However objectionable, the inegalitarian features of Aristotle's thought are consistent with the moderate-individualist interpretation, which requires that justice protect each and every citizen. The theory of natural justice yields the principle of universal human rights (that all human beings have equal natural rights) only if it is conjoined with the additional premiss that all human beings are by nature equal, a premiss which Aristotle regrettably does not accept.

The problem of ostracism

Ostracism was mainly used in democracies in order to expel citizens with outstanding wealth, numerous friends, or other sources of political power (III 13 1284^{a}17–22). The Athenian law permitting ostracism was enacted under Cleisthenes in 508/7 BC and remained in effect until the fourth century, but it was evidently used in Athens only from 487 to 415 (before

---

[132] Cf. Irwin (1988), sect. 222, who points out that Aristotle maintains that the citizens must be soldiers (when they are younger), although he also recognizes that a purely military life can be morally debilitating (see p. 621 n. 23). It is not clear why he does not make a similar concession for productive activities.

Aristotle's lifetime).[133] Ostracism was also practised in other polises during the fifth century. In Athens it involved the following procedure: once a year the assembly could vote on whether to conduct an ostracism, which was conducted in the market-place with each citizen having the right to vote. The ballot was a potsherd (*ostrakon*) on which was written the name of the citizen to be banished. Provided 6,000 ballots were cast, the citizen named on the most ballots was banished for ten years. Ostracism differed from other punishments such as exile or dishonour (*atimia*), in that the ostracized citizen retained his citizenship and property rights and had the right to return to the polis and resume active citizenship after the term of banishment. None the less, ostracism is problematic from the standpoint of legal justice, because it does not require that a citizen be convicted of any offence. Hence, it would seem to involve punishing a person who has not violated the rights of anyone else. It is hard to see how this can be justified on the basis of corrective justice.

Aristotle remarks that ostracism is used in deviant constitutions in order to further the private advantage of the rulers, but adds that it has a place in constitutions that aim at 'the common good':

This is clear also in the case of the other crafts and sciences; for neither would a painter permit a painted animal to have a foot which exceeded [the limits of] proportion, even if it was superior in beauty, nor would a shipbuilder permit the stern or any other part of the ship [to exceed this limit], nor would the teacher of the chorus permit a person who sang louder and more beautifully than the rest of the chorus to sing with the chorus. Hence for this reason nothing prevents monarchs from being in concord with their polises if they do this when their own rule is beneficial to their polises. Therefore, in regard to the accepted types of superiority, the argument for ostracism has a sort of political justice. It is better if the lawgiver establishes the constitution from the beginning so that it does not need this sort of remedy; but the 'second sailing', if it occurs, is to try to correct it in some such manner ... (1284^b7–20)

This passage asserts that ostracism is just, and the supporting argument seems to assume the holistic view of the polis for which he takes the *Republic* to task in *Politics*, II 5. The analogy to the crafts suggests that just as a doctor may be justified in amputating a leg in order to save the patient, the ruler may be justified in sacrificing one or more citizens for the sake of the whole polis. This presents a fundamental challenge to my

---

[133] See Raubitschek (1991), 58.

interpretation, because it implies that justice is the overall advantage, rather than the mutual advantage. This is especially the case if Aristotle means that it is unqualifiedly just to ostracize fully virtuous citizens in case they possess so much wealth or so many friends that the opportunity of others to exercise their virtue is thereby diminished.[134]

It should be noted, however, that this is to read more into the text than Aristotle actually says. Indeed, the above passage contains some important qualifications. Most importantly, it implies that ostracism will not be needed in the best constitution, but only in the 'second sailing' (*deuteros plous*) or second-best constitution. This suggests that the best constitution is *best* because it avoids genuine conflicts of interest among the citizens. Moreover, the concessive statement at 1284^{b}16 that the case for ostracism has 'a sort of (*ti*) political justice', uses a phrase which is sometimes contrasted with unqualified justice (see 9 1280^{a}9–11), so that it could here mean a second-best form of justice. Ostracism may be justified in a suboptimal situation where some citizens possess so much wealth or so many friends that they threaten to make themselves tyrants (13 1284^{a}19–22; cf. VI 8 1308^{b}16–19). The other citizens justifiably regard this as a threat to their own political rights. It is noteworthy that Cleisthenes introduced ostracism in order to prevent the restoration of tyranny in Athens (*Ath. Pol.* XXII).[135] This interpretation is also suggested by the allusion to the fable of the lions and the hares which prefaces Aristotle's discussion of ostracism: when the hares engaged in demagoguery and advanced a merit-based claim of everyone to equality, the lions retorted, 'Where are your claws and teeth?'[136]

To sum up, Aristotle's concessions to ostracism (although they offend modern liberal notions of due process) are consistent with an individualistic construal of his theory of justice. If someone becomes so wealthy and powerful that he threatens the political rights of other citizens, they may justly ostracize him. Ostracism does, however, imply a conflict of interests which is inconsistent with the 'correct' constitution and which, therefore, the Aristotelian lawgiver should avert through a more judicious assignment of political and property rights.

---

[134] This is the interpretation of Kraut (1989), 90–7, who contends that ostracism illustrates the more general point that for Aristotle 'justice does not demand that the community always act in ways that promote the best interests of everyone'. Cf. Mulgan (1977), 33.

[135] Raubitschek (1991) argues that this was, as a matter of historical fact, the purpose of ostracism.

[136] The answer is found in Aesop's *Fables*, 241 (ed. C. Halm). On the lost passage of Antisthenes cited by Aristotle see Newman (1887), iii. 243.

Limits on liberty

Aristotle is not a totalitarian who advocates total governmental authority
at the expense of individual liberty. He defends individual property rights
and private families against the communistic scheme of Plato's *Republic*
(see Sections 6.4 and 9.6). He thinks it a sign of the correct constitution
that the citizens are ruled *voluntarily*, whereas the subjects of despotic
rules are involuntary (see II 11 1272^{b}30–1; III 14 1285^{a}27–8).[137] Also, in
the best constitution the citizen *chooses* to be ruled and to rule in order to
live a virtuous life (III 13 1284^{a}1–3).[138] Further, individuals must attain
happiness through their own efforts (VII 1 1323^{b}25).[139] Accordingly,
political justice presupposes that the citizens are free (*EN* V 6 1134^{a}26–
8).[140] None the less, this endorsement of freedom and liberty is severely
qualified, and Aristotle's sketch of the best constitution in *Politics*, VII–
VIII, contains many restrictions on individual liberty, including the
following:[141]

- The citizens should not live a vulgar or a merchant's or a farmer's
  way of life (VII 9 1328^{b}39–40).
- All the citizens ought to share in common meals (10 1330^{a}3–8).
- Expenditures concerning the gods should be common to the entire
  polis (1330^{a}8–9).
- The laws should regulate sexual reproduction, the ages when mar-
  riages are permissible, and the conduct of parents: e.g. pregnant

---

[137] This idea is already in Plato's *Laws*, III 690^{b}7–^{c}3, where the Athenian Stranger,
opposing Pindar, identifies voluntary rule with natural rule. Keyt (1993) argues persuasively
that the connections between the voluntary and the natural and between the coerced and the
unnatural are deeply rooted in Aristotle's thought. Cole (1988) also argues that *autarkeia* in
Aristotle corresponds to the modern idea of autonomy, but this interpretation is convincingly
criticized by Kelley (forthcoming).

[138] A voluntary (*hekōn*) act has its source in the agent; i.e. it is done without outside force
or coercion and with knowledge of the particular circumstances (*EN* III 1 1111^{a}22–4).
Choice (*prohairesis*) involves voluntariness, as well as prior deliberation about what acts will
promote the ends of the agent (see III 2 1112^{a}14–15; cf. 1111^{b}26–7).

[139] See Cooper (1975), 122–3.

[140] Arendt (1958), 29–33, contends that 'all Greek philosophers . . . took for granted . . . that
freedom is exclusively located in the political realm, that necessity is primarily a pre-
political phenomenon, characteristic of the private household organization'. This
interpretation, which she extends to Aristotle, involves an exaggerated dichotomy between
the public and private realms, and also neglects the paramount place of the philosophical life
in Aristotle's ethics. Arendt's interpretation of Aristotle is criticized by Salkever (1990),
173–4, Swanson (1992), and Yack (1993), 11–13.

[141] Other curbs on individual freedom are approved elsewhere by Aristotle, for example
in his examination of other candidates for the best constitution in *Politics*, II. His recommended
restrictions on the possession and use of private property are also discussed in Sects. 9.5, 7.

women might be required to get exercise by walking to the temple of the goddess of fertility (16 1335^{a}4–^{b}19).

- The number of citizens should be limited and abortion within prescribed limits should be used to limit population (16 1335^{b}22–5; cf. II 6 1265^{a}38–^{b}16).
- The play of children should be overseen, especially so that they will not be in the company of slaves (17 1336^{a}39–^{b}3).
- The lawgiver ought to banish shameful speech, especially among the young, so that they will not be induced to speak in a similar way; an offending free person should be punished with dishonour (along with a beating if it is a younger person); similarly the lawgiver ought to prohibit one from looking at indecent paintings and writings (1336^{b}3–14).
- Obscene statues and paintings should be restricted to the temples of the appropriate gods; the law may permit full-grown citizens to witness them but the young should be excluded until they are mature and education makes them unaffected by the harm from such objects (1336^{b}14–23).
- All children should be educated in common under the supervision of the appropriate officials (VIII 1 1337^{a}8–32).

It is not always clear whether these are intended as written laws or as unwritten customs, and the punishment for violation and the mode of enforcement is often unstated. However, it is obvious that Aristotle thinks that the conduct of the citizens should be made to conform to these rules.[142] These provisions therefore provide abundant evidence that Aristotle would reject 'the night-watchman state of classical liberal theory limited to the function of protecting all of its citizens against violence, theft, fraud and to the enforcement of contracts, and so on'.[143]

However, Aristotle does not justify such measures on the holistic grounds that individual interests may be sacrificed in order to promote the general good. Rather, he justifies them on the ground that the aim of the polis is to promote moral perfection in the individual citizens. To achieve this goal the citizens must perform only those functions which are conducive

---

[142] e.g. Mayhew (1993a), 823–5, argues that the common meal (*sussitia*) pertains only to the main meal of the day, and that it is unclear whether attendance was legally compulsory. Keyt (1993), 152, argues that Aristotle views coercion as unnatural and accordingly de-emphasizes it. Although he accepts defence and punishment as necessary (VII 8 1328^{b}7–10), 'it would be more choiceworthy if neither man nor polis had any need of such things' (13 1332^{a}12–15, 17 1336^{b}3–12). Compliance with the strictures enumerated above is preferably voluntary and induced by education.   [143] Nozick (1974), 26.

to their mutual happiness. Aristotle maintains that they should in some cases be required to perform these functions, including the holding of political offices (see II 9 1271ª11–12; cf. IV 9 1294ª35–ᵇ1 and 13 1297ª34–6), and that they should in some cases be prohibited from acting in a matter detrimental to their own moral development. Moreover, an individual should be prohibited from actions impeding the moral development of others. Hence, adults are not permitted to marry or bear children or raise them however they wish, or to use foul language or otherwise corrupt impressionable young persons. On the other hand, there is no indication that the prohibitions will impede an individual's own moral development.

To some extent Locke agrees with Aristotle that freedom is justly subject to certain constraints. For he rejects Edward Filmer's definition of freedom as 'a Liberty for everyone to do what he lists, to live as he pleases, and not to be tyed by any Laws'. This is mere licence. Freedom, for Locke, is instead 'Liberty to follow my own Will in all things, where the Rule prescribes not; and not to be subject to the inconstant, uncertain, unknown, Arbitrary Will of another Man. As Freedom of Nature is to be under no other restraint but the Law of Nature.' However, Locke departs from Aristotle in making freedom central to natural rights, when he characterizes the state of nature as '*a state of perfect Freedom* to order their Actions, and dispose of their Possessions, and Persons as they think fit, within the bonds of the Law of Nature, without asking leave, or depending upon the will of any other Man'.¹⁴⁴ Locke implies that freedom is a central defining condition of the human end. Thus, for Locke natural rights provide a self-limiting, inalienable sphere of liberty for the individual right-holder.

For Aristotle, also, freedom has its place, but its place is far more modest than for Locke. For Aristotle liberty is an external good necessary for virtuous activity but which can be possessed in excess (see *EN* X 8 1178ª28–33). However, when it is defined by the ancient democrats as 'doing whatever one wishes' (*Pol.* V 10 1310ª31–2), it becomes an impediment to personal moral perfection and a threat to constitutional order (see V 12 1316ᵇ21–7; VI 4 1318ᵇ38–1319ª1). Aristotle's critique of democratic freedom is revealing. 'So that in such democracies each person lives as he wishes and "for what he craves", as Euripides says; but this is base; for [he] should not believe that living in relation to the constitution is slavery, but preservation' (V 10 1310ª32–6). The aim of the individual

---

¹⁴⁴ Locke, *Second Treatise*, II. 6, IV. 22, II. 4.

should not be unlimited liberty but moral perfection, which is achieved through conformity to the constitution. Freedom is an external good subject to the Aristotelian mean.

Hence, Aristotle's repudiation of the democratic ideal of liberty (and the implied rejection of the modern ideal of purely 'negative' freedom[145] is entirely consistent with the interpretation defended throughout this chapter: that justice, the political good, consists in the mutual advantage, i.e. the perfection of each of the citizens. Here again, illiberal features of Aristotle's best constitution result from controvertible premisses which are logically distinct from his theory of justice.

---

[145] Cf. Berlin (1969), 122–31, on the modern principle of 'negative' freedom, i.e. the non-interference by others with an agent's activity.

The Second-Best Constitution

7.1. THE 'SECOND SAILING' OF POLITICS

The 'constitution of our prayers', though possible in principle, was unattainable in practice on Aristotle's view. For, owing to nature and fortune, the polises of his day possessed neither the population nor the resources required to secure the best way of life for each and every citizen (cf. *Pol.* VII 4 1325^{b}33–40). However, Aristotle also endorses the normative principle of proximity: it is best to attain the end, but, failing that, a thing is better in proportion as it is near to the end (see *DC* II 12 292^{b}17–19). He accordingly proposes an alternative constitution in which he thinks most polises could partake (*Politics*, IV 11 1295^{a}30–1). He remarks that Plato had a similar aim in the *Laws* (*Pol.* II 2 1265^{a}3; cf. *Laws*, V 739^{a}1–^{b}7). Such a constitution is the 'second sailing' or second-best solution.[1] The leading example of this is polity, which, despite its shortcomings, Aristotle includes as one of the three types of correct constitution in *Politics*, III. *Politics*, IV, in effect extends the 'second-best' category to include a group of mixed constitutions which are not deviations but fall short of the most correct constitution (IV 8 1293^{b}22–7).[2] This chapter will argue that the second-best constitution resembles the best constitution in that it promotes a form of justice and mutual advantage for the citizens.

It is necessary to begin with Aristotle's terms for the second-best constitutions. First is the term *politeia*, which Aristotle uses in two senses: a general sense, ordinarily translated as 'constitution' or 'regime'; and a

---

[1] 'Second sailing' (*deuteros plous*) refers to the use of oars when there is no wind to fill the sails. See *Pol.* III 13 1284^{b}19; *EN* II 9 1109^{a}34–5; Plato, *Statesman*, 300^{c}2; cf. Plato, *Phdo.* 99^{c}9–^{d}1 and *Phlb.* 19^{c}2–3. A related idea is found in Plutarch, *Lives*, Solon, XV 2, which impressed Pierce Butler, one of the American founders, who remarked in the debates on the US Constitution in 1787, 'We must follow the example of Solon who gave the Athenians not the best Government he could devise; but the best they would receive' (reported by James Madison (1984); echoed by Madison himself in *The Federalist*, no. 38, in Cooke (1961), 241).

[2] I use 'second-best constitution' (not Aristotle's term, though suggested by 'second sailing') for this group, which includes polity, so-called aristocracy, and their variants, and I shall distinguish among these specific forms where appropriate.

specific sense, as 'polity' or 'republic' (cf. III 7 1279ᵃ37–9; IV 7 1293ᵃ39– 40).³ This ambiguity sometimes gives rise to difficulties of interpretation, but it is generally clear which sense is intended.⁴ Aristotle sometimes marks this distinction by referring to polity as 'the so-called *politeia*', which implies that the use of *politeia* for a specific constitution was not his innovation.⁵ Second is the term *aristokratia*, which Aristotle uses not only for true aristocracy (described in *Politics*, III 7), but also for an inferior form (IV 7 1293ᵇ1–21). Just as the term 'polity' is used commonly for certain constitutions which resemble or tend towards democracy, constitutions which are commonly called 'aristocracy' tend towards oligarchy (IV 8 1293ᵇ34–8; V 7 1307ᵃ15–16). A second designation is thus 'so-called aristocracy', distinguished both from true aristocracy and from other inferior forms (IV 7 1293ᵇ7–12).⁶ Aristotle speaks of the attainable aristocracies as bordering on polity (or so-called *politeia*) in IV 11 1295ᵃ31– 4 and includes them as a form of second-best constitution.

Regarding the historicity of polity Aristotle says that it has either not occurred or has not often existed (IV 7 1293ᵃ40–1; cf. 11 1296ᵃ36–8), although he does cite some historical examples: Mali (IV 13 1297ᵇ14), Tarentum (V 3 1303ᵃ3), Oreus (1303ᵃ18), and Syracuse (4 1304ᵃ27). Further, he says, 'the polises which we now call polities were earlier called democracies' (IV 13 1297ᵇ24–5), where the hoplites replaced cavalry as the dominant military force. *Politics*, IV 11 1295ᵃ31–4, also implies that polity (or so-called constitution) is within the grasp of most polises.⁷ Examples of so-called aristocracy include Carthage and Sparta (IV 7 1293ᵇ15–17), as well as Thurii and Locris (V 7 1307ᵃ27, 38).

³ He prefers Plato's term 'timocracy' (*Rep.* VIII 545ᵇ6) to 'polity' for this specific constitution at *EN* VIII 10 1160ᵃ33–5, although 'polity' is the uncontested term at *EE* VII 9 1241ᵇ30–1. Plato, *Statesman*, 302ᵈ3–5, distinguishes between a good and bad form of democracy, the former corresponding to Aristotle's polity, the latter to his democracy. Polybius, VI 4 6, uses 'democracy' for the good form and 'ochlocracy' for the deviation.
⁴ An added complication is that Aristotle sometimes distinguishes between monarchy and *politeia*, i.e. the other constitutions (V 10 1310ᵃ39–ᵇ2; 1311ᵃ22–5, ᵇ37; 12 1315ᵇ40–1; cf. III 15 1286ᵇ8–13). Newman (1887), i. 251; ii, p. xxvii, notes that Aristotle is here following common Greek usage.
⁵ The phrase *hē kaloumenē* occurs, for example, at *Pol.* IV 7 1293ᵇ9, 20; 9 1294ᵃ31. The phrase suggests that the use of *politeia* for a specific constitution is common. This is also indicated in the *EN* passage cited in the previous note.
⁶ Sometimes *aristokratia* refers to a so-called aristocracy: cf. V 7 1307ᵃ6 and 12. The referents of *aristokratia* and *politeia* in the *Politics* must be determined, as far as possible, by the context.
⁷ Robinson (1962), 24, 94, states that 'while constitutions called polities had often occurred, Aristotle was changing the meaning of "polity" to something that had not often or ever occurred'. This is, however, consistent with polity being in principle attainable by most polises.

One historical example of polity often cited by commentators is described in the *Constitution of Athens*, although it is not mentioned in the *Politics*: the Athenian constitution of the Five Thousand (411 BC) which was established primarily at the instigation of Theramenes after the disastrous expedition to Sicily.[8] The Constitution was dominated by the 'Five Thousand' who were heavily armed soldiers or hoplites. This number may be contrasted with 40,000 citizens in the earlier Athenian democracy. Another example was the regime established by Antipater, the Macedonian governor, in 321 BC, shortly after Aristotle's death (Diodorus Siculus, XVIII 18). This constitution confined political rights to those who possessed a property qualification of 2,000 drachmas, thus reducing the citizen body from 21,000 to 9,000. These constitutions bear interesting similarities to Aristotle's polity, including the fact that they concentrated political power in the hands of the moderately wealthy.

Aristotle offers several criteria for a polity: It is

(1) rule by the multitude (*plēthos*) for the common advantage (III 7 1279^a37-9);

(2) a mixed constitution (IV 8 1293^b33-4, 1294^a22-3; 9 1294^a41-^b1);

(3) a middle constitution (cf. IV 11 1295^a31-4 with 1296^a7, 37–8);

(4) based upon the middle class,[9] those between the rich and poor (IV 11 $1295^b34-1296^a9$); and

(5) based on hoplites or soldiers with heavy armour (IV 13 1297^b1-2; II 6 1265^b28-9; III 7 1279^b2-4).

The relations among these criteria have perplexed commentators. The first concerns one of the three correct constitutions concerned with the common advantage in *Politics*, III 7. However, as noted in Section 5.2 above, polity takes different forms in *Politics*, IV, with democratic, oligarchic, and aristocratic casts, under the rubric of 'mixed constitutions'.

---

[8] *Ath. Pol.* XXIX–XXXIII. See also Thucydides, VIII 67–98, which may be a source for the *Ath. Pol.*

[9] 'Middle class' has anachronistic connotations. Barker (1906), 474, describes these citizens as leading the 'life of a quiet *bourgeoisie*'. However, Mulgan (1977), 106–7, properly cautions us against importing 'any modern, Marxist connotations of the *bourgeoisie* or of a specific relation to the means of production. "Those in the middle" are simply those of moderate or medium wealth. They are the men who could afford the amount of the hoplite or heavy-armed infantryman and thus formed the core of the city's military power on land.' It should also be noted that the middle class on Aristotle's view enjoys a moderate amount of the goods of fortune generally, including good looks, strength, and good breeding as well as wealth (cf. IV 11 1295^b6-7).

In *Politics*, IV, the focus of discussion seems to shift from the mixed constitution in IV 7–9 to the middle constitution in IV 11–12 and back to the mixed in IV 13. Aristotle in general takes it for granted that the mixed and middle constitutions are equivalent, although IV 9 evidently contains an argument of sorts that the mixed constitution is a middle one (see 1284^{a}41, ^{b}2, 5). In IV 11 he seems to argue that polity is a middle constitution and is based upon the middle class. The relation between the middle class and the hoplites is also not made explicit, although they are clearly intended as equivalent. Aristotle also speaks of so-called aristocracy in passing in *Politics*, IV, suggesting that it is a mixed constitution in IV 7–9 and that it is (or is akin to) a middle constitution in IV 11. Presumably, a so-called aristocracy meets criteria (1) and (2), and satisfies (3)–(5) to the extent that political rights are ceded to the middle class.

The first criterion is that polity is a correct constitution because it aims at the common advantage. This chapter considers the status of this claim in *Politics*, IV, and how it is related to the other four criteria. The previous chapter has argued that the best polis aims at the happiness of each of the members of the polis rather than merely at their overall happiness. This chapter considers the extent to which the second-best constitution realizes this ideal. This question arises because, as noted above, Aristotle denies that polity and so-called aristocracy are deviations but also says they 'fall short of' the best (IV 8 1293^{b}22–7), suggesting some ambivalence towards this second-best group.[10] This prompts the question: To what extent does Aristotle remain committed in *Politics*, IV, to the claim that the second-best constitution is a correct form? And does the second-best constitution, like the true aristocracy of *Politics*, VII–VIII, aim at the *mutual* advantage of all of the citizens? I shall concentrate on three major themes. Section 7.2 considers the analysis of the mixed constitution. Section 7.3 examines the defence of the middle constitution. Section 7.4 examines the practical maxims which Aristotle invokes in support of the second-best constitution and considers how these maxims relate to considerations of justice.

---

[10] This unclarity is reflected in Newman (1887) who says that Aristotle treats polity as one of the 'failures' and not a 'really normal constitution' (i. 218), and, on the other hand, that 'Aristotle is far from holding his best constitution to be the only normal (*orthē*) constitution' (i. 423). Again, says Newman, 'there are in fact constitutions which are partly normal, partly deviation forms' (i. 491). Some other commentators contend, implausibly, that Aristotle regards polity as on a par with the most correct constitution: e.g. Bluhm (1962), Johnson (1990), and Nichols (1992). Nn. 26 and 27 below state my reasons for rejecting this interpretation.

7.2. THE MIXED CONSTITUTION

Polity is described by Aristotle as a mixed constitution[11] in several different ways, as

(a) a mixture of oligarchy and democracy (IV 8 1293ᵇ34; cf. V 7 1307ᵃ11–12);

(b) a mixture of the wealthy and the poor (IV 8 1294ᵃ16–17, 22–3);

(c) a mixture of wealth and freedom (IV 8 1294ᵃ16–17);

(d) a mixture or synthesis of the institutions of oligarchy and democracy (IV 9 1294ᵃ36).

Description (a) has been criticized as an unhelpful metaphor: 'You cannot mix democracy and oligarchy like gin and vermouth in a glass. In a cocktail gin and vermouth are both actually present. In a mixture of democracy and oligarchy neither is present.'[12] Thus (a) needs to be explicated in other terms, and Aristotle does so, in terms of (b) and (c) in *Politics*, IV 8, and in terms of (d) in *Politics*, IV 9.

Newman plausibly argues that (c) reveals the essence of the mixed constitution: 'it is rather a combination of social elements—virtue, wealth, free birth—than a combination of constitutions.' On this account, 'it is mixed, not because it divides power between king, nobles and people, but because two or more of the social elements which can justly claim power in a State share power within it.'[13] In the mixed constitutions more than one standard of justice is used to distribute political rights among the inhabitants of the polis. When the standards of wealth and freedom are well mixed, the result is polity. In addition, the standards of virtue may be combined with either or both of the others, issuing in so-called aristocracy (IV 8 1294ᵃ19–25). This explains how the sixfold classification of constitutions in *Politics*, III 7, gives way to the much more complicated classification of Book IV. Aristotle distinguishes several mixed constitutions on the basis of the following standards:

Constitution	*Standards*
Aristocratic democracy	Virtue, freedom
Aristocratic oligarchy	Virtue, wealth

---

[11] The idea of a mixed constitution is expounded by Aristotle's predecessors, including Plato in *Laws*, III 693ᵈ2–ᵉ3 and VI 756ᵉ9–10; cf. *Pol.* II 6 1265ᵇ33–1266ᵃ3. The elements mixed in the *Laws* are monarchy and democracy. On Plato's conception of the mixed constitution, see Morrow (1960), ch. 10. On the evolution of this idea in antiquity, see von Fritz (1954).   [12] Robinson (1962), 90.

[13] Newman (1887), 264–5, 498.

Aristocratic polity   Virtue, wealth, freedom
Democratic polity   Freedom, wealth
Oligarchic polity   Wealth, freedom

In oligarchic polity there is a slight tilt in favour of wealth, and in democratic polity, of freedom. In the ideal case, polity would involve a perfect balance between these standards. The three aristocratic forms are 'so-called' aristocracies, because virtue is diluted with other criteria of merit and because their standard of virtue falls short of the complete and unqualified moral virtue of the ideal polis (IV 7 1293^{b}1–7). The virtuous persons in the mixed constitution are described as reasonable, reputable, refined, notable, and noble-and-good; but they are not characterized as excellent or great-souled as are the citizens of the best constitution.[14] This description of so-called aristocracy is consistent with the observation in III 7 1279^{a}40–^{b}2 that the citizens of polity possess not virtue in its entirety but 'military virtue', i.e. the virtue characteristic of the hoplite class. Presumably, so-called aristocracy 'borders on' polity (see IV 11 1295^{a}31–4) because there is a trade-off between the standard of virtue and the standards of wealth and freedom which are in force in polity.

There remains the question of how description (*d*) of polity as a mixture of political institutions is related to the other three descriptions. Aristotle illustrates three sorts of mixture in *Politics*, IV 9, showing how features of democracy and oligarchy might be combined within the constitution of a sample polity: (i) by combining features from each; (ii) by taking a mean between features of each; and (iii) by selecting features from both. He provides an example of each sort of mixture in polity: (i) *Combination* Regarding the juries, the rich are fined for not attending as in oligarchy, and the poor are paid to attend as in democracy (1294^{a}37–^{b}2; cf. 13 1297^{a}38–^{b}1). (ii) *Moderation* Regarding the assembly the right to attend is conditional on an assessment which is moderate rather than large as in oligarchy or small to non-existent as in democracy (9 1294^{b}2–6). (iii) *Selection* Regarding special offices citizens are chosen by election rather than by lot as in oligarchy, but no assessment is required as in democracy (1294^{b}6–13).

The bridge between descriptions (*c*) and (*d*) is provided by Aristotle's theory of political justice. As we saw in Sections 5.3–5 above, he

---

[14] The best citizens of the mixed constitutions are reasonable (*epieikeis*, IV 7 1293^{b}14), reputable (*eudokimountes*, 1293^{b}13), refined (*charienteis*, 13 1297^{b}9), notable (*gnōrimoi*, 4 1291^{b}28–30), and noble-and-good (*kaloi kagathoi*, 8 1293^{b}39). The citizens of true aristocracy are excellent (*spoudaioi*, VII 13 1332^{a}34) and great-souled (*megalopsuchoi*, VIII 3 1338^{b}3). On the scarcity of the virtuous see also V 4 1304^{b}4–5.

distinguishes among three patterns for distributing political rights: (1) the democratic pattern which disperses authority equally throughout the entire citizenry; (2) the oligarchic pattern which concentrates authority unequally in the hands of a few; and (3) the mixed pattern which divides authority, assigning some of it to a few and distributing the rest to everyone. Pattern (1) is justified by the democratic standard of merit as free birth; pattern (2) by the oligarchic standard of merit as personal wealth; and pattern (3) by a 'mixed' standard which appeals to freedom and wealth—and, in the case of so-called aristocracy, also to virtue. The specific mixture of political institutions is thus determined by the principle of distributive justice. In each part of the constitution—the deliberative, adjudicative, and magistracies—political rights are assigned on the basis of distributive justice and the distinctive standards of the constitution; in the case of polity, wealth and freedom.[15]

The interpretation of the mixed constitution is a subject of disagreement. According to Barker, Aristotle views the mixed constitution as a harmonious and homogeneous social union:

in a properly mixed government each separate function would, in Aristotle's conception, bear the impress of the same mixed character: in a polity the legislative, executive and judicature would each be entrusted to the mixed or middle class; but mixture would *not* be attempted on the plan of making one part black, another white, and trusting the whole to come out gray. It follows from this that for Aristotle there is no idea of a check exercised by one department (or even class) on another: the different departments will work harmoniously together, because each is permeated by the same spirit as the rest.[16]

This interpretation contains an important kernel of truth: the middle class does have a central place in Aristotle's defence of polity (as we shall see in the following section). However, it is implausible to suppose that polity will be composed *exclusively* of the middle class. It is true that he says that a polity (or constitution) should only be composed of hoplites (IV 13 1297^{b}1–2; cf. II 6 1265^{b}28–9), but even this statement is followed by the admission that the amount of the property assessment cannot be defined without qualification, and by the recommendation that it be fixed at such a level that those who share in the constitution outnumber those who do not, which provides no guarantee that citizenship will be confined to the moderately wealthy (1297^{b}2–6). Moreover, Barker implies that the rich are excluded from political offices, which is such an extraordinary

[15] Cf. Newman (1887), i. 265 n. 1, and Barker (1906), 481–5.
[16] Barker (1906), 485.

proposal that one would have expected Aristotle to state it unequivocally.[17] Further, at IV 11 1295^{b}34–9 he indicates that the citizen body may include both the wealthy and the poor, as long as the middle class has a superior position. In addition, immediately before the exclusionary passage IV 13 1297^{b}1–2 noted above, he states that it is characteristic of a 'justly mixed' constitution that it permits *all* the citizens to participate:

So it is evident that if one wishes to mix justly, one ought to bring together features from each [viz., democracy and oligarchy], for example, paying some for attending, and fining others for not attending; for thus all persons would have [governing] in common, whereas in the other case the constitution comes to belong to only one group of them. (1297^{a}38–^{b}1)

In order to reconcile Aristotle's different statements about the social composition of polity, one must suppose that although the hoplite group is composed predominately of moderately wealthy citizens, it also includes rich persons and even some poor (see also VI 7 1321^{a}12–13),[18] although the poor would for the most part not share in offices (*timai*, see IV 13 1297^{b}6–7). Therefore, although the middle, moderately wealthy group possesses greater authority than the other groups within the polity, the rich and the poor also have political rights within the mixed constitution of polity.

It is also an exaggeration to deny that Aristotle has any idea of checks and balances. Although he does not propose a system of separate, counterpoised branches of government of the sort found in later constitutional theories, he describes techniques for partitioning political rights among different groups of the polis and of instituting limits upon the exercise of political power so as to prevent the excesses characteristic of tyranny and the extreme forms of democracy and oligarchy. These modes are discussed systematically in *Politics*, IV 14–16, and mentioned elsewhere throughout the middle books. Since this is discussed in some detail in Sections 5.3–5 above, a few examples will suffice here. In mixed constitutions deliberative rights are typically partitioned. The authority over certain matters (e.g. to declare war or peace, and to audit officials) belongs to all the citizens, whereas other authority (e.g. to form or dissolve alliances, to pass laws, to execute or exile citizens) belongs to only some of them, i.e. to a smaller deliberative body. In addition, to offset the power of the poor majority, some deliberative officials are elected rather

---

[17] See Robinson (1962), 100. *Pol*. IV 9 describes provisions in polity and so-called aristocracy to ensure participation of both rich and poor.

[18] Cf. Newman (1887), i. 503 n. 1; iv. 201.

than chosen by lot.[19] It is also characteristic of a polity to assign to the popular assembly the authority to pass decrees, but also to confer on a small body (e.g. the 'law guardians') the power to veto them (IV 14 1298^{b}38–1299^{a}1). These features limit the exercise of authority by any particular individual or group, and thus hinder any single group (e.g. the rich or poor) from gaining exclusive control over public deliberation. Further, in regard to the election of magistrates, the mixed constitutions circumscribe either the eligibility to hold office or the right to elect officials.[20] Similarly polity and so-called aristocracy employ mixed modes for selecting jurors.[21]

In all three parts of the mixed constitution, then, an effort is made to divide authority by distributing political rights among different parts of the citizen body, and by providing checks and balances on the exercise of power, for example by having the deliberative part select and audit officials. There is also a concern that the political authority of all of the citizens not be exercised simultaneously. Aristotle argues that this is inconsistent with the rule of law: 'where the laws are not authoritative, there arise demagogues; for the people becomes a monarch, one combined out of many; for the many are authoritative not as individuals but all collectively' (IV 4 1292^{a}10–13). Mode (1.1.4) of extreme democracy is dangerous because the populace exercises its political authority without restraint. Such a collective is susceptible to flattery and other forms of persuasion in much the same way as a tyrant. Aristotle is generally fearful of an assembly that meets continually or frequently, because the multitude will come to have authority over the constitution and will ignore the constraints characterized by the rule of law (IV 6 1292^{b}41–1293^{a}10). Nothing would prevent the majority from committing acts of injustice against other members of the

---

[19] These are the mixed deliberative modes (1.3.X), discussed in Sect. 5.3. In addition, so-called aristocracies tend to place greater authority in the hands of elected officials. For in mode (1.3.3) of polity, elected officials and those chosen by lot deliberate about the same things in common; whereas, in modes (1.3.1) and (1.3.2) of so-called aristocracy, elected officials and those selected by lot preside over different spheres. The aristocratic procedure is presumably warranted on the grounds that election singles out more qualified and virtuous candidates.

[20] See Sect. 5.4: in modes (2.1.1.Z) of democratic polity, all the citizens have the right to choose officials, but they do not exercise this right at the same time but have to do so in shifts. In modes (2.2.1.Z) of oligarchic polity, the right to elect magistrates is confined to some of the citizens, although all are eligible to stand for election. In modes (2.1.3.Z) of aristocratic polity, all can elect, but the eligibility for office is mixed, in that all citizens are eligible for some of the offices, but only some are eligible for others.

[21] See Sect. 5.5: in modes (3.3.X) on some courts all the citizens are eligible to serve, on others only some of them are eligible, and some courts are composed of members chosen from the entire citizenry as well as from a select group.

polis, just as occurs in tyranny and extreme oligarchy. The various provisions which partition and limit the political rights of the citizens of the mixed constitutions are clearly designed to prevent such excesses. If Aristotle were as sanguine about the exercise of political power by the citizens of polity as Barker's interpretation suggests, these constitutional provisions would be unnecessary.

Aristotle offers a defence of a mixed democratic constitution in *Politics*, III 11, where he allows that the claim 'that the multitude ought to be in authority rather than the few best persons might seem ... to contain some difficulty but perhaps also some truth' (1281^a40-2).[22] There follows the 'summation' argument that many individuals may possess a collective wisdom exceeding that of the excellent few:

> For the many, each of whom is not an excellent man, none the less by coming together can be better (not individually but collectively) than those [i.e. the excellent], just as a feast to which many contribute is better than one equipped out of a single purse. For each individual among the many has a portion of virtue and practical wisdom, and when they come together the multitude becomes like one human being, having many feet, hands, and senses, so also regarding character and thought. (1281^a42-^b7)

This argument gives us a special application of Aristotle's aristocratic standard of justice.[23] In this case the principle is applied to an excellent person (E) and to the multitude of citizens (M) treated collectively as if it were a single person:

$$(\text{AR}) \quad \frac{\text{The virtue of } E}{\text{The virtue of } M} = \frac{\text{The political rights of } E}{\text{The political rights of } M}$$

The virtue of E exceeds that of each individual in M, so that each individual in M has a weaker claim than E to an office of deliberation and judgement (see 1281^b25). None the less, when all the members of M come together, they may be a better judge or no worse than E (1282^a16-17). If so, and given that virtue is the standard of justice, the multitude will have a greater or equal merit-based just-claim right to authority (cf. 13 1283^b21-7). The many discharge their offices not as individuals but as members of bodies such as the assembly, council, or jury. 'Therefore, the multitude justly has authority over greater things; for the people [sc. assembly], the council, and the jury are composed of many persons' (11 1282^a38-9). The individuals in question will accordingly not have rights

---

[22] I delete *luesthai* found in the manuscripts.   [23] See Keyt (1991a), 270–2.

to hold higher offices but only to serve in bodies such as the assembly or jury.

Aristotle does not indicate the range of constitutions he has in view. He does not use the summation argument to defend democracy explicitly, although he does mention the *dēmos* (1281^{b}16, 1282^{a}28, 35–6, 39). The proviso that the multitude not be overly slavish seems intended to rule out extreme democracy (1282^{a}15–16; cf. 1281^{b}15–21).[24] It is noteworthy that his main illustration of the summation argument is the 'nobly mixed' democratic constitution of Solon in which the many have the right in the assembly to choose officials and to audit them and the right in juries to pass judgement, but they do not have the right to hold important offices such as treasurer or general by themselves (III 11 1281^{b}32–4, 1282^{a}25–32; II 12 1273^{b}41–1274^{a}3, 15–17).[25] Aristotle adds that the constitution 'mixes' the many who have an adequate perception when they come together with the few who are better, whereas each group separately is incomplete (III 11 1281^{b}34–8). It might be objected against Aristotle's summation argument that it fails to take into account problems of collective irrationality, but it can be replied that the mixed constitution provides a check on the rule of the many which prevents the sort of irrational excesses perpetrated under extreme democracy.

In conclusion, the mixed constitutions of *Politics*, IV, conform to the requirements of justice in two ways: they assign political rights to citizens on the basis of a mixed standard of distributive justice, and they do so in such a way that no group of citizens is able to take unfair advantage of other citizens. Hence, it is clearly Aristotle's intention that the mixed constitution aims at justice in the sense of the mutual advantage of the citizens.

7.3. THE MIDDLE CONSTITUTION

Politics, IV 11, defends the 'middle' constitution, understood to include so-called aristocracy and polity (see 1295^{a}31–4).[26] The preamble to this

---

[24] He adds later that 'the multitude must be free persons acting in no way contrary to law, except where it necessarily falls short' (15 1286^{a}36–7). The summation argument here is used to defend the rule of law (see Sect. 3.4 above).

[25] This constitution combines the moderate democratic mode of deliberative rights (1.1.2) and the democratic mode of judicial rights (3.1.X) with the mixed mode of official rights which conjoins universal electoral rights with property assessments for eligibility (2.1.2.2).

[26] Johnson (1990), ch. 8, contends that the middle constitution is distinct from polity and the other mixed constitutions, but his arguments are not convincing: (i) Johnson contends

defence (1295^a25-34) makes clear that it concerns the second-best constitution and way of life. It will not assume moral capacities beyond the reach of private persons and an extraordinary level of education and equipment due to nature and fortune. Happiness and virtue of the highest sort are the object of the best constitution of Books VII–VIII, whereas the second-best constitution of IV 11 aims at the ordinary happiness attainable by most persons in most polises.[27]

The argument of IV 11 is in five stages: 1295^a34-^b1 argues that the standards of virtue and vice are the same for the polis as for the individual person; $1295^b1-1296^a6$ presents several arguments in favour of the constitution based on the middle persons (i.e. where the middle class possesses the greatest political authority); 1296^a6-21 argues that the middle constitution (identified with the constitution based on the middle persons) is the best; 1296^a22-^b2 tries to explain why democracies and oligarchies are more prevalent even though the middle constitution is better; finally, 1296^b2-12 claims that the middle serves as a standard for the other constitutions.

The defence begins with claims made 'in the *Ethics*':

(1)   The happy life is virtuous and unimpeded (cf. *EN* VII 13 1153^b9- 21).

(2)   Virtue is a mean (cf. *EN* II 6 $1106^b36-1107^a2$; *EE* II 10 1227^b5- 11).

that because Aristotle uses 'the middle constitution' as a separate name, he must intend it to refer to a separate constitutional form. This argument is weak because Aristotle does not elsewhere distinguish the middle constitution from the other constitutions; nor does he describe institutions peculiar to this form as he does for the others, e.g. in *Pol.* IV 14–16. (ii) Johnson argues that the middle constitution is described differently from polity: for example, in polity offices are distributed to the rich and poor in some combination, but in the middle state all the offices are monopolized by the middle class. However, the middle class *is* a 'mixture' of rich and poor in one of Aristotle's senses (i.e. moderation: cf. IV 9 1294^b2-3). Moreover, Aristotle does not say that the middle constitution 'excludes' both poor and rich from political rights (*pace* Johnson (1990), 154 n. 21). Rather, his constitution depends on the middle class and requires only that the middle class have a superior position in relation to the other classes (IV 11 1295^b34-9).

[27] This passage distinguishes the constitution to be defended from that which is 'according to our prayers [*kat' euchēn*]' (1295^a29). But the constitution described in *Pol.* VII–VIII is 'according to our prayers' (VII 4 1325^b36, 5 1327^a4, 12 1331^b21). Johnson (1990), ch. 9, argues, unconvincingly, that the constitution defended in *Pol.* IV 11 is the same as that described in Books VII–VIII. He fails to recognize that 'the best', in the context of *Pol.* IV 11, really means 'second best' (1295^b4, 34, 35; 1296^a7, $^b2$, 7). The claim of Nichols (1992), 88, that 'polity is the best regime simply' faces similar difficulties; likewise Bluhm (1962). Nichols relies also on the implausible claim that Aristotle's account of the best constitution in *Pol.* VII–VIII is deliberately ironic (criticized in Sect. 6.9 above).

(3) Therefore, the middle life must be best, the mean which each person is able to attain.

The preamble has made clear that this is the ordinary happiness and virtue which is attainable by most human beings. Aristotle proceeds to argue that the same standards are applicable to the polis and its constitution:

(4) The constitution is a certain way of life of the polis (cf. VII 8 1328^a41-^b2; Plato, *Laws*, VII 817^b3-4).

(5) Therefore, the same standards must also belong to virtue and vice of a polis and a constitution (as to each individual) (cf. VII 1 1323^b33-2 1324^a13).

As with the best constitution, it is tempting to see Aristotle here as endorsing the holistic theory that the polis has a life of its own over and above the lives of its citizens.[28] If Aristotle were arguing this way, he would be guilty of the fallacy of composition. From the fact that the good life of individual members of the polis consists in activity conforming to the mean, it does not follow that the good life of a collection of such individuals, i.e. the polis, is a collective activity conforming to the mean. However, there is an alternative, individualistic interpretation of step (5), along the lines of the individualistic interpretation of the best constitution defended in Chapter 6: the polis as a whole exhibits the middle way of life in so far as its individual citizens do so.

There follow ($1295^b1-1296^a6$) arguments that the constitution based on the middle class is best, and that those polises can be well governed in which the middle class is numerous (especially if it is greater than the rich and the poor combined, but if not, if it is greater than either part).[29] The thesis is that moderately wealthy persons have the following three attributes which qualify them to be citizens of the second-best constitution.

Rationality (1295^b5-11) Those who possess the goods of fortune in moderation find it easier to follow (practical) reason than do the very well off or the very poor. Hence, the middle persons are less inclined to insolence (*hubris*) than are the rich or to malice (*kakourgia*) than are the

---

[28] Robinson (1962), 103, objects that this would not give Aristotle what he wants, for 'the conclusion will be that the happy and good city is one that is active in a mean and not an extreme way. It will, for example, conquer the right amount of other cities, neither too many nor too few. What Aristotle draws from the analogy, however, is that the happy and good city will have a large and politically influential middle class. This does not follow because it is nothing to do with action.'

[29] See 1295^b34-6: *ara*, 'therefore', at $^b35$ indicates that these claims follow from the preceding passage.

poor. Insolence and malice produce unjust acts. The implied conclusion is that the moderately wealthy are more apt to treat their fellow citizens justly.

The claim that those of moderate means are less disposed to exhibit insolence or malice and thus are more inclined to treat one another justly is also made in Plato's *Laws*, III 679^{b}7–^{e}4. Elsewhere Aristotle observes that great wealth presents many temptations which tend to corrupt character and inhibit the formation of moral virtue (*Rhet.* II 16; cf. *Laws*, V 742^{c}4–743^{c}4).

Aptitude for political rule (1295^{b}13–28) The distinctive virtue of a citizen is the capacity to rule and be ruled nobly (III 4 1277^{a}25–7). Those who enjoy a great excess of the goods of fortune tend to become tyrannical and despotic, whereas the disadvantaged tend to be intimidated and slavish. The former are not habituated to being ruled by others and the latter are incapable of exercising such rule. A polis composed of the rich and poor will thus tend to consist of master and slaves, who regard each other, respectively, with contempt and envy, which are far removed from friendship. However, a community, and hence a polis, requires friendship among its members. In his ethical works Aristotle endorses the adage that equality is friendship (*EN* IX 8 1168^{b}8, *EE* VII 6 1240^{b}2). Friendships are generally vitiated by wide disparities in virtue and in goods of fortune such as wealth (*EN* VIII 7 1158^{b}33–1159^{a}5). Hence, the polis is by nature composed of persons who are equal and similar. But when the citizens are in the middle class rather than divided into rich and poor they are equal and similar to a greater degree. Consequently, they are more capable of friendship and have a greater aptitude for participating in a political community.

The constitution based on the middle class resembles the best constitution in this fundamental respect, that the citizens are by nature equal to each other and are thus able to share in political rule. As Aristotle says of the best constitution: '[I]t is evident that for many causes it is necessary for everyone to share [*koinōnein*] similarly in ruling, and being ruled, in turn. For the equal is the same for similar persons, and it is difficult for the constitution which is established contrary to justice to survive' (VII 14 1332^{b}25–9). However, Aristotle implies that the citizens of the middle constitution fall short of the best, for the citizens of the best are great-souled persons (VII 7 1328^{a}9–10; VIII 3 1338^{b}2–4), but great-souled persons are not middle persons (*EN* IV 3 1124^{b}17–23). There is no suggestion in *Politics*, IV 11, that the middle citizens will enjoy the leisure and equipment necessary for the completely virtuous life of the ideal state, where all production and exchange are carried out by slaves and foreigners.

Non-covetousness ($1295^b28–34$) The moderately wealthy do not desire the things of others, as the poor do, nor do they possess so much as to inspire envy. Because they do not plot against each other, they are secure and free from danger to a greater extent than city-states divided into rich and poor. The third point resembles the first, but the first argues that the middle class is not inclined to injustice as a result of insolence or malice, whereas the third argues that they present less of a threat of excessive possessiveness (*pleonexia*). The three points together show that the middle class exhibits justice, friendship, and mutual respect. As Phocylides prays: 'Many things are best for those in the middle; I would be in the middle in my polis' (1295^b34; fr. 12 Diehl).

The conclusion ($1295^b34–1296^a6$) is that the (second-)best constitution will be found where the middle class is dominant rather than where the polis is divided into rich and poor. In the most favourable situation the middle class outnumbers both the rich and the poor. In a less favourable situation it outnumbers one of these classes so that it can be 'added to' the other, either to the rich or to the poor. Hence, political rights should be assigned so that the middle class, in alliance with one of the other groups, possesses greater political authority. Where the middle class is numerous and shares in political rights (*timai*), factional strife and battles over the constitution occur least of all ($1296^a6–21$; cf. V 8 $1308^b30–1$). Those of moderate means are most inclined to treat their fellow citizens with justice and friendship and to share political rule with them. Therefore, if they have an absolute majority, they will tend not to promote their own advantage at others' expense; and if they are more powerful than either the poor or the wealthy, they can prevent either group from establishing a constitution to its own advantage. The rich and poor mistrust each other, but they both regard the middle class as an arbitrator they can trust (12 $1296^b38–1297^a7$).

Aristotle proceeds ($1296^a22–^b2$) to explain the prevalence of democracy and oligarchy in spite of the inherent superiority of polity. Because the middle class is often small, whichever of the other two groups, the poor or rich, gains the upper hand, rules according to its own lights, so that it becomes a democracy or oligarchy. 'Moreover, because of factions and fights between the people and the well to do, whichever happens to gain power over its opponents does not establish a common or equal constitution but takes the superior share of the constitution as its prize of victory, and creates either a democracy or oligarchy' ($1296^a27–32$). It is clear from the context that by 'a common or equal constitution' Aristotle means a constitution in which there is a just and equal distribution of political rights.

The concluding section (1296^{b}2–12) puts the middle constitution forward as the standard by which the other constitutions are to be evaluated. Noting that there are several sorts of democracies and oligarchies, he states: 'after the best constitution has been defined it is not difficult to see what sort of constitution should be placed first, what sort second, and which next in this manner, on account of being better or worse; for the one closest to the best must always be better, and the one further away from the middle must be worse . . .' (1296^{b}5–9). This is an instance of Aristotle's principle of proximity: it is best to attain perfection, but, failing that, a thing is better in proportion as it is nearer to the end (see *DC* II 12 292^{b}17–19). This passage might suggest a simple ordinal ranking of constitutions in which the middle constitution is best and each of the others is ranked first, second, third, and so forth. Another passage suggests, however, that Aristotle has something different in mind: after noting that proponents of the deviant constitutions overlook the middle class and fail to grasp the analogy between noses and constitutions, he says,

just as a nose deviating from the most beautiful straightness towards being hooked or snubbed is still beautiful and agreeable to the eye, yet if one increases it further towards an extreme he will first lose the moderateness of the part and finally will make it not even appear to be a nose due to the excess and deficiency of the opposites . . . , so this also happens concerning constitutions also. For it is possible for an oligarchy or democracy to be satisfactory, even if it departs from the best order, but if one increases either of them further, he will first make the constitution worse, and finally not even a constitution. (V 9 1309^{b}23–35)

This passage combined with IV 11 1296^{b}5–9 indicates that the middle or mixed constitution represents a norm from which the other constitutions deviate in either of two directions: democratic and oligarchic. It also implies that if a deviant constitution reasonably approximates the norm, it may be satisfactory. This suggests the layout of constitutions shown in Fig. 7.1. It is only if the constitution diverges significantly from the norm that it becomes unacceptable. If it deviates sufficiently, like tyranny, it does not even qualify as a constitution.

A strength of the foregoing argument is the plausible empirical claim that states containing a strong middle class tend to be more stable and less prone to exploitation and conflict between classes. However, the argument also contains an obvious weakness: the allegation that the middle class is

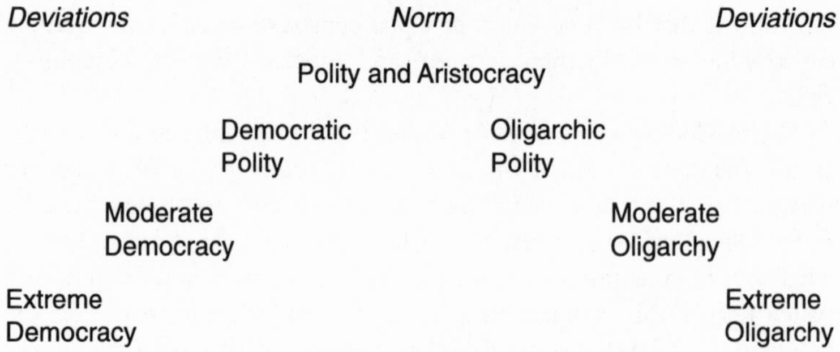

Deviations	Norm	Deviations
	Polity and Aristocracy	

Democratic Polity	Oligarchic Polity

Moderate Democracy   Moderate Oligarchy

Extreme Democracy   Extreme Oligarchy

FIG. 7.1. Constitutional Norms and Deviations

morally superior to the other two classes. The argument would be most implausible if it inferred from the mere fact that citizens possessed moderate wealth that they also possessed moral virtue, whereas deficient or excessive wealth excluded virtue. This would assume a kind of economic determinism which Aristotle himself rejects in his criticisms of Phaleas's proposal for an egalitarian redistribution of property (II 7 1266^{b}28–1267^{a}9) and of the communistic scheme in Plato's *Republic* (II 5 1263^{b}22–1264^{a}1). In both instances he argues that moral virtue is the result of the proper moral habituation rather than of level of personal wealth. It is doubtful, however, whether Aristotle would have made such an inconsistent claim, since he recognizes the importance of education even for the deviant constitutions (V 9 1310^{a}12–36). His point seems rather to be that the middle class faces fewer obstacles to the virtuous life than the poor, who become slavish and debilitated, and the rich, who are corrupted by temptation. Even so, his claim is not substantiated, and it seems open to the same general objections as his other sweeping claims regarding the innate superiority of a particular group (see Section 6.9 above).

The fact that societies with a strong middle class tend to be more stable and less prone to conflict does not have to be explained in terms of the moral superiority of the middle class. It can be explained instead in terms of the strategic relationships among the classes. The middle class serves as a buffer between the other two groups, because its interests are less opposed to either of theirs than theirs are to each other's. The moderately wealthy are less likely to arouse envy in the poor or to feel resentment towards the rich. If either the rich or poor attempts to seize power, the middle class can form an alliance with the other to prevent them.[30] Even

---

[30] See Mulgan (1977), 108–11.

if a middle class has this sort of stabilizing influence, it does not follow that this group is any more virtuous than the rich or poor. In fact, the moderately wealthy may have a common set of interests as a class and consequently their own political agenda which they seek to advance at the expense of other groups, if they can get away with it—although this class may be less in a position to use political means for self-aggrandizement because it is hemmed in by the other two classes.

7.4. THE MAXIM OF UNANIMITY

Aristotle argues that the mixed constitution is inherently stable: 'the better the constitution is mixed, the more lasting it will be' (IV 2 1297^a6–7). He also contends that stability is a consequence of constitutional justice (V 7 1307^a26–7), and, conversely, instability of injustice ($1\ 1301^b26$–7, 7 1307^a5–7). The connection between justice and stability may be illuminated by a practical principle regarding the preservation of constitutions which I shall call *the maxim of unanimity*.[31] This maxim, which is reiterated throughout the *Politics*, is complex, assuming positive as well as negative forms. The positive version is stated in *Politics*, II 9 1270^b21–2, in connection with the Spartan constitution: 'if a constitution is going to be preserved, all the parts ought to wish that it exist and continue in the same respects.' Another, negative version is found in the following passage:

In the nobly mixed constitution both [democratic and oligarchic features] ought to seem to exist, yet neither [of these features should be dominant], and it ought to be preserved on account of itself and not from outside—and on account of itself not because those who wish it[32] are more numerous (for this might hold even of a wicked constitution) but because no portion of the polis generally would wish another constitution. (IV 9 1294^b34–40)

The negative maxim (contained in the final clause of this passage) is logically weaker and less restrictive than the positive maxim, since 'everyone supports this constitution' entails 'nobody wishes another constitution', but the reverse entailment does not hold (e.g. there may be some alienated citizens who are anarchists or simply apathetic). An apparently parallel thought is expressed in the following clause:

[31] The maxim formalizes the ideal of unanimity (*homonoia*) or political friendship as described at *EN* IX 6 1167^a26–$^b4$ (cf. Sect. 4.7 above).
[32] I delete *exōthen* with Thurot.

all the citizens ought to be well disposed towards the constitution, but if this is not the case, they ought not to regard the authorities as their enemies. (VI 5 1320ᵃ14–17)[33]

Here the negative maxim takes the form 'nobody opposes this constitution'. This is slightly stronger than the previous negative formulation, since it rules out anarchists as well as partisans of other constitutions. In summary, the general maxim of unanimity takes the following specific forms, in order from stronger to weaker:

Positive: All the members of the polis ought to support the constitution.
Negative (1): No members ought to oppose the constitution.
Negative (2): No members ought to wish for another constitution.

The maxim of unanimity in these different forms may be regarded as a corollary of the principle of justice, or the mutual advantage. For rational citizens will each wish for the continued existence of the constitution if it promotes the good life for each of them. They will accede voluntarily to authority and will not resist it as long as they deem it as serving their interests. Thus, although Aristotle does not invoke the maxim of unanimity in *Politics*, VII–VIII,[34] it will be satisfied by the best constitution described there, because this system aims at the happiness of each and every citizen (VII 9 1329ᵃ23–4). However, the maxim of unanimity is a weaker requirement than justice because the former can also be satisfied even if it is impossible to promote the highest form of happiness for each and every citizen. Hence, we find that the maxim of unanimity *is* explicitly invoked in connection with the second-best, mixed constitutions. The strongest, positive form of the maxim, as cited above in *Politics*, II 9, is allegedly satisfied by the Spartan constitution, because all the free members of the polis possess political rights: the kings have the highest honour, the nobles are senators, and the people are eligible to be ephors (II 9 1270ᵇ21–6; cf. 10 1272ᵃ31–3). The Spartan constitution is said to be well mixed in that it combines democratic and oligarchic features (IV 9 1294ᵇ16–19).

It is noteworthy that the Spartan constitution of Lycurgus satisfies the unanimity requirement because it provides for political participation (in

---

[33] I read *dei de tēi politeiai*, etc., with Ross. On this reading the clause enunciates a general norm applicable more widely than the form of democracy under consideration in the immediate context. See Braun (1973), 395–6.

[34] Something like the first negative maxim may be implicit at VII 9 1329ᵃ9–12: viz., the polis should not contain armed enemies, because they have authority over whether the constitution lasts or not. Hence, those who bear arms should be citizens.

some form or other) for all the citizens. Aristotle's view seems to be that universal participation is the most reliable means to unanimity. In addition to the Spartan example, he mentions Solon's constitution in Athens. Solon reserved the higher offices for the three higher classes which could meet the property assessments, but ceded to the people the authority to elect officials and to audit them, on the grounds that the people would be opposed to the constitution otherwise (II 12 1274^{a}15–21; III 11 1281^{b}32–4; cf. VI 4 1318^{b}21–6). The rationale for this, as we have noted above, is that the auditing of officials ensures that they will rule justly (cf. VI 4 1318^{b}32–8). None the less, universal participation must be distinguished from unanimous support. Aristotle believed that a constitution might avoid internal discord by chance: this was the case in Carthage, where ambitious members of the people could easily emigrate to colonies. However, Aristotle thinks it better to achieve peace through proper legislation (II 11 1273^{b}18–22). Again, he states that a constitution controlled by hoplites can satisfy the negative unanimity maxim, because the poor will remain peaceful even when they do not possess honours (i.e. offices), if no one abuses them insolently or takes their property. However, he adds a caveat: 'But this is not easy; for it does not always happen that those who partake in the government are refined persons' (IV 13 1297^{b}6–10). Presumably, the support of the people would be more secure if they had some constitutional protections of the sort provided by Solon or Lycurgus.

The maxim of unanimity in its various forms must be carefully distinguished from another precept alluded to in IV 9 1294^{b}34–40 (cited above). The other rule may be called *the maxim of superiority*—which Aristotle elsewhere refers to as 'the great preserving principle': to make sure that the multitude which wishes the constitution to last is superior to that not wishing it (V 9 1309^{b}16–18).[35] Aristotle's view seems to be that the well-mixed constitutions will satisfy the maxim of unanimity. The best forms of democracy and oligarchy will also meet this requirement (at least in its negative form of universal non-opposition). However, for the most part the deviant constitutions will satisfy at best the maxim of superiority. Accordingly, this weaker requirement will be examined in the next chapter which is concerned with the deviant constitutions.

Aristotle's principle of unanimity (especially in its strongest form) bears a superficial resemblance to modern theories of popular sovereignty, in that it requires that the constitution must have the consent of the

---

[35] Braun (1973) offers an illuminating discussion of these two precepts.

governed.[36] However, the doctrine of popular sovereignty holds that the people, those who are governed, have ultimate authority over those who govern them. The most common form of this doctrine is that the government must rest upon the will of the people and that those who govern are representatives of the people. To most modern theorists this implies that the best political system is democracy, in which the people express their will through voting (either directly on issues or indirectly for legislators and officials who are authorized to act on their behalf). Underlying many versions of popular sovereignty is the reasoning that a government is legitimate only if its subjects are obligated to obey its rules and regulations and that such an obligation can arise only if each of the subjects makes a voluntary agreement to obey the government. Underlying this in turn is the thesis that the subjects of government are autonomous agents who can acquire political and other obligations only through their own consent. This is the view expounded by Hobbes:

The only way to erect such a Common Power . . . is, to conferre all their power and strength upon one Man, or upon one Assembly of men, that may reduce all their Wills, by plurality of voices, unto one Will: which is as much as to say, to appoint one man, or Assembly of men, to beare their Person; and every one to owne, and acknowledge himselfe to be Author of whatsoever he that so beareth their Person, shall Act, or cause to be Acted, in those things which concerne the Common Peace and Safetie; and there to submit their Wills, every one to his Will, and their Judgements, to his Judgment . . . This done, the Multitude so united in one Person, is called a COMMON-WEALTH, in latine CIVITAS.[37]

Similarly, Locke states,

Every Man being . . . *naturally free*, and nothing being able to put him into sub-jection to any Earthly Power, but only his own Consent; it is to be considered, what shall be understood to be *a sufficient Declaration of* a Man's *Consent to make him subject* to the Laws of any Government.[38]

The idea that political authority can be justified on the basis of an agreement made by those who are subject to the authority is also suggested

---

[36] Barker (1946), 80 n. L, goes so far as to refer to the 'important Aristotelian idea' that 'will is the basis of the state'.   [37] Hobbes, *Leviathan*, II. 17 (1968: 87).

[38] *Second Treatise*, VIII. 119. Cf. Pufendorf, *On the Duty of Man and Citizen According to Natural Law*, II. 10. 1: 'Consent of subjects is required to constitute any legitimate government . . .' Rousseau covers the following account of the social compact: 'Each of us places his person and all his power in common under the supreme direction of the general will; and as one we receive each member as an indivisible part of the whole', *On the Social Contract*, I. 6 (1983: 24).

by various ancient thinkers. The doctrine is at any rate implied by state-ments attributed to sophists such as Hippias and Lycophron that the laws are based on agreement.[39] This view is also attributed by Glaucon in Plato's *Republic* to 'Thrasymachus and countless others', who say that individuals in a state of nature 'make an agreement with each other neither to do nor to suffer injustice. Henceforth they begin to lay down laws and contracts of their own, and they name what is commanded by the law "lawful" and "just"; and this is the origin and being of justice . . .' (II 359^{a}2–5). A related view is found in Plato's *Crito*, in Socrates' argument that he should not escape from prison because he has agreed to obey the laws of Athens. The crucial premisses of the argument are that one ought to enact those agreements which are just (49^{c}5–8) and that since the citizens are at liberty to leave, whoever of them remains, when he sees how the laws conduct trials and manage the other affairs of the polis, has in fact made an agreement with the laws to obey their commands (51^{c}8–^{e}4). However, Socrates' reasoning seems to differ from the modern view that consent is a *necessary* condition for justified political authority. Socrates apparently assumes, instead, that agreement is a *sufficient* condition. For he also offers an argument that he stands to the laws as a child to its parents and is obligated to obey the laws just as a child is (50^{d}1–^{e}3; cf. 51^{e}4–52^{a}3); but the obligation of a child to its parents is obviously not based on an agreement.

However, Aristotle gives no indication of going even as far as Socrates in treating the consent of the governed as a *justification* for political au-thority. Rather, his view is that the voluntary compliance of the subjects to political rule is *evidence* that the political rule is justified.[40] The justifiability of a constitution rests ultimately on whether it promotes the ends of its citizens. Presumably this is why Aristotle reiterates that a kingship (as opposed to a tyranny) has voluntary subjects (see III 14 1285^{a}27; ^{b}3, 5, 8, 21). Thus, the subjects of tyranny are ruled over invol-untarily *because* the tyrant aims at his own advantage rather than at theirs:

[39] Hippias in Xenophon, *Mem.* IV 4 13: the laws are 'what the citizens have enacted after they have agreed about what they ought to do and what they ought to refrain from'. Lycophron in Aristotle, *Pol.* III 9 1280^{b}10–11: 'the law is a contract and a guarantee of mutual rights'.

[40] See *Pol.* II 11 1272^{b}30–2: 'A sign (*sēmeion*) of a constitution which has been put in order is that the people voluntarily (*hekousion*) remain in the order of the constitution and there is no faction deserving mention nor a tyranny.' Spengel here reads *hekousion*, instead of *echousan* found in the π^2 manuscripts. Although Dreizehnter (1970), Immisch (1929), and various commentators accept Spengel's emendation, Ross (1957) does not, and it would be inadvisable to place much weight on this passage as an explicit reference to consent. However, the passage does at least express a negative form of the maxim of unanimity.

'for no free person voluntarily endures such rule' (V 10 1295^{a}19–23).[41] Aristotle's theory ultimately bases political authority on a teleological, perfectionist principle rather than on the dictum that power must be derived from the people by an act of will.

Postscript on classical republicanism

In Aristotle's second-best constitution, just as in his best, political offices must be assigned to those possessing moral virtue and wisdom; and for Aristotle (as for Socrates and Plato) this has the aristocratic corollary that political authority must be confined to a privileged set of individuals within the polis. In what he calls the middle constitution, moderately wealthy landholders will hold sway on the grounds that it is morally superior to the other classes. The fundamental thesis that political offices should be based on virtue continued to be accepted by modern theorists in the tradition called 'classical republicanism'.[42] A number of scholars have argued that this tradition had an important influence on Renaissance and then on Enlightenment political theorists in England and America, who drew on Aristotle along with Plato, Cicero, Polybius, Plutarch, and other ancient authors in a defence of a republican form of government.[43] Especially notable in this regard is John Adams, second president of the United States, whose *A Defence of the Constitutions of Government of the United States of America* was published in 1787 in support of the ratification of the US Constitution. Adams and other classical republicans were very sympathetic to the classical ideals of the rule of law, the mixed constitution, and political virtue. However, they generally rejected the aristocratic corollary that virtue is necessarily confined to a privileged few. In particular, many of them rejected Aristotle's arguments for excluding farmers,

[41] The criterion of voluntary subjects is also found in Plato, *Statesman*, 291^{c}10–292^{a}8, and Laws, VIII 832^{c}2–7; and Xenophon, *Mem.* IV 6 12 and I 2 44–5. See Schütrumpf (1990), ii. 457–8. Cf. also Keyt (1993), 143, on the 'anti-coercion principle' in Aristotle.

[42] The argument of this paragraph is developed more fully in F. D. Miller (forthcoming).

[43] The rise of classical republicanism (or civic humanism) and more generally the influence of Aristotle and other ancient authors on English and American political theorizing in the 17th and 18th cents. is documented in Fink (1945); Gummere (1963); Robbins (1959); and Wood (1969). Pocock (1975) traces the evolution of classical republicanism through the Italian Renaissance. Richard (1994), ch. 5, discusses the influence of Aristotle's ideal of 'mixed government' on the American founders. Pangle (1988), ch. 4, challenges the classical-republican interpretation of the American Revolution. However, Pangle's thesis that Locke's natural-rights theory was a more important philosophical influence than the classics is consistent with the observation that the American founders and their English contemporaries were eclectic thinkers who readily combined Locke with Aristotle and other classical sources. See also McDonald (1985), ch. 3.

manufacturers, and merchants from citizenship, objecting that Aristotle's arguments for the psychological and moral inferiority of persons engaged in these professions depended more on prejudice than evidence. John Adams, for example, maintained that moral virtue and practical wisdom could be found in the husbandmen, artificers, and merchants of eighteenth-century America.[44] The classical republican theorists were sympathetic to Aristotle's view that the holders of higher office should be exemplars of virtue. Although Adams was conspicuous and somewhat controversial in his support of traditional, aristocratic ideals, other American founders such as James Madison agreed with him on a number of points, especially on the dangers of direct democracy and omnipotent popular assemblies.[45] However, rather than concentrating authority in the hands of a perpetual minority distinguished by birth or wealth, they proposed the device of representative government as a means by which the mass of citizens could select their leaders from among themselves. They thus trusted the people at large to be sufficiently virtuous to be capable of electing qualified officials. (The American electorate was, however, originally limited to free, property-owning males.) As we have seen, a number of Aristotle's constitutional modes provide for election of officials, but the American founders differed in excluding the people in their collective capacity from *any* share in the federal government. In addition, a judicious arrangement of separation of powers and of checks and balances was intended to prevent elected officials from exercising excessive and arbitrary authority. In this way the government could be relied upon to promote 'the public happiness' and to respect the rights of individuals and minorities. However, the US Constitution was ratified only on the condition that it included in the form of amendments the Bill of Rights. This enumerated a set of rights which Congress (and, implicitly, other branches of government) were barred from infringing. The notion that a constitution must explicitly provide for the protection of enumerated civil and legal rights was an American innovation, added to the classical republican ideals of the rule of law, a mixed constitution, and a virtuous citizenry.

---

[44] Adams (1787), iii. 162–74.
[45] See *The Federalist*, particularly the papers written by Madison, e.g. Nos. 45, 51, 55, and 63.

8

Deviant Constitutions

8.1. THE BEST AND THE WORST

In addition to his study of correct constitutions, Aristotle investigated with relish the entire spectrum of regimes existing throughout the ancient Greek world. This is in keeping with his admonition to study all forms of life in the *Parts of Animals*: 'All natural things contain something wonderful . . . so we should approach the inquiry into each [kind of] animal without bashfulness, on the grounds that all contain something natural and noble' (*PA* I 5 645ª16–17, 21–3). *Politics*, IV–VI, makes frequent references to the political practices of ancient Greece. Aristotle and his associates in the Lyceum also prepared detailed descriptions of 158 constitutions (see *EN* X 9 1181ᵇ17; Diogenes Laertius, V 27). Hence, Aristotle may be regarded as a pioneer of political science as an empirical discipline. None the less, politics is in Aristotle's view primarily a practical science, and the study of the inferior constitutions is intended to equip the politician and lawgiver to be an effective practitioner. Accordingly, *Politics*, IV 1–2, includes prominently among the functions of political science the study of the inferior constitutions and of how to establish, preserve, and correct them (1289ª1–7).

Aristotle is not very clear about the relations among the various functions of politics, and, in particular, about the connection between its inquiries into the best constitution and the inferior regimes. He implies that the study of the better constitutions precedes the study of the worse, but he does not give an explicit reason for this priority (IV 2 1289ᵇ12–26; see Section 5.6 above). This raises the question of whether or not an understanding of the best constitution is supposed to provide guidance for the activities of establishing, preserving, and reforming the deviant constitutions.

This issue is closely connected with another: What is the role of justice in the various applications of politics? The best constitution represents the fullest application by the lawgiver of Aristotle's aristocratic theory of justice, on the level of universal justice. The lawgiver should promote the good life for each and every citizen, and of distributive justice, by assigning political rights to fully equipped, virtuous citizens. Because they have excellent souls, there is no factional conflict in the best polis (III 15 1286^{b}1–3). The second-best constitution is also based on the theory of justice, but the standard is lowered in the face of necessity: a more ordinary sort of happiness is promoted for all the citizens, and rights are accorded to those of middling virtue and middling wealth. This is also without faction (IV 11 1296^{a}7–9). What norms guide the work of political science in connection with deviant systems? Does justice have any role here? Aristotle makes frequent mention of injustice as a cause of faction and political change,[1] but it may be objected that these passages only refer to *perceived* injustice, which may involve defective, hypothetical, mistaken conceptions of justice.

Another factor suggests that Aristotelian politics is not guided by the theory of justice when it turns to the deviant systems. Aristotle invokes a principle in these contexts which seems to run counter to justice, which I shall call *the maxim of superiority*: viz., that the part of the polis that supports the constitution ought to be superior to the part that does not (see e.g. V 9 1309^{b}16–18; IV 12 1296^{b}15–16). Unlike the maxim of unanimity which implies that the mutual advantage will be promoted (see Section 7.4 above), superiority seemingly is compatible with a state of affairs in which one group benefits at the expense of another.

The shift has led some commentators to postulate different 'strata' (conceptual and probably also chronological) in Aristotle's *Politics* (see Section 5.6 above). Against this view, I shall argue that, although Aristotle's constitutional theory is fundamentally consistent, he regards different normative principles as appropriate for different political settings. Just as he is prepared to relax the strict requirements of justice and the common advantage in the case of the second-best constitution, he is willing to make much deeper concessions where necessity requires. None the less, I shall argue, this pragmatic policy has the guiding principle that the politician should strive for the closest feasible approximation to justice which is attainable under variable and often adverse circumstances.

8.2. THE PROBLEMS OF JUSTICE IN DEVIANT CONSTITUTIONS

According to Aristotle, the diversity of political constitutions stems from the diversity of human beings (see Section 5.2 above). Different polises

---

[1] See V 1 1301^{b}26–9; 2 1302^{a}40–^{b}2; 6 1305^{a}38; 7 1307^{a}5–7, 23–7; cf. Plato, *Rep.* I 351^{d}4–6.

have widely varying demographic profiles, containing in different proportions classes with different occupations, economic status, and ways of life. This leads to moral dissensus: i.e. disagreement over the end of the polis and the standard of justice.[2] Aristotle's account of diversity is not pluralistic, in the sense of acknowledging many equally valid conceptions of the good. Rather it is perfectionistic, recognizing only one conception as the best and treating the others as inferior or mistaken (VII 8 1328ª35–41). The deviant constitutions rest on an erroneous conception of the ultimate good: in oligarchy the end is wealth and personal wealth is also the standard of merit; in democracy, freedom is the end and free birth is the standard.

In a deviant constitution a mistaken hypothesis of the good life and an erroneous standard of justice produce an aberrant distribution with political rights in the hands of one group. In an oligarchy, political authority is concentrated in the hands of the few who can meet stringent property qualifications (IV 4 1290ᵇ1–2, 19–20). The process is less direct but equally inexorable in a democracy: 'It results [*sumbainei*] that in democracies the poor have more authority than the well off, for they are the majority, and the opinion of the majority has authority' (VI 2 1317ᵇ8–10). Here the fact that democracy is rule by the poor is a 'result'; it is essentially rule by the free.[3] When the poor are in this position they also abuse their authority, promoting their own advantage at the expense of the rich.[4]

The lawgiver is like a craftsman who must provide a form (the con-

---

[2] Yack (1993), 6, emphasizes Aristotle's preoccupation with political conflict, especially in *Pol.* III–VI, and remarks that this aspect of Aristotle's political theory has not been fully appreciated by some recent communitarian interpreters, e.g. MacIntyre (1981), 153.

[3] Aristotle grapples with the question of whether democracy should be defined as rule by the poor in other passages. This seems definitely his view at III 8 1279ª35–6, where rule by the many is a result or 'accident' (*sumbebēkos*). He apparently revises the definition in IV 4 1290ᵇ17–20 to rule by the free and poor when they have a majority. If *Pol.* VI 2 presents his final view of the matter, he is saying that democracy essentially accords equal authority rights to the free. Since there are more of the poor, free persons, they have more authority rights and thus end up 'more authoritative' than the wealthy.

[4] Aristotle recognizes two apparent exceptions to this. First, in *Pol.* III 11 he grants credence to the 'summation argument' for popular rule, allowing that the multitude taken collectively might have more virtue than the excellent few. In this case it would appear that Aristotle's aristocratic standard could be used to justify democracy. However, as noted in Sect. 7.2 above, Aristotle's concession to popular rule is carefully hedged. It is true only for 'a certain kind of multitude' (1281ᵇ20–1), viz., one which has some share in virtue, and the sort of constitution he thinks the argument supports is evidently a mixed constitution in which the many have collective deliberative rights but not eligibility to high offices (cf. 1281ᵇ21–38, 1282ª32–41). Second, the most moderate type of democracy mentioned in *Pol.* IV 4 does not put the poor in authority over the rich: 'The law in this sort of democracy states that there is equality when the poor are no more pre-eminent than the wealthy, and neither have authority, but both are similar' (1291ᵇ31–4). This seems more like a democratic polity than a deviant constitution.

stitution) which is appropriate for its matter (its population and territory). However, the special difficulties which the lawgiver encounters with human 'matter' indicate that the analogy to crafts such as pottery and shipbuilding is only partially revealing. It is true that the clay has a material nature which limits in definite ways the kinds of pots the potter can produce. But the members of a polis are not like clay which is inert and waiting for the potter to impose on it a shape of his choosing. They have their own views of the good life and justice which may be mistaken or only partially true, but they do have them and are not inclined to relinquish them. Here the analogy of the gymnastics trainer of *Politics*, IV 1, is more apt: just as trainers have to proceed from the particular goal of their pupils which may fall short of excellence in athletic contests, lawgivers and politicians must deal with the ends of a given population, ends which may fall well short of human excellence. The attempt to impose perfectionist political goals upon a population which is unwilling and incapable of realizing them would be futile if not disastrous.

The constraints upon the lawgiver are especially pressing in view of the fact that 'those who have authority over arms also have authority over whether or not the constitution will last' (VII 9 1329ᵃ11–12). In classical Greece there were four principal kinds of warrior: cavalry, hoplites, light-armed infantrymen, and sailors (see *Politics*, VI 7). Soldiers had to provide their own equipment. Cavalry was associated with oligarchy because it required considerable land to support horses. Hoplites had to be rich enough to afford the heavy arms and shields needed for the phalanx. In contrast, the light-armed soldiers (they were called 'naked', *psiloi*) needed a weapon such as a bow or sling. Service in the navy required only an oar. Not surprisingly, oligarchies tended to excel in land warfare relying on horse and heavy arms. However, in warfare a government had to employ whatever resources were available: a polis with large estates could use cavalry quite effectively, whereas one with a large population could be expected to make greater use of light-armed infantry. Athens with its strategic location and port of Piraeus relied on its navy. According to Aristotle, because the people were responsible for Athens's naval victories in the Persian War, they became presumptuous and supported the demagogues who instituted extreme democracy (II 12 1274ᵃ12–15). In sufficiently desperate circumstances governments permitted the lower classes and even slaves to bear arms. These policies, though unavoidable, carried a price: 'the light-armed and naval force is entirely popular [*dēmotikē*]. Now, therefore, wherever such a multitude is great, when they divide in faction [the oligarchs] often do worse in the struggle' (VI 7 1321ᵃ13–16).

In dealing with polarized and refractory populations, the lawgiver must take care that the deviant constitution be stable and long lasting:

But it is not the greatest or the only function of the lawgiver and of those who wish to establish a constitution of this sort [i.e. democracy], to establish it but rather to ensure that it is preserved; for it is not difficult to remain governed in any manner whatsoever for one, two, or three days. Therefore, [the lawgiver] ought to proceed from the preservation and destruction of constitutions studied earlier [in *Politics*, V], and try to fashion stability, being wary of destructive factors and enacting those sorts of laws, unwritten as well as written, which encompass most of all the things that preserve the constitutions; and he ought not to regard as populist [*dēmotikon*] or oligarchic that which will make the polis democratically or oligarchically governed to the greatest extent, but what will make it last for the greatest time. (VI 5 1319^{b}33–1320^{a}4)

This passage emphasizes the stability and durability of the constitution rather than its justice. This suggests that when Aristotle turns to the deviant constitutions, justice ceases to be his primary concern, in favour of expedience and necessary evils (see Sections 5.6, 8.1 above).

However, this interpretation, despite its seeming plausibility, overlooks a primary concern of Aristotle, which is implicit throughout *Politics*, IV–VI, but is expressed clearly in *Politics*, VI 3 1318^{a}18–26. After reiterating that the democrats and oligarchs base their claims to political authority upon their different standards of justice, Aristotle adds, 'but both involve inequality and injustice'. The oligarchic standard leads to tyranny, for if one person were richer than all the other landowners put together, it would be just for him to rule alone and disenfranchise the others. Since the democratic conception reduces justice to the decision of the numerical majority, 'they will do injustice by public confiscation of the belongings of the rich and few, as was said earlier' (a back reference to III 10 1281^{a}17–21). This passage employs a commonplace notion of injustice as harming others and of justice as mutual deference and respect for rights.[5] This is a notion of justice and injustice which is shared by the different parties to the political dispute. The rich and the poor alike fear that their rights will be violated if the other side controls the levers of power.

---

[5] Remedying injustices in this sense is the concern of corrective justice (*EN* V 4 1132^{a}5–7). These types of injustice fall under the heading of universal injustice because they are unlawful and detrimental to the political community (see Sect. 3.2 above). Hippodamus of Miletus proposed a minimal constitution in which the laws were restricted to punishing insolent abuse (*hubris*), harm (*blabē*), and killing (*thanatos*) (II 8 1267^{b}37–9). Although Aristotle rejects this minimalist view of law, he himself regards justice in the sense of mutual respect for rights as a necessary but not definitive function of the polis (*Pol.* III 9 1280^{b}25–36).

Hence, this notion of justice provides common ground for the partisans of divergent conceptions of justice: democratic, oligarchic, and aristocratic.

This notion of justice is exhibited in the earlier discussion referred to above, *Politics*, III 10, which is written in the style of a public dispute. Aristotle speaks in turn on behalf of the partisans:[6]

[OLIGARCHS]. If the poor possess authority by being more numerous and distribute among themselves the belongings of the wealthy, is this not unjust?

[DEMOCRATS]. By Zeus, it was enacted justly by the authority.

[OLIGARCHS]. If this is not extreme injustice, what is? Again . . . if the majority distribute among themselves the belongings of the minority, this will destroy the polis; but virtue does not destroy what has it and justice is not destructive of the polis; so it is clear that this law cannot be just. Further, [on this argument] whatever actions a tyrant performs are necessarily all just, for he uses force being superior, just as the multitude [uses force against] the rich.

[DEMOCRATS]. But is it just for the few rich to rule? If they do these things and rob and seize the property of the multitude, is this just? If so, then the other also. It is evident, therefore, that all these things are base and unjust.

[ARISTOCRATS]. But ought the reasonable persons to rule and have authority over all things [or over everyone]?

[DEMOCRATS]. But then all the other persons will necessarily be dishonoured because they will not be honoured by receiving offices. For we say that offices are honours, and if the same persons always rule the others necessarily are dishonoured.

[MONARCHISTS]. But is it better for the most excellent person to rule?

[DEMOCRATS]. But this is even more oligarchic; for those who are dishonoured are more numerous.

[PROPONENTS OF RULE OF LAW]. But it is generally bad if the authority [i.e. sovereign] is not law but a human being, who has in his soul the passions resulting [from humanness].

[MONARCHISTS]. But if the law is oligarchic or democratic, what difference will it make regarding the aforementioned difficulties?

In this interchange the parties are concerned lest they be treated unjustly. Such injustice takes a number of different forms, but the most familiar and non-controversial are insolence (*hubris*), excessive possession (*pleonexia*), and dishonour (*atimia*).

Hubris, 'insolence', is typically displayed in wanton or abusive behaviour. Insolence is doing or saying things to cause shame to a victim, not in order that some benefit will accrue to the perpetrator or to exact retribution, but simply for the pleasure involved in the action (*Rhet.* II 3 1378^{b}23–5).

---

[6] *Pol.* III 10 1281^{a}11–38 is here recast as a dialogue.

An example of insolence was the invasion of Odysseus' defenceless household by Penelope's suitors 'whose insolence and violence reach their own heaven' (Homer, *Odyssey*, XV 329). Thus insolence is 'especially' (*malista*) a cause of injustice (*Pol.* V 10 1311ᵃ27; IV 11 1295ᵇ10–11; cf. Plato, *Laws*, III 691ᶜ4). Insolence was a category of legal offence for which one could be prosecuted in Athens.[7] Plato's *Laws* distinguishes five types of insolent acts in order of seriousness: against sacred things such as statues (especially when they are also public), against tombs, against one's parents, against the rules, and against the political rights of individual citizens (X 884ᵃ6–885ᵃ7). Those who are blessed with the goods of fortune have a tendency to behave insolently towards those who are less fortunate (*EN* IV 3 1124ᵃ29–30).[8] Thus the insolent person typically has the advantages of wealth, noble birth, strength, friends, and political power, whereas the typical victim is poor, base-born, young or female, and relatively defenceless (IV 11 1295ᵇ5–11). *Hubris* is the distinctive trait of tyrants, as Sophocles observes: 'Insolence breeds the tyrant' (*Oedipus Tyrannus*, 873.) The typical response to insolence, not surprisingly, is anger or outrage (*EN* VII 6 1149ᵃ32–4), so that such offences frequently incite faction and revolution (*Pol.* V 10 1311ᵃ27).

Pleonexia, 'excessive possessiveness', is commonly translated as 'graspingness', 'greed', 'covetousness', or 'selfishness', but, literally, it means 'having more'. Sometimes the term has a morally neutral sense of 'having more' than someone else, which may be just or unjust (V 2 1302ᵇ1; cf. III 12 1282ᵇ31–4). The vice of excessive possessiveness is opposed to the particular virtue of distributive justice (see Section 3.2 above). The verb *pleonektein*, 'to take more', denotes taking or claiming more than one's due. The excessively possessive person (*pleonektēs*) wants more than his share of good things and less of bad things (*EN* V 1 1129ᵇ1–10). In general, then, 'taking more' involves unjust taking, either of private or of public property (*Pol.* V 3 1302ᵇ9–10). Most typically, such a taking is concerned with pecuniary gain; e.g. committing adultery in order to make a profit rather than for pleasure. However, the objects taken can also be honour, reputation, and pleasures (*EN* IX 8 1168ᵇ15–23). Hence, *pleon echein* or *pleonektein* can refer to 'overreaching' or 'outdoing' others (Plato, *Rep.* I 349ᵇ3, 8). Because of the value which they place upon wealth, the oligarchs are especially prone to excessive possessiveness. In general, the unjust takings by the wealthy ruin the

---

[7] See MacDowell (1978), 129–32.

[8] However, an undisciplined slave or helot could become insolent (*hubrizousi*) and unjustly claim equality with those in authority (II 9 1269ᵇ9–11).

constitution more than those by the poor (*Pol.* IV 12 1297ᵃ11–13). However, as noted above, in the extreme democracy, the poor egged on by demagogues also confiscate and redistribute the properties of wealthy citizens.⁹

Atimia, literally 'dishonour', is the political counterpart to having one's property taken. The honouring or dishonouring of a person is either just or unjust, depending on whether it is in accord with or contrary to that person's merit (V 3 1302ᵇ12–14). Unjust dishonouring is thus a special case of unjustly taking honours that another deserves (2 1302ᵃ38–ᵇ2). But Aristotle usually confines *pleonexia* to the unjust taking of money or property, and treats *atimia* as a distinct form of injustice. Dishonour is not merely a loss of self-esteem or even of social status. Because honour is also tied to political rights and a citizen is by definition one who possesses political rights, 'one who partakes of honours is especially spoken of as a citizen; thus for example, Homer said, "like some wanderer without honour". For one who does not partake of honours is like a metic' (III 5 1278ᵃ35–8). To lose honour in the legal sense was to cease to be a full member of the polis, for 'dishonour' denoted a legal punishment in ancient Athens and elsewhere. In early times a person who was dishonoured was an outlaw who could be killed or robbed with impunity. By Aristotle's time it had come to mean 'disenfranchisement' or the loss of political rights.¹⁰ This punishment was generally reserved for crimes against the polis (failure to pay debts, refusing military service, rebelling against the government, etc.) and had the following implications:

A disenfranchised citizen was not allowed to enter temples or the agora. He could not hold any public office, nor be a member of the *boulē* or a juror. He could not speak in *ekklēsia* [assembly] or in a law-court (though he could be present in a court without speaking). But it is not clear that he lost any of the other rights and duties of a citizen; probably he could still marry an Athenian wife and own land in Attika, and was still liable to pay taxes and perform military service.¹¹

For noble persons dishonour is catastrophic because it entails a loss of social status.¹² In addition to punishment of individuals for wrongs against

---

⁹ The pernicious effects of *pleonexia* are noted by Plato, e.g. at *Laws*, X 906ᶜ2–6. Hobbes recalls and endorses the Greek condemnation of *pleonexia* at *Leviathan*, v. 15 (1968: 78).

¹⁰ e.g. in the Athenian law against tyranny (337/6 BC) members of the Council and Areopagus do not have the liberty (*mē exeinai*) to meet or deliberate if the democracy has been overthrown. If anyone breaks the law, he and his descendants will lose their civil rights (*atimos*) and their property will be subject to public confiscation. Cf. Meritt (1952), 355–9.

¹¹ MacDowell (1978), 74; cf. Hansen (1991), 99.

¹² Sophocles' tragedy *Ajax* depicts the psychological ramifications of dishonour: 'I perish dishonoured by the Argives' (440).

the polis, the term *atimia* also refers in the *Politics* to the wholesale deprivation of social classes of their political rights (III 10 1281^{a}29–32). For well-born and virtuous individuals this is intolerable (V 7 1306^{b}26–36). The lower classes are also resentful if they are totally disenfranchised: 'when there are present many dishonoured and poor persons, this polis is necessarily full of enemies' (III 11 1281^{b}29–30). Aristotle thinks, however, that the many desire profit above honour, so that they are more inclined to tolerate disenfranchisement than loss of their property, and more content with limited political rights (VI 4 1318^{b}16–22).

We are now able to describe the problem confronted by the lawgiver: the population of many polises is heterogeneous and divided into opposed groups of rich and poor. The opposing groups cannot agree upon a specific conception of justice to serve as the basis for political authority. However, the different groups do share a commonplace notion of justice as mutual deference and respect for rights. Injustices in this sense are violations of rights such as taking the property of others, treating others insolently, and dishonouring them. After Aristotle notes in *Politics*, VI 3, that the rich and poor are both fearful of being treated unjustly in this sense, he states the first problem of the lawgiver: 'What sort of equality both groups will agree on should be investigated by proceeding from both of their definitions of justice' (1318^{a}27–8). A few lines later Aristotle identifies a second, even more intractable problem: 'However, although it is very difficult to find the truth concerning equality and justice, it is still easier to attain this than to persuade those who are able to take more [than their share] [*pleonektein*]. For the weaker always seek equality and justice, but the stronger have no concern about them' (1318^{b}1–5).

Thus the first problem faced by the lawgiver is: *What type of justice or equality might there be on which opposed groups could agree?* How can one find a basis for political co-operation when there is no moral consensus among the members of the population? Even if they share a formal principle of justice by which political rights should be distributed according to merit, they do not agree on the standard by which merit is to be determined. However, they would be disposed to accept as just a scheme of co-operation which ensured a reasonable degree of mutual deference. The problem for the lawgiver, then, is to define the basis for such co-operation in adverse circumstances of disagreement, mistrust, and enmity.

But then the lawgiver faces the second, even more difficult problem: *How can the groups be persuaded to co-operate with others and to refrain from injustice?* Even if it is possible in theory to identify a basis for just co-operation among the divergent groups which make up the polis, how can these groups, especially the group which is more powerful, be persuaded to comply with this? This is akin to Glaucon's problem in the *Republic*: those who are in a superior position ask why they should treat the inferior justly. The task of political persuasion is also emphasized by Aristotle when he criticizes political theorists who either focus on Utopian ideals or those who 'though speaking of an attainable sort of constitution, disregard those that exist and instead praise the Spartan or some other. But one ought to introduce an order such that under existing circumstances they [the leaders of existing regimes] will easily be persuaded and will be able to participate, since to reform a constitution is no less a task than to establish one from the beginning . . .' (IV 1 $1288^b39–1289^a4$).[13]

Although Aristotle explicitly states these two problems in *Politics*, VI, they are implicit concerns throughout the discussion of the deviant constitutions in Books IV and V also. As I shall now argue, in answer to the first problem Aristotle tries to show that it is possible for groups with opposed partial conceptions of justice to find a stable basis of co-operation, namely, through the maxim of superiority, which is the closest feasible approximation to justice under adverse circumstances. In answer to the second problem, he argues that any significant departure by the rulers from such a co-operative basis or from justice in the ordinary sense of mutual deference and respect for rights is destabilizing and ultimately self-defeating.

8.3. THE MAXIM OF SUPERIORITY

In most cases politicians seeking a basis for political co-operation are not able to satisfy the maxim of unanimity, which requires that all parts of the polis wish for the continued existence of the constitution (see Section 7.4 above). They can at best meet the maxim of superiority, viz., that the multitude wishing that the constitution continue to exist ought to be superior (*kreitton*) to the multitude that does not (IV 12 $1296^b15–16$; V 9 $1309^b16–18$).[14] This precept clearly diverges from justice correctly understood because it provides no guarantee that the interests of the inferior group will be protected. However, the maxim can be regarded as defining a fallback position if a correct constitution is unattainable: viz., establish a constitution which enables a superior portion of the polis to

[13] I follow the translation of Curren (forthcoming), who rightly emphasizes the importance of political persuasion in *Pol.* IV–VI.

[14] The latter passage evidently contains a reference back to the former.

co-operate for mutual advantage. Aristotle intends the maxim for general application:

What constitution is advantageous for what persons and what sort of constitution for what sort of persons is to be discussed next. One must first grasp the same thing universally concerning all [constitutions]: for the part of the polis that wishes the constitution to remain ought to be superior to the part which does not wish it. (IV 12 1296^{b}13–16)

However, to apply the principle to a particular case, one must interpret the term *kreittōn*, 'superior'. The word can mean either 'stronger' (see II 8 1268^{a}25; III 10 1281^{a}23) or 'better' (see II 3 1262^{a}7, 9 1271^{b}9).[15] Given that Aristotle is concerned with the survival of the constitution, *kreittōn* must imply 'stronger'. However, Aristotle also evidently sees superiority as involving a qualitative as well as a quantitative element. For *Politics*, IV 12, points out that the groups making up the polis may be compared in terms of quantity or quality. Quantity pertains to the sheer number of claimants, and quality to the attributes which enable them to rule properly, viz., freedom, wealth, education, and good birth. Although the majority exceeds the minority in quantity, the minority excels in quality:[16] for example, the base born may be more numerous than the well born, and the poor than the rich. But it is possible that the multitude does not excel in quantity to the extent that it is lacking in quality. 'Therefore these two things [quantity and quality] should be judged together' (1296^{b}24). The maxim of superiority is not tantamount to 'the greatest happiness for the greatest number', because a mere majority may be outweighed by a large minority of higher quality. Putting it another way, the poor have a comparative advantage in terms of numbers and the rich in terms of quality. The question is which group is superior all things considered.

Aristotle's analysis assumes that there is a trade-off between quantity and quality which enables one to determine which group is superior. Granted this assumption, one can make a comparison between the two measures, e.g.:

$$\frac{\text{Quantity of the poor}}{\text{Quantity of the rich}} > \frac{\text{Quality of the rich}}{\text{Quality of the poor}}$$

[15] Keyt (1991a), 272–3, notes that the ambiguity can be removed by qualifying *kreittōn* with *kata dunamin* ('in strength') or *kata aretēn* ('in virtue'), in order to signify 'stronger' and 'better', respectively. Both qualifications appear at VII 3 1325^{b}10–12.

[16] Strictly, 1296^{b}19–21 says that quantity belongs to one group and quality to another, but the example makes clear that he means pre-eminence in quantity and quality.

In this case the poor would be deemed superior. Aristotle does not, unfortunately, tell us how to make this comparative judgement. But he presumably has it in mind that just as the poor may be two or three times as numerous as the rich, the better off may as a group be twice or three times as wealthy as the poor (and similarly possessed of other meritorious qualities). According to the maxim of superiority, the constitution should be a form of democracy in the case described above. Note that this is equivalent by cross multiplication to the following:

$$(\text{Quantity} \times \text{quality of the poor}) > (\text{Quantity} \times \text{quality of the rich})$$

On each side we have the *product* of quantity and quality for each group. This product is equivalent to a summation of the quality of the individual members of each group. In this case, Aristotle says, there will *naturally* (*pephuken*) be a democracy (1296^b26). This might be expected in the Athens of Aristotle's day, where the 30,000 citizens included only 1,000 to 1,200 rich citizens.[17] On the other hand, there will (naturally) be an oligarchy (cf. 1296^b32-3 with 26) when

$$(\text{Quantity} \times \text{quality of the rich}) > (\text{Quantity} \times \text{quality of the poor})$$

The general maxim of superiority that these cases illustrate may be expressed as follows for a given constitution C:

$$(\text{Quantity} \times \text{quality for } C) > (\text{Quantity} \times \text{quality against } C)$$

A constitution will be 'natural' in the sense of *Politics*, IV 12, if it satisfies this principle. These deviant constitutions are not 'natural' in the same strict sense as the constitutions which seek the advantage of all the citizens. But by satisfying the superiority maxim these deviant constitutions do attain a quasi-natural condition enabling at least a superior portion of the polis to co-operate. They can be seen as mimicking the correct constitution, which is unattainable under the circumstances. Democracy can be expected to result 'always or for the most part' in cases like the first, and oligarchy 'always or for the most part' in cases like the second. Hence, the maxim of superiority defines quasi-natural, stable points of co-operation, which can be expected to obtain always or for the most part given specific social conditions.

Any deviation from the outcome specified by the maxim of superiority leads to instability. For example, a democratic constitution is unlikely to

[17] See Hansen (1991), 110–15, who cites evidence of special taxes and liturgies (public services) imposed on the rich. Only about 300 Athenian citizens were wealthy enough to equip and command a warship.

T A B L E 8.1. *Example of Weighted Voting*

Outcome	Rich	Poor	Total
For	4 × 2	15	23
Against	6 × 2	5	17

endure if there are a sufficient number of wealthy persons opposed to it. On the other hand, if the poor are superior in Aristotle's sense, an oligarchy will be unstable even if it resorts to various contrivances to deceive or intimidate the poor. Those possessing political authority will face faction and dissension and will be under pressure to make concessions in order to retain their authority.

The maxim also explains why the stablest forms of democracy and oligarchy are well mixed (IV 12 1297^{a}6–7). In *Politics*, VI 3, he describes how the democratic and oligarchic standards of justice might be combined with each other, for example, in a system of weighted voting. If there are ten rich and twenty poor, each might have a vote weighted on the basis of the property assessment. Suppose a rich vote counts twice as much as a poor vote. Then if the votes are cast as in Table 8.1, 'The [side] whose assessment predominates when those of both are added up has authority' (1318^{a}37–8). This procedure for tallying votes provides an analogue to the maxim of superiority:

$$(\text{Quantity} \times \text{quality for}) > (\text{Quantity} \times \text{quality against})$$

This example differs from the cases considered above in that the product of quantity and quality on each side of the issue is an aggregate of products for the rich and the poor. The maxim of superiority can be applied in an analogous way in the case of moderate or mixed constitutional forms of democracy and oligarchy. If neither the rich nor the poor is superior, one group should try to include members of the other so that the entire group supporting the constitution is in a superior position.

The superiority maxim is also applicable to cases in which there are three contending classes: the rich, the poor, and the middle class (IV 12 1296^{b}23–1297^{a}13). The latter, being moderately wealthy, are important players when they are more numerous than the rich and of higher quality than the poor. Aristotle advises that the lawgiver ought to include the middle class in the constitution. For even if the middle class is inferior to the other groups, it can serve as a 'swing' group that could ally itself to the other side. For example, if the rich are superior to the poor but not to the poor and the middle taken together, the maxim of superiority prescribes a moderate oligarchy supported by the rich and the middle.

$$\frac{\text{Quantity of poor}}{\text{Quantity of rich and middle}} < \frac{\text{Quality of rich and middle}}{\text{Quality of poor}}$$

On the other hand, if the poor are superior to the rich but inferior to the rich allied with the middle, the maxim supports a moderate democracy supported by the poor and the middle. In the unusual case in which the middle class is superior to both the other groups combined, there will be a lasting polity. If it is superior to one of the other groups, it can form a coalition with this group against the third. The rich and poor find it harder to form an alliance with each other because of their opposed interests and mutual distrust. In all of these cases adding the middle class will help to satisfy the maxim of superiority.[18] 'The better the constitution is mixed the more lasting it is' (IV 12 1297^{a}6–7), because the mixture guarantees that the constitution has the allegiance of the superior portion of the polis. The mixed constitution thus finds a basis for co-operation which is, under the circumstances, natural and stable.

The superiority maxim also provides guidance in screening potential citizens: in the case of democracy 'one ought to deviate in succession and always separate out the worse multitude' (VI 4 1319^{a}40–^{b}1). For the many can be segmented into distinct groups of descending quality: farmers, herdsmen, vulgar artisans, merchants, hired labourers, illegitimate sons of citizens, sons of foreigners, and sons of slaves (VI 1 1317^{a}24–6; 4 1319^{a}19–28, ^{b}9–10; III 5 1278^{a}32–4). If the worse groups have political rights, they are apt to abuse them. Because they live in a disorderly way they make the constitution more disordered (*ataktoteran*), and the notable class will no longer submit to their rule (VI 4 1319^{b}14–17). For example, in his democratic reform of 507 BC Cleisthenes granted citizenship to a large number of metics and foreigners, so that the citizen population rose to an unwieldy total of 60,000 by the mid-fifth century BC (cf. *Pol.* III 2 1275^{b}35–7, *Ath. Pol.* XXI 4; see Section 5.1 above). The maxim of superiority accordingly counsels the lawgiver to apportion political rights first to the best layer of the poor, then to the next best layer, and so forth: 'but one ought to add [citizens] up to the point where the multitude predominates over the notables and middle class and not go beyond this'

---

[18] If the lawgiver were able to establish a 'justly mixed' constitution which involved all three classes, the maxim of unanimity could be satisfied, as in the second-best constitution discussed in the previous chapter (IV 13 1297^{a}38–^{b}1).

(VI 4 1319^{b}12–14).[19] Conversely, if the mass of poor is inordinately large, it should be discouraged from exercising its political rights (IV 14 1298^{b}23–6) or even removed from the citizen rolls, layer by layer starting from the worst. In the case of oligarchy the lawgiver should proceed in the opposite manner, since the more extreme forms of oligarchy are increasingly selective:

[T]he first and best blended [form of] oligarchy is near to polity. In it one ought to divide the property assessments making some lower and others higher. Those with the lower assessments will partake [only] of the necessary offices, and those with the higher will partake of offices with more authority; and one who possesses the assessment ought to have the liberty [*exeinai*] to partake of the constitution, and the multitude of people admitted [ought to] be such that [the citizens] are superior [*kreittones*] to those not partaking; and they always ought to take the participants [*koinōnous*] from the better people. (VI 6 1320^{b}19–29)[20]

The next form of oligarchy involves tightening the property requirement so that the poorer layer of citizens is excluded. In general, the lawgiver should follow the procedure of assigning political rights to the best strata of the many until he reaches the point at which the enfranchised group is superior to the non-citizens. This enables the constitution to endure while minimizing the number of citizens who would abuse their political rights and produce disorder.

The maxim of superiority thus provides the lawgivers with guidance as they select among the various political modes which are described in *Politics*, IV 14–16, and elsewhere (see Sections 5.3–5 above). In the example just given, the lawgiver might combine two oligarchic modes: (1.2.1) which assigns the right to deliberate to everyone who meets a low property requirement, with (2.2.2.2), which confines the right to elect and hold office to the few who meet a higher requirement.

Conversely, a constitution will be worse and more unstable if the superior portion of the polis is deprived of their political rights. Aristotle observes that this often results from deception. He offers as illustrations

---

[19] Newman (1887), iv. 521–2, alleges a conflict between this statement and IV 11 1296^{a}16–18: 'When the poor predominate numerically [*plēthei*] without [the middle class], they do badly and quickly perish.' However, the latter adds the qualification *plēthei*, indicating the comparison is purely numerical, in contrast to 1319^{b}12–14 where the superiority involves quality as well as quantity.

[20] Cf. IV 5 1292^{a}39–41 which states that the disenfranchised poor are a majority. This shows that *kreittones* at 1320^{b}27 does not mean a majority, as translated by Rackham (1932). Newman (1887), iv. 538–9, has a good note on this passage, and also (i. 491) suggests that the maxim of superiority can be traced back to Theramenes, who established the constitution of the Five Thousand in Athens in 411 BC. See Xenophon, *Hell.* II 3 42.

various pretexts (*prophaseis*) or devices (*sophismata*) the oligarchs use against the people (IV 12 1297^{a}7–13 1297^{a}35). The constitution contains apparently democratic modes which are nugatory because the many do not exercise their political rights:[21] regarding deliberative rights, every citizen has the liberty (*exeinai*) to attend the assembly, but only the wealthy receive a fine for not attending (or the wealthy are liable to a much larger fine). Regarding official rights, the wealthy do not have the liberty to decline (*mē exeinai exomnusthai*),[22] but the poor do have this liberty (*exeinai*). Regarding judicial rights, the wealthy are fined if they do not attend, but the poor have immunity (*adeia*) (or the wealthy receive a larger fine). Again in some oligarchies, every citizen who has registered[23] has the liberty (*exesti*) to attend the assembly and jury courts, but if they have registered and do not attend the assembly and jury courts they receive large fines. (The law is intended to discourage the poor from registering and thus from participating at all.) Finally, regarding military rights, the poor have the liberty not to possess arms (*exesti mē kektēsthai*),[24] but the wealthy are liable to a fine (*epizēmion*) if they do not possess them; similarly, if the wealthy do not engage in gymnastic training they are liable to a fine, but the poor receive no fine. Against these devices, Aristotle remarks, democracy has its own counter-devices (*antisophizontai*), assignments of political rights which will encourage the participation of the poor and discourage the rich, for example, paying the poor for attending assemblies and juries, and not fining the rich for failing to do so (1297^{a}35–8).

The 'justly mixed constitutions' differ from these because they combine these devices so as to encourage participation by all of the citizens, for example, paying the poor for participating and fining the rich for shirking (1297^{a}38–^{b}1, 9 1294^{a}36–^{b}13). He recommends similar combinations as advantageous in reforming extreme democratic constitutions (1298^{b}13–26). One such reform is to adopt an oligarchic device of fining the wealthy for not attending the assembly, 'for everyone will deliberate better if they deliberate in common, the people with the notables and these with the multitude'. Aristotle also recommends as advantageous a representational

[21] Cf. IV 9 1294^{a}36–^{b}13. Aristotle at II 9 1266^{a}5–22 points out similar oligarchic devices in Plato's *Laws*, V 756^{b}7–^{c}8, VI 764^{a}3–^{b}1.

[22] This entailed taking an oath that one did not have the health or financial means to perform the office.

[23] At 1297^{a}24–5 Lord (1984) translates 'it is open to all to enroll themselves for the assembly and courts . . .' However, *apograpsamenois* modifies *pasin*, requiring, 'it is open to all who have enrolled . . .'

[24] Rackham (1932) translates '. . . the poor are not allowed to possess arms . . .' One would expect *mē exesti kektēsthai* if that were what Aristotle intended (cf. VI 4 1319^{a}8). Also, it would hardly be a 'pretext' to prohibit the poor from bearing arms.

scheme, in which deliberative officials are chosen by election or lot in
equal numbers out of the different classes. Moreover, if the poor greatly
exceed those with political ability, the lawgiver ought to find ways of
reducing the participation of the former: 'it is also advantageous . . . either
not to pay a fee to all but only to as many as will balance the multitude
of notables, or else to exclude by lot the excess [from pay].'[25] He makes
similar recommendations for oligarchy, that the poor be included in
deliberation to a greater extent, so that 'the people will have a share in
deliberation but will not be able to undo the constitution' (1298^b26-34).[26]

The maxim of superiority thus defines a basis for political co-operation
among groups who are otherwise unable to agree upon a conception of
the good or a standard of justice. In effect, it shows the lawgiver how
to combine opposed standards of justice in assigning political rights to
the population. For example, the democratic lawgiver should temper the
democratic standard, by which political rights are distributed solely on
the basis of free birth, with the oligarchic standard, assigning rights
also assigned on the basis of wealth or noble birth, until superiority is
satisfied. The result is, in effect, a mixed standard of distributive justice.
The oligarchic lawgiver should proceed in a similar fashion, tempering
the pure oligarchic standard with the democratic until superiority is
attained. Therefore, just as the maxim of unanimity provides the basis
for the nobly mixed, second-best constitution, the maxim of superiority
provides a way of mixing and thus correcting the deviant constitutions.

Aristotle describes these suggested reforms as 'advantageous' (*sumpherei*)
for the constitution in question. Because the constitutions are deviant, the
reforms cannot result in a constitution which is fully just in the sense of
promoting the *mutual* advantage. For even if an oligarchic constitution
is moderated so as to cede political rights to the more highly qualified
segment of the poor, many persons will still lack political rights and
hence may not support the constitution. However, if the reforms result
in a constitution which passes the test of superiority it has come closer to
the ideal of the mutual advantage; and it may well be that the polis can
come no closer than this if its members disagree deeply over the conception of the good and the standard of justice.

As we have seen the maxim of superiority requires the inclusion of a

---

[25] I read *politikōn* at 1298^b24 with the manuscripts and understand it to refer to those who
have political skill (i.e. the notables) and I take *moriōn* at 1298^b23 to refer to the two classes
under discussion (the notables and the popular multitude). Cf. Newman (1887), iv. 250.

[26] *Pol.* IV 14–15 have other suggestions regarding representative government and
constitutional checks and balances, discussed in Sects. 5.3–5 above.

superior portion of the polis in the political process (VI 6 1320^{b}25–8). However, we should be careful to distinguish between two different versions of the maxim of superiority:

Superior support: The portion supporting the constitution is superior to the portion not supporting it (or opposing it).
Superior participation: The portion exercising political rights is superior to the portion not doing so.[27]

Aristotle clearly thinks that in practice superior participation is the surest way to secure superior support, because it is obvious that individuals are more disposed to support a system in which they have a stake and to resent being excluded from the process. On the other hand, he allows that the poor may be content even when they are excluded from the government, provided those in power do not treat them insolently or take their property. They may even be willing to fight in defence of the polis if they are given rations (IV 13 1297^{b}6–12). Hence, there may be superior support without superior participation, if the disenfranchised group trusts its rights are being respected. Even a tyrant may succeed in attracting the allegiance of a superior part of the polis by protecting it from injustice (V 11 1315^{a}31–7).

In most cases, however, superior participation is needed to ensure just treatment of members of the polis. For unrestrained rulers tend to abuse their power: 'those who are wealthy, when the constitution gives them pre-eminence, seek to act insolently and have excessive possessions' (V 7 1307^{a}19–20). Similarly in extreme democracy the demagogues attack the rich and confiscate their property (5 1305^{a}3–7).

8.4. THE PRESERVATION OF THE POLIS

The previous section considered Aristotle's answer to the question: Upon what basis can the opposing parties in a deviant polis agree to co-operate?

---

[27] Another distinct but closely related maxim is *majority participation*: those who participate in the constitution should be more numerous (*pleious*) than those who do not (IV 13 1297^{b}4–5). The disenfranchised group presumably includes only free native men (not slaves, foreigners, and women), since first-class citizens were a minority of the total population even in extreme democracies. This maxim is satisfied by democracies, some mixed constitutions, and no oligarchies. Superior participation will of course imply majority participation if the free native men are roughly equal in terms of quality. Note further that majority participation differs from *majority rule*, the principle that the majority of those with political rights should prevail, which is found in aristocracy and oligarchy as well as democracy (IV 8 1294^{a}11–14).

His maxim of superiority falls short of justice in the sense of the mutual advantage but is intended to locate a point at which opposing parties can co-operate. It is also the closest feasible approximation to a just constitution because at last a superior part of the polis can co-operate for mutual advantage. But there remains the even more challenging question: How can those who possess political power be persuaded to co-operate and respect the rights of others? The problem is unavoidable if a part of the polis remains disenfranchised. Because the question concerns persuasion it is a problem of rhetoric (*Rhet.* I 2 1355^b26–7). The political scientist must direct arguments against the democrats, oligarchs, and tyrants, who do not accept or even understand the correct theory of justice. In order to persuade them, he must direct his arguments to *their* concern, which is to maintain their own political authority. Aristotle, however, holds that 'rhetoric is useful because things that are true and things that are just are by nature superior to their opposites' (I 1 1355^a20–2). The problem is thus one of truth and justice as well, hence a problem of political philosophy (cf. *Pol.* III 9 1282^b22–3). Aristotle believes that in political affairs the morally justified solution is also the practical one. The inferior constitutions which are the closest feasible approximations to justice, as defined by the maxim of superiority, exhibit a natural resiliency, and to the extent that constitutions deviate from this point the more unstable they become. Hence, the maxim is also 'the greatest elementary principle' for preserving constitutions (cf. V 9 1309^b16–18). This theme runs throughout his diagnoses of constitutional change and his prescriptions for the preservation of the polis in *Politics*, V.[28]

Aristotle proceeds from the observation that 'many types of constitutions have arisen because, although everybody agrees about justice and proportionate equality, they are mistaken about this' (1 1301^a26–8). The poor and the rich agree that justice should be based on merit, but favour opposing standards of merit, respectively, free birth and personal wealth. Because these constitutions are based on contested standards of justice, 'when either does not share in the constitution according to the hypothesis it happens to have, they engage in faction' (1301^a37–9). Revolution and constitutional change (*metabolē*) usually involve faction (*stasis*)[29] so that a

[28] *Pol.* V offers a general theory of political change, including change in aristocracies and polity (discussed in *Pol.* V 7). But the treatise is mainly concerned with deviant constitutions because, on Aristotle's view, they are most prone to faction and instability. References in this section are to *Pol.* V unless otherwise noted.

[29] The terms *metabolē* and *stasis* are difficult to translate. *Metabolē* is often translated as 'revolution'. However, *metabolē* is also used by Aristotle for peaceful and subtle changes in the constitutions (1303^a13–14), so that 'change' is a preferable translation: see Polansky

treatment of change must take justice and injustice into account. 'Faction is everywhere the result of inequality,' remarks Aristotle, 'for in general they engage in faction [*stasiazousin*] because they seek the equal' (1301^b26-9). But 'the equal' (*to ison*) is understood in two different ways. The democrats understand it as numerical equality, the oligarchs as proportionate equality. Thus although 'there is agreement that justice in an unqualified sense is according to merit', the democrats and oligarchs differ: the former regarding themselves as numerically equal with the rich because they are equal in one respect [namely, freedom] and the latter claiming to be unequal with [i.e. greater than] the poor because they are unequal in one respect [namely, wealth] (1301^b29-39).

Aristotle views disagreements over justice and injustice as the 'chief and universal cause' of revolutionary tendencies:[30]

For some engage in faction because they aim at equality, if they believe that they have less although they are equal to those who take more [*pleonektousin*]; and others, who aim at inequality and pre-eminence, engage in faction if they suppose that even though they are unequal [i.e. better], they do not have more [*pleon echein*], but [only] an equal [amount] or less. (It is possible to strive for these things justly, and also to do so unjustly.) For the inferior engage in faction in order that they might be equal; those who are equal, in order that they might be greater. . . . The things over which they engage in faction are gain and honour and their opposites (for they engage in faction in polises to avoid dishonour or punishment either for their own sake or that of their friends). (2 1302^a24-34)

In these cases the malcontents may claim that they are victims of injustice because others are taking an unfair share of political power or property, or they may claim that they have a right to higher offices or more property

(1991). This also preserves the connection with *metabolē* (translated as 'change') in Aristotle's *Physics*. None the less, in *Pol.* V many of the examples of *metabolē* are clearly what we would call revolutions. I translate *stasis* as 'faction' and the related verb *stasiazein* as 'to engage in faction'. (Both are related to the verb *histasthai*, 'to make to stand'.) Plato describes *stasis* as 'war within the polis' (*Rep.* V 470^b4-9; *Laws* I 628^b1-2), and often it describes what we would call 'rebellion'. However, a *stasis* may arise within the governing body (6 1306^a31-4) or may aim solely at seizing power without a change in the constitution (1 1301^b10-13). In addition, *stasis* can refer to a party attempting to gain political power through illegal and violent means if necessary.

[30] In addition, he takes into account a wide range of causes of constitutional change and faction, a number of which involve developments relating to the 'material causes' of the constitution, such as population and geography: e.g. the disproportionate growth of a group; chance events (e.g. war, pestilence, economic developments) affecting the size of fortunes of a social class; ethnic differences among the citizens; geographical differences (e.g. urban and rural); etc. The Aristotelian politician should take into account such contingencies as well as political factors such as scheming and negligence (see *Pol.* V $3-4$).

than the constitution allows. Such claims may in fact be just or unjust, depending upon whether their appeal to justice is correct or mistaken. But faction arises from the perception that they are victims of injustice. This is especially likely to occur when they see those in office committing acts of insolence or taking unfair advantage, or if they feel they have been unfairly dishonoured or disenfranchised (1302^a38-^b3, 3 1302^b6-14). He applies this general explanation to each constitution, e.g. democracy:

Democracies undergo changes especially due to the wantonness of the demagogues. For sometimes they make false accusations as individuals against property owners and unite them (for common fear brings together even the greatest enemies); and other times in public they set the multitude upon them . . . Sometimes, in order to curry favour with [the people, the demagogues] do injustice to the notables and this unites them, either by making a redistribution of their wealth or taking their income for public services; sometimes they slander the wealthy in order to be able to impose a public confiscation of their goods. (V 5 1304^b20-4, 1305^a3-7)

Oligarchies also suffer revolutions when the wealthy treat the multitude unjustly. Also, sometimes wealthy citizens who have been deprived of political rights (*timai*) in a more extreme oligarchy themselves protest and topple the constitution (6 1305^a37-^b22).

Moreover, even the mixed constitutions may become infected with injustice:

Polities and aristocracies are overthrown especially because of a deviation from justice in the constitution itself. The source in polity is that democracy and oligarchy have not been nobly mixed, and in aristocracy that these [two] things and also virtue have not been nobly mixed, though above all the two (by the two I mean [rule of] the people and oligarchy); for polities and most of the so-called aristocracies attempt to mix these things. (7 1307^a5-12)

So-called aristocracies are especially vulnerable because of the tendency of the affluent to indulge in insolence and excessive possession when they hold positions of dominance (7 1307^a19-20; cf. IV 13 1297^b6-10). Whichever group holds the upper hand continues to press its advantage until it provokes rebellion. He cites the example of Thurii in which the notables managed to acquire all of the land contrary to the law until eventually the people revolted (1307^a27-33).

A central thesis of Book V, therefore, is that the further a constitution deviates from justice the less it is able to last. Accordingly, Aristotle recommends a number of remedies which have the effect of making the constitution more just.[31] He argues that the constitution will be more secure if the authorities treat citizens and noncitizens alike in a just and equal manner:

[One ought] to see that not only some aristocracies but even some oligarchies last, not because the constitutions are stable, but because the office-holders treat well both those outside the constitution and those in the government: by not doing injustice to those who do not partake [in the constitution]; by admitting into the constitution those among them who have the capacity to be leaders; not doing injustice to ambitious persons by dishonouring them or to the many by profiting at their expense; and by treating one another, themselves and those who partake [in the constitution] in a mutual popular [*dēmotikōs*] way. For the equality that the populists [*dēmotikoi*] seek for the multitude is not only just but advantageous for persons who are similar. (8 1308ᵃ3–13)

Democracies should take measures to protect the wealthy, and oligarchies likewise to protect the poor. For example, in democracies the properties of the wealthy should be protected from public confiscation and from onerous liturgies, i.e. mandatory public services such as presenting a chorus, feast, or festival, or commanding and financing a warship.[32] Likewise, in oligarchies the poor should be cared for, for example, assigned less important offices, granted privileges, and protected from acts of insolence and unjust takings by the wealthy. Generally, 'it is advantageous both in a democracy and in an oligarchy to distribute equality or precedence in other things to those who partake least in the constitution (in democracy to the wealthy and in oligarchy to the poor), except for the offices that have authority over the constitution; these should be entrusted only, or mostly, to those from the constitution' (1309ᵃ27–32).

Aristotle also emphasizes the importance of moderation in a constitution.

---

[31] Again, he also offers various other remedies of a more pragmatic sort (see *Pol.* V 8). For example, to be on guard against unconstitutional change (*paranomia*), even in slight forms, perhaps by means of an office such as the law-guardians; to encourage the fears of the citizens against external enemies so that they will be more concerned with defending the constitution than with overturning it; to revise property-requirements and other regulations periodically to take into account the effects of inflation and the like; to prevent the disproportionate rise of individuals or groups by regulation or even laws, lest they become corrupted and threaten the constitution; to institute offices to regulate people's private lives so that they do not live in a manner disadvantageous to the constitution; to prevent officials from profiting from their offices, through audits and the like. Mayhew and Smith (1994) point out that Aristotle also discusses questionable techniques, in part on the principle that the political reformer should 'know the strengths and weaknesses of such constitutions, so that he will be in the best position to advise *against* the evil forms of constitution and their abuses of power'.

[32] On the institution of liturgy (*leitourgia*) see Hansen (1991), 110–12, and Stockton (1991), 107–9.

The extreme oligarch or democrat who insists upon defining the virtue of the constitution exclusively in terms of the oligarchic or democratic standard of justice ultimately destroys the constitution, just as a sculptor who overemphasizes the concavity or convexity of a nose destroys its beauty and ultimately its function as a nose.[33] Although it falls short of the best, even a deviant constitution can be brought into an adequate condition by moving towards a more mixed constitution, while still relying mainly on an oligarchic or democratic standard of justice. The adequate condition involves satisfying the maxim of superiority: For 'neither of these constitutions can exist and last without the wealthy and the multitude' (1309^b38–9; cf. 7 1307^a16–20, VI 4 1318^b32–8).

A further recommendation is that those who possess greater political authority should serve as spokesmen and advocates of those who do not:

> Moreover, a mistake is made in both democracies and oligarchies. In democracies the demagogues, where the multitude has authority over the laws, [make a mistake], for by fighting with the wealthy they forever divide the polis into two, but they ought to do the opposite and always seem to speak on behalf of the wealthy. And in oligarchies the oligarchs ought to seem to speak on behalf of the people and to swear oaths which are the opposite of what the oligarchs swear now. For now in some [oligarchies] they swear, 'I will bear malice against the people and will devise whatever harm I can against them.' But they should take the opposite view and act[34] accordingly, affirming in their oaths: 'I shall not do injustice to the people.' (1310^a2–12)

To speak on behalf of (*legein huper*) someone is not to represent that person, in the sense of being authorized as that person's agent. It is, however, to be an advocate, i.e. to articulate and defend that person's rights. Aristotle's proposal that the oligarch swear an oath not to act unjustly towards the poor implies that, more generally, there should be a covenant between ruler and ruled that the latter will not be subjected to rights-violating acts of insolence or dispossession. Only by upholding this covenant can the deviant government maintain long-lasting and stable authority.

In addition, Aristotle prescribes habituation and education 'relative to the constitution', be it oligarchic or democratic (9 1310^a12–38).[35] Even

---

[33] As argued in the nose analogy (9 1309^b21–35), quoted in Sect. 7.3 above.

[34] The term *hupokrinesthai* (act) refers to playing a part on a stage. It may imply dissembling, but one may seem to do action A by actually doing A, as we see in Aristotle's 'advice to the tyrant' (discussed below).

[35] This advice is obviously intended for the well-mixed constitutions such as polity and aristocracy as well.

though such education is aimed at promoting the ends of the constitution, it serves to constrain the behaviour of the citizen: 'But to be educated relative to the constitution is not to do the things enjoyed by oligarchs or proponents of democracy, but rather to do the things that will enable them, respectively, to govern in an oligarchic or democratic way' (1310^a19–22). If the scions of the wealthy wallow in luxury, they will become unfit to defend their constitution, whereas the children of the poor will be industrious and hence become rebellious and capable of overthrowing their masters. On the other hand, in a democracy, if the principle of freedom is applied without restraint, the progeny of the poor will tend to become licentious as 'each person lives as he wishes and for the sake of whatever he relishes' (1310^a32–3). Aristotle admonishes the democrats, 'This is base; for one ought not to believe that it is slavery to live relative to the constitution; rather [it is one's] preservation' (1310^a34–6).

Although the ends of democracy and oligarchy are, respectively, freedom and wealth, each constitution will be destroyed if every citizen single-mindedly pursues, respectively, freedom or wealth. Oligarchy faces a paradox[36] because a life devoted solely to the acquisition and consumption of wealth leaves no room for the cultivation of political virtues such as temperance and courage which are necessary to preserve and protect the oligarchic constitution. The continued existence of any constitution depends upon widespread political virtue, i.e. upon *most* of the citizens virtuously exercising their political rights. However, the development of political virtue is an arduous, prolonged undertaking which would detract from the enjoyment of wealth. Any oligarch would be better off if he could enjoy his wealth all the time while others took time to cultivate virtue, i.e. if he could 'free ride' on others' efforts. The problem is represented by Fig. 8.1 below. The first number in each cell represents the individual oligarch's ordinal ranking of outcomes as more or less choiceworthy from first to fourth. The second number is the ordering for the other citizens. Each oligarch has the following ordering from best to worst:

I always pursue wealth while others sometimes cultivate political virtue. > All (including me) sometimes cultivate political virtue. > None of us sometimes cultivate virtue. > I cultivate virtue sometimes while others always pursue wealth.

The individual calculates that if the others take time to be virtuous, his best option is to pursue wealth single-mindedly; but if others eschew

[36] The argument for the democratic paradox takes a similar form.

OTHER CITIZENS

		Virtue	Wealth
OLIGARCH	Virtue	(2, 2)	(4, 1)
	Wealth	(1, 4)	(3, 3)

FIG. 8.1. The Oligarch's Dilemma

virtue, he would obviously be better off pursuing wealth single-mindedly and neglecting virtue. Either way he should always pursue wealth. Unfortunately every other oligarch will reason the same way. The paradoxical outcome is that even though reciprocated virtue is more choiceworthy for each oligarch than reciprocated vice, the latter is what they collectively end up with.

Aristotle's problem resembles what is now known as a public goods problem: everyone would benefit if a common resource (here a virtuous citizenry) existed, but individuals acting separately do not have an incentive to contribute to the good's production. Aristotle's proposed solution to the oligarchic's dilemma is to institute a system of moral education to ensure that the citizens acquire the virtues necessary to sustain the oligarchic constitution. Having been morally habituated, the individual oligarchs prefer to act virtuously, provided that they are assured that others will do likewise. The existence of the educational system ensures that all, or most, of the oligarchs will co-operate, develop virtue, and support the constitution. Aristotle can therefore argue plausibly that the end of the oligarchic constitution is not being compromised ('it is not slavery to live with a view to the constitution'), because moral education leaves all citizens better off from the standpoint of the oligarchic hypothesis: because it is mutually advantageous for all the oligarchic citizens to have such an educational system, it is consistent with oligarchic justice and rights to establish it.

The controversial treatment of tyranny in *Politics*, V 10–11, presents the most serious challenge for the interpretation that Aristotelian lawgivers combine moral with practical concerns when they turn to deviant constitutions. For *Politics*, V 11, offers an extended discussion of how to preserve a tyrannical regime without apparent concern for justice. However, it is necessary to consider the discussion of tyranny in its proper context. Aristotle begins by reiterating the claim of *Politics*, III 7, that tyranny is a deviant constitution opposed to kingship: 'Whereas kingship is based on aristocracy, tyranny is composed of the extreme types of oligarchy and democracy. And, indeed, therefore, it is the most harmful to the ruled, because it is composed out of two bad constitutions and possesses the deviations and mistakes of both' (10 1310^{b}2–7). Ironically, however, both kingship and tyranny arise out of a concern for justice: kingship is established in order to protect reasonable (*epieikeis*) individuals, i.e. the virtuous, against the people or multitude; the former elect as king one of their members who is outstanding in virtue or who belongs to an outstanding family. On the other hand, the tyrant is elected to protect the multitude from injustices by the notables (1310^{b}9–14). However, the two forms of government diverge because only kingship involves aristocratic justice, so that only kings are capable of truly benefiting their polis (1310^{b}31–40).

The king is inclined to be a guardian, ensuring that property holders do not suffer expropriation and the people do not suffer insolent abuse, for the king has a noble end and looks to the common advantage. Consequently, the citizens support and defend their constitution. In contrast, the tyrant's end is not nobility but his own gratification (and, consequently, the power to secure this: 11 1314^{a}36). Concerned with his private benefit, he heeds the common advantage only as a means to this end. Lacking the support of the governed, tyrannies are typically defended by foreign mercenaries (10 1310^{b}31–1311^{a}8).

Among the causes of revolution against monarchies is injustice: 'For due to injustice, fear, and contempt, many of the ruled attack monarchies, and regarding injustice it is due to insolence especially, but sometimes also due to the taking of private property' (1311^{a}25–8). For example, Pausanias assassinated King Philip of Macedon for letting him suffer insolent treatment (1311^{b}1–3). Characteristically, Aristotle considers a number of other causes of revolution, including other motivations by the ruled and attacks by foreign city-states. However, he concludes that the greatest threats to kingship are internal, for example, when factional strife breaks out within the royal family itself, or when the kings try to extend their authority in a tyrannical way contrary to law. The monarchies of Aristotle's day are tyrannies rather than kingships (including Macedon?). Aristotle says, 'because kingship is a voluntary type of rule', but where there are many similar persons and nobody is so superior as to be able to have a meritorious claim to rule,[37] the subjects will not voluntarily endure this sort of constitution, and they regard anyone who becomes ruler through force or fraud as a tyrant (1312^{b}38–1313^{a}10). A parallel passage

---

[37] The meritorious claim to rule (*to axiōma tēs archēs*) is based on the aristocratic standard of justice: cf. III 5 1278^{a}19–20 and see Sect. 4.6 above.

in *Politics*, IV, remarks that tyrants rule over persons equal to themselves or better than themselves for their own advantage not that of their subjects. Therefore, tyranny is involuntary (*akousios*); i.e. the subjects do not give their consent, 'for no free person would voluntarily endure this sort of rule' (IV 10 1295ᵃ19–23).³⁸ Monarchy thus loses the support of its subjects when it departs from justice and the common advantage (see Section 7.4 above). Aristotle accordingly recommends that kingships be preserved by moving them towards a more moderate condition, in particular by limiting the king's authority through various checks and balances such as the divisions of kingship and Theopompus' institution of ephors in Sparta (11 1313ᵃ18–33).

Next, however, Aristotle commences a controversial discussion of how tyrannies are preserved. He distinguishes two opposite 'modes', or strategies, the first being the traditional method used by most tyrants (11 1313ᵃ34–1314ᵃ29). Techniques include the removal of high-minded persons and the prohibition of common messes, clubs, education, leisurely conversations, or anything else that encourages confidence and trust among their subjects (1313ᵃ34–ᵇ6). These and other techniques have been used throughout the ages by tyrants, aimed especially at repressing 'any expression of freedom' (1314ᵃ1–10). Aristotle sums them up in three guiding precepts (or hypotheses) of the tyrant: that the subjects not trust each other, that they lack the ability (including the knowledge) to act against the tyrant, and that they lose self-confidence (1314ᵃ14–29). Aristotle does not disguise his contempt for such techniques which are 'lacking no sort of evil' (1314ᵃ13–14). He also implies that these stratagems can only succeed in the short run, because they incite the animosity which most often undermines tyrannies. It is only by moderating the excesses of tyranny that it can be made longer lasting.³⁹

The second strategy of preserving tyranny is 'almost the opposite' of the first, since it tries to preserve tyranny by making it 'more kingly', although it safeguards the tyrant's power, 'so that he rules not only willing subjects, but also unwilling; for if this is conceded, so is the tyranny' (1314ᵃ29–38). In addition to holding on to power he should give a noble performance of a king in everything he does or appears to do. First of all, he should appear to be concerned about public revenues. For

---

³⁸ Cf. Socrates in Xenophon, *Mem.* IV 6 12: 'He thought that rule over willing [*hekontōn*] human beings and according to law was kingship, whereas rule of unwilling [*akontōn*] persons and not according to law was despotism.'

³⁹ See 11 1313ᵃ30–3 and cf. 12 1315ᵇ11–18, two passages which frame the discussion of the two modes of preserving tyranny.

example, he should not offend the working poor by taking their income and transferring it to prostitutes, foreigners, and artisans. He should also give an account of public revenues and expenditures (1314^a38-^b6). Also, the tyrant should try to inspire awe rather than fear in his subjects, for example by fostering, at least, military virtue (1314^b18-23). 'Further, neither he nor his associates ought to appear to abuse anyone he rules insolently, whether boys or girls' (1314^b23-5). This appearance, it becomes evident, requires actual self-constraint by the tyrant: a safeguard of monarchy is that the ruler 'abstain from any sort of insolence and above all from two: towards the bodies and towards youth'; i.e. from bodily violence and sexual abuse (1315^a14-16). Moreover, he should himself distribute honours to his subjects who are deserving 'in such a way that they believe they would not have been honoured more by citizens [governing themselves] under their own laws' (1315^a4-6).

Hence, among the specific prescriptions which belong to the second mode of preserving tyranny, Aristotle emphasizes those which create the appearance that the tyrant is respecting their rights by not dispossessing them, treating them insolently, or dishonouring them. It is evident from the whole tenor of the discussion that the tyrant can create the appearance of justice successfully only by, for the most part, actually respecting their rights.[40] Of the tyrant's subjects, both the rich and the poor ought to suppose that they are being preserved because of his rule and that neither group has its rights violated: '. . . but whichever is superior, he should make these especially partial to his rule, so that, if they support his interests, it will not be necessary for him to emancipate slaves or to take away [citizens'] arms; for adding either part [i.e. rich or poor] to his power is sufficient to make him superior to his attackers' (1315^a31-40). Thus, Aristotle assumes that the subjects will accept the tyrant's rule if they believe their rights are respected. At least, the tyrant should satisfy the maxim of superiority by enlisting the superior segment of the polis in his support. Otherwise, his regime will be unstable and short-lived.

By adopting the second strategy, the tyranny would become the closest approximation of a just kingly constitution. According to this mode, then, the ruler ought to appear to his subjects as a king rather than as a tyrant, as a trustee rather than as an expropriator. He should pursue a moderate way of life and avoid extremes. He should try both to conciliate the notables by companionship and to be a leader of the people.

---

[40] Cf. Nichols (1992), 110: the tyrant 'should, in other words, appear to serve the city, and the way to do so is actually to do so'.

Consequently, his rule is necessarily nobler and more to be emulated not only because he rules over better persons who have not been humiliated without his being hated or feared, but also because his rule is longer lasting. Further, with respect to his character he will either have a noble and virtuous disposition, or be half-benevolent, and he will be not wicked but half-wicked. ($1315^{b}4$-10)

Aristotle here emphasizes two features of the second mode of preserving tyranny: it conduces to greater nobility and virtue, and it makes his rule longer lasting. Thus, even in the case of tyranny, Aristotle offers a way to persuade those in power to tend towards justice rather than injustice.

8.5. ARISTOTLE ON REVOLUTION

It is often noted that Aristotle seems to anticipate Karl Marx (1818–83) in so far as he emphasizes conflicts between opposed social classes. However, Aristotle does not define classes, as Marx does, in terms of methods of production.[41] Aristotle's 'classes' consist of groups performing various functions for the polis: productive, military, political, religious (see Section 5.2 above). It would be particularly misleading to identify Aristotle's 'middle class' with an economic class like the modern sense of the *bourgeoisie*. For Aristotle's middle class is defined not in terms of mercantile or capitalistic economic activities, but in terms of a military function which it can perform within the polis: viz., to serve as hoplites or heavily armed infantry (see Section 7.3 above). Although Aristotle places great weight upon factors such as relative wealth and poverty in accounting for social conflict and revolution, he does not conceive of productive forces as constituting a 'base' which determines political or other factors as part of a 'superstructure'. Rather, as we have seen, economic factors help to determine the 'matter' upon which the lawgiver acting like a craftsman (an efficient cause) imposes the formal structure of a constitution. The material factors importantly limit or constrain the lawgiver's work but do not determine the outcome.

Further, Aristotle's orientation differs from that of Marx and Locke, who are writing for aspiring revolutionaries. The argument of *Politics*, IV–VI, is directed to political scientists who may be in a position to offer practical advice, as well as to enlightened lawgivers and politicians, whose aim it is to establish, preserve, or reform constitutions. Thus Aristotle's

---

[41] On the difficulties of applying Marx's theory of class conflict to the ancient Greek polis, see Irwin (1988), 637 n. 37, and Yack (1993), 210–15.

prescriptions are intended to reform existing regimes or make them more lasting, even in the case of tyrannies which are indisputably unjust, rather than with toppling them. Even recommendations for reform tend to be guarded, in view of the political instability which might result. Yet Aristotle's viewpoint is far from that of Hobbes, who insists on unquestioning obedience to the sovereign except when this would require suicide. For Aristotle seems to imply that citizens may have a right to engage in faction and revolution.[42] At any rate, he remarks that when dissidents strive for equality or pre-eminence, 'it is possible to strive for these things justly, and also it is possible to do so unjustly' (1302^a28-9; cf. 1302^b12-14). Moreover, he says, 'Those who excel in virtue would engage in faction most justly of all, but they do this the least; for these alone have the best reason to be unequal without qualification' (V 1 $1301^a39-{}^b1$). However, virtuous persons seldom exercise this right: '[I]f either of the parts [of the polis, i.e. the rich or the poor] is very pre-eminent, the remaining part is unwilling to run the risk [of rebelling] against one that is clearly superior. Thus, those who excel in virtue do not engage in faction generally speaking; for they are a few against many' (V 4 1304^b2-5). Even though the virtuous few have the right to carry out a revolution and take control of the constitution, they are unable to do so because of their relative weakness. This is, undeniably, a pragmatic argument, which implicitly assures Aristotle's second preserving principle, the maxim of superiority. A truly aristocratic regime could not survive if the superior part of the polis were opposed to its continued existence. The closest approximation to justice which a viable political system can satisfy in such a case is defined by the maxim of superiority.

Yet Aristotle's approach still seems to contain a basic difficulty. There is the possibility that an existing regime, particularly a tyranny, might be fundamentally at variance with even the maxim of superiority. In such a case revolution would seem to be the only just course. In providing advice as to how to prop up such a regime, the political scientist would be acting contrary to justice. Aristotle does not satisfactorily confront this possibility. He has also been criticized for inconsistently applying his own political theory to the problems of social conflict and constitutional change. Newman, for example, complains that

---

[42] Hobbes in *Leviathan*, II. 21, IV. 46 (1968: 110–1, 377) complains that Aristotle is over sympathetic to democracy, and that the reading of Aristotle and other classical authors has had a subversive, detrimental effect on 17th-cent. politics. However, Hobbes does not distinguish between Aristotle and the neo-Aristotelians of Hobbes's day who drew anti-monarchical lessons from Aristotle's texts.

We might have expected . . . that constitutional change, though often for the worse, would sometimes be for the better, and that we should learn in [*Pol.* V] how to help forward changes for the better, and to prevent or delay changes for the worse. [Book V], however, sets itself to show how all constitutional change is to be avoided, and we are taught to view it as arising only partly from changes in the composition of society—ethical changes seem to escape notice—and far more often from faults committed by the holders of power. We learn here the wholesome lesson that, if constitutions '*habent sua fata*', much may still be done by watchfulness, fairness to those excluded from power, and moderation to preserve them even under unfavourable circumstances.[43]

At the same time, curiously, Newman accuses Aristotle of underestimating the difficulty of bringing about fundamental change:

Aristotle's analysis of the causes of *stasis* and constitutional change reveals, in fact, the existence of causes with which it is extremely difficult for the statesman to deal, however great his skill and watchfulness. Aristotle himself seems, indeed, to be hardly conscious of this. He hardly realizes how difficult it is to prevent *stasis* and constitutional change when they are brought about by changes in the size or credit of classes, or other changes not easily guided or controlled.[44]

Although Newman's criticisms are not without justification, they tend to neglect what I have argued are Aristotle's fundamental concerns in *Politics*, IV–VI: viz., finding a justice-approximating basis of co-operation among widely opposed social groups, and persuading those with political power to comply with the requirements of justice. The political scientist confronts the brute fact that certain groups occupy positions of superiority and want to promote their own advantage at the expense of others. The recommendations must take this reality into account and provide a credible reason for the stronger to treat the weak justly. In order to be persuasive Aristotle's proposed reforms must be justified on the basis of the preserving principles, and in most cases on the maxim of superiority (rather than unanimity). Moreover, although the constitution can have some effect upon the character of the population (e.g. by fostering the rise or decline of a given group), he views demographic material as largely a given. Hence, his conservative stance is in fundamental accord with the theoretical framework of Books IV–VI.

It is instructive to contrast Newman's charge of excessive conservatism (albeit qualified with a 'wholesome lesson') with Mulgan's complaint that Aristotle's prescriptions are in fact subversive: although purporting to

---

[43] Newman (1887), i. 527.   [44] Ibid., iv. 276.

preserve constitutions by reforming them, his recommendations sometimes have the effect of changing the fundamental character of the constitution; for example, changing a tyranny into a type of kingship.[45] This criticism correctly points out the meliorist agenda running through many of Aristotle's prescriptions. Mulgan also complains that Aristotle's pose as a preserver of constitutions is exaggerated if not disingenuous, but Aristotle does not go so far as to allege that he can preserve any constitution no matter how bad without in any way improving it (see Section 5.6 above). On Aristotle's behalf, we may recall the very fine-grained character of his analysis of constitutions. Each of these constitutions embodies various specific modes of deliberative, official, and adjudicative institutions. There is a continuum of such constitutions which differ among each other often only in quite subtle ways. Aristotle can justifiably distinguish between the sort of fine-tuned reforms he recommends from political change which alters the fundamental character of the constitution.

However, Aristotle's own maxim of superiority would sometimes support deeper fundamental change, for example, when the existing constitution assigns political authority to a group which is not in fact in a superior position in terms of quantitative and qualitative measures. There might be an oligarchy controlled by the wealthy although the poor actually have a superior position in terms of numbers as well as quality. It is difficult to see how the politician could make the constitutional changes required to stabilize the regime without changing its fundamental constitutional form from oligarchy to democracy or at least to polity. For the rich minority merely to co-opt a few of the more ambitious members of the poor while retaining the real political authority would not be a stable solution if the preponderance of the poor still opposed the regime.

Aristotle is rather vague as to how and to what extent his maxim supports specific constitutional reforms. For example, an oligarchic regime might be advised to seek superiority by including the middle class in the governing body. However, it is not clear how extensive the rights are which should be ceded to the middle group in such a case. The maxim implies that the middle group's share of political rights should be proportionate to its combination of quantity and quality as compared to the rich and the poor. However, because the middle class is a 'swing' group, it might be able to bargain for a disproportionate share of political power. Generally, one would expect that the actual institutional arrangement which resulted from inclusion of the middle group would be the result of

[45] Mulgan (1977), 137.

strategic bargaining between the different parties. Moreover, a constitutional outcome might tend to be more open to revision as a result of changing social conditions and renewed bargaining than Aristotle is inclined to recognize.

Finally, granted the interpretation defended in this chapter is correct, it might be questioned whether Aristotle's maxim of superiority and the principle of mutual deference provide a satisfactory approximation to justice. It might be objected in the first place that mutual deference may simply reflect status quo arrangements which are in fact unjust (i.e. unjust without qualification though just in relation to a hypothesis). A large proportion of the population may in fact be unjustly enslaved, suppressed, exploited, or disenfranchised—as was the case in actual city-states. Second, to embrace the maxim of superiority is to forsake the principle of the mutual advantage, since the maxim permits the superior part of the polis to benefit at the expense of the inferior part. However, Aristotle holds that the maxim of unanimity should be satisfied if at all possible, and the maxim of superiority is a fall-back position, for deeply divided societies, in which *faute de mieux* a superior part of the polis can co-operate for mutual advantage. On Aristotle's behalf it may be argued that he has seriously considered the unavoidable cases where the polis cannot reach a moral consensus and that he has tried to offer a solution which attempts to approximate justice in adverse political climates.

9

Property Rights

9.1. PROBLEMS OF PROPERTY

The members of Aristotle's polis are private individuals with households
of their own in addition to being citizens who share in the common life
of politics. Although the *Politics* is primarily occupied with constitutional
issues, Aristotle is also concerned with the private sphere and its relation
to the common or public sphere, as is evident in *Politics*, II 1:

> of as many things as it is possible to have in common is it better for the polis that
> is going to be nobly administered to have them all in common, or is it better to
> have some [in common] but not others? For it is possible for the citizens to have
> children, wives, and possessions in common with each other, as in Plato's *Republic*;
> for there Socrates says that children, women, and property ought to be common.
> Are things better as they are now or as they are according to the law written in
> the *Republic*? (1261ᵃ2–9)

This chapter focuses on Aristotle's remarks about property, on the grounds
that private property necessarily has a central place in any account of
the private sphere, since it defines the location and means of private activities. Moreover, the arguments concerning private property parallel the
main points which he makes concerning children and wives. He discusses
property in several different contexts throughout the *Politics* as well as in
other works, most notably the *Rhetoric* and *Nicomachean Ethics*. These
discussions, when taken together, provide the basic materials of a theory
of property rights. Here I follow the lead of Barker, who refers to 'the
vindication of the right of private property which appears in the second
book of the *Politics*'.[1]

---

[1] Barker (1906), 248, here, as in many other instances, was following the lead of Newman
(see 1887: i. 167–8). Cf. also Swanson (1992), who argues that Aristotle is concerned to
defend a sphere of privacy for the sake of individual virtue. Swanson convincingly criticizes
the thesis of Arendt (1958) that Aristotle depreciates the private (as a realm of violence and
necessity) in contrast to the public (as a realm of freedom and virtue). However, as we shall
see, property rights do not play as central a role in Aristotle's political theory as they do in
Locke's. None the less, I have found it necessary to devote an entire chapter to this topic
in order to correct the erroneous view that Aristotle does not recognize individual property
rights at all.

I shall begin by indicating in quite general terms how I am using the expression 'property rights'. Property rights are complex legal or moral relationships involving individuals and objects, concerning different sorts of rights or their correlatives.[2] For example, the right of Coriscus to an object such as a jar of olive oil typically involves both a liberty to possess it and to put it to various uses as well as a claim right imposing duties of non-interference on the part of others with its possession or use. This typically implies the right to compensation or restitution if there is inter- ference or harm to the object by others. It also typically involves the authority to offer the object for sale or to give it away, which changes the legal or moral relationships of others. And it typically involves an immunity against others putting the object up for sale or giving it away without the owner's consent. This repeated use of 'typically' is deliberate. The various elements into which the relations of ownership and property have been analysed are not necessarily present in all cases. Thus, although Honoré[3] distinguishes eleven such elements—the right to possess, to use, to manage, the right to the income, to the capital, to security, to transmissibility, the absence of term, the prohibition of harmful use, the liability to execu- tion, and the residual character of property—he contends that while all of these elements are required for full ownership, none is a necessary condi- tion for 'owning' something. In ascribing a concept of property rights to Aristotle, I am claiming that such elements play an important role in his normative assertions about property and wealth in the *Politics* and other works. The following section proposes a working concept of property rights in Aristotle's own terms.

A theory of property rights should provide answers to a number of problems about property rights: What sorts of individuals can properly hold rights to property? To what sorts of objects can they have property rights? In what ways are property rights exercised? What is the general moral justification for the thesis that individuals should have property rights? Under what circumstances do individuals justly acquire objects and under what circumstances do they come to possess them unjustly? What specific public policies are implied by property rights; i.e. in what way should property rights be protected and what constraints, if any, do individual property rights place upon the conduct of government? And in what ways may individual property rights be restricted or regulated by government? In ascribing to Aristotle a theory of property rights, I am claiming that Aristotle offers answers to questions such as these.

---

[2] See Becker (1977), 21.   [3] Honoré (1961).

The test of this interpretation is whether it does indeed provide a way of connecting Aristotle's scattered claims about property into a more comprehensible whole. Accordingly, this chapter examines his main discussions of property, and Section 9.8 considers his answers to the foregoing questions concerning property rights.

9.2. A WORKING CONCEPT OF PROPERTY RIGHTS

The ancient Greeks recognized a distinction which is fundamental to the conception of property rights: the distinction between the mere possession of an object and the ownership of it. Socrates acknowledges this juridical distinction in Plato's *Republic* when he says that the goal of the rulers in conducting law suits will be 'that individuals should neither have [*echōsi*] another's things [*t'allotria*] nor be deprived of their own things [*tōn hautōn*]' (IV 433ᶜ6–8).[4] Similarly, the Athenian orator Hegesippus (*c*.390–*c*.325 BC) states that 'it is possible to have [*echein*] another's things; and not all those who have, have their own things, but many have acquired [*kektēntai*] another's things'.[5] Again, Theophrastus (*c*.320–*c*.288 BC) asserts that even if goods for sale have changed hands, the seller remains the owner of the property (*kurios tou ktēmatos*) until he receives the payment.[6]

There were elaborate legal procedures through which property owners could seek protection and compensation; this is especially evident in the Athenian legal system, about which the most is known. Nevertheless, the Greeks did not have an abstract term which unambiguously stood for legal ownership as such.[7] *Ousia*, for example, is used for the concrete property which an individual owns[8] rather than to designate ownership as such. The verbs *echein*, *kratein*, and *kektēshai* do not have special legal or moral implications. This underscores the importance of Aristotle's attempt in *Rhetoric*, I 5 1361ᵃ12–25 to offer a *general* treatment of the notion of wealth (*ploutos*). (The argument to which this passage belongs is examined in the following section.) This treatment is of special interest here because it mentions central elements of the concept of property rights.

The treatment begins with an enumeration of the parts (*merē*) of wealth: plenty of money; possession (*ktēsis*) of land and estates; possession of movable objects, animals, and slaves. Since the Greeks typically include

---

[4] See Vlastos (1977), 4–11.   [5] [Demosthenes], VII 26.

[6] Stobaeus, *Florileg.* XLIV 22; see Harrison (1971), i. 204.

[7] See Jones (1956), 201 n. 4, Harrison (1971), i. 201, and MacDowell (1978), 133.

[8] See Plato, *Rep.* VIII 551ᵇ3.

with land ownership the buildings and crops on it, Aristotle has enumerated the main types of property recognized by Greek law.[9] In this passage Aristotle states a number of conditions which must be met if one is fully to qualify as being wealthy (*ploutein*):

(1) the properties are numerous, large, and beautiful;
(2) the properties are liberal (*eleutheria*) or useful (*chrēsima*);[10]
(3) the properties are secure (*asphalē*);
(4) the properties are one's own (*oikeia*);[11]
(5) one is actually using the property rather than merely owning it.

The conditions especially important for a right of property are (3) and (4). Aristotle explains what he means by each at 1361ᵃ19–23: 'A criterion of "security" is possession [*kektēshai*] in a given place and in such a manner that the use of the objects is up to oneself [*eph' hautōi*]; and a criterion of "being one's own or not"[12] is when the alienation of it is up to oneself; I mean by "alienation" [*apallotriōsis*] giving and selling.' So defined, (3) and (4) differ importantly from (1) which distinguishes wealth from more modest levels of property possession; and from (5) which distinguishes leading an actually wealthy life from being materially capable of doing so. In contrast, (3) and (4) are preconditions not only of wealth but of ownership in general.

A historian of Athenian law finds it 'noteworthy that Aristotle should single out the power to alienate as the true sign of a thing being one's own [*oikeion*]'.[13] It is also important to note that (3) and (4) correspond to central elements in the modern Anglo-American concept of property rights.[14] In the light of this parallel, (3) and (4) may be taken to constitute an Aristotelian working concept of property rights, viz.:

> X has a property right in P if, and only if, X possesses P in such a way that the use of P is up to X, and the alienation of P (giving P away or selling P) is up to X.

[9] See Harrison (1971), i. 202, and MacDowell (1978), 133.

[10] I understand *kai* at 1361ᵃ15 as disjunctive because Aristotle defines the two conditions so that they are mutually exclusive: useful properties are productive, those from which we derive income or rents; whereas liberal properties are employed in intrinsically valuable activities. All references to Aristotle in this and the following section are to *Rhet*. I 5 unless otherwise indicated.   [11] Understanding <*oikeia*> at 1361ᵃ15; cf. ᵃ21.

[12] On the location of *ē mē* see Grimaldi (1980).

[13] Harrison (1971), i. 202; cf. Jones (1956), 198, on the place of this power in ownership for Greek law generally.

[14] Becker (1977), 20, argues that among Honoré's elements the right to the capital is 'the most fundamental of the elements, if only because it includes the right to destroy, consume, and alienate. (Alienation is understood to include exchanges, gifts, and just "letting go".)'

It is reasonable to suppose that this analysis has a force comparable to the conjunction of the following rights claims: '*X* has the liberty to use *P* in one way or in another way, and *X* has a just claim against others not to be interfered with in his use of *P*.[15] *X* has the authority to transfer ownership of *P* to *Y* by giving it or selling it to *Y*, and *X* has immunity against others alienating *P*.'[16]

The remainder of this chapter argues that good sense can be made of Aristotle's discussions of property in the *Politics* if he is understood as using the working concept of property rights just described.

9.3. THE EUDAIMONISTIC JUSTIFICATION OF PROPERTY

One important form of justification of property concerns its relationship to happiness (*eudaimonia*). In the context of such a justification, the analysis of wealth discussed in the preceding section occurs. *Rhetoric*, I 5, commences with an assertion of the principle of *eudaimonia* similar to the openings of the *Politics* and *Nicomachean Ethics*. Everybody, individually and collectively, has a goal, and this is happiness and its parts. We should understand what happiness is and what its parts are, because all those who try to persuade others presuppose the principle of *eudaimonia*:

One ought to do the things which provide happiness or any of its parts, or increase rather than decrease it, and ought not to do those things which destroy or hinder it or make those things that are contrary to it. ($1360^{b}11-14$)

Like the *Politics* (cf. Section 6.6 above), *Rhetoric*, I 5 prescribes happiness as an end for public policy as well as for individual decision-making ($1360^{b}4$, $^{b}31-1361^{a}12$). Aristotle then offers an account of happiness:

Let then happiness be [*a*] doing well with virtue, or [*b*] self-sufficiency of life, or [*c*] the most pleasant way of life with security, or [*d*] a thriving state of possessions and bodies with the power to protect and put them into action. ($1360^{b}14-17$)[17]

Aristotle is, in effect, treating happiness as a cluster concept, which includes both common notions and philosophical ideas. It is not clear whether these are meant to be necessary or sufficient conditions of

---

[15] Cf. $1360^{b}16-17$: the defining conditions of happiness include 'the power to protect and put to use' one's possessions.

[16] See Grimaldi (1980), 112, who remarks that *apallotriōsai* 'Aristotle defines immediately as the right to give or to sell (what one possesses)'.

[17] For (*a*) cf. *Pol.* VII 1 $1323^{b}21-3$; 3 $1325^{a}32-4$, $^{b}12-16$. For (*b*) cf. *EN* I 5 $1097^{b}7-21$; X 7 $1177^{a}27-^{b}4$; *Rhet.* I 5 $1360^{b}23$. For (*c*) cf. *Rhet.* I 5 $1360^{b}28$.

happiness. Nevertheless, on the basis of this account, Aristotle infers that happiness has numerous parts,[18] including external goods, such as wealth or property ($1360^{b}20$, 28).

The eudaimonistic justification is a straightforward application of the eudaimonistic principle of *eudaimonia*:

(1) One should do the things which provide happiness or any of its parts, or increase rather than decrease it, and should not do those things which destroy or hinder it or make those things that are contrary to it.

(2) Wealth is a part of happiness.

(3) Therefore, one should do the things which provide wealth or increase rather than decrease it and should not do those things which destroy or impede its use.

Premiss (2) is based on two of the disjunctive conditions of happiness: (*b*) self-sufficiency of life and (*d*) a thriving state of possessions and bodies with the power to protect and put them into action. Moreover, as noted in the previous section, Aristotle states that wealth must satisfy the conditions of being secure and being one's own, conditions which are central elements of property rights: the use and alienation of the possessions are up to the owner.

To be sure, care must be taken with an argument from the first book of the *Rhetoric* which is generally regarded as early in composition,[19] and which is more prone than other Aristotelian compositions to draw uncritically upon common-sense views. Both premisses of the above argument seem to be open to objection. (1) speaks of 'parts' of happiness, a usage which he avoids in the discussion of happiness in the *Nicomachean Ethics*, I and X.[20] Even more controversially, (2) makes wealth a part of happiness. Not only do the ethical works not treat wealth as a part of happiness, but they point out a serious mistake which (2) might be taken to commit, of confusing a necessary condition of happiness with a part of happiness (cf. *EE* I 2 $1214^{b}24$–7; *Pol.* VII 1 $1323^{b}24$–9; 13 $1332^{a}25$–7).

Nevertheless, it seems possible to reformulate this argument of the

---

[18] Commentators have remarked that Aristotle's enumeration of these parts is complicated, seemingly redundant, and possibly inconsistent. On the ways of counting and classifying these parts see Grimaldi (1980), 106–7.   [19] See Düring (1966), 118.

[20] Aristotle indeed speaks in this way in *EE* I 2 $1214^{b}26$–7; 5 $1216^{a}39$–40; II 1 $1219^{b}11$–13; cf. *MM* I 2 $1184^{a}18$–19, 26–9, 30–1; but he does not use this sort of language in the *Nicomachean Ethics*, except for the common books; e.g. parts of happiness are mentioned in the common books at *EN* V 1 $1129^{b}18$. Cf. Cooper (1975), 122.

Rhetoric in terms of the doctrines stated in Aristotle's ethical works. Wealth is one of the external goods (*ta ektos agatha*) which a human being needs in order to be happy (*EN* I 8 1099ᵃ31–4, VII 13 1153ᵇ14–19, X 8 1178ᵃ23–31; *MM* II 8 1206ᵇ33–4; *Pol.* VII 13 1331ᵇ41–1332ᵃ1). Perhaps the strongest affirmation of this comes in the definition of happiness at *EN* I 10 1101ᵃ14–16: 'that person is happy who is active in accordance with complete virtue and is sufficiently equipped with external goods not for any chance period of time but for a complete life.' The claim that the happy person requires equipment (*kechorēgēmenos*) also occurs at *Politics*, VII 1 1323ᵇ40–1324ᵃ1. Elsewhere Aristotle suggests that the value of external goods derives from that of virtuous activities: 'no activity is complete when it is impeded, and happiness is a complete thing; this is why the happy person needs the goods of the body and external goods, i.e. those of fortune, in order that he may not be impeded in these ways.'[21] Aristotle thus maintains that wealth, like other external goods, is indispensable for complete human happiness.[22] However, the *Rhetoric*'s justification of property would still need to be corrected to say that wealth is a necessary condition for happiness rather than a 'part' of it. And the justification would be restricted to property which plays an essential role in the activities of happiness, e.g. property used in acts of generosity.

9.4. THE INSTRUMENTALIST JUSTIFICATION OF PROPERTY

Politics, I 4–10, offers a justification of property rights based on Aristotle's teleological view of nature. This justification is part of a general effort in *Politics*, I, to show that the polis arises out of basic natural communities: ultimately, those of master and slave, husband and wife, and parent and child. Hence, his treatment of property is closely bound up with his highly objectionable defence of slavery, but it includes arguments concerning property in general, which can be disentangled from his concerns about slavery. He begins with a loosely structured argument (4 1253ᵇ23–1254ᵃ17) which I reconstruct as follows:

---

[21] *EN* VII 13 1153ᵇ17–19; cf. *EN* I 8 1099ᵃ31–ᵇ8; X 8 1178ᵃ23–ᵇ7. Jost (forthcoming) points out a similar treatment of the natural goods (*phusei agatha*), which include wealth, in *EE* VIII 3.

[22] The exact significance of this claim is a subject of controversy. Cooper (1985) and White (1992) take external goods to be valuable for Aristotle only in so far as they permit virtuous activity; Irwin (1985*b*) and Nussbaum (1986), ch. 11, think that they are intrinsically valuable; and Annas (1988) finds Aristotle's account ambivalent on this issue.

(1) Just as the specialized crafts need their proper instruments (*organa*) to fulfil their function (*ergon*), the householder needs the proper instruments to fulfil his function.

(2) [The function of the householder is to maintain life.]

(3) A possession (*ktēma*) is an instrument for life, which is separable from the possessor, and property (*ktēsis*) is a number of such instruments.

(4) One cannot live or live well without the necessary things.

(5) Therefore, the householder needs property to fulfil his function.

(6) A part is not only a part of something else but wholly belongs to it, and this is also true of a possession.

(7) [The part belongs by nature to the whole].

(8) Similarly, therefore,[23] property belongs by nature to the household.

(9) [Whatever belongs by nature belongs justly (cf. 1254^{a}17–18).]

(10) [Therefore, it is just for property to belong to the household.]

This justification of property resembles the eudaimonistic justification of *Rhetoric*, I 5, in so far as it proceeds from the view of property as a necessary means to the attainment of the natural end of human beings, but it differs in important details. A central role is assumed for the household (*oikia*), the householder (*oikonomikos*), and household management (*oikonomia*), which have the function of fulfilling daily needs. In contrast to the eudaimonistic justification, this argument covers possessions necessary for everyday subsistence. However, the scope of the conclusion is narrowed: it establishes only the property rights of individuals *qua* householders, not *qua* human beings or under any other description.[24] The inference that property is a 'part' of the household also seems unwarranted, since on Aristotle's view the fact that X is a necessary condition for Y does not entail that X is a part of Y.[25]

The central point, however, is that the householder has a just claim to property because he has it by nature. That this is intended is clear from the immediate context, because *Politics*, I 4, defends slave-holding as a

---

[23] 'Therefore' (*oun*) at 1254^{a}13 implies that (8) is an inference, and I take it to follow from the analogy to parts which precedes it.

[24] Aristotle makes another distinction (which I have ignored in the above reconstruction) between property defined as a 'practical instrument' and instruments used for production. A cloak or bed which one uses in one's daily life is an example of the former (because life is action not production), a shuttle an example of the latter. This special sense of *ktēma* and *ktēsis* seems not only unnecessary but also confusing. Note that if (1) were narrowed to practical instruments, the conclusion would not apply to any of the productive implements belonging to the household.   [25] See VII 8 1328^{a}21–^{b}37; cf. Newman (1887), ii. 135.

form of property ownership, and it follows directly in response to the objection that slave-holding is 'against nature' and 'not just, for it is due to force' (3 1253^{b}20–3). This argument, of course, rests upon the principle that human relationships which are by nature or according to nature are just and those which are against nature are unjust (see Section 3.3 above). Apart from this, a major difficulty with the argument as it stands is the weakness of the argument for (8) that the household possesses property 'by nature'. Aristotle has previously argued that the household exists by nature (2 1252^{b}12–14) and he can perhaps infer that its parts belong to it by nature. But even so, it does not follow that *everything* which the household possesses belongs to it by nature. The household might acquire things which it is against nature, and consequently unjust, for it to possess—for example, naturally free human beings. Aristotle must therefore supplement this argument with an account of what the household may acquire according to nature and against nature.

9.5. JUSTICE AND INJUSTICE IN ACQUISITION

Aristotle distinguishes natural (just) and unnatural (unjust) forms of his general discussion of the acquisitive craft (*chrēmatistikē* [*sc. technē*]) in *Politics*, I 8–11. This craft is distinct from household management in that it is for the acquisitive craft to supply and for household management to use, because the former studies where possessions (*chrēmata*) and property (*ktēsis*) come from (I 8 1256^{a}10–12, 15–16). The defensible (natural) form of the acquisitive craft is alternatively described as a part of householding (I 8 1256^{b}26–7) or as a subordinate art which provides the resources which the householder uses (I 10 1258^{a}34).

In *Politics*, I 8, Aristotle offers a rather loosely organized argument for the conclusion that one form of the acquisitive art is natural. It advances two lines of argument, both of which assume the teleological principle that 'nature makes nothing incomplete and does nothing in vain' (1256^{b}20–1). The argument may be summarized as follows: *Part I* (1256^{a}19–^{b}7) There are many kinds of food. It is impossible to live without food. [Nature makes nothing incomplete and does nothing in vain.] Therefore, nature has differentiated the ways of life of animals for their convenience and preference. Similarly, humans have many different modes of life which involve self-generated (*autophuton*) industry, not exchange or commerce—viz., the shepherd, husbandman, brigand, fisherman, and hunter. [Therefore, nature has differentiated these modes of human life.] *Part II* (1256ᵇ7–30) Nature makes nothing incomplete and does nothing in vain. The yolks, milk, etc. needed by the young at birth are given to them by nature. Similarly, [since animals need plants for food,] plants exist for the sake of animals. Humans need animals for food, clothing, and instruments, and as beasts of burden. Therefore, animals exist for the sake of man. The argument as a whole has two major conclusions (1256ᵇ7–10, 26–30):[26]

(C 1) Therefore, such property (*ktēsis*) is given by nature to all both at birth and when grown (cf. 10 1258ᵃ34–7).

(C 2) Therefore, one kind of acquisitive craft is by nature a part of household management and must be present (or householding must provide that it be present), and this acquisitive art has to do with those storable things which are necessary and useful for the community of the polis or household.

If Aristotle's teleological principle that 'nature makes nothing incomplete and does nothing in vain' is understood to imply that what is needed to make a substance complete exists for its sake and is thus given to it by nature, then his argument appears to be valid.[27] But, unfortunately, this principle would also seem to support the conclusion that human beings exist for the sake of, and are given by nature to, carnivorous beasts or intestinal parasites. However, Aristotle is probably assuming another principle such as that at *Pol.* VII 14 1333ᵃ21–4: 'The inferior always exists for the sake of the superior, and this is manifest in matters of art as well as of nature. And the superior is that which possesses reason.' This principle would postulate a hierarchy of natural kinds along the following lines:

If natural kind K_1 has end E_1 and natural kind K_2 has end E_2 and E_1 is superior to E_2, then entities of kind K_2 exist for the sake of, and are given by nature to, entities of kind K_1.

These teleological principles regarding the gift of nature have a place in Aristotle's theory of natural acquisition comparable to the principles underlying Locke's theory: viz., from the view of 'Revelation' that God 'has given the Earth to the Children of Men'; or from the view of 'natural

---

[26] See Newman (1887), ii. 179. I treat (C 1) as following from both parts because the *men oun* at 1256ᵇ7 indicates that (C 1) follows in some way from Part I, and because the *gar* at ᵇ10 implies that Part II is also intended to support (C 1). The *men oun* at ᵇ26 implies that (C 2) follows at least from Part II.

[27] On Aristotle's teleology see Sects. 1.4 and 2.1 above and Sect. 10.2 below.

Reason' that 'Men, being once born, have a right to their Preservation, and consequently to Meat and Drink, and such other things, as Nature affords for their Subsistence.'[28]

Natural acquisition as limited (1256ᵇ30–9)

However, Aristotle wants to establish that the acquisitive craft is natural without establishing too much: he wants to establish that it is a natural art *only in so far as* it provides the necessary means for the natural ends of householding management and politics. This argument proceeds as follows: no instrument (*organon*) belonging to any craft is without a limit (*apeiron*) in number or in size. True wealth is the amount of property sufficient for the good life. The householder and politician use property as an instrument for the good life. True wealth is the instrument of household management and politics. Therefore, true wealth has a limit (cf. 9 1257ᵇ19–20). The natural acquisitive craft provides true wealth. Therefore, the natural acquisitive craft is constrained by a limit.

Natural acquisition has a limit resulting from its subordination to household management or politics. The basis for the premiss that the instrument of a craft has a limit is suggested later at 9 1257ᵇ27–8: the end of a craft may be unlimited but not the means, for the end is the limit (*peras*) for all crafts. But the idea of a 'limit' as used in this argument is unclear because a limit may be understood as a baseline (minimum) or a ceiling (maximum). Does the end require that a certain baseline of resources be acquired or a certain ceiling? If the end is 'the good life' it would seem possible to interpret the limit as a baseline, but Aristotle interprets it as a ceiling as well as a baseline.

His reason for this becomes somewhat clearer in *Politics*, I 9 (see also VII 4 1326ᵃ35–40). Aristotle contrasts the natural acquisitive craft with another acquisitive craft which has no limit (1256ᵇ40–1257ᵃ1) and is due to experience and craft rather than to nature (1257ᵃ4–5). This unnatural acquisitive craft is one of two arts of exchange (*metablētikē*). It is commerce (*kapēlikē*), 'retail exchange', and the other, unobjectionable type of exchange is barter (*allagē*), 'simple exchange'. The following argument involves three stages: an analysis of the proper use of property, a defence of barter, and a critique of commerce.

(1) *Proper use* He begins by distinguishing two uses of a piece of property such as a shoe: to be worn and to be exchanged. The proper use of

[28] Locke, *Second Treatise*, v. 25.

a possession is that for the sake of which it came into existence. But such a piece of property did not come into existence for the sake of barter. Therefore, barter is not its proper use (cf. *EE* III 4 1231^{b}39–1232^{a}4).

(2) *Defence of barter* However, activities carried out in order to replenish one's natural self-sufficiency are the result of the natural fact that humans have more or less than what they need. Because barter is carried out in order to replenish the natural self-sufficiency of individuals, it is not against nature.

(3) *The critique of commerce* Commerce is the art of producing wealth by exchanging things with money. The other crafts (e.g. medicine) have no limit regarding their end (e.g. health). Similarly, this acquisitive craft, whose end is wealth and the possession of things, has no limit to its end. But for the natural acquisitive craft, all wealth has a limit. Therefore, commerce is an unnatural acquisitive craft.

The critique of commerce raises the question: Why is commerce, but not medicine, an unnatural art? It is not that commerce employs a perverted instrument, filthy lucre, because it uses the same instrument as the natural art (1257^{b}35–8).[29] Aristotle attempts to distinguish them by arguing that the unlimited end of commerce is due to a false view of the good life: viz., the unlimited gratification of desires, which requires unlimited wealth. This leads to a vicious disposition towards unlimited acquisition and a tendency to use one's faculties in an unnatural way (1257^{b}32–1258^{a}14; cf. *EN* I 5 1096^{a}5–10). This argument seems open to the objection that the definition of commerce—the art of making an exchange in order to make a profit (1257^{b}4–5)—no more entails that a practitioner must pursue wealth in an excessive manner than the definition of medicine entails that one must pursue health in an excessive manner. Aristotle seems to dismiss without argument the possibility that one could observe the mean while engaging in commerce, or that one might have other motives aside from profit seeking.[30]

Apart from these objections, Aristotle's prescription of a limit for natural acquisition offers an interesting parallel to the Lockian proviso for just

---

[29] Sinclair's (1983) suggestion that Aristotle means to contrast commerce with medicine runs afoul of the *houtō kai* at ^{b}28 which he infelicitously translates as 'but'.

[30] Aristotle's argument has also been criticized from the Platonist side: Why does not *all* private acquisition have this corrupting influence? In *Pol.* II 5 Aristotle suggests that the acknowledged evils associated with private property such as lawsuits and flattery of the rich are due to moral vice and thus curable through moral education. But this raises such obvious questions as why these evils are curable by education, but those associated with commerce or those associated with Plato's communism are not similarly curable. See Irwin (1991*a*), 219–20.

acquisition, viz., that there must be 'enough, and as good left in common for others'.[31] To be sure, Aristotle's arguments in *Politics*, I 8 and I 9, for a limit are based upon self-regarding considerations: excessive acquisition will prevent the *agent* from achieving the good life. However, it is noteworthy that when Aristotle sums up his conclusions in *Politics*, I 10, he says that commerce or exchange is justly censured 'for it is not according to nature but from one another' ($1258^{b}1-2$). This very brief remark does not obviously follow from the critique and requires considerable speculative unpacking. One way of reconstructing his argument is that commerce is a 'zero-sum game', in which there is a loser for every gainer, so that any person can exceed his limit only by taking something which others need in order to attain their natural ends. In this sense people would be making unnatural, hence unjust, gains 'from one another'.[32]

9.6. DEFENCE OF PRIVATE PROPERTY

While *Politics*, I, is concerned with the property rights of a person *qua* householder or statesman, *Politics*, II, deals with the property of individual citizens. Should property (along with wives and children) be held by all the citizens in common (as Socrates advocates for the guardian class in Plato's *Republic*), or should it be privately owned?

Although *Politics*, II 5, aims to defend individual ownership, it is an oversimplification to treat his argument *simply* as a 'vindication of private property rights'. For he only takes into account three possible property schemes: (i) private property, common use; (ii) common property, private use; and (iii) common property, common use. He omits from discussion another option: (iv) private property, private use. He is not defending a system of unqualified privatization.[33] Hence, we should take careful note of the proviso he adds when he expresses a preference for the 'present

---

[31] Locke, *Second Treatise*, v. 27.

[32] Cf. *Oec.* I 2 $1343^{a}27-30$ (perhaps by Theophrastus): 'Agriculture is the most just [occupation]; for it does not take from human beings, either voluntarily, as do commerce and wage-earning, or involuntarily, as does military occupation.' Although Aristotle's account of commercial exchange certainly reflects ancient Greek popular attitudes (see Dover (1974), 172–4), it has been criticized by modern theorists for failing to recognize the mutual gains from voluntary trade and the positive contributions made by profit-seeking entrepreneurs: see Susemihl and Hicks (1976), 23–31, and Flew (1981), 148–54. Meikle (1991), Lewis (1978), and McNeill (1990) offer more sympathetic views of Aristotle's arguments. (These articles also include references to the extensive secondary literature.)

[33] Cf. Grunebaum (1987), 35–46. References to Aristotle in this section are to *Pol.* II 5 unless otherwise indicated.

mode, if improved by custom and correct legal order' (1263ᵃ22–3; cf. 1 1261ᵃ8 where there is no proviso).

Aristotle's way of defending his preferred option is not deductive but is deliberative (seeking the better of three options) and dialectical (appealing to accepted opinions related to property). He offers five different criteria for evaluating a property arrangement:

(1) it does not give rise to quarrels and complaints (1263ᵃ8–21, 27–8, ᵇ23–7);

(2) it leads to improvement in the care devoted to the property (1263ᵃ28–9; cf. 3 1261ᵇ33–40; IV 15 1299ᵃ38–ᵇ1; cf. *Oec.* I 6 1344ᵇ35–1345ᵃ1);

(3) it facilitates friendship (1263ᵃ29–40; cf. VII 8 1328ᵃ25–8; 10 1329ᵇ41–1330ᵃ2);

(4) it fosters natural pleasures, in particular self-love (1263ᵃ40–ᵇ5);

(5) it makes possible the exercise of virtues such as generosity and moderation (1263ᵇ5–14; 6 1265ᵃ28–38).

It is noteworthy that criteria (3)–(5) presuppose the moderate-individualistic view that political institutions should promote the advantages of individual citizens, understood to include virtuous activity (cf. Section 6.2).

Aristotle's thesis is that these criteria taken together show that mode (i) private property, common use, is better than the other modes. The omitted option (iv) would presumably be ruled out by appeal to criteria (3) and (5).[34] Plato's scheme (iii) is ruled out by all the criteria in Aristotle's view, except perhaps (3). Unfortunately, Aristotle is rather unclear about how these modes differ in practice and what exactly his distinction between 'common property' and 'common use' comes to. This has to be gathered from the criteria on which he bases his argument. For example, both (ii) and (iii) allegedly fail criterion (1) because conflict is unavoidable under these schemes; but Aristotle does not explain how his own scheme (i) does any better. Why does not the 'common use' of slaves, horses, dogs, or crops lead to the same sorts of conflicts as those for which he indicts (ii) and (iii)?

A straightforward and plausible explanation of why Aristotle does not think that this problem will arise for (i) is that he takes for granted the working concept of property rights defined in *Rhetoric*, I 5, including the requirements that the use and the alienation of the object are up to

[34] Cf. Dobbs (1985), 39–40.

the owner. In the case of a piece of property P and two individuals, X, who wants P put to use U_1, and Y, who wants to put P to use U_2, if U_1 and U_2 are incompatible and if neither X nor Y has the right to decide in this matter, conflict is the likely result. This is what happens in schemes (ii) and (iii), according to Aristotle. But in his scheme (i) for any object P there is some individual X such that it is up to X to decide how P will be used, so that conflict can be avoided. Thus, although Aristotle recognizes that conflicts can arise in systems of private property, he still maintains that conflict is far more pervasive in common property arrangements.[35]

Criterion (2) should be understood along similar lines. If, as seems plausible, Aristotle is tacitly assuming the property rights concept of *Rhetoric*, I 5, his point is that an individual X will take better care of object P to the extent that the use of P is up to X; if its use is up to many individuals in addition to X, X will tend to neglect P on the grounds that other people can bear the cost of caring for P. Some commentators find a parallel between Aristotle's argument that individuals tend to take better care of their own personal possessions than of common property and explanations by modern economists of the function of private property. In general, privatization gives individuals a much greater incentive to use property efficiently. Also, the costs involved in using resources are more fully taken into account when they are 'internalized' in private possessions. Property which is commonly owned tends to be overused, abused, or neglected, resulting in 'the tragedy of the commons'.[36] However, it should also be noted that Aristotle agrees in *Politics*, VII, that part of the land should be common, to be used for public religious cults and to cover the expenses of common meals for the citizens (10 1330^{a}9–13). Perhaps he thinks these functions are sufficiently circumscribed to avoid the problems associated with criteria (1) and (2).

This interpretation is also consistent with criterion (3) and can be used to explain how he can reconcile a defence of private property with the common use characteristic of friendship. Although private property implies that particular individuals have rights over particular objects, Aristotle also claims that they should place these objects at the disposal of their friends. As long as some individual has the final say over what friend uses what property, criterion (3) is consistent with criterion (1). It is the

---

[35] Similarly, Steiner (1977) argues that a system of private property is necessary if individual rights are to be compossibly realizable.

[36] See Hardin (1973). Machan (1975), 206, notes the parallel of Hardin and Aristotle. Also, Aristotle's argument for private property is acknowledged in modern economics texts, e.g. Gwartney and Stroup (1990), 718–19. See also Sect. 10.5 below.

function of the educational system to habituate individuals to share their property as well as to observe limits on acquisition of the sort discussed in Section 9.5 (5 1263ᵃ38–40, ᵇ36–7; 7 1267ᵇ5–9). Therefore, this criterion rules out a scheme of (iv) private property, private use, but it is consistent with a scheme like (i) in which educated adults retain property rights.

Criteria (4) and (5) can also be better appreciated from the standpoint of the property rights interpretation. Criterion (4) introduces a new line of teleological argument: a property scheme is according to nature to the extent that it fosters natural pleasures of self-love. True self-love is embodied in persons who act according to their own rational judgement (cf. *EN* IX 8 1168ᵇ34–1169ᵃ3). True self-love thus requires that persons be able to act according to their own judgement, and the existence of private property provides them the sphere in which they can do so.³⁷

Criterion (5) concerns moral virtues such as generosity or liberality, the function of which is in the use of possessions (1263ᵇ13–14). Aristotle evidently intends an argument of the following sort: a property scheme should permit the exercise of generosity, which involves the use and alienation of property (cf. *EN* IV 1 1119ᵇ23–6). Since one can act generously only if one acts voluntarily and by choice, one can act generously only if the use and alienation of property is up to oneself, and this is the case only in a system of private ownership.

Whether Aristotle's argument based on generosity is sound continues to be debated. Against Aristotle and in defence of common ownership, T. H. Irwin has objected that generosity does not require that agents have resources under their exclusive control.

Even if we think the practice of generosity requires me to be free to dispose of some resources under my own initiative, it does not follow that the resources must be under my exclusive control. The state might loan them to me, and allow me to dispose of them as I please within certain limits and in certain circumstances; such an arrangement would leave ample room for the exercise of generosity.³⁸

Aristotle might regard this as a pallid form of generosity, because the virtue involves actions that cost the agent something and hence it entails giving away something that is the agent's own. Hence, virtuous agents should have a stronger right to property on the grounds that it is more noble to give up something more valuable, for example property that

---

³⁷ Mayhew (1993*a*), 239, also mentions *Rhet.* I 11 1371ᵇ12–28 which states that 'since everyone is a lover of self, one's things (*ta hautōn*) are necessarily pleasant to everyone [individually], e.g. deeds and words', and plausibly suggests that the inference can be extended to physical objects. Cf. also *Pol.* II 4 1262ᵇ22–3.

³⁸ Irwin (1991*a*), 222–3.

would otherwise be one's own in perpetuity, than an object which one is merely borrowing for a while. However, Irwin responds,

[T]his objection seems to overlook the virtuous person's attachment to the common good. He will regard the distribution of his friend's resources as a cost to himself, because he regards his friend's resources as his own; and he will take the same view of the community's resources. We might object that such identification of one's own interest with the interests of others is impossible or undesirable; but Aristotle should not be easily persuaded by any such objection, since it would undermine his whole account of friendship.[39]

On Aristotle's behalf, Robert Mayhew offers two objections:

First, . . . according to Aristotle we will not and indeed cannot attend to common things very well—in fact we tend to neglect them. For this and other reasons, I cannot feel for the community's resources what I feel for myself and my own things; I cannot really regard the former as my own. Second, I *might* regard the distribution of a close friend's (or family member's) resources as a cost to me, since, in a sense, the goods of such friends are common. But I do not have the same relationship with the community, and thus neither do I view the community's resources in this way.[40]

Mayhew's first point gains support from the aforementioned economists' argument that individuals have more incentive to take care of objects when they own them. The second point is supported by Aristotle's arguments that political friendship falls short of virtue-based friendship and is too diluted to support a genuine identification of interests (see Section 6.4 above). Hence, Aristotle would seem to have good reasons for concluding that private property is necessary for full generosity.

9.7. CITIZENSHIP AND PROPERTY

In *Politics*, VII 9–10, Aristotle also discusses property in connection with the best constitution. As we have seen in Section 6.6 above, the discussion of property is preceded by an account of who the citizens of the best constitution are. In brief, they must perform a necessary function of the polis and must be capable of participating in the common end of the polis. Aristotle argues that citizenship should be confined to those who have the natural capacity, the virtue, and leisure to carry out the military and deliberative-juridical functions of the best polis.

---

[39] Ibid. 224.   [40] Mayhew (1993a), 814–15.

The argument (1329ᵃ17–26) for universal property rights may be reconstructed as follows:

(1) The lawgiver should promote the happiness of the polis.

(2) 'A polis should be called happy not by viewing part of it but by viewing all the citizens' (1329ᵃ23–4).

(3) [Happiness requires equipment (cf. VII 1 1323ᵇ40–1324ᵃ21).]

(4) Therefore, all citizens have a right to property.

Aristotle's application of this argument is not without difficulty. He claims that 'no group partakes of the [best] polis which is not a craftsman of virtue' (1329ᵃ20–1) and obviously wants the conclusion to be that property belongs *exclusively* to the soldiers and councillors, but this does not follow from his premisses. This would follow only if (4) stated, 'Only citizens have a right to property', but that would not follow from (1)–(3). Hence, his premisses in fact leave open the possibility that noncitizens could possess property as well (although 1329ᵃ25–6 implies noncitizens are slaves).⁴¹

Aristotle applies conclusion (4), when he argues in favour of a proposal (adopted from Plato's *Laws*, V 745ᶜ3–ᵈ4) that each person's property should be divided into two lots, one near the frontier and one near the city, 'in order that two lots may be distributed to each person and everyone may have a share of both districts. For in this way there is equality (*to ison*) and justice (*to dikaion*) and greater unanimity regarding border wars' (*Pol.* VII 10 1330ᵃ14–18). Thus Aristotle argues that property should be distributed not only on the basis of considerations of expediency or security but also on the basis of considerations of distributive justice.⁴² Hence, this argument makes it explicit that in the best polis each citizen has a right to a share of property based on distributive justice.

The argument of *Politics*, VII 9–10, also differs from the preceding arguments in the importance which it places upon citizenship as a basis for property rights. For Aristotle here treats political rights as more basic than property rights. The most basic rights are justified directly on the

---

⁴¹ Morrow (1960), 112, remarks that Aristotle appears to follow Plato's *Laws* in restricting land ownership to citizens. The issue is further complicated by the fact that the summary in *Pol.* VII 10 describes the previous argument as dealing with 'land' (*chōra*, 1329ᵇ36–8), prompting the question of whether the earlier argument was intended to be restricted to land rather than to the movable property, including tools of the trade, which might belong to artisans and labourers (cf. Newman (1887), i. 198 n. 3). However, the summary may not be Aristotle's (see Susemihl and Hicks (1894), 516).

⁴² Cf. VI 3 1318ᵇ1–5 where *to ison kai to dikaion* is similarly applied to political rights, viz., voting.

basis of a person's well-being or objective interests, whereas the justification of derivative rights includes the assertion of more basic rights.[43] In *Politics*, VII 9–10, Aristotle clearly regards the right to be a citizen and participate in government as a more basic right, because ethical virtues are most fully exercised in political activity. Since citizenship can be exercised only by those who have sufficient property, citizens also have a derivative right to property. When Aristotle implicitly concludes in *Politics*, VII 9, that property should belong exclusively to citizens, and not to those who are incapable of political virtue, he may simply be taking it for granted that if property rights cannot be justified as derivative from political rights they cannot be justified at all. This priority of political over property rights in Aristotle is fundamentally at variance with the priority of property to government in Locke[44] and is rooted in the basic principles of the *Politics*—most importantly, that human beings are political animals and that the polis is prior to the individual.

9.8. SUMMARY AND APPLICATIONS

The first section introduced a number of questions which a theory of property rights might be expected to answer. I take Aristotle's theory to be offering, briefly, the following answers to these questions:

(1) *What sorts of individuals have rights to property?* He offers two different answers in the *Politics*: it is the citizen of the best polis in *Politics*, VII, and the householder in *Politics*, I. However, in the best constitution every citizen is a landholding householder. In the second-best constitutions, also, the citizens have moderate and sufficient property (IV 11 1295^b39–40). Moreover, in democracy he suggests that 'the surplus from public revenues should be collected and distributed among the poor, especially if one can collect such quantities as may enable them to acquire a piece of land, or, if not, to make a beginning in trade or farming . . .' (VI 5 1320^a35–^b1). The focus in these discussions is on land. It is presumably taken for granted, but not stated, that artisans and other lower classes possess movable property.[45]

(2) *To what sorts of objects do they have property rights?* The answer given in *Rhetoric*, I 5, is land (including dwellings), movable objects, animals, and slaves. Although this answer is accepted in the *Politics*,

---

[43] Cf. Raz (1986), 168–70, who calls the set of most basic rights 'core rights'.
[44] Cf. Mathie (1979), 17.   [45] Cf. Newman (1887), i. 198 n. 3.

Aristotle seems to assume an important distinction between land and other forms of property.

(3) *What form does the exercise of property rights take?* According to *Rhetoric*, I 5, this consists of two elements: X possesses P in such a way that the use of P is up to X and the alienation of P (giving it away or selling it) is up to X. I have argued that this concept is presupposed throughout Aristotle's treatments of private property in the *Politics*.

(4) *What is the justification for the thesis that individuals generally have property rights?* I have surveyed four principal strands of argument. These rely upon a number of Aristotelian principles: for example, the principle of *eudaimonia* that happiness and its parts should be protected and promoted, the teleological principle that nature provides all living things with what is necessary for living and attaining their natural ends, and the principle of justice that every citizen should have the things necessary for happiness and the exercise of moral virtue. They also employ Aristotelian dialectic, appealing to accepted opinions. In *Politics*, VII 9–10, Aristotle attempts to combine the principles of *eudaimonia* and distributive justice, but he does not indicate what he would say if the two principles came into conflict. Another apparent tension is that the *Rhetoric* argument suggests that property rights are basic rights because the use of property is itself a part of the human end of happiness, and *Politics*, II 5, also claims that private property is indispensable for virtuous conduct; but the argument of *Politics*, VII 9, suggests that property rights are derivative rights because property is a necessary condition for exercising a more basic right (viz., to membership in the polis). Alternatively, he may mean that membership in a polis is a precondition for entitlement to property because it is a necessary condition for the acquisition and practice of virtue. This might resolve the apparent conflict.

(5) *Under what circumstances do individuals justly acquire title to specific objects and under what circumstances do they come to possess them unjustly?* Aristotle recognizes a number of different ways in which property can be justly acquired: original acquisition from nature (hunting, farming, etc.), barter, cash exchange, gifts, inheritance, and distribution by the government. He does not, however, endorse a Locke-style labour theory of acquisition.[46] Although he does not offer a complete set of sufficient conditions for the just acquisition of property, he does indicate some important necessary conditions: an individual X can justly acquire object P only if (i) the natural end of X is superior to the natural end of P (if P

---

[46] See e.g. Susemihl and Hicks (1894), 28.

has one), (ii) in acquiring P, X does not exceed his natural limit, and (iii) X does not unjustly take P from another person equal to X. I see no evidence, however, that Aristotle is committed to the view that X owns P only if X uses P to perform a virtuous act or puts P to common use (e.g. shares it with a friend). To be sure, Aristotle argues that individuals should be able to acquire property because they need it in order to perform virtuous and friendly acts; and he directs the legislators to institute public education to habituate the citizens to this end. But it does not follow from this that the just acquisition of each piece of property is contingent on the performance of a virtuous and friendly act.[47]

(6) *What are the implications of the theory of property rights for public policy?* As noted in question (1) above, Aristotle's theory has important implications for the distribution of property to the citizens. Property rights also place certain constraints upon the conduct of governments according to Aristotle. In particular, he criticizes confiscation by democratic majorities of the property of wealthier citizens (VI 3 1318ᵃ24–6; cf. III 10 1281ᵃ17–21).[48] He explicitly rejects the conventionalist argument that whatever law the majority decides to enact is just, objecting that even if the majority wants it, such confiscation is *unjust* (*adikēsousi dēmeuontes*). Thus, the property owner has a claim of justice, a right, against other citizens which is violated by the law of confiscation. It is implicit that the magistrates in the best constitution will respect the property of the citizens. *Politics*, V, especially is filled with warnings that those with political power should not deprive others of their property (see Section 8.4 above).

Aristotle's theory of property rights also allows for the regulation of property. Newman remarks that the defence of private property in *Politics*, II 5, is not expressly coupled with qualifications,[49] but Aristotle elsewhere

---

[47] Dobbs (1985), 40 n. 9, interprets Aristotle as here maintaining, 'paradoxically, only if one shares his property with another can it be said that he has truly acquired it. This is the insight that lies beneath Aristotle's otherwise puzzling use of the verbal and substantive forms of "possession." In other words, it is in a liberal action that it first comes to light that a possession (*ktēma*) can be one's apart from the active possessing (*ktēsis*) or hoarding of it. Thus only the liberal man will feel genuine, natural pleasure in ownership.' Aristotle would agree with the conclusion, but not, I think, with the premises which Dobbs attributes to him. For the uses of *ktēsis* and *ktēma* indicate that liberality or generosity is concerned with both of them. Recall also the definitions at I 4 1253ᵇ31–2 which imply that *ktēsis* is a collection of *ktēmata*. Aristotle's point is not that X can acquire P only if X shares it with Y but that X ought to share P with Y and that in order to do so X must be able to acquire title to P.

[48] See Jones (1956), 198, who also cites *Ath. Pol.* LVI 2 and Demosthenes, XVII 15, for the historical importance of this issue. Aristotle also recommends that confiscation in democracies be discouraged by limiting the uses to which the confiscated property can be put (*Pol.* VI 5 1320ᵃ4–11). [49] Newman (1887), i. 199–200.

endorses various social policies which limit private property rights. The qualifications upon private property rights should probably be understood in the light of the fact that they are, for Aristotle, subordinate to political rights. His defence of private property is not intended as a case for total privatization. Presumably on similar grounds, he advocates coercive taxation for the purposes of defence and internal needs (VII 8 1328^{b}10–11; III 12 1283^{a}17–18). He also recommends support for needy citizens, as virtuous acts carrying out his policy of 'private ownership, common use' (VII 10 1329^{b}41–1330^{a}2; VI 6 1320^{b}2–11). The provisos which he attaches to natural acquisition can explain his advocacy of legal limits on the amount of land any citizen can own (see VI 4 1319^{a}8–10). He also recommends that individuals do not have the liberty to sell and bequeath land however they please (II 9 1270^{a}18–21). He even admits that the ostracism of very rich or powerful citizens may be justified by a sort of political justice (see III 13 1284^{b}15–34; VI 8 1308^{b}19). The point here is probably that the excessive exercise of property and other rights by some persons jeopardizes the political rights of the other citizens, and that the political rights of the latter should override the property rights of the former (see Section 6.8 above). Further, the citizens of the best constitution should not be merchants because this is a morally degrading profession (VII 9 1328^{b}39–40) and the 'free market' of citizens should be separate from the commercial *agora* regularly frequented by farmers and merchants (12 1331^{a}30–^{b}4). He also recommends market magistrates to supervise transactions. In Athens such officials ensured that commodities were pure and unadulterated, that merchants used fair weights and measures, and that foodstuffs were not unjustly priced (*Ath. Pol.* LI; cf. Plato, *Laws*, XI 917^{c}2–918^{a}1). However, he assumes elsewhere that traders generally have immunity (*adeia*) to set their own terms (EN V 4 1132^{b}15–16; see Section 4.3 above). In sum, the rationale for these restrictions upon individual property rights involves features of the general theory discussed above: the provisos on the acquisition of property, the precedence of political rights and duties over property rights, and the prescription of 'private property, common use'.

However, it would be a mistake to ascribe to Aristotle a theory resembling modern socialism or social democracy. For 'private ownership, common use' implies that property owners ought to put their property to virtuous uses, thereby benefiting others. He does not mean by this to create entitlements on the part of others to this property. If others have a legally enforceable right to help themselves to one's crops, it is not an act of generosity to permit them to do so.[50] Aristotle holds that no citizen should lack sustenance, and that all of the citizens should be included in common meals (VII 10 1330ª2–8). He approves of the Cretan system for providing common meals for everyone including women and children out of the proceeds from common property (II 5 1272ª16–21). However, there is no indication that Aristotle advocates a general policy of redistribution of wealth. The rudimentary social safety net for the unfortunate which Aristotle admits is a far cry from the modern egalitarian welfare state.

In conclusion, Aristotle addresses the questions that must be answered by a theory of property rights. His way of developing, justifying, and qualifying his views on wealth and property can be interpreted in terms of a property rights theory, and the policies he recommends for both the best polis and for deviant constitutions are illuminated by this interpretation. Although there are a number of respects in which Aristotle's arguments appear to be objectionable or underdeveloped, and undoubtedly his theory would be unacceptable to many modern theorists (either of a *laissez-faire* capitalist perspective or of a socialist perspective), his theory of property rights is, none the less, comprehensible and worthy of further investigation.

---

[50] Nussbaum (1990), 232, comments on Aristotle's example of sharing one's crops with the needy, 'One might fruitfully compare to this housing policies that have been adopted in some socialist and social democratic countries, giving the homeless certain rights towards unoccupied or luxury housing.' Mayhew (1993a), 819–21 argues convincingly that Nussbaum has 'failed to grasp the essential nature of Aristotle's view that property should be private generally, but common in use': the policies indicated by Nussbaum would effectively negate the owner's right of use and alienation. Also, her translation (Nussbaum, 1990: 203) of Aristotle's statement that property should have a 'common use, in a friendly way (*philikōs*)' (VII 10 1329ᵇ41–1330ª2) as 'common by way of a use that is agreed upon in mutuality' seems in conflict with Aristotle's reasons for rejecting common property.

Conclusion

10

Aristotle's *Politics* Reconsidered

10.1. INTRODUCTION

The central argument of Aristotle's *Politics*, as reconstructed in Part I, had three main stages. The first concluded with political naturalism, consisting of four claims: human beings are by nature political, in that only they are naturally able and disposed to live together and co-operate in political communities; the polis exists by nature, in that it arises from natural potentials and serves natural ends; the polis is prior by nature to its individual members, in that they can realize their natural ends only if they belong to a polis; however, the polis also arises from human practical wisdom collaborating with nature. The second stage was the theory of political justice: human beings can attain their natural ends only if they co-operate in a specific way, viz., according to universal justice and for the common (i.e. mutual) advantage. The theory of justice yielded principles of particular justice (i.e. distributive, corrective, and reciprocal) which may be used to guide the lawgiver in establishing, maintaining, assessing, and reforming particular constitutions. The third stage was the derivation of a theory of political rights and associated responsibilities which secure the advantage of the individual members of the political community. A correct theory bases political rights on nature, i.e. merit, and ethical virtue is the correct standard of merit.

Part II considered the applications of this argument to political constitutions. Presupposing a particular theory of justice, a constitution imposes on the polis a certain order, consisting of modes that assign specific rights and responsibilities to the citizens. Aristotle's theory of nature, justice, and rights is supposed to guide the politician in dealing not only with the best constitution, but also with the second-best and even inferior constitutions, as well as institutions such as private property.

This concluding chapter reconsiders in a more speculative manner the main presuppositions underlying Aristotle's argument, taking into account some major objections which have been levelled against them by others.

This discussion reconsiders the prospects for neo-Aristotelian[1] political philosophy, i.e. the attempt to recover important Aristotelian insights and apply them to modern issues of political philosophy. The presuppositions under examination are: (1) the principle of teleology, i.e. that human beings have distinctive natural ends, in terms of which their origin, development, and behaviour is to be understood; (2) the principle of perfection, i.e. that the good for human beings consists in the attainment of these ends; (3) the principle of community, i.e. that individuals can attain the good only if they belong to and are subject to the authority of the political community; and (4) the principle of rulership, i.e. that the community can function only if an order is imposed on it by rational agents. The final section reconsiders the contribution which Aristotle makes to our understanding of the justification and scope of human rights, and in the light of the foregoing, the prospects for a neo-Aristotelian theory of rights.

10.2. NATURAL TELEOLOGY

Aristotle's natural teleology was of course challenged by early modern scientists and philosophers and was almost universally repudiated as a part of physical science.[2] In modern biology, however, the relevance of Aristotelian teleology is still the subject of debate. To the extent that his biological views are bound up with obsolete physical theories—e.g. that sublunary matter is a mixture of earth, air, fire, and water; that forms are transmitted by means of motions through these material elements; and that a *sui generis* form of 'vital heat', distinct from fiery heat, is essential

---

[1] I use 'neo-Aristotelian' for modern theorizing which incorporates some central doctrines of Aristotle, e.g. teleology (see Sect. 1.5 above). Such theorizing should critically assess his claims in the light of modern philosophical theory, scientific research, and practical experience, revise or reject them where necessary, and consider their applications to social and political contexts not envisioned by him. One should try to distinguish Aristotle exegesis from neo-Aristotelian theorizing, although the two activities are frequently interconnected.

[2] e.g. Hobbes, in *Leviathan*, IV. 46, declares that 'scarce anything can be more absurdly said in naturall Philosophy, than that which now is called *Aristotles Metaphysiques*; nor more repugnant to Government, than much of that he hath said in his *Politiques*; nor more ignorantly, than a great part of his *Ethiques*'. Hobbes complains that the schools of his day are 'rife with a Vain Philosophy' derived from Aristotle that is 'a handmaid to the Romane Religion'. Among other doctrines, Hobbes attacks the Aristotelian theory of natural place, according to which 'the cause why things sink downward, is an Endeavor to be below: which is as much as to say, that bodies descend, or ascend, because they doe. Or they will tell you the center of the earth is the place of rest, and conservation for Heavy things; and therefore they endeavour to be these: As if Stones, and Metalls had a desire, or could discern the place they would be at . . .' (1968: 370, 375).

for life—they have been rejected by modern biologists. Further, to the extent that his views depend on cosmological and metaphysical postulates such as the eternity of species and the *scala naturae* ascending from the simple elements to the unmoved mover, they have also been discredited. On the basis of considerations such as these, MacIntyre states that 'Aristotle's teleology presupposes his metaphysical biology', which is no longer tenable, and that 'any adequate generally Aristotelian account [of the virtues] must supply a teleological account which can replace Aristotle's metaphysical biology'. In a similar vein Strauss remarks that 'the teleological view of the universe, of which the teleological view of man forms a part, would seem to have been destroyed by modern science', because it entails an outmoded view of the heavenly bodies and their motions.[3]

It is also widely held that biological accounts in terms of final causes have been superseded by efficient-cause explanations in terms of molecular chemistry. The growth of an organism to maturity is explained in terms of physical processes involving the interaction of its DNA with other molecules. The zygote does not have an 'end' which literally causes it to develop into an embryo, and ultimately an organism, in the way that a person's conscious goal causes him to go on a journey. The zygote has an 'end' only in a metaphorical sense, and, it is often argued, the metaphor should not mislead us into thinking that the end literally causes the outcome.[4]

However, some theorists find agreement between Aristotle and modern biology. The biologist Max Delbrück (1906–81), a founder of molecular genetics, describes the discovery of DNA as a confirmation of Aristotle's biological theory:

What strikes the modern reader most forcibly is his insistence that in the generation of animals the male contributes, in the semen, a *form principle*, not a mini-man . . . The form principle is likened to a carpenter. The carpenter is a moving force which changes the substrate, but the moving force is not materially contained in the finished product . . . Put into modern language, [what Aristotle says] is this: The form principle is the information which is stored in the semen. After fertilization it is read out in a preprogrammed way; the readout alters the matter upon which it acts, but it does not alter the stored information, which is not, properly speaking, part of the finished product. In other words, if that committee in Stockholm, which has the unenviable task each year of pointing out the most creative scientists, had the liberty of giving awards posthumously, I think they should consider Aristotle for the discovery of the principle implied in DNA.[5]

---

[3] MacIntyre (1981), 152, and Strauss (1953), 7.   [4] Cf. Paul (1993), 108–9.
[5] Delbrück (1971), 54–5; cf. (1976), 127–9.

Delbrück discerns a close analogy between DNA theory and Aristotle's teleology: the form or information encoded in the DNA molecule guides the development of the embryo without the form being altered. The implication is that a merely material account of DNA would not adequately explain the process of growth.

Delbrück's assessment suggests the possibility of a 'neo-Aristotelian' teleology, i.e. a theory which contains essential components of Aristotle's teleology but from which the objectionable features of his physics and cosmology have been expunged along with factual errors (viz., his claim that the form of the offspring derives only from the male parent). A reconsideration of teleology would have to address a number of difficult issues including the following two. First, is a teleological explanation of living systems compatible with a materialistic account of these same systems? And second, if there is no incompatibility between teleology and a materialistic account, can the ascription of final causes or natural ends *add* anything to such a materialistic account; i.e. can teleology really *explain* living processes, or is it unavoidably metaphorical to speak of a seed as having the 'end' of growing into an olive tree? An assessment of neo-Aristotelian teleology would, of course, have to consider these issues in connection with the sort of materialistic explanations offered by modern biochemistry and physiology. However, before any such undertaking, formidable in itself, could be undertaken, it is necessary to have a clear understanding of Aristotle's own teleological theory, since what is envisaged is an extrapolation of this theory to a modern scientific framework. To begin with, it must be stressed that Aristotle does not assert the sorts of teleology which modern scientists have found egregious: for example, natural theology (explanation in terms of a conscious design) or vitalism (explanation in terms of occult forces beyond the reach of empirical research).[6]

It is noteworthy that Aristotle himself discusses the relationship between his use of final causes and the putative explanations offered by early natural scientists:

We must explain then first that nature is one of the causes that are for the sake of something; then about the necessary and its place in natural things, for everyone refers the cause to this, saying that since the hot and the cold and so forth are naturally such and such, certain things are and come to be out of necessity . . . (*Phys.* II 8 198^{b}10–14)

---

[6] Cf. Lennox (1992).

Aristotle here contrasts nature as the final cause with the material cause, which he later calls 'necessary nature' (*anagkaia phusis*, 9 200^{a}8–9), because he is viewing the matter of a thing as an internal cause of movement or rest. However, there are conflicting interpretations of his views on the issues mentioned above: viz., are final causes compatible with material causes of the same systems, and, if so, do teleological accounts add anything of explanatory value?

Regarding the first issue, Aristotle explicitly holds that many biological phenomena involve both final causes and natural necessity, for example:

No animal has as much hair on the head as man. This, in the first place, is the necessary result of the fluid character of his brain, and of the presence of so many sutures in his skull. For wherever there is the most fluid and the most heat, there also must necessarily occur the greatest outgrowth. But, secondly, [hair is present] in order to protect the head, by preserving it from excess of either heat or cold. And as the brain of man is larger and more fluid than that of any other animal, it requires a proportionately greater amount of protection. For the more fluid a substance is, the more readily it becomes excessively heated or excessively chilled, while substances of an opposite character are less liable to such affections. (*PA* II 14 658^{b}2–10)[7]

Aristotle thus clearly thinks that final causes are compatible with natural necessity, in the sense that living systems have teleological properties and also contain material components which are governed by natural necessity.[8]

Granted this compatibility, there remains the second issue of whether teleological accounts have any independent explanatory power and, if so, what they might add. Aristotle's discussions of final causes are quite complex and not always clear, so that several different interpretations are possible. These may be divided into two main groups: (1) Aristotle regards teleology as supererogatory; i.e. material-cause accounts are complete and final-cause accounts add nothing indispensable, although they may

---

[7] Trans. from Barnes (1984). For other examples see *PA* I 1 642^{a}1–2, 13–24, ^{a}31–^{b}2; II 14 658^{b}2–13; III 2 663^{b}12–14, ^{b}22–664^{a}11; IV 3 677^{b}16–35, 4 678^{a}3–6, 5 679^{a}25–30, 13 694^{a}22–^{b}12; *GA* II 4 738^{a}33–^{b}4, 739^{b}20–30; II 6 743^{a}36–^{b}18; III 4 755^{a}21–5.

[8] See Bradie and Miller (1984), 144, and Meyer (1992), 792 n. 3. A former proponent of the incompatibilist interpretation was Balme (1972), 76–80, who argued that natural necessity was not absolute but merely hypothetical. However, Balme (1987) abandoned this interpretation through a consideration of passages such as those cited above. As Irwin (1988), 526 n. 29, remarks, this interpretation seems to have arisen from a confusion of the claim that the same process cannot have teleological and non-teleological explanations with the claim that the same *property* of a process cannot have both types of explanation. On the compatibility of teleology with modern science see Block (1971) and Lennox (1992).

serve certain practical human purposes, by indicating the significance of certain processes from our point of view.[9] (2) Aristotle regards teleology as indispensable because biological phenomena possess features which cannot be fully explained in terms of natural necessity. A leading spokesman for (2) is Allan Gotthelf, who argues that final causality, for Aristotle, involves 'irreducible potential for form'. Gotthelf cites persuasive evidence against the supererogatory view, including the following passage from *Generation of Animals*:

[W]e may allow that hardness and softness, stickiness and brittleness, and whatever other qualities are found in the parts that have life and soul, may be caused by mere heat and cold, yet, when we come to the principle in virtue of which flesh is flesh and bone is bone, that is no longer so; what makes them is the movement set up by the male parent, who is in actuality what that out of which the offspring is made is in potentiality. (II 1 734^b31-6)[10]

Type (2) interpretations agree that, for Aristotle, teleological systems have certain features which cannot be fully accounted for in terms of natural necessity and the material elements; however, they differ over which feature is most fundamental in Aristotle's analysis of final causation. The following teleological features have been imputed to Aristotle: (*a*) involving a potential for form which cannot be reduced to the powers of the material elements; (*b*) happening for the sake of something good; (*c*) having intrinsic causes and hence not being mere chance outcomes; and (*d*) involving an inherent self-regulating principle. Different interpretations take one or another of these features as more fundamental in Aristotle's analysis of teleology. I shall briefly review each of these approaches.

(*a*) *Irreducible potential for form*[11] The form or potential for form has a real causal role in the generation, growth, and life of organisms. Interpretations which emphasize the irreducible role of the form as efficient cause in Aristotle's teleology are committed to the view that the sum of actualizations of element-potentials in the organism and its environment

---

[9] See Wieland (1975), 155, Nussbaum (1978), 60, 74–6, 91–2, and Sorabji (1980), 162–6, for variants of this line of interpretation.

[10] Trans. from Barnes (1984). I am indebted to Allan Gotthelf for showing me notes on the interpretations of Aristotle's teleology and for discussion of these matters. The following taxonomy of different interpretations of Aristotle derives from Gotthelf, 'Understanding Aristotle's Teleology', in *Final Causality in Nature and Human Affairs*, ed. R. F. Hassing (Washington DC, forthcoming).

[11] In addition to *GA* II 1 734^b31-6 quoted above, see I 21 729^b25-30, 22 730^b8-32; II 2 $735^b37-736^a1$, with 737^a7-9, 4 740^b25-9.

cannot be sufficient for the generation, growth, and life of the organism.[12] According to Gotthelf 'the irreducibility thesis' is 'at the core of the concept of [Aristotle's] concept of final causality'.[13]

(*b*) *For the sake of the good* Teleological explanations are often stated in terms of goodness (*Phys.* II 2 194^{a}32–3, 7 198^{b}8–9; *Met.* I 3 983^{a}31–2, V 2 1013^{b}25–7). For example, Aristotle explains that animals sleep *because* this is beneficial for them (*Somn.* 2 455^{b}17–18).[14] This goodness consists in the fact that these features promote the survival of the organism and, secondarily, its replacement by other organisms of the same kind (*Phys.* II 8 198^{b}29–31; *DA* II 4 415^{a}26–^{b}7; *GA* II 1 731^{b}24–732^{a}3; *Pol.* II 2 1261^{b}9). Some interpreters emphasize this feature, contending that the goodness of outcomes such as the existence of organisms and of their organs requires the use of teleological explanations. Of these interpreters, some deny that the potentials of the elements are sufficient to determine the existence of living systems, whereas others hold that teleology is compatible with the biological phenomena resulting of necessity from the activities of the material elements.[15]

(*c*) *Result of intrinsic (efficient) causation, not of chance* Aristotle argues against Empedocles and other natural philosophers who claim that the existence of living things results from chance or as an accidental by-product of material processes: 'for example, that our teeth should come up of necessity—the front teeth come up sharp, suitable for tearing, and the molars come up flat and suitable for grinding food—they did not arise for the sake of this, but it was an accidental result' (*Phys.* II 8 198^{b}23–7). Aristotle reasons that such events must either be by accident (the result of chance or spontaneity), or else due to teleology; and that they cannot be accidental because they happen always or for the most part. The implication is that teleology involves causes which are intrinsic (*kath'*

---

[12] Cf. Meyer (1992), 703 n. 3, 5), who refers to the claim that elemental processes *are* sufficient for biological processes as 'the thesis of necessity'. She distinguishes interpreters who find teleology incompatible with the thesis of necessity (Cooper (1982), Gotthelf (1987), Lear (1988), Waterlow (1982)) from those who regard them as compatible (Charles (1991), Irwin (1988), Nussbaum (1978), Sorabji (1980)).

[13] Gotthelf (1987), 254. Other interpretations emphasizing the irreducibility of teleology to material causation are offered by Waterlow (1982), Lennox (1982), Code (1987), and Lear (1988), 22.

[14] See also passages cited in n. 7 above and *Phys.* II 3 195^{a}23–6, cited by Charles (1991), 108 n. 7.

[15] For the latter interpretation see Charles (1991) and Salkever (1990), ch. 1. Cooper (1982) favours the former view, rejecting the thesis of necessity; but he also contends that if, *per impossibile*, organisms and their organs came to be from natural necessity, this would not explain the fact that the arrangement of the parts is *good*.

hauto) rather than accidental, i.e. causes which determine their outcomes and are not merely sufficient. (For example, although the same person may be a housebuilder, pale, and musical, the housebuilder is the intrinsic cause of the house, whereas the pale or musical thing is merely an accidental cause (5 196^{b}26–7).) Interpretations which emphasize this feature see Aristotle as arguing that living things come to be by nature rather than by chance, if they are to be substances. He is, on this view, concerned not with whether or not living things come to be by natural necessity, but with whether they have intrinsic efficient causes. His main concern is to combat a version of eliminativism which 'proposes to eliminate from the ontological category of substance all entities other than the material elements (*Phys.* II 1 193^{a}21–5)'.[16]

(*d*) *Internal directive principle* According to Aristotle, growth involves the self-replication of a formal structure or proportion (*logos*) of materials, although particular bits of matter may come and go (*GC* I 5 321^{b}16–322^{a}4; II 6 333^{a}35–^{b}16). There is in the seed a 'programme' which determines that a certain form develops, survives, and replicates itself *ad infinitum*. According to an interpretation which identifies the final cause with such an internal directive principle, Aristotle is only committed to a weaker or relative version of irreducibility (i.e. the potential for form is irreducible to element-potentials).[17] There is no need to ascribe to him the stronger thesis that the potential for form is irreducible to *any* potential on *any* level of explanation (absolute irreducibility). Indeed, such an interpretation would require taking him to rule out in advance theories (e.g. molecular biology) which had not occurred to him.

An apparent advantage of the latter interpretation, which emphasizes feature (*d*), is that it can arguably account for the other three features. Feature (*a*), irreducibility, is evident from the fact that simple elemental processes cannot account for the fact that living things contain an internal directive principle which is self-replicating and self-limiting:

[The element fire] is in a sense a co-operating cause, but not the cause without qualification; that is rather the soul; for the increase of fire goes on without limit as long as there is combustible [material], but of all things which are established by nature there is a limit or proportion of their size and increase; and these are features of soul but not of fire, and of a proportion rather than of matter. (*DA* II 4 416^{a}13–18)

---

[16] Meyer (1992). Cf. Irwin (1988), sects. 55–60, and Matthen (1989).
[17] Bradie and Miller (1984).

The existence of flesh and bone depends upon a specific proportion (*logos*) of the elements, and such a proportion is continued throughout the growth process; and it is due not to the elements themselves but to the essential nature of the organism. Feature (*b*), goodness or benefit, can seemingly also be accounted for. As remarked above this goodness consists in the fact that living things have traits which are suited to their survival as things of a specific kind. The Presocratic materialists held that this goodness is solely due to chance: if the materials combine spontaneously in a suitable way, like animals with teeth for chewing, they will survive; otherwise they will perish like Empedocles' 'man-faced oxprogeny' (*Phys.* II 8 198^{b}29–31). Aristotle argues that a directive principle must be present within living systems to explain why the outcomes are beneficial 'always or for the most part'. Also, feature (*c*), intrinsic causation, can seemingly be accounted for. Substances as teleological systems have intrinsic rather than accidental causes and the internal directive principle is a feature of such an intrinsic cause: 'For not any chance [living being] comes to be from a seed, nor does a chance seed come to be from any chance body; but a definite thing comes from a definite thing. Therefore, the seed is the principle and maker of what comes from it.' He adds that the seed is prior to the offspring in generation, but the living thing, as a substance, is prior in completeness or perfection. 'Prior to both, however, is the [living being] from which the seed comes to be' (*PA* I 1 641^{b}26–33). The seed thus contains a nature, understood as a principle at work within the thing which is analogous to thought in purposeful action directing and limiting the outcome (*Phys.* II 5 196^{b}21–2). The presence of this principle in a human being but not in a bed explains why a human being comes to be from a human being, but a bed does not come to be from a bed (*Phys.* II 1 193^{b}8–9; cf. *PA* I 1 640^{a}25–^{b}4). The form of the offspring which is the final cause of the seed is identical in kind with the form of the parent which is the efficient cause. The intrinsic cause of the living organism must contain the internal directive principle and cannot be a mere chance confluence of material elements.

But of what relevance is Aristotelian teleology, so understood, to modern biology? First, it is necessary to distinguish two claims about teleological processes:

(T_1) In a life process the goal is produced by means of a potential existing from the outset, through movement conforming to a formal principle.

(*T*₂)   The source of movement through which life processes occur is vital heat, which cannot be identified with the potentials of the simpler sublunary elements.

Claim (*T*₂) has been discredited by modern biology: Aristotle was mistaken to think that the form was transmitted by means of motions through bodily fluids due to vital heat. However, (*T*₁), which is the theoretical core of Aristotle's teleology, has been arguably vindicated by modern biology. For the point of (*T*₁) is that life processes are self-directing in virtue of inherent forms or structures. The type of movement required on Aristotle's account for a potential for form is the type of movement exemplified by the DNA molecule. The genetic 'programme' contained in the molecule's structure directs and limits the organism's growth in the manner set forth in Aristotle's biological writings.

As noted above, Delbrück has observed this parallel between Aristotle and DNA theory. Ernst Mayr, a historian of biology, concurs, 'Aristotle's *eidos* (even though considered immaterial, because invisible) was conceptually virtually identical with the ontogenetic programme of the developmental physiologist.' He observes that the nature of the genetic programme required the collaboration of molecular biology and computer science. 'What is particularly important is that the genetic program itself remains unchanged while it sends out its instructions to the body. The whole concept of program is so novel that it is still resisted by many philosophers.' Biological processes may thus be described as 'teleonomic' (lawlike and goal directed). Providing a teleonomic account is tantamount to providing a 'mechanistic' explanation of at least one class of teleological phenomena. The 'movements' which Aristotle took to be the physiological correlates of the action of final causality have turned out to be complex material natures. Have final causes, thus, been eliminated? Some might suppose so, yet it seems more reasonable on Mayr's account to conceptualize the action of genetic programmes in terms of the assimilation of final causes into the rubric of material and efficient causation. Thus, the concept of natural necessity in modern biology, which includes principles of both material and efficient causation, also incorporates elements which are distinctly teleological in character.[18]

The modern theory of evolution was of course in fundamental disagreement with Aristotle's doctrine of the eternity of the species. In *The Origin of Species*, Charles Darwin (1809–82) observes that the principle of

---

[18]   Mayr (1982), 48, 56; cf. Mayr (1988). Does this leave open the possibility that a robot, a self-directing machine of sufficient complexity, could count as a teleological system? This seems possible, although Aristotle would no doubt have found it utterly paradoxical.

natural selection is 'shadowed forth' in Empedocles' explanation of the formation of teeth:

Wheresoever, therefore, all things together (that is all the parts of one whole) happened like as if they were made for the sake of something, these were preserved, having been appropriately constituted by an internal spontaneity; and whatsoever things were not thus constituted, perished, and still perish. (*Phys.* II 8 198^{b}29–31; C. Grece trans. consulted by Darwin)

Darwin complains of 'how little Aristotle fully comprehended the principle', as shown by his rejection of Empedocles' account of the origin of teeth.[19] However, Darwin's theory of natural selection does offer an interesting parallel to Aristotle. Most organisms produce more offspring than can survive to the age of adulthood and reproduction, and their progeny exhibit many variations in their parts and functionings. Some variations give their possessors a comparative advantage in the struggle for existence in specific environments, so that they are able to produce more offspring which tend to inherit the advantageous traits. Natural selection thus favours those characters which have survival and reproductive value. Although Aristotle is mistaken about the ultimate origin of such adaptive traits, he correctly understands that they are transmitted as formal principles from parents to offspring of the same kind (see *PA* I 1 641^{b}26–9). Meyer points out the parallel in Aristotelian teleology: 'if the parent had not survived to maturity, it would not have reproduced its species-typical parts in the offspring. So if such parts were not good for a member of the species, they would not have been reproduced in the offspring. The offspring therefore has such parts because such parts are good'.[20] Thus Aristotle's final cause is not a paradoxical sort of retroactive efficient cause. The form of the offspring (the final cause) is identical in kind with the form of the parent (the efficient cause).

It has been objected that evolutionary biology cannot provide any answer to the question about the well-being of individuals and about its possible relation to the ethical life, because 'evolutionary biology is not at all concerned with the well-being of the individual, but with fitness, which is the likelihood of that individual's leaving offspring'.[21] It is certainly correct that one cannot deduce a set of moral principles valid for civilized human beings from a theory about how the human species evolved. However, evolutionary theory might have an indirect relevance

---

[19] 'An Historical Sketch of the Progress of Opinion on the Origin of Species' in Darwin (1859).

[20] Meyer (1992), 811. See also Irwin (1988), 524–5 n. 5, on the parallels (and differences) between Darwin and Aristotle.   [21] Williams (1985), 44.

to ethics. The forces of natural selection might well have favoured the evolution of intelligent organisms which are both concerned with their own well-being and disposed to co-operate with others for mutual advantage. Darwin himself argued that sociability is an adaptive trait of many animals and that human beings specifically possessed 'social instincts', associated with what modern philosophers call 'sympathy' and 'the moral sense'. These basic social instincts, when combined with rationality, language, and social habituation, enable individuals to co-operate in communities and to express 'the common opinion how each member ought to act for the public good' and to abide by this understanding.[22] Although such organisms would not be genetically 'programmed' to be virtuous or ethical, virtue could be viewed as a natural extension of potentials deeply rooted in their biological nature. One would expect, however, that the resulting theory would allow for much greater variability and diversity among the forms of virtue that could be admitted as 'according to nature' than Aristotle himself recognized. Given the genetic diversity among individuals, the natural ends of individuals should be expected to differ considerably in detail. However, it would be expected that individuals would also share important common traits such as rationality and co-operativeness.[23]

In summary, Aristotle was completely mistaken in his account of the physical mechanism through which the final cause takes effect, viz., through the operation of vital heat and wave-like movements transmitted through the blood and semen. He did not anticipate the direction taken by modern science—explanation in terms of complex, *molecular* structures—because he saw materialist theories as hopelessly mired in a commitment to simple elemental properties. Yet, according to neo-Aristotelian teleology, he correctly characterized the kind of process required to sustain the development, survival, and reproduction of living organisms, viz., as requiring an appeal to internal directing principles. This claim is controversial, and it would obviously require extensive investigation to determine whether it can be ultimately validated by modern scientific research.

10.3. PERFECTION

The principle of perfection identifies the human good with the actualization of natural potentials. It holds that objects of desire are good apart

---

[22] Darwin (1871), ch. 4. See also Sect. 2.6 above on Darwin and recent social theorists influenced by him.

[23] Arnhart (1984), 1994, argues that Darwinian evolutionary biology can be used to support neo-Aristotelian political naturalism.

from subjective considerations such as whether they result in pleasure or satisfaction or are viewed with a favourable attitude. A perfectionist theory may hold that a self-actualizing condition is intrinsically pleasant or that pleasure supervenes on complete self-realization, but it does not concede that the mere enjoyment of an activity makes it good. For one may erroneously find pleasure in the wrong sorts of activity. Perfection, instead, provides an objective standard by which individual practices, ways of life, social customs, and political institutions may be evaluated. To the extent that these frustrate self-realization they may be justifiably condemned as 'against nature'. Aristotle's theory is perfectionist in the sense that it presupposes a theory of human nature and identifies the good with the fullest possible development of this nature.[24]

Before proceeding it is necessary to avoid some misconceptions about the principle of perfection. First, the translation 'perfection' has misleading connotations, such as the pursuit (or pretence) of absolute perfection. For Aristotle, 'perfection' (*teleiotēs*) refers to the full actualization of natural potentials and is understood as the normal functioning of an organism over an entire life. Aristotle is not a 'perfectionist' in the unreasonable sense of insisting that anything short of perfection is unacceptable. For he also asserts a principle of proximity: i.e. a thing is better the closer it is to perfection.

Second, the principle is sometimes taken to assert that certain objects are good or bad for agents regardless of whether they want them or not. By totally sundering the good from human desires, this doctrine would make itself irrelevant or oppressive. Alternatively, perfectionism may be understood as the paradoxical claim that everyone desires true perfection most of all but falls short due to ignorance. Neither of these accurately depicts Aristotle's principle of perfection. He expresses agreement with the statement that 'the good is that for which everything strives' (*EN* I 1 1094[a]3), but denies that the good is simply that which one desires. This is evident when he argues that the object of wishing cannot be identified with either the good, without qualification, or the apparent good (III 4 1113[a]15–22). His own view is that among the things we wish for some are more choiceworthy than others and hence better, not merely in that they appear so to us but 'without qualification and in truth'. The excellent

---

[24] Hurka (1993), 4, distinguishes this narrow sense of 'perfectionism' from the broader sense which merely identifies the good with the development of capacities or the achievement of excellence without necessarily assuming a theory of human nature. Rawls's 'Aristotelian principle' appears to be perfectionist in the broad sense (1971: 424–33). The Marxist notion of self-realization is also perfectionist in a broad sense: cf. Elster (1985), 82–92, 521–5, and (1986).

virtuous person (*spoudaios*) is a reliable judge of what is objectively good or bad, whereas the many mistakenly identify the pleasant, the apparent good, with the objective good ($1113^{a}22-^{b}2$). Hence, for Aristotle, the good is both desirable *and* choiceworthy.

Third, although Aristotle's account of human perfection is based on his natural teleology, in the sense that happiness is the natural end of human beings, he does not hold that the meaning of happiness can be discovered solely through a scientific study of human nature. It would be surprising if he did think this, in view of his sharp distinction between the contemplative natural sciences and practical sciences such as politics (see Section 1.2 above). Further, given his view that human beings are by nature political, a full understanding of human perfection will also require an investigation of political affairs. As we have seen, the general technique of Aristotle's ethics and political science is to combine general claims about nature with common-sense observations about the requirements and conditions of human choice and action. The principle of perfection will, therefore, be based on, but not totally defined by, a scientific theory of human nature.

Aristotle's account of happiness is based on the premiss that human beings have a proper function (*idion ergon*) which is based on their essence or nature (*EN* I 7 $1097^{b}22-1098^{a}20$; *EE* II 1 $1218^{b}37-1219^{a}39$). By this he does not mean that human beings like tools have instrumental functions; rather he is speaking of a function in the sense in which it is identified with an end (*EE* II 1 $1219^{a}8$). In speaking of the function as *idion*, he does not mean that it is 'peculiar' or 'unique' to humans,[25] but, instead, that it is 'proper', in the sense of 'essential', to human beings.[26] However, he makes the strong claim that rationality is the proper function of a human being. Hence, he dismisses the vegetative part of the soul when he defines the excellence of the human soul (*EE* II 1 $1219^{b}26-1220^{a}4$, *EN* I 1 $1097^{b}33-1098^{a}1$). Moreover, Aristotle holds that promoting the function is good for the organism which has it in the sense that it promotes the life or being of an organism of that kind (cf. *EE* II 1 $1219^{a}24$). In terms of this function it is possible to define things which are good without qualification for the organism in contrast to things which are good for particular

---

[25] This is assumed by many critics, e.g. Williams (1972), 64: 'one could as well, on these principles, end up with a morality which exhorted men to spend as much time as possible in making fire; or developing peculiarly human physical characteristics; or having sexual intercourse without regard to season; or despoiling the environment and upsetting the balance of natur; or killing things for fun.'

[26] See Whiting (1988), 35–6. For this use of *idion* cf. *Top.* I 4 $101^{b}19-20$. See also Irwin (1988), sect. 194.

persons in particular circumstances. Thus we can speak of what is advantageous to a body in health as good without qualification for a body, in contrast to what is good for a sick body, such as drugs or a scalpel. We can make a similar distinction for pleasures: seeing in the light is pleasant without qualification, i.e. for a healthy eye, but painful for a particular eye, i.e. a diseased one (*EE* VII 2 1235^b30–8; cf. *EN* VII 12 1152^b26–1153^a7). According to Aristotle human nature includes a number of functions, which can be arranged in a hierarchy:

CONTEMPLATIVE RATIONALITY

PRACTICAL RATIONALITY, subsuming productive

PERCEPTION, with imagination, appetite, locomotion

VEGETATION, including nutrition, growth, reproduction

Among living organisms a function F_1 is higher than F_2 if, and only if, all normal members of species with F_1 also have F_2 but there are normal members of species with F_2 that do not have F_1. For example, all normal animals with sense-perception also have vegetative functions, but normal plants with the latter do not have the former; hence, sense-perception is higher than vegetative function. Correspondingly, the living species form a hierarchy: plants, beasts, and humans.[27] Aristotle also implies that some human beings are not capable of the contemplative function (*Pol.* VII 14 1333^a27–9), suggesting that there will also be a stratification within the human race. Given that the end of human beings is life or activity, Aristotle maintains that they should perform the highest possible level of activity: 'what is most choiceworthy for each individual is always the highest it is possible for him to attain' (1333^a29–30). Since for human beings the highest function is rationality, Aristotle's perfectionism leads to an intellectualism advocating the philosophical life or the life of the intellect as the best life for human beings (X 7 1177^a12–18, 1178^a4–8, 8 1178^b7–32).

Aristotle's argument for the superiority of intellectual activity appeals to a number of criteria:

... the activity of the intellect seems to be superior in excellence because it is contemplative, and to aim at nothing apart from itself, and to have its own proper pleasure (and this enhances the activity), and to be self-sufficient and leisurely and unwearied, so far as this is possible for a human being; and whatever else is

[27] See Keyt (1983), 366–7.

ascribed to the blessed person, is evidently connected with this activity. This, then, will be the complete happiness of a human being, which receives a complete term of life; for nothing incomplete belongs to happiness. (X 7 1177^{b}19–26)

The features which distinguish the contemplative life from the political and lesser forms are that it is most of all self-contained and self-sufficient, thus depending to the least extent on external resources for its realization. It is thus also a leisurely activity, carried out for its own sake and not for the sake of other activities. A modern perfectionist would have to extend and buttress arguments of this sort, or mount an alternative defence of a determinate conception of the good life.

In keeping with Aristotle's teleology, a neo-Aristotelian theory of the good would understand it as the condition to which an organism tends, to which it reflectively refers, and from which it will not depart, unless it is impeded by external factors or is suffering from an internal incapacity or disease. By extension, external conditions would be called good or bad to the extent that they promote or frustrate the organism's natural development. A modern psychological theory which is broadly Aristotelian in character has been advanced by Abraham Maslow.[28] Maslow's theory incorporates three Aristotelian principles. First, individuals have essential natures of their own, which are genetically based and which result in part not only in physical characteristics but also in psychological needs, capacities, and tendencies. Second, that individuals are in a healthy and normal way, to the extent that they develop their nature and actualize their potentialities. Third, most psychopathology results from the frustrating or twisting of essential human nature. Maslow's theory also resembles Aristotle's in that he recognizes a natural hierarchy of needs. The most basic needs are shared by all animals and must be met before the others. The higher needs are the most individualized but are also the most satisfying and characteristic of healthy functioning. The hierarchy of needs, from basic to highest, is as follows: physiological, safety, belongingness, esteem, self-actualization. The latter Maslow defines as 'people's desire for self-fulfillment, namely the tendency for them to become actualized in what they are potentially'. Maslow believes that this theory yields a theory of value which is objective and cuts across different cultures. Although he acknowledges that his theory has much in common with the philosophy of Aristotle as well as Spinoza, Maslow departs from Aristotle on many particulars. This is not surprising. Even if one follows Aristotle in basing a theory of value on a theory of human nature, the content of

---

[28] Maslow (1987), 15–26, 115–16, makes evident his debt to Aristotle.

such a theory must depend upon the results of empirical investigation combining the methods of biology, psychology, and the social sciences.[29]

It has seemed implausible, however, even to most sympathetic modern commentators that such a method could vindicate the specific version of perfectionism which Aristotle himself advocates; i.e. that it could support intellectualism to the exclusion of other ways of life and Aristotle's particular scheme of the ethical virtues.[30] Aristotle is cognizant of the great diversity of ways of life but he characterizes them as variations on imperfection and deviations from the good (*Pol.* VII 8 1328^{a}37–^{b}2). Indeed, any neo-Aristotelian attempt to revive perfectionism must cope with a dilemma: Is perfection to be understood in a monistic way (the human good consists in a single kind of activity) or an inclusivistic way (different kinds of activity constitute the good)? If a monistic account of the good seems unreasonably exclusionary and arbitrary, the inclusivistic account runs the risk of incoherence. On the monistic horn of the dilemma, because humans are complex beings with a wide repertoire of potentials, it seems arbitrary to identify the human good with the exercise of only one of them, for example, with the life of contemplation.[31] But if the human good becomes more expansive, there looms the other horn: How can one satisfy the demands of all the potentials of a human being, especially when the full actualization of the different potentials requires incompatible courses of action? Or if one must choose among goods, what guidance would such an open-minded perfectionism provide?

This problem arises to some extent even in Aristotle's own theory of perfection. As I have pointed out above (Sections 4.7, 6.8), there are two opposed lines of interpretation of Aristotle's theory, one of which is monistic and the other inclusivistic. The monistic view, or strict intellectualism, holds that contemplative or theoretical activity is the sole component of the best life for man and that anything else has value only as a means to contemplative activity. Some commentators are reluctant to attribute this view to Aristotle because 'contemplate at any cost' would lead to immoral consequences.[32] The inclusivist view admits at least one

---

[29] Hurka (1993), ch. 2–4, also defends a neo-Aristotelian theory of human essence in which physical embodiment and theoretical and practical rationality have the central place, although he eschews Aristotle's teleology.

[30] For criticism of Aristotle's intellectualism, see Maslow (1987), 116. On the alleged parochialism of Aristotle's theory of virtue, see MacIntyre (1981), 152, and Williams (1985), 43–7.

[31] Cooper (1975), 175–7, finds an argument for such an identification in Aristotle, maintaining that Aristotle identifies the human being with the contemplative intellect. Whiting (1986) criticizes this interpretation.   [32] Ackrill (1980), 32.

other activity as intrinsically valuable. A leading inclusivist candidate, moderate intellectualism, holds that theoretical activity is the primary but not the sole component of the best life for a human being, the practically wise and ethically virtuous activity being a secondary component.[33] This exegetical issue is exceedingly complex and continues to be disputed in numerous articles and books on Aristotle's ethics, so it must suffice to mention a few salient points.[34]

The primary evidence for strict intellectualism is found in *Nicomachean Ethics*, X. Here Aristotle argues that the activity of intellect is superior (to political and military actions) because it has no end beyond itself, has its own proper pleasure which increases the activity, and is self-sufficient, leisurely, and unwearied in so far as this is possible for a human being; and he concludes that 'this is the complete [or perfect] happiness for a human being, if it receives a complete term of life (for nothing incomplete belongs to happiness)' (7 1177[b]16–26, summarizing preceding arguments). 'However, such a life would be superior to the human; but not in so far as he is a human being will one live thus, but in so far as something divine is present in him.' None the less, Aristotle offers a perfectionist prescription: 'We must not follow those who advise us being human to think human things and being mortal to think mortal things, but in so far as we can, we must make ourselves immortal and do everything in order to live according to the best thing in us; for even if this is small in bulk, it surpasses everything in power and worth.' He adds that a person might be identified with his intellect (*nous*) since this is his authoritative and better part. This leads to another argument for intellectualism: 'For what is proper to each thing by nature is best and pleasantest for it; and the life according to the intellect is, then, [best and pleasantest by nature], since this [viz., intellect] is most of all a human being. Therefore, this life is also the happiest' (1177[b]26–1178[a]8).

Although this might seem to endorse a strict-intellectualist ideal, Aristotle immediately seems to qualify it: 'But, secondarily, the life according to the other kind of virtue [viz., ethical], is happy' (8 1178[a]9). Aristotle

---

[33] For these terms and definitions see Keyt (1983), 368, which also offers a valuable taxonomy of interpretations.

[34] Different commentators have offered many variations and refinements of this basic distinction which cannot be examined here (see Hardie (1980), 420–4). Proponents of the strict-intellectualist interpretation include Kenny (1978), 203–6; (1992), ch. 8; Cooper (1975), chs. 2–3—Cooper (1975) finds strict intellectualism in *EN* I and X, but a more inclusive view in the rest of the *EN*, the *MM*, and *Pol.*; Kraut (1989); Heinaman (1988); and Larmore (1993), 70–4. The inclusivist view, in various forms, is defended by Ackrill (1980); Keyt (1983; 1989); Engberg-Pedersen (1983), ch. 4; Nussbaum (1986), 373–7; Cooper (1987); White (1990; 1992: 11 n. 13); Rasmussen and Den Uyl (1991), 36–8; and Irwin (1991*b*). This is only a partial list of items published to date.

adds that ethical virtue is inextricably linked to practical wisdom and that these are connected with the passions and thus are tied to the compound nature of human beings. 'Since the virtues of the compound are human, the life and happiness according to these virtues are also [human]' (1178^a19–22). He reiterates that contemplative activity is independent and self-sufficient in a way that ethically virtuous activity is not, since it does not require the use of external goods; but he also says of the person who is contemplating, 'in so far as he is a human being and lives together with a number [of other human beings], he chooses to do acts according to virtue; for he will need such things [viz., external goods] to lead a human life' (1178^b3–7). This suggests that because human nature is complex, including the passionate and political nature along with the intellect, the person leading the contemplative life will, *qua* human being, choose to be ethically virtuous. This agrees with other unqualified statements that good action is an end (VI 5 1140^b6–7) and that virtuous acts are chosen for themselves (II 4 1105^a32). Commentators who favour the strict-intellectualist interpretation fail to distinguish between two questions: 'What is the best life for me?' to which Aristotle's answer is 'the contemplative or philosophical life'; and 'What is the best life for me *in so far as I am a human being*?' to which 'a mixed life with contemplation as a primary component and ethically virtuous activity as a secondary element' is Aristotle's answer (cf. 7 1177^b27–8, 8 1178^b5–8, 1179^a22–32). On this moderate-intellectualist interpretation, then, human perfection will consist of both contemplative activity and ethically virtuous action.[35]

However, even if Aristotle's theory of the human good is inclusivistic to this extent, it would seem that any defensible form of perfectionism must be more pluralistic (countenancing alternative valid forms of perfection) than Aristotle's in order to avoid the charge of invoking an arbitrarily narrow conception of human nature.[36] A modern version of perfectionism that is both inclusivistic and pluralistic was espoused by

---

[35] Even among those who agree that the human being leading the best life, on Aristotle's view, will be ethically virtuous, there are important disagreements: for example, whether it is possible for the same person to lead both a philosophical and a political way of life. Keyt (1983; 1989) and Engberg-Pederson (1983) argue that it is, whereas Cooper (1987) and Broadie (1991) disagree. Lawrence (1993) views the purely contemplative life as Utopian, the best albeit humanly unattainable.

[36] Gray (1989), 257, remarks, 'it should be evident to any eye that is not blinkered by the local connections of our culture that human flourishing can come in many different forms. The form of life of a troubadour poet, of a Japanese *bushido* warrior, of a Desert Father, or a Renaissance courtesan are in no obvious sense lesser forms of human flourishing than that of Aristotle's leisured, contemplative gentleman.' Even if one were to take exception to one or another of these examples, Gray's general contention that flourishing is multiform is plausible. George (1993) also defends a pluralistic form of perfectionism.

Wilhelm von Humboldt (1767–1835): 'The true end of Man, or that which is prescribed by the eternal and immutable desires of reason, and not suggested by vague and transient desires, is the highest and most harmonious development of his powers to a complete and consistent whole.' For Humboldt 'the highest ideal . . . of the co-existence of human beings seems to me to consist in a union in which each strives to develop himself from his inmost nature, and for his own sake'.[37] The best life is one of self-development (*Bildung*) in which one develops all of one's natural capacities: intellectual, artistic, physical, social, etc.

Such an account faces the inclusivist horn of the dilemma mentioned above. How can the natural human end accommodate a wide plurality of ends so that they fit together into a harmonious whole? Two strategies suggest themselves: the perfectionist might permit trade-offs of some sort between the competing conceptions of the good, or else, following Aristotle, seek a way of prioritizing or ranking the conceptions of the good.[38] Both approaches face prima-facie difficulties. It has been objected that it is impossible to resolve the conflicting demands between different components of human flourishing. For example, the life of Gauguin suggests that the full expression and development of one's artistic genius might entail the repression or hypertrophy of one's domestic or civic potentialities.[39] As Isaiah Berlin maintains:

There are many objective ends, ultimate values, some incompatible with others, pursued by different societies at different times, or by different groups in the same society, by entire classes or churches or races, or by particular individuals within them, any one of which may find itself subject to conflicting claims of uncombinable, yet equally ultimate and objective, ends.[40]

On the other hand, one might try to rank these components, but it has also been objected that the attempt to advance one component of perfection ahead of another implicitly assumes another set of undefended values,

[37] Humboldt (1993), 10, 13.

[38] Hurka (1993), ch. 7, adopts the trade-off approach and criticizes the attempt to establish a lexical ordering among the human excellences. Den Uyl (1991), 203, argues that 'the moral virtues are traits of character the possession of which allows the "first order" or specified generic goods . . . to be compossibly enjoyed'. First-order goods include intellectual activity, artistic pursuits, beauty, health, wealth, humour, friendship, etc. Practical wisdom plays a comparable role in Nussbaum (1986), 374.

[39] See Williams (1972), 61; (1985), 47; and MacIntyre (1988), 142.

[40] Berlin (1990), 79–80, followed by Gray (1993), 290–9, espouses objective value pluralism: there are many incommensurable and incompatible ultimate values grounded in human nature. See also Hampshire (1971), 79; (1983), 31.

and consequently that the theory of perfection would lose its putative status as an objective ethic, reducing itself to a version of moral relativism.[41]

Alternatively, the perfectionist might follow in Rawls's footsteps, eschewing the task of selecting a unique form of perfection and instead seeking to identify a set of 'primary goods'.[42] On this approach, even though individuals differ in their natures from one another and thus may vary considerably in their modes of perfection, there may be one or more goods which are indispensable for all forms of self-perfection. It could be argued that practical wisdom and ethical virtue as described by Aristotle can play this role, since they permit the compossible realization of human potentialities and thus must range over all the potentialities, including themselves. Thus individuals can ascertain what their distinctive potentialities are and how best to realize them under the circumstances.[43] It might be objected that such an argument ignores the fact of human tragedies, where human beings face moral conflicts which force them to make tragic choices between conflicting values. Aristotle recognizes that such cases may arise, for example, when a tyrant commands you to do a shameful act or else he will kill your parents and children (*EN* III 1 1110^{a}5–7),[44] where one must follow a course of action which is frustrating and leaves one with a deep sense of regret. However, Aristotle regards such tragic dilemmas as unfortunate but unusual. His view is that in the normal state of affairs the theory of the mean will enable a virtuous agent to satisfy a wide range of competing demands and attain a level of flourishing.

Similarly, in the social sphere, one might try to define primary goods which permit the compossible perfection of different individuals. This seems in fact to be Humboldt's strategy, because he follows the statement, regarding 'the true end of Man' with the following: 'Freedom is the first and indispensable condition which the possibility of such a development presupposes; but there is besides another essential—intimately connected with freedom, it is true—a variety of situations.' This sentence

---

[41] This sort of objection is offered in Harman (1983); for a reply see Norton (1985) as well as Harman's rejoinder (1986). See also Norton (1976) for a defence of a perfectionist ethical theory.

[42] Rawls (1971), 62, defines primary goods as 'things that every rational man is presumed to want' since they 'normally have a use whatever a person's rational plan of life'. Some primary goods are 'natural' (e.g. health, vigour, intelligence, imagination), others are 'social' (e.g. rights and liberties, powers and opportunities, income and wealth).

[43] Cf. Den Uyl (1991), ch. 8.

[44] The case is cited by Stocker (1990), ch. 3, and Yack (1993), 259–67, who offer persuasive treatments of moral conflicts from an Aristotelian standpoint.

was quoted with approval by John Stuart Mill who followed Humboldt in arguing that liberty along with variety is necessary for self-development, which in turn is necessary for human happiness.[45] In order to uphold such a requirement perfectionism would have to secure for autonomy or self-directedness an essential and central place in the good life.

This was not, however, the view of Aristotle himself, who evidently relegated liberty to the status of a mere external good and who prescribed frequent intrusions on individual freedom of choice in the pursuit of virtue.[46] None the less, it has been argued that Aristotle provided the theoretical basis for a more central role for self-directedness or autonomy.[47] Happiness is not for Aristotle the mere satisfaction of one's desires and appetites; rather it is an *activity* of the soul in accordance with virtue. Further, one must achieve happiness through one's own efforts and not through external goods or chance (*Pol.* VII 2 1323^{b}24–9; *EN* I 9 1099^{b}18–25). Moreover, virtuous acts must be *chosen* by the agent for their own sakes (*EN* II 4 1105^{a}31–2). Further, true self-love is embodied in persons who act according to their own rational judgement and voluntary acts are most of all those involving reason (*EN* IX 8 1168^{b}34–1169^{a}3). The exercise of reason, in contrast to perception, is voluntary and up to the agent (*DA* II 5 417^{b}18–26).[48] These claims together seem to imply that rationality, virtue, and happiness are essentially free and voluntary.

Apart from Aristotle's exegesis, whether these general claims about human nature are true is an issue for empirical psychology. If they are true, rationality and freedom could be defended as goods grounded in human nature as such, and not merely culture-specific values. This might in turn provide a naturalistic foundation for social or political freedom, as a necessary condition for individual self-realization. This would lend support to Humbolt's argument for individual liberty:

freedom is undoubtedly the indispensable condition, without which even the pursuits most congenial to individual human nature can never succeed in producing such salutary influences. Whatever does not spring from a man's free choice, or

---

[45] Mill (1989), 58. Raz (1986) also defends a version of liberal perfectionism in which personal autonomy has a leading role.

[46] Cf. Barnes (1990a), 251–2, Gray (1989), 254–7, Irwin (1988), sects. 225–7, and Sect. 6.9 above. Galston (1980), 97–9, and George (1993), ch. 6, agree with Aristotle that freedom is only instrumentally valuable.

[47] See Whiting (1988), 47–8, and Nichols (1992), 197 n. 33. Cf. Rasmussen and Den Uyl (1991), who offer a neo-Aristotelian theory of rights for which self-directedness or autonomy has the central role in human flourishing; also Den Uyl (1991), 181–6, and Machan (1975), 1989.

[48] See also Keyt (1993) who argues that Aristotle is theoretically committed to the principle that force and coercion are unnatural and unjust.

is only the result of instruction and guidance, does not enter into his very being, but still remains alien to his true nature; he does not perform it with truly human energies, but merely with mechanical exactness.[49]

Humboldt's argument was accepted not only by Mill but also by Hegelian perfectionists like T. H. Green, who argued, 'It is the business of the state, not indeed to promote moral goodness, for that from the very nature of moral goodness, it cannot do, but to maintain the conditions without which a free exercise of the human faculties is impossible.' Hence, the proper role of government 'seems necessarily confined to the removal of obstacles'.[50]

However, contemporary neo-Aristotelian theorists are not agreed that autonomy is a necessary ingredient of every good life, or that the best human lives are the most autonomous ones. Both claims are questioned by John Gray, who avers that flourishing takes many forms and that people may flourish just as well, if not better, in societies in which autonomy is inconspicuous or lacking (e.g. medieval Christendom) as in the open, pluralistic societies of the modern world. On Gray's pluralistic neo-Aristotelian view, 'the virtue of autonomy is a local affair'. In support of this he approvingly quotes Joseph Raz: 'I do not see that the absence of choice diminishes the value of human relations or the display of excellence in technical skills, physical ability, spirit and enterprise, leadership, scholarship, creativity or imaginativeness.'[51] On the opposing view, the rational forms of perfection require voluntary choice, especially activities involving invention, creativity, and imaginativeness. Even in relatively unfree societies the most fulfilling activities open to agents are voluntary and open to choice. The point is not that choosing activities makes them more valuable, but that the most choiceworthy activities are inherently voluntary. However, the issue of how important freedom of choice in fact is for human perfection remains to be settled by the human sciences.

10.4. COMMUNITY

According to the principle of community, individuals ought to be subject to the authority of the community. This doctrine underlies Aristotle's

---

[49] Humboldt (1993), 23.

[50] Green, quoted by Hurka (1993), 153. Hurka offers a perfectionist case for autonomy. See also Veatch (1985) and Rasmussen and Den Uyl (1991).

[51] Gray (1993), 308, citing Raz, 'Facing Up: A Reply', *University of Southern California Law Review*, 62 (1989), 1227.

argument for the priority of the polis to the individual because he maintains that individuals can attain perfection only if they are morally habituated under the polis and its laws (see Section 2.4). In addition, his description of the best constitution includes extensive controls over the conduct of the citizens in order to improve their moral conduct, including a system of public education (see Sections 6.7, 8.4).

However, Aristotle's argument seems open to criticism even on his own grounds. From the claim that the polis is the most inclusive of communities, he infers that it has the most authority (*Pol.* I 1 1252ᵃ1–7; see Section 1.4 above). This inference seems plausible only because two notions which are distinguished by modern political theorists are fused together in his conception of a polis: viz., the state and society. A state in the modern sense is an association which possesses a monopoly over the legitimized use of coercive force within a definite geographical area. It discharges narrowly political functions (those of deliberation, officiation, and adjudication in Aristotle's theory), maintains internal order, and defends against external enemies. In contrast, a society includes the full range of associations which human beings need to meet their basic needs and to flourish: including households, personal friendships, fraternal clubs, religious cults, schools (including Plato's Academy and Aristotle's Lyceum), and business relations organizations. This all-inclusive community contains an intricate web of human relationships, voluntary as well as coercive, private as well as public, through which individuals can find sustenance, companionship, and happiness.

The argument in *Politics*, I 2, that the polis exists by nature depends to a large extent on the identification of the polis with society, since it attains 'the limit of self-sufficiency' for the good life. The polis is thus alleged to be lacking in nothing the citizens require for the good life. The polis, so understood, is not confined to narrowly political relationships but is understood as the whole society in which the individual is able to flourish. However, when Aristotle studies the polis in *Politics*, III, he is concerned with a political entity, the state, rather than with the community. For, when he applies the method of analysis to the polis at III 1 1274ᵇ38–41, the basic constituent he arrives at is a citizen rather than a member of a basic social relationship (husband–wife, parent–child, master–slave), as was the case in Book I. The citizen is defined as the possessor of political rights in a narrow sense (see Section 5.1 above); for the polis is defined as 'a community of citizens in a constitution' (3 1276ᵇ1–2), and it is the function of the constitution to distribute offices and define authority (see IV 1 1289ᵃ15–20).

Similarly, in *Politics*, III 3, when Aristotle deals with the question of the identity of the polis over time, he holds that if there is a change of constitutions (e.g. if an oligarchy is overthrown, and a new democratic regime is established), a new polis comes into existence. His criterion for the continued existence of a polis over time is thus identity in constitution. Aristotle has been criticized for taking this stand on the grounds that 'the absurd consequence would follow that a city would not change its constitution without committing suicide' and also on the grounds that it 'seems quite inharmonious' with the rest of the *Politics*: 'It is particularly discordant with the emphasis in Book I on the city's being a natural growth.'[52] The appearance of discordance between Books I and III disappears, however, once it is recognized that in Book I it is the polis in the sense of a society which is treated as a natural growth, whereas in Book III the focus is on the state, which is just one aspect of the total community. It would be absurd to say a society could not change its constitution without ceasing to exist, but it would not be at all absurd to say this in regard to the state. Indeed, revolutionary states often refuse to shoulder the obligations of their predecessors, on the grounds that *they* did not originally assume them.

However, the waters become choppier in *Politics*, III 9, where Aristotle is trying to given an account of 'justice in the authoritative sense' and of the true polis. He criticizes one conception of the polis which, he maintains, cannot be correct. 'It is clear, therefore, that the polis is not a community [of persons] in a territory with the aim of not doing injustice to themselves and of promoting exchange' (1280ᵇ29–31). Here the polis is understood in the narrow sense of a political state because he is concerned with legislation (see 1280ᵇ6). The view which Aristotle is criticizing is that the purpose of the polis *qua* state is to prevent anyone from doing injustice to others and to protect contracts. The state seeks to prevent individuals from doing physical injury and perpetrating fraud against others as well as to protect its citizenry from foreign invaders. Aristotle contends that such a scheme is a polis in name only, not in reality (1280ᵇ7–8). It is a mere defensive alliance among parties which happen to reside in the same locality, and the law is a mere contract for this purpose.

Aristotle associates this theory with Lycophron, who calls the law 'a guarantee of mutual rights' (1280ᵇ10–11; cf. Sections 4.3, 7 above). Aristotle also mentions Hippodamus of Miletus (born *c*.500 BC), who evidently professed similar views. Especially noteworthy is Hippodomas' proposal

---

[52] Robinson (1962), 10.

that there be only three kinds of laws concerning which lawsuits should take place: laws against *hubris* or insolent assault, *blabē* (damage, as to property), and *thanatos* (homicide) (II 8 1276^{b}37–9). The proposals of Lycophron and Hippodamus tend to disconfirm the claim that 'the "limit of state interference" never suggested itself to the Greek philosophers as a problem for their consideration'.[53] These thinkers evidently proposed to limit the scope of the laws to the protection of rights, and it is for this very reason that Aristotle is attacking them. For their polis is not concerned with making its citizens virtuous. 'Whoever is concerned with good law must pay attention to political virtue and vice. It is thereby evident that the polis ought to care about virtue in so far as it is truly called a polis, and not merely so-called' (III 9 1280^{b}5–8). The laws must aim not merely at requiring the citizens to treat one another justly, but also at making them virtuous. This dictum is derived from the premiss that the polis 'exists for the sake not merely of life, but, more so, of the good life' (1280^{a}31–2). Although there is not an explicit cross-reference to Book I here, the statement of this premiss clearly echoes I 2 1252^{b}29–30. Thus, the refutation of the limited polis is evidently supposed to derive from the theory defended in *Politics*, I 2.

But, if so, Aristotle's opponents would seem to have a reply. The end of the polis *qua* society is the virtuous and happy life, but it does not follow that the function of the polis *qua* state is to use coercive force against its citizens so as to make them virtuous and happy. Aristotle, in making such an inference, is confusing the two senses of 'polis' and is assigning to the polis *qua* state a function which properly belongs only to the polis *qua* society.[54] Lycophron could argue that the proper function of the polis *qua* state is to use force only to prevent its citizens from harming each other, but it should be limited to this, because virtue and happiness are achieved through non-political private associations which are a part of the polis *qua* society. The state is necessary for virtue and happiness, but only in the sense that by protecting individual rights it provides the legal framework within which individuals can perfect themselves.

Aristotle might respond that the polis resembles an organism in that

[53] Barker (1946), li.

[54] Cf. Mulgan (1977), 16–17. Many historians have held that Aristotle's concept of the polis as a fusion of state and society reflects historical reality. For example, Fustel de Coulanges (1864) argued that the polis was an all-embracing state in which all social spheres (religion, family, marriage, education, production, and trade) were politicized. Although this thesis has been repeated many times, a dissenting note is sounded by Hansen (1991), 61–4, and Humphreys (1978), 256–64, who argue that, in fact, many Greek social activities were essentially non-political.

when it has a function it always has a part whose function it is to realize that end. 'For example, one end of every plant and animal is to generate another like itself, and to realize this end every plant and animal has a reproductive soul' (*DA* II 4 416^{b}23–5; *GA* II 1 735^{a}17–19).[55] Aristotle suggests such an analogy when he says that just as the soul is more a part of an animal than the body, the governing body is more a part of the polis than the other parts such as slaves and vulgar workers (*Pol.* IV 4 1291^{a}24– 8; cf. *EN* IX 8 1168^{b}31–3). However, Lycophron could object again that the polis is not a natural whole in the same way as an organism. It is, instead, a community all of whose parts partake of the end. Even if the members of the polis share in the functions of governing, they also belong to many other non-political associations including family life, business, personal friendships, and leisurely pursuits such as philosophy. Further, Aristotle's argument for public education assumes precisely what he needs to prove, viz., that it is the business of the polis *qua* state to inculcate morality in the citizens. Thus, Lycophron might conclude, Aristotle's principle of community results from a confused view of the polis and is not entailed by his principles of teleology and perfection.

In recent years, the principle that the community has the right to enforce its moral values upon its members has been defended by a group of theorists collectively referred to as 'communitarians', who attack the modern liberal theory that individuals have rights to 'negative' liberty: i.e. the rights to act free of coercion or harm from others, so long as their actions do not coerce or harm others. Liberals generally hold that the state must respect and protect the rights of individuals. Although there is a spectrum of modern liberals ranging from libertarians to welfare liberals, nearly all liberals concur that the state should be prohibited from violating individual rights such as freedom of thought, speech, the press, religion, and privacy; but libertarians argue further that the state should also respect private-property rights and freedom of enterprise, whereas welfare liberals will sanction governmental interference with economic liberties in order to promote welfare or equality (i.e. by using taxation to transfer wealth). However, liberals of both forms oppose the principle of community on the grounds that the state would violate the rights of individuals if it forced them to conform to an official code of morality.

Consequently, liberalism in both forms is criticized by the new communitarians, who frequently invoke Aristotle as an authority (along with Hegel and Rousseau).[56] For example, MacIntyre argues that there is a

---

[55] Keyt (1991*a*), 256.   [56] Gutmann (1985), 308.

'crucial moral opposition . . . between liberal individualism in some version or other and the Aristotelian tradition in some version'. He draws from Aristotle the ideal of 'a community whose shared aim is the realisation of the human good', presupposing 'a wide range of agreement in that community on goods and virtues'. He remarks that 'this notion of the political community as a common project is alien to the modern liberal individualistic world'. Aristotle would regard a modern political society not as a genuine polis but 'only as a collection of citizens of nowhere who have banded together for their common protection', for he regards the true polis as a community 'in which men in company pursue *the* human good and not merely as—what the modern liberal state takes itself to be—providing the arena in which each individual seeks his or her own private good'.[57]

The communitarians argue that individuals are deeply dependent on the community for their moral development, their sense of self-identity and self-esteem, and their ability to lead lives with unity and meaning. Their arguments are varied and complex, but they include the ideas that individuals come to understand themselves through words and concepts which they acquire through 'communities such as those of the family, the neighbourhood, the city, and the tribe', and that they come to lead lives which have meaning and unity through customs, practices, and virtues which they have learned from the community.[58] Hence, many communitarians also endorse a virtue ethics. Because of this alleged utter dependence of the individual on the community, it is argued that the individual has an obligation to belong to the community and obey its dictates.[59] Thus the communitarians hold that the community is not bound by the individual rights championed by liberals. For example, on the economic front, the authorities might 'enact laws regulating plant

---

[57] MacIntyre (1981), 241, 146–7, 160. Similarly, Sandel (1984a), 87, accuses Rawls and other liberals of presupposing 'the unencumbered self', a person 'freed from the dictates of nature and the sanction of social roles', and 'free to choose our purposes and ends unbound by [an order of value antecedently given by the community], or by custom or tradition or inherited status'.

[58] MacIntyre (1981), 205–6. See also Sandel (1982), 172–3, for the argument that individuals are defined by their socially derived self-understandings.

[59] See F. H. Bradley (1927), 166, 173: 'what we call an individual man is what he is because of and by virtue of community'; and: 'what [a man] has to do depends on what his place is, what his function is, and that all comes from his station in the [social] organism.' Cf. Taylor (1985) who appeals to Aristotle. However, Yack (1993), 30, objects that modern communitarians and 'civic republicans' in the Rousseauian or Hegelian traditions go far beyond Aristotle. According to Yack, Aristotle's doctrine of the priority of the polis to the individual entails 'the necessary role that communities play in the full development of the natural capacities of human beings, not the subordination of individuals to collective identities'. This section is concerned only with the implications of the former claim.

closings, to protect their communities from the disruptive effects of capital mobility and sudden industrial change'. As for civil liberties such as freedom of speech, 'communitarians would be more likely than liberals to allow a town to ban pornographic bookstores, on the grounds that pornography offends its way of life and the values that sustain it'.[60] The principle that the community has the right to exercise this sort of moral authority over its members and to override their liberties is a common thread throughout the coalition of communitarians, ranging from traditional conservative to radical, religious to secular, national to local. Communitarians of different stripes might or might not agree on particular applications of this principle. Religious conservatives and radical feminists (reasoning from their respective moral premises) might agree that the sale of pornographic books and films should be banned in a particular community, although they would probably disagree on whether abortions should be prohibited.

A central feature of the communitarian critique[61] is that liberalism misconstrues the nature of the community, as MacIntyre asserts:

For liberal individualism a community is simply an arena in which individuals each pursue their own self-chosen conception of the good life, and political institutions exist to provide that degree of order which makes such self-determined activity possible. Government and law are, or ought to be, neutral between rival conceptions of the good life for man, and hence, although it is the task of government to promote law-abidingness, it is on the liberal view no part of the legitimate function of government to inculcate any one moral outlook.[62]

It is noteworthy that this description shifts between two different concepts: community and government. However, there is a fundamental difference between the state (understood as the association which successfully asserts a monopoly on the legitimate use of force) and the community in the broader sense of society (comprised of many different forms of association). To advocate a limited state dedicated to the protection of individual rights is not to declare that society as a whole must resemble a liberal state (in the sense that its components must be value-free and neutral). Rather, the proponent of the limited state can maintain that the community in the broader sense should be a civil society, i.e. a community which consists of

[60] Sandel (1984*b*), 17, for both examples.

[61] The new communitarians, of course, have other arguments (some of them quite sound) and differ among themselves on many particulars. This section focuses on the disputed concept of community. See Paul and Miller (1990) for a critique of the communitarian theories of the good proposed by MacIntyre and Sandel.

[62] MacIntyre (1981), 182.

many different semi-autonomous associations, in addition to the government, which has the task of protecting these associations.

Although earlier the idea of a civil society was a popular theme during the eighteenth-century Scottish Enlightenment, it was not clearly defined;[63] and the distinction between civil society and the state was made for the first time by Hegel (1770–1831), who treated civil society (*bürgerliche Gesellschaft*) as a form of association distinct from both the family and the state.[64] Further illumination is afforded by Oakeshott who distinguishes a civil association from an enterprise association such as a fire station or a religious order, where the members pursue a substantive common purpose under a common authority. In a civil association the members do not have common substantive ends but co-operate and coexist under non-instrumental rules. Modern totalitarian regimes are an extreme example of the attempt to force societies into the mould of enterprise associations.[65] Oakeshott proposes the civil association as a more defensible model for modern society. Following Oakeshott, a liberal conception of a civil society would be of a community which consists of many different semi-autonomous associations, which is governed by the rule of law, and has the institution of private property, thereby permitting the compossible exercise of individual rights.[66] On the limited-government view, the essential functions of Aristotle's best polis—viz., moral education and the direct facilitation of the good life—would be the aim of non-governmental sectors of civil society, just as the formation and use of economic capital is the proper function of private associations. Thus one could agree with Aristotle's arguments for the need for moral education without agreeing that there must be a centralized system of compulsory moral education. The state as the most authoritative association makes other functions such as moral education possible by upholding the rule of law and protecting individual freedoms, but it is not properly assigned these other functions.[67] The active participation in government may be an important

---

[63] Civil society was the subject of *An Essay on the History of Civil Society* published in 1767 by Adam Ferguson (1723–1816), who left unclear the relation between this concept and other notions such as the state and government: see Ferguson (1966), pp. xix–xx. On the historical development of the idea of civil society see Seligman (1992), chs. 1–2.

[64] Hegel, *Philosophy of Right* sects. 182–229 on civil society, 230–56 on the police, 257–71 on the Hegelian state and its relation to civil society and the 'political state'. Hegel's analysis contains many difficulties which are discussed by Plamenatz (1991–2), iii. 111–16.

[65] Oakeshott (1975), 108–84, 313–15. Oakeshott (109–10) credits Aristotle with anticipating to a great extent his own analysis of the 'civil condition'.

[66] See Gray (1993), 314–20, for the concept of a civil society.

[67] e.g. Simpson (1990), proposes a neo-Aristotelian theory in which the modern democratic state does not directly try to make its citizens good but instead provides a framework within which some community could directly promote lives of moral and intellectual virtue.

part of the good life and not merely of value to secure non-political goods. However, the right to participate in government should not take precedence over other rights. Individuals possess a number of civil rights, including property rights, which should constrain the exercise of political rights *per se*.

Just as Aristotle makes the mistake of conflating two concepts of the polis, modern communitarian theorists run the risk of committing a similar error in connection with the community in so far as they treat it as a state or a quasi-state with an authoritative structure and a collective voice.[68] This obscures the fundamental complexity of civil society, which is composed of diverse associations which differ widely in purpose, structure, longevity, and conditions of entry and exit. (Compare a family, a business corporation, a religious congregation, a love affair, an amateur football team, or a philosophy discussion group.)

There are good reasons to think that a civil society would be more congenial than an authoritarian community to individual flourishing. First, a defensible account of perfection cannot ignore the wide range of human diversity (see Section 5.3). Even if we grant the existence of universal human characteristics such as rationality and voluntariness, individuals also vary widely in their genetic endowment, hence in their aptitudes and dispositions, so that it is *natural* for different individuals to have different values. Aristotle's ideal polis and its modern communitarian counterparts presuppose too narrow an end to accommodate the robust diversity of human flourishing. The communitarian attempt to inculcate a common set of values and virtues by means of public institutions will, therefore, tend to produce repression, frustration, and resentment, if not outright rebellion. Diversity was already evident to Aristotle, albeit as an unfortunate deviation, but it is far more extensive in modern times due to the complexity of modern society and the all-pervasive communications and interactions among different societies throughout the world. Given this, the attempt to impose a single moral order on the community is likely to result in ceaseless wrangling among opposing interest groups over the levers of authority.

An even stronger argument against communitarianism is available if those neo-Aristotelian theorists are correct who maintain that the perfection of individuals requires the exercise of free choice, because the higher levels of human functioning, whatever their specific form, consist of continuing, voluntary mental acts (see Section 10.3). Individual perfection

---

[68] Some communitarians (including civic republicans and social democrats) identify the community with the state. Others like MacIntyre (1981), 182, deny that the modern state can be a genuine community.

thus requires that agents be able to define and pursue projects of their own choice. A society congenial to this ability would provide private property, a liberal market order, and protection of civil liberties. Conversely, the communitarian attempt to impose preordained socially assigned roles on individuals would be oppressive and stultifying to the extent that it frustrated their autonomous pursuit of perfection. If individuals must conform to their social roles involuntarily or without reflection or by repressing any objections they may have, this can scarcely promote the full actualization of their human potentials.

This suggests a possible way for a neo-Aristotelian political theorist to reconcile the demands of perfection and liberty.[69] By endorsing justice and liberty as primary goods a liberal perfectionist would be willing to tolerate the practice of many competing conceptions of the good, without endorsing these other conceptions or taking the neutralist stance that all lifestyles are equally valid. This view need not exclude the practice of other conceptions which are mutually tolerant. Such a liberal perfectionism could not, however, countenance conceptions of final ends which require that the personal liberty of some be compromised in order to advance the aims of others. Despotic plans of life such as Leninism and Fascism would be ruled out as acceptable for just this reason, for the realization of such plans would require the obstruction of the plans of most other people. Provided that a perfectionist theory can prohibit such interference by insisting that among its catalogue of primary social goods is the greatest equal liberty of each agent, a requirement which may not be traduced by the plans of any individual, it will be liberal as well as perfectionist.[70]

10.5. RULERSHIP

According to the principle of rulership, a community can have order only through the exercise of political rule by an individual or group of individuals. In Homer's words, 'The rule of many is not good; let there be one ruler' (*Iliad*, II 204, cited at *Met.* XII 10 1076ᵃ4). The principle was endorsed by many ancient Greek thinkers, and, indeed, the notion that all order must be due to a ruler seemed self-evident to most philosophers until modern times. It is made explicit by St Thomas Aquinas (*c*.1225–74):

[69] On the alleged incompatibility of perfectionism and the equal liberty principle, see Rawls (1971), 327–8.
[70] See Paul and Miller (1990) for a more general statement of this argument.

If, then, it is natural for man to live in the society of many, it is necessary that there exist among men some means by which the group may be governed. For where there are many men together and each one is looking after his own interest, the multitude would be broken up and scattered unless there were also an agency to take care of what appertains to the common weal. In like manner, the body of a man or any other animal would disintegrate unless there were a general ruling force within the body which watches over the common good of all members. With this in mind, Solomon says: 'Where there is no governor, the people shall fail.'

Indeed it is reasonable that this should happen, for what is proper and what is common are not identical. Things differ by what is proper to each; they are united by what they have in common. But diversity of effects is due to diversity of causes. Consequently, there must exist something which impels towards the common good of the many, over and above that which impels towards the particular good of each individual. Wherefore also in all things that are ordained towards one end, one thing is found to rule the rest. Thus in the corporeal universe, by the first body, i.e. the celestial body, the other bodies are regulated according to the order of divine providence; and all bodies are ruled by a rational creature. So, too, in the individual man, the soul rules the body; and among the parts of the soul, the irascible and the concupiscible parts are ruled by reason. Likewise, among the members of a body, one, such as the heart or the head, is the principal and moves all the others. Therefore, in every multitude there must be some governing power.[71]

The argument from order retained its appeal for modern philosophers such as Descartes (1596–1650):

Among the first that occurred to me was the thought that there is not usually so much perfection in works composed of several parts and produced by various different craftsmen as in the works of one man. Thus we see that buildings undertaken and completed by a single architect are usually more attractive and better planned than those which several have tried to patch up by adapting old walls built for different purposes. Again, ancient cities which have gradually grown from mere villages into large towns are usually ill-proportioned, compared with those orderly towns which planners lay out as they fancy on level ground ... Again, I thought, peoples who have grown gradually from a half-savage to a civilized state, and have made their laws only in so far as they were forced to by the inconvenience of crimes and quarrels, could not be so well governed as those who from the beginning of their society have observed the basic laws laid down by some wise lawgiver.[72]

Descartes follows with praise of the ancient Spartan constitution which was the work of one man, Lycurgus.

[71] Aquinas, *De regimine principum*, I 1 8–9 (1949: 5–6).
[72] Descartes (1984), 116–17.

However, the premiss that 'there must exist something which impels towards the common good of the many, over and above that which impels towards the particular good of each individual' was challenged by Bernard de Mandeville (1670–1733) and the theorists of the Scottish Enlightenment.[73] The economist Adam Smith (1723–1790) observes that each individual uses his capital 'so that its produce may be of the greatest possible value'. The greater the value of the product the greater the profits the individual reaps, but an object is valuable to the extent that the producer can exchange it with someone else for money or for other goods.

As every individual, therefore, endeavours as much as he can both to employ his capital in the support of domestick industry, and so to direct that industry that its produce may be of the greatest value; every individual necessarily labours to render the annual revenue of the society as great as he can. He generally, indeed, neither intends to promote the publick interest, nor knows how much he is promoting it. By preferring the support of domestick to that of foreign industry, he intends only his own security; and by directing that industry in such a manner as its produce may be of the greatest value, he intends only his own gain, and he is in this, as in many other cases, led by an invisible hand to promote an end which was no part of his intention. Nor is it always the worse for the society that it was no part of it. By pursuing his own interest he frequently promotes that of the society more effectually than when he really intends to promote it. I have never known much good done by those who affected to trade for the publick good.[74]

According to Smith, therefore, individuals are able to co-operate for the common advantage without having to be commanded to do so.

Smith's embryonic account is developed more fully in the economic theory of spontaneous order, a leading exponent of which is F. A. Hayek,[75] who distinguishes between two types of order, using classical Greek terms for each: *taxis* is a consciously created order, whereas *kosmos* is a spontaneously developed order.[76] However, this distinction is not found in Aristotle, who is unable to conceive of an effective co-ordination of human activities without deliberate organization by a commanding intel-

---

[73] See Barry (1982) and Hamowy (1987).
[74] Smith, *Wealth of Nations*, IV. ii. 9 (1979: i. 456); cf. *Theory of Moral Sentiments*, IV. i. 1. 10. The idea is also found in Adam Ferguson (1966), 187: '. . . the result of human action but not the execution of any human design'.
[75] See Hayek (1973; 1976; 1979; 1960). Hayek builds upon the work of earlier economists such as Eugen von Böhm-Bawerk, Carl Menger, and Ludwig von Mises, although he borrowed the expression 'spontaneous order' from Michael Polanyi. See also Ullman-Margalit (1978) and Sowell (1980).   [76] Hayek (1973), i. 37.

ligence.[77] Hayek observes, 'One of the achievements of economic theory has been to explain how such a mutual adjustment of the spontaneous activities of individuals is brought about by the market, provided that there is a known delimitation of the sphere of control of each individual.'[78] For example, price theory explains how the individual decisions of individuals to exchange goods in a competitive, unregulated market (assuming private property and voluntary exchange) result in the most efficient distribution of goods. As one economist remarks, 'The normal economic system works itself. For its current operation it is under no central control, it needs no central survey. Over the whole range of human activity and human need, supply is adjusted to demand, and production to consumption, by a process that is automatic, elastic and responsive.'[79]

Adam Smith also contends that the effort to impose an order upon society which is contrary to the spontaneous order which would otherwise emerge, generally often has unanticipated, untoward consequences:

The man of system . . . is often so enamoured with the supposed beauty of his own ideal plan of government, that he cannot suffer the smallest deviation from any part of it. . . . He seems to imagine that he can arrange the different members of a great society with as much ease as the hand arranges the different pieces upon a chess-board. He does not consider that the pieces upon the chess-board have no other principle of motion besides that which the hand impresses upon them; but that, in the great chess-board of human society, every single piece has a principle of motion of its own, altogether different from that which the legislature might chuse to impress upon it. If those two principles coincide and act in the same direction, the game of human society will go on easily and harmoniously, and is very likely to be happy and successful. If they are opposite or different, the game will go on miserably, and the society must be at all times in the highest degree of disorder.[80]

Economists have argued that the attempt to regulate the market by stipulating certain prices often has the effect of disrupting equilibrium and impeding co-ordination. If the price is set below the market-clearing price, there will tend to be more people who want to buy the good than those who are willing to sell, resulting in a perceived 'shortage' of the good. If the price is pegged higher than the market-clearing price, sellers

---

[77] e.g. both good order (*eutaxia*) and regularity (*kosmos*) are connected with rule at *Pol.* VI 8 1321^{b}6–8.　　　　　　　　　　　　　　　　　　[78] Hayek (1967), 167.
[79] J. A. Salter, *Allied Shipping Control* (Oxford, 1921), 16–17, cited by Coase (1988).
[80] Smith (1982), pt. 6, sect. 2, ch. 2.

will find that they cannot find buyers for all of the goods at the higher price, resulting in a perceived 'glut'. Other misallocations of goods may result. If the price of bread is fixed so low that it is cheaper than the same quantity of wheat, farmers will feed bread rather than wheat to their livestock. The example of pricing illustrates a general point that the spontaneous order which arises in an unregulated market economy is more efficient (i.e. able to yield greater benefits at a lower cost) than the order which is imposed by an official in a command economy. The economist Ludwig von Mises (1881–1973) argued that centralized economic planning of the sort envisaged by modern socialists was impossible on the grounds that facts relevant to planning could be taken into account in an efficient manner only by means of the pricing problems of a competitive market economy. The prices of natural resources and production goods are the result of the interactions of individual entrepreneurs, who place their capital at risk in production and exchange and adjust their activities to the activities of consumers and other entrepreneurs.[81] The widespread collapse of command economies in the late twentieth century is confirmation of the Misesian thesis.

The theory of spontaneous order presents a serious challenge to Aristotle's principle of rulership. Many types of social order, e.g. in the economic sphere, will neither exist by nature nor as the result of the deliberate act of a legislator. They will instead be the predictably regular— hence in a way 'natural'—result of the intentional interactions of human beings pursuing their individual goals in a deliberate manner. This type of order is also the result of human rationality, but it is an unintended result of the sort indicated by the metaphor of the 'invisible hand'.[82] Aside from economics, it has also been argued that other orderly social phenomena, such as languages, customs, systems of private property, common law, and even money, have emerged spontaneously. These, it is alleged, are not the creations of a primordial Prometheus, but are the complex result of human interactions over many generations.

Hayek makes the general point that 'under the enforcement of universal rules of just conduct, protecting a recognizable private domain of individuals, a spontaneous order of human activities of much greater complexity will form itself than could ever be produced by deliberative

---

[81] See Lavoie (1985) and Steele (1992) for overviews of the socialist calculation debate. Mises (1920) was a seminal essay, incorporated in Mises (1936). Waldron (1988), 9, points out that Mises developed a line of argument implicit in Aristotle's defence of private property (see Sect. 9.6 above). [82] See especially Hayek (1948).

arrangement . . .'[83] There is considerable justification for this claim, especially in the economic realm, but the status of 'universal rules of just conduct' is a subject of some debate. Aristotle, following Plato, clearly sees the establishment of a constitution and a system of laws as a job for the lawgiver. Some modern theorists such as Hume and Hayek have taken the view that rules and laws evolve in an unintended fashion out of human co-operation, and that any attempt to replace them with a rationally constructed set of laws will result in disruption more far-reaching than that caused by the example of the setting of prices discussed above.

On the other hand, it has been argued that the theory of spontaneous order does not apply to all aspects of a capitalistic economy. For example, the organization of activities within a business firm or corporation is evidently not the result of the automatic functioning of the price mechanism. Employees move between different departments not because they are responding to the price mechanism but because they are ordered to do so. The firm is governed by someone who exercises controlling authority, rationally allocating resources and directing production. There are different reasons why business firms emerge in an unregulated economy, but one reason, observed by Ronald H. Coase, is that it is costly for isolated individuals to co-ordinate their activities with each other in the production of certain commodities and that in many cases it is more efficient for them to participate in hierarchically managed firms.[84]

The price system and the business firm exemplify two different types of order, spontaneous and authoritarian (i.e. the application of human reason). In the economic sphere which type of order is justified depends upon particular circumstances. Economists generally address such questions in terms of efficiency, considering, for example, the costs which individual agents incur in trying to co-ordinate their activities with each other. In the political sphere, it also needs to be considered which type of order is justified, and we may expect, analogously, that this will depend upon particular circumstances.

It might be plausibly argued that a case can be made for Aristotle's principle of rulership, provided that it is appropriately restricted, in particular, to establishing constitutions and enforcing principles of justice and the protection of rights. Here there is a plausible analogy with Coase's rationale for the firm. The Aristotelian lawgivers and politicians have the political virtue and wisdom needed to establish, reform, or maintain

---

[83] Hayek (1967), 162. [84] Coase (1988), esp. 37–47.

constitutions and political institutions. The constitution of the United States was designed by men who possessed a rare combination of practical political experience, theoretical and historical knowledge, and sound moral judgement.

In the case of public goods it is also argued that the unregulated market does not always produce a satisfactory type of order. Familiar cases of public goods are defence against foreign invaders and police protection. Although everyone would benefit from the good, an unregulated market does not provide sufficient incentives for individuals to produce it. Because individuals can benefit from the good regardless of whether they contribute to its production, there are pervasive free-rider problems. It is commonly argued that governmental provision of the good is justified because its existence is advantageous to everyone. It might be argued that political virtue is such a public good along the lines of *Politics*, V 9 (see Section 8.4 above). Individual citizens acting separately would face a collective-action problem in providing this good, for even though they might all recognize the value of moral virtue, each of them would as individuals find it more advantageous to cultivate their personal wealth (or freedom) instead of promoting the development of virtue. Hence, the state should undertake the task of inculcating virtue in the citizens through a system of public education.

However, a public-goods defence of public moral education would have to answer many questions, one of which Aristotle anticipates with the remark, 'One ought to think that living for the constitution is not slavery but salvation' (1310ᵃ34–6). Is Aristotle right to think that a system of public education would not impose inordinately high costs on individual citizens by invading their individual freedom in the attempt to make them virtuous? The question is more pressing if perfectionism takes a pluralistic form and emphasizes the centrality of autonomy in the human good. Further, does not civil society contain private associations which could provide moral education, for example, families, private schools, clubs, and religious organizations?[85] Is there convincing evidence that the graduates of private schools today display less 'civic virtue' than do the products of state-operated schools?[86] Finally, a proponent of public moral education should take into account the findings of the public-

---

[85] Schmidtz (1991), chs. 4–5, discusses devices used by non-governmental associations to provide public goods, e.g. assurance contracts and fringe benefits, to offset free-rider incentives. See also Sugden (1986).

[86] Lieberman (1993), 152–3, argues that there is no such evidence for public and private schools in the United States.

choice school of economics,[87] which proceeds from the premiss that persons in political authority are motivated by the same considerations as ordinary citizens. Is there any guarantee that public officials will not suffer from the same failings of human nature which Aristotle thinks necessitates political action? Might the public providers tend to overestimate the importance of their own contributions and to underestimate the costs which are borne by the public rather than themselves? Might the agencies providing the public goods be vulnerable to capture by special-interest groups who find it advantageous to define the agenda for coercive moral education? For example, 'right-to-life' groups might want public schools to teach that abortion is immoral, whereas 'pro-choice' groups might want them to endorse a woman's right to abortion.

On the whole, the twentieth century has taught that the common good is often better promoted by *kosmos* than by *taxis*, and the attempt by the bureaucratic state to impose a rational order on all aspects of society has had disastrous consequences. In contrast, a system of democratic capitalism is, arguably, a viable synthesis of the two types of order: political order is subject to representative democratic rule, whereas economic order is largely the result of decisions by individuals possessing rights of property, contract, and enterprise. If this is correct, a tenable neo-Aristotelian political theory would need narrowly to circumscribe the permissible sphere of political authority.

10.6. ARISTOTLE'S CONTRIBUTION TO THE THEORY OF RIGHTS

This book has argued that Aristotle's theory of rights is based on a conception of justice which is moderately individualistic. If this interpretation is correct, Aristotle offers an alternative worth considering to the extreme-individualistic theories of rights which are offered by many modern philosophers. Although many different defences of natural rights have been attempted, they often contain serious flaws. One recurring difficulty is apparent in a derivation offered by Herbert Spencer (1820–1903):

Those who hold that life is valuable, hold, by implication, that men ought not to be prevented from carrying on life-sustaining activities. In other words, if it is said to be 'right' that they should carry them on, then, by permutation, we get the

---

[87] See Buchanan and Tullock (1962) and Schmidtz (1991), 88–91.

assertion that they 'have a right' to carry them on. Clearly the conception of 'natural rights' originates in recognition of the truth that if life is justifiable, there must be a justification for the performance of acts essential to its preservation; and, therefore, a justification for those liberties and claims which makes such acts possible.[88]

The difficulty with such an argument is that from the fact that it is right for individual X to do act A, it does not follow that individual X has *a* right against some other individual Y to do that act—at least if we are to understand X's 'right' as sufficiently robust to include a Hohfeldian claim right, i.e. to entail an obligation or duty on the part of Y to X. The argument appears to be a *non sequitur*: the premiss has to do with what it is right for individual X to do and implies nothing whatsoever about what it is right or wrong for any other individual Y to do. Robert Nozick has made a similar point against Ayn Rand:

> If we assume that rights are not to be violated, and others should not forcibly intervene in the exercise of someone's rights, then argument is needed to the conclusion that a person does have a right to his own life, that is, that *others* shouldn't forcibly intervene in it, even granting that its maintenance is *his* highest value.[89]

However, Nozick can be fairly criticized himself for failing to provide such an argument.[90] Although his theory in *Anarchy, State, and Utopia* rests on the thesis that individuals are ends in themselves and thus have rights to life, liberty, and private property, he scarcely argues for this premiss. This is crucial because his neo-Lockian theory of justice requires that rights existing in a state of nature are inviolable side constraints on the morally permissible actions of the individuals and of the political states they establish. He gestures towards an argument which would supposedly connect moral constraints with characteristics of persons. 'It would appear that a person's characteristics, by virtue of which others are constrained in their treatment of him, must themselves be valuable characteristics. How else are we to understand why something so valuable emerges from them?'[91] Nozick's candidate is the capacity for a meaningful life:

---

[88] Spencer (1981), 150.

[89] Nozick (1981), 227 n. 7. Nozick evidently interprets Rand (1964) as offering an argument like Spencer's. It should be noted, however, that Rand (1964), 92, holds that the concept of rights is 'the concept that preserves and protects individual morality in a social context'. The reference to 'a social context' suggests that Rand's theory of rights assumes that human nature and morality have a social dimension.   [90] See e.g. Nagel (1981).

[91] Nozick (1974), 48.

I conjecture that the answer is connected with that elusive and difficult notion: the meaning of life. A person's shaping his life in accordance with some overall plan is his way of giving meaning to his life; only a being with the capacity to so shape his life can have or strive for meaningful life.[92]

Nozick does not in fact offer a derivation connecting the meaning of life to the right to life. Indeed, it is difficult to see how such a derivation could overcome the difficulty raised by Nozick himself: Why should the value to X of having a meaningful life give rise to any sort of obligation on the part of *anyone else* not to frustrate this value?

This suggests a serious difficulty for any derivation of natural rights which takes extreme individualism as its starting-point. Such natural rights would have to belong to individuals intrinsically, with no bearing on others. But if the point of such a justification is to provide individuals with agent-relative reasons for recognizing and respecting the rights of others, extreme individualism, which defines the end of the individual agent entirely in terms related to the agent, does not have the resources to support moral side constraints on individual action. The most the extreme individualist could derive would be some form of 'rule egoism' or a contractarian argument for mutual deference, which faces the familiar problem that rational individuals, so understood, should break the rule or fail to comply with the bargain whenever it is advantageous for them to do so.

This is where Aristotle's theory of nature, justice, and rights seems relevant, because it holds that a defensible theory of rights must appeal to some version of the thesis that humans are by nature political animals. This means not that humans are programmed to perform 'political' tasks in a narrow sense, but that they need to participate in a community of a certain sort in order to fulfil their natures. According to Aristotle, because human beings are perfected or fully developed in part by entering into friendships or co-operative relations with others, they are not self-sufficient as individuals: they cannot achieve their ends in isolation from one another. This does not mean that they are interdependent in a merely instrumental sense. Since it is part of their nature to live in communities, they find being friends, i.e. co-operators and contributors (as opposed to parasites or predators), to be intrinsically valuable and indispensable to their sense of self-esteem. But justice is a necessary precondition for such co-operation: 'all justice is in relation to a friend' (*EE* VII 10 1242ª20–1) and 'in every community there seems to be a sort of justice, and a sort of friendship

---

[92] Ibid. 50.

also' (*EN* VIII 9 1159^{b}26–7). So understood justice is necessary for the individual good, but not merely instrumentally; for justice is a necessary feature of co-operative activity which is a constituent of the good life. Therefore, a practically rational agent pursuing the good life ought to choose to enter into a just system of co-operation.[93] I have argued that Aristotle understands justice in terms of moderate individualism: i.e. the just constitution will aim at the perfection of each individual and hence will respect the rights of each individual. At the same time, the perfection of each individual includes other-regarding virtues such as friendship, generosity, and justice. A neo-Aristotelian argument for rights would jettison the hypothetical state of nature and proceed instead from the social and political conditions which are indispensable for reasonable persons to exist in a natural condition. The reasonable person for Aristotle is disposed to lead a virtuous life and to abide by a just constitution which guarantees the rights of its individual members. Reasonable persons can thus reach unanimity or agreement on a standard of justice and on a political system. Since the terms of agreement are in accord with their own conception of the good life, they can rely upon one another and maintain a stable and durable constitution of justice and rights.[94]

Such a theory of rights could be an appealing alternative to other theories in currency, if it could surmount the obstacles (which are indeed formidable) to establishing that the human good has a basis in human nature and that human beings are by nature political animals (in a broad sense of 'political'). It could offer an agent-relative alternative to both neo-Hobbesian theory, which is constricted by a minimalist starting-point of extreme individualism, and to neo-Kantian theory, which is wedded to an impersonal, agent-neutral perspective alien to actual agents. On a neo-Aristotelian account (in contrast, for example, to Nozick's)

---

[93] Cf. Taylor (1985) who criticizes 'primacy-of-right theories' such as Nozick's for presupposing anthropological 'atomism': i.e. for assuming that individuals are self-sufficient in the very sense denied by Aristotle. Taylor (197) points out that the case for natural rights must rest on the argument that certain natural capacities are of great moral worth, but 'then any proof that these capacities can only develop in society or in a society of a certain kind is a proof that we ought to belong to or sustain society or this kind of society'. So far Taylor is persuasive. But he tries to derive from this 'an obligation to belong' to society which is more sweeping than can be supported by his premiss. The 'obligation' which follows is a qualified agent-relative ought: to belong to a civil society which protects the right to the pursuit of happiness (and hence to life and liberty) of every agent to whom the argument is supposed to apply.

[94] Cf. Everson (1988), 100, who argues that Aristotle's '*Politics* provides a better foundation for the development of rights' than do state-of-nature extreme individualist theories like Nozick's. Everson's further inference that one cannot have rights against the state is, however, vitiated by a shift between 'society' and 'state' of the sort noted in Sect. 10.4.

claims of rights would not be theoretically primary or fundamental, but would be based upon a theory of justice; and it would not attempt to demonstrate the existence of rights in a pure state of nature, but would regard rights as normative relations between members of a community. However, such a theory would be strongly committed to individual rights in so far as justice is concerned with the mutual advantage, i.e. the good life for each and every member of the community.[95]

Given this framework, it would remain to develop the theory in detail, drawing upon empirical sciences such as biology, psychology, and the social sciences. However, for reasons discussed in Sections 10.4–5, it does seem likely that the principles of community and rulership would have to be greatly circumscribed. Moreover, there seem to be good reasons to distinguish between the state and civil society: the coercive apparatus of government should have the function of maintaining the rule of law and protecting the civil liberties and property rights of the citizens, whereas the multifarious private associations and corporations that comprise civil society should carry out the complex tasks of directly promoting human development and flourishing. How central freedom or autonomy is in fact to human perfection and flourishing remains a contested issue (see Section 5.3). The extent to which a neo-Aristotelian theory turns out to have a 'liberal' character would seem to depend on this issue to a large extent.

The practical policy implications of the theory for a given society would also depend upon actual circumstances, such as prevailing customs and economic practices, technological level, demographic diversity, geography, and climate. For purposes of legislation the theory of justice as mutual advantage would be an ideal or regulative principle that actual constitutions and laws should satisfy as far as actual circumstances permit, even when it was necessary to settle for second-best or worse solutions. If it followed Aristotle, the theory would place greater weight on individual virtue, merit, and responsibility than have many recent egalitarian theories of justice.[96] Constitutions would have to be adapted to particular circumstances, but, in a modern social and economic context, the theory would probably support some form of democratic capitalism.[97] However,

---

[95] For a recent argument along these lines, see Rasmussen and Den Uyl, who treat rights as 'meta-normative' or 'foundational principles for political order' (1991), 83 n. 20, 105–6, 111.

[96] Recent neo-Aristotelian theories predicated on need-based distributive justice depart from Aristotle in this regard, e.g. Galston (1980) and Nussbaum (1988; 1990; 1992).

[97] See Novak (1982).

the theory would also imply that political institutions should protect the rights of all of the citizens and not become vehicles for special-interest groups (the modern counterpart to Greek factions). Hence, it would continue to endorse Aristotle's ideal of a 'mixed constitution', i.e. a political order which is, as far as possible, inclusive of diverse constituencies and which has internal mechanisms to prevent any one group from gaining supreme control and inflicting injustice on others.

In the end, however, a neo-Aristotelian theory will have to stand on its own two legs—philosophical argument and empirical evidence—and not fall back on quotations from Aristotle. None the less, for those engaged in such a project, the texts of Aristotle will undoubtedly continue to be a source of inspiration and insight.

Bibliography

ACKRILL, J. L. (1980), 'Aristotle on *Eudaimonia*', in Rorty (1980), 15–33.

ADAMS, J. (1787), *A Defence of the Constitutions of Government of the United States of America*, 3 vols. (London).

ADKINS, A. W. H. (1991), 'The Connection Between Aristotle's *Ethics* and *Politics*', in Keyt and Miller (1991), 75–93.

ALLAN, D. J. (1952), *The Philosophy of Aristotle* (London).

—— (1953), 'Aristotle's Account of the Origin of Moral Principles', *Actes du XIe Congrès International de Philosophie*, 12. 120–7; repr. Barnes *et al.* (1977), ii. 72–8.

—— (1964), 'Individual and State in the *Ethics* and *Politics*', *Entretiens sur l'Antiquité Classique IX, La 'Politique' d'Aristote*, Fondation Hardt (Geneva), 53–95.

AMBLER, W. (1985), 'Aristotle's Understanding of the Naturalness of the City', *Review of Politics*, 47. 163–85.

ANNAS, J. (1988–9), 'Aristotle on Virtue and Happiness', *University of Dayton Review*, 19: 3. 7–22.

—— (1990), 'Comments on J. Cooper', in Patzig (1990), 242–8.

—— (1993), *The Morality of Happiness* (New York).

AQUINAS, T. (1949), *On Kingship, to the King of Cyprus*, trans. G. B. Phelan, introd. and notes I. T. Eschmann (Toronto).

—— (1966), *In octo libris Politicorum Aristotelis expositio*, ed. R. M. Spiazzi (Turin).

—— (1993), *Commentary on Aristotle's Nicomachean Ethics*, trans. C. I. Litzinger (Notre Dame, Ind.).

ARENDT, H. (1958), *The Human Condition* (Chicago).

ARNHART, L. (1984), 'Darwin, Aristotle, and the Biology of Human Rights', *Social Science Information*, 23. 493–521.

—— (1988), 'Aristotle's Biopolitics: A Defense of Biological Teleology against Biological Nihilism', *Politics and the Life Sciences*, 6. 173–229.

—— (1993), *Political Questions: Political Philosophy from Plato to Rawls*, 2nd edn. (Prospect Heights, Ill.).

—— (1994), 'The Darwinian Biology of Aristotle's Political Animals', *American Journal of Political Science*, 38. 464–85.

AUBONNET, J. (1968), *Aristote, Politique*, 3 vols., text, trans., and notes (Paris).

BADHWAR, N. K. (1985), 'Friendship, Justice, and Supererogation', *American Philosophical Quarterly*, 22. 123–31.

BALME, D. (1972), *Aristotle's De partibus animalium I and De generatione animalium I*, trans. and notes (Oxford).

—— (1987), 'Teleology and Necessity', in A. Gotthelf and J. Lennox (eds.), *Philosophical Issues in Aristotle's Biology* (Cambridge).

BARKER, E. (1906, repr. 1959), *The Political Thought of Plato and Aristotle* (London).
—— (1931), 'The Life of Aristotle and the Composition and Structure of the *Politics*', *Classical Review*, 45. 162–72.
—— (1946), *The Politics of Aristotle*, trans. with introd., notes, and appendices (Oxford).
BARNES, J. (1982), *Aristotle* (Oxford).
—— (1984), *The Complete Works of Aristotle*, the rev. Oxford trans., 2 vols. (Princeton, NJ).
—— (1990a), 'Aristotle and Political Liberty', in Patzig (1990), 249–63.
—— (1990b), 'Partial Wholes', *Social Philosophy & Policy*, 8: 1. 1–23.
—— Schofield, M., and Sorabji, R. (1977), *Articles on Aristotle*, 4 vols. (London).
BARNETT, R. E. (1977), 'Restitution: A New Paradigm of Criminal Justice', *Ethics*, 87. 279–301.
—— (1980), 'The Justice of Restitution', *American Journal of Jurisprudence*, 25. 117–32.
BARRY, N. (1982), 'The Tradition of Spontaneous Order', *Literature of Liberty*, 5: 2. 7–58.
BECKER, L. (1977), *Property Rights: Philosophical Foundations* (London).
BEKKER, I. (1960), *Aristotelis Opera*, 2nd edn., rev. O. Gignon, 2 vols. (Berlin).
BERLIN, I. (1969), *Four Essays on Liberty* (London).
—— (1990), *The Crooked Timber of Humanity: Chapters in the History of Ideas* (London).
BERNS, L. (1984), 'Spiritedness in Ethics and Politics: A Study in Aristotelian Psychology', *Interpretation*, 12. 335–48.
BLOCK, N. (1971), 'Are Mechanistic and Teleological Explanations of Behaviour Incompatible?', *The Philosophical Quarterly*, 21. 109–17.
BLUHM, W. T. (1962), 'The Place of the "Polity" in Aristotle's Theory of the Ideal State', *Journal of Politics*, 24. 743–53.
BODÉÜS, R. (1993), *The Political Dimensions of Aristotle's Ethics*, trans. J. E. Garrett (Albany, NY).
BORNEMANN, E. (1923), 'Aristoteles' Urteil über Platons politische Theorie', *Philologus*, 79. 70–111, 113–58, 234–57.
BRADIE, M., and Miller, F. D. (1984), 'Teleology and Natural Necessity in Aristotle', *History of Philosophy Quarterly*, 1. 133–46.
BRADLEY, A. C. (1991), 'Aristotle's Conception of the State', in Keyt and Miller (1991), 13–56; orig. (1880) in E. Abbott (ed.), *Hellenica* (London), 181–243.
BRADLEY, F. H. (1927), 'My Station and Its Duties', in *Ethical Studies*, 2nd edn. (Oxford), 160–213.
BRAUN, E. (1965), *Das dritte Buch der aristotelischen 'Politik': Interpretation* (Vienna).
—— (1973) 'Eine Maxime der Staatskunst in der Politik des Aristoteles', in P. Steinmetz, *Schriften zu den Politika des Aristoteles* (Hildesheim), 424–30.
BROADIE, S. W. (1991), *Ethics with Aristotle* (New York).
BUCHANAN, J. M., and Tullock, G. (1962), *The Calculus of Consent: Logical Foundations of Constitutional Democracy* (Ann Arbor, Mich.).

BUCKLE, S. (1991), *Natural Law and the Theory of Property: Grotius to Hume* (Oxford).

BURCKHARDT, J. (1960), *The Civilization of the Renaissance in Italy*, 6th edn., ed. I. Gordon, trans. S. G. C. Middlemore (New York).

BURNET, J. (1900), *The Ethics of Aristotle*, text with introd. and notes (London).

BUSOLT, G., and Swoboda, H. (1920–6), *Griechische Staatskunde*, 2 vols. (Munich).

BYWATER, I. (1984), *Aristotelis Ethica Nicomachea*, text with introd. (Oxford).

CHAMBERS, M. (1990), *Aristoteles Staat der Athener*, trans. with notes (Berlin).

—— (1986), *Aristoteles Athēnaiōn Politeia*, text with introd. (Teubner, Leipzig).

CHARLES, D. (1984), *Aristotle's Philosophy of Action* (Ithaca, NY).

—— (1988), 'Perfectionism in Aristotle's Moral Theory: Reply to Martha Nussbaum', *Oxford Studies in Ancient Philosophy*, suppl. vol., 185–206; repr. in Patzig (1990), 187–201.

—— (1991), 'Teleological Causation in the *Physics*', in Lindsay Judson (ed.), *Aristotle's Physics: A Collection of Essays* (Oxford), 101–28.

COASE, R. (1988), 'The Nature of the Firm', in *The Firm, the Market, and the Law* (Chicago), 33–55.

CODE, A. (1987), 'Soul as Efficient Cause in Aristotle's Embryology', *Philosophical Topics*, 15. 51–9.

COLE, E. B. (1988–9), '*Autarkeia* in Aristotle', *University of Dayton Review*, 19. 7–22.

COOKE, J. E. (1961) (ed.), *The Federalist* (Middletown, Conn.).

COOPER, J. M. (1975), *Reason and Human Good in Aristotle* (Cambridge, Mass.).

—— (1977), 'Aristotle on the Forms of Friendship', *Review of Metaphysics*, 30: 4. 619–48.

—— (1982), 'Aristotle on Natural Teleology', in M. Schofield and M. Nussbaum (eds.), *Language and Logos* (Cambridge), 197–222.

—— (1985), 'Aristotle on the Goods of Fortune', *Philosophical Review*, 94. 173–96.

—— (1987), 'Contemplation and Happiness: A Reconsideration', *Synthese*, 72. 187–216.

—— (1990), 'Political Animals and Civic Friendship', in Patzig (1990), 221–48.

CURREN, R. (forthcoming), *Aristotle on the Necessity of Public Education* (Totowa, NJ).

DARWIN, C. (1859), *On the Origin of Species by Means of Natural Selection or the Preservation of Favoured Races in the Struggle for Life* (London).

—— (1871), *The Descent of Man and Selection in Relation to Sex* (London).

DELBRÜCK, M. (1971), 'Aristotle-totle-totle', in Jacques Monod and Ernest Borek (eds.), *Of Microbes and Life* (New York), 50–5.

—— (1976), 'How Aristotle Discovered DNA', in K. Huang (ed.), *Physics and Our World: A Symposium in Honor of Victor F. Weisskopf*, AIP Conference Proceedings No. 28 (New York), 123–30.

DEN UYL, D. J. (1991), *The Virtue of Prudence* (New York).

DEPEW, D. J. (1991), 'Politics, Music, and Contemplation in Aristotle's Ideal State', in Keyt and Miller (1991), 346–80.

—— (forthcoming*a*) 'Does Aristotle's Political Philosophy Rest on a Contradiction?'.

—— (forthcoming*b*), 'Political Animals'.

DESCARTES, R. (1984), *Discourse on Method*, in *The Philosophical Writings of Descartes*, trans. J. Cottingham, R. Stoothoff, and D. Murdoch (Cambridge, Mass.).

DIRLMEIER, F. (1963), *Aristoteles, Eudemische Ethik*, trans. and comm. (Berlin).

—— (1964), *Aristoteles, Magna Moralia*, trans. and comm. (Berlin).

—— (1983), *Aristoteles, Nikomachische Ethik*, trans. and comm. (Berlin).

DOBBS, D. (1985), 'Aristotle's Anti-Communism', *American Journal of Political Science*, 29. 29–46.

DOVER, K. J. (1974), *Greek Popular Morality in the Time of Plato and Aristotle* (Berkeley, Calif.).

DREIZEHNTER, A. (1970), *Aristoteles' Politik*, text and introd. (Munich).

DÜRING, I. (1966), *Aristoteles, Darstellung und Interpretation seines Denkens* (Heidelberg).

EHRENBERG, V. (1964), *The Greek State* (New York).

ELSTER, J. (1985), *Making Sense of Marx* (Cambridge, Mass.).

—— (1986), 'Self-Realization in Work and Politics: The Marxist Conception of the Good Life', *Social Philosophy & Policy*, 3: 2. 97–126.

ENGBERG-PEDERSEN, T. (1983), *Aristotle's Theory of Moral Insight* (Oxford).

ENGLAND, E. B. (1921) *The Laws of Plato*, text with introd. and notes, 2 vols. (London).

EVERSON, S. (1988), 'Aristotle on the Foundations of the State', *Political Studies*, 36. 89–101.

FARRAR, C. (1988), *The Origins of Democratic Thinking: The Invention of Politics in Classical Athens* (Cambridge, Mass.).

FERGUSON, A. (1966), *An Essay on the History of Civil Society* (1767), ed. D. Forbes (Edinburgh).

FINK, Z. S. (1945), *The Classical Republicans: An Essay in the Recovery of a Pattern of Thought in Seventeenth Century England* (Evanston, Ill.).

FINLEY, M. I. (1977), 'Aristotle and Economic Analysis', in Barnes *et al.*, ii. 140–58.

—— (1985), *Studies in Land and Credit in Ancient Athens, 500–200 B.C.*, repr. (New Brunswick).

FINNIS, J. (1980), *Natural Law and Natural Rights* (Oxford).

FLEW, A. G. N. (1981), *The Politics of Procrustes* (Buffalo).

FORREST, W. G. (1968), *A History of Sparta, 950–192 B.C.* (London).

FORTENBAUGH, W. (1977), 'Aristotle on Slaves and Women', in Barnes *et al.*, ii. 135–9.

—— (1991), 'Aristotle on Prior and Posterior, Correct and Mistaken Constitutions', in Keyt and Miller (1991), 226–37.

FRITZ, K. V. (1954), *The Theory of the Mixed Constitution in Antiquity* (New York).

FUSTEL DE COULANGES, N. D. (1864), *La Cité antique* (Paris).

GALSTON, W. A. (1980), *Justice and the Human Good* (Chicago).

GAUTHIER, D. (1986), *Morals by Agreement* (Oxford).

—— (1990), 'David Hume, Contractarian', in *Moral Dealing: Contract, Ethics, and Reason* (Ithaca, NY), 45–76.

GAUTHIER, R. A., and Jolif, J. Y. (1958), *Aristotle: L'Éthique à Nicomaque*, introd., trans., and comm. (Louvain).

GEORGE, R. P. (1993), *Making Men Moral: Civil Liberties and Public Morality* (Oxford).

GEWIRTH, A. (1978), *Reason and Morality* (Chicago).

GOLDING, M. (1978), 'The Concept of Rights: A Historical Sketch', in E. L. Bandman and B. Bandman (eds.), *Bioethics and Human Rights* (Boston), 44–61.

—— (1981), 'Justice and Rights: A Study in Relationship', in E. Shelp (ed.), *Justice and Health Care* (Dordrecht), 23–36.

—— (1982), review of R. Tuck (1979), *Natural Rights* (Cambridge, Mass.), in *Political Theory*, 10. 152–7.

—— (1984), 'The Primacy of Welfare Rights', *Social Philosophy & Policy*, 1: 2. 119–36.

GOMME, A. W. (1933), *The Population of Athens in the Fifth and Fourth Centuries, B.C.* (Oxford).

GOTTHELF, A. (1987), 'Aristotle's Conception of Final Causality', in id. and J. Lennox (eds.), *Philosophical Issues in Aristotle's Biology* (Cambridge), 204–42.

—— (1988), 'The Place of the Good in Aristotle's Natural Teleology', in J. J. Cleary (ed.), *Proceedings of the Boston Area Colloquium in Ancient Philosophy* (Lanham, Md.), 4. 113–35.

GRANT, A. (1885), *The Ethics of Aristotle: Illustrated with Essays and Notes*, 4th edn. (London).

GRAY, J. (1986), *Liberalism* (Minneapolis).

—— (1989), *Liberalisms* (London).

—— (1993), *Post-Liberalism* (London).

GREEN, T. H. (1937), *Lectures on the Principles of Political Obligation* (London).

GRIMALDI, W. M. A. (1980), *Aristotle, Rhetoric I, A Commentary* (New York).

GRUNEBAUM, J. (1987), *Private Ownership* (London).

GROTE, G. (1883), *Aristotle*, 3rd edn. (London).

GUMMERE, R. M. (1963), *The American Colonial Mind and the Classical Tradition* (Cambridge, Mass.).

GUTHRIE, W. K. L. (1962–81), *A History of Greek Philosophy*, 6 vols. (Cambridge).

GUTMANN, A. (1985), 'Communitarian Critics of Liberalism', *Philosophy & Public Affairs*, 14. 308–22.

GWARTNEY, J. D., and Stroup, R. L. (1990), *Economics: Private and Public Choice*, 5th edn. (San Diego).

HAMOWY, R. (1987), *The Scottish Enlightenment and the Theory of Spontaneous Order* (Carbondale, Ill.).

HAMPSHIRE, S. (1971), *Freedom of Mind* (Princeton, NJ).

—— (1983), *Morality and Conflict* (Cambridge, Mass.).

HAMPTON, J. (1986), *Hobbes and the Social Contract Tradition* (Cambridge, Mass.).

HANSEN, M. H. (1989), *Was Athens a Democracy: Popular Rule, Liberty, and Equality in Ancient and Modern Political Thought* (Copenhagen).

—— (1991), *The Athenian Democracy in the Age of Demosthenes: Structure, Principles and Ideology*, trans. J. A. Crook (Oxford).

HARDIE, W. F. R. (1980), *Aristotle's Ethical Theory*, 2nd edn. (Oxford).

HARDIN, G. (1973), 'The Tragedy of the Commons', in id. (ed.), *Exploring New Ethics of Survival* (Baltimore), 250–64.

HARMAN, G. (1983), 'Human Flourishing, Ethics, and Liberty', *Philosophy and Public Affairs*, 12. 307–22.

—— (1986), 'Troubles with Flourishing: Comments on David Norton', *Reason Papers*, 11. 69–71.

HARRISON, A. R. W. (1957), 'Aristotle's *Nicomachean Ethics*, Book V, and the Law of Athens', *Journal of Hellenic Studies*, 77. 42–7.

—— (1968, 1971), *The Law of Athens*, 2 vols. (Oxford).

HART, H. L. A. (1984), 'Are There Any Natural Rights?', in J. Waldron (ed.), *Theories of Rights* (Oxford), 71–90.

HAVELOCK, E. A. (1957), *The Liberal Temper in Greek Politics* (New Haven, Conn).

HAYEK, F. A. (1948), *Individualism and Economic Order* (Chicago).

—— (1960), *The Constitution of Liberty* (Chicago).

—— (1967), 'The Principles of a Liberal Social Order', *Studies in Philosophy, Politics, and Economics* (Chicago), 160–77.

—— (1973–9), *Law, Legislation, and Liberty*, 3 vols. (Chicago).

HEADLAM, J. W. (1933), *Election by Lot at Athens*, 2nd edn. rev. D. C. MacGregor (Cambridge).

HEGEL, G. W. F. (1955), *Lectures in the History of Philosophy*, trans. E. S. Haldane and Frances H. Simson (London).

—— (1991), *Elements of the Philosophy of Right*, ed. A. W. Wood, trans. H. B. Nisbet (Cambridge).

HEINAMAN, R. (1988), 'Eudaimonia and Self-Sufficiency in the *Nicomachean Ethics*', *Phronesis*, 33. 31–53.

HOBBES, T. (1949), *De Cive or the Citizen*, ed. S. P. LAMPRECHT (New York).

—— (1986), *Leviathan*, ed. C. B. Macpherson (Harmondsworth) (with pagination of 1651 edn.).

HOHFELD, W. N. (1923), *Fundamental Legal Conceptions as Applied in Judicial Reasoning* (New Haven, Conn.).

HOLMES, S. T. (1979), 'Aristippus in and out of Athens', *American Political Science Review*, 73. 113-28.

HONORÉ, A. M. (1961), 'Ownership', in A. G. Guest (ed.), *Oxford Essays in Jurisprudence* (Oxford), 107-47.

HUMBOLDT, W. v. (1993), *Limits of State Action*, ed. J. W. Burrow (Indianapolis).

HUME, D. (1978), *A Treatise of Human Nature*, ed. L. A. Selby-Bigge (Oxford).

HUMPHREYS, S. C. (1978), *Anthropology and the Greeks* (London).

HURKA, T. (1993), *Perfectionism* (New York).

IMMISCH, O. (1929), *Aristotelis Politica*, text with scholia and glosses (Leipzig).

IRWIN, T. H. (1977), *Plato's Moral Theory* (Oxford).

—— (1985*a*), 'Moral Science and Political Theory in Aristotle', in P. A. Cartledge and F. D. Harvey (eds.), *Crux* (London), 150-68.

—— (1985*b*), 'Permanent Happiness: Aristotle and Solon', in *Oxford Studies in Ancient Philosophy*, 3, ed. J. Annas (Oxford), 89-124.

—— (1985*c*), *Aristotle, Nicomachean Ethics*, trans., introd., and notes (Indianapolis).

—— (1985*d*), 'Aristotle's Conception of Morality', in *Proceedings of the Boston Area Colloquium in Ancient Philosophy*, 1, ed. J. J. Cleary (Lanham, Md.), 115-43.

—— (1988), *Aristotle's First Principles* (Oxford).

—— (1990), 'The Good of Political Activity', with commentary by G. Striker, in Patzig (1990), 73-101.

—— (1991*a*), 'Aristotle's Defense of Private Property', in Keyt and Miller (1991), 200-25.

—— (1991*b*), 'The Structure of Aristotelian Happiness', *Ethics*, 101. 382-91.

JACKSON, H. (1879), *Peri Dikaiosynēs: The Fifth Book of the Nicomachean Ethics of Aristotle*, text with notes (London).

JAEGER, W. (1948), *Aristotle: Fundamentals of the History of His Development*, trans. R. Robinson, 2nd edn. (Cambridge).

JAFFA, H. (1968), s.v. 'Natural Rights', *International Encyclopedia of the Social Sciences*, 11 (New York), 85-90.

—— (1972), 'Aristotle', in L. Strauss and J. Cropsey (eds.), *History of Political Philosophy*, 2nd edn. (Chicago), 64-129.

JOACHIM, H. H. (1951), *Aristotle, The Nicomachean Ethics: A Commentary* (Oxford).

JOHNSON, C. N. (1990), *Aristotle's Theory of the State* (New York).

JONES, J. W. (1956), *The Law and Legal Theory of the Greeks: An Introduction* (Oxford).

JOST, L. (forthcoming), 'Moral Luck and External Goods in the *Eudemian Ethics*'.

KAGAN, D. (1987), *The Fall of the Athenian Empire* (Ithaca, NY).

KAHN, C. H. (1990), 'The Normative Structure of Aristotle's *Politics*', in Patzig (1990), 369-84.

KANGER, S., and Kanger, H. (1966), 'Rights and Parliamentarianism', *Theoria*, 32. 85-115.

KASSEL, R. (1976), *Aristotelis Ars Rhetorica* (Berlin).

KAVKA, G. (1986), *Hobbesian Moral and Political Theory* (Princeton, NJ).

KELLEY, M. (forthcoming), 'Aristotle on Self-Sufficiency'.

KELSEN, H. (1937), 'The Philosophy of Aristotle and the Hellenic-Macedonian Policy', *Ethics*, 48. 1–64; partially repr. in Barnes *et al.* (1977), ii. 170–94.

KENNY, A. (1978), *The Aristotelian Ethics* (Oxford).

—— (1992), *Aristotle on the Perfect Life* (Oxford).

KENYON, F. G. (1920), *Aristotelis Atheniensium Respublica* (Oxford).

KERFERD, G. B. (1981), *The Sophistic Movement* (Cambridge, Mass.).

KEYT, D. (1983), 'Intellectualism in Aristotle', in J. P. Anton and A. Preus (eds.), *Essays in Ancient Greek Philosophy*, (Albany), ii. 364–87.

—— (1987), 'Three Fundamental Theorems in Aristotle's *Politics*', *Phronesis*, 32. 54–79; rev. as (1991*b*).

—— (1989), 'The Meaning of *Bios* in Aristotle's *Ethics* and *Politics*', *Ancient Philosophy*, 9. 15–21.

—— (1991*a*), 'Aristotle's Theory of Distributive Justice', in Keyt and Miller (1991), 238–78.

—— (1991*b*), 'Three Basic Theorems in Aristotle's *Politics*', in Keyt and Miller (1991), 118–41; rev. of (1987).

—— (1993), 'Aristotle and Anarchism', *Reason Papers*, 18. 133–52.

—— and Miller, F. D. (1991), *A Companion to Aristotle's Politics* (Oxford).

KHAWAJA, I. (1991), 'The Concept of the Individual in Aristotle's Ethics', Princeton University BA thesis.

KRAUT, R. (1989), *Aristotle on the Human Good* (Princeton, NJ).

KULLMANN, W. (1991), 'Man as a Political Animal in Aristotle', in Keyt and Miller (1991), 94–117.

LARMORE, C. (1993), 'Pluralism and Reasonable Disagreement', *Social Philosophy & Policy*, 11: 1. 61–79.

LAVOIE, D. C. (1985), *Rivalry and Central Planning: The Socialist Calculation Debate Reconsidered* (Cambridge, Mass.).

LAWRENCE, G. (1993), 'Aristotle and the Ideal Life', *The Philosophical Review*, 102. 1–34.

LEAR, J. (1988), *Aristotle: The Desire to Understand* (Cambridge, Mass.).

LENNOX, J. G. (1982), 'Teleology, Chance, and Aristotle's Theory of Spontaneous Generation', *Journal of the History of Philosophy*, 20. 219–38.

—— (1992), 'Teleology', in E. F. Keller and E. A. Lloyd (eds.), *Keywords in Evolutionary Biology* (Cambridge, Mass.), 324–33.

LERNER, M. P. (1969), *Recherches sur la notion de finalité chez Aristote* (Paris).

LEWIS, T. J. (1978) 'Acquisition and Anxiety: Aristotle's Case Against the Market', *Canadian Journal of Economics*, 11. 69–90.

LIDDELL, H. G., Scott, R., and Jones, H. S. (1976), *A Greek–English Lexicon* (Oxford).

LIEBERMAN, M. (1993), *Public Education: An Autopsy* (Cambridge, Mass.).

LOCKE, J. (1954), *Essays on the Law of Nature*, ed. W. von Leyden (Oxford).

—— (1960), *Two Treatises of Government*, ed. P. Laslett (New York).

—— (1990), *Questions concerning the Law of Nature*, ed. R. Horwitz, J. S. Clay, and D. Clay (Ithaca, NY).

LORD, C. (1982), *Education and Culture in the Political Thought of Aristotle* (Ithaca, NY).

—— (1984), *Aristotle, The Politics*, trans. with introd., notes, and glossary (Chicago).

McDONALD, F. (1985), *Novus Ordo Seclorum: The Intellectual Origins of the Constitution* (Lawrence, Kan.).

MacDOWELL, D. M. (1978), *The Law in Classical Athens* (Ithaca, NY).

McGRADE, A. S. (1980), 'Ockham and the Birth of Individual Rights', in B. Tierney and P. Linehan (eds.), *Authority and Power: Studies on Medieval Law and Government* (Cambridge, Mass.), 149–65.

—— (1982), 'Rights, Natural Rights, and the Philosophy of Law', in N. Kretzmann, A. Kenny, and J. Pinborg (eds.), *The Cambridge History of Later Medieval Philosophy* (Cambridge, Mass.), 738–56.

MacINTYRE, A. (1981), *After Virtue* (Notre Dame).

—— (1988) *Whose Justice? Which Rationality?* (Notre Dame).

McNEILL, D. (1990), 'Alternative Interpretations of Aristotle on Exchange and Reciprocity', *Public Affairs Quarterly*, 4. 55–68.

McSHEA, R. J. (1990), *Morality and Human Nature: A New Route to Ethical Theory* (Philadelphia).

MACHAN, T. R. (1975), *Human Rights and Human Liberties* (Chicago).

—— (1989), *Individuals and Their Rights* (LaSalle, Ill.).

MACK, E. (1989), 'Moral Individualism: Agent-Relativity and Deontic Restraints', *Social Philosophy & Policy*, 7: 1. 81–111.

MACKIE, J. L. (1984), 'Can There be a Right Based Moral Theory?', in J. Waldron (ed.), *Theories of Rights* (Oxford), 168–81.

MADIGAN, A. (1991), '*Eth. Nic.* 9.8: Beyond Egoism and Altruism?', in J. P. Anton and A. Preus (eds.), *Essays in Ancient Greek Philosophy*, iv. *Aristotle's Ethics* (Albany, NY).

MADISON, J. (1984), *Notes of Debates in the Federal Convention of 1787* (Athens, Ohio).

MARTIN, R., and Nickel, J. W. (1978), 'A Bibliography on the Nature and Foundation of Rights 1947–1977', *Political Theory*, 6. 395–413.

—— (1980), 'Recent Work on the Concept of Rights', *American Philosophical Quarterly*, 17. 165–80.

MASLOW, A. (1987), *Motivation and Personality*, 3rd edn. (New York).

MASTERS, R. D. (1975), 'Politics as a Biological Phenomenon', *Social Science Information*, 14. 7–63.

—— (1987), 'Evolutionary Biology and Natural Rights', in W. Soffer and K. Deutsch (eds.), *The Crisis of Liberal Democracy* (Albany, NY), 48–66.

—— (1989*a*), 'Classical Political Philosophy and Contemporary Biology', in K. Moors (ed.), *Politikos*, 1 (Pittsburgh), 1–44.

MASTERS, R. D. (1989*b*), *The Nature of Politics* (New Haven, Conn.).

—— (1990), 'Evolutionary Biology and Political Theory', *American Political Science Review*, 84. 195–210.

MATHIE, W. (1979), 'Property in the Political Science of Aristotle', in A. Parcel and T. Flanagan (eds.), *Theories of Property: Aristotle to the Present* (Waterloo, Ont.), 13–32.

MATTHEN, M. (1989), 'The Four Causes in Aristotle's Embryology', in T. Penner and R. Kraut (eds.), *Nature, Knowledge, and Virtue: Essays in Memory of Joan Kung, Apeiron*, 22. 159–79.

MAYHEW, R. A. (1993*a*), 'Aristotle on Property', *Review of Metaphysics*, 46. 803–31.

—— (1993*b*), 'Aristotle on the Extent of the Communism in Plato's *Republic*', *Ancient Philosophy*, 13. 323–40.

—— (forthcoming), 'Part and Whole in Aristotle's Political Philosophy'.

—— and Smith, N. D. (1994), 'Aristotle on What the Political Scientist Needs to Know', in K. Boudouris (ed.), *Proceedings of the Sixth International Conference on Greek Philosophy, 'Aristotelian Political Philosophy'* (Athens).

MAYR, E. (1982), *The Growth of Biological Thought* (Cambridge, Mass.).

—— (1988), 'The Multiple Meanings of Teleological', in *Towards a New Philosophy of Biology* (Cambridge, Mass.), 38–66.

MEIER, C. (1990), *The Greek Discovery of Politics*, trans. D. McLintock (Cambridge, Mass.).

MEIKLE, S. (1991), 'Aristotle and Exchange Value', in Keyt and Miller (1991), 156–81.

MERITT, B. D. (1955), 'Greek Inscriptions', *Hesperia*, 21. 340–59.

MEYER, S. S. (1992), 'Aristotle, Teleology, and Reduction', *Philosophical Review*, 101. 791–825.

MILL, J. S. (1969), 'Utilitarianism', in *Collected Works of John Stuart Mill*, x, ed. J. M. Robson (Toronto and London), 203–59.

—— (1989), *On Liberty with the Subjection of Women and Chapters on Socialism*, ed. Stefan Collini (Cambridge, Mass.).

MILLER, E. F. (1979), 'Prudence and the Rule of Law', *American Journal of Jurisprudence*, 24. 181–206.

MILLER, F. D. (1974), 'The State and the Community in Aristotle's *Politics*', *Reason Papers*, 1. 61–9.

—— (1983), 'Rationality and Freedom in Aristotle and Hayek', *Reason Papers*, 9. 29–36.

—— (1984), 'Aristotle on Rationality in Action', *The Review of Metaphysics*, 38. 499–520.

—— (1988), 'Aristotle and the Natural Rights Tradition', *Reason Papers*, 13. 166–81.

—— (1991), 'Aristotle on Natural Law and Justice', in Keyt and Miller (1991), 279–306.

—— (forthcoming), 'Aristotle and American Classical Republicanism'.

MILLER, R. W. (1981), 'Marx and Aristotle: A Kind of Consequentialism', in K. Nielson and S. C. Patten (eds.), *Marx and Morality, Canadian Journal of Philosophy*, supplementary vol. 7. 323–52.

MILNE, A. J. M. (1986), *Human Rights and Human Diversity* (Albany, NY).

MISES, L. v. (1920), 'Die Wirtschaftsrechnung im sozialistischen Gemeinwesen', *Archiv für Sozialwissenschaft und Sozialpolitik*, 47. 86–121.

—— (1937), *Socialism: An Economic and Sociological Analysis*, trans. J. Kahane (London).

MOORE, G. E. (1903), *Principia Ethica* (Cambridge, Mass.).

MORRIS, C. W. (1988), 'The Relation between Self-Interest and Justice in Contractarian Ethics', *Social Philosophy & Policy*, 5: 2. 119–53.

MORROW, G. R. (1960), *Plato's Cretan City: A Historical Interpretation of the Laws* (Princeton, NJ).

MULGAN, R. G. (1977), *Aristotle's Political Theory* (Oxford).

—— (1990), 'Aristotle and the Value of Political Participation', *Political Theory*, 18. 195–215.

MURPHY, J. B. (1993), *The Moral Economy of Labor: Aristotelian Theories in Economic Theory* (New Haven, Conn.).

NAGEL, T. (1981), 'Libertarianism without Foundations', in J. Paul (ed.), *Reading Nozick* (Totowa, NJ), 191–205.

NARVESON, J. (1988), *The Libertarian Idea* (Philadelphia).

—— (forthcoming), 'Rights, Laws, and the Common Good'.

NEWMAN, W. L. (1887–1902; repr. 1973), *The Politics of Aristotle*, text, introd., notes, critical and explanatory, 4 vols. (Oxford).

NICHOLS, M. P. (1992), *Citizens and Statesmen: A Study of Aristotle's Politics* (Lanham, Md.).

NORTON, D. L. (1976), *Personal Destinies* (Princeton, NJ).

—— (1985), 'Is "Flourishing" a True Alternative Ethics?', *Reason Papers*, 10. 101–5.

NOVAK, M. (1982), *The Spirit of Democratic Capitalism* (New York).

NOZICK, R. (1974), *Anarchy, State, and Utopia* (New York).

—— (1981), 'On the Randian Argument', in J. Paul (ed.), *Reading Nozick* (Totowa, NJ), 206–31.

NUSSBAUM, M. C. (1978), *Aristotle's De Motu Animalium*, text, trans., commentary, and essay (Princeton, NJ).

—— (1980), 'Shame, Separateness, and Political Unity: Aristotle's Criticism of Plato', in Rorty (1980), 395–435.

—— (1986), *The Fragility of Goodness* (Cambridge, Mass.).

—— (1988), 'Nature, Function, and Capability: Aristotle on Political Distribution', with commentary by D. Charles and reply by Nussbaum, *Oxford Studies in Ancient Philosophy*, suppl. vol., 148–214; repr. in Patzig (1990), 152–201.

—— (1990), 'Aristotelian Social Democracy', in R. B. Douglass, G. M. Mara, and H. S. Richardson (eds.), *Liberalism and the Good* (London).

NUSSBAUM, M. C. (1992), 'Human Functioning and Social Justice: In Defense of Aristotelian Essentialism', *Political Theory*, 20. 202–46.

OAKESHOTT, M. (1975), *On Human Conduct* (Oxford).

OPPERMANN, H. (1928), *Aristotelis Athēnaion Politeia* (Stuttgart).

OSTWALD, M. (1986), *From Popular Sovereignty to the Sovereignty of Law: Law, Society, and Politics in Fifth-Century Athens* (Berkeley, Calif.).

PANGLE, T. L. (1980), *The Laws of Plato*, trans. with notes and an interpretative essay (New York).

—— (1988), *The Spirit of Modern Republicanism: The Moral Vision of the American Founders and the Philosophy of Locke* (Chicago).

PARFIT, D. (1986), *Reasons and Persons* (Oxford).

PATZIG, G. (1990), *Aristoteles' 'Politik': Akten des XI. Symposium Aristotelicum 1987* (Göttingen).

PAUL, J. (1993), 'Natural Ends and Natural Rights', *Reason Papers*, 18. 107–13.

—— and Miller, F. D. (1990), 'Communitarian and Liberal Theories of the Good', *Review of Metaphysics*, 43. 803–30.

PELLEGRIN, P. (1987), 'La *Politique* d'Aristote: unité et fractures', *Revue philosophique*, 177. 129–59.

PLAMENATZ, J. (1991–2), *Man and Society*, rev. M. E. Plamenatz and R. Wokler, 3 vols. (New York).

POCOCK, J. G. A. (1975), *The Machiavellian Moment: Florentine Political Thought and the Atlantic Republican Tradition* (Princeton, NJ).

POLANSKY, R. (1991), 'Aristotle on Political Change', in Keyt and Miller (1991), 323–45.

—— (unpublished), 'What Aristotle Means by the Naturalness of the Polis'.

POPPER, K. R. (1962), *The Open Society and Its Enemies*, 4th edn., 2 vols. (Princeton, NJ).

PUFENDORF, S. von (1934), *De jure naturae et gentium libri octo*, trans. C. H. and W. A. Oldfather (Oxford).

—— (1991), *On the Duty of Man and Citizen According to Natural Law*, trans. M. Silverthorne, ed. J. Tully (Cambridge).

RACKHAM, H. (1932), *Aristotle, Politics*, text and trans. (Cambridge, Mass.).

—— (1934), *Aristotle, Nicomachean Ethics*, text and trans., rev. edn., Loeb (Cambridge, Mass.).

RAND, A. (1964), 'Man's Rights', in *The Virtue of Selfishness* (New York), 92–100.

RASMUSSEN, D. B. (1984), 'Conceptions of the Common Good and the Natural Right to Liberty', in R. Porreco (ed.), *The Georgetown Symposium on Ethics: Essays in Honor of Henry Babcock Veatch* (Lanham, Md.), 185–93.

—— and Den Uyl, D. J. (1991), *Liberty and Nature: An Aristotelian Defense of Liberal Order* (LaSalle, Ill.).

RAUBITSCHEK, A. E. (1991), 'Ostracism: The Athenian Ostraca', in id., *The School of Hellas* (Oxford).

RAWLS, J. (1971), *A Theory of Justice* (Cambridge, Mass.).

RAZ, J. (1986), *The Morality of Freedom* (Oxford).

REES, D. A. (1990), 'Comments on C. Lord', in Patzig (1990), 216–19.

REEVE, C. D. C. (1992), *Practices of Reason: Aristotle's Nicomachean Ethics* (Oxford).

RHODES, P. J. (1981; 1993 edn. with addenda), *A Commentary on the Aristotelian Athēnaiōn Politeia* (Oxford).

—— (1984), *The Athenian Constitution*, trans. with introd. and notes (Harmondsworth).

—— (1986), *The Greek City States: A Sourcebook* (Norman, Okla.).

RICHARD, C. J. (1994), *The Foundations and the Classics: Greece, Rome, and the American Enlightenment* (Cambridge, Mass.).

RICHARDSON, H. S. (1992), 'Degrees of Finality and the Highest Good in Aristotle', *Journal of the History of Philosophy*, 30. 327–52.

ROBBINS, C. (1959), *The Eighteenth-Century Commonwealth: Studies in the Transmission, Development, and Circumstance of English Liberal Thought from the Restoration of Charles II until the War with the Thirteen Colonies* (Cambridge, Mass.).

ROBINSON, R. (1962), *Aristotle's Politics Books III and IV*, trans., introd., and notes (Oxford).

ROGERS, K. (1993), 'Aristotle's Conception of *To Kalon*', *Ancient Philosophy*, 13. 355–71.

RORTY, A. O. (1980), *Essays on Aristotle's Ethics* (Berkeley, Calif.).

ROSE, V. (1886), *Aristotelis qui ferebantur Librorum Fragmenta* (Leipzig).

ROSHWALD, M. (1959), 'The Concept of Human Rights', *Philosophy and Phenomenological Research*, 19. 354–79.

ROSS, W. D. (1948), *Aristotle's Metaphysics*, 2 vols., rev. text with introd. and comm. (Oxford).

—— (1949), *Aristotle* (5th edn., London).

—— (1957), *Aristotelis Politica* (Oxford).

—— (1966) *Aristotle's Physics*, rev. text with introd. and comm. (Oxford).

ROUSSEAU, J. J. (1983), *On the Social Contract*, trans. D. A. Cress (Indianapolis).

ROWE, C. J. (1977), 'Aims and Methods in Aristotle's *Politics*', *Classical Quarterly*, 27. 159–72; rev. as Rowe (1991).

—— (1989), 'Reality and Utopia', *Elenchos*, fasc. 2. 317–36.

—— (1991), 'Aims and Methods in Aristotle's *Politics*', in Keyt and Miller (1991), 57–74; rev. of Rowe (1977).

RUSE, M. (1990), 'Evolutionary Ethics and the Search for Predecessors: Kant, Hume, and All the Way Back to Aristotle?', *Social Philosophy & Policy*, 8: 1. 59–85.

SABINE, G. H. (1973), *A History of Political Theory* (4th edn., Fort Worth, Texas).

SALKEVER, S. G. (1990), *Finding the Mean: Theory and Practice in Aristotelian Political Philosophy* (Princeton, NJ).

SANDEL, M. (1982), *Liberalism and the Limits of Justice* (Cambridge, Mass.).

—— (1984*a*), 'The Procedural Republic and the Unencumbered Self', *Political Theory*, 12. 81–96.

—— (1984*b*), 'Morality and the Liberal Ideal', *New Republic*, 190. 15–17.

SAUNDERS, T. J. (1975), *Plato, The Laws*, trans., introd., corr. edn. (Harmondsworth).

SAXONHOUSE, A. W. (1982), 'Family, Polity, and Unity: Aristotle on Socrates' Community of Wives', *Polity*, 15. 202–19.

SCHEFFLER, S. (1982), *The Rejection of Consequentialism* (Oxford).

SCHLAIFER, R. O. (1936), 'Greek Theories of Slavery from Homer to Aristotle', *Harvard Studies in Classical Philology*, 47. 165–204.

SCHMIDTZ, D. (1991), *The Limits of Government: An Essay on the Public Goods Argument* (Boulder, Col.).

SCHOFIELD, M. (1990), 'Ideology and Philosophy in Aristotle's Theory of Slavery', with commentary by C. H. Kahn, in Patzig (1990), 1–31.

SCHÜTRUMPF, E. (1980), *Die Analyse der Polis durch Aristoteles* (Amsterdam).

—— (1991), *Aristoteles Politik*, i, general introd., trans. with notes of Book I; ii, trans. with notes of Books II–III (Berlin).

SEALEY, R. (1976), *A History of the Greek City States, 700–338 BC* (Berkeley, Calif.).

SEEL, G. (1990), 'Die Rechtfertigung von Herrschaft in der Politik des Aristoteles', with commentary by T. Ebert, in Patzig (1990), 32–72.

SELIGMAN, A. B. (1992), *The Idea of Civil Society* (New York).

SHIELDS, C. (1990), 'The First Functionalist', in J. C. Smith (ed.), *Historical Foundations of Cognitive Science* (Dordrecht), 19–33.

SIMMONS, A. J. (1992), *The Lockean Theory of Rights* (Princeton, NJ).

SIMPSON, P. (1990), 'Making the Citizens Good: Aristotle's City and Its Contemporary Relevance', *Philosophical Forum*, 22. 149–66.

SINCLAIR, R. K. (1988), *Democracy and Participation in Athens* (Cambridge).

SINCLAIR, T. A. (1983), *Aristotle, The Politics*, trans., rev. edn. by J. T. Saunders (Harmondsworth).

SMITH, A. (1979), *An Inquiry Into the Nature and Causes of the Wealth of Nations*, ed. R. K. Campbell and A. S. Skinner, 2 vols. (Oxford).

—— (1982), *The Theory of Moral Sentiments*, ed. D. D. Raphael and A. L. Macfie (Oxford).

SMITH, N. D. (1991), 'Aristotle's Theory of Natural Slavery', in Keyt and Miller (1991), 142–55.

SOLMSEN, F. (1964), 'Leisure and Play in Aristotle's Ideal State', *Rheinische Museum*, 107. 193–220.

SORABJI, R. (1980), *Necessity, Cause, and Blame* (Ithaca, NY).

SOWELL, T. (1980), *Knowledge and Decisions* (New York).

SPENCER, H. (1981), 'The Great Political Superstition', in *The Man versus the State* (Indianapolis), 123–66.

STALLEY, R. F. (1991), 'Aristotle's Criticism of Plato's *Republic*', in Keyt and Miller (1991), 182–99.

STEELE, D. R. (1992), *From Marx to Mises: Post-Capitalist Society and the Challenge of Economic Calculation* (LaSalle, Ill.).

STEINER, H. (1977), 'The Structure of Compossible Rights', *Journal of Philosophy*, 74. 767–75.

STEWART, J. A. (1892), *Notes on the Nicomachean Ethics of Aristotle*, 2 vols. (Oxford).

STOCKER, M. (1990), *Plural and Conflicting Values* (Oxford).

STOCKTON, D. (1991), *The Classical Athenian Democracy*, corr. edn. (Oxford).

STRAUSS, L. (1953), *Natural Right and History* (Chicago).

SUGDEN, R. (1986), *The Economics of Rights, Co-operation, and Welfare* (Oxford).

SUSEMIHL, F. (1884), *Aristotelis, Ethica Eudemia* (Leipzig).

—— (1912), *Aristotelis, Ethica Nicomachea* (3rd edn., Leipzig).

—— and Hicks, R. D. (1894; repr. 1976), *The Politics of Aristotle*, text, introd., analysis, and comm. to Books I–V (I–III, VII–VIII) (London).

SWANSON, J. A. (1992), *The Public and the Private in Aristotle's Political Philosophy* (Ithaca, NY).

TAYLOR, C. (1985), 'Atomism', in *Philosophy and the Human Sciences* (Cambridge, Mass.), 187–210.

TIERNEY, B. (1983), 'Tuck on Rights: Some Medieval Problems', *History of Political Thought*, iv. 429–41.

—— (1988), 'Villey, Ockham and the Origin of Individual Rights', in J. Witte and F. S. Alexander (eds.), *The Weightier Matters of the Law: A Tribute to Harold J. Berman* (Atlanta), 1–31.

—— (1989), 'Origins of Natural Rights Language: Texts and Contents, 1150–1250', *History of Political Thought*, x. 615–46.

—— (1991), 'Aristotle and the American Indians—Again: Two Critical Discussions', *Cristianesimo nella storia*, 12. 295–322.

—— (1992), 'Natural Rights in the Thirteenth Century: A *Quaestio* of Henry of Ghent', *Speculum*, 67. 58–68.

TUCK, R. (1979), *Natural Rights Theories: Their Origin and Development* (Cambridge).

TULLY, J. (1980), *A Discourse on Property: John Locke and His Adversaries* (Cambridge).

ULLMANN-MARGALIT, E. (1978), 'Invisible Hand Explanations', *Synthese*, 39. 263–92.

VANDER WAERDT, P. A. (1985), 'Kingship and Philosophy in Aristotle's Best Regime', *Phronesis*, 30. 249–73.

VEATCH, H. B. (1985), *Human Rights: Fact or Fancy?* (Baton Rouge, La.).

VERBEKE, G. (1990), *Moral Education in Aristotle* (Washington, DC).

VILLEY, M. (1946), 'L'Idée du droit subjectif et les systèmes juridiques romains', *Revue historique de droit*, ser. 4, 24–5, 201–27.

—— (1962), *Leçons d'histoire de la philosophie du droit* (Paris).

—— (1964), 'Le Genèse du droit subjectif chez Guillaume d'Occam', *Archives de philosophie du droit*, 9. 97–127.

—— (1969), *Seize essais de philosophie du droit* (Paris).

—— (1975), *La Formation de la pensée juridique moderne* (4th edn., Paris).

VLASTOS, G. (1977), 'The Theory of Social Justice in the *Polis* in Plato's *Republic*', in H. North (ed.), *Interpretations of Plato*, suppl. vol. of *Mnemosyne* (1977), 1–40.

VLASTOS, G. (1978), 'The Rights of Persons in Plato's Conception of the Foundations of Justice', in H. T. Engelhardt and D. Callahan (eds.), *Morals, Science and Sociality* (New York), 172–214.

—— (1981), '*Isonomia Politikē*', in *Platonic Studies* (2nd edn., Princeton, NJ), 164–203.

WALDRON, J. (1988), *The Right to Private Property* (Oxford).

WALZER, R. R., and Mingay, J. M. (1991), *Aristotelis Ethica Eudemia* (Oxford).

WATERLOW, S. (1982), *Nature, Change, and Agency in Aristotle's Physics* (Oxford).

WEBER, M. (1947), *Theory of Social and Economic Organization* (New York).

WHITE, S. A. (1990), 'Is Aristotelian Happiness a Good Life or the Best Life?', *Oxford Studies in Ancient Philosophy*, 8. 97–137.

—— (1992), *Sovereign Virtue: Aristotle on the Relation between Happiness and Prosperity* (Stanford, Calif.).

WHITING, J. (1986), 'Human Nature and Intellectualism in Aristotle', *Archiv für Geschichte der Philosophie*, 68. 70–95.

—— (1988), 'Aristotle's Function Argument: A Defense', *Ancient Philosophy*, 8. 33–48.

WIELAND, W. (1975), 'The Problem of Teleology', in Barnes *et al.* (1977), i. 141–60.

WIGGINS, D. (1975–6), 'Deliberation and Practical Wisdom', *Proceedings of the Aristotelian Society*, 76. 29–51.

—— (1978), 'Weakness of the Will, Commensurability, and the Objects of Deliberation and Desire', *Proceedings of the Aristotelian Society*, 79. 251–77.

WILAMOWITZ-MOELLENDORFF, U. v. (1893), *Aristoteles und Athen*, 2 vols. (Berlin).

WILLIAMS, B. (1972), *Morality: An Introduction to Ethics* (New York).

—— (1980), 'Justice as a Virtue', in Rorty (1980), 189–99.

—— (1985), *Ethics and the Limits of Philosophy* (Cambridge, Mass.).

WILSON, E. O. (1975), *Sociobiology: The New Synthesis* (Cambridge, Mass.).

WILSON, J. Q. (1993), *The Moral Sense* (New York).

WOOD, G. S. (1969), *The Creation of the American Republic, 1776–1787* (Chapel Hill, NC).

WOODRUFF, P. (1982), *Hippias Major, Plato*, trans. with commentary and essay (Indianapolis).

WOODS, M. (1982), *Aristotle's Eudemian Ethics, Books I, II, and VIII*, trans. with commentary (Oxford).

YACK, B. (1993), *The Problems of a Political Animal: Community, Justice, and Conflict in Aristotelian Political Thought* (Berkeley, Calif.).

ZELLER, E. (1897), *Aristotle and the Earlier Peripatetics*, trans. B. F. C. Costelloe and J. H. Muirhead (London).

ZUCKERT, C. H. (1983), 'Aristotle on the Limits and Satisfactions of Political Life', *Interpretation*, 11. 185–206.

ZUCKERT, M. P. (1989), 'Bringing Philosophy Down from the Heavens: Natural Right in the Roman Law', *The Review of Politics*, 51. 70–85.

General Index

abortion 229, 249, 373
acquisition, art of (*chrēmatistikē*) 317–21,
    328–9
action (*praxis*) 9, 186, 215–16, 238,
    244–5, 316 n, 348
activity (*energeia*) 225–6, 233, 264, 315,
    347–57, 369–70
agent-relativity 131, 375–6
aggression 64–5
agriculture 317–21
Alexander the Great 3, 192 n
alienation 312–14, 322–4, 328, 331 n
aliens, *see* foreigners *and* metics
altruism 194 n, 198, 200–3
animals 311, 318, 327
    analogous to polis 47–9, 54–6, 160,
        173
    compared to humans 30–1, 44,
        317–18
    contrasted with humans 32–4, 64–6,
        318
Antipater 254
Areopagus 283 n
aretē, *see* virtue
Arginousai 167 n
aristocracy 153–6, 159, 192–3, 203,
    223–4, 235 n, 253, 257 n
    causes of change in 296–7
    definition of 192
    so-called aristocracy 164–5, 171–2,
        179–80, 182–3, 223 n, 235 n, 252–3,
        255–8, 260, 296–7
Aristotle:
    interpretation of 21–4, 192 n
    writings of 3, 22–3
art, *see* craft
artefact, and polis 29–30, 38–42, 56,
    59–60
artisan 149, 161, 219–20, 244, 327
Assembly (*ekklēsia*) 145–6, 150, 167–8,
    175–6, 224, 257, 261–2, 291
assessment, *see* property
association, *see* community
Athens, Attica 4, 145–50, 167, 172, 174 n,
    182, 245–6, 271, 279, 282–3, 287,
    330

atomism, *see* individualism
auditing 108, 167, 171, 259–62, 271
autarkeia, *see* self-sufficiency
authority (*to kurion*) 20–1, 104–8, 145,
    151, 166–83 *passim*, 243, 256–75
    passim, 276–308 *passim*, 357–73
    passim
    and rights 104–7, 115, 125, 146, 311
    and sovereignty 104 n, 149–50, 271–4
    without authority (*akuros*) 106, 115,
        243
autonomy 113–17, 248 n, 355–7, 365–6,
    372, 377

banausos, *see* vulgar
barter 319–20
base 136–7
best constitution, *see* constitution
Bill of Rights 275
biology 18, 27–8, 160, 276, 336–46
body 47–8, 53–5, 228, 245, 349, 367
boulē, *see* Council
business firm 371

capacity 33–4, 36, 160, 347 n, 354, 362 n,
    376 n
capitalism 105 n, 331, 371, 373, 377
Carthage 146, 164, 271
cause (*aitia*) 27
    efficient 28, 337, 340–5
    final 27, 28, 45, 150–2, 204, 337–46
    formal 28, 151–2
    material 27–8, 338–40, 344
    of political change 185–6, 295–6,
        306
cavalry 253, 279
Chaeronea, battle of 3
chance (*tuchē*) 341–3, 356
change, political (*metabolē*) 294, 307–8
    causes of 185–6, 295–6, 306
    prevention of 186, 297, 306
    and revolution 186, 294–6
    see also faction *and* revolution
character (*ēthos*) 230, 234, 265
checks and balances 172, 259–60, 275,
    292 n, 302

Index Nominum

This index includes authors other than Aristotle and Plato, for whom see the Index Locorum.
For other names, see the General Index

Index Locorum